American Book Company
Meeting Standards, Exceeding Expectations

MW00974331

Dear Educator,

Thank you for your interest in American Book Company's state-specific test preparation resources. We commend you for your interest in pursuing your students' success. Feel free to contact us with any questions about our books, software, or the ordering process.

Our Products Feature	Your Students Will Improve
Multiple-choice and open-ended diagnostic tests	Confidence and mastery of subjects
Step-by-step instruction	Concept development
Frequent practice exercises	Critical thinking
Chapter reviews	Test-taking skills
Multiple-choice practice tests	Problem-solving skills

American Book Company's writers and curriculum specialists have over 100 years of combined teaching experience, working with students from kindergarten through middle, high school, and adult education.

Our company specializes in effective test preparation books and software for high stakes graduation and grade promotion exams across the country.

How to Use This Book

Each book:

*contains a chart of standards which correlates all test questions and chapters to the state exam's standards and benchmarks as published by the state department of education. This chart is found in the front of all preview copies and in the front of all answer keys.

*begins with a full-length pretest (diagnostic test). This test not only adheres to your specific state standards, but also mirrors your state exam in weights and measures to help you assess each individual student's strengths and weaknesses.

*offers an evaluation chart. Depending on which questions the students miss, this chart points to which chapters individual students or the entire class need to review to be prepared for the exam.

*provides comprehensive review of all tested standards within the chapters. Each chapter includes engaging instruction, practice exercises, and chapter reviews to assess students' progress.

*finishes with two full-length practice tests for students to get comfortable with the exam and to assess their progress and mastery of the tested standards and benchmarks.

While we cannot <u>guarantee</u> success, our products are designed to provide students with the concept and skill development they need for the graduation test or grade promotion exam in their own state. We look forward to hearing from you soon.

Sincerely,

The American Book Company Team

PO Box 2638★Woodstock, GA 30188-1383★Phone: 1-888-264-5877★Fax: 1-866-827-3240

Standards Covered on the ACT Mathematics Test

Pre-Algebra (PA) – 23% of the test

Questions in this content area are based on basic operations using whole numbers, decimals, fractions, and integers; place value; square roots and approximations; the concept of exponents; scientific notation; factors; ratio, proportion, and percent; linear equations in one variable; absolute value and ordering numbers by value; elementary counting techniques and simple probability; data collection, representation, and interpretation; and understanding simple descriptive statistics.

Elementary Algebra (EA) – 17% of the test

Questions in this content area are based on properties of exponents and square roots, evaluation of algebraic expressions through substitution, using variables to express functional relationships, understanding algebraic operations, and the solution of quadratic equations by factoring.

Intermediate Algebra (IA) – 15% of the test

Questions in this content area are based on an understanding of the quadratic formula, rational and radical expressions, absolute value equations and inequalities, sequences and patterns, systems of equations, quadratic inequalities, functions, modeling, matrices, roots of polynomials, and complex numbers.

Coordinate Geometry (CG) – 15% of the test

Questions in this content area are based on graphing and the relations between equations and graphs, including points, lines, polynomials, circles, and other curves; graphing inequalities; slope; parallel and perpendicular lines; distance; midpoints; and conics.

Plane Geometry (PG) – 23% of the test

Questions in this content area are based on the properties and relations of plane figures, including angles and relations among perpendicular and parallel lines; properties of circles, triangles, rectangles, parallelograms, and trapezoids; transformations; the concept of proof and proof techniques; volume; and applications of geometry to three dimensions.

Trigonometry (T) – 7% of the test

Questions in this content area are based on understanding trigonometric relations in right triangles; values and properties of trigonometric functions; graphing trigonometric functions; modeling using trigonometric functions; use of trigonometric identities; and solving trigonometric equations.

Chart of Standards

Standard	Chapter Number	Diagnostic Test Question Number	Practice Test 1 Question Number	Practice Test 2 Question Number
Pre-Algebra (PA) (23% of the test)	2, 3, 4, 5, 15, 16	1, 9, 13, 19, 25, 30, 33, 37, 40, 42, 44, 50, 52, 60	1, 3, 4, 5, 6, 7, 8, 9, 10, 11, 12, 13, 20, 32	1, 8, 10, 20, 25, 31, 36, 38, 41, 44, 47, 54, 57, 60
Elementary Algebra (EA) (17% of the test)	2, 3, 4, 8, 9, 10	2, 6, 14, 20, 26, 31, 36, 41, 56, 57	14, 15, 16, 17, 18, 19, 21, 22, 23, 30	6, 12, 17, 24, 29, 35, 48, 53, 56, 59
Intermediate Algebra (IA) (15% of the test)	4, 6, 7, 8, 9, 10, 14	3, 7, 15, 21, 27, 28, 43, 47, 55	2, 24, 25, 26, 27, 28, 29, 31, 33	3, 9, 11, 21, 27, 28, 33, 45, 58
Coordinate Geometry (CG) (15% of the test)	10, 11, 12, 13	10, 12, 16, 22, 32, 32, 38, 45, 48	48, 49, 50, 51, 52, 53, 54, 55, 56	5, 15, 18, 23, 30, 34, 40, 51, 52
Plane Geometry (PG) (23% of the test)	17, 18, 19, 20, 21, 22	5, 11, 17, 23, 29, 34, 39, 46, 49, 51, 53, 54, 58, 59	34, 35, 36, 37, 38, 39, 40, 41, 42, 43, 44, 45, 46, 47	4, 13, 19, 22, 26, 32, 37, 39, 42, 43, 46, 49, 50, 55
Trigonometry (T) (7% of the test)	23	4, 8, 18, 24	57, 58, 59, 60	2, 7, 14, 16

American Book Company's

ACT® Mathematics

Test Preparation Guide

ERICA DAY

COLLEEN PINTOZZI

TIMOTHY TROWBRIDGE

AMERICAN BOOK COMPANY

P. O. BOX 2638

WOODSTOCK, GEORGIA 30188-1383

TOLL FREE 1 (888) 264-5877 PHONE (770) 928-2834

TOLL FREE FAX 1 (866) 827-3240

WEB SITE: www.americanbookcompany.com

Acknowledgements

In preparing this book, we would like to acknowledge Mary Stoddard and Eric Field for their contributions in developing graphics for this book and Samuel Rodriguez and Camille Woodhouse for their contributions in editing this book. We would also like to thank our many students whose needs and questions inspired us to write this text.

P.O. Box 2638
Woodstock, GA 30188-1383

Printed in the United States of America
07/08

Contents

Preface

ACT Mathematics Test Preparation Guide will help you review and learn important concepts and skills related to high school mathematics. To help identify which areas are of greater challenge for you, first take the diagnostic test, and then complete the evaluation chart with your instructor in order to help you identify the chapters which require your careful attention. When you have finished your review of all of the material your teacher assigns, take the practice tests to evaluate your understanding of the material presented in this book. **The materials in this book are based on the standards in mathematics published by ACT, Inc.**

This book contains several sections. These sections are as follows: 1) A Diagnostic Test; 2) Chapters that teach the concepts and skills for the ACT Mathematics Test; 3) Two Practice Tests. Answers to the tests and exercises are in a separate manual.

ABOUT THE AUTHORS

Erica Day has a Bachelor of Science Degree in Mathematics and is working on a Master of Science Degree in Mathematics. She graduated with high honors from Kennesaw State University in Kennesaw, Georgia. She has also tutored all levels of mathematics, ranging from high school algebra and geometry to university-level statistics, calculus, and linear algebra. She is currently writing and editing mathematics books for American Book Company, where she has coauthored numerous books, such as ***Passing the Georgia Algebra I End of Course***, ***Passing the Georgia High School Graduation Test in Mathematics***, ***Passing the Arizona AIMS in Mathematics***, and ***Passing the New Jersey HSPA in Mathematics***, to help students pass graduation and end of course exams.

Colleen Pintozzi has taught mathematics at the middle school, junior high, senior high, and adult level for 22 years. She holds a B.S. degree from Wright State University in Dayton, Ohio and has done graduate work at Wright State University, Duke University, and the University of North Carolina at Chapel Hill. She is the author of many mathematics books including such best-sellers as ***Basics Made Easy: Mathematics Review***, ***Passing the New Alabama Graduation Exam in Mathematics***, ***Passing the Louisiana LEAP 21 GEE***, ***Passing the Indiana ISTEP+ GQE in Mathematics***, ***Passing the Minnesota Basic Standards Test in Mathematics***, and ***Passing the Nevada High School Proficiency Exam in Mathematics.***

Timothy Trowbridge graduated with summa cum laude honors from Hawaii Loa College with a Bachelor of Arts degree in Mathematics. He taught in Japan as a participant in the Japan Exchange and Teaching (JET) Program, and he has written and edited parts of various mathematics textbooks for several major educational publishers.

Diagnostic Test

60 Minutes – 60 Questions

DIRECTIONS: Solve each problem and then choose the correct answer.

Do not linger over problems that take too much time. Solve as many as you can, then return to the others in the time you have left for this test.

You are permitted to use a calculator on this test. You may use your calculator for any problems you choose, but some of the problems may best be done without using a calculator.

Note: Unless otherwise stated, all of the following should be assumed.

1. Illustrative figures are NOT necessarily drawn to scale.
2. Geometric figures lie in a plane.
3. The word *line* indicates a straight line.
4. The word *average* indicates arithmetic mean.

---

1. Cam has just completed her first year of college, and she has decided to put her possessions in a self-storage facility while she is visiting her family during summer vacation. She will be charged a flat fee of \$35.00 plus \$0.45 for each day of storage. If Cam stores her possessions for d days and is charged a total of \$63.80, which of the following equations can be used to solve for d?

A. $35 + 0.45 + d = 63.80$
B. $35 + 0.45 = d + 63.80$
C. $35 = 0.45 + d + 63.80$
D. $35 + 0.45d = 63.80$
E. $35 + 0.45 = 63.80d$

PA

2. If $3x^2 - 2x - 16 = 0$, then $x =$?

F. $-\frac{8}{3}$ or -2
G. $\frac{3}{8}$ or 2
H. -2 or $\frac{8}{3}$
J. -2 or $\frac{3}{8}$
K. 2 or $\frac{8}{3}$

EA

3. Jimmy is playing a computer game, and his score on the game has improved each time he has played. In his first attempt at the game, he had a score of $20,017$, and his subsequent scores have been $20,183$; $20,349$; $20,515$; and $20,681$. If the pattern in Jimmy's scores continues, what can Jimmy expect his score to be the next time he plays the game?

A. $20,747$
B. $20,748$
C. $20,774$
D. $20,784$
E. $20,847$

IA

4. The positive x-axis of a unit circle and a ray from the origin of the unit circle to a point in the second quadrant form an angle measuring θ degrees. If $\sin\theta = -\cos\theta$, what is the value of θ?

F. 130°
G. 135°
H. 140°
J. 145°
K. 150°

T

5. A rectangle is graphed on a coordinate grid and has the vertices $(-5,8), (-5,2), (1,2)$, and $(1,8)$. The rectangle is then reflected in the x-axis of the coordinate grid. Which of the following points is not a vertex of the reflected rectangle?

A. $(-1,-2)$
B. $(1,-2)$
C. $(1,-8)$
D. $(-5,-2)$
E. $(-5,-8)$

PG

6. $\frac{b^6}{a^6} + \frac{a^6}{b^6} = ?$

F. 1
G. $\frac{a^{12}+b^{12}}{a^6b^6}$
H. $\frac{a^{12}+b^{12}}{a^{12}b^{12}}$
J. a^6b^6
K. $a^{12}b^{12}$

EA

7. A traveller has some Japanese yen and some Thai baht left over from a trip to Asia five years ago, when one yen was worth 0.02 dollars and one baht was worth 0.02 dollars. Today one yen is worth 0.01 dollars, and one baht is worth 0.03 dollars. If the money was worth 800 dollars five years ago and is worth 1000 dollars today, how many yen does the traveller have?

A. 1000
B. 3000
C. 10,000
D. 20,000
E. 30,000

IA

8. In the triangle shown below, what is the tangent of $\angle ACB$?

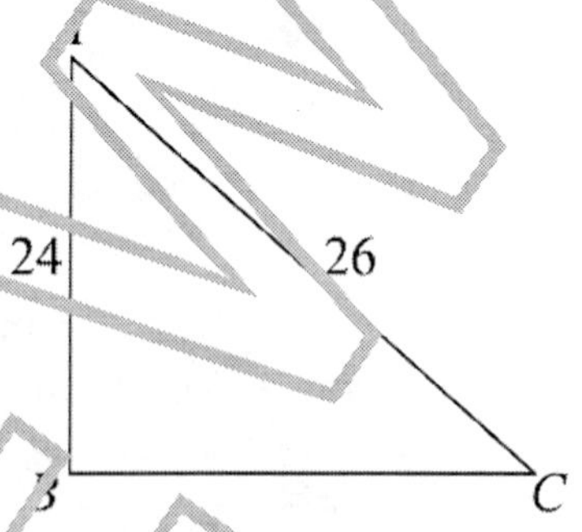

F. $\frac{5}{13}$
G. $\frac{5}{12}$
H. $\frac{12}{13}$
J. $\frac{12}{5}$
K. $\frac{13}{5}$

T

9. Roberto started with 12 blue ties, 7 red ties, and 17 green ties in his closet. He then randomly chose a blue tie from his closet, but he didn't put it back. What is the probability that if Roberto randomly chooses another tie from his closet that it will be a blue tie?

A. $\frac{11}{36}$
B. $\frac{1}{3}$
C. $\frac{11}{35}$
D. $\frac{12}{35}$
E. [illegible]

PA

10. The parabola shown below is the graph of the equation $y = x^2 + kx - 48$. What is the value of k?

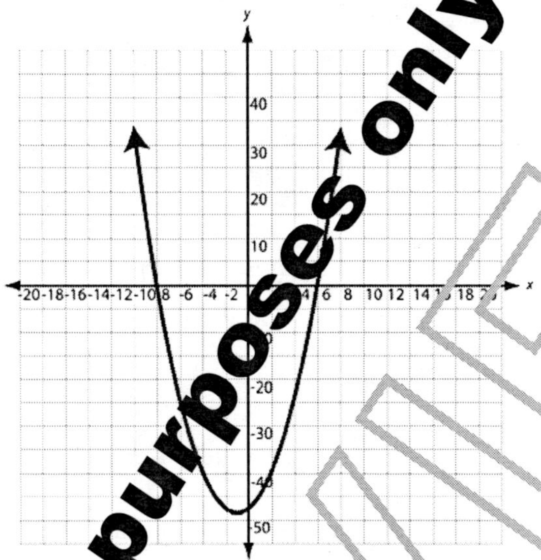

F. −[illegible]
G. −2
H. [illegible]
J. 6
K. 8

CG

11. Cylinder A and cylinder B are congruent. If cylinder A has its height reduced by $\frac{1}{3}$, while cylinder B has its radius reduced by $\frac{1}{3}$, which of the following statements is now true?

A. The volume of cylinder A is greater than the volume of cylinder B.

B. The volume of cylinder B is greater than the volume of cylinder A.

C. The volume of cylinder A is $\frac{4}{9}$ of what it was previously.

D. The volume of cylinder B is $\frac{1}{3}$ of what it was previously.

E. The volume of cylinder B is $\frac{2}{3}$ of what it was previously.

PG

12. Which of the following statements is true about the line shown below?

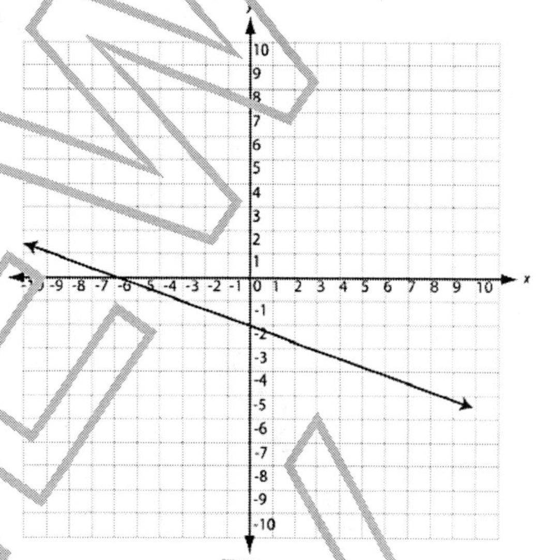

F. This line has a slope of $\frac{1}{3}$.
G. This line has a y-intercept of -6.
H. This line has an x-intercept of -2.
J. A line that is perpendicular to this line would have a slope of -3.
K. A line that is parallel to this line would have a slope of $-\frac{1}{3}$.

CG

13. So far Jessica has had scores of 72, 88, 90, and 92 on the tests in her algebra class. She has one more test to take, and she then has the option of choosing the mean, median, or mode of the scores to determine her grade. Which of the following choices would be in Jessica's best interest?

A. If her next score is 72, choose the mode.
B. If her next score is 72, choose the mean.
C. If her next score is 88, choose the mean.
D. If her next score is 92, choose the median.
E. If her next score is 92, choose the mode.

PA

14. If $x = 169$ and $y = 9$, then $\frac{\sqrt{y}}{\sqrt{x}} - \frac{\sqrt{x}}{y} =$

F. $-\frac{169}{117}$

G. $-\frac{142}{117}$

H. $-\frac{27}{117}$

J. $\frac{27}{117}$

K. 13

EA

15. Which of the following quadratic functions has the complex roots $3 + \frac{i}{2}$ and $3 - \frac{i}{2}$?

A. $f(x) = x^2 + 6x + 37$

B. $f(x) = x^2 - 6x + 37$

C. $f(x) = x^2 + 6x - \frac{37}{4}$

D. $f(x) = x^2 - 6x + \frac{37}{4}$

E. $f(x) = x^2 + 6x - 4$

EA

16. Peter and Paul are hunting for morel mushrooms in the forest, and they start out at the same spot. Peter walks 400 yards directly south, turns, and walks 600 yards directly west. Paul walks 300 yards directly east, turns, and walks 900 yards directly north. What is the distance between Peter and Paul?

F. $200\sqrt{13} + 300\sqrt{10}$ yards

G. 900 yards

H. 1300 yards

J. $500\sqrt{10}$

K. $300\sqrt{10}$ yards

CG

17. Which of the following is a counterexample to the statement, "The sum of the interior angles of any regular polygon is equal to that of any other regular polygon."

A. The sum of the exterior angles of any regular polygon is equal to 360°.

B. An exterior angle of a regular pentagon is equal to 72°

C. An interior angle of a regular decagon is equal to 144°.

D. The sum of the interior angles of a regular hexagon is equal to 720°.

E. The sum of the interior angles of an equilateral triangle is equal to 180°, while the sum of the interior angles of a square is equal to 360°.

PG

18. The curve shown below is the graph of which of the following trigonometric functions?

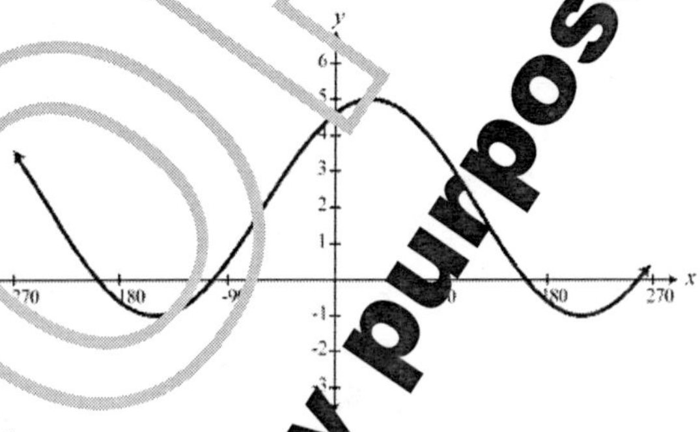

F. $f(x) = 3\sin(x - 30) + 2$

G. $f(x) = 3\cos(x - 30) + 2$

H. $f(x) = 3\sin(x + 30) + 2$

J. $f(x) = 3\cos(x + 30) + 2$

K. $f(x) = 3\cos(x - 30) - 2$

T

19. Whitney just read about a new scientific study, which revealed that for every 3 left-handed people, there are 32 right-handed people. If there are 1365 people in Whitney's school, how many can she expect to be left-handed based on the study?

A. 117
B. 118
C. 120
D. 127
E. 128

PA

20. Simplify: $\dfrac{y}{7x+1} \cdot \dfrac{3x-4}{y^3}$

F. $\dfrac{3x-4}{y^2(7x+1)}$

G. $\dfrac{y^2(7x+1)}{3x-4}$

H. $\dfrac{y^4}{21x^2-25x-4}$

J. $\dfrac{y^4}{21x^2-31x-4}$

K. $\dfrac{21x^2-25x-4}{y^4}$

EA

21. Sriram has written a computer program that randomly substitutes a value of x into a relation and produces one value for y. So far his computer program has generated the following data points:

$(5, 2), (10, -3), (17, -4), (37, 6), (65, -8)$

Which of the following data points produced by the computer program would show that the relation it is using is not a function?

A. $(1, 0)$
B. $(2, 1)$
C. $(26, -5)$
D. $(37, -6)$
E. $(50, 7)$

IA

22. Which of the following equations represents the circle shown below?

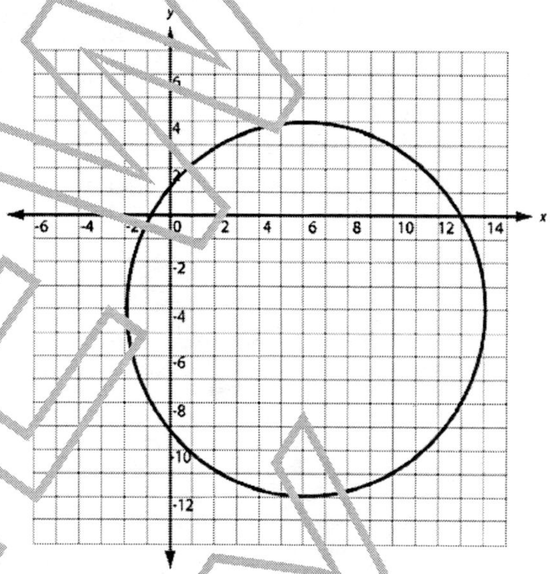

F. $\dfrac{x^2}{6} - \dfrac{y^2}{4} = 64$

G. $\dfrac{x^2}{6} + \dfrac{y^2}{4} = 64$

H. $(x^2+6)+(y^2-4)=64$
J. $(x+6)^2+(y-4)^2=64$
K. $(x-6)^2+(y+4)^2=64$

23. Which of the following three-dimensional geometric objects consists of the line segments joining a single point in space to every point on a circle, with the line segment joining the point in space to the center of the circle being perpendicular to the plane of the circle?

A. Triangular prism
B. Cone
C. Cylinder
D. Sphere
E. Cube

PG

24. A game show requires contestants to spin a circular wheel that is parallel to the ground. The pegs the contestants must grab to make their spins is along the circumference of the wheel. The following graph shows the distance a specific peg travels from the contestant versus the distance the peg travels total as the wheel rotates. What is the radius of the wheel?

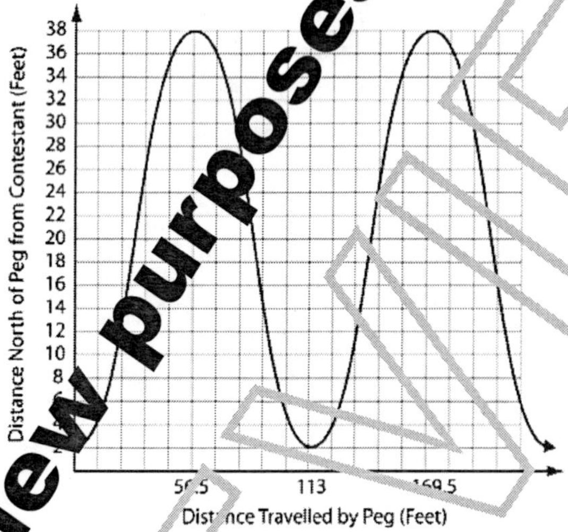

F. 18 feet
G. 19 feet
H. 38 feet
J. 56.5 feet
K. 113 feet

T

25. Which of the following groups of numbers is not in order from least to greatest?

A. $-\frac{7}{8}, -\frac{4}{5}, \frac{4}{5}, \frac{7}{8}, \frac{7}{6}$

B. $-\frac{21}{4}, -5, -\frac{18}{4}, -4, -\frac{15}{4}$

C. $\frac{1}{9}, \frac{1}{8}, \frac{1}{7}, \frac{1}{6}, \frac{1}{5}$

D. $-\frac{1}{24}, -\frac{1}{22}, -\frac{1}{20}, -\frac{1}{18}, -\frac{1}{16}$

E. $3, \frac{19}{5}, 4, \frac{25}{6}, 5$

PA

26. Leila, Lola, and Leiani collect butterflies. Leila has five times as many butterflies as Lola, and Lola has $\frac{2}{5}$ as many butterflies as Leiani. If Leila has b butterflies, how many butterflies does Leiani have?

F. $\frac{b}{5}$

G. $\frac{2b}{5}$

H. $\frac{b}{2}$

J. $2b$

K. $5b$

EA

27. $\begin{bmatrix} -13 & 2 \\ 5 & 8 \end{bmatrix} \times \begin{bmatrix} 3 & 6 \\ -7 & 11 \end{bmatrix} = ?$

A. $\begin{bmatrix} -53 & -41 \\ -56 & 118 \end{bmatrix}$

B. $\begin{bmatrix} -53 & -56 \\ -41 & 118 \end{bmatrix}$

C. $\begin{bmatrix} -41 & -53 \\ 118 & -56 \end{bmatrix}$

D. $\begin{bmatrix} -56 & -53 \\ 118 & -41 \end{bmatrix}$

E. Undefined

IA

28. If $|9x - 7| \leq 26$, which of the following statements is false?

F. $9x - 7 \leq 26$

G. $-(9x - 7) \leq 26$

H. $9x - 7 \geq -26$

J. $x \leq \frac{11}{3}$

K. $x \geq -\frac{19}{9}$

IA

29. A line and a plane exist in space. Which of the following scenarios is not possible?

A. The line and the plane do not intersect.
B. The line is contained in the plane.
C. The line is perpendicular to the plane.
D. The line and the plane intersect at one point.
E. The line and the plane intersect at two points.

PG

30. A high school decided to switch its school colors, so it sent out a survey to all of its 1600 students with the following choices:

1. Red and gold
2. Blue and gold
3. Blue and white
4. White and green

95 percent of the students responded, with 76 students choosing white and green. What percentage of the students who responded chose white and green?

F. 4.75 percent
G. 5 percent
H. 5.25 percent
J. 5.5 percent
K. 5.75 percent

PA

31. $\left(\dfrac{a^{-2}}{b^2c^{-1}} \times \dfrac{b^5c^{-2}}{a^4}\right)^{-4} = ?$

A. $\dfrac{b^{12}c^4}{a^{24}}$

B. $\dfrac{b^{12}}{a^{24}c^4}$

C. $\dfrac{a^{24}c^4}{b^{12}}$

D. $\dfrac{a^{24}}{b^{12}c^4}$

E. $\dfrac{c^4}{a^{24}b^{12}}$

EA

32. Which of the following inequalities is represented by the graph shown below?

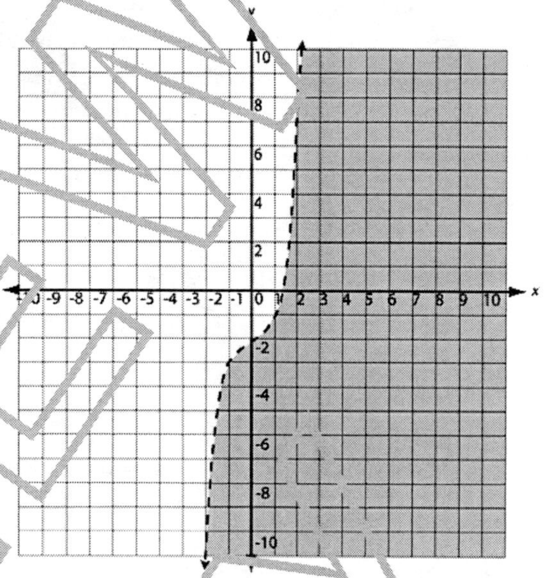

F. $y < x^2 - 2$
G. $y > x^2 - 2$
H. $y < x^3 - 2$
J. $y > x^3 - 2$
K. $y > x^3 + 2$

CG

33. Astronomers have computed the length of Neptune's semi-major axis to be 4,503,443,661 km. Which of the following values best represents the length of Neptune's semi-major axis in scientific notation?

A. 4.5×10^9 km
B. 4.5×10^{10} km
C. 4.5×10^{11} km
D. 4.5×10^{-9} km
E. 4.5×10^{-10} km

PA

34. An isosceles trapezoid is a four-sided geometric figure with one pair of parallel sides and one pair of non-parallel, congruent sides. If one of the internal angles of an isosceles trapezoid measures 79 degrees, what are the measures of its other internal angles?

F. 90°, 90°, and 101°
G. 79°, 79°, and 123°
H. 79°, 101°, and 101°
J. 11°, 135°, and 135°
K. 90°, 95.5°, and 95.5°

PG

35. Each of four convenience stores is located at the midpoint of a line segment joining two towns. The first convenience store is between the towns of Westerville and South Hampton, the second is between South Hampton and North Liberty, the third is between Easton and Westerville, and the fourth is between North Liberty and Easton. Based on the map shown below, which of the following points does not represent one of the convenience stores?

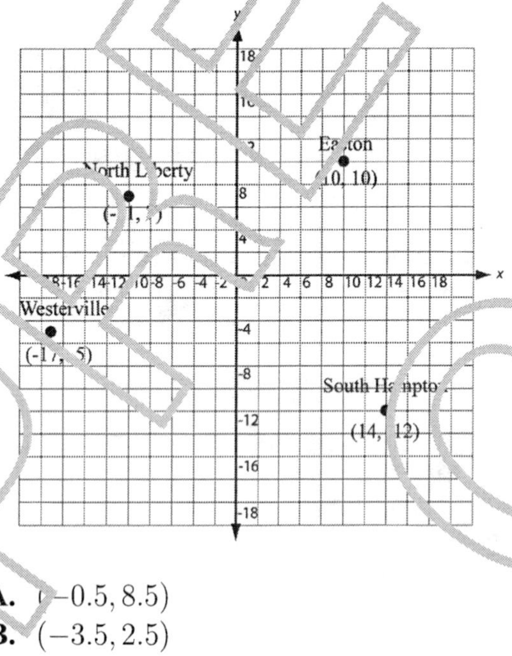

A. $(-0.5, 8.5)$
B. $(-3.5, 2.5)$
C. $(1.5, -2.5)$
D. $(0.5, -8.5)$
E. $(-1.5, -8.5)$

CG

36. Bradley computed the product of 3 and $\sqrt{5}$ with his calculator by pressing the appropriate keys and then pressing the = key. He noticed that when he pressed the = key a second time, the product of 3 and $\sqrt{5}$ that he had already computed was multiplied by $\sqrt{5}$ again. He then pressed the = key some more times, and the pattern continued. After Bradley pressed the = key a total of eight times (including the first time), what number was showing on his calculator's screen?

F. 375
G. 625
H. 1875
J. 390, 625
K. 1, 171, 875

EA

37. The following bar graph shows the percent increase in sales of a company over the previous year for the years 2001 through 2006.

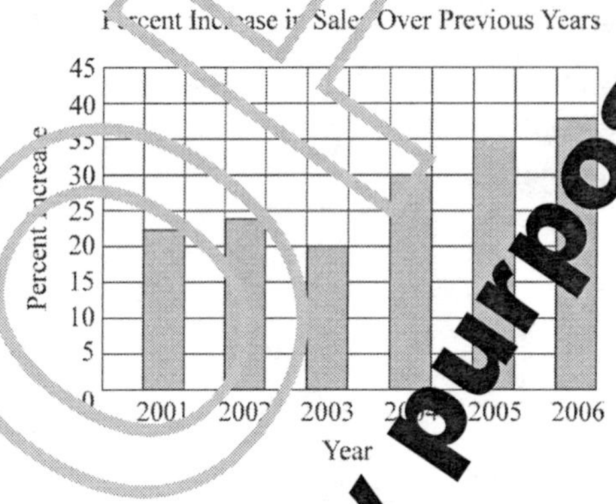

Which of the following conclusions cannot be drawn from the graph?

A. Sales increased from 2003 to 2004.
B. Sales did not decrease from 2001 to 2002.
C. Sales increased from 2005 to 2006.
D. Sales did not decrease from 2000 to 2001.
E. Sales did not decrease from 2002 to 2003.

PA

38. Which of the following equations could possibly represent the ellipse shown below?

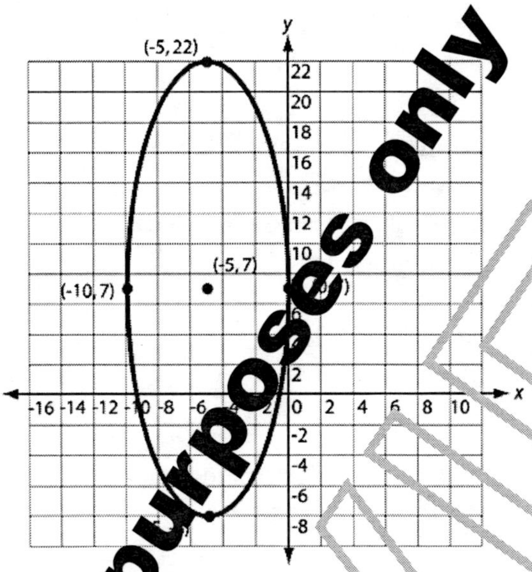

F. $(x+5)^2 + (y-7)^2 = 225$

G. $\frac{(x-5)^2}{25} + \frac{(y-7)^2}{225} = 1$

H. $\frac{(x+5)^2}{25} + \frac{(y+7)^2}{225} = 1$

J. $\frac{(x+5)^2}{25} + \frac{(y-7)^2}{225} = 1$

K. $\frac{(x-5)^2}{25} + \frac{(y+7)^2}{225} = 1$

CG

39. When the diagonals of a parallelogram are drawn, four triangles are formed. For any of the four triangles, how many of the other three triangles must be congruent to it? Hint: All rectangles are parallelograms, and all squares are rectangles.

A. Zero
B. At least one
C. Exactly one
D. At least two
E. Exactly three

PG

40. Solve for x:

$2(x+5) + 4(2x-1) = -14$

F. $x = -1\frac{1}{2}$
G. $x = -2$
H. $x = -1$
J. $x = -1\frac{4}{5}$
K. $x = -1\frac{2}{10}$

PA

41. To solve the quadratic equation $\frac{7}{12}x - x^2 = -1$, an algebra student went through a number of steps. Which of the following equations could not be the result of one of those steps?

A. $x^2 - \frac{7}{12}x = 1$
B. $12x^2 - 7x = -12$
C. $x^2 - \frac{7}{12}x - 1 = 0$
D. $12x^2 - 7x - 12 = 0$
E. $(3x-4)(4x+3) = 0$

EA

42. An e-retailer has a total of 150 food items listed in its catalog. 30 percent of the items are different varieties of jams, 20 percent are varieties of syrups, 40 percent are varieties of nuts, and 10 percent are varieties of cheeses. If a gift basket consists of one choice each of jam, syrup, nut, and cheese, how many possible gift baskets does the e-retailer offer?

F. $12,150$
G. $24,000$
H. $121,500$
J. $240,000$
K. $1,215,000$

PA

43. The following graph was constructed to help solve the quadratic inequality $x^2 - x - 42 < 0$. Which of the following conclusions can be drawn?

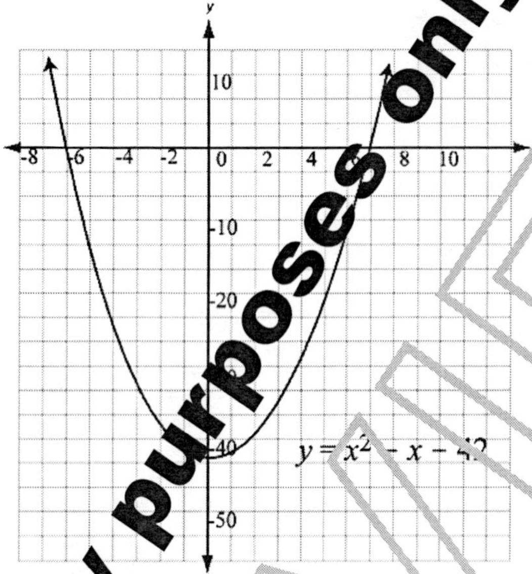

A. Because the parabola is below the x-axis between $x = -6$ and $x = 7$, the solution is $x < -6$ and $x > 7$.
B. Because the parabola is below the x-axis between $x = -6$ and $x = 7$, the solution is $-6 < x < 7$.
C. Because the parabola intersects the x-axis at $x = -6$ and $x = 7$, the solution is $x = -6$ and $x = 7$.
D. Because the parabola is above the x-axis when $x < -6$ and $x > 7$, the solution is $x < -6$ and $x > 7$.
E. Because the parabola is above the x-axis when $x < -7$ and $x > 6$, the solution is $x < -7$ and $x > 6$.

IA

44. $(8.16 \times 10^{-3}) + (8.16 \times 10^{-4}) + (8.16 \times 10^{-5}) = ?$

F. 0.000000000000816
G. 0.00000000000816
H. 0.000090576
J. 0.00090576
K. 0.0090576

PA

45. The relations $x = 6y^2 + 5$, $x = 6y^2 - 5$, $x = -6y^2 - 5$, $y = 6x^2 + 5$, and $y = -6x^2 - 5$ are graphed on a coordinate grid. Which of the relations has a graph that lies in all four quadrants?

A. all of the relations except $y = 6x^2 + 5$ and $y = -6x^2 - 5$
B. $y = 6x^2 + 5$ and $y = -6x^2 - 5$
C. only $x = 6y^2 - 5$
D. $x = 6y^2 + 5, x = 6y^2 - 5$, and $y = 6x^2 + 5$
E. only $y = -6x^2 - 5$

CG

46. What can be determined about the two triangles shown below?

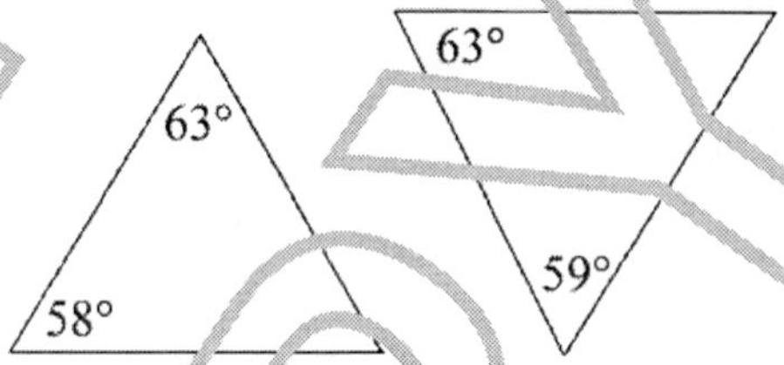

F. They are similar.
G. They are congruent.
H. They are equilateral.
J. They are isosceles.
K. Nothing.

47. Ryan is using the quadratic formula to find the roots of a quadratic equation. After he plugged the appropriate numbers into the formula, he was left with the following:

$$x = \frac{-6 \pm \sqrt{6^2 - 4(11)(-1)}}{2(11)}$$

For which of the following quadratic equations is Ryan finding the roots?

A. $11x^2 - 6x - 1 = 0$
B. $11x^2 + 6x - 1 = 0$
C. $11x^2 - 6x + 1 = 0$
D. $11x^2 + 6x - 4 = 0$
E. $11x^2 - 6x - 4 = 0$

IA

48. Which of the following statements accurately describes the lines $y = \frac{1}{5}x + 1$, $y = -\frac{1}{2}x + 8$, and $y = 2x - 17$?

F. All three lines intersect at a point in the first quadrant.
G. All three lines intersect at a point in the second quadrant.
H. All three lines intersect at a point in the third quadrant.
J. All three lines intersect at a point in the fourth quadrant.
K. The three lines do not all intersect at one point.

CG

49. A large, rectangular public aquarium has been built with a tunnel in the shape of a half cylinder going through it so that people may view the marine life. The aquarium has a height of 40 meters, a width of 60 meters, and a length of 30 meters, while the tunnel has a maximum height of 15 meters. A cross-section of the aquarium appears as follows:

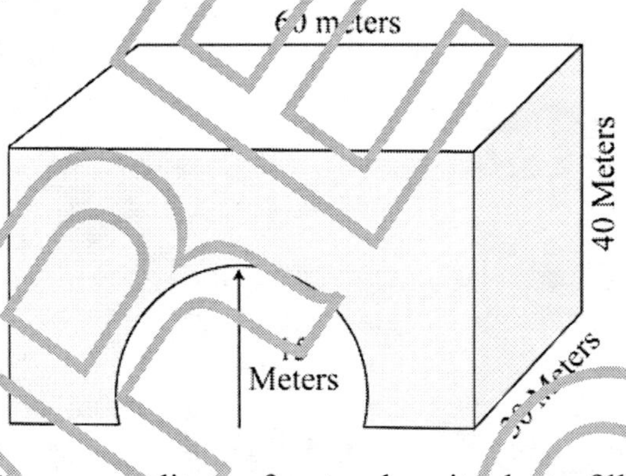

How many liters of water does it take to fill the aquarium if the space taken up by the objects inside of it is not taken into account? ($1\text{ L} = 0.001\text{ m}^3$)

A. $72,000 - 6750\pi$
B. $72,000 - 3375\pi$
C. $72,000,000 - 6,750,000\pi$
D. $72,000,000 - 3,375,000\pi$
E. $72,000,000 - 450,000\pi$

PG

50. If 8 percent of the cars sold in a particular country are hybrid cars, what is the ratio of hybrid cars sold to non-hybrid cars sold?

F. $23 : 2$
G. $25 : 2$
H. $25 : 8$
J. $2 : 23$
K. $2 : 25$

PA

51. In three dimensions, which of the following scenarios is not possible for two lines?

A. They are not parallel and intersect.
B. They are not parallel and do not intersect.
C. They are parallel and intersect.
D. They are parallel and do not intersect.
E. They are perpendicular and intersect.

PG

52. The amount of an annuity can be determined with the following formula:

$$A = \frac{R[(1+i)^n - 1]}{i}$$

Where A is the amount, R is the regular deposit, i is the interest rate per compounding period, and n is the total number of deposits. If annual deposits of \$100 are made into an annuity for 3 years at 10% compounded annually, what is the amount of the annuity?

F. \$133.10
G. \$300
H. \$330
J. \$331
K. \$399.30

PA

53. A rectangle has a base measuring 16 units and a height measuring 6 units. If it is translated 3 units down and 2 units to the right, what will be its area?

A. 42 units^2
B. 52 units^2
C. 96 units^2
D. 104 units^2
E. 126 units^2

PG

54. Edna and her young son are rearranging their living room, which has a clock hanging normally from the wall. Edna tells her son, "Please rotate that clock hanging on the wall counterclockwise 90 degrees about the point that is 10 inches directly left of the 9." Edna's son is a good boy and does as he is told. Which of the numbers on the clock is now highest on the wall?

F. 3
G. 6
H. 9
J. 10
K. 12

PG

55. Which of the following expressions is not rational?

A. $\frac{-9}{\sqrt{196}} - 15.43$

B. $14.106735979665 - \frac{22}{7}$

C. $\frac{289}{\sqrt{289}} \times -\frac{7}{\sqrt{324}}$

D. $3.141592653589 \div \frac{1}{3}$

E. $\frac{1}{7} + 8.185352771872\ldots$

IA

56. $\left(\frac{64^{\frac{1}{3}}}{4^{\frac{3}{2}}}\right)^{-5} = ?$

F. $\frac{1}{32}$

G. $\frac{1}{16}$

H. $\frac{1}{8}$

J. 16

K. 32

EA

57. What is the value of $\frac{98x^2 - 162}{49x^2 - 126x + 81} \div \frac{49x^2 + 126x + 81}{7x + 9}$?

A. $\frac{1}{7x+9}$

B. $\frac{2}{7x+9}$

C. $\frac{1}{7x-9}$

D. $\frac{2}{7x-9}$

E. $\frac{7x-9}{2}$

58. A piece of hard candy in the shape of a small sphere has a spherical chocolate ball at its center. If the radius of the piece of candy is 3 centimeters, and the radius of the chocolate ball at its center is 1 centimeter, what is the ratio of the volume of the non-chocolate part of the candy to the volume of the chocolate part?

F. 2 : 1
G. 9 : 4
H. 3 : 1
J. 26 : 1
K. 27 : 1

PG

59. Which of the following arguments is not enough to prove that a right triangle has an angle measuring 90 degrees?

A. If it does not have an angle measuring 90 degrees, it is not a right triangle.

B. If it is a right triangle, it has two sides that are perpendicular. If it has two sides that are perpendicular, it has an angle measuring 90 degrees.

C. A right triangle has an external angle measuring 90 degrees. An external angle and its adjacent internal angle are supplementary.

D. A certain polygon has an angle measuring 90 degrees. A right triangle is a polygon.

E. If it is a right triangle, it adheres to the Pythagorean Theorem. If it adheres to the Pythagorean Theorem, it has an angle measuring 90 degrees.

PG

60. What is the prime factorization of the number 39,312?

F. $2^4 \times 3^3 \times 7 \times 13$

G. $2^4 \times 3 \times 7 \times 9 \times 13$

H. $2^5 \times 3^3 \times \frac{7}{2} \times 13$

J. $3 \times 7 \times 9 \times 13 \times 16$

K. $3^3 \times 4^2 \times 7 \times 13$

PA

Evaluation Chart for the Diagnostic Mathematics Test

Directions: On the following chart, circle the question numbers that you answered incorrectly. Then turn to the appropriate topics (listed by chapters), read the explanations, and complete the exercises. Review the other chapters as needed. Finally, complete ***ACT Mathematics Test Preparation Guide*** Practice Tests for further review.

		Questions	Pages
Chapter 2:	Pre-Algebra Review	1, 25, 30, 55, 60	22–42
Chapter 3:	Exponents and Square Roots	14, 31, 33, 36, 44, 56	43–55
Chapter 4:	Solving Multi-Step Equations, Inequalities, and Patterns	3, 28, 40	56–79
Chapter 5:	Ratios and Proportions	7, 19, 50	80–85
Chapter 6:	Matrices	27	86–100
Chapter 7:	Polynomials		101–107
Chapter 8:	Factoring	6, 20, 57	108–117
Chapter 9:	Solving Quadratic Equations and Inequalities	2, 15, 41, 47	118–133
Chapter 10:	Relations and Functions	21, 52	134–157
Chapter 11:	Graphing and Writing Linear Equations and Inequalities	12, 35	158–173
Chapter 12:	Applications of Linear Graphs	12	174–184
Chapter 13:	Graphing Non-Linear Equations	10, 22, 32, 38, 43, 45	185–204
Chapter 14:	Systems of Equations and Systems of Inequalities	26, 48	205–222
Chapter 15:	Statistics	13, 37	223–231
Chapter 16:	Probability and Counting	9, 42	232–243
Chapter 17:	Angles	29, 51	244–251
Chapter 18:	Triangles	16, 46	252–263
Chapter 19:	Plane Geometry	17, 34, 39, 53	264–281
Chapter 20:	Solid Geometry	11, 23, 49, 58	282–296
Chapter 21:	Logic and Geometric Proofs	59	297–304
Chapter 22:	Transformations	5, 54	305–318
Chapter 23:	Trigonometry	4, 8, 18, 24	319–341

Chapter 1
About The ACT Mathematics Test

1.1 Description of the ACT Math Test

The ACT Mathematics Test is a 60-item, 60-minute test. The following six categories represent content areas of the ACT Mathematics Test commonly taught by the end of grade 11 that are important to success in entry-level college mathematics courses:

- **Pre-Algebra**
- **Elementary Algebra**
- **Intermediate Algebra**
- **Coordinate Geometry**
- **Plane Geometry**
- **Trigonometry**

You will receive a score for all 60 questions and three subscores: a Pre-Algebra/Elementary Algebra subscore based on 24 questions, an Intermediate Algebra/Coordinate Geometry subscore based on 18 questions, and a Plane Geometry/Trigonometry subscore based on 18 questions.

The problems assume knowledge of basic formulas and computational skills but do not require memorization of complex formulas or extensive computation. The material covered on the test emphasizes the major content areas that are prerequisite to successful performance in entry-level courses in college mathematics. The test offers a wide range of questions to ensure that students continually will be challenged with new situations.

The items in the ACT Mathematics Test cover four cognitive levels: **knowledge and skills**, , **understanding concepts** and **integrating conceptual understanding**. **Knowledge and skills items** require the student to use one or more facts, definitions, formulas, or procedures to solve straightforward problems set in real-world situations. **Direct application items** are word problems from everyday life that need mathematics to solve. **Understanding concepts items** test the student's depth of understanding major concepts by requiring reasoning from a concept to reach an inference or a conclusion. **Integrating conceptual understanding items** test the student's ability to achieve an integrated understanding of two or more major concepts to solve nonroutine problems. The approximate percentage of the test devoted to each cognitive level is given in the table below. The number of questions in each cognitive level may vary slightly from the number of questions shown in the table.

ACT Mathematics Test Cognitive Levels

Cognitive Level	**Proportion of Test**	**Number of Items**
Knowledge and Skills	0.50	30
Direct Application	0.28	17
Understanding Concepts, Integrating Conceptual Understanding	0.22	13
Total	1.00	**60**

1.2 Content of the Test

Items are classified according to the six content areas mentioned in the previous section. These categories and the approximate proportion of the test devoted to each are given in the following table.

ACT Mathematics Test 60 items, 60 minutes		
Content Area	**Proportion of Test**	**Number of Items**
Pre-Algebra	0.23	14
Elementary Algebra	0.17	10
Intermediate Algebra	0.15	9
Coordinate Geometry	0.15	9
Plane Geometry	0.23	14
Trigonometry	0.07	4
Total	**1.00**	**60**

1. **Pre-Algebra.** Items in this content area are based on basic operations using whole numbers, decimals, fractions, and integers; place value; square roots and approximations; the concept of exponents; scientific notation; factors; ratio, proportion, and percent; linear equations in one variable; absolute value and ordering numbers by value; elementary counting techniques and simple probability; data collection, representation, and interpretation; and understanding simple descriptive statistics.

2. **Elementary Algebra.** Items in this content area are based on properties of exponents and square roots, evaluation of algebraic expressions through substitution, using variables to express functional relationships, understanding algebraic operations, and solving quadratic equations by factoring.

3. **Intermediate Algebra.** Items in this content area are based on an understanding of the quadratic formula, rational and radical expressions, absolute value equations and inequalities, sequences and patterns, systems of equations, quadratic inequalities, functions, modeling, matrices, roots of polynomials, and complex numbers.

4. **Coordinate Geometry.** Items is this content area are based on graphing and the relations between equations and graphs, including points, lines, polynomials, circles, and other curves; graphing inequalities; slope; parallel and perpendicular lines; distance; midpoints; and conics.

5. **Plane Geometry**. Items in this content area are based on the properties and relations of plane figures, including angles and relations among perpendicular and parallel lines; properties of circles, triangles, rectangles, parallelograms, and trapezoids; transformations; the concept of proof and proof techniques; volume; and applications of geometry to three dimensions.

6. **Trigonometry**. Items in this content area are based on understanding trigonometric relations in right triangles; values and properties of trigonometric functions; graphing trigonometric functions; modeling using trigonometric functions; use of trigonometric identities; and solving trigonometric equations.

1.3 Frequently Asked Questions

What is the ACT?

The ACT is a national college admission examination which is accepted by virtually all US colleges and universities. The exam measures the knowledge, understanding, and skills that you have gained throughout your education.

How long is the exam?

The full ACT includes 215 multiple-choice questions and takes approximately three hours and thirty minutes to complete (just over four hours if you are taking the optional Writing Test). Actual testing time is two hours and fifty-five minutes (plus thirty minutes if you are taking the Writing Test).The exam has four sections: English, Math, Reading, and Science.

When do I take the ACT?

The ACT is administered in October, December, February, April, and June (in some states, it is also offered in September). When you take the ACT will depend on both when you feel ready and when you need test scores to include with applications to colleges.

Is there a fee?

Yes. The basic registration fee (currently $30.00 for the basic test or $44.50 if also taking the writing test) includes score reports for up to four colleges for which a valid code is listed at the time that you register.

For more details about the ACT, please visit ACT, Inc. at www.actstudent.org.

1.4 ACT Preparation

The ACT measures your overall learning, so if you have paid attention in school, you should do well. It would be difficult to "cram" for an exam as comprehensive as this. However, you can study wisely by using an ACT-specific guide and practice answering questions of the type that will be asked on the ACT.

Believe in yourself! Attitude plays a big part in how well you do in anything. Keep your thoughts positive. Tell yourself you will do well on the exam.

Be prepared. Get a good night's sleep the day before your exam. Eat a well-balanced meal, one that contains plenty of proteins and carbohydrates, prior to your exam.

Arrive early. Allow yourself at least 15-20 minutes to find your room and get settled. Then you can relax before the exam, and you won't feel rushed.

Practice relaxation techniques. Many students become stressed, and they begin to worry too much about the exam. They may perspire heavily, experience upset stomach, or have shortness of breath. If you feel any of these symptoms, talk to a close friend or see your counselor. They will suggest ways to deal with your test anxiety.

1.5 Taking the ACT Mathematics Test

Read the instructions on the ACT test booklet carefully. To ensure that you will understand the instructions, you can read them at www.actstudent.org prior to taking the test.

Once you are told that you may open the booklet, read the directions thoroughly for the test before beginning to mark your answers.

Read each question carefully enough so that you know what you're trying to find, and use your best approach for answering the questions.

Use your calculator wisely and sparingly. Remember, some problems can be solved without using a calculator. In fact, some of the problems are best done without a calculator. Use good judgment to decide whether or not you need to use your calculator.

Solve the problems. For working out the solutions to the problems, you may usually do scratch work in the space provided in the test booklet, or you will be given scratch paper to use.

Answer every question on the exam. Your score is based on the number of questions you answer correctly. There is no penalty for guessing and no penalty for wrong answers, but every spot left blank is an automatic zero. A guess has a 20% chance of being correct, whereas a blank has no chance of being correct. So, if you are unsure about an answer, take an educated guess. Eliminate choices that are definitely wrong, and then choose from the remaining answers.

Use your answer key correctly. Make sure the number on your question matches the number on your answer sheet. If you need to change an answer, erase it completely. Use a number two pencil. The computerized scanner may skip over answers that are too light so make sure the answers are dark.

Check your answers. Make sure your answers make sense. If you finish the test before time is called, review your exam to make sure you have chosen the best responses. Change answers only if you are sure they are wrong.

Be sure to pace yourself. Since you will have a limited amount of time, be careful not to spend too much time on one problem, leaving no time to complete the rest of the test. Keep an eye on the clock to make sure that you are working at a pace that will allow you to finish the test in the 60 minutes given. Listen for announcement of five minutes remaining on the test.

When time is called for the test, put your pencil down. If you continue to write or erase, you run the risk of being dismissed and your test being disqualified from scoring.

1.6 Types of Questions on the ACT Mathematics Test

The content of the ACT Mathematics Test will vary. The questions vary in difficulty and complexity. The type of questions include basic math problems, basic math problems in settings, very challenging problems, and question sets.

Basic Math Problems

Basic math problems are simple and straightforward. They usually have very few words, no extra information, and a numeric solution. Question 1 is an example of a basic pre-algebra math problem.

1. What is 6% of $1,000$?

   A. 6
   B. 6.6
   C. 60
   D. 66
   E. 660

This problem has few words, a direct question is asked, and its answer is numeric. The solution is simple: change 6% to a decimal and multiply by $1,000$ to get $(0.06)(1,000) = 60$ (**C**).

Basic Math Problems in Settings

Basic math problems in settings are often called **word problems** or **story problems**. They describe situations from everyday life where you need to apply mathematics to find an answer to a question. Question 2 is an example of a basic elementary algebra problem in a setting.

2. The relationship between temperature expressed in degrees Fahrenheit (F) and degrees Celsius (C) is given by the formula

   $F = \frac{9}{5}C + 32$

   If the temperature is 50 degrees Fahrenheit, what is the degrees Celsius?

   F. 0°
   G. 10°
   H. 20°
   J. 30°
   K. 40°

In this problem, you're given an equation between temperatures expressed in degrees Fahrenheit (F) and degrees Celsius (C). You're also given a temperature of 50 degrees Fahrenheit and asked what that temperature would be in degrees Celsius. First, you would substitute 50 into the given equation in place of F. Now you must solve the equation $50 = \frac{9}{5}C + 32$ in order to find C. It would be wise to check your answer before moving on to the next problem. The answer should be C $= 10°$ (**G**). By putting 10 in for C, multiplying it by $\frac{9}{5}$ and then adding 32, the answer should be 50.

Very Challenging Problems

These problems are not like the problems you usually see. They test your ability to reason and appear in all different forms. These challenging problems will show up in all six categories of the test. Question 3 is an example of a very challenging intermediate algebra problem.

3. If $\left(\frac{2}{5}\right)^x = \sqrt{\left(\frac{5}{2}\right)^3}$, then $x = ?$

   A. $\frac{2}{3}$
   B. $\frac{3}{2}$
   C. $-\frac{2}{3}$
   D. $-\frac{3}{2}$
   E. $\frac{1}{2}$

In this problem, you are asked to find the value of x. Remember that the square root is the same as $\frac{1}{2}$ power. After using properties of exponents, put the left side in the same form of the right side, $\sqrt{\left(\frac{5}{2}\right)^3} = \left(\left(\frac{5}{2}\right)^3\right)^{\frac{1}{2}} = \left(\frac{5}{2}\right)^{\frac{3}{2}}$. Both sides are now in the same form, but the bases are not the same, they're reciprocals. Using the connection between reciprocals and exponents, we know that taking the opposite of the exponent will flip the base. This means $\left(\frac{5}{2}\right)^{\frac{3}{2}} = \left(\frac{2}{5}\right)^{-\frac{3}{2}}$. So with $\left(\frac{2}{5}\right)^x = \left(\frac{2}{5}\right)^{-\frac{3}{2}}$, $x = -\frac{3}{2}$ (D).

Question Sets

The test contains sets of questions that all relate to the same information. There are usually two question sets on the test, with two or four questions on each set. Questions 4–5 show a group of questions that use the same information. This is called a question set.

Use the following information to answer questions 4 and 5.

The city of Seneca, South Carolina is adding a swimming pool to its park. The dimensions of the pool are shown in the diagram below.

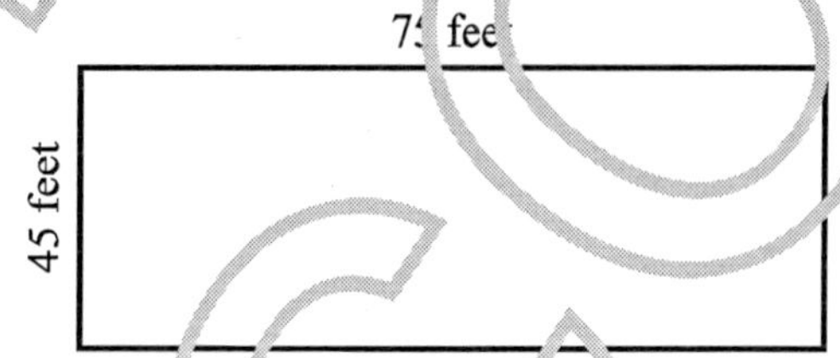

4. The park service commissioners are planning on putting up a fence around the pool. They want the fence to be set 40 feet out from the edge of the pool all the way around the pool. How many feet of fencing will they need?

   F. 240 feet
   G. 280 feet
   H. 400 feet
   J. 560 feet
   K. 620 feet

5. The park officials also want to pour concrete between the pool and the fence. How many square feet of concrete would be between the pool and the fence?

   A. 3,375 ft^2
   B. 6,400 ft^2
   C. 16,000 ft^2
   D. 19,375 ft^2
   E. 6,400 ft^2

Question 4 requires you to find the length of the fence. To find this you need to add 40 to all four sides of the pool. The new width would be $45+40+40=125$ feet. (Remember, you must add 40 to both sides of the width.) The new length is $75+40+40=155$ feet. Then substitute your new values for the length and width into the formula for perimeter: $P=2l+2w=2(155)+2(125)=560$ feet (**J**).

Question 5 requires you to find the area between the pool and the fence. To find this, you must find the area enclosed by the fence, and then subtract the area of the pool. Using your dimensions of the fence, find the area inside the fence. $A=lw=155\times125=19,375$ ft^2. Then use the dimensions of the pool to find the area of the pool. $A=lw=75\times45=3,375$ ft^2. Now subtract the area of the pool from the fenced in area to find the area between the pool and fence. $19,375$ $ft^2-3,375$ $ft^2=16,000$ ft^2 (**C**).

The diagnostic test at the beginning and two practice tests at the end of the book are simulated ACT tests. They are the same length and contain questions comparable to those you will see on the ACT. Review your scores on the diagnostic test and the practice tests with your teacher or tutor to determine if there are skill areas you need to focus on before taking the ACT.

For practice with other sections of the ACT, refer to these titles from American Book Company:

ACT English Test Preparation Guide
ACT Reading Test Preparation Guide
ACT Science Test Preparation Guide

Chapter 2
Pre-Algebra Review

2.1 Number Systems Review

Write the value of the number 4.

1. 14   2. 4,689.108   3. 12,047,622

Use the number below to answer the following questions.
425,006
Which number is in the

4. Tens place?   5. Ones place?   6. Hundred thousands place?

Find the opposite of the numbers below.

7. -42 8. $\frac{1}{16}$ 9. $-\frac{5}{8}$ 10. 26.1

Find the reciprocal of the following numbers.

11. -3 12. 5   13. $\frac{4}{5}$ 14. -72

Identify the following numbers as rational (R) or irrational (I).

15. $\sqrt{42}$ 16. 7.8383   17. 16π 18. $\sqrt{64}$

Find the GCF of each set of numbers.

19. $18, 27$ 20. $14, 21$ 21. $18, 45$ 22. $16, 28$

Find the LCM of each set of numbers.

23. $9, 6$ 24. $18, 30$ 25. $12, 15$ 26. $16, 64$

Solve the following absolute value problems.

27. $|4|$ 28. $|-6|$ 29. $|-3| + |7|$ 30. $|-2| - |-6|$ 31. $|8| - |-5|$

Solve the following word problems.

32. Concession stand sales for a football game totaled $1,563. The actual cost for the food and beverages was $395. How much profit did the concession stand make?

33. Use a factor tree to find the prime factorization of 96.

34. Tom has 155 head of cattle. Each eats 8 pounds of grain per day. How many pounds of grain does Tom need to feed his cattle for 10 days?

35. When you grind [illegible] cups of grain, you get 5 cups of flour. How many cups of grain must you grind to get 40 cups of flour?

36. The Beta Club is raising money by selling boxes of candy. It sold 152 boxes on Monday, 236 boxes on Tuesday, 107 boxes on Wednesday, and 93 boxes on Thursday. How many total boxes did the Beta Club sell?

37. Mrs. Jones waters the plants on her porch every 5 days. She waters the vegetable garden every 2 days. If she waters them both today, how many days will pass before she will water both of them on the same day again?

38. Katey passed around a plate of cookies to 4 friends. Before the party she ate 4 cookies and dropped 2. When Katey passed the cookies, her first friend took one cookie, the second friend took 2, and so on. When the plate came back around to Katey there was 1 cookie left. How many cookies did Katey start with?

39. Mr. Gonzalez opened a new account in April with $100. He recorded the following deposits in April: $45, $57, $69. He recorded the following withdrawals: −$[illegible], −$9, −$17. What is his balance after these transactions?

40. Brittany measured the temperature of the liquid in the beaker and found it to be 22°C. During her experiment, she recorded the following temperature changes: +7, +2, +1, −1, −4. What was the temperature of the liquid at the end of her experiment?

2.2 Number Systems Test

1. The common factors of 45 and 60 are:

   A. $\{1, 2, 3, 4, 5, 20, 30, 45, 60\}$
   B. $\{1, 3, 5, 15\}$
   C. $\{1, 3, 5, 15, 45\}$
   D. $\{1, 2, 3, 4, 5, 6, 9, 15, 20, 30, 45, 60\}$
   E. $\{1, 2, 3, 5\}$

2. Anna and Josh are putting up lights for a party. For every 4 blue lights, they put up 2 red lights. If they put up 120 lights, how many are blue?

   F. 30
   G. 40
   H. 80
   J. 100
   K. 140

3. During the summer months, one ice cream truck visits Madeline's neighborhood every [illegible] days, and another ice cream truck visits her neighborhood every 5 days. If both trucks visited today, when is the next time both trucks will visit on the same day?

   A. in 20 days
   B. in 5 days
   C. in 8 days
   D. in 2 days
   E. in 15 days

4. Robert's teacher assigns math homework due every 2 days and vocabulary homework due every 4 days. If he turned in both assignments today, how many days until he will have to turn in both again?

   F. [illegible] days
   G. 6 days
   H. 4 days
   J. 8 days
   K. none of the above

5. What is the smallest number that has 4 different prime factors (not including 1)?

   A. 60
   B. 210
   C. 6
   D. 30
   E. 120

6. What is the LCM of 7 and 3?

   F. 1
   G. 10
   H. 21
   J. 42
   K. 63

7. What is the prime factorization of 245?

   A. 5×72
   B. 52×7
   C. $5 \times 7 \times 7$
   D. $5 \times 3 \times 7$
   E. $5 \times 3 \times 7 \times 7$

8. What is the GCF of 12 and 33?

   F. 66
   G. 9
   H. 6
   J. 3
   K. 7

9. What is the place value of the underlined digit?

   4,[illegible]19,612

   A. millions
   B. ten-thousands
   C. hundreds
   D. thousands
   E. hundred-thousands

10. Which pair contains an even and an odd number?

- **F.** 106 and 48
- **G.** 205 and 37
- **H.** 444 and 555
- **J.** 360 and 440
- **K.** 465 and 917

11. What is the opposite of -9?

- **A.** 9
- **B.** $\frac{1}{9}$
- **C.** -9
- **D.** $-\frac{1}{9}$
- **E.** 3

12. What is the reciprocal of $\frac{1}{3}$?

- **F.** $-\frac{1}{3}$
- **G.** -3
- **H.** $\frac{1}{3}$
- **J.** -9
- **K.** 3

13. $|-55| \div -5 =$

- **A.** 11
- **B.** -11
- **C.** 50
- **D.** -60
- **E.** -275

14. Which of the following numbers is irrational?

- **F.** $\sqrt{169}$
- **G.** $\sqrt{100}$
- **H.** 7π
- **J.** $\frac{1}{3}$
- **K.** 17.984

15. Mrs. Campbell's 5th grade class is going on a field trip. There are 29 children in the class. Parents are driving, and there will be 4 students per car. What is the smallest number of cars they will need for the children?

- **A.** 6
- **B.** 7
- **C.** 8
- **D.** 9
- **E.** 10

16. Jed has 155 head of cattle. Each eats 31 pounds of silage every day. How much silage does Jed feed his cattle every day?

- **F.** 5 lb
- **G.** 186 lb
- **H.** 3,705 lb
- **J.** 4,705 lb
- **K.** 4,805 lb

17. Jerry set up 18 rows of chairs and put 9 chairs in each row. How many chairs did he set up?

- **A.** 18
- **B.** 27
- **C.** 81
- **D.** 162
- **E.** 189

18. Eric's mom drove 11 miles each way to bring Eric to school in the morning and back home in the afternoon. How many miles did she drive for 10 days of school?

- **F.** 110 miles
- **G.** 220 miles
- **H.** 330 miles
- **J.** 440 miles
- **K.** 550 miles

2.3 Fraction and Decimal Review

Perform the following operations and simplify.

1. $\frac{5}{9} + \frac{7}{9}$
2. $7\frac{1}{2} + 3\frac{3}{8}$
3. $4\frac{4}{15} + \frac{1}{5}$
4. $\frac{1}{7} + \frac{3}{7}$
5. $10 - 5\frac{1}{8}$
6. $3\frac{1}{3} -$ [illegible]
7. $9\frac{3}{4} - 2\frac{3}{8}$
8. [illegible] $1\frac{3}{10}$
9. $1\frac{1}{3} \times 3\frac{1}{2}$
10. $5\frac{[illegible]}{7} \times \frac{7}{8}$
11. $4\frac{[illegible]}{6} \times 1\frac{5}{[illegible]}$
12. $\frac{2}{[illegible]} \times \frac{5}{6}$
13. $\frac{1}{2} \div \frac{4}{5}$
14. $6\frac{6}{7} \div 2\frac{2}{3}$
15. $3\frac{5}{6} \div 11\frac{1}{2}$
16. $1\frac{1}{3} \div 3\frac{1}{5}$

Perform the following operations.

17. $12.589 + 5.62 + 0.$[illegible]
18. $7.8 + 10.24 + 1$[illegible]
19. $152.64 + 12.$[illegible] $+ 0.024$
20. $18.547 -$ [illegible]
21. $1.85 - 0.093$
22. $45.2 - 37.9$
23. 4.5[illegible] $\times 0.025$
24. 0.879×1.7
25. 30.7×0.0041
26. $17.28 \div 0.054$
27. $174.66 \div 1.23$
28. $2.115 \div 9$

Change to a fraction.

29. 0.5[illegible]
30. 0.[illegible]4
31. 0.32

Change to a mixed number.

32. [illegible].375
33. 9.6
34. 1[illegible].25

Change to a decimal.

35. $5\frac{3}{25}$
36. $\frac{7}{100}$
37. $10\frac{2}{3}$

Circle the greatest fraction and underline the least in each group below.

38. $\frac{1}{3}, \frac{3}{5}, \frac{10}{16}, \frac{15}{32}$
39. $\frac{1}{2}, \frac{17}{36}, \frac{25}{4[illegible]}, \frac{40}{81}$

Put in order from GREATEST to LEAST.

40. 0.[illegible], 0.55, 0.5[illegible]5, 0.05
41. [illegible].89, 1.08, 0.98, [illegible]

Put in order from LEAST to GREATEST.

42. 0.19, 0.2, 0.109, 0.22
43. 1.[illegible]5, 0.79, [illegible].709, 1.8

Order the following from LEAST to GREATEST.

44. $0.4, -\frac{1}{3}, \frac{1}{4}, -0.5, 3$
45. $\frac{1}{1[illegible]}$, [illegible]%, $\frac{1}{9}$, 0.12, 1.12

Solve the following word problems.

46. The Vargas family is hiking a $23\frac{1}{3}$-mile trail. The first day, they hiked $10\frac{1}{2}$ miles. How much further do they have to go to complete the trail?

47. Jena walks $\frac{1}{5}$ of a mile to a friend's house, $1\frac{1}{[illegible]}$ miles to the store, and $\frac{3}{4}$ of a mile back home. How far does Jena walk?

48. Cory uses $2\frac{4}{5}$ gallons of paint to mark one mile of this year's spring road race. How many gallons will he use to mark the entire $6\frac{1}{4}$ mile course?

49. Gene works for his father sanding wooden rocking chairs. He earns \$6.35 per chair. How many chairs does he need to sand in order to buy a portable radio/CD player for \$146.05?

50. Margo's Mint Shop has a machine that produces 4.35 pounds of mints per hour. How many pounds of mints are produced in each 8-hour shift?

51. Carter's Junior High track team runs the first leg of a 400-meter relay race in 10.2[illegible] seconds, the second leg in 11.4 seconds, the third leg in 10.77 seconds, and the last leg in 9.[illegible] seconds. How long does it take for them to complete the race?

52. Spaulding High School decided to sell boxes of oranges to earn money for new football uniforms. They ordered a truckload of 500 boxes of oranges from a California grower for \$15.00 per box. They sold 450 boxes for \$19.00 per box. On the last day of the sale, they sold the oranges they had left for \$17.00 per box. How much profit did they make?

2.4 Fraction and Decimal Test

1. Simplify the improper fraction.

$\frac{27}{5}$

A. $5\frac{4}{5}$

B. $5\frac{1}{5}$

C. $5\frac{2}{5}$

D. $5\frac{3}{5}$

E. $5\frac{7}{5}$

2. Put the following fractions in order from least to greatest.

$\frac{5}{7}, \frac{2}{3}, \frac{3}{4}, \frac{8}{11}$

F. $\frac{3}{4}, \frac{8}{11}, \frac{5}{7}, \frac{2}{3}$

G. $\frac{3}{4}, \frac{5}{7}, \frac{8}{11}, \frac{2}{3}$

H. $\frac{2}{3}, \frac{5}{7}, \frac{8}{11}, \frac{3}{4}$

J. $\frac{2}{3}, \frac{3}{4}, \frac{5}{7}, \frac{8}{11}$

K. $\frac{2}{3}, \frac{8}{11}, \frac{5}{7}, \frac{3}{4}$

3. Ayesha's dog weighs $40\frac{1}{4}$ lbs. He weighed $8\frac{1}{2}$ lbs as a puppy. How much weight did her dog gain?

A. $31\frac{1}{2}$ lbs

B. 32 lbs

C. $30\frac{1}{4}$ lbs

D. $48\frac{3}{4}$ lbs

E. $31\frac{3}{4}$ lbs

4. Melissa's books weigh 14.5 lbs, Jonathan's weigh 12.5 lbs, and Cindy's books weigh 7.25 lbs. What is the combined weight of all of the books?

F. $34\frac{1}{4}$ lbs

G. $33\frac{2}{3}$ lbs

H. 34 lbs

J. $34\frac{1}{2}$ lbs

K. $33\frac{1}{2}$ lbs

5. Which fraction below is greater than $\frac{2}{3}$?

A. $\frac{5}{8}$

B. $\frac{1}{2}$

C. $\frac{6}{10}$

D. $\frac{7}{9}$

E. $\frac{5}{9}$

6. Convert $6\frac{2}{4}$ to an improper fraction.

F. $6\frac{1}{2}$

G. $\frac{24}{4}$

H. $\frac{26}{4}$

J. $\frac{12}{4}$

K. $\frac{16}{4}$

7. Add: $\frac{1}{2} + \frac{5}{8} =$

A. $\frac{7}{12}$
B. $\frac{7}{8}$
C. $1\frac{3}{8}$
D. $1\frac{1}{8}$
E. $1\frac{2}{8}$

8. Order the following numbers from least to greatest:

$5.7, 0.57, \frac{5}{7}, -5.7, -\frac{5}{7}$

F. $-\frac{5}{7}, -5.7, \frac{5}{7}, 0.57, 5.7$
G. $-5.7, -\frac{5}{7}, 0.57, \frac{5}{7}, 5.7$
H. $-\frac{5}{7}, -5.7, \frac{5}{7}, 5.7, 0.57$
J. $-\frac{5}{7}, -5.7, 0.57, \frac{5}{7}, 5.7$
K. $-5.7, -\frac{5}{7}, \frac{5}{7}, 5.7, 0.57$

9. Order the following decimals from greatest to least:

1.011, 101.1, 1.101, 10.11, 1.111

A. 101.1, 10.11, 1.011, 1.101, 1.111
B. 101.1, 1.111, 10.11, 1.101, 1.011
C. 101.1, 10.11, 1.111, 1.011, 1.101
D. 101.1, 10.11, 1.111, 1.101, 1.011
E. 101.1, 10.11, 1.101, 1.111, 1.011

10. Grandma made a candy cane 39.75 inches long. If she divides it equally among her 3 grandchildren, how long will each piece be?

F. 11.6 inches
G. 10.25 inches
H. 13.25 inches
J. 13 inches
K. 12.2 inches

11. Richard buys a camcorder for \$229.95, which is now on sale for \$207.99. How much could he have saved if he waited to buy the camcorder on sale?

A. \$21.96
B. \$21.04
C. \$22.04
D. \$22.06
E. \$22.96

12. What is the value of 1.875 in fractional form?

F. $\frac{7}{5}$
G. $\frac{9}{8}$
H. $\frac{15}{8}$
J. $\frac{13}{8}$
K. $\frac{7}{6}$

13. What is the value of $12\frac{2}{3}$ in decimal form?

A. 12.25
B. 12.50
C. 12.75
D. $12.\overline{33}$
E. $12.\overline{66}$

14. What is the value of 0.78 as a fraction?

F. $\frac{39}{100}$
G. $\frac{78}{100}$
H. 78
J. $\frac{39}{50}$
K. $\frac{78}{\text{[illegible]}}$

15. What is the value of $\frac{5}{16}$ in decimal form?

A. 0.3125
B. 0.3025
C. 3.2
D. 3.125
E. 31.25

16. Multiply: $6.27 \times 0.43 =$

F. 2.5961
G. 2.6971
H. 2.9661
J. 2.6961
K. 2.6981

17. Divide: $124 \div 6.2 =$

A. 20.12
B. 20
C. 20.2
D. 20.02
E. 2.2

18. If 15 pencils cost $1.20, what is the cost of one pencil?

F. $0.80
G. $0.18
H. $0.15
J. $0.09
K. $0.08

19. Hanna bought 3 pairs of socks priced at 3 for $5.00 and shoes for $45.95. She paid $2.55 sales tax. How much change did she receive from $100.00?

A. $36.50
B. $55.50
C. $46.50
D. $51.50
E. $53.50

20. Subtract: $12\frac{1}{2} - 6\frac{2}{3} =$

F. $5\frac{1}{6}$
G. $5\frac{2}{6}$
H. $6\frac{1}{6}$
J. $5\frac{5}{6}$
K. $6\frac{1}{3}$

21. Find the product: $\frac{6}{8} \times \frac{16}{4}$

A. $\frac{22}{12}$
B. 3
C. $\frac{96}{28}$
D. 4
E. $\frac{192}{8}$

22. Find the quotient: $\frac{2}{10} \div \frac{8}{5}$

F. $\frac{16}{50}$
G. $\frac{7}{18}$
H. $\frac{1}{8}$
J. $\frac{3}{8}$
K. 8

2.5 Percent Review

Change the following percents to decimals.

1. 45% 2. 219% 3. 22% 4. 1.25%

Change the following decimals to percents.

5. 0.52 6. 0.64 7. 1.09 8. 0.625

9. What is 1.65 written as a percent?

10. Change 5.65 to a percent.

Change the following percents to fractions.

11. 25% 12. 3% 13. 68% 14. 102%

Change the following fractions to percents.

15. $\frac{9}{10}$ 16. $\frac{5}{16}$ 17. $\frac{1}{8}$ 18. $\frac{1}{4}$

19. A school receives 56% of the total sale at the end of a fund-raiser. If a fund-raiser makes $564,000, how much money does the school receive?

20. Peeler's Jewelry is offering a 30% off sale on all bracelets. How much will you save if you buy a $45.00 bracelet during the sale?

21. How much would an employee pay for a $724 stereo if the employee gets a 15% discount?

22. Misha buys a CD for $14.95. If sales tax is 7%, how much does she pay total?

23. The Pep band made $640 during a fund-raiser. The band spent $400 of the money on new uniforms. What percent of the total did the band members spend on uniforms?

24. Hank gets 10 hours per week to play his video games. Since he made straight A's last semester, his parents increased his playing time to 16 hours per week. What percent increase in time does he get?

25. Patton, Patton, and Clark, a law firm, won a malpractice lawsuit for $4,500,000. Sixty-eight percent went to the law firm. How much did the law firm make?

26. A department store is selling all swimsuits for 40% off in August. How much would you pay for a swimsuit that is normally priced at $35.80?

27. High school students voted on where they would go on a field trip. For every 3 students who wanted to see Calaveras Big Trees State Park, 8 students wanted to see Columbia State Historic Park. What percent of the students wanted to go to Columbia State Historic Park?

28. An increase from 20 to 36 is what percent of increase?

2.6 Percent Test

1. Which decimal best represents 27.2%?

   A. 2,720
   B. 272.0
   C. 2.72
   D. 0.272
   E. 27.2

2. Carlos earned 76.9 points out of 100 for his science fair project. What is his score written as a percentage?

   F. 0.769%
   G. 76.9%
   H. 7,690%
   J. 769%
   K. 7.69%

3. Rosalita earns 5% of the total sales for her company each month as a bonus. If her company has total sales of $15,980, what is Rosalita's bonus rounded to the nearest hundred?

   A. $8,000
   B. $400
   C. $700
   D. $800
   E. $1,600

4. What is 10% as a fraction in simplest form?

   F. $\frac{2}{5}$
   G. $\frac{1}{20}$
   H. $\frac{10}{100}$
   J. $\frac{1}{10}$
   K. 10

5. What would be a 15% tip for a total bill of $45?

   A. $5.50
   B. $4.50
   C. $7.75
   D. $6.75
   E. $1.50

6. What is 25% of 136?

   F. 30.4
   G. 34
   H. [illegible]
   J. [illegible]
   K. 27.2

7. Emily buys two pairs of shoes, each costing $18. Sales tax is 7%. What is her total?

   A. $1.26
   B. $18.07
   C. $36.14
   D. $38.52
   E. $19.26

8. What is 33.3% of 1,000?

   F. 3.33
   G. 33.3
   H. 33.0
   J. 333
   K. 3,333

9. Which fraction best represents 34%?

   A. $\frac{17}{100}$
   B. $\frac{17}{25}$
   C. $\frac{12}{50}$
   D. $\frac{17}{50}$
   E. $\frac{34}{[illegible]}$

2.7 Introduction to Algebra Review

Solve the following problems using $x = 2$.

1. $3x + 4 =$
2. $\frac{6x}{4} =$
3. $x^2 - 5 =$
4. $\frac{x^3 + 8}{[illegible]} =$
5. [illegible]$2 - 3x =$
6. $x - 5 =$
7. $-5x + 4 =$
8. $9 - x =$
9. $2x + 2 =$

Solve the following problems. Let $w = -1$, $y = 3$, $z = 5$.

10. $5w - y =$
11. $wyz + 2 =$
12. $z - 2w =$
13. $\frac{3z + 5}{wz} =$
14. $\frac{6w}{y} + \frac{z}{w} =$
15. $25 - 2yz =$
16. $-2y + 3 =$
17. $4w - (yz) =$
18. $7y - 5z =$

For questions 19–21, write an equation to match the problem.

19. Calista earns \$450 per week for a 40-hour work week plus \$16.83 per hour for each hour of overtime after 40 hours. Write an equation that would be used to determine her weekly wages where w is her wages and v is the number of overtime hours worked.

20. Daniel purchased a 1 year CD, c, from a bank. He bought it at an annual interest rate of 6%. After 1 year, Daniel cashes in the CD. What is the total amount it is worth?

21. Omar is a salesman. He earns an hourly wage of \$8.00 per hour, plus he receives a commission of 7% on the sales he makes. Write an equation which would be used to determine his weekly salary, w, where x is the number of hours worked and y is the amount of sales for the week.

Answer each of the following questions.

22. Juan sells a boat that he bought 5 years ago. He sells it for 60% less than he originally paid for it. If the original cost is b, write an expression that shows how much he sells the boat for.

23. Toshi is going to get a 7% raise after he works at his job for 1 year. If [illegible] represents his starting salary, write an expression that shows how much he will make after his raise, x.

24. Lumber is measured with the following formula:

    Number of board feet $= \frac{LWT}{12}$

    L = Length of the board in feet
    W = Width of the board in feet
    T = Thickness of the board in feet
    Find the number of board in feet if $L = 12$ feet, $W =$ [illegible] feet, and $T = 6$ feet.

2.8 Introduction to Algebra Test

1. Numbers or variables separated by a + or − are called

   A. coefficients.
   B. degrees.
   C. expressions.
   D. bases.
   E. terms.

2. More, plus, and total are words that indicate

   F. addition.
   G. subtraction.
   H. division.
   J. multiplication.
   K. substitution.

3. A constant is

   A. the number multiplied by the highest power.
   B. a term that does not have a variable.
   C. a sentence with an equal sign.
   D. a letter that can be replaced by a number.
   E. the number used as a factor.

4. Rosa has to pay the first \$100 of her medical expenses each year before she qualifies for her insurance company to begin paying. After paying the \$100 "deductible," her insurance company will pay 80% of her medical expenses. This year, her total medical expenses came to \$960.00. Which expression below shows how much her insurance company will pay?

   F. $0.80\,(960 - 100)$
   G. $100 + (960 \div 0.80)$
   H. $960\,(100 - 0.80)$
   J. $0.80\,(960 + 100)$
   K. $0.80\,(960) + 100$

5. Eight times the sum of x and three divided by five.

   A. $8\left(x + \frac{3}{5}\right)$
   B. $8x + \frac{3}{5}$
   C. $\frac{8(x+3)}{5}$
   D. $\frac{8x+3}{5}$
   E. $\frac{8x}{5} + 3$

6. Write the equation from the following word problem.
   Sixteen times two plus a number equals seven.

   F. $16 \times 2 + x = 7$
   G. $16 \times 2 = 7x$
   H. $16 \times (2 + x) = 7$
   J. $16 + 2 \times x = 7$
   K. $16 + 2 + x = 7$

7. Product, times, and half are words that indicate

   A. addition.
   B. subtraction.
   C. division.
   D. multiplication.
   E. substitution.

8. Seven times x minus eleven equals seventeen

   F. $7(x - 11) = 17$
   G. $7x = 17 - 11$
   H. $7x - 77 = 119$
   J. $7x - 77 = 17$
   K. $7x - 11 = 17$

9. A plumber charges \$45 per hour plus a \$25.00 service charge. If a represents his total charges in dollars and b represents the number of hours worked, which formula below could the plumber use to calculate his total charges?

A. $a = 45 + 25b$
B. $a = 45 + 25 + b$
C. $a = (45)(25) + b$
D. $b = 45a + 25$
E. $a = 45b + 25$

10. In 2009, Bell Computers informed its sales force to expect a 2.6% price increase on all computer equipment in the year 2010. A certain sales representative wanted to see how much the increase would be on a computer, that sold for \$2200 in 2009. Which expression below will help him find the cost of the computer in the year 2010?

F. $0.026(2200)$
G. $2200 - 0.026(2200)$
H. $2200 + 0.026(2200)$
J. $0.026(2200) - 2200$
K. $0.026(2200) + 2.6$

11. Write the expression from the following word problem.

Fifteen minus a number, then divided by two equals eleven.

A. $\dfrac{15 - y}{2} = 11$
B. $11 - \dfrac{y}{2} = 15$
C. $15 - \dfrac{y}{2} = 11$
D. $2 - \dfrac{y}{15} = 11$
E. $\dfrac{15 - 2y}{2} = 11$

12. The difference of x and five divided by the sum of x and two.

F. $\dfrac{x - 5}{x + 2}$
G. $x - \dfrac{5}{x + 2}$
H. $\dfrac{x}{x + 2} - 5$
J. $\dfrac{x}{2} - \dfrac{5}{x}$
K. $x - 5x \div 2$

13. Write the expression from the following word problem.

Five less than x plus seven.

A. $5 - (x + 7)$
B. $(x + 5) - 7$
C. $(x + 7) - 5$
D. $(x - 7) + 5$
E. $5 - (x - 7)$

14. Solving the following expression using $a = 4$.

$3a - 2$

F. 14
G. 10
H. 16
J. 12
K. 6

15. Stacey bought her car at a certain price, x. After some years she wishes to sell her car, but sells it for 40% less than the price she paid for it. Which equation represents the amount of money she got for selling her car?

A. $0.6x$
B. $0.4x$
C. $0.6x - 0.4x$
D. $x - 0.6x$
E. $1 - 0.4x$

16. Solving the following expression using $y = 3$.

$8y \div 3$

F. 8
G. 21
H. 24
J. 72
K. 16

17. A box has length of 20 inches, the height of 12 inches, and the width of 38 inches. What is the volume of the box using the formula $V = lwh$?

A. 70 inches
B. 240 inches
C. 9,120 inches
D. 2,912 inches
E. 560 inches

18. Solving the following expression using $x = 2$ and $y = 5$.

$3x + 4y - 1$

F. 22
G. 13
H. 25
J. 10
K. 26

19. Tom earns $500 per week before taxes are taken out. His employer takes out a total of 33% for state, federal, and Social Security taxes. Which expression below will help Tom figure his net pay?

A. $500 - 0.33$
B. $500 \div 0.33$
C. $500 + 0.33\,(500)$
D. $500 - 0.33\,(500)$
E. 500×0.33

20. Together John, Brian, and Devin spent $29.00 on a movie. Brian spent three more dollars than John. Devin spent twice as much as Brian. Which equation best represents this situation?
j = amount of money John spent

F. $\$29 = j + j + 3 + 2j$
G. $\$29 = j + j - 3 + 2j$
H. $\$29 = j - j + 3 - 2\,(j + 3)$
J. $\$29 = j + j + 3 + 2\,(j + 3)$
K. $\$29 = j + j + 3 + 2j + 3$

2.9 Distance Between Points on a Number Line

A **number line** is a horizontal line with integers evenly spaced on the line and an arrow at each end. Negative integers are on the left side of zero on the line, while positive integers are on the right side of zero. The arrows at the ends of the line are meant to indicate that the line goes on forever in each direction. Even though only integers are shown on a number line, the number line represents all real numbers. As one goes from left to right on a number line, the numbers will always become greater. That is, if $a < b$, then a will be to the left of b on the number line, and b will be to the right of a. The distance between two points on a number line can be obtained by finding the absolute value of the difference of the numbers representing those points. In other words, the distance between a and b on a number line is $|a - b|$.

Example 1: On the number line shown below, find the lengths of the line segments DA, DC, DB, AC, AB, and CB.

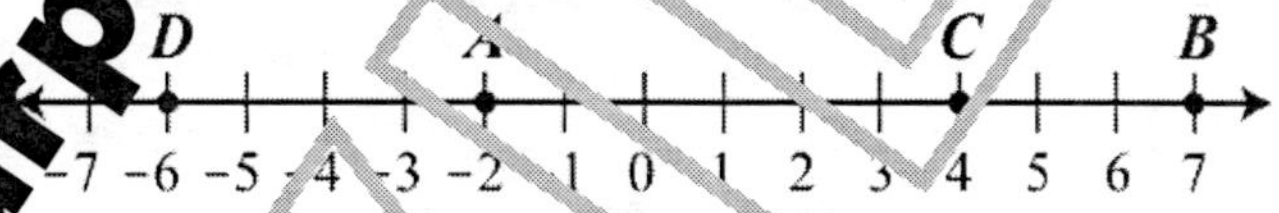

Step 1: Since the distance between a and b on a number line is $|a - b|$, the distance between point D and point A is $|-6 - (-2)| = |-6 + 2| = |-4| = 4$. Therefore, the length of line segment DA is 4.

Step 2: The lengths of line segments DC, DB, AC, AB, and CB can be found in a similar fashion as follows:

$\overline{DC} = |-6 - 4| = |-10| = 10$ $\quad$ $\overline{AB} = |-2 - 7| = |-9| = 9$
$\overline{DB} = |-6 - 7| = |-13| = 13$ $\quad$ $\overline{CB} = |4 - 7| = |-3| = 3$
$\overline{AC} = |-2 - 4| = |-6| = 6$

For questions 1–6, find the lengths of each of the following line segments based on the number line shown below.

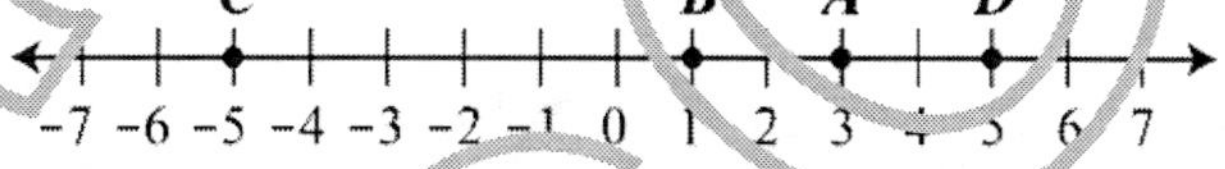

1. $\overline{BD}$ 2. $\overline{BA}$ 3. $\overline{CA}$ 4. $\overline{CD}$ 5. $\overline{AD}$ 6. $\overline{CB}$

7. Points A, B, C, and D are located on a number line. Point D is to the left of point C, point B is to the left of point A, point A is to the left of point C, and point D is to the left of point B. If it can be determined, state whether the lengths of the line segments DB, DA, DC, BC, and AC are greater than, less than, or equal to the length of the line segment BA.

8. Points F, G, H, and K are located on a number line. Point H is to the right of point G, point F is to the right of point G, point G is to the right of point K, and point H is to the right of point F. If it can be determined, state whether the lengths of the line segments KG, KF, KH, GF, and FH are greater than, less than, or equal to the length of the line segment GH.

Example 2: The points A, B, C, and D are located on a number line as shown below. The distance between A and C is $\frac{88}{15}$, the distance between B and D is $\frac{128}{15}$, and the distance between A and D is $\frac{176}{15}$. What is the distance between point B and point C?

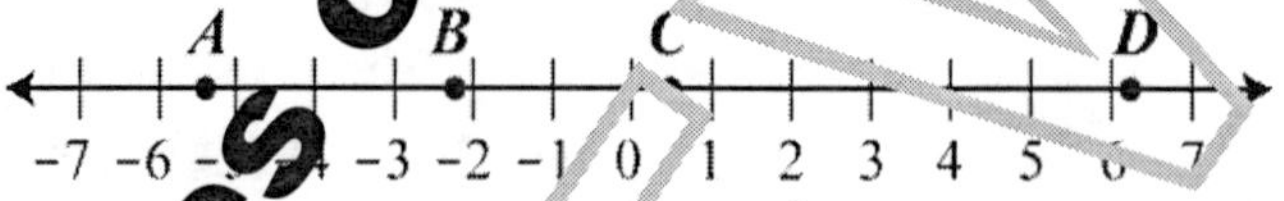

Step 1: Think of the distance between point B and point C as the length of line segment BC. The lengths of line segments AC, BD, and AD are given, and if the length of $\overline{AC}$ is added to the length of $\overline{BD}$, the result will be the length of $\overline{AD}$ plus the length of $\overline{BC}$. The reason for this is because when adding $\overline{AC}$ and $\overline{BD}$, $\overline{BC}$ is counted twice, since $\overline{BC}$ is the intersection of $\overline{AC}$ and $\overline{BD}$. Therefore, $\overline{BC} = \overline{AC} + \overline{BD} - \overline{AD}$

Step 2: Plug values into the equation $\overline{BC} = \overline{AC} + \overline{BD} - \overline{AD}$

$\overline{BC} = \frac{88}{15} + \frac{128}{15} - \frac{176}{15} = \frac{216}{15} - \frac{176}{15} = \frac{40}{15} = \frac{8}{3}$

The distance between point B and point C is $\frac{8}{3}$.

For the number line shown below, find the distance between point G and point H if the values of $\overline{FH}$, $\overline{GK}$, and $\overline{FK}$ are the given values in questions 1–6.

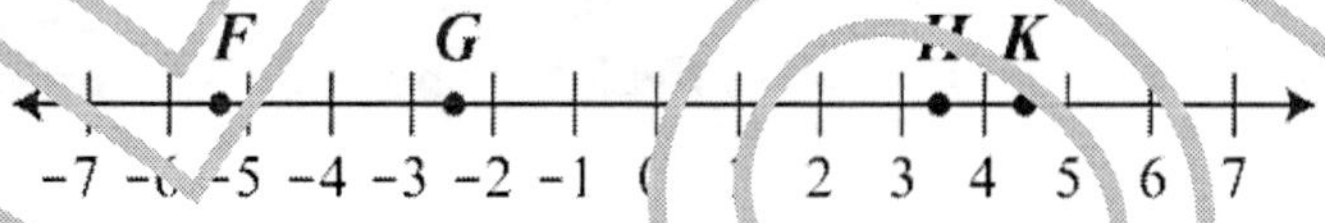

1. $\overline{FH} = \frac{62}{7}; \overline{GK} = 7; \overline{FK} = \frac{137}{14}$
2. $\overline{FH} = 9; \overline{GK} = \frac{34}{5}; \overline{FK} = \frac{146}{15}$
3. $\overline{FH} = 9; \overline{GK} = \frac{29}{4}; \overline{FK} = \frac{79}{8}$
4. $\overline{FH} = \frac{79}{9}; \overline{GK} = \frac{62}{9}; \overline{FK} = \frac{87}{9}$
5. $\overline{FH} = \frac{89}{10}; \overline{GK} = 7; \overline{FK} = \frac{97}{10}$
6. $\overline{FH} = 9; \overline{GK} = 7; \overline{FK} = \frac{119}{12}$

7. Points A, B, C, and D are located on a number line. Point A is to the left of point B, point C is to the left of point D, point B is to the left of point D, and point C is to the left of point B. $\overline{AB} = 66$, $\overline{CD} = 31$, and $\overline{AD} = 89$. If the value of point B is $-\frac{3}{2}$, what is the value of point C?

2.10 Cartesian Coordinates

A **Cartesian coordinate plane** allows you to graph points with two values. A Cartesian coordinate plane is made up of two number lines. The horizontal number line is called the x-**axis**, and the vertical number line is called the y-**axis**. The point where the x and y axes intersect is called the **origin**. The x and y axes separate the Cartesian coordinate plane into four quadrants that are labeled I, II, III, and IV. The quadrants are labeled and explained on the graph below. Each point graphed on the plane is designated by an **ordered pair** of coordinates. For example, $(2, -1)$ is an ordered pair of coordinates designated by point B on the plane below. The first number, 2, tells you to go over positive two on the x-axis. The -1 tells you to then go down negative one on the y-axis.

Remember: The first number always tells you how far to go right or left of 0, and the second number always tells you how far to go up or down from 0.

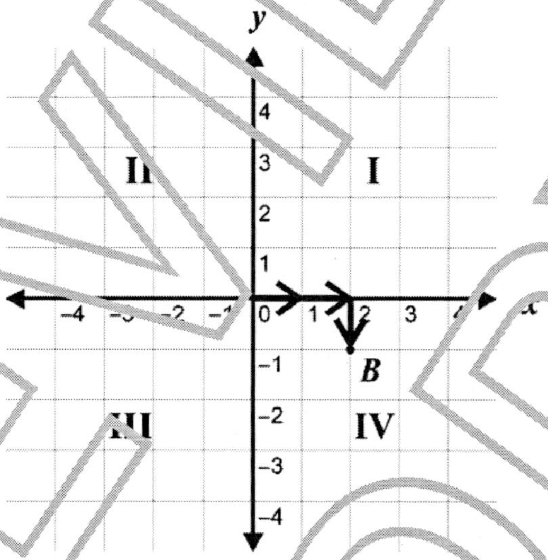

Quadrant II:
The x-coordinate is negative, and the y-coordinate is positive $(-, +)$.

Quadrant I:
Both coordinates in the ordered pair are positive $(+, +)$.

Quadrant III:
Both coordinates in the ordered pair are negative $(-, -)$.

Quadrant IV:
The x-coordinate is positive and the y-coordinate is negative $(+, -)$.

Plot and label the following points on the Cartesian coordinate plane provided.

A. $(2, 4)$
B. $(-1, 5)$
C. $(3, -4)$
D. $(-5, -2)$
E. $(5, 3)$
F. $(-3, -5)$
G. $(-2, 5)$
H. $(5, -1)$
I. $(4, -4)$
J. $(6, 2)$
K. $(-1, -1)$
L. $(3, -3)$
M. $(5, 5)$
N. $(-2, -2)$
O. $(0, 0)$
P. $(0, 4)$
Q. $(2, 0)$
R. $(-4, 0)$
S. $(0, -2)$
T. $(5, 1)$

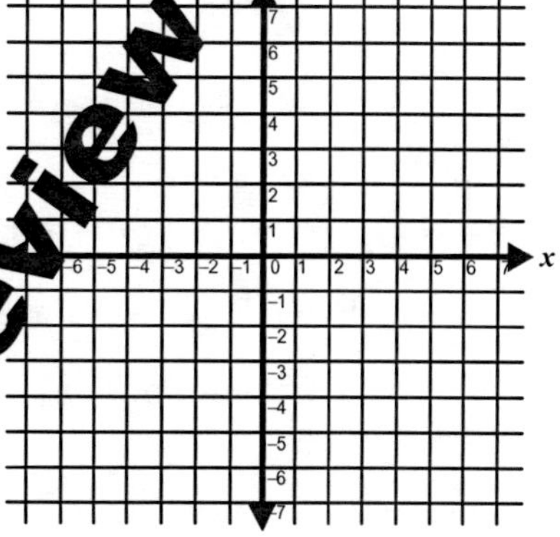

2.11 Introduction to Graphing Review

1. 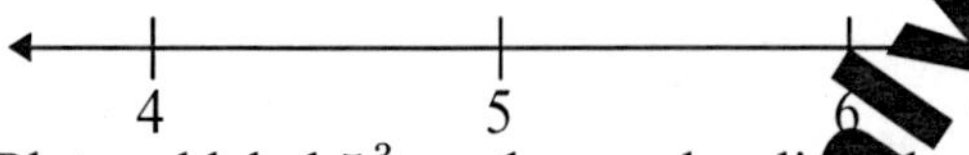

Plot and label $5\frac{3}{5}$ on the number line above.

2. 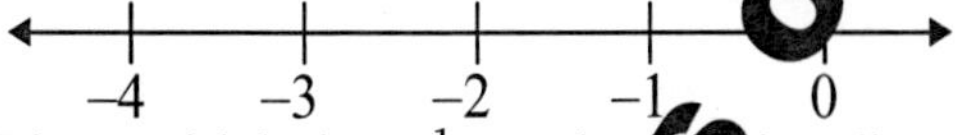

Plot and label $-3\frac{1}{2}$ on the number line above.

3. 

Plot and label 7.8 on the number line above.

4. 

Plot and label −2.3 on the number line above.

Record the value represented by the point on the number line for questions 5–10.

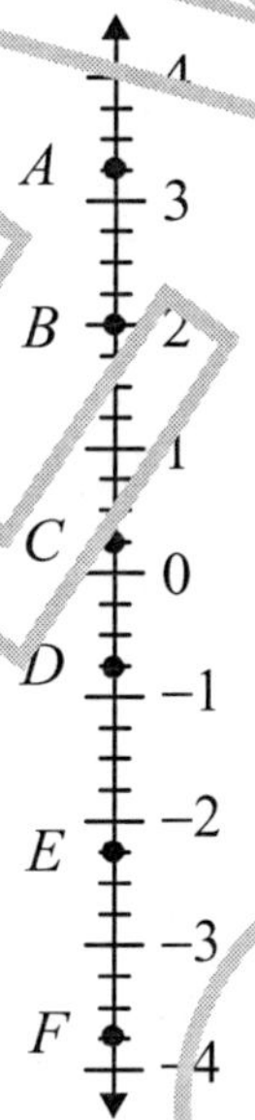

5. $A =$ _____

6. $B =$ _____

7. $C =$ _____

8. $D =$ _____

9. $E =$ _____

10. $F =$ _____

Answer the following questions.

11. In which quadrant does the point $(2, 3)$ lie?

12. In which quadrant does the point $(-5, -2)$ lie?

Record the coordinates and quadrants of the following points.

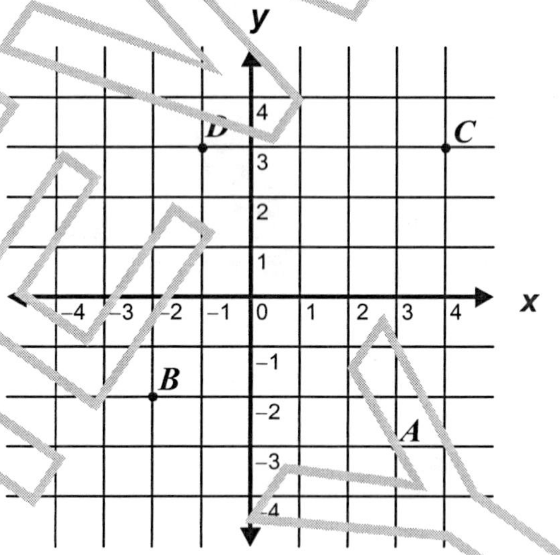

	Coordinates	Quadrants
13. $A =$	_____	_____
14. $B =$	_____	_____
15. $C =$	_____	_____
16. $D =$	_____	_____

On the same plane above, label these additional coordinates.

17. $E = (0, -3)$

18. $F = (-3, -1)$

19. $G = (\ ,\ )$

20. $H = (2, 2)$

Find the lengths of each of the following line segments based on the number line shown below.

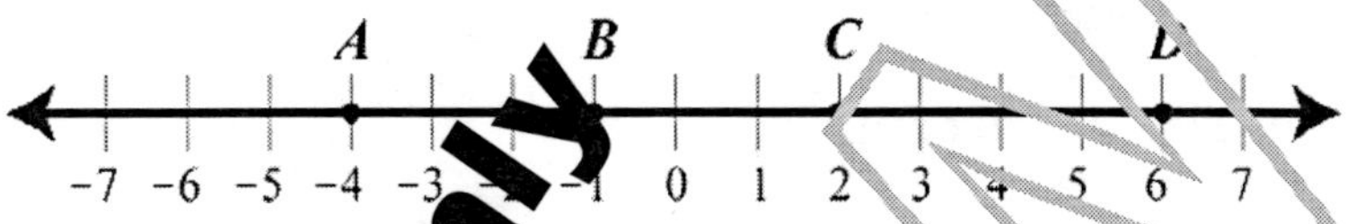

21. $\overline{AC}$

22. $\overline{BC}$

23. $\overline{BD}$

For the number line shown below, find the distance between point G and point H if the values of $\overline{FH}$, $\overline{GK}$, and $\overline{FK}$ are given values.

24. $\overline{FH} = \frac{26}{3}; \overline{GK} = \frac{85}{12}; \overline{FK} = \frac{117}{12}$

25. $\overline{FH} = \frac{133}{15}; \overline{GK} = 7; \overline{FK} = \frac{147}{15}$

2.12 Introduction to Graphing Test

1. According to the number line, which point is $\sqrt{3}$?

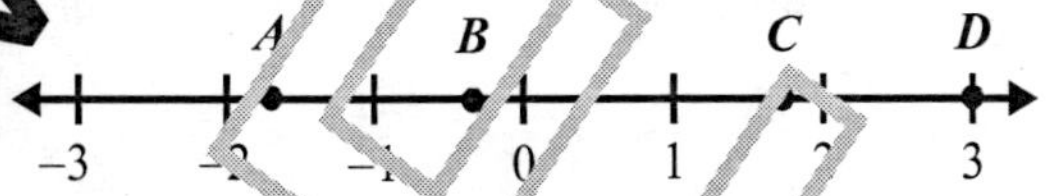

A. A
B. B
C. C
D. D
E. None of the above

2. Which point on the number line represents -1.4?

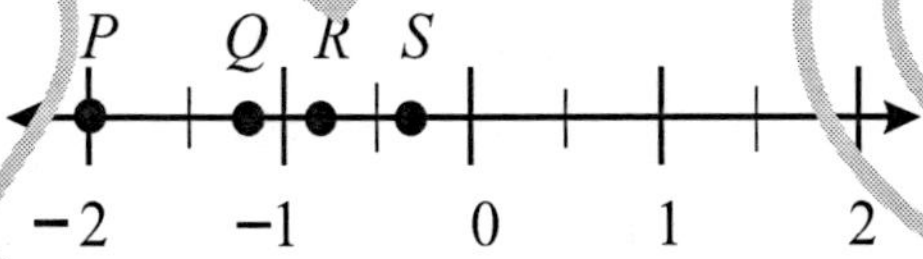

F. P
G. Q
H. R
J. S
K. None of the above

3. Which point on the number line represents $-2\frac{3}{4}$?

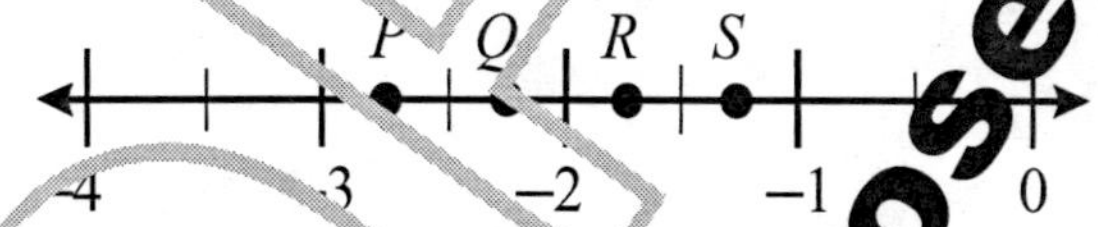

A. P
B. Q
C. R
D. S
E. None of the above.

4. Points D, C, A, and B are located in that order from left to right on a number line. Which of the following statements might not be true?

F. $\overline{DC} < \overline{DA}$
G. $\overline{CB} > \overline{CA}$
H. $\overline{DB} > \overline{CB}$
J. $\overline{DC} < \overline{AB}$
K. $\overline{DA} < \overline{DB}$

5. Points A, B, C, and D are located in that order from left to right on a number line. $\overline{AC} = 9$, $\overline{BD} = 95$, and $\overline{AD} = 99$. If the value of point C is 2, what is the value of point B?

A. -5
B. -3
C. -2
D. 3
E. 5

6. The point $(1, -8)$ is in what quadrant?

F. I
G. II
H. III
J. IV
K. V

7. According to the number line, which point is $\sqrt{2}$?

A. A
B. B
C. C
D. D
E. None of the above

8. Which point on the number line represents $-\frac{12}{16}$?

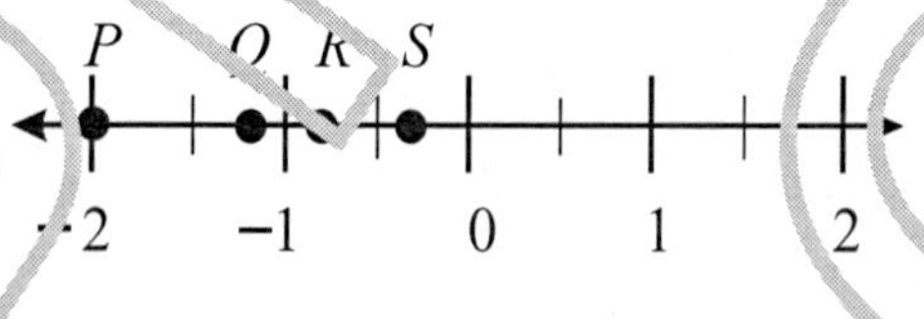

F. P
G. Q
H. R
J. S
K. None of the above

9. What are the coordinates of point P?

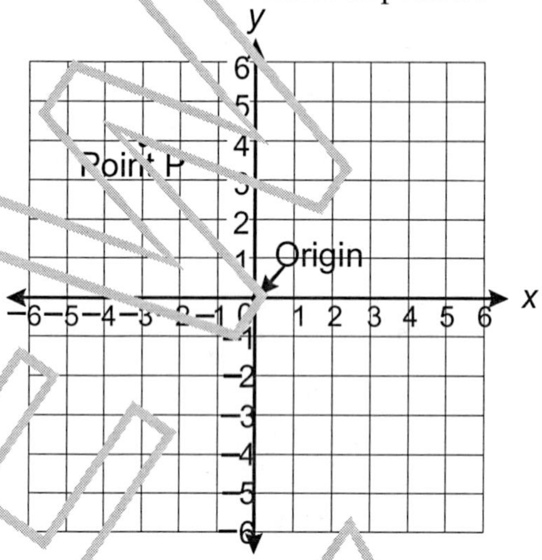

A. $(4, -3)$
B. $(-4, 3)$
C. $(-3, 4)$
D. $(-3, -4)$
E. $(4, 3)$

10. Which of these is the best estimate of the coordinate of Point P on the number line?

F. $-1\frac{1}{8}$
G. $-1\frac{3}{8}$
H. $-1\frac{5}{8}$
J. $-2\frac{3}{8}$
K. $-2\frac{3}{8}$

Chapter 3
Exponents and Square Roots

3.1 Numbers Raised to Positive Integer Powers

The number a raised to the positive integer power n results in the multiplication of the number a with itself (except when $n = 1$, in which case the number a raised to the positive integer power n results in the number a, itself). The term a^n is equal to the expression $a \times . . . \times a$, with the number of terms in the expression equal to n.

If a is positive, a^n will always be positive.

If a is negative, a^n will be positive only when n is even; if n is odd, a^n will be negative.

If $a > 1$, a^n will become larger as n becomes larger.

If $0 < a < 1$, a^n will become smaller as n becomes larger.

If $a < 0$, no such relationships exist for a^n and n, since a^n alternates between negative and positive as n becomes larger.

However, relationships do exist for $|a^n|$ and n; if $a < -1$, $|a^n|$ will become larger as n becomes larger, but if $-1 < a < 0$, $|a^n|$ will become smaller as n becomes larger.

Example 1: Put the expressions a^1, a^2, a^3, a^4, a^5, and a^6 in order from least to greatest for each of the following conditions:
i) $a > 1$ ii) $0 < a < 1$ iii) $a < -1$ iv) $-1 < a < 0$

For the condition $a > 1$, a^n will become larger as n becomes larger, so the correct order is a^1, a^2, a^3, a^4, a^5, a^6.

For the condition $0 < a < 1$, a^n will become smaller as n becomes larger, so the correct order is a^6, a^5, a^4, a^3, a^2, a^1.

For the condition $a < -1$, if n is even, a^n will become larger as n becomes larger. However, if n is odd, a^n will become smaller as n becomes larger. Also, any value for a^n when n is even is greater than any value for a^n when n is odd. Therefore, the correct order is a^5, a^3, a^1, a^2, a^4, a^6.

For the condition $-1 < a < 0$, if n is even, a^n will become smaller as n becomes larger. However, if n is odd, a^n will become larger as n becomes larger. Also, any value for a^n when n is even is greater than any value for a^n when n is odd. Therefore, the correct order is a^1, a^3, a^5, a^6, a^4, a^2.

For each of the following values of a, put the expressions a^1, a^2, a^3, a^4, a^5, and a^6 in order from least to greatest.

1. $a = -3$
2. $a = -\frac{3}{4}$
3. $a = \frac{2}{5}$
4. $a = \frac{1}{6}$
5. $a = 9$
6. $a = -\frac{4}{9}$
7. $a = 12$
8. $a = -7$
9. $a = -2$

Example 2: The expression 603^{91} would have 254 digits if it were simplified. What would be the value of the ones digit (the digit farthest to the right)?

It's impractical to find the value of the ones digit by simplifying 603^{91} by hand, and a calculator does not have enough space to display all 254 digits. Therefore, it's necessary to find another way to solve the problem. A good way to start would be to find the value of the ones digit of 603^n for the first few positive integer values of n. First of all, it's easy to calculate that $603^1 = 603$, so the ones digit is 3. As for 603^2, the ones digit would have to be 3^2, or 9, because the ones digit of 603 is multiplied by itself once. For 603^3, the ones digit is that of the expression 3^3, since the ones digit of 603 is multiplied by itself twice. In other words, the ones digit is that of 27, which is 7. The pattern continues with 603^4, with the ones digit being that of the expression 3^4, or 81, which is 1. The information that has been determined so far, as well as the ones digit of 603^n for the next few values of n, is summarized in the table below.

n	3^n	Ones digit of 3^n	Ones digit of 603^n
1	3	3	3
2	9	9	9
3	27	7	7
4	81	1	1
5	243	3	3
6	729	9	9
7	2187	7	7
8	6561	1	1
9	19683	3	3
10	59049	9	9
11	177147	7	7

It's clear that a pattern for the ones digit of 603^n has emerged. It is 3, 9, 7, 1, 3, 9, 7, 1, . . . In other words, the ones digit of 603^n repeats itself every 4 values of n. Since the ones digit of 603^{91} is being sought, it's necessary to find the ones digit of 603^n for the 91st value of n. Because the ones digit of 603^n repeats itself every 4 values of n, it repeats itself 22 times for the first 88 values of n, since $88 \div 4 = 22$. From this point, the ones digit of 603^n for the 89th value of n would be 3, that for the 90th value of n would be 9, and that for the 91st value of n would be 7. Therefore, the ones digit of 603^{91} is 7.

What would the value of the ones digit be for the simplified version of each of the following expressions?

10. 222^{801}
11. 537^{111}
12. 145^{99}
13. 423^{133}
14. 561^{1001}
15. 319^{210}
16. 244^{443}
17. 196^{213}
18. 308^{307}

3.2 Order of Operations

In long math problems with +, −, ×, ÷, (), and exponents in them, you have to know what to do first. Without following the same rules, you could get different answers. If you will memorize the silly sentence, Please Excuse My Dear Aunt Sally, you can memorize the order you must follow.

Please — **"P"** stands for parentheses. You must get rid of parentheses first.
Examples: $3(1+4) = 3(5) = 15$
$6(10-6) = 6(4) = 24$

Excuse — **"E"** stands for exponents. You must eliminate exponents next.
Example: $4^2 = 4 \times 4 = 16$

My Dear — **"M"** stands for multiply. **"D"** stands for divide. Start on the left of the equation and perform all multiplications and divisions in the order in which they appear.

Aunt Sally — **"A"** stands for add. **"S"** stands for subtract. Start on the left and perform all additions and subtractions in the order they appear.

Example 3: $12 \div 2(6-3) + 3^2 - 1$		
Please	Eliminate **parentheses**. $6 - 3 = 3$ so now we have	$12 \div 2 \times 3 + 3^2 - 1$
Excuse	Eliminate **exponents**. $3^2 = 9$ so now we have	$12 \div 2 \times 3 + 9 - 1$
My Dear	**Multiply** and **divide** next in order from left to right	$12 \div 2 = 6$ then $6 \times 3 = 18$
Aunt Sally	Last, we **add** and **subtract** in order from left to right.	$18 + 9 - 1 = 26$

Simplify the following problems.

1. $6 + 9 \times 2 - 4$
2. $3(4+2) - 6^2$
3. $3(6-3) - 2^3$
4. $49 \div 7 - 3 \times 3$
5. $10 \times 4 - (7-2)$
6. $2 \times 3 \div 6 \times 4$
7. $4^3 \div 8(4+2)$
8. $7 + 8(14-6) \div 4$
9. $(2 + 8 - 12) \times 4$
10. $4(8-13) \times 4$
11. $8 + 4^2 \times 2 - 6$
12. $3^2(4+6) + 3$
13. $(12-6) + 27 \div 3^2$
14. $8\,2$[illegible] $- 1 + 4 \div 2^2$
15. 1[illegible] $- (2-3) + 8$
16. $12 - 4(7-2$[illegible]
17. $18 \div (6 +$ [illegible] $) - 12$
18. $10^2 + 3$[illegible] $- 2 \times 3$
19. $4^2 + (7+2) \div 3$
20. 7 [illegible] $- 9 \div 3$

When a problem has a fraction bar, simplify the top of the fraction (numerator) and the bottom of the fraction (denominator) separately using the rules for order of operations. You treat the top and bottom as if they were separate problems. Then reduce the fraction to lowest terms.

Example 4: $\dfrac{2(4-3)-6}{5^2+3(2+1)}$

Please	Eliminate **parentheses**. $(4-3)=1$ and $(2+1)=3$	$\dfrac{2\times 1-6}{5^2+3\times 3}$
Excuse	Eliminate **exponents**. $5^2=25$	$\dfrac{2\times 1-6}{25+3\times 3}$
My **D**ear	**Multiply** and **divide** in the numerator and denominator separately. $3\times 3=9$ and $2\times 1=2$	$\dfrac{2-6}{25+9}$
Aunt **S**ally	**Add** and **subtract** in the numerator and denominator separately. $2-6=-4$ and $25+9=34$	$\dfrac{-4}{34}$

Now reduce the fraction to lowest terms. $\dfrac{-4}{34}=\dfrac{-2}{17}$

Simplify the following problems.

1. $\dfrac{2^2+4}{5+3(8+1)}$
2. $\dfrac{8^2-(4+11)}{4^2-3^2}$
3. $\dfrac{5-2(4-3)}{2(1-8)}$
4. $\dfrac{10+(2-4)}{4(2+6)-2^2}$
5. $\dfrac{3^3-8(1+2)}{-10-(3+8)}$
6. $\dfrac{(9-3)+3^2}{-5-2(4+1)}$
7. $\dfrac{16-3(10-6)}{(13+15)-5^2}$
8. $\dfrac{(2-5)-11}{12-2(3+1)}$
9. $\dfrac{7+(8-16)}{6^2-5^2}$
10. $\dfrac{16-(12-3)}{8(2+3)-5}$
11. $\dfrac{-3(9-7)}{7+9-2^3}$
12. $\dfrac{4-(2+7)}{3+(6-9)}$
13. $\dfrac{5(3-8)-2^2}{7-3(6+1)}$
14. $\dfrac{2(3-8)+5}{8^2-(5+9)}$
15. $\dfrac{6^2-4(7+3)}{8+(9-3)}$

3.3 Logarithms

The **logarithm** of the number x to the base b is the power y to which b must be raised in order to produce x. The logarithm just described is written as follows: $\log_b x = y$. A logarithmic equation such as this is the inverse of a corresponding exponential equation, and vice versa. The corresponding exponential equation for $\log_b x = y$ is $b^y = x$. Oftentimes the base b of a logarithm is not explicitly stated. That is, the logarithm will be written as $\log x = y$. In this case, the base b is assumed to be 10, so $\log 10 = 1$, $\log 100 = 2$, $\log 1000 = 3$, and so on. Logarithms result in many interesting identities. One of these is the product identity, which states that $\log_b mn = \log_b m + \log_b n$. Another is the quotient identity, which states that $\log_b \frac{m}{n} = \log_b m - \log_b n$. Still another is the power identity, which states that $\log_b m^a = a \log_b m$. Finally, there is the change of base identity, which states that $\log_a b = \frac{\log_c b}{\log_c a}$. All of these identities can be used to help simplify logarithmic expressions and solve exponential and logarithmic equations.

Example 5: Simplify the logarithmic expression $2\log_7 18 - \log_7 2 + \log_7 18 - 2\log_7 2$.

Step 1: First, like terms should be grouped together and combined.

$$2\log_7 18 - \log_7 2 + \log_7 18 - 2\log_7 2$$
$$= (2\log_7 18 + \log_7 18) - (\log_7 2 + 2\log_7 2)$$
$$= 3\log_7 18 - 3\log_7 2$$

Step 2: Next, 3 should be factored from both terms of the expression.

$$3\log_7 18 - 3\log_7 2 = 3(\log_7 18 - \log_7 2)$$

Step 3: Now the quotient identity should be used to further simplify the expression.

$$3(\log_7 18 - \log_7 2) = 3(\log_7 \tfrac{18}{2}) = 3(\log_7 9)$$

Step 4: Finally, the power identity should be applied.

$$3(\log_7 9) = \log_7 9^3 = \log_7 729$$

Simplify each of the following logarithms expressions.

1. $\log_6 44 + \log_6 4$
2. $8(\log_5 8 - \log_5 4)$
3. $\dfrac{\log_8 14}{\log_8 10}$
4. $\log_6 5 + 2\log_6 9 + \log_6 5$
5. $\dfrac{\log_9 21}{\log_9 7} + \dfrac{\log_9 2}{\log_9 7}$
6. $5\log_2 35 - 4\log_2 7 - \log_2 35$
7. $a(\log_f g + \log_f h)$
8. $u\log_w z - v\log_w z$
9. $t\log_q r - t\log_q s$

Example 6: The amount of money A in a bank account can be calculated with the equation $A = P\left(1 + \frac{r}{n}\right)^{nt}$, where P is the amount initially deposited, r is the annual interest rate expressed as a decimal, n is the number of compounding periods per year, and t is the number of years that have passed since the initial deposit. \$650 was deposited 4 years ago into a bank account that compounds interest quarterly, and no additional deposits or withdrawals have been made. If the amount of money now in the bank account is \$824.84, what is the annual interest rate to the nearest percent?

Step 1: First, the information given should be substituted into the equation, and the equation should be simplified.

$$824.84 = 650\left(1 + \frac{r}{4}\right)^{(4)(4)} = 650\left(1 + \frac{r}{4}\right)^{16}$$

$$\frac{824.84}{650} = \frac{650}{650}\left(1 + \frac{r}{4}\right)^{16}$$

$$1.26898 = \left(1 + \frac{r}{4}\right)^{16}$$

Step 2: Next, the log should be taken of both sides of the equation, the power identity should be applied, and the equation should be simplified further. Note: The base used when taking the log of both sides of the equation can be any number, as long as it is the same for both sides of the equation. For this example, a base of 10 will be used, since it makes calculations with a calculator the easiest.

$$\log 1.26898 = \log\left(1 + \frac{r}{4}\right)^{16} = 16\log\left(1 + \frac{r}{4}\right)$$

$$0.10346 = 16\log\left(1 + \frac{r}{4}\right)$$

$$\frac{0.10346}{16} = \frac{16}{16}\log\left(1 + \frac{r}{4}\right)$$

$$0.00647 = \log\left(1 + \frac{r}{4}\right)$$

Step 3: At this point, it's useful to remember that $0.00647 = \log\left(1 + \frac{r}{4}\right)$ means that 10 raised to the power 0.00647 equals $1 + \frac{r}{4}$. Since 10 raised to the power 0.00647 equals 1.0150, the equation can be rewritten as follows: $1.0150 = 1 + \frac{r}{4}$.

Step 4: Finally, it's possible to solve for r.

$$1.0150 - 1 = 1 + \frac{r}{4} - 1$$

$$0.0150 = \frac{r}{4}$$

$$(0.0150)(4) = \left(\frac{r}{4}\right)(4)$$

$$r = 0.06$$

Therefore, the annual interest rate of the bank account is 6 percent.

For each of the following sets of conditions, an amount of money was deposited into a bank account, and no additional deposits or withdrawals were made. Determine the annual interest rate for each bank account to the nearest percent.

1. Initial deposit: \$1750; Compounding period: semi-annually; Amount of money in bank account after 3 years: \$2029.46

2. Initial deposit: \$800; Compounding period: monthly; Amount of money in bank account after 7 years: \$920.11

3. Initial deposit: \$2[illegible]0; Compounding period: annually; Amount of money in bank account after 5 years: \$3[illegible]72.08

4. Initial deposit: \$1200; Compounding period: weekly; Amount of money in bank account after 9 years: \$2695.60

5. Initial deposit: \$1600; Compounding period: quarterly; Amount of money in bank account after 8 years: \$2199.91

6. Initial deposit: \$2200; Compounding period: daily; Amount of money in bank account after 6 years: \$3348.18

7. A country expects its population to increase by a certain percent per year between the years 2005 and 2025. In 2005 the country's population was 20, 000, 000, and it is expected that in 2025, the population will be 60, 000, 000. At what percent per year to the nearest tenth of a percent is the country's population expected to grow?

8. The total number of profiles created on a social networking website quadrupled in the last 18 months. If the total number of profiles increased at a certain percent per month, what was that percent to the nearest tenth?

3.4 Simplifying Square Roots

Square roots can sometimes be simplified even if the number under the square root is not a perfect square. One of the rules of roots is that if a and b are two positive real numbers, then it is always true that $\sqrt{a \cdot b} = \sqrt{a} \cdot \sqrt{b}$. You can use this rule to simplify square roots. Remember every positive number has two roots of opposite signs.

Example 7: $\sqrt{100} = \sqrt{4 \cdot 25} = \sqrt{4} \cdot \sqrt{25} = \pm 2 \cdot \pm 5 = \pm 10$

Example 8: $\sqrt{200} = \sqrt{100 \cdot 2} = \pm 10\sqrt{2} \leftarrow$ Means 10 multiplied by the square root of 2

Example 9: $\sqrt{160} = \sqrt{10 \cdot 16} = \pm 4\sqrt{10}$

Simplify. Be sure to include the positive and negative roots.

1. $\sqrt{98}$
2. $\sqrt{600}$
3. $\sqrt{50}$
4. $\sqrt{27}$
5. $\sqrt{8}$
6. $\sqrt{63}$
7. $\sqrt{48}$
8. $\sqrt{75}$
9. $\sqrt{54}$
10. $\sqrt{40}$
11. $\sqrt{72}$
12. $\sqrt{80}$
13. $\sqrt{90}$
14. $\sqrt{175}$
15. $\sqrt{18}$
16. $\sqrt{20}$

Chapter 3 Review

Write using exponents.

1. $3 \times 3 \times 3 \times 3$
2. $6 \times 6 \times 6 \times 6 \times 6 \times 6$
3. $11 \times 11 \times 11$
4. $2 \times 2 \times 2 \times 2 \times 2 \times 2 \times 2 \times 2$

Simplify the following expressions. Simplify the answers. Make all exponents positive.

5. $5^2 \times 5^3$
6. $(4^4)^5$
7. $(4y^3)^3$
8. $6x^{-3}$
9. $(3a^2)^{-2}$
10. $(b^3)^{-4}$
11. $\frac{4^6}{4^4}$
12. $\left(\frac{3}{5}\right)^2$
13. $x^3 \cdot$ [illegible]
14. $(2x)^{-4}$
15. $3^3 \times 3^2$
16. $(2$[illegible]$)^2$
17. $5^7 \times 5^{-4}$
18. $\frac{(3a^2)^3}{a^3}$
19. $(4^2)^{-2}$
20. $(5^{-9} \times$ [illegible]
21. $\frac{(2^3)\text{[illegible]}}{\text{[illegible]}}$
22. $\frac{\text{[illegible]}}{3y^4}$
23. $(6x)^{-3}$
24. $(4d^5)^{-3}$

Convert the following numbers to scientific notation.

25. $5,340,000$
26. 0.00000005874
27. $1,451$
28. 0.0000041
29. 0.0004178
30. $105,000$

Convert the following numbers from scientific notation to conventional numbers.

31. 5.204×10^{-5}
32. 1.02×10^{7}
33. 8.1×10^{5}
34. $2.0678 \times 10^{-}$[illegible]
35. 4.7×10^{-3}
36. 7.75×10^{-8}

For each of the following values of a, put the expressions a^1, a^2, a^3, a^4, a^5, and a^6 in order from least to greatest.

37. $a = -88$
38. $a = -\frac{2}{75}$
39. $a = \frac{1}{30}$

What would the value of the ones digit be for the simplified version of each of the following expressions?

40. [illegible]34^{105}
41. 887^{99}
42. 783^{43}[illegible]

Simplify each of the following logarithmic expressions.

43. $2(\log_{11} 17 + \log_{11} 20)$
44. $\frac{\log_3 16}{\log_3 6}$
45. $5(\log_2 9 - \log_2 3)$

For each of the following sets of conditions, an amount of money was deposited into a bank account, and no additional deposits or withdrawals were made. Determine the annual interest rate for each bank account to the nearest percent.

46. Initial deposit: \$5800; Compounding period: quarterly; Amount of money in bank account after 6 years: \$10, 490.61

47. Initial deposit: \$2700; Compounding period: semi-annually; Amount of money in bank account after 4 years: \$2923.71

48. Initial deposit:\$8200; Compounding period: weekly; Amount of money in bank account after 8 years: \$12, 230.61

Simplify the following square root expressions. Be sure to include the positive and negative roots.

49. $\sqrt{50}$
50. $\sqrt{44}$
51. $\sqrt{12}$
52. $\sqrt{18}$
53. $\sqrt{8}$
54. $\sqrt{48}$
55. $\sqrt{75}$
56. $\sqrt{200}$
57. $\sqrt{32}$
58. $\sqrt{20}$
59. $\sqrt{63}$
60. $\sqrt{80}$

Simplify the following square root problems.

61. $5\sqrt{27} + 7\sqrt{3}$
62. $\sqrt{40} - \sqrt{10}$
63. $\sqrt{64} + \sqrt{81}$
64. $8\sqrt{50}$ [illegible] $3\sqrt{32}$
65. $14\sqrt{5} + 8\sqrt{80}$
66. $\sqrt{63} \times \sqrt{28}$
67. $\dfrac{\sqrt{56}}{\sqrt{35}}$
68. $\sqrt{8} \times \sqrt{56}$
69. $\dfrac{\sqrt{20}}{\sqrt{45}}$
70. $5\sqrt{40} \times 3\sqrt{20}$
71. $2\sqrt{48} - \sqrt{12}$
72. $\dfrac{2\sqrt{5}}{\sqrt{30}}$
73. $\dfrac{3\sqrt{22}}{2\sqrt{3}}$
74. $\sqrt{72} \times 3\sqrt{27}$
75. $4\sqrt{5} + 8\sqrt{45}$

Estimate the following square root solutions.

76. Is $\sqrt{5}$ closer to 2 or 3?
77. Is $\sqrt{52}$ closer to 7 or 8?
78. Is $\sqrt{130}$ closer to 11 or 12?
79. Is $\sqrt{619}$ closer to 24 or 25?
80. Is $\sqrt{79}$ closer to 8 or 9?
81. Is $\sqrt{106}$ closer to 10 or 11?
82. Is $\sqrt{160}$ closer to 12 or 13?
83. Is $\sqrt{29}$ closer to 5 or 6?

Chapter 3 Test

1. What is $x^3 + x^3$ in simplest terms?

A. $2x^9$
B. $2x^6$
C. x^6
D. x^9
E. $2x^3$

2. What is $(x^7)^{-2}$ in simplest terms?

F. $\frac{1}{x^{14}}$
G. x^{-14}
H. x^5
J. x^9
K. $\frac{1}{x^9}$

3. What is $\frac{x^5}{y^2}$ in simplest terms?

A. x^3
B. xy^3
C. $\frac{x^5}{y^2}$
D. x^5y^2
E. $\frac{y^2}{x^5}$

4. What is $a^4 \times a^7$ in simplest terms?

F. a^{28}
G. a^{-3}
H. a^{-28}
J. a^{11}
K. a^3

5. What is $1,777,901$ in scientific notation?

A. $1.777901 \times 10^?$
B. 1.78×10^6
C. 1.77×10^7
D. 1.77×10^6
E. $1,777,901.0 \times 10^6$

6. What is 0.0000249 in scientific notation?

F. 2.49×10^{-5}
G. 2.49×10^5
H. 24.9×10^{-6}
J. 249×10^{-7}
K. 2.49×10^6

7. Which is the possible expansion of $(xy)^{12}$?

A. x^4x^3
B. $x^{12}y^{12}$
C. x^6y^2
D. x^4y^3
E. xy^{12}

8. What is $(ac)^2$ in simplest terms?

F. ac^4
G. a^2c^2
H. $(ac)^2$
J. a^4c^4
K. ac^2

9. What is 6.34 × [illegible] in standard form?

A. 0.0634
B. 6.34
C. 63,400
D. 0.0000634
E. 0.000634

10. What is 706, 000 in scientific notation?

F. 706.0×10^3
G. 7.06×10^5
H. 7.06×10^{-5}
J. 7.06×10^{-3}
K. 7.06×10^6

11. What is $\frac{x^{100}}{x^{50}}$ in simplest terms?

A. x^2
B. x^{150}
C. x^{50}
D. $\frac{x^{100}}{x^{50}}$
E. x^{5000}

12. What is ([illegible]) in simplest terms?

F. x^{12}
G. [illegible]
H. [illegible]
J. $(x^4)^3$
K. x^{-1}

13. What is $\frac{x^5}{x^3}$ in simplest terms?

A. x^2
B. x^8
C. x^5x^{-3}
D. $\frac{x^5}{x^3}$
E. $x^{5/3}$

14. If 843^{843} were simplified, what would be the value of the ones digit?

F. 1
G. [illegible]
H. 5
J. 7
K. 9

15. If $-1 < a < 0$, which of the following statements is true for the expressions a^m and a^n?

A. If m and n are both positive and odd, and if $m > n$, then $a^n > a^m$.
B. If m and n are both positive and even, and if $m > n$, then $a^n > a^m$.
C. If m and n are both positive and odd, and if $m > n$, then $a^n = a^m$.
D. If m and n are both positive and even, and if $m > n$, then $a^n < a^m$.
E. If m and n are both positive and even, and if $m > n$, then $a^n = a^m$.

16. What is $x^4 \times y^4$ in simplest terms?

F. xy^8
G. $(xy)^4$
H. $2x^4y^4$
J. xy^4
K. x^4y^4

17. Which of the following logarithms is equivalent to the expression $8\log_{12} 26 - 5\log_{12} 13 - 3\log_{12} 26$?

A. $\log_{12} \frac{1}{32}$
B. $\log_{12} 12$
C. $\log_{12} 2$
D. $\log_{12} 16$
E. $\log_{12} 32$

18. $\frac{3[(-6) \cdot (5) + 15]}{10 + (-5)} =$

F. -15
G. -9
H. -45
J. 15
K. [illegible]

19. What is the proper name for the square root sign?

A. radical
B. radicand
C. quotient
D. square root sign
E. root symbol

20. What is the $\sqrt{100}$?

F. 100
G. 50
H. 20
J. 25
K. 10

21. What is $\sqrt{3} \times \sqrt{5}$?

A. 15
B. $\sqrt{15}$
C. $3\sqrt{5}$
D. $5\sqrt{3}$
E. You cannot multiply these two numbers.

22. Which number is $\sqrt{53}$ closest to?

F. 4
G. 6
H. 8
J. 7
K. 50

23. What is the estimated value of $\sqrt{3}$?

A. 1.75
B. 2
C. 1.25
D. 3
E. 1.5

24. Which number is $\sqrt{66}$ closest to?

F. 7
G. 8
H. 9
J. 66
K. 33

25. What is $7\sqrt{3} + 4\sqrt{3}$?

A. $11\sqrt{6}$
B. $28\sqrt{9}$
C. 33
D. $74\sqrt{6}$
E. $11\sqrt{3}$

26. What is $\sqrt{60}$ in simplest terms?

F. $\sqrt{60}$
G. $2\sqrt{15}$
H. $\sqrt{4}\sqrt{15}$
J. $5\sqrt{2}$
K. $15\sqrt{2}$

27. What is $3\sqrt{32} - 2\sqrt{2}$?

A. $10\sqrt{2}$
B. $\sqrt{2} \times \sqrt{32}$
C. $\sqrt{64}$
D. $12 - 2\sqrt{2}$
E. $\sqrt{30}$

28. What is $\frac{\sqrt{3}}{\sqrt{7}}$?

F. 21
G. $\frac{3}{7}$
H. $\frac{7}{3}$
J. $\frac{\sqrt{21}}{7}$
K. You cannot divide these numbers.

Chapter 4
Solving Multi-Step Equations, Inequalities, and Patterns

4.1 Two-Step Algebra Problems

In the following two-step algebra problems, **additions** and **subtractions** are performed first and then **multiplication** and **division**.

Example 1: $-4x + 7 = 31$

Step 1: Subtract 7 from both sides.

$$\begin{array}{rl} -4x + 7 & = 31 \\ -7 & \;\; -7 \\ \hline -4x & = 24 \end{array}$$

Step 2: Divide both sides by -4.

$$\frac{-4x}{-4} = \frac{24}{-4} \qquad \text{so } x = -6$$

Example 2: $-8 - y = 12$

Step 1: Add 8 to both sides.

$$\begin{array}{rl} -8 - y & = 12 \\ +8 \quad & \;\; +8 \\ \hline -y & = 20 \end{array}$$

Step 2: To finish solving a problem with a negative sign in front of the variable, multiply both sides by -1. The variable needs to be positive in the answer.

$(-1)(-y) = (-1)(20)$ so $y = -20$

Solve the two-step algebra problems below.

1. $6x - 4 = -34$	6. $4x - 12 = 24$	11. $-g - 24 = -17$	16. $21t + 17 = 80$
2. $5y - 3 = 32$	7. $3x - 17 = -41$	12. $-7k - 12 = 30$	17. $20y + 9 = 149$
3. $8 - t = 1$	8. $9d - 5 = 49$	13. $9 - 5r = 64$	18. $15p - 27 = 33$
4. $10p - 6 = -36$	9. $10h + 8 = 78$	14. $6y - 14 = 34$	19. $22h + 9 = 97$
5. $11 - 9m = -70$	10. $-6b - 8 = 10$	15. $12t + 15 = 51$	20. $-5 + 36w = 175$

4.2 Two-Step Algebra Problems with Fractions

An algebra problem may contain a fraction. Study the following example to understand how to solve algebra problems that contain a fraction.

Example 3: $\frac{x}{2} + 4 = 3$

Step 1:

$$\begin{array}{r} \frac{x}{2} + 4 = 3 \\ -4 \quad -4 \\ \hline \frac{x}{2} = -1 \end{array}$$

Subtract 4 from both sides.

Step 2: $\frac{x}{2} = -1$ Multiply both sides by 2 to eliminate the fraction.

$\frac{x}{2} \times 2 = -1 \times 2,\ x = -2$

Simplify the following algebra problems.

1. $4 + \frac{y}{3} = 7$
2. $\frac{a}{2} + 5 = 12$
3. $\frac{w}{5} - 3 = 6$
4. $\frac{x}{9} - 3 = -5$
5. $\frac{b}{6} + 2 = -4$
6. $7 + \frac{z}{2} = -13$
7. $\frac{x}{2} - 7 = 3$
8. $\frac{c}{5} + 6 = -2$
9. $3 + \frac{x}{11} = 7$
10. $16 + \frac{m}{6} = 14$
11. $\frac{p}{3} + 5 = -2$
12. $\frac{t}{8} + 9 = 3$
13. $\frac{v}{7} - 8 = -1$
14. $5 + \frac{h}{10} = 8$
15. $\frac{k}{7} - 9 = 1$
16. $\frac{y}{4} + 13 = 8$
17. $15 + \frac{z}{14} = 13$
18. $\frac{b}{6} - 9 = -14$
19. $\frac{d}{3} + 7 = 12$
20. $10 + \frac{b}{6} = 4$
21. $2 + \frac{p}{4} = 6$
22. $\frac{t}{7} - 9 = -5$
23. $\frac{a}{10} - 1 = 3$
24. $\frac{a}{8} + 16 = 9$

4.3 Combining Like Terms

In algebra problems, separate **terms** by + and − signs. The expression $5x - 4 - 3x + 7$ has 4 terms: $5x$, 4, $3x$, and 7. Terms having the same variable can be combined (added or subtracted) to simplify the expression. $5x - 4 - 3x + 7$ simplifies to $2x + 3$.

$$5x - 3x \quad - 4 + 7 \quad = 2x + 3$$

Simplify the following expressions.

1. $7x + 12x$
2. $8y - 5y + 8$
3. $4 - 2x + 9$
4. $11a - 16 - a$
5. $9w + 3w - 8$
6. $-5x + x + 2x$
7. $w - 15 + 9w$
8. $21 - 10t + 9 - 2t$
9. $-3 + x - 4x + 9$
10. $7b + 12 + 4b$
11. $4h - h + 2 - 5$
12. $-6k + 10 - 4k$
13. $2a + 12a - 5 + a$
14. $5 + 9c - 10$
15. $-d + 1 + 2d - 4$
16. $-8 + 4h + 1 - h$
17. $12x - 4x + 7$
18. $10 + 3z + z - 5$
19. $14 + 3y - y - 2$
20. $11p - 4 + p$
21. $11m + 2 - m + 1$

4.4 Solving Equations with Like Terms

When an equation has two or more like terms on the same side of the equation, combine like terms as the **first** step in solving the equation.

Example 4: $7x + 2x - 7 = 21 + 8$

Step 1: Combine like terms on both sides of the equation.

Step 2: Solve the two-step algebra problem as explained previously.

$$\begin{aligned} 7x + 2x - 7 &= 21 + 8 \\ 9x - 7 &= 29 \\ +7 \quad & \quad +7 \\ 9x \div 9 &= 36 \div 9 \\ x &= 4 \end{aligned}$$

Solve the equations below combining like terms first.

1. $3w - 2w + 4 = 6$
2. $7x + 3 + x = 16 + 3$
3. $5 - 6y + 9y = -15 + 5$
4. $-14 + 7a + 2a = -5$
5. $-2t + 4t - 7 = 9$
6. $9d + d - 3d = 14$
7. $-6c - 4 - 5c = 10 + 8$
8. $15m - 9 - 6m = 9$
9. $-4 - 3x - x = -16$
10. $9 - 12p + 5p = 14 + 2$
11. $10y + 4 - 7y = -17$
12. $-8a - 15 - 4a = 9$

4.5 Solving for a Variable

Sometimes an equation has two variables and you may be asked to solve for one of the variables.

Example 5: If $5x + y = 19$, then $y =$

Solution: The goal is to have only y on one side of the equation and the rest of the terms on the other side of the equation. Follow order of operations to solve.

$5x + y - 5x = 19 - 5x$ Subtract $5x$ from both sides of the equation.
$y = 19 - 5x$

Example 6: If $7m + n = 30$, then $m =$

Solution: The goal is to have only m on one side of the equation and the rest of the terms on the other side of the equation. Follow order of operations to solve.

$7m + n = 30$ Subtract n from both sides of the equation.

$7m + n - n = 30 - n$

$\frac{7m}{7} = \frac{30 - n}{7}$ Divide both sides of the equation by 7.

$m = \frac{30 - n}{7}$

Solve each of the equations below for the variable indicated. Be sure to follow order of operations.

1. If $4a + b = 12$, then $a =$
2. If $6c - d = 17$ [illegible], then $d =$
3. If $3m - n = 11$, then $m =$
4. If $7r + 5s = 35$, then $r =$
5. If $8m - 9n - 2m = 6n$, then $m =$
6. If $-10y - 3x - x = -12y$, then $x =$
7. If $-4t + 4t - 2s = 8$, then $s =$
8. If $5x - 7y +$ [illegible]$y = -9x + 3$, then $y =$
9. If $-10b +$ [illegible]$a + 3a = -4b$, then $a =$
10. If $7x$ [illegible] $8y + x = 5y + 3$, then $x =$

4.6 Removing Parentheses

The distributive principle is used to remove parentheses.

Example 7: $2\,(a+6)$

You multiply 2 by each term inside the parentheses. $2 \times a = 2a$ and $2 \times 6 = 12$. The 12 is a positive number so use a plus sign between the terms in the answer.

$2\,(a+6) = 2a + 12$

Example 8: $4\,(-5c+2)$

The first term inside the parentheses could be negative. Multiply in exactly the same way as the examples above. $4 \times (-5c) = -20c$ and $4 \times 2 = 8$

$4\,(-5c+2) = -20c + 8$

Remove the parentheses in the problems below.

1. $7\,(n+6)$	6. $4\,(d-8)$	11. $10\,(9-y)$
2. $8\,(2g-5)$	7. $2\,(-4x+6)$	12. $9\,(c-9)$
3. $11\,(5$[illegible]$2)$	8. $7\,(4+6p)$	13. $12\,(-3t+1)$
4. $6\,($[illegible]$-4)$	9. $5\,(-4w-8)$	14. $3\,(4y+9)$
5. $2\,(-3k+5)$	10. $6\,(11x+2)$	15. $8\,(t+3)$

The number in front of the parentheses can also be negative. Remove these parentheses the same way.

Example 9: $-2\,(b-4)$

First, multiply $-2 \times b = -2b$

Second, multiply $-2 \times -4 = 8$

Copy the two products. The second product is a positive number so put a plus sign between the terms in the answer.

$-2\,(b-4) = -2b + 8$

Remove the parentheses in the following problems.

16. $-7\,(x+2)$	21. $-3\,(4x-2)$	26. $-8\,(9-7p)$
17. $-5\,(4-y)$	22. $-2\,(-z+2)$	27. $-9\,(-k-3)$
18. $-4\,(2b-2)$	23. $-4\,(7p+7)$	28. $-1\,(7b-9)$
19. $-2\,(8c+6)$	24. $-9\,(t-6)$	29. $-6\,(-5t-2)$
20. $-5\,(-w-8)$	25. $-10\,(2w+4)$	30. $-7\,(-v+4)$

4.7 Multi-Step Algebra Problems

You can now use what you know about removing parentheses, combining like terms, and solving simple algebra problems to solve problems that involve three or more steps. Study the examples below to see how easy it is to solve multi-step problems.

Example 10: $3(x+6) = 5x - 2$

Step 1: Use the distributive property to remove parentheses.

Step 2: Subtract $5x$ from each side to move the terms with variables to the left side of the equation.

Step 3: Subtract 18 from each side to move the integers to the right side of the equation.

Step 4: Divide both sides by -2 to solve for x.

$$\begin{aligned} 3x + 18 &= 5x - 2 \\ -5x \quad & \quad -5x \\ \hline -2x + 18 &= -2 \\ -18 \quad & \quad -18 \\ \hline \frac{-2x}{-2} &= \frac{-20}{-2} \\ x &= 10 \end{aligned}$$

Example 11: $\dfrac{3(x-3)}{2} = 9$

Step 1: Use the distributive property to remove parentheses.

Step 2: Multiply both sides by 2 to eliminate the fraction.

Step 3: Add 9 to both sides, and combine like terms.

Step 4: Divide both sides by 3 to solve for x.

$$\begin{aligned} \frac{3x-9}{2} &= 9 \\ \frac{2(3x-9)}{2} &= 2(9) \\ 3x - 9 &= 18 \\ +9 \quad & \quad +9 \\ \hline \frac{3x}{3} &= \frac{27}{3} \\ x &= 9 \end{aligned}$$

Example 12: $4(x-2) = 4x - 8$

Step 1: Use the distributive property to remove parentheses.
$4x - 8 = 4x - 8$

Step 2: Both sides of the equation are the same, so when you finish solving you will get $0 = 0$. In this specific case, any real number would make this equation true. Therefore, all real numbers are solutions for x.

Example 13: $x - 12 = x + 2$

Step 1: Subtract x from both sides.
$x - x - 12 = x - x + 2$
$-12 = 2$

Step 2: The result $-12 = 2$ is false. This means the equation has no solution. Therefore, there are no solutions for x. $x = \emptyset$.

Solve the following multi-step algebra problems.

1. $2(y-3) = 4y + 6$

2. $\dfrac{2(a+4)}{2} = 12$

3. $\dfrac{10(x-2)}{5} = 14$

4. $\dfrac{12y-18}{6} = 4y + 3$

5. $2x + 3x = 30 -$ [illegible]

6. $\dfrac{2a+1}{3} = a + 5$

7. $5(b-4) = 10b + 5$

8. $-8(y+4) = 10y + 4$

9. $\dfrac{x+4}{-3} = 6 - x$

10. $\dfrac{4(n+3)}{4} = n + 3$

11. $3(2x-5) = 8x - 9$

12. $7 - 9a = 9 - 9a$

13. $7 - 5x = 10 - (6x + 7)$

14. $4(x-3) - x = x - 6$

15. $4a + 4 = 3a - 4$

16. $-3(x-4) + 5 = -2x - 2$

17. $5b - 11 = 13 - b$

18. $\dfrac{-4x+3}{2x} = \dfrac{7}{2x}$

19. $-(x+1) = -2(5-x)$

20. $4(2c+3) - 7 = 13$

21. $6 - 3a = 9 - 2(2a+5)$

22. $-5x + 9 = -3x + 11$

23. $3y + 2 - 2y - 5 = 4y + 3$

24. $3y - 10 = 4 - 4y$

25. $-(a+3) = -(a+1) - 2$

26. $5m - 2(m+1) = m - 10$

27. $\dfrac{1}{2}(b-2) = 5$

28. $-3(b-4) = -2b$

29. $4x + 12 = -2(x+3)$

30. $\dfrac{7x+4}{3} = 2x - 1$

31. $9x - 5 = 8x - 7$

32. $4x - 5 = 4x + 10$

33. $\dfrac{4x+8}{2} = 6$

34. $2(c+4) +$ [illegible] $= 10$

35. $y - (y+3) = y + 6$

36. 4[illegible] $- 2(x-6) = 8$

4.8 Solving Radical Equations

Some multi-step equations contain radicals. An example of a radical is a square root, $\sqrt{}$.

Example 14: Solve the following equation for x. $\sqrt{4x-3}+2=5$

Step 1: The first step is to get the constants that are not under the radical on one side. Subtract 2 from both sides of the equation.

$\sqrt{4x-3}+2-2=5-2$
$\sqrt{4x-3}+0=3$
$\sqrt{4x-3}=3$

Step 2: Next, you must get rid of the radical sign by squaring both sides of the equation.

$\left(\sqrt{4x-3}\right)^2=\left((4x-3)^{1/2}\right)^2=(4x-3)^{(1/2)\times 2}=(4x-3)^1=4x-3$
$4x-3=(3)^2$
$4x-3=9$

Step 3: Add 3 to both sides of the equation to get the constants on just one side of the equation.

$4x-3+3=9+3$
$4x+0=12$
$4x=12$

Step 4: Last, get x on one side of the equation by itself by dividing both sides by 4.

$\frac{4x}{4}=\frac{12}{4}$
$x=3$

Solve the following equations.

1. $\sqrt{x+3}-13=-8$
2. $3+\sqrt{7t-3}=5$
3. $\sqrt{3q+12}-4=5$
4. $\sqrt{11f+3}+2=8$
5. $5=\sqrt{6g-5}+(-2)$
6. $2=\sqrt{x-3}$
7. $\sqrt{-8t}-3=1$
8. $\sqrt{-a+1}-9=-6$
9. $10-\sqrt{8x+2}=9$
10. $\sqrt{15y+4}+4=12$
11. $\sqrt{r+14}-1=9$
12. $3-\sqrt{2q-1}=0$
13. $\sqrt{5t+16}+4=13$
14. $17=\sqrt{23-f}+15$
15. $19-\sqrt{7x-5}=16$

4.9 Multi-Step Inequalities

Remember that adding and subtracting with inequalities follow the same rules as equations. When you multiply or divide both sides of an inequality by the same positive number, the rules are also the same as for equations. However, when you multiply or divide both sides of an inequality by a **negative** number, you must **reverse** the inequality symbol.

Example 15:

$-x > 4$

$(-1)(-x) < (-1)(4)$

$x < -4$

Example 16:

$-4x < 2$

$\frac{-4x}{-4} > \frac{2}{-4}$

$x > -\frac{1}{2}$

Reverse the symbol when you multiply or divide by a negative number.

When solving multi-step inequalities, first add and subtract to isolate the term with the variable. Then multiply and divide.

Example 17: $2x - 8 > 4x + 1$

Step 1: Add 8 to both sides.

$2x - 8 + 8 > 4x + 1 + 8$

$2x > 4x + 9$

Step 2: Subtract $4x$ from both sides.

$2x - 4x > 4x + 9 - 4x$

$-2x > 9$

Step 3: Divide by -2. Remember to change the direction of the inequality sign.

$\frac{-2x}{-2} < \frac{9}{-2}$

$x < -\frac{9}{2}$

Solve each of the following inequalities.

1. $8 - 3x \leq 7x - 2$

2. $3(2x - 5) \geq 8x - 5$

3. $\frac{1}{3}b - 2 > 5$

4. $7 + 3y > 2y - 5$

5. $3a + 5 < 2a -$ [illegible]

6. $3(a - 2) > 5a - 2(3 - a)$

7. $2x - 7 \geq 4(x - 3) + 3x$

8. $6x - 2 \leq 5x + 5$

9. $-\frac{x}{4} > 12$

10. $-\frac{2x}{3} \leq 6$

11. $3b + 5 < 2b - 8$

12. $4x - 5 \leq 7x + 13$

13. $4x + 5 < -2$

14. $2y - 5 > 7$

15. $4 + 2(3 - 2y) < 5y - 20$

16. $-4c + 6 \leq 3$

17. $-\frac{1}{2}x + 2 > 9$

18. $\frac{1}{4}y - 3 \leq 1$

19. $-3x + 4 > 5$

20. $\frac{y}{2} - 2 \geq 10$

21. $7 + 4c < -2$

22. $2 - \frac{a}{2} > 1$

23. $10 + 4b \leq -2$

24. $-\frac{1}{2}x + 3 > 4$

4.10 Solving Equations and Inequalities with Absolute Values

When solving equations and inequalities which involve variables placed in absolute values, remember that there will be two or more numbers that will work as correct answers. This is because the absolute value variable will signify both positive and negative numbers as answers.

Example 18: $5 + 3|k| = 8$ Solve as you would any equation.

Step 1: $3|k| = 3$ Subtract 5 from each side.

Step 2: $|k| = 1$ Divide by 3 on each side.

Step 3: $k = 1$ or $k = -1$ Because k is an absolute value, the answer can be 1 or -1.

Example 19: $2|x| - 3 < 7$ Solve as you normally would an inequality.

Step 1: $2|x| < 10$ Add 3 to both sides.

Step 2: $|x| < 5$ Divide by 2 on each side.

Step 3: $x < 5$ or $x > -5$ or $-5 < x < 5$ Because x is an absolute value, the answer is a set of both positive and negative numbers.

Read each problem and write the number or set of numbers which solves each equation or inequality.

1. $7 + 2|y| = 15$
2. $4|x| - 9 < 3$
3. $6|k| + 2 = 14$
4. $10 - 4|n| > -14$
5. $-3 = 5|z| + 12$
6. $-4 + 7|m| < 10$
7. $5|x| - 12 > 13$
8. $21|g| + 7 = 49$
9. $-9 + 6|x| = 15$
10. $12 - 6|w| > -12$
11. $31 > 13 + 9|r|$
12. $-30 = 21 - 3|t|$
13. $9|x| - 19 < 35$
14. $-13|c| + 21$ [illegible]
15. $5 - 11|k| < -17$
16. $-42 + 14|p|$ [illegible]4
17. $15 < 3$[illegible]$+ 6$
18. 9 [illegible] $|q| = 29$
19. $-14|y| - 38 < -45$
20. $36 = 4|s| + 20$
21. $20 \leq -60 + 8|e|$

4.11 More Solving Equations and Inequalities with Absolute Values

Now, look at the following examples in which numbers and variables are added or subtracted within the absolute value symbols ($||$).

Example 20: $|3x - 5| = 10$

Remember an equation with absolute value symbols has two solutions.

Step 1:

$$3x - 5 = 10$$
$$3x - 5 + 5 = 10 + 5$$
$$\frac{\not{3}x}{\not{3}} = \frac{15}{3}$$
$$x = 5$$

To find the first solution, remove the absolute value symbol and solve the equation.

Step 2:

$$-(3x - 5) = 10$$
$$-3x + 5 = 10$$
$$-3x + 5 - 5 = 10 - 5$$
$$-3x = 5$$
$$x = -\tfrac{5}{3}$$

To find the second solution, solve the equation for the negative of the expression in absolute value symbols.

Solutions: $x = \{5, -\frac{5}{3}\}$

Example 21: $|5z - 10| < 20$

Remove the absolute value symbols and solve the inequality.

Step 1:

$$5z - 10 < 20$$
$$5z - 10 + 10 < 20 + 10$$
$$\frac{\not{5}z}{\not{5}} < \frac{30}{5}$$
$$z < 6$$

Step 2:

$$-(5z - 10) < 20$$
$$-5z + 10 < 20$$
$$-5z + 10 - 10 < 20 - 10$$
$$\frac{-\not{5}z}{\not{5}} < \frac{10}{5}$$
$$-z < 2$$
$$z > -2$$

Next, solve the equation for the negative of the expression in the absolute value symbols.

Solution: $-2 < z < 6$

Example 22: $|4y + 7| - 5 > 18$

Step 1:
$4y + 7 - 5 + 5 > 18 + 5$
$4y + 7 > 23$
$4y + 7 - 7 > 23 - 7$
$4y > 16$
$y > 4$

Remove the absolute value symbols and solve the inequality.

Step 2:
$-(4y + 7) - 5 > 18$
$-4y - 7 - 5 + 5 > 18 + 5$
$-4y - 7 + 7 > 23 + 7$
$-4y > 30$
$y < -7\frac{1}{2}$

Solve the equation for the negative of the expression in the absolute value symbols.

Solutions: $y > 4$ or $y < -7\frac{1}{2}$

Solve the following equations and inequalities below.

1. $-4 + |2[illegible] + 4| = 14$
2. $|4b - 7| + 3 > 12$
3. $6 + |12e + 3| < 39$
4. $-15 + |8f - 14| > 35$
5. $|-9b + 13| - 12 = 10$
6. $-25 + |7b + 11| < 35$
7. $|7w + 2| - 50 > 30$
8. $63 + |3d - 12| = 21$
9. $|-23 + 8x| - 12 > +37$
10. $|61 + 20x| + 32 > 51$
11. $|4a + 13| + 31 = 50$
12. $4 + |4k - 32| < 51$
13. $8 + |4x + 3| = 21$
14. $|28 + 7v| - 28 < 77$
15. $|62p + 31| + 43 = 136$
16. $18 + |6v + 22| < 22$
17. $12 = 4 + |42 + 10m|$
18. $53 < 18 + |12e + 31|$
19. $38 > -39 + |7j + 14|$
20. $9 = |14 + 15u| + 7$
21. $11 + |2j + 50| > 45$
22. $|35 + 6[illegible]| - 3 = 14$
23. $|26 - 8[illegible]| - 9 > 41$
24. $|25 + 6z| - 21 = 28$
25. $12 < |2t + 6| - 4$
26. $50 > |9q - [illegible]| + 6$
27. $12 + |8v - 18| > 26$
28. $-38 + |16i - 33| = 41$
29. $|-14 + 6p| - 9 < 7$
30. $28 > |25 - 5f| - 12$

4.12 Graphing Inequalities

An inequality is a sentence that contains a $\neq$, $<$, $>$, $\leq$, or $\geq$ sign. Look at the following graphs of inequalities on a number line.

NUMBER LINE

$x < 3$ is read "x is less than 3."

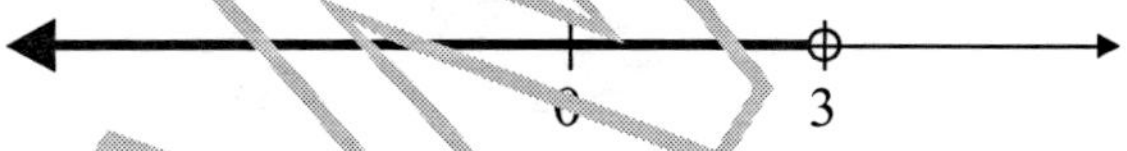

There is no line under the $<$ sign, so the graph uses an **open** endpoint to show x is less than 3 but does not include 3.

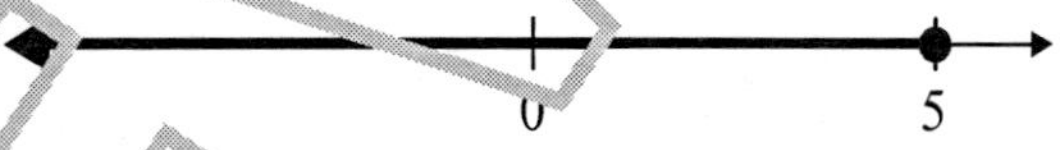

$x \leq 5$ is read "x is less than or equal to 5."

If you see a line under $<$ or $>$ ($\leq$ or $\geq$), the endpoint is filled in. The graph uses a **closed** circle because the number 5 is included in the graph.

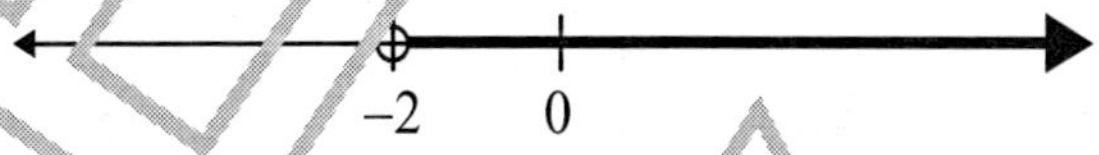

$x > -2$ is read "x is greater than -2."

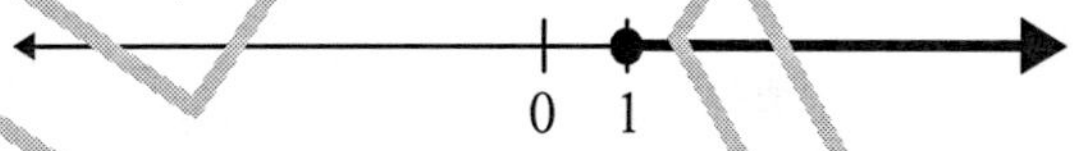

$x \geq 1$ is read "x is greater than or equal to 1."

There can be more than one inequality sign. For example:

$-2 \leq x < 4$ is read "-2 is less than or equal to x and x is less than 4."

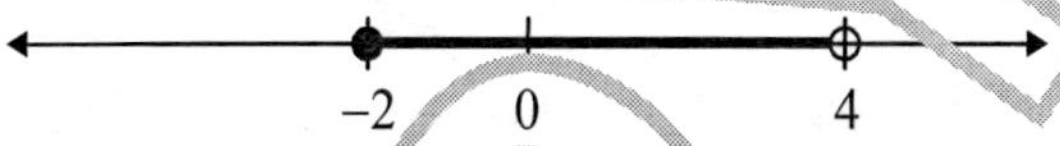

$x < 1$ or $x \geq 4$ is read "x is less than 1 or x is greater than or equal to 4."

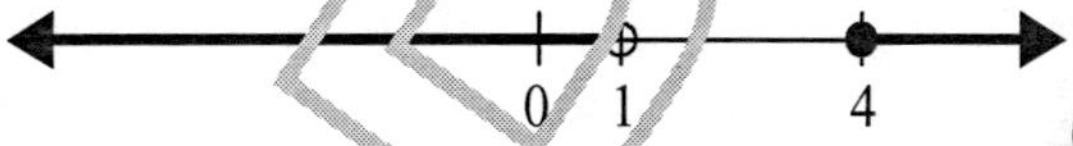

Graph the solution sets of the following inequalities.

1. $x > 8$
2. $x \leq 5$
3. $-5 < x < 1$
4. $x > 7$
5. $1 < x < 4$
6. $x < -2$ or $x > 1$
7. $x \geq 10$
8. $x < 4$
9. $x < 3$ or $x \geq 5$
10. $x < -1$ or $x > 1$

Give the inequality represented by each of the following number lines.

11. 

____

12. 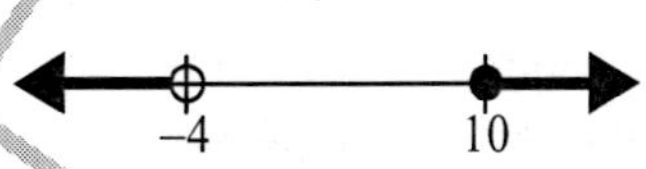

____

13. 

____

14. 

____

15. 

____

16. 

____

17. 

____

18. 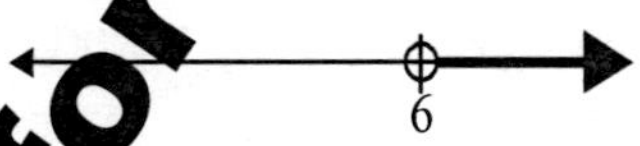

____

4.13 Inequality Word Problems

Inequality word problems involve staying under a limit or having a minimum goal one must meet.

Example 23: A contestant on a popular game show must earn a minimum of 800 points by answering a series of questions worth 40 points each per category in order to win the game. The contestant will answer questions from each of four categories. Her results for the first three categories are as follows: 160 points, 200 points, and 240 points. Write an inequality which describes how many points, (p), the contestant will need on the last category in order to win.

Step 1: Add to find out how many points she already has. $160 + 200 + 240 = 600$

Step 2: Subtract the points she already has from the minimum points she needs. $800 - 600 = 200$. She must get at least 200 points in the last category to win. If she gets more than 200 points, that is okay, too. To express the number of points she needs, use the following inequality statement:

$p \geq 200$ The points she needs must be greater than or equal to 200.

Solve each of the following problems using inequalities.

1. Sheila wants to place her money in a high interest money market account. However, she needs at least $1,000 to open an account. Each month, she set aside some of her earnings in a savings account. In January through June, she added the following amounts to her savings: $121, $205, $138, $212, $109, and $134. Write an inequality which describes the amount of money she can set aside in July to qualify for the money market account.

2. A high school band program will receive $2,000.00 for selling $10,000.00 worth of coupon books. Six band classes participate in the sales drive. Classes 1–5 collect the following amounts of money: $1,400, $2,600, $1,800, $2,450, and $1,550. Write an inequality which describes the amount of money the sixth class must collect so that the band will receive $2,000.

3. A small elevator has a maximum capacity of 1,000 pounds before the cable holding it in place snaps. Six people get on the elevator. Five of their weights follow: 146, 180, 130, 262, and 135. Write an inequality which describes the amount the sixth person can weigh without snapping the cable.

4. A small high school class of 9 students were told they would receive a pizza party if their class average was 92% or higher on the next exam. Students 1–8 scored the following on the exam: 86, 91, 98, 83, 97, 89, 99, and 96. Write an inequality which describes the score the ninth student must make for the class to qualify for the pizza party.

5. Raymond wants to spend his entire credit limit on his credit card. His credit limit is $2,000. He purchases items costing $600, $800, $50, $168, and $3. Write an inequality which describes the amounts Raymond can put on his credit card for his next purchases.

4.14 Number Patterns

In each of the examples below, there is a sequence of numbers that follows a pattern. Think of the sequence of numbers like the output for a function. You must find the pattern (or function) that holds true for each number in the sequence. Once you determine the pattern, you can find the next number in the sequence or any number in the sequence.

	Sequence	Pattern	Next Number	20th number in the sequence
Example 24:	$3, 4, 5, 6, 7$	$n + 2$	8	22

In number patterns, the sequence is the output. The input can be the set of whole numbers starting with 1. But, you must determine the "rule" or pattern. Look at the table below.

input	sequence
1 →	3
2 →	4
3 →	5
4 →	6
5 →	7

What pattern or "rule" can you come up with that gives you the first number in the sequence, 3, when you input 1? $n + 2$ will work because when $n = 1$, the first number in the sequence = 3. Does this pattern hold true for the rest of the numbers in the sequence? Yes, it does. When $n = 2$, the second number in the sequence = 4. When $n = 3$, the third number in the sequence = 5, and so on. Therefore, $n + 2$ is the pattern. Even without knowing the algebraic form of the pattern, you could determine that 8 is the next pattern in the sequence. To find the 20th number in the pattern, use $n = 20$ to get 22.

	Sequence	Pattern	Next Number	20th number in the sequence
Example 25:	$1, 4, 9, 16, 25$	n^2	36	400
Example 26:	$-2, -4, -6, -8, -10$	$-2n$	-12	-40

Find the pattern, the next number, and the 20th number in each of the sequences below.

	Sequence	Pattern	Next Number	20th number in the sequence
1.	$-2, -1, 0, 1, 2$	_____	_____	_____
2.	$5, 6, 7, 8, 9$	_____	_____	_____
3.	$3, 7, 11, 15, 19$	_____	_____	_____
4.	$-3, -6, -9, -12, -15$	_____	_____	_____
5.	$3, 5, 7, 9, 11$	_____	_____	_____
6.	$2, 4, 8, 16, 32$	_____	_____	$1,048,576$
7.	$1, 8, 27, 64, 125$	_____	_____	_____
8.	$0, -1, -2, -3, -4$	_____	_____	_____
9.	$2, 5, 10, 17, 26$	_____	_____	_____
10.	$4, 6, 8, 10, 12$	_____	_____	_____

4.15 Real-World Patterns

Humans have always observed what happened in the past and used these observations to predict what would happen in the future. This is called **inductive reasoning**. Although mathematics is referred to as the "deductive science," it benefits from inductive reasoning. We observe patterns in the mathematical behavior of a phenomenon, then find a rule or formula for describing and predicting its future mathematical behavior. There are lots of different kinds of predictions that may be of interest.

Example 27: Nancy is watching her nephew, Drew, arrange his marbles in rows on the kitchen floor. The figure below shows the progression of his arrangement.

Assuming this pattern continues, how many marbles would Drew place in a fifth row?

Solution: It appears that Drew doubles the number of marbles in each successive row. In the 4th row he had 8 marbles, so in the 5th row we can predict 16 marbles.

Example 28: Manuel drops a golf ball from the roof of his high school while Carla video tapes the motion of the ball. Later, the video is analyzed and the results are recorded concerning the height of each bounce of the ball.

What height do you predict for the fifth bounce?

Initial height	1st bounce	2nd bounce	3rd bounce	4th bounce
30 ft	18 ft	10.8 ft	6.48 ft	3.888 ft

To answer this question, we need to be able to relate the height of each bounce to the bounce immediately preceding it. Perhaps the best way to do this is with **ratios** as follows:

$$\frac{\text{Height of 1st bounce}}{\text{Initial bounce}} = 0.6 \qquad \frac{\text{Height of 2nd bounce}}{\text{Height of 1st bounce}} = 0.6$$

$$\frac{\text{Height of 4th bounce}}{\text{Height of 3rd bounce}} = 0.6$$

Since the ratio of the height of each bounce to the bounce before it appears constant, we have some basis for making predictions.

Using this, we can reason that the fifth bounce will be equal to 0.6 of the fourth bounce.
Thus we predict the fifth bounce to have a height of $0.6 \times 3.888 = 2.3328$ ft.

Which bounce will be the last one with a height of one foot or greater?

For this question, keep looking at predicted bounce heights until a bounce of less than 1 foot is reached.

The sixth bounce is predicted to be $0.6 \times 2.3328 = 1.399768$ ft.
The seventh bounce is predicted to be $0.6 \times 1.399768 = 0.839808$ ft.

Thus, the last bounce with a height greater than 1 ft is predicted to be the sixth one.

Read the following questions carefully. Use inductive reasoning to answer each question. You may wish to make a table or a diagram to help you visualize the pattern in some of the problems.

1. Bob and Alice have designed and created a website for their high school. The first week they had 5 visitors to the site; the second week, they had 10 visitors; and during the third week, they had 20 visitors.

   (A) If current trends continue, how many visitors can they expect in the fifth week?

   (B) How many in the nth week?

   (C) How many weeks will it be before they get more than 500 visitors in a single week?

2. In 1979 (the first year of classes), there were 500 students at Brookstone High. In 1989, there were 1000 students. In 1999, there were 2000 students. How many students would you predict at Brookstone in 2009 if this pattern continues (and no new schools are built)?

3. The average combined (math and verbal) SAT score for students at Brookstone High was 1000 in 2003, 1100 in 2004, 1210 in 2005, and 1331 in 2006. Predict the combined SAT score for Brookstone seniors in 2007.

4. Marie has a daylily in her mother's garden. Every Saturday morning in the spring, she measures and records its height in the table below. What height do you predict for Marie's daylily on April 29? (Hint: Look at the *change* in height each week when looking for the pattern).

April 1	April 8	April 15	April 22
12 in	18 in	21 in	22.5 in

5. Bob puts a glass of water in the freezer and records the temperature every 15 minutes. The results are displayed in the table below. If this pattern of cooling continues, what will be the temperature at 2:15 P.M.? (Hint: Again, look at the changes in temperature in order to see the pattern.)

1:00 P.M.	1:15 P.M.	1:30 P.M.	1:45 P.M.
92° F	60° F	44° F	36° F

Example 29: Mr. Applegate wants to put desks together in his math class so that students can work in groups. The diagram below shows how he wishes to do it.

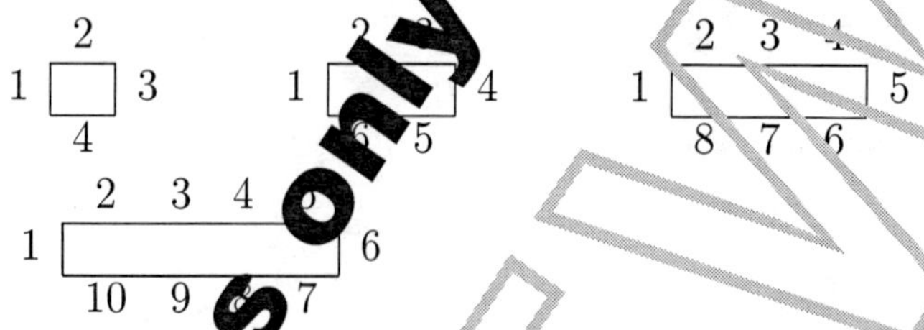

With one table he can seat 4 students, with two tables he can seat 6, with three tables 8, and with four tables 10.

How many students can he seat with 5 tables?

With 5 tables he could seat 5 students along the sides of the tables and 1 student on each end; thus, a total of 12 students could be seated.

Write a rule that Mr. Applegate could use to tell how many students could be seated at *n* tables. Explain how you got the rule.

For n tables, there would be n students along each of 2 sides and 2 students on the ends (1 on each end); thus, a total of $2n + 2$ students could be seated at n tables.

Example 30: When he isn't playing football for the Brookstone Bears, Tim designs web pages. A car dealership paid Tim \$500 to start a site with photos of its cars. The dealer also agreed to pay Tim \$50 for each customer who buys a car first viewed on the website.

Write and explain a rule that tells how much the dealership will pay Tim for the design of the website and the sale of *n* cars from the website.

Tim's payment will be the initial \$500 plus \$50 for each sale. Translated into mathematical language, if Tim sells n cars he will be paid a total of $500 + 50n$ dollars.

How many cars have to be sold from his site in order for Tim to get \$1000 from the dealership?

He earned \$500 just by establishing the site, so he only needs to earn an additional \$500, which at \$50 per car requires the sale of only 10 cars. (Note: Another way to solve this problem is to use the rule found in the first question. In that case, you simply solve the equation $500 + 50n = 1000$ for the variable n.)

Example 31: Eric is baking muffins to raise money for the Homecoming dance. He makes 18 muffins with each batch of batter, but he must give one muffin each to his brother, his sister, his dog, and himself each time a batch is finished baking.

Write a rule for the number of muffins Eric produces for the fund-raiser with n batches. He makes 18 muffins with each batch, but only 14 are available for the fund-raiser. Thus with n batches he will produce $14n$ muffins for Homecoming. **The rule** $= 14n$.

Use your rule to determine how many muffins he will contribute if he makes 7 batches. The number of batches, n, equals 7. Therefore, he will produce $14 \times 7 = 98$ muffins with 7 batches.

Determine how many batches he must make in order to contribute at least 150 muffins. Ten batches will produce $10 \times 14 = 140$ muffins. Eleven batches will produce $11 \times 14 = 154$ muffins. To produce at least 150 muffins, he must bake at least 11 batches.

Determine how many muffins he would actually bake in order to contribute 150 muffins. Since Eric actually bakes 18 muffins per batch, 11 batches would result in Eric baking $11 \times 18 = 198$ muffins.

Carefully read and solve the problems below. Show your work.

1. Tito is building a picket fence along both sides of the driveway leading up to his house. He will have to place posts at both ends and at every 10 feet along the way because the fencing comes in prefabricated ten-foot sections.
   (A) How many posts will he need for a 180-foot driveway?
   (B) Write and explain a rule for determining the number of posts needed for n ten-foot sections.
   (C) How long of a driveway can he fence with 32 posts?
2. Dakota's beginning pay at his new job is \$300 per week. For every three months he continues to work there, he will get a \$10 per week raise.
   (A) Write a formula for Dakota's weekly pay after n three-month periods.
   (B) After n years?
   (C) How long will he have to work before his pay gets to \$400 per week?
3. Amanda is selling shoes this summer. In addition to her hourly wages, Amanda got a \$100 bonus just for accepting the position, and she gets a \$2 bonus for each pair of shoes she sells.
   (A) Write and explain a rule that tells how much she will make in bonuses if she sells n pairs of shoes.
   (B) How many pairs of shoes must she sell in order to make \$200 in bonuses?
4. The table below displays data relating temperature in degrees Fahrenheit to the number of chirps per minute for a cricket.

Temp (°F)	50	52	55	58	60	64	68
Chirps/min	40	48	60	72	80	96	112

Write a formula or rule that predicts the number of chirps per minute when the temperature is n degrees.

Chapter 4 Review

Solve each of the following equations.

1. $4a - 8 = 28$
2. $5 + \frac{x}{8} = -4$
3. $-$[illegible] $+ 2$[illegible]$w = 108$
4. $\frac{y - 8}{6} = 7$
5. c [illegible] $13 = 5$
6. $\frac{b + \text{[illegible]}}{12} = -3$

Simplify the following expressions by combining like terms.

7. $-4a + 8 + 3a - 9$
8. $14 + 2z - 8 + 5z$
9. $-7 - 7x - 2 - 9x$

Solve.

10. $19 - 8d = d - 17$
11. $7w - 8w = -4w - 30$
12. $6 + 16x = 16x - 12$
13. $6(b - 4) = 6b - 24$
14. $4x - 16 = 7x + 2$
15. $9w - 2 =$ [illegible]$w - 22$

Remove parentheses.

16. [illegible]$(-4x + 7)$
17. $11(2y + 5)$
18. $6(8 - 9b)$
19. $-8(-2 + 3a)$
20. $-2(5c - 3)$
21. $-5(7y - 1)$

Solve for the variable.

22. If $3x - y = 15$, then $y =$
23. If $7a + 2b = 1$, then $b =$

Solve each of the following equations and inequalities.

24. $\frac{-11c - 35}{4} = 4c - 2$
25. $5 + x - 3(x + 4) = -17$
26. $4(2x + 3) \geq 2x$
27. $7 - 3x \leq 6x - 2$
28. $\frac{5(n + 4)}{3} = n - 8$
29. $-y > 14$
30. $2(3x - 1) \geq 3x - 7$
31. [illegible]$(x + 2) = 3x - 10$
32. $-11|k| < -22$
33. $18 - 3|w|$ [illegible] -18
34. $21 = -4 + |5x + 5|$
35. $|3x + 2| - 4 \geq -2$

Graph the solution sets of the following inequalities.

36. $x \leq -3$

37. $x > 6$

38. $x < -2$

39. $x \geq 4$

Give the inequality represented by each of the following number lines.

40. 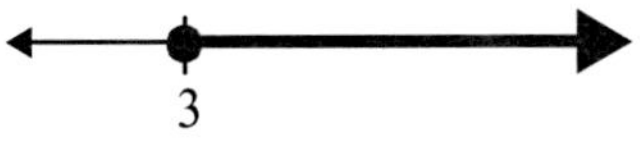 ________

41. 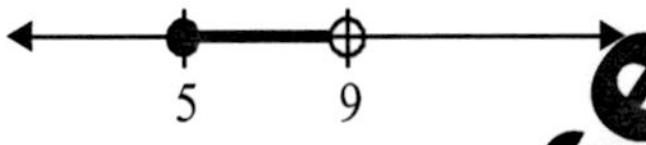 ________

42. 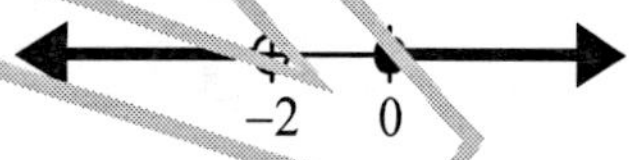 ________

43.  ________

Find the pattern for the following number sequences, and then find the nth number requested.

44. 0, 1, 2, 3, 4 pattern________

45. 0, 1, 2, 3, 4 20th number________

46. 1, 3, 5, 7, 9 pattern________

47. 1, 3, 5, 7, 9 25th number________

48. 3, 6, 9, 12, 15 pattern________

49. 3, 6, 9, 12, 15 30th number________

Justin receives a bill from his internet service provider. The first four months of service are charged according to the table below:

	January	February	March	April
Hours	0	10	5	25
Charge	$4.95	$14.45	$9.70	$28.70

50. Write a formula for the cost of n hours of internet service.

51. What is the greatest number of hours he can get on the internet and still keep his bill under $20.00?

Lisa is baking cookies for the Fall Festival. She bakes 27 cookies with each batch of batter. However, she has a defective oven, which results in 5 cookies in each batch being burnt.

52. Write a formula for the number of cookies available for the festival as a result of Lisa baking n batches of cookies.

53. How many batches does she need in order to produce 300 cookies for the festival?

54. How many cookies (counting burnt ones) will she actually bake?

55. Jim takes great pride in decorating his float for the homecoming parade for his high school. With the $5,000 he has to spend, Jim bought 5,000 carnations at $0.25 each, 4,000 tulips at $0.50 each, and 300 irises at $0.90 each. Write an inequality which describes how many roses, r, Jim can buy if roses cost $0.80 each.

56. Mr. Chan wants to sell some or all of his shares of stock in a company. He purchased the 80 shares for $0.50 last month, and the shares are now worth $4.50 each. Write an inequality which describes how much profit, p, Mr. Chan can make by selling his shares.

Chapter 4 Test

1. Find the value of n. $19n - 57 = 76$

A. 1

B. 2

C. 3

D. 5

E. 7

2. Solve: $3(x - 2) - 1$[illegible]$6(x + 5)$

F. -4

G. $-\frac{37}{3}$

H. $\frac{23}{3}$

J. 4

K. $\frac{[illegible]}{3}$

3. [illegible]$(2x + 11) - 3 \times 5 = ?$

A. $7x + 40$

B. $7x + 20$

C. $10x + 40$

D. $10x - 4$

E. $10x + 26$[illegible]

4. Which inequality correctly depicts the following graph?

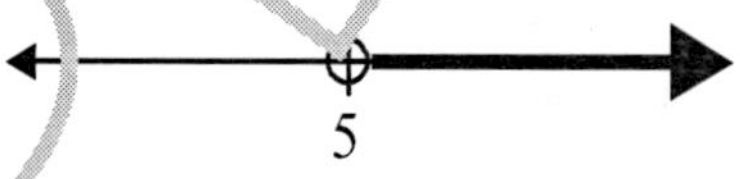

F. $x < 5$

G. $x \leq 5$

H. $x \geq 5$

J. $x > 5$

K. $x \geq 6$

5. Solve: $29 + |10x - 8| > 41$

A. $x = 1$

B. $x > 1$ or $x < \frac{2}{5}$

C. $x > \frac{3}{5}$

D. $x > 1$ or $x < -1$

E. $1 < x <$ [illegible]1

6. Solve: $4b - 8 < 56$

F. $b > 16$

G. $b < 12$

H. $b < -12$

J. $b < -16$

K. $b < 16$

7. Which of the following is equivalent to $3(2x - 5) - 4(x - 3) = 7$?

A. $x + 27 = 7$

B. $2x - 3 = 7$

C. $x - 27 = 7$

D. $10x - 27 = 7$

E. $2x - 8 = 7$

8. Which of the following describes the solution set for $3(x - 2) + 1$ [illegible] $3x = -5$?

F. $x = -5$

G. $x = 0$

H. $x = -\frac{5}{3}$

J. There are no solutions for x.

K. All real numbers are solutions for x.

9. Solve for x. $14x + 84 = 154$

A. 4

B. 5

C. 11

D. 17

E. 28

10. Which of the following is equivalent to $4 - 5x > 3(x - 4)$?

F. $4 - 5x > 3x - 4$
G. $4 - 5x > 3x - 12$
H. $4 - 5x > 3x - 1$
J. $4 - 5x > 3x - 7$
K. $4 - 5x > 3x + 12$

11. What is the next number in this sequence?
$0.03, 0.12, 0.48, 1.92,$ ____

A. 1.95
B. 3.36
C. 5.08
D. 7.68
E. 5.92

12. What is the next number in this sequence?
$2, 16, 128, 1024,$ ____

F. 1,[illegible]20
G. 8,192
H. 9,050
J. 11,586
K. 16,384

13. As shown in the table, the monthly rent of an apartment depends on the number of bedrooms.

MONTHLY RENT

Bedrooms	Rent
1	\$550
2	\$625
3	\$700

If the pattern is extended, which of these is the likely cost of a 4-bedroom apartment?

A. \$715
B. \$725
C. \$750
D. \$775
E. \$800

14. During a science experiment, Kyle counted the number of bacteria present in a petri dish after every minute.

Number of Minutes	Number of Bacteria
1	1
2	4
3	9
4	16

Assuming the pattern continues, how many bacteria will there be after 20 minutes?

F. 400
G. 200
H. 100
J. 80
K. 60

15. There is a new bike that Bianca has had her eye on for a few weeks. The bike costs \$75. Her allowance is 10 dollars per week. If she saves 60% of her allowance each week, write an inequality that describes the minimum amount of weeks, y, that Bianca must save in order to buy that bike.

A. $y > 75 - 0.6(10)$

B. $y > 45(10)$

C. $y > \dfrac{75}{0.6(10)}$

D. $10 > \dfrac{75}{0.6y}$

E. $10 > \dfrac{75}{y}(0.6)$

Chapter 5
Ratios and Proportions

Ratio Problems

In some word problems, you may be asked to express answers as a **ratio**. Ratios can look like fractions. Numbers must be written in the order they are requested. In the following problem, 8 cups of sugar is mentioned before 6 cups of strawberries. But in the question part of the problem, you are asked for the ratio of STRAWBERRIES to SUGAR. The amount of strawberries IS THE FIRST WORD MENTIONED, so it must be the **top** number of the fraction. The amount of sugar, THE SECOND WORD MENTIONED, must be the **bottom** number of the fraction.

Example 1: The recipe for jam requires 8 cups of sugar for every 6 cups of strawberries. What is the ratio of strawberries to sugar in this recipe?

First number requested	6	cups strawberries
Second number requested	8	cups sugar

Answers may be reduced to lowest terms. $\frac{6}{8} = \frac{3}{4}$

Practice writing ratios for the following word problems and reduce to lowest terms. DO NOT CHANGE ANSWERS TO MIXED NUMBERS. Ratios should be left in fraction form.

1. Out of the 248 seniors, 112 are boys. What is the ratio of boys to the total number of seniors?

2. It takes 7 cups of flour to make 2 loaves of bread. What is the ratio of cups of flour to loaves of bread?

3. A skyscraper that stands 620 feet tall casts a shadow that is 125 feet long. What is the ratio of the shadow to the height of the skyscraper?

4. Twenty boxes of paper weigh 520 pounds. What is the ratio of boxes to pounds?

5. The newborn weighs 8 pounds and is 22 inches long. What is the ratio of weight to length?

6. Jack paid $6.00 for 10 pounds of apples. What is the ratio of the price of apples to the pounds of apples?

7. Jordan spends $[illegible] on groceries. Of that total, $23 is for steaks. What is the ratio of steak cost to the total grocery cost?

8. Madison's flower garden measures 8 feet long by 6 feet wide. What is the ratio of length to width?

5.2 Writing Ratios Using Variables

Ratios can be written using variables instead of just numbers.

Example 2: Timothy has a bag of marbles. He only has red, r, marbles and blue, b, marbles. If he gives three of the blue marbles to his little brother, what fractional part of the marbles remaining in the bag are blue?

Step 1: The total number of marbles in the bag before Timothy gives three to his brother is $r + b$. So the fractional part of the marbles that are blue before Timothy gives some away is $\frac{b}{r+b}$.

Step 2: Since Timothy takes three blue marbles out of the bag, the total number of marbles that are left are $r + b - 3$. The total number of blue marbles left is $b - 3$. So, the fractional part of the marbles that are blue after Timothy gives three to his brother is $\frac{b-3}{r+b-3}$.

Use the following for questions 1 through 4.

Sancho has a box of bouncy balls. He has green, g, bouncy balls, yellow, y, bouncy balls, and blue-and-white striped, b, bouncy balls. He gives four yellow bouncy balls and 1 green bouncy ball to a friend.

1. What is the ratio of green bouncy balls to the total number of bouncy balls after he gave the 4 yellow balls and 1 green ball to a friend?
2. What is the ratio of yellow and blue and white striped bouncy balls to the total number of bouncy balls after he gave the 4 yellow balls and 1 green ball to a friend?
3. If Sancho originally had 5 green bouncy balls, 7 yellow bouncy balls, and 3 blue and white striped bouncy balls, what is the numerical ratio of yellow bouncy balls to the total number of bouncy balls after he gave the 4 yellow balls and the 1 green ball to a friend?
4. Using variables, what fractional part of the remaining bouncy balls are yellow?

Use the following for questions 5 and 6.

Callie has a bag of lollipops. She has cherry lollipops, designated by the letter c, and blue raspberry lollipops, designated by the letter b. She gave two cherry lollipops to her best friend.

5. What fractional part of the remaining lollipops are cherry?
6. If Callie originally had 8 cherry lollipops and 3 blue raspberry lollipops, what is the numerical ratio of blue raspberry to the total number of lollipops after she gave two cherry lollipops to her best friend?

5.3 Solving Proportions

Two **ratios (fractions)** that are **equal** to each other are called **proportions. For example, $\frac{1}{4} = \frac{2}{8}$. Read the following example to see how to find a number missing from a proportion.**

Example 3: $\frac{5}{15} = \frac{8}{x}$

Step 1: To find x, you first multiply the two numbers that are diagonal to each other.

$\frac{5}{\{15\}} = \frac{\{8\}}{x}$

$15 \times 8 = 120$

$5 \times x = 5x$

Therefore, $5x = 120$

Step 2: Then divide the product (120) by the other number in the proportion (5).

$120 \div 5 = 24$

Therefore, $\frac{5}{15} = \frac{8}{24}$ **and** $x = 24$.

Practice finding the number missing from the following proportions. First, multiply the two numbers that are diagonal from each other. Then divide by the other number.

1. $\frac{2}{5} = \frac{6}{x}$
2. $\frac{9}{3} = \frac{x}{5}$
3. $\frac{x}{12} = \frac{3}{4}$
4. $\frac{7}{x} = \frac{3}{9}$
5. $\frac{12}{x} = \frac{2}{5}$
6. $\frac{12}{x} = \frac{4}{3}$
7. $\frac{27}{3} = \frac{x}{2}$
8. $\frac{1}{x} = \frac{3}{12}$
9. $\frac{15}{2} = \frac{x}{4}$
10. $\frac{7}{14} = \frac{x}{6}$
11. $\frac{5}{6} = \frac{10}{x}$
12. $\frac{4}{x} = \frac{3}{6}$
13. $\frac{x}{5} = \frac{9}{15}$
14. $\frac{9}{18} = \frac{x}{2}$
15. $\frac{5}{7} = \frac{35}{x}$
16. $\frac{x}{[illegible]} = \frac{8}{4}$
17. $\frac{15}{20} = \frac{x}{8}$
18. $\frac{x}{40} = \frac{5}{100}$

5.4 Proportion Word Problems

Example 4: A stick one meter long is held perpendicular to the ground and casts a shadow 0.4 meters long. At the same time, an electrical tower casts a shadow 112 meters long. Use ratio and proportion to find the height of the tower.

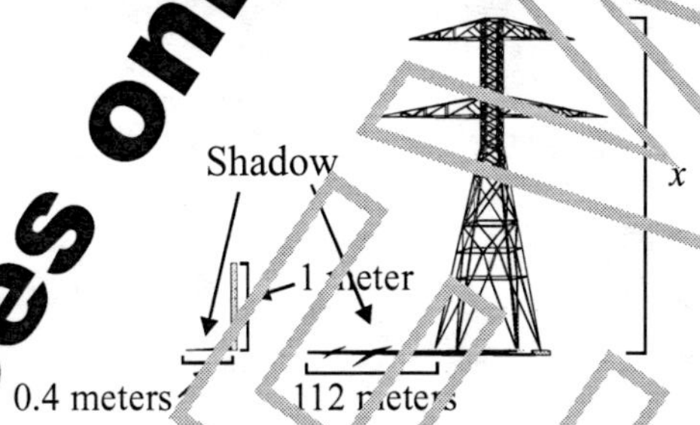

Step 1: Set up a proportion using the numbers in the problem. Put the shadow lengths on one side of the equation and put the heights on the other side. The 1 meter height is paired with the 0.4 meter length, so let them both be top numbers. Let the unknown height be x.

$$\begin{array}{ccc} \text{shadow length} & & \text{object height} \\ \frac{0.4}{112} & = & \frac{1}{x} \end{array}$$

Step 2: Solve the proportion as you did on page 82.

$112 \times 1 = 112 \qquad 112 \div 0.4 = 280$

Answer: The tower height is 280 meters.

Use ratio and proportion to solve the following problems.

1. Rudolph can mow a lawn that measures $1,000$ square feet in 2 hours. At that rate, how long would it take him to mow a lawn 3,500 square feet?
2. Faye wants to know how tall her school building is. On a sunny day, she measures the shadow of the building to be 6 feet. At the same time she measures the shadow cast by a 5-foot statue to be 2 feet. How tall is her school building?
3. Out of every 5 students surveyed, 2 listen to country music. At that rate, how many students in a school of 800 listen to country music?
4. Butterfly, a Labrador retriever, has a litter of 8 puppies. Four are black. At that rate, how many puppies in a litter of 10 would be black?
5. According to the instructions on a bag of fertilizer, 5 pounds of fertilizer are needed for every 100 square feet of lawn. How many square feet will a 25-pound bag cover?
6. A race car can travel 2 laps in 5 minutes. At this rate, how long will it take the race car to complete 100 laps ?
7. If it takes 7 cups of flour to make 4 loaves of bread, how many loaves of bread can you make from 35 cups of flour?
8. If 3 pounds of jelly beans cost \$6.30, how much would 2 pounds cost?
9. For the first 4 home football games, the concession stand sold a total of 600 hotdogs. If that ratio stays constant, how many hotdogs will sell for all 10 home games?

Chapter 5 Review

Solve the following proportions and ratios.

1. $\frac{8}{x} = \frac{1}{2}$ 2. $\frac{2}{5} = \frac{x}{10}$ 3. $\frac{x}{6} = \frac{3}{9}$ 4. $\frac{4}{9} = \frac{8}{x}$

5. Out of 100 coins, 45 are in mint condition. What is the ratio of mint condition coins to the total number of coins?

6. The ratio of boys to girls in the ninth grade is 6 : 5. If there are 135 girls in the class, how many boys are there?

7. Twenty out of the total 235 seniors graduate with honors. What is the ratio of seniors graduating with honors to the total number of seniors?

8. Aunt Bess uses 3 cups of oatmeal to bake 6-dozen oatmeal cookies. How many cups of oatmeal would she need to bake 15-dozen cookies?

9. On a map 2 centimeters represents 150 kilometers. If a line between two cities measures 5 centimeters, how many kilometers apart are they?

10. When Jack measures the shadow of a yard stick, it is 5 inches. At the same time, the shadow of the tree he would like to chop down is 45 inches. How tall is the tree in yards?

11. Jamal wonders how many ants are in his ant farm. He puts a stick in the container, and when he pulls it out, there are 15 ants on it. He gently sprays these ants with a mixture of water and green food coloring, then puts them back into the container. The next day his stick draws 20 ants, 1 of which is green. Estimate how many ants Jamal has.

12. The animal keeper feeds Mischief, the monkey, 5 pounds of bananas per day. The gorilla eats 4 times as many bananas as the monkey. How many pounds of bananas does the animal keeper need to feed both animals for a week?

13. Jonathan can assemble 47 widgets per hour. How many can he assemble in an 8-hour day?

14. Jacob drove 252 miles, and his average speed was 42 miles per hour. How many hours did he drive?

15. The Jones family traveled 300 miles in 5 hours. What was their average speed?

16. Aisha climbed a mountain that was 4,760 feet high in 14 hours. What was her average speed per hour?

17. Last year Rikki sang 960 songs with his Latin rock band. How many songs did he sing per month?

18. Connie drove for 2 hours at a constant speed of 55 miles per hour. How many total miles did she travel?

Chapter 5 Test

1. In a animal shelter, there are 5 black and 13 multi-colored cats. What is the ratio of multicolored cats to total number of cats?

A. $\frac{13}{18}$
B. $\frac{13}{5}$
C. $\frac{5}{13}$
D. $\frac{5}{18}$
E. $\frac{18}{13}$

2. Solve for x. $\frac{x}{2} = \frac{91}{7}$

F. 13
G. 26
H. 52
J. 91
K. 182

3. Scott has typed 4 pages of a term paper in 15 minutes. At the same rate, approximately how long should it take him to type the remaining 25 pages?

A. 24 minutes
B. 40 minutes
C. 67 minutes
D. 78 minutes
E. 94 minutes

4. Solve for x. $\frac{2}{18} = \frac{6}{x}$

F. 6
G. 9
H. 18
J. 36
K. 54

5. A school bus is carrying 13 boys and 18 girls to school. What is the ratio of girls to boys?

A. $\frac{13}{18}$
B. $\frac{18}{31}$
C. $\frac{18}{13}$
D. $\frac{13}{31}$
E. $\frac{31}{18}$

6. Monique is examining a scale model of an ancient building as a part of her research for a history project. If the scale is $\frac{1}{4}$ inch to one foot and the model is 24 inches long, what is the actual length of the building?

F. 6 feet
G. 20 feet
H. 28 feet
J. 16 feet
K. 96 feet

7. Alisha climbed a mountain that was 4,760 feet high in 14 hours. What was her average speed per hour?

A. 476 ft/hr
B. 4,774 ft/hr
C. 340 ft/hr
D. 0.003 ft/hr
E. 66,640 ft/hr

Chapter 6
Matrices

A **matrix** (plural: **matrices**) is a rectangular or square ordered array of numbers, and each number in a matrix is called an **element**. The matrix shown below contains six elements: 3, −1, 2, 4, 0, and 1. It is arranged in two rows and three columns and, therefore, is referred to as a 2 × 3 matrix. When describing a matrix, always give the number of rows and then the number of columns.

2 Rows $\begin{bmatrix} 3 & -1 & 2 \\ 4 & 0 & 1 \end{bmatrix}$

3 Columns

Since their invention in 1858, matrices have played a role in such fields as economics, engineering, and quantum mechanics. This chapter will cover the use of basic operations on matrices.

6.1 Addition of Matrices

In order to add matrices, they must be of the same size; they need to have the same number of rows and columns. A 2 × 3 matrix can only be added to another 2 × 3 matrix.

To add two matrices of the same size, add the corresponding elements of the two matrices. The resulting matrix is the same size as each of the two matrices that were added together.

Example 1: $\begin{bmatrix} 7 & -2 \\ -1 & 4 \end{bmatrix} + \begin{bmatrix} -6 & 2 \\ 4 & 0 \end{bmatrix} = \begin{bmatrix} 7+(-6) & (-2)+2 \\ (-1)+4 & 4+0 \end{bmatrix} = \begin{bmatrix} 1 & 0 \\ 3 & 4 \end{bmatrix}$

Note that the resulting matrix is a 2 × 2 matrix, as are the matrices added together.

Example 2: $\begin{bmatrix} 7 & -2 \\ -1 & 4 \\ 5 & -3 \end{bmatrix} + \begin{bmatrix} -6 & 2 & 2 \\ 4 & 0 & 0 \end{bmatrix} =$

The matrices to be added are not of the same size. The first matrix is a 3 × 2 matrix, and the second matrix is 2 × 3. Therefore, these two matrices cannot be added. It is not possible to add these matrices.

Note: Any number of matrices of the same size can be added together.

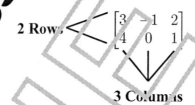

Add the matrices together when possible. When the matrices cannot be added, write NP.

1. $\begin{bmatrix} 8 & 4 \\ 5 & -3 \end{bmatrix} + \begin{bmatrix} 0 & -7 \\ -4 & -9 \end{bmatrix}$

2. $\begin{bmatrix} 6 \\ -4 \\ 5 \end{bmatrix} + \begin{bmatrix} 2 \\ -9 \\ -8 \end{bmatrix} + \begin{bmatrix} 9 \\ -1 \\ -3 \end{bmatrix} + \begin{bmatrix} 5 \\ -1 \\ \text{[illegible]} \end{bmatrix}$

3. $\begin{bmatrix} 3 & -1 & 2 \\ 4 & 0 & 1 \end{bmatrix} + \begin{bmatrix} 6 & 0 & 5 \\ 4 & 0 & 1 \end{bmatrix}$

4. $\begin{bmatrix} -6 \\ -2 \end{bmatrix} + \begin{bmatrix} -4 & -1 \end{bmatrix}$

5. $\begin{bmatrix} -5 & -2 \\ 9 & -7 \\ 3 & 6 \end{bmatrix} + \begin{bmatrix} 1 & -2 \\ -8 & 7 \\ 9 & -4 \end{bmatrix}$

6. $\begin{bmatrix} 8 & -1 & -6 & 3 \\ 0 & -7 & -5 & -4 \end{bmatrix} + \begin{bmatrix} -8 & 1 & 5 & -2 \\ 1 & 6 & 6 & 5 \end{bmatrix}$

6.2 Multiplication of a Matrix by a Constant

A matrix can be multiplied by a constant. The constant is multiplied by each element in the matrix. The resulting matrix is the same size as the matrix being multiplied.

Example 3: $4\begin{bmatrix} 1 & 0 \\ 3 & 4 \end{bmatrix} =$

Step 1: Multiply every number in the matrix by 4.

$$\begin{bmatrix} (4 \times 1) & (4 \times 0) \\ (4 \times 3) & (4 \times 4) \end{bmatrix} = \begin{bmatrix} 4 & 0 \\ 12 & 16 \end{bmatrix}$$

Step 2: The solution of $4\begin{bmatrix} 1 & 0 \\ 3 & 4 \end{bmatrix}$ is $\begin{bmatrix} 4 & 0 \\ 12 & 16 \end{bmatrix}$.

Example 4: $-3\begin{bmatrix} -8 & 1 & 5 & -2 \\ 1 & 6 & 6 & 5 \end{bmatrix} =$

Step 1: Multiply every number in the matrix by -3.

$$\begin{bmatrix} (-3 \times -8) & (-3 \times 1) & (-3 \times 5) & (-3 \times -2) \\ (-3 \times 1) & (-3 \times 6) & (-3 \times 6) & (-3 \times 5) \end{bmatrix} = \begin{bmatrix} 24 & -3 & -15 & 6 \\ -3 & -18 & -18 & -15 \end{bmatrix}$$

Step 2: The solution of $-3\begin{bmatrix} -8 & 1 & 5 & -2 \\ 1 & 6 & 6 & 5 \end{bmatrix}$ is $\begin{bmatrix} 24 & -3 & -15 & 6 \\ -3 & -18 & -18 & -15 \end{bmatrix}$

Multiply each of the following.

1. $-2\begin{bmatrix} -8 & 1 \\ 6 & 7 \\ -5 & -4 \end{bmatrix}$

2. $5\begin{bmatrix} 3 \\ 0 \\ -1 \end{bmatrix}$

3. $\frac{1}{2}\begin{bmatrix} 2 & -4 & -9 & 7 \\ -1 & 6 & 3 & -8 \end{bmatrix}$

4. $-\frac{1}{4}\begin{bmatrix} -1 & -6 & 4 & 2 \\ 8 & 0 & 3 & -8 \\ 4 & 6 & \text{[illegible]} & 12 \end{bmatrix}$

5. $-9\begin{bmatrix} -10 & -1 & \frac{1}{3} & 7 & -\frac{3}{4} \end{bmatrix}$

6. $6\begin{bmatrix} -4 & -5 \\ 1 & 0 \end{bmatrix}$

6.3 Subtraction of Matrices

Subtraction of matrices is similar to addition of matrices in that the matrices to be subtracted must be the same size. Suppose x and y represent two different matrices of the same size. $x - y$ can also be written $x + (-1)\,y$. Therefore, subtraction of matrices involves two steps: multiplying the second matrix by -1 and then adding it to the first matrix.

Example 5: $\begin{bmatrix} 4 & -6 \\ 9 & -5 \end{bmatrix} - \begin{bmatrix} 3 & -1 \\ -4 & 7 \end{bmatrix}$ can also be written as $\begin{bmatrix} 4 & -6 \\ 9 & -5 \end{bmatrix} + (-1)\begin{bmatrix} 3 & -1 \\ -4 & 7 \end{bmatrix}$

Step 1: Multiply the second matrix by -1.

$$(-1)\begin{bmatrix} 3 & -1 \\ -4 & 7 \end{bmatrix} = \begin{bmatrix} -3 & 1 \\ 4 & -7 \end{bmatrix}$$

Step 2: Add the first matrix and the product from step 1.

$$\begin{bmatrix} 4 & -6 \\ 9 & -5 \end{bmatrix} + \begin{bmatrix} -3 & 1 \\ 4 & -7 \end{bmatrix} = \begin{bmatrix} 1 & -5 \\ 13 & -12 \end{bmatrix}$$

Subtract the matrices when possible. When the matrices cannot be subtracted, write NP.

1. $\begin{bmatrix} 1 & 2 \\ 6 & 0 \\ -1 & 4 \end{bmatrix} - \begin{bmatrix} 3 & 2 \\ 1 & -3 \\ 5 & 1 \end{bmatrix}$

2. $\begin{bmatrix} 1 & 2 & 3 \\ 4 & 5 & 6 \end{bmatrix} - \begin{bmatrix} 3 & 2 & 1 \\ 5 & 4 & 6 \end{bmatrix}$

3. $\begin{bmatrix} 6 & 2 & 2 \\ -4 & -3 & -9 \\ 5 & 1 & -8 \end{bmatrix} - \begin{bmatrix} 6 & 9 & -4 \\ -4 & 0 & -8 \\ 2 & 3 & -7 \end{bmatrix}$

4. $\begin{bmatrix} 2 & 3 \\ 1 & 5 \end{bmatrix} - \begin{bmatrix} 1 & 3 \\ -2 & 1 \end{bmatrix}$

5. $\begin{bmatrix} 8 & -1 & -6 & 3 \\ 0 & -7 & -5 & -4 \end{bmatrix} - \begin{bmatrix} -8 & 1 & 5 & 2 \\ 1 & 6 & 6 & 5 \end{bmatrix}$

6. $\begin{bmatrix} 1 & 2 & 5 & 5 \\ 7 & 9 & 1 & -8 \\ -3 & 2 & 5 & -7 \end{bmatrix} - \begin{bmatrix} 1 & 3 & 1 \\ -1 & 0 & -8 \\ 0 & 1 & -7 \end{bmatrix}$

Perform the proper operation(s) on each set of matrices.

7. $\begin{bmatrix} 4 & -1 & 2 & 7 \\ -3 & 1 & -5 & -4 \end{bmatrix} + \frac{1}{2}\begin{bmatrix} 6 & 8 & 10 & -2 \\ -4 & 2 & 0 & -6 \end{bmatrix}$

8. $4\begin{bmatrix} -1 & 2 & -\frac{1}{2} & 0 & -\frac{3}{4} \end{bmatrix} - \begin{bmatrix} -1 & 0 & -5 & 6 & -3 \end{bmatrix}$

6.4 Multiplying Matrices

Example 6: Multiply: $\begin{bmatrix} 9 & 1 & 6 \\ 8 & 2 & 7 \\ 7 & -3 & 8 \\ 6 & 4 & 9 \\ 5 & 5 & 0 \end{bmatrix} \times \begin{bmatrix} 4 & 1 \\ 6 & 0 \\ 8 & -1 \end{bmatrix} =$

Step 1: Determine the size of the resulting matrix.
When multiplying matrices, the number of columns in the first matrix must equal the number of rows in the second matrix. The resulting matrix will consist of the number of rows in the first matrix by the number of columns in the second matrix.
The first matrix is a 5×3 matrix and the second matrix is a 3×2 matrix, so the resulting matrix will be a 5×2 matrix.

$$\begin{bmatrix} 9 & 1 & 6 \\ 8 & 2 & 7 \\ 7 & -3 & 8 \\ 6 & 4 & 9 \\ 5 & 5 & 0 \end{bmatrix} \times \begin{bmatrix} 4 & 1 \\ 6 & 0 \\ 8 & -1 \end{bmatrix} = \begin{bmatrix} \_ & \_ \\ \_ & \_ \\ \_ & \_ \\ \_ & \_ \\ \_ & \_ \end{bmatrix}$$

Step 2: Multiply the first row in the first matrix by the first column in second matrix.

$$\begin{bmatrix} 9 & 1 & 6 \end{bmatrix} \times \begin{bmatrix} 4 \\ 6 \\ 8 \end{bmatrix} = (9 \times 4) + (1 \times 6) + (6 \times 8) = 36 + 6 + 48 = 90$$

The number, 90, will go in the first row and first column of the resulting matrix.

$$\begin{bmatrix} 90 & \_ \\ \_ & \_ \\ \_ & \_ \\ \_ & \_ \\ \_ & \_ \end{bmatrix}$$

Step 3: Next multiply the second row in the first matrix by the first column in the second matrix.

$$\begin{bmatrix} 8 & 2 & 7 \end{bmatrix} \times \begin{bmatrix} 4 \\ 6 \\ 8 \end{bmatrix} = (8 \times 4) + (2 \times 6) + (7 \times 8) = 100$$

The number, 100, will go in the second row and first column of the resulting matrix.

$$\begin{bmatrix} 90 & \_ \\ 100 & \_ \\ \_ & \_ \\ \_ & \_ \\ \_ & \_ \end{bmatrix}$$

Step 4: Continue multiplying in the same manner for rows three through five of the first matrix.

Row 3 by column 1: $\begin{bmatrix} 7 & -3 & 8 \end{bmatrix} \times \begin{bmatrix} 4 \\ 6 \\ 8 \end{bmatrix} = (7 \times 4) + (-3 \times 6) + (8 \times 8) = 74$

Row 4 by column 1: $\begin{bmatrix} 6 & 4 & 9 \end{bmatrix} \times \begin{bmatrix} 4 \\ 6 \\ 8 \end{bmatrix} = (6 \times 4) + (4 \times 6) + (9 \times 8) = 120$

Row 5 by column 1: $\begin{bmatrix} 5 & 5 & 0 \end{bmatrix} \times \begin{bmatrix} 4 \\ 6 \\ 8 \end{bmatrix} = (5 \times 4) + (5 \times 6) + (0 \times 8) = 50$

Plug the values into the appropriate spaces: $\begin{bmatrix} 90 & \_ \\ 100 & \_ \\ 74 & \_ \\ 120 & \_ \\ 50 & \_ \end{bmatrix}$

Step 5: Now multiply all of the rows in the first matrix by the second column in the second matrix.

Row 1 by column 2: $\begin{bmatrix} 9 & 1 & 6 \end{bmatrix} \times \begin{bmatrix} 1 \\ 0 \\ -1 \end{bmatrix} = (9 \times 1) + (1 \times 0) + (6 \times -1) = 3$

Row 2 by column 2: $\begin{bmatrix} 8 & 2 & 7 \end{bmatrix} \times \begin{bmatrix} 1 \\ 0 \\ -1 \end{bmatrix} = (8 \times 1) + (2 \times 0) + (7 \times -1) = 1$

Row 3 by column 2: $\begin{bmatrix} 7 & -3 & 8 \end{bmatrix} \times \begin{bmatrix} 1 \\ 0 \\ -1 \end{bmatrix} = (7 \times 1) + (-3 \times 0) + (8 \times -1) = -1$

Row 4 by column 2: $\begin{bmatrix} 6 & 4 & 9 \end{bmatrix} \times \begin{bmatrix} 1 \\ 0 \\ -1 \end{bmatrix} = (6 \times 1) + (4 \times 0) + (9 \times -1) = -3$

Row 5 by column 2: $\begin{bmatrix} 5 & 5 & 0 \end{bmatrix} \times \begin{bmatrix} 1 \\ 0 \\ -1 \end{bmatrix} = (5 \times 1) + (5 \times 0) + (0 \times -1) = 5$

Step 6: Plug all of the values found in step 4 in column 2 of the resulting matrix to find the answer.

$$\begin{bmatrix} 9 & 1 & 6 \\ 8 & 2 & 7 \\ 7 & -3 & 8 \\ 6 & 4 & 9 \\ 5 & 5 & 0 \end{bmatrix} \times \begin{bmatrix} 4 & 1 \\ 6 & 0 \\ 8 & -1 \end{bmatrix} = \begin{bmatrix} 90 & 3 \\ 100 & 1 \\ 74 & -1 \\ 120 & -3 \\ 50 & 5 \end{bmatrix}$$

Example 7: Multiply: $\begin{bmatrix} -1 & 0 \\ 0 & -1 \end{bmatrix} \times \begin{bmatrix} -4 & -3 & 3 & -7 \\ 2 & -6 & -5 & 8 \end{bmatrix} =$

Step 1: Determine the size of the resulting matrix.
The first matrix is a 2 × 2 matrix and the second matrix is a 2 × 4 matrix, so the resulting matrix will be a 2 × 4 matrix.

$$\begin{bmatrix} -1 & 0 \\ 0 & -1 \end{bmatrix} \times \begin{bmatrix} -4 & -3 & 3 & -7 \\ 2 & -6 & -5 & 8 \end{bmatrix} = \begin{bmatrix} \_ & \_ & \_ & \_ \\ \_ & \_ & \_ & \_ \end{bmatrix}$$

Step 2: Now multiply all of the rows in the first matrix by the first column in the second matrix.

Row 1 by column 1: $\begin{bmatrix} -1 & 0 \end{bmatrix} \times \begin{bmatrix} -4 \\ 2 \end{bmatrix} = (-1 \times -4) + (0 \times 2) = 4$

Row 2 by column 1: $\begin{bmatrix} 0 & -1 \end{bmatrix} \times \begin{bmatrix} -4 \\ 2 \end{bmatrix} = (0 \times -4) + (-1 \times 2) = -2$

Plug the values into the appropriate spaces: $\begin{bmatrix} 4 & \_ & \_ & \_ \\ -2 & \_ & \_ & \_ \end{bmatrix}$

Step 3: Now multiply all of the rows in the first matrix by the first column in the second matrix.

Row 1 by column 2: $\begin{bmatrix} -1 & 0 \end{bmatrix} \times \begin{bmatrix} -3 \\ -6 \end{bmatrix} = (-1 \times -3) + (0 \times -6) = 3$

Row 2 by column 2: $\begin{bmatrix} 0 & -1 \end{bmatrix} \times \begin{bmatrix} -3 \\ -6 \end{bmatrix} = (0 \times -3) + (-1 \times -6) = 6$

Plug the values into the appropriate spaces: $\begin{bmatrix} 4 & 3 & \_ & \_ \\ -2 & 6 & \_ & \_ \end{bmatrix}$

Step 4: Now multiply all of the rows in the first matrix by the first column in the second matrix.

Row 1 by column 3: $\begin{bmatrix} -1 & 0 \end{bmatrix} \times \begin{bmatrix} 3 \\ -5 \end{bmatrix} = (-1 \times 3) + (0 \times -5) = -3$

Row 2 by column 3: $\begin{bmatrix} 0 & -1 \end{bmatrix} \times \begin{bmatrix} 3 \\ -5 \end{bmatrix} = (0 \times 3) + (-1 \times -5) = 5$

Plug the values into the appropriate spaces: $\begin{bmatrix} 4 & 3 & -3 & \_ \\ -2 & 6 & 5 & \_ \end{bmatrix}$

Step 5: Now multiply all of the rows in the first matrix by the first column in the second matrix.

Row 1 by column 4: $\begin{bmatrix}-1 & 0\end{bmatrix} \times \begin{bmatrix}-7\\8\end{bmatrix} = (-1 \times -7) + (0 \times 8) = 7$

Row 2 by column 4: $\begin{bmatrix}0 & -1\end{bmatrix} \times \begin{bmatrix}-7\\8\end{bmatrix} = (0 \times -7) + (-1 \times 8) = -8$

Plug the values into the appropriate spaces: $\begin{bmatrix}4 & 3 & -3 & 7\\-2 & 6 & 5 & -8\end{bmatrix}$

Step 6: $\begin{bmatrix}-1 & 0\\0 & -1\end{bmatrix} \times \begin{bmatrix}-4 & -3 & 3 & -7\\2 & -6 & -5 & 8\end{bmatrix} = \begin{bmatrix}4 & 3 & -3 & 7\\-2 & 6 & 5 & -8\end{bmatrix}$

Multiply the following matrices.

1. $\begin{bmatrix}4 & 2\\1 & 3\end{bmatrix} \times \begin{bmatrix}2 & -6 & 8\\-4 & 3 & 1\end{bmatrix} =$

2. $\begin{bmatrix}1 & 0\\0 & 1\end{bmatrix} \times \begin{bmatrix}-4 & 8 & 7\\2 & 3 & -5\end{bmatrix} =$

3. $\begin{bmatrix}-5 & 4 & 3\\2 & -1 & 6\end{bmatrix} \times \begin{bmatrix}1\\2\\3\end{bmatrix} =$

4. $\begin{bmatrix}8 & 9 & 0\\-1 & -2 & 3\end{bmatrix} \times \begin{bmatrix}4\\5\\6\end{bmatrix} =$

5. $\begin{bmatrix}0 & -1\\-1 & 0\end{bmatrix} \times \begin{bmatrix}-4 & 2 & 2 & -4\\5 & 3 & -3 & 5\end{bmatrix} =$

6. $\begin{bmatrix}3 & 6 & 9 & -4\\8 & 1 & -5 & 2\end{bmatrix} \times \begin{bmatrix}-8\\-4\\-1\\2\end{bmatrix} =$

7. $\begin{bmatrix}4 & 2 & 6 & 1 & 9\\1 & 3 & 4 & 1 & 2\end{bmatrix} \times \begin{bmatrix}5 & 6\\3 & 2\\1 & 7\\ \text{[illegible]} & 9\\2 & 4\end{bmatrix} =$

8. $\begin{bmatrix}1 & -1\\-1 & 1\end{bmatrix} \times \begin{bmatrix}4 & 3 & 1\\2 & 1 & 2\end{bmatrix} =$

6.5 Determinants of Matrices

The **determinant** of the 2×2 matrix $\begin{bmatrix} a & b \\ c & d \end{bmatrix}$ is $ad - bc$, while the determinant of the 3×3 matrix $\begin{bmatrix} a_1 & b_1 & c_1 \\ a_2 & b_2 & c_2 \\ a_3 & b_3 & c_3 \end{bmatrix}$ is $a_1b_2c_3 + b_1c_2a_3 + c_1a_2b_3 - a_3b_2c_1 - b_3c_2a_1 - c_3a_2b_1$. Determinants of matrices are used for many purposes, including the calculation of inverses. If $A = \begin{bmatrix} a & b \\ c & d \end{bmatrix}$, and if the determinant of A (written $\det A$) does not equal 0, the inverse of A (written A^{-1}) is $\frac{1}{\det A}\begin{bmatrix} d & -b \\ -c & a \end{bmatrix}$, or $\frac{1}{ad - bc}\begin{bmatrix} d & -b \\ -c & a \end{bmatrix}$.

Note: It's not necessary to memorize the formulas for calculating the determinants of matrices, as they will be given.

Example 8: Find the inverse of the matrix $A = \begin{bmatrix} -5 & 2 \\ 3 & -4 \end{bmatrix}$.

Step 1: First, the determinant of A is calculated with the formula $\det A = ad - bc$ as follows: $(-5)(-4) - (2)(3) = 20 - 6 = 14$.

Step 2: Next, the determinant of A and the values of d, $-b$, $-c$, and a are substituted into the formula for the inverse of matrix A:
$A^{-1} = \frac{1}{\det A}\begin{bmatrix} d & -b \\ -c & a \end{bmatrix} = \frac{1}{14}\begin{bmatrix} -4 & -2 \\ -3 & -5 \end{bmatrix}$

Step 3: Finally, each element of the matrix $\begin{bmatrix} -4 & -2 \\ -3 & -5 \end{bmatrix}$ is multiplied by $\frac{1}{14}$, and the result is
$\begin{bmatrix} -\frac{2}{7} & -\frac{1}{7} \\ -\frac{3}{14} & -\frac{5}{14} \end{bmatrix}$.

Calculate the determinant of each of the following matrices.

1. $\begin{bmatrix} 3 & 8 \\ -1 & 2 \end{bmatrix}$
3. $\begin{bmatrix} 10 & 6 \\ 1 & 4 \end{bmatrix}$
5. $\begin{bmatrix} -9 & [illegible] \\ -8 & 2 \end{bmatrix}$
2. $\begin{bmatrix} 5 & -2 \\ -3 & 9 \end{bmatrix}$
4. $\begin{bmatrix} -4 & 7 \\ -5 & -7 \end{bmatrix}$
6. $\begin{bmatrix} -6 & -3 \\ -10 & 8 \end{bmatrix}$

Find the inverse of each of the following matrices.

7. $\begin{bmatrix} 4 & 3 \\ 2 & -1 \end{bmatrix}$
8. $\begin{bmatrix} 8 & -9 \\ 3 & -8 \end{bmatrix}$
9. $\begin{bmatrix} 11 & -1 \\ -2 & 3 \end{bmatrix}$

Example 9: Calculate the determinant of the matrix $A = \begin{bmatrix} 7 & -9 & 1 \\ 4 & -3 & 2 \\ -5 & 6 & 8 \end{bmatrix}$.

Step 1: To calculate the determinant of matrix A, use the formula
$\det A = a_1b_2c_3 + b_1c_2a_3 + c_1a_2b_3 - a_3b_2c_1 - b_3c_2a_1 - c_3a_2b_1$.

Step 2: Substitute known values into the formula as shown.

$\det A = (7)(-3)(8) + (-9)(2)(-5) + (1)(4)(6) - (-5)(-3)(1) - (6)(2)(7) - (8)(4)(-9)$

Step 3: Solve.

$\det A = -168 + 90 + 24 - 15 - 84 - (-288) = 135.$

Therefore, the determinant of matrix A is 135.

Calculate the determinant of each of the following matrices.

10. $\begin{bmatrix} 11 & 7 & 4 \\ -2 & -8 & 3 \\ 6 & 9 & 2 \end{bmatrix}$

11. $\begin{bmatrix} 3 & -5 & 9 \\ 2 & -6 & 8 \\ 1 & -7 & 7 \end{bmatrix}$

12. $\begin{bmatrix} 9 & 3 & 9 \\ 10 & 5 & 7 \\ -1 & -7 & -5 \end{bmatrix}$

13. $\begin{bmatrix} 6 & 3 & 7 \\ 7 & 2 & 6 \\ -8 & -3 & 5 \end{bmatrix}$

14. $\begin{bmatrix} 1 & 4 & 7 \\ -2 & -5 & -8 \\ -3 & -6 & -9 \end{bmatrix}$

15. $\begin{bmatrix} -1 & 2 & 11 \\ 5 & 10 & -2 \\ 12 & -3 & 3 \end{bmatrix}$

16. $\begin{bmatrix} 5 & -10 & 3 \\ 10 & 1 & -5 \\ -4 & 2 & 4 \end{bmatrix}$

17. $\begin{bmatrix} 9 & 6 & -3 \\ 3 & 7 & 2 \\ 1 & -12 & -2 \end{bmatrix}$

18. $\begin{bmatrix} 8 & -5 & 2 \\ -7 & 4 & -1 \\ 6 & -3 & 2 \end{bmatrix}$

19. The area of a triangle with vertices at the points (a, b), (c, d), and (e, f) is $\frac{1}{2}|\det A|$, where
$A = \begin{bmatrix} a & b & 1 \\ c & d & 1 \\ e & f & 1 \end{bmatrix}$.

What is the area of a triangle with vertices at the points $(3, 8)$, $(-5, 14)$ and $(6, 9)$?

6.6 Applications with Matrices

Example 10: Find a, b, c, and d such that

$$\begin{bmatrix} 2 & -1 \\ 4 & 3 \end{bmatrix} + \begin{bmatrix} a & b \\ c & d \end{bmatrix} = \begin{bmatrix} 3 & -1 \\ 2 & 2 \end{bmatrix}$$

Step 1: Write the equation for the four sets of corresponding elements.

$$2 + a = 3 \qquad -1 + b = -1$$

$$4 + c = 2 \qquad 3 + d = 2$$

Step 2: Solve each of the four equations.

$$a = 1 \qquad b = 0$$

$$c = -2 \qquad d = -1$$

Example 11: Lucie and her friend Laura are shopping for a new cellular phone plan. Plan A offers 400 minutes per month for \$60, plus another 200 night and weekend minutes for an extra \$20. Plan B offers 500 monthly minutes for \$50, plus 150 night and weekend minutes for an extra \$20. The two plans can be represented in the following matrices:

$$\begin{bmatrix} \$60 & \$20 \\ 400 & 200 \end{bmatrix} = \text{A} \qquad \begin{bmatrix} \$50 & \$20 \\ 500 & 150 \end{bmatrix} = \text{B}$$

If Lucie chooses Plan A and Laura chooses Plan B, what will the total cost of their services be if they also select the night and weekend minutes, and how many total minutes will they receive? What is the average cost and minutes of the plans?

Step 1: To determine the total of the two plans, add the two matrices together, A + B.

$$\begin{bmatrix} \$60 + \$50 & \$20 + \$20 \\ 400 + 500 & 200 + 150 \end{bmatrix} = \begin{bmatrix} \$110 & \$40 \\ 900 & 350 \end{bmatrix}$$

Step 2: Calculate the average cost and minutes by multiplying the total matrix by $\frac{1}{2}$ (or dividing it by 2):

$$\frac{1}{2} \times \begin{bmatrix} \$110 & \$40 \\ 900 & 350 \end{bmatrix} = \begin{bmatrix} \$55 & \$20 \\ 450 & 175 \end{bmatrix}$$

Solve the following matrix problems.

1. $\begin{bmatrix} d & 3 \\ e & 1 \end{bmatrix} + \begin{bmatrix} 2 & f \\ 2 & g \end{bmatrix} = \begin{bmatrix} 5 & 3 \\ 1 & 2 \end{bmatrix}$

2. $\begin{bmatrix} 3d & 1 \\ 2 & 3g \\ 1 & f \end{bmatrix} - \begin{bmatrix} 2d & 0 \\ e & g \\ 1 & 2 \end{bmatrix} = \begin{bmatrix} -2 & 1 \\ 4 & 4 \\ 0 & 1 \end{bmatrix}$

3. $3\begin{bmatrix} 1 & 0 \\ 2 & 1 \end{bmatrix} + \frac{1}{2}\begin{bmatrix} 4 & 6 \\ 0 & 2 \end{bmatrix} = \begin{bmatrix} d & f \\ e & g \end{bmatrix}$

4. A computer company with one plant in the West and one plant in the East produces monitors and printers. The production for January and February are give as follows:

$$\text{January} = \begin{array}{c} \text{West Plant} \quad \text{East Plant} \\ \begin{bmatrix} 2000 & 1710 \\ 800 & 650 \end{bmatrix} \end{array} \qquad \text{February} = \begin{array}{c} \text{West Plant} \quad \text{East Plant} \\ \begin{bmatrix} 2300 & 1850 \\ 950 & 800 \end{bmatrix} \end{array} \begin{array}{l} \text{Monitors} \\ \text{Printers} \end{array}$$

(A) What is the average monthly production of the monitors and printers?
(B) What is the increase from January to February?
(C) What is the total production for January and February?

5. The Yummy Candy Company produces a variety of candy products and packages them for various holidays. The Christmas package consists of three pieces of chocolate, two pecan candies, one peppermint twist, and four chocolate-covered cherries. The Valentine package consists of the same package, but contains three times as many pieces of each candy. Write the number of candies in both the Christmas and Valentine packages in matrix form.

6. What are the total numbers of candies contained in one Christmas package and one Valentine package from problem 5?

Chapter 6 Review

Solve each matrix. If not possible, write not possible.

1. $2\begin{bmatrix} -5 & -1 \\ 4 & -7 \\ 9 & 6 \end{bmatrix} + \begin{bmatrix} -1 & -5 \\ -8 & 7 \\ 1 & -4 \end{bmatrix} =$

2. $\begin{bmatrix} 4 \\ -1 \end{bmatrix} + \begin{bmatrix} -7 & -1 \end{bmatrix} =$

3. $\begin{bmatrix} 9 & -1 & -6 & 3 \\ 0 & -5 & -5 & -4 \end{bmatrix} + \begin{bmatrix} -8 & 1 & 2 & -3 \\ 1 & 6 & 11 & 5 \end{bmatrix} =$

4. $-\frac{1}{4}\begin{bmatrix} -1 & -6 & 4 & -8 \\ 12 & 0 & 3 & -2 \\ 4 & 6 & -4 & 16 \end{bmatrix} =$

Subtract the following matrices. If not possible, write not possible.

5. $\begin{bmatrix} 2 & 4 \\ 0 & 5 \end{bmatrix} - \begin{bmatrix} 1 & 7 \\ -3 & 1 \end{bmatrix} =$

6. $\begin{bmatrix} 1 & 2 & 5 & 4 \\ 7 & 0 & 1 & 8 \\ -3 & 2 & [illegible] & -2 \end{bmatrix} - \begin{bmatrix} 1 & [illegible] & 13 \\ -1 & 0 & -11 \\ 0 & [illegible] & -7 \end{bmatrix} =$

7. $\begin{bmatrix} -1 & 0 \\ 0 & 1 \end{bmatrix} \times \begin{bmatrix} 5 & 6 & 7 \\ 8 & 1 & 3 \end{bmatrix} =$

8. $\begin{bmatrix} 1 & 2 & 5 & 4 \\ 7 & 0 & 1 & -8 \end{bmatrix} \times \begin{bmatrix} 1 & 2 & 3 & 4 \\ 2 & 3 & 4 & 1 \\ 3 & 4 & 1 & 2 \\ 4 & 3 & 2 & 1 \end{bmatrix} =$

9. Mr. Thompson goes on two road trips per year. His two favorite places to go are Dallas, TX and Atlantic City, NJ. When he went to Dallas last year, he spent $3,000 and drove 1,235 miles, and when he went to Atlantic City last year, he spent $5,500 and drove 786 miles. This year when he goes on vacation, he will have $4,300 to spend in Dallas and $4,900 in Atlantic City. He will drive 200 more miles because he is picking up his sister for both trips.
   (A) Write two 2×2 matrices that include miles and price for the Dallas trip and Atlantic City trip.
   (B) What is the difference in the amount of money Mr. Thompson will spend this year compared to last year?

For questions 10 and 11, find a, b, c, and d.

10. $\begin{bmatrix} a & 4 \\ b & 5 \end{bmatrix} + \begin{bmatrix} 2 & c \\ 0 & d \end{bmatrix} = \begin{bmatrix} 5 & 3 \\ 1 & 7 \end{bmatrix}$

11. $5\begin{bmatrix} 8 & 0 \\ 1 & 3 \end{bmatrix} + \frac{1}{2}\begin{bmatrix} 10 & 8 \\ 0 & 2 \end{bmatrix} = \begin{bmatrix} [illegible] & c \\ [illegible] & d \end{bmatrix}$

Calculate the determinant of each of the following matrices.

12. $\begin{bmatrix} -7 & 4 \\ 5 & 8 \end{bmatrix}$

13. $\begin{bmatrix} -9 & 9 & 5 \\ 13 & 7 & 6 \\ 2 & -6 & -7 \end{bmatrix}$

14. $\begin{bmatrix} -3 & 2 \\ 20 & -4 \end{bmatrix}$

15. $\begin{bmatrix} 1 & 6 & 5 \\ -6 & -8 & -4 \\ 12 & 7 & 2 \end{bmatrix}$

16. $\begin{bmatrix} 14 & 3 \\ -2 & 1 \end{bmatrix}$

17. $\begin{bmatrix} 6 & 9 & 6 \\ 7 & -8 & 5 \\ 8 & 7 & -4 \end{bmatrix}$

Chapter 6 Test

1. $-2\begin{bmatrix}-5 & -2\\ 9 & -7\\ 3 & 6\end{bmatrix} + \begin{bmatrix}-1 & -2\\ -8 & 7\\ 9 & -4\end{bmatrix} =$

A. $\begin{bmatrix}-6 & -4\\ 1 & 0\\ 12 & 2\end{bmatrix}$

B. $\begin{bmatrix}-12 & -8\\ 1 & 0\\ 12 & 2\end{bmatrix}$

C. $\begin{bmatrix}9 & 2\\ -26 & 21\\ 3 & -16\end{bmatrix}$

D. $\begin{bmatrix}9 & -26 & 3\\ 2 & 21 & -16\end{bmatrix}$

E. $\begin{bmatrix}9 & -4\\ 1 & 0\\ 12 & 2\end{bmatrix}$

2. The local hardware store has four different style grills for the summer sale. The price of the four grills are listed from least to greatest, and they are represented in the 2 × 2 matrix below.

$\begin{bmatrix}\$120 & \$155\\ \$160 & \$230\end{bmatrix}$

If the store is having a sale where everything is 20% off, what is the new price of the grill that is the second most expensive?

F. \$32
G. \$124
H. \$184
J. \$128
K. \$31

3. $-1\begin{bmatrix}1 & -6\\ 2 & -3\end{bmatrix} + 3\begin{bmatrix}3 & -1\\ 0 & -3\end{bmatrix} =$

A. $\begin{bmatrix}8 & 3\\ -2 & -6\end{bmatrix}$

B. $\begin{bmatrix}11 & 6\\ 1 & 9\end{bmatrix}$

C. $\begin{bmatrix}4 & -7\\ 2 & -6\end{bmatrix}$

D. $\begin{bmatrix}10 & -9\\ 2 & -12\end{bmatrix}$

E. $\begin{bmatrix}8 & -7\\ 2 & 0\end{bmatrix}$

4. The discount store next to the mall is having a huge sale. All pants normally priced \$25.95 are now 40% off, and all shoes normally priced \$14.95 are now 60% off. Which of the following best represents this information in a matrix?

F. $\begin{bmatrix}\$25.95 & 40\%\\ \$14.95 & 60\%\end{bmatrix}$

G. $\begin{bmatrix}\$25.95 & 60\%\\ \$14.95 & 40\%\end{bmatrix}$

H. $\begin{bmatrix}\$25.95 & \$14.95\\ 40\% & 60\%\end{bmatrix}$

J. Both F and H represent the data correctly.

K. None of the matrices above represent the data correctly.

5. $\begin{bmatrix} 1 & 3 \\ 1 & -4 \end{bmatrix} + 3\begin{bmatrix} 3 & -1 & 0 \\ 6 & 5 & 2 \end{bmatrix} =$

A. $\begin{bmatrix} 10 & 0 & 0 \\ 19 & 11 & 6 \end{bmatrix}$

B. $\begin{bmatrix} 10 & -3 & 0 \\ 19 & 15 & 2 \end{bmatrix}$

C. $\begin{bmatrix} 10 & 0 \\ 19 & 11 \end{bmatrix}$

D. $\begin{bmatrix} 10 & 2 & 0 \\ 7 & 1 & 2 \end{bmatrix}$

E. Not possible

6. $\begin{bmatrix} 0 & -2 \\ 4 & 5 \end{bmatrix} + \begin{bmatrix} -2 & -1 \\ 6 & 14 \end{bmatrix} =$

F. $\begin{bmatrix} [illegible] & 1 \\ [illegible]2 & 9 \end{bmatrix}$

G. $\begin{bmatrix} -2 & 2 \\ 24 & [illegible] \end{bmatrix}$

H. $\begin{bmatrix} -2 & -3 \\ 10 & 19 \end{bmatrix}$

J. $\begin{bmatrix} 2 & 3 \\ 10 & 19 \end{bmatrix}$

K. $\begin{bmatrix} -4 & -1 \\ 11 & 14 \end{bmatrix}$

7. If a 2×4 matrix was multiplied by a 4×2 matrix, the resulting matrix would be what type of matrix?

A. 2×8
B. 2×4
C. 2×2
D. 4×8
E. 8×8

8. $\dfrac{1}{2}\begin{bmatrix} 5 & 8 & -4 \\ -1 & 12 & 6 \end{bmatrix} =$

F. $\begin{bmatrix} 2.5 & 8 & -4 \\ -1 & 12 & 6 \end{bmatrix}$

G. $\begin{bmatrix} 10 & 16 & -8 \\ -2 & 24 & 12 \end{bmatrix}$

H. $\begin{bmatrix} 2.5 & 4 & -2 \\ -\frac{1}{2} & 6 & 3 \end{bmatrix}$

J. $\begin{bmatrix} 2.5 & 4 & -2 \\ -1 & 12 & 6 \end{bmatrix}$

K. Not possible

9. $\begin{bmatrix} 2 & 4 & 6 \\ 8 & 0 & -2 \end{bmatrix} \times \begin{bmatrix} -6 \\ 7 \\ 8 \end{bmatrix} =$

A. $\begin{bmatrix} -64 \\ 64 \end{bmatrix}$

B. $\begin{bmatrix} 64 \\ -64 \end{bmatrix}$

C. $\begin{bmatrix} 98 \\ -64 \end{bmatrix}$

D. $\begin{bmatrix} 98 \\ 64 \end{bmatrix}$

E. $\begin{bmatrix} -96 \\ -32 \end{bmatrix}$

10. The area of a triangle with vertices at the points (a, b), (c, d), and (e, f) is $\frac{1}{2}|\det A|$, where $A = \begin{bmatrix} a & b & 1 \\ c & d & 1 \\ e & f & 1 \end{bmatrix}$.

If $\det A = ad + be + cf - ed - af - bc$ and the vertices of a triangle are at the points $(-7, 5)$, $(3, $ [illegible]$)$, and $(1, 9)$, what is the area of the triangle?

F. -64
G. -32
H. 32
J. 64
K. 128

11. The inverse of the matrix $\begin{bmatrix} a & b \\ c & d \end{bmatrix}$ is $\dfrac{1}{ad-bc}\begin{bmatrix} d & -b \\ -c & a \end{bmatrix}$.

What is the inverse of $\begin{bmatrix} -4 & 7 \\ 6 & -10 \end{bmatrix}$?

A. $\begin{bmatrix} -10 & -7 \\ -6 & -4 \end{bmatrix}$

B. $\begin{bmatrix} 10 & 7 \\ 6 & 4 \end{bmatrix}$

C. $\begin{bmatrix} -5 & -\frac{7}{2} \\ -3 & -2 \end{bmatrix}$

D. $\begin{bmatrix} 5 & \frac{7}{2} \\ 3 & 2 \end{bmatrix}$

E. $\begin{bmatrix} 5 & 7 \\ \text{[illegible]} & 2 \end{bmatrix}$

12. $\begin{bmatrix} 1 & 3 \\ 0 & -1 \end{bmatrix} \times \begin{bmatrix} 4 & -1 \\ 2 & 0 \end{bmatrix} =$

F. $\begin{bmatrix} -2 & -1 \\ 2 & 0 \end{bmatrix}$

G. $\begin{bmatrix} 1 & 1 \\ 0 & 0 \end{bmatrix}$

H. $\begin{bmatrix} 10 & -1 \\ 0 & 0 \end{bmatrix}$

J. $\begin{bmatrix} 4 & -3 \\ 6 & 0 \end{bmatrix}$

K. $\begin{bmatrix} 10 & -1 \\ -2 & 0 \end{bmatrix}$

Chapter 7
Polynomials

7.1 Adding Polynomials

When adding **polynomials,** make sure the exponents and variables are the same on the terms you are combining. The easiest way is to put the terms in columns with **like exponents** under each other. Each column is added as a separate problem. Fill in the blank spots with zeros if it helps you keep the columns straight. You never carry to the next column when adding polynomials.

Example 1: Add $3x^4 + 25$ and $7x^4 + 4x$

$$\begin{array}{r} 3x^4 + 0x + 25 \\ (+)\ 7x^4 + 4x + 0 \\ \hline 10x^4 + 4x + 25 \end{array}$$

Add the following polynomials.

1. $y^4 + 3y + 4$ and $4y^4 + 5$
2. $(7y^4 + 5y - 6) + (4y^4 - 7y + 9)$
3. $3x^4 + 25x^3 + 27$ and $8x^3 - 24$
4. $(-x^4 + 4x - 5) + (3x^4 - 3)$
5. $(y^4 - 22y + 20) + (-23y^4 + 7y - 5)$
6. $40b^3 + 27b$ and $-5b^4 - 7b + 25$

7.2 Subtracting Polynomials

When you subtract polynomials, it is important to remember to change all the signs in the subtracted polynomial (the subtrahend) and then add.

Example 2: $(5y^4 + 9y + 20) - (4y^4 + 6y - 5)$

Step 1: Copy the subtraction problem into vertical form. Make sure you line up the terms with like exponents.

$$\begin{array}{r} 5y^4 + 9y + 20 \\ (-)\ 4y^4 + 6y - 5 \\ \hline \end{array}$$

Step 2: Change the subtraction sign to addition and all the signs of the subtracted polynomial to the opposite sign.

Step 3: Add:

$$\begin{array}{r} 5y^4 + 9y + 20 \\ (+) - 4y^4 - 6y + 5 \\ \hline y^4 + 3y + 25 \end{array}$$

Subtract the following polynomials.

1. $(4x^4 + 7x + 4) - (x^4 + 3x + 2)$
2. $(8g + 3) - (g^4 + 5g - 7)$
3. $(-9w^3 + 5w) - (-5w^4 - 20w^3 - w)$
4. $(x^4 + 24x^3 - 20) - (4x^4 + 3x^3 + 2)$
5. $(4a^4 + 4a + 4) - (-a^4 + 3a + 3)$
6. $(7x^4 + 27x^3 - 5) - (-5x^4 + 5x^3)$
7. $(9y^4 - 4) - (22y^4 - 4y - 3)$
8. ([illegible]$z^4 - 7z - 9) - (3z^4 - 7z + 7)$

7.3 Multiplying Monomials

When two monomials have the **same variable**, you can multiply them. Then, add the **exponents** together. If the variable has no exponent, it is understood that the exponent is 1.

Example 3: $5x^5 \times 3x^4 = 15x^9$ $\quad$ $4y \times 7y^4 = 28y^5$

Multiply the following monomials.

1. $6a \times 20a^7$ $\quad$ 2. $4d^9 \times 20d^{[illegible]}$ $\quad$ 3. $9w^8 \times w$

When problems include negative signs, follow the rules for multiplying integers.

4. $-8s^5 \times 7s^3$ $\quad$ 5. $-6a \times -20a^7$ $\quad$ 6. $-8s^5 \times 8s^3$

7.4 Multiplying Monomials with Different Variables

Warning: You cannot add the exponents of variables that are different.

Example 4: $(-5wx)(6w^3x^4)$

To work this problem, first multiply the whole numbers: $-5 \times 6 = -30$. Then multiply the w's: $w \times w^3 = w^4$. Last, multiply the x's: $x \times x^4 = x^5$. The answer is $-30w^4x^5$.

Multiply the following monomials.

1. $(4x^4y^4)(-5xy^3) =$ $\quad$ 3. $(6f^3g^7)(-f^3g) =$ $\quad$ 5. $(20p^4y)(7p^7y^3) =$

2. $(20x^5y^4)(3x^3y) =$ $\quad$ 4. $(-5a^3v^5)(9a^5v) =$ $\quad$ 6. $(-4a^8x^4)(6ax^4) =$

Multiplying three monomials works the same way. The first one is done for you.

7. $(3st)(5s^3t^4)(4s^4t^5) = 60s^8t^{10}$ $\quad$ 9. $(4a^4b^4)(a^3b^3)(4ab) =$

8. $(xy)(x^4y^4)(4x^{[illegible]}y^4) =$ $\quad$ 10. $(5y^4z^5)(4y^3)(4z^4) =$

7.5 Dividing Monomials

Simplify the expressions below. All answers should only have positive exponents.

1. $\dfrac{(6x^3y^5)^4}{(4x^7y)^3}$ $\quad$ 3. $\dfrac{33x^7y^3}{44x^8y^7}$ $\quad$ 5. $\dfrac{30x^5y^4}{6(x^4y^4)^4}$ $\quad$ 7. $\dfrac{20x^{20}y^8}{57x^7y^3}$

2. $\dfrac{27a^4b^3}{3a^7b^6}$ $\quad$ 4. $\dfrac{27(4a^6b^8)}{42a^3b^6}$ $\quad$ 6. $\dfrac{20(9ab^{[illegible]})}{40a^{[illegible]}b^4}$ $\quad$ 8. $\dfrac{(a^5b^8)^5}{a^9b^8}$

7.6 Extracting Monomial Roots

When finding the roots of monomial expressions, you must first divide the monomial expression into separate parts. Then, simplify each part of the expression.

Note: To find the square root of any variable raised to a positive exponent, simply divide the exponent by 2. For example, $\sqrt{y^{10}} = y^5$.

Example 5: $\sqrt{25x^6y^4z^6}$

Step 1: Break each component apart. $(\sqrt{25})\left(\sqrt{x^6}\right)\left(\sqrt{y^4}\right)\left(\sqrt{z^6}\right)$

Step 2: Solve for each component. $(\sqrt{25} = 5)\left(\sqrt{x^6} = x^3\right)\left(\sqrt{y^4} = y^2\right)\left(\sqrt{z^6} = z^3\right)$

Step 3: Recombine the simplified expressions. $(5)(x^3)(y^2)(z^3) = 5x^3y^2z^3$

Example 6: Simplify $\sqrt{40x^7y^{11}z^{23}}$

Step 1: Begin by simplifying the coefficient. $\sqrt{40} = (\sqrt{4})(\sqrt{10})$, $\sqrt{4} = 2$, so $\sqrt{40} = 2\sqrt{10}$

Step 2: Simplify the variable with exponents.

$$\sqrt{x^7} = \left(\sqrt{x^6}\right)(\sqrt{x}),\ \sqrt{x^6} = x^3, \text{ so } \sqrt{x^7} = x^3\sqrt{x}$$

$$\sqrt{y^{11}} = \left(\sqrt{y^{10}}\right)(\sqrt{y}),\ \sqrt{y^{10}} = y^5, \text{ so } \sqrt{y^{11}} = y^5\sqrt{y}$$

$$\sqrt{z^{23}} = \left(\sqrt{z^{22}}\right)(\sqrt{z}),\ \sqrt{z^{22}} = z^{11}, \text{ so } \sqrt{z^{23}} = z^{11}\sqrt{z}$$

Step 3: Recombine the simplified expressions. $2x^3y^5z^{11}\sqrt{10xyz}$

Simplify the problems below.

1. $\sqrt{4a^2b^4c^8}$
2. $\sqrt{49h^{24}i^6j^4}$
3. $\sqrt{121p^{20}q^{24}r^6}$
4. $\sqrt{36a^{28}b^{10}c^6}$
5. $\sqrt{144t^{44}u^{30}v^2}$
6. $\sqrt{36k^6l^{26}m^{20}}$
7. $\sqrt{900l^{50}m^{26}n^4}$
8. $\sqrt{400g^{40}h^{26}i^{36}}$
9. $\sqrt{25a^{54}b^6c^{46}}$
10. $\sqrt{16j^{24}k^8l^{20}}$
11. $\sqrt{57d^{25}e^{27}f^{22}}$
12. $\sqrt{140h^{26}i^{20}j^9}$
13. $\sqrt{27x^{44}y^{42}z^9}$
14. $\sqrt{75p^{22}q^8r^{21}}$
15. $\sqrt{4[illegible]k^{[illegible]7}l^{27}m^3}$
16. $\sqrt{75s^{23}t^7u^{28}}$
17. $\sqrt{50d^7e^9f^{23}}$
18. $\sqrt{45x^{28}y^6z^{23}}$
19. $\sqrt{32a^6b^{23}c^7}$
20. $\sqrt{74j^{24}k^{27}m^7}$
21. $\sqrt{20q^{24}r^{27}s^7}$

7.7 Multiplying Monomials by Polynomials

In the chapter on solving multi-step equations, you learned to remove parentheses by multiplying the number outside the parentheses by each term inside the parentheses: $4(5x - 8) = 9x - 25$. Multiplying monomials by polynomials works the same way.

Example 7: $-7t\,(4t^4 - 8t + 20)$

Step 1: Multiply $-7t \times 4t^4 = \mathbf{-28t^5}$

Step 2: Multiply $-7t \times -8t = \mathbf{56t^2}$

Step 3: Multiply $-7t \times 20 = \mathbf{-140t}$

Step 4: Arrange the answers horizontally in order: $-28t^5 + 56t^2 - 140t$

Remove parentheses in the following problems.

1. $3x\,(3x^4 + 5x - 2)$
2. $5y\,(y^3 - 8)$
3. $8a^4\,(4a^2 + 3a + 4)$
4. $-7d^3\,(d^4 - 7d)$
5. $4w\,(-5w^4 + 3w - 9)$
6. $9p\,(p^3 - 6p + 7)$
7. $-20b^4\,(-4b + 7)$
8. $4t\,(t^4 - 5t - 20)$
9. $20c\,(5c^4 + 3c - 8)$

7.8 Dividing Polynomials by Monomials

Example 8: $\dfrac{-8wx + 6x^2 - 16wx^2}{2wx}$

Step 1: Rewrite the problem. Divide each term from the top by the denominator, $2wx$.

$$\frac{-8wx}{2wx} + \frac{6x^2}{2wx} + \frac{-16wx^2}{2wx}$$

Step 2: Simplify each term in the problem. Then combine like terms.

$$-4 + \frac{3x}{w} - 8x$$

Simplify each of the following.

1. $\dfrac{bc^4 - 9bc - 4b^4c^4}{4bc}$
2. $\dfrac{3jk^4 + 24k + 20j^4k}{3jk}$
3. $\dfrac{7x^4y - 9xy^4 + 4y^3}{4xy}$
4. $\dfrac{5wx^4 + 6wx - 24w^3}{4wx}$
5. $\dfrac{cd^4 + 20cd^3 + 26c^4}{4cd}$
6. $\dfrac{y^4z^3 - 4yz - 9z^4}{-4yz^4}$
7. $\dfrac{[illegible] + 4ab^4 - 25ab^3}{4a^4}$
8. $\dfrac{pr^4 + 6pr + 9p^4r^4}{4pr^4}$
9. $\dfrac{7jk^2 - 14jk - 63j^2}{7jk}$

Chapter 7 Review

Simplify.

1. $3a^4 + 20a^4$
2. $(8x^4y^5)(20xy^7)$
3. $-6z^4(z+3)$
4. $(5b^4)(7b^3)$
5. $8x^4 - 20x^4$
6. $(7p-5) - (3p$ [illegible]
7. $-7t(3t+2$[illegible]
8. $(3w^3y^4)(5$[illegible]$y^7)$
9. $3(4$[illegible]$3)^2$
10. [illegible]$d^5 - 20d^5$
11. $(8w-5)(w-9)$
12. $27t^4 + 5t^4$
13. $(8c^5)(20c^4)$
14. $(20x+$[illegible]$)($[illegible]$+$[illegible]$)$
15. $5y(5y^4 - 20y + 4)$
16. $(9a^5b)(4ab^$[illegible]$)(ab)$
17. $(7w^6)(20w^{20})$
18. $9x^3 + 24x^3$
19. $27p^7 - 22p^7$
20. $(3s^5t^4)(5st^3)$
21. $(5$[illegible]$)(4d+8)$
22. [illegible]$(-3w^4 + 8$[illegible]$- 7)$
23. $45z^6 - 20$[illegible]
24. $-8y^3 - 9y^3$
25. $(8x^5)(8x^7)$
26. $28p^4 + 20p^4$
27. $(a^4v)(4av)(a^3v^6)$
28. $5($[illegible]$- 7)^2$
29. $(3c^4)(6c^9)$
30. $(5x^7y^3)(4xy^3)$
31. Add $4x^4 + 20x$ and $7x^4 - 9x + 4$
32. $5t(6t^4 + 5t - 6) + 9t(3t+3)$
33. Subtract $y^4 + 5y - 6$ from $3y^4 + 8$
34. $4x(5x^4 + 6x - 3) + 5x(x+3)$
35. $($[illegible]$- 5) - (6t^4 + t + 4)$
36. $(5x+6) + (8x^4 - 4x + $[illegible]$)$
37. Subtract $7a - 4$ from [illegible]$+ 20$
38. $(-4y+5) + (5y$[illegible]$6)$
39. $4t(t+6) - 7t(4t+8)$
40. Add $3c$[illegible]$- 5$ and $c^4 - 3c - 4$
41. $4b(b-5) - (b^4 + 4b + 2)$
42. $(6k^4 + 7k) + (k^4 + k + 20)$
43. $(q^4r^3)(3qr^4)(4q^5r)$
44. $(7df)($[illegible]$f^4)(4df)$
45. $(8g^4h^3)(g^3h^6)(6gh^3)$
46. [illegible]$(3v^6x^4)(4v^5x^5)$
47. $(3n^4m^4)(20n^4m)(n^3m^8)$
48. $(2$[illegible]$t^4a^4)(5t^3a^9)(4t^6a)$
49. $\frac{24(4a^3)b}{2a^4b^{-}\text{[illegible]}}$
50. $\frac{8(g^3h^3)}{5(g^4h)^{-4}}$
51. $\frac{26(m^4\text{[illegible]})}{5(m^4n)^{-}\text{[illegible]}}$
52. $\frac{\text{[illegible]}p^3q^3}{\text{[illegible]}p^4q}$
53. $\frac{9(e^5h^{-4})^{-4}}{36e^4h^7}$
54. $\frac{44x^3y^5}{154(x^{-3}y^8)^4}$

Chapter 7 Test

1. $2x^2 + 5x^2 =$

A. $10x^4$
B. $7x^4$
C. $7x^2$
D. $10x^2$
E. $7x$

2. $-8m^3 + m^3 =$

F. $-8m^6$
G. $-8m^9$
H. $-9m^6$
J. $-7m^3$
K. $-7m^6$

3. $(6x^3 + x^2 - 5) + (-3x^3 - 2x^2 + 4) =$

A. $3x^3 - 3x^2 - 1$
B. $3x^3 - 3x^2 - 9$
C. $-3x^3 - 3x^2 - 1$
D. $-3x^3 - x^2 - 1$
E. $3x^3 - x^2 - 1$

4. $(-7c^2 + 5c + 3) + (-c^2 - 7c + 2) =$

F. $-3x^3 - 3x^2 - 1$
G. $-8c^2 - 2c + 5$
H. $-6c^2 - 12c + 5$
J. $-8c^2 - 12c + 5$
K. $-8c^2 + 12c + 5$

5. $(5x^3 - 4x^2 + 5) - (-2x^3 - 3x^2) =$

A. $3x^3 + x^2 + 5$
B. $3x^3 - 7x^2 + 5$
C. $7x^3 - x^2 + 5$
D. $7x^3 - 7x^2 + 5$
E. $7x^3 - 7x^2$

6. $(-z^3 - 4z^2 - 6) - (3z^3 - 6z + 5) =$

F. $-4z^3 - 4z^2 + 6z - 11$
G. $-2z^3 - 10z - 1$
H. $-4z^3 - 10z^2 - 1$
J. $-2z^2 + 2z - 11$
K. $-4z^2 - 10z - 11$

7. $(-7d^5)(-3d^2) =$

A. $-21d^7$
B. $21d^{10}$
C. $21d^7$
D. $-21d^{10}$
E. $-10d^7$

8. $(-5c^3d)(3c^5d^3)(2cd^4) =$

F. $30c^{15}d^8$
G. $15c^8d^{12}$
H. $-17c^{15}d^{12}$
J. $-30c^{15}d^{12}$
K. $-30c^9d^8$

9. $-11j^2 \times -j^4 =$

A. $11j^6$
B. $11j^8$
C. $-11j^6$
D. $-11j^8$
E. You cannot multiply these monomials.

10. $-6m^2(7m^2 + 5m - 6) =$

F. $-42m^2 - 30m^3 - 36$
G. $-42m^4 - 30m^3 + 36m^2$
H. $-13m^4 - m^2 + 36m^2$
J. $42m^4 - 30m^3 - 36m^2$
K. $-42m^4 + 5m - 6$

11. $-h^2(-4h + 5) =$

A. $-4h^3 - 5h^2$
B. $4h^3 - 5h^2$
C. $-5h^2 - 5h^2$
D. $-5h^3 - 5h^2$
E. $4h^2 - 5h^2$

12. $\dfrac{4xy^2 - 6xy + 8x^2y}{2xy} =$

F. $2xy - 3 + 4x$
G. $2y - 3 + 4xy$
H. $2y - 3 + 4x$
J. $2xy - 3 + 4x^2$
K. $2xy - 3 + 4x$

13. $\dfrac{3cd^3 + 6c^2d - 12cd}{3cd} =$

A. $cd + 3c - 4cd$
B. $d^2 + 2c - 4cd$
C. $cd + 2c - 4cd$
D. $d^2 + 2c - 4$
E. $3d^2 + 2c - 4cd$

14. $4m(m - 5) - 3m(2m^2 - 6m + 4) =$

F. $6m^3 - 14m^2 - 8m$
G. $-8m^2 - 8m - 1$
H. $7m - 14m^2 - 1$
J. $10m^2 - 26m - 20$
K. $10m^2 - 14m - 1$

15. $2h(3h^2 - 5h - 2) + 4h(h^2 + 6h + 8) =$

A. $6h^3 + 19h^2 + 28h$
B. $-8m^2 - 8m - 1$
C. $7m - 14m^2 - 1$
D. $10h^3 + 14h^2 + 28h$
E. $10h^3 + h + 6$

16. Multiply the following binomials and simplify.

$(x - 3)(x + 3)$

F. $x^2 - 3x + 3x - 9$
G. $x^2 - 9$
H. $x^2 + 9$
J. $x^2 + 6x + 9$
K. $x^2 - 3x + 9$

17. Multiply the following binomials and simplify.

$(x + 9)(x + 1)$

A. $x^2 + 10x + 9$
B. $x^2 + 10x + 10$
C. $x^2 + 9x + 9$
D. $x^2 + 9x + x + 9$
E. $x^2 + 9x + 10$

18. Multiply the following binomials and simplify.

$(x - 2)^2$

F. $x^2 - 4x - 4$
G. $x^2 - 2x + 4$
H. $x^2 + 2x - 4$
J. $x^2 - 4x + 4$
K. $x^2 + 4$

Chapter 8
Factoring

8.1 Finding the Greatest Common Factor of Polynomials

Example 1: Find the greatest common factor of $4a^3b^2 - 6a^2b^2 + 2a^4b^3$

Step 1: The greatest common factor of the whole numbers is 2.

$$4a^3b^2 - 6a^2b^2 + 2a^4b^3 = 2\left(2a^3b^2 - 3a^2b^2 + a^4b^3\right)$$

Step 2: Find the lowest power of each variable that is in each term. Factor them out of each term. The lowest power of a is a^2. The lowest power of b is b^2.

$$4a^3b^2 - 6a^2b^2 + 2a^4b^3 = 2a^2b^2\left(2a - 3 + a^2b\right)$$

Factor each of the following polynomials.

1. 3[illegible]$^2 - 6a^3b^4 + 9a^2b^3$
2. $12x^4y^3 + 18x^3y$[illegible]$ - 24x$[illegible]$y^3$
3. $20x^2y - 25x^3y^3$
4. $12x$[illegible]$y - 20x^2y^2 + 16xy$[illegible]
5. $8a$[illegible]$b + 12a^2b + 20a^2b^3$
6. $36c^4 + 42c^3 + 24c^2 - 18c$
7. $14m^3n^4 - 28m^3n^2 + 42m^2n^3$
8. $16x^4y^2 - 24x^3y^2 + 12x^2y^2 - 8xy^2$
9. $32c^3d^4 - 56c^2d^3 + 64c^3d^2$
10. $21a^4b^3 + 27a^2b^3 + 15a^3b^2$
11. $4w^3t^2 + 6w^2t - 8wt^2$
12. $5pq^3$ [illegible] $2p^2q^2 - 9p$[illegible]q
13. $49x^3t^3 + 7xt^2 - 14xt^3$
14. $9cd^4 - 3d$[illegible]$ - 6c^2d^3$
15. $12a^2b^3 - 14ab + 10ab^2$
16. $25x^4 + 10x - 20x^2$
17. $bx^3 - b^2x^2 + b^3x$
18. $4k^3a$[illegible]$ + 22ka$ [illegible] $16k^2a^2$
19. $33w^4y^2 -$ [illegible]$w^3y^2 + 24w^2y^2$
20. $18x^3$ [illegible] $9x^5 + 27x^2$

8.2 Factoring Trinomials

Sometimes a trinomial has a greatest common factor which must be factored out first.

Example 2: Factor $4x^2 + 8x - 32$

Step 1: Begin by factoring out the greatest common factor, 4.

$4\left(x^2 + 2x - 8\right)$

Step 2: Factor by finding a pair of numbers whose sum is 2 and product is -8. 4 and -2 will work, so

$4\left(x^2 + 2x - 8\right) = 4\left(x + 4\right)\left(x - 2\right)$

Check: Multiply to check. $4\left(x + 4\right)\left(x - 2\right) = 4x^2 + 8x - 32$

Factor the following trinomials. Be sure to factor out the greatest common factor first.

1. $2x^2 + 6x + 4$
2. $3y^2 - 9y + 6$
3. $2a^2 + 2a - 12$
4. $4b^2 + 28b + 40$
5. $3y^2 - 6y - 9$
6. $10x^2 + 10x - 200$
7. $5c^2 - 10c - 40$
8. $6d^2 + 30d - 36$
9. $4x^2 + 8x - 60$
10. $6a^2 - 18a - 24$
11. $5b^2 + 40b + 75$
12. $3c^2 - 6c - 24$
13. $2x^2 - 18x + 28$
14. $4y^2 - 20y + 16$
15. $7a^2 - 7a - 42$
16. $6b^2 - 18b - 60$
17. $11d^2 + 66d + 88$
18. $3x^2 - 24x + 45$

8.3 Simplifying Rational Expressions

We will use what we learned so far in this chapter to factor the terms in the numerator and the denominator when possible, then simplify the rational expression.

Example 3: Simplify $\frac{c^2 - 25}{c^2 + 5c}$

Step 1: The numerator is the difference of two perfect squares, so it can be easily factored as in the previous section. Use the square root of each of the terms in the parentheses, with a plus sign in one and a minus sign in the other.
$c^2 - 25 = (c - 5)(c + 5)$

Step 2: Find the greatest common factor in the denominator and factor it out. In this case, it is the variable c.
$c^2 + 5c = c(c + 5)$

Step 3: Simplify $\frac{c^2 - 25}{c^2 + 5c} = \frac{(c - 5)(c + 5)}{c(c + 5)} = \frac{c - 5}{c}$

Simplify the rational expressions. Check for perfect squares and common factors.

1. $\frac{25x^2 - 4}{5x^2 - 2x}$
2. $\frac{64c^2 - 25}{8c^2 + 5c}$
3. $\frac{36a^2 - 49}{6a^2 - 7a}$
4. $\frac{x^2 - 9}{x^2 + 3x}$
5. $\frac{9a^2 - 16}{3a^2 - 4a}$
6. $\frac{16x^2 - 81}{4x^2 - 9x}$
7. $\frac{49x^2 - 100}{7x^2 + 10x}$
8. $\frac{x^4 - 16}{x^2 + 2x}$
9. $\frac{4y^2 - 36}{2y^2 + 6y}$
10. $\frac{81y^4 - 16}{9y^2 + 4}$
11. $\frac{25x^2 - 225}{5x + 15}$
12. $\frac{3y^3 + 9}{y^9 - 9}$

8.4 Adding Rational Expressions

Rational expressions are fractions that can have variables in the numerator and/or the denominator. Adding rational expressions is similar to adding fractions.

Example 4: Add: $\frac{x-3}{x-2} + \frac{5}{x+3}$

Step 1: Just like adding fractions, we must find a common denominator by the finding the least common multiple of the denominators. The least common multiple of $x-2$ and $x+3$ is $(x-2)(x+3)$.

Step 2: Set up the algebra problem like a fraction problem and find the numerators.

$$\frac{x-3}{x-2} = \frac{(x-3)(x+3)}{(x-2)(x+3)}$$

$$+\ \frac{5}{x+3} = \frac{5x-10}{(x+3)(x-2)}$$

Step 3: Add: $\frac{(x-3)(x+3)+5x-10}{(x+3)(x-2)}$

Step 4: Simplify: $\frac{x^2-9+5x-10}{(x+3)(x-2)} = \frac{x^2+5x-19}{(x+3)(x-2)}$

Add the following rational expressions.

1. $\frac{x^2-9x-22}{x^2-8x-33} + \frac{x^2+12x+35}{x^2+10x+21}$
2. $\frac{1}{x^3} + \frac{x-9}{x^2}$
3. $\frac{1}{2x} + \frac{x^2-3}{2x}$
4. $\frac{y^3}{x} + \frac{x^3}{y}$
5. $\frac{(x-2)(x+13)}{x^2-4} + \frac{(x-3)(x+1)}{x^2-x-6}$
6. $\frac{a}{b^2} + \frac{b^3}{a-b}$
7. $\frac{5}{y^3} + \frac{7}{y^3}$
8. $\frac{12b}{a^2} + \frac{31c}{a^2}$
9. $\frac{y}{x^2} + \frac{3}{y^2} + \frac{x}{x^2y^2}$
10. $\frac{r}{q^{12}} + \frac{s}{r^{15}} + \frac{q}{s^5}$
11. $\frac{x}{x+y} + \frac{y}{x+y}$
12. $\frac{9b^{-1}}{a} + \frac{[illegible]}{b}$

8.5 Subtracting Rational Expressions

Subtracting rational expressions is similar to subtracting fractions.

Example 5: Subtract: $\frac{x^2}{5} - \frac{9}{x+3}$

Step 1: Just like adding you must find a common denominator. The common denominator of the rational expressions is $5(x+3)$.

Step 2: Set up the algebra problem like a fraction problem and find the numerators.

$$\frac{x^2}{5} = \frac{x^2(x+3)}{5(x+3)}$$

$$-\frac{9}{x+3} = \frac{45}{5(x+3)}$$

Step 3: Subtract: $\frac{x^2(x+3) - 45}{5(x+3)}$

Step 4: Simplify: $\frac{x^2(x+3) - 45}{5(x+3)} = \frac{x^3 + 3x^2 - 45}{5(x+3)}$

Subtract the following rational expressions.

1. $\frac{x}{3y} - \frac{2}{3y}$
2. $\frac{7}{5c} - \frac{2}{c}$
3. $\frac{x}{y^2} - \frac{x^2}{y^2}$
4. $\frac{x+1}{y+1} - \frac{y+1}{x+1}$
5. $\frac{1}{x} - \frac{2x^2}{y}$
6. $\frac{2a^2}{bc} - \frac{a^5}{bc}$
7. $\frac{d-c}{a+b} - \frac{5}{a+b}$
8. $\frac{x}{5y^2} - \frac{y}{5x^2}$
9. $\frac{c^2}{3b} - \frac{b^2}{4a}$
10. $\frac{2x+5}{y} - \frac{5x^3 - x^2}{y}$
11. $\frac{2d}{3c^5} - \frac{a^5}{2b^2}$
12. $\frac{5x}{y} - \frac{2x}{y}$

8.6 Multiplying Rational Expressions

Multiplying rational expressions is similar to multiplying fractions because a rational expression is a fraction.

Example 6: Multiply: $\frac{x^4 - x^3}{y^3} \times \frac{y^4}{x^2}$

Step 1: When you multiply a rational expression, you must multiply the numerators together and multiply the denominators together.

$$\frac{x^4 - x^3}{y^3} \times \frac{y^4}{x^2} = \frac{(x^4 - x^3) \times y^4}{y^3 \times x^2} = \frac{x^4y^4 - x^3y^4}{x^2y^3}$$

Step 2: Simplify the resulting rational expression. You can factor x^3y^4 out of the numerator.

$$\frac{x^4y^4 - x^3y^4}{x^2y^3} = \frac{x^3y^4(x - 1)}{x^2y^3}$$

Step 3: You can also cancel x^2y^3 because it is in the numerator and denominator of the expression.

$$\frac{x^3y^4(x - 1)}{x^2y^3} = \frac{xy(x - 1)}{1} = xy(x - 1)$$

Therefore, $\frac{x^4 - x^3}{y^3} \times \frac{y^4}{x^2} = xy(x - 1)$.

Multiply the following rational expressions.

1. $\frac{-b}{2a} \times \frac{-a}{3b}$
2. $\frac{4x}{y} \times \frac{1}{2y}$
3. $\frac{5a}{3b} \times \frac{4a}{3b}$
4. $\frac{a + b}{a - b} \times \frac{c + b}{c - b}$
5. $\frac{c}{a} \times \frac{c - a}{b - c}$
6. $\frac{y^2}{x^3} \times \frac{y^2 + 2y + 1}{x^2 - y}$
7. $\frac{x^2 - 2x - 3}{x^2 - 5x - 14} \times \frac{x^2 - 2x - 35}{x^2 + 6x - 27}$
8. $\frac{9}{x} \times \frac{x^5}{y}$
9. $\frac{a^2 - b}{a - b^2} \times \frac{7c}{b}$
10. $\frac{5}{x^2y} \times \frac{4}{xy^2}$
11. $\frac{5x^3}{2} \times \frac{2x^3}{5}$
12. $\frac{x + 7}{x - 1} \times \frac{x - 3}{x + 5}$
13. $\frac{3c}{a^2} \times \frac{2ba}{c}$
14. $\frac{c^5 - a^2}{b^3} \times \frac{c^4}{a^2}$
15. $\frac{b - 17}{c^2 + 2} \times \frac{a}{b^3} \times \frac{c^3}{b - 17}$
16. $\frac{hk}{[illegible]} \times \frac{16}{m}$

8.7 Dividing Rational Expressions

Dividing rational expressions is similar to dividing fractions because a rational expression is a fraction.

Example 7: Divide: $\frac{2a^3}{b} \div \frac{5}{b^2}$

Step 1: Just like dividing fractions, you must flip the second expression to get it's reciprocal, then multiply.

$$\frac{2a^3}{b} \div \frac{5}{b^2} = \frac{2a^3}{b} \times \frac{b^2}{5}$$

Step 2: Multiply the two rational expressions together just like you did in the previous section.

$$\frac{2a^3}{b} \times \frac{b^2}{5} = \frac{2a^3 \times b^2}{b \times 5} = \frac{2a^3b^2}{5b}$$

Step 3: Simplify: $\frac{2a^3b^2}{5b} = \frac{2a^3b}{5}$

Therefore, $\frac{2a^3}{b} \div \frac{5}{b^2} = \frac{2a^3b}{5}$.

Divide the following rational expressions.

1. $\frac{x}{y} \div \frac{y}{x}$
2. $\frac{2x}{y^3} \div \frac{x}{y}$
3. $\frac{x-1}{y+2} \div \frac{y-5}{x+7}$
4. $\frac{a-2}{c-1} \div \frac{c-2}{c+3}$
5. $\frac{x^2+2x+1}{y^2+8y+15} \div \frac{x^2+10x+9}{y^2+10y+21}$
6. $\frac{a}{c} \div \frac{c}{b}$
7. $\frac{c}{a} \div \frac{c}{b}$
8. $\frac{2x+3}{x+3} \div \frac{x+3}{2x+3} \div \frac{x}{y}$
9. $\frac{ac}{b^2} \div \frac{c^2}{ab}$
10. $\frac{b^2}{a} \div \frac{a^2}{c}$
11. $\frac{c^2}{3b} \div \frac{16}{a}$
12. $\frac{20ca}{b} \div \frac{2ac}{d}$
13. $\frac{x+4}{x+2} \div \frac{x-1}{x-3}$
14. $\frac{y}{3x^2} \div \frac{2y}{x^3}$
15. $\frac{y^3-1}{x^2+1} \div \frac{x-7}{y+2}$
16. $\frac{20[illegible]}{10[illegible]} \div \frac{10a}{b}$

Chapter 8 Review

Factor the following polynomials completely.

1. $8x - 18$
2. $6x^2 - 18x$
3. $16b^3 + 8b$
4. $15a^3 + 40$
5. $20y^6 - 12y^4$
6. $5a - 15a^2$
7. $4y^2 - 36$
8. $25a^4 - 49b^2$
9. $3ax + 3ay + 4x + 4y$
10. $ax - 2x + ay - 2y$
11. $2bx + 2x - 2by - 2y$
12. $4b^2 - 2b - 12$
13. $7x^3 + 14x - 3x^2 - 6$
14. $3a^3 + 4a^2 + 9a + 12$
15. $27y^2 + 42y - 5$
16. $12b^2 + 25b - 7$
17. $c^2 + cd - 20d^2$
18. $x^2 - 4xy - 21y^2$
19. $6y^2 + 30y + 36$
20. $2b^2 + 6b - 20$
21. $16b^4 - 81d^4$
22. $9w^2 - 54w - 63$
23. $m^2p^2 - 5mp + 2m^2p - 10m$
24. $12x^2 + 27x$
25. $2xy - 36 + 8y - 9x$
26. $2a^4 - 32$
27. $21c^2 + 41c + 10$
28. $x^2 - y + xy - x$
29. $2b^3 - 24 + 16b - 3b^2$
30. $5 - 2a - 25a^2 + 10a^3$

Simplify the following rational expressions by performing the appropriate operation.

31. $\frac{a^{-1}}{b^{-1}} + \frac{b}{a}$
32. $\frac{x}{y} + \frac{y}{x}$
33. $\frac{x}{x+y} - \frac{y}{x+y}$
34. $\frac{3x+5}{x+1} - \frac{3x-1}{x-1}$
35. $\frac{-b}{ac} \times \frac{3b}{a-2} \times \frac{c}{b+1}$
36. $\frac{x}{y^3} \times \frac{3y^2}{x^2}$
37. $\frac{-b}{5ac} \div \frac{d}{b^2}$
38. $\frac{5}{a+3} \div \frac{7a+21}{b^2+b}$

Chapter 8 Test

1. What is the greatest common factor of $4x^3$ and $8x^2$?
   - **A.** $4x^2$
   - **B.** $4x$
   - **C.** x^2
   - **D.** $8x$
   - **E.** $4x^3$

2. Factor: $8x^4 - 7x^2 + 4x$
   - **F.** $4x\left(2x^3 - 7x + 1\right)$
   - **G.** $x\left(8x^4 - 7x^2 + 4x\right)$
   - **H.** $x\left(8x^3 - 7x + 4\right)$
   - **J.** $4x\left(2x^3 - 7x + 1\right)$
   - **K.** $4x\left(2x^3 + 1\right)$

3. Subtract: $\dfrac{1}{7x} - \dfrac{13y}{x}$
   - **A.** $\dfrac{14y}{6x}$
   - **B.** $-\dfrac{13y}{7x}$
   - **C.** $\dfrac{1 - 13y}{6x}$
   - **D.** $\dfrac{1 - 91y}{7x}$
   - **E.** $\dfrac{1 - 91y}{6x}$

4. Simplify: $\dfrac{36x^4 - 16}{6x^3 + 4x}$
   - **F.** $\dfrac{\left(6x^2 - 4\right)\left(6x^2 + 4\right)}{x}$
   - **G.** $\dfrac{6x^2 - 4}{x}$
   - **H.** $6x^2 - 4$
   - **J.** $\dfrac{\left(3x - 2\right)\left(3x + 2\right)}{x}$
   - **K.** $\dfrac{6x^2 - 8}{2x}$

5. Divide: $\dfrac{5}{2x} \div \dfrac{5x}{y}$
   - **A.** $\dfrac{y}{2x}$
   - **B.** $\dfrac{25}{2x^2y}$
   - **C.** $\dfrac{y}{2x^2}$
   - **D.** $\dfrac{25x}{2y}$
   - **E.** $\dfrac{5y}{10x^2}$

6. Factor: $x^2 + 6x + 8$
   - **F.** $(x + 3)(x + 3)$
   - **G.** $(x + 1)(x + 8)$
   - **H.** $(x - 2)(x - 4)$
   - **J.** $(x - 1)(x - 8)$
   - **K.** $(x + 2)(x + 4)$

7. Simplify: $\dfrac{c^2 + 10c + 24}{c^3 + 4c^2}$
   - **A.** $\dfrac{c + 6}{c}$
   - **B.** $\dfrac{c + 4}{c^2}$
   - **C.** $\dfrac{c + 6}{c^2}$
   - **D.** $\dfrac{(c + 6)(c + 4)}{c^2(c + 4)}$
   - **E.** $\dfrac{c + 4}{4c}$

8. Factor: $4x^2 - 64$
   - **F.** $(x - 8)(x + 8)$
   - **G.** $(4x - 8)(4x + 8)$
   - **H.** $(2x - 16)(2x + 16)$
   - **J.** $(2x - 8)(2x + 8)$
   - **K.** $(4x - 8)(x + 8)$

9. Add: $\dfrac{11x - y}{y} + \dfrac{2}{xy^2}$

A. $\dfrac{11x^2y - xy^2 + 2}{xy^3}$

B. $\dfrac{11x^2y - xy^2 - 2}{xy^2}$

C. $\dfrac{22x - 2y}{y + xy^2}$

D. $\dfrac{11x^2y - xy^2 + 2}{xy^2}$

E. $\dfrac{11x^2y - xy^2 - 2}{2xy^2}$

10. Subtract: $\dfrac{x + 2}{x^2 - 4} - \dfrac{x}{x - 2}$

F. $\dfrac{1 - x}{x - 2}$

G. $\dfrac{[illegible]}{x^2 - 4}$

H. $\dfrac{2x - 2}{x^2 - 4}$

J. $\dfrac{x + 2}{x^2 - x - 6}$

K. undefined

11. Multiply: $\dfrac{x + 3}{2x} \times \dfrac{x(y - 1)}{y}$

A. $\dfrac{xy - x + 3y - 3}{2x}$

B. $\dfrac{xy - x + 3y - 3}{2xy}$

C. $\dfrac{xy - x + 3y - 3}{xy}$

D. $\dfrac{xy - x + 3y - 3}{2y}$

E. $\dfrac{xy - x + 3y - 3}{4xy}$

12. Factor: $2x^2 - 2x - 84$

F. $(2x + 7)(x - 12)$
G. $(2x - 12)(x + 7)$
H. $(2x - 7)(x + 12)$
J. $(2x + 12)(x - 7)$
K. $(2x + 7)(x + 12)$

13. Factor by grouping: $xy + 2x + 3y + 6$

A. $(x + 2)(y + 3)$
B. $(x + 3)(y + 2)$
C. $x(y + 2) + 3(y + 2)$
D. $(2x + 3)(3y + 2)$
E. This problem cannot be factored.

14. Multiply: $\dfrac{12y}{x} \times \dfrac{y^3}{x}$

F. $\dfrac{12y^4}{x^2}$

G. $\dfrac{12y}{x^3}$

H. $\dfrac{36y^4}{x^2}$

J. $\dfrac{12y^3}{x}$

K. $\dfrac{12y^4}{x}$

15. Divide: $\dfrac{x - 2}{y} \div \dfrac{7}{x + 3}$

A. $\dfrac{7x - 14}{y + x + 3}$

B. $\dfrac{x^2 + x - 6}{7y}$

C. $\dfrac{7x - 14}{xy + 3y}$

D. $\dfrac{x^2 + x - 6}{y}$

E. $\dfrac{x - 2}{7y}$

Chapter 9
Solving Quadratic Equations and Inequalities

In the previous chapter, we factored polynomials such as $y^2 - 4y - 5$ into two factors:

$$y^2 - 4y - 5 = (y + 1)(y - 5)$$

In this chapter, we learn that any equation that can be put in the form $ax^2 + bx + c = 0$ is a quadratic equation if a, b, and c are real numbers and $a \neq 0$. $ax^2 + bx + c = 0$ is the standard form of a quadratic equation. To solve these equations, follow the steps below.

Example 1: Solve $y^2 - 4y - 5 = 0$

Step 1: Factor the left side of the equation.

$$\begin{aligned} y^2 - 4y - 5 &= 0 \\ (y + 1)(y - 5) &= 0 \end{aligned}$$

Step 2: If the product of these two factors equals zero, then the two factors individually must be equal to zero. Therefore, to solve, we set each factor equal to zero.

$$\begin{array}{rcl} (y + 1) & = & 0 \\ -1 & & -1 \\ \hline y & = & -1 \end{array} \qquad \begin{array}{rcl} (y - 5) & = & 0 \\ +5 & & +5 \\ \hline y & = & 5 \end{array}$$

The equation has two solutions: $y = -1$ and $y = 5$

Check: To check, substitute each solution into the original equation.

When $y = -1$, the equation becomes:

$$\begin{aligned} (-1)^2 - (4)(-1) - 5 &= 0 \\ 1 + 4 - 5 &= 0 \\ 0 &= 0 \end{aligned}$$

When $y = 5$, the equation becomes:

$$\begin{aligned} 5^2 - (4)(5) - 5 &= 0 \\ 25 - 20 - 5 &= 0 \\ 0 &= 0 \end{aligned}$$

Both solutions produce true statements.
The solution set for the equation is $\{-1, 5\}$

Solve each of the following quadratic equations by factoring and setting each factor equal to zero. Check by substituting answers back in the original equation.

1. $x^2 + x - 6 = 0$
2. $y^2 - 2y - 8 = 0$
3. $a^2 + 2a - 15 = 0$
4. $y^2 - 5y + 4 = 0$
5. $b^2 - 9b + 14 = 0$
6. $x^2 - 3x - 4 = 0$
7. $y^2 + y - 20 = 0$
8. $d^2 + 6d + 8 = 0$
9. $y^2 + 7y + 12 = 0$
10. $x^2 - 3x - 28 = 0$
11. $a^2 - 5a + 6 = 0$
12. $b^2 + 3b - 10 = 0$
13. $a^2 + 7a - 8 = 0$
14. $x^2 + 3x + 2 = 0$
15. $x^2 - x - 42 = 0$
16. $a^2 + a - 6 = 0$
17. $b^2 + 7b + 12 = 0$
18. $y^2 + 2y - 15 = 0$
19. $a^2 - 3a - 10 = 0$
20. $d^2 + 10d + 16 = 0$
21. $x^2 - 4x - 12 = 0$

Quadratic equations that have a whole number and a variable in the first term are solved the same way as the previous page. Factor the trinomial, and set each factor equal to zero to find the solution set.

Example 2: Solve $2x^2 + 3x - 2 = 0$

$(2x - 1)(x + 2) = 0$

Set each factor equal to zero and solve:

$$\begin{aligned} 2x - 1 &= 0 \\ +1 &\quad +1 \\ \hline \frac{2x}{2} &= \frac{1}{2} \\ x &= \frac{1}{2} \end{aligned} \qquad \begin{aligned} x + 2 &= 0 \\ -2 &\quad -2 \\ \hline x &= -2 \end{aligned}$$

The solution set is $\left\{\frac{1}{2}, -2\right\}$

Solve the following quadratic equations.

22. $3y^2 + 4y - 32 = 0$
23. $5c^2 - 2c - 16 = 0$
24. $7d^2 + 18d + 8 = 0$
25. $3a^2 - 10a - 8 = 0$
26. $11x^2 - 31x - 6 = 0$
27. $5b^2 + 17b + 6 = 0$
28. $3x^2 - 11x - 20 = 0$
29. $5a^2 + 47a - 30 = 0$
30. $2c^2 - 5c - 25 = 0$
31. $2y^2 + 11y - 21 = 0$
32. $5a^2 + 23a - 42 = 0$
33. $3d^2 + 11d - 20 = 0$
34. $3x^2 - 10x + 8 = 0$
35. $7b^2 + 23b - 20 = 0$
36. $9a^2 + 58a + 24 = 0$
37. $4c^2 - 25c - 21 = 0$
38. $8d^2 + 53d + 30 = 0$
39. $4y^2 + 37y - 30 = 0$
40. $8a^2 + 37a - 15 = 0$
41. $3x^2 - 41x + 26 = 0$
42. $8b^2 + 2b - 3 = 0$

9.1 Solving the Difference of Two Squares

To solve the difference of two squares, first factor. Then set each factor equal to zero.

Example 3: $25x^2 - 36 = 0$

Step 1: Factor the left hand side of the equation.

$25x^2 - 36 = 0$

$(5x + 6)(5x - 6) = 0$

Step 2: Set each factor equal to zero and solve.

$$\begin{array}{rcl} 5x + 6 & = & 0 \\ -6 & & -6 \\ \hline \frac{5x}{5} & = & \frac{-6}{5} \\ x & = & -\frac{6}{5} \end{array} \qquad \begin{array}{rcl} 5x - 6 & = & 0 \\ +6 & & +6 \\ \hline \frac{5x}{5} & = & \frac{6}{5} \\ x & = & \frac{6}{5} \end{array}$$

Check: Substitute each solution in the equation to check.

for $x = -\frac{6}{5}$:

$$25x^2 - 36 = 25\left(-\frac{6}{5}\right)\left(-\frac{6}{5}\right) - 36 = 25\left(\frac{36}{25}\right) - 36 = 36 - 36 = 0$$

$x = -\frac{6}{5}$ is a solution.

for $x = \frac{6}{5}$:

$$25x^2 - 36 = 25\left(\frac{6}{5}\right)\left(\frac{6}{5}\right) - 36 = 25\left(\frac{36}{25}\right) - 36 = 36 - 36 = 0$$

$x = \frac{6}{5}$ is a solution.

The solution set is $\left\{\frac{-6}{5}, \frac{6}{5}\right\}$.

Find the solution sets for the following.

1. $25a^2 - 16 = 0$
2. $c^2 - 36 = 0$
3. $9x^2 - 64 = 0$
4. $100y^2 - 49 = 0$
5. $4b^2 - 81 = 0$
6. $d^2 - 25 = 0$
7. $9x^2 - 1 = 0$
8. $16a^2 - 9 = 0$
9. $36y^2 - 1 = 0$
10. $36y^2 - 25 = 0$
11. $d^2 - 16 = 0$
12. $64b^2 - 9 = 0$
13. $81a^2 - 4 = 0$
14. $64y^2 - 25 = 0$
15. $4c^2 - 49 = 0$
16. $x^2 - 81 = 0$
17. $49b^2 - 9 = 0$
18. $a^2 - 64 = 0$
19. $x^2 - 1 = 0$
20. $4y^2 - 9 = 0$
21. $t^2 - 100 = 0$
22. $16k^2 - 81 = 0$
23. $a^2 - 4 = 0$
24. $36b^2 - 16 = 0$

9.2 Solving Perfect Squares

When the square root of a constant, variable, or polynomial results in a constant, variable, or polynomial without irrational numbers, the expression is a **perfect square**. Some examples are 49, x^2, and $(x-2)^2$.

Example 4: Solve the perfect square for x. $(x-5)^2 = 0$

Step 1: Take the square root of both sides.

$\sqrt{(x-5)^2} = \sqrt{0}$

$(x-5) = 0$

Step 2: Solve the equation.

$(x-5) = 0$

$x - 5 + 5 = 0 + 5$

$x = 5$

Example 5: Solve the perfect square for x. $(x-5)^2 = 64$

Step 1: Take the square root of both sides.

$\sqrt{(x-5)^2} = \sqrt{64}$

$(x-5) = \pm 8$

$(x-5) = 8$ and $(x-5) = -8$

Step 2: Solve the two equations.

$(x-5) = 8$	and	$(x-5) = -8$
$x - 5 + 5 = 8 + 5$	and	$x - 5 + 5 = -8 + 5$
$x = 13$	and	$x = -3$

Solve the perfect square for x.

1. $(x-2)^2 = 0$
2. $(x+1)^2 = 0$
3. $(x+11)^2 = 0$
4. $(x-4)^2 = 0$
5. $(x-1)^2 = 0$
6. $(x+8)^2 = 0$
7. $(x+2)^2 = 4$
8. $(x-5)^2 = 16$
9. $(x-10)^2 = 100$
10. $(x+9)^2 = 9$
11. $(x-4.5)^2 = 25$
12. $(x+7)^2 = 36$
13. $(x+$[illegible]$)^2 = 49$
14. $(x-1)^2 = 4$
15. $(x+8.9)^2 = 49$
16. $(x-6)^2 = 81$
17. $(x-12)^2 = 121$
18. $(x+2.5)^2 = 64$

9.3 Completing the Square

"Completing the Square" is another way of factoring a quadratic equation. To complete the square, convert the equation into a perfect square.

Example 6: Solve $x^2 - 10x + 9 = 0$ by completing the square.

Completing the square:

Step 1: The first step is to get the constant on the other side of the equation. Subtract 9 from both sides:
$x^2 - 10x + 9 - 9 = -9$
$x^2 - 10x = -9$

Step 2: Determine the coefficient of the x. The coefficient in this example is 10. Divide the coefficient by 2 and square the result.
$(10 \div 2)^2 = 5^2 = 25$

Step 3: Add the resulting value, 25, to both sides:
$x^2 - 10x + 25 = -9 + 25$
$x^2 - 10x + 25 = 16$

Step 4: Now factor the $x^2 - 10x + 25$ into a perfect square:
$(x - 5)^2 = 16$

Solving the perfect square:

Step 5: Take the square root of both sides.
$\sqrt{(x-5)^2} = \sqrt{16}$
$(x - 5) = \pm 4$
$(x - 5) = 4$ and $(x - 5) = -4$

Step 6: Solve the two equations.

$(x - 5) = 4$	and	$(x - 5) = -4$
$x - 5 + 5 = 4 + 5$	and	$x - 5 + 5 = -4 + 5$
$x = 9$	and	$x = 1$

Solve for x by completing the square.

1. $x^2 + 2x - 3 = 0$
2. $x^2 - 8x + 7 = 0$
3. $x^2 + 6x - 7 = 0$
4. $x^2 - 16x - 36 = 0$
5. $x^2 - 14x + 49 = 0$
6. $x^2 - 4x = 0$
7. $x^2 + 12x + 27 = 0$
8. $x^2 + 2x - 24 = 0$
9. $x^2 + 12x - 85 = 0$
10. $x^2 - 8x + 15 = 0$
11. $x^2 - 16x + 60 = 0$
12. $x^2 - 8x - 48 = 0$
13. $x^2 + 24x + 44 = 0$
14. $x^2 + 6x + 5 = 0$
15. $x^2 - 11x + 5.25 = 0$

9.4 Using the Quadratic Formula

You may be asked to use the quadratic formula to solve an algebra problem known as a **quadratic equation**. The equation should be in the form $ax^2 + bx + c = 0$.

Example 7: Using the quadratic formula, find x in the following equation: $x^2 - 8x = -7$.

Step 1: Make sure the equation is set equal to 0.

$x^2 - 8x + 7 = -7 + 7$
$x^2 - 8x + 7 = 0$

The quadratic formula, $\dfrac{-b \pm \sqrt{b^2 - 4ac}}{2a}$, will be given to you on your formula sheet with your test.

Step 2: In the formula, a is the number x^2 is multiplied by, b is the number x is multiplied by and c is the last term of the equation. For the equation in the example, $x^2 - 8x + 7$, $a = 1$, $b = -8$, and $c = 7$. When we look at the formula we notice a $\pm$ sign. This means that there will be two solutions to the equation, one when we use the plus sign and one when we use the minus sign. Substituting the numbers from the problem into the formula, we have:

$$\frac{8 + \sqrt{8^2 - (4)(1)(7)}}{2(1)} = 7 \qquad \text{or} \qquad \frac{8 - \sqrt{8^2 - (4)(1)(7)}}{2(1)} = 1$$

The solutions are $\{7, 1\}$

For each of the following equations, use the quadratic formula to find two solutions.

1. $x^2 + x - 6 = 0$
2. $y^2 - 2y - 8 = 0$
3. $a^2 + 2a - 15 = 0$
4. $y^2 - 5y + 4 = 0$
5. $b^2 - 9b + 14 = 0$
6. $x^2 - 3x - 4 = 0$
7. $y^2 + y - 20 = 0$
8. $d^2 + 6d + 8 = 0$
9. $y^2 - 7y + 12 = 0$
10. $x^2 - 3x - 28 = 0$
11. $a^2 - 5a + 6 = 0$
12. $b^2 + 3b - 10 = 0$
13. $a^2 + 7a - 8 = 0$
14. $c^2 + 3c + 2 = 0$
15. $x^2 - x - 42 = 0$
16. $a^2 + 5a - 6 = 0$
17. $b^2 + 7b + 12 = 0$
18. $y^2 + y - 12 = 0$
19. $a^2 - 3a - 10 = 0$
20. $d^2 + 10d + 16 = 0$
21. $x^2 - 4x - 12 = 0$

9.5 Discriminant

The **discriminant**, D, is determined from the coefficients of the quadratic equation $ax^2 + bx + c = 0$. The formula for the discriminant is shown below.

$$D = b^2 - 4ac$$

The discriminant illustrates how many real roots the quadratic equation has. Look at the table below:

Discriminant	Roots
$D < 0$	no real roots
$D = 0$	one real root
$D > 0$	two real roots

Example 8: Find the discriminant, D, of the equation $x^2 + 7x + 12 = 0$.

Step 1: Determine what a, b, and c are in the quadratic equation $x^2 + 7x + 12 = 0$.
$a = 1, b = 7, c = 12$

Step 2: Plus the values for a, b, and c into the formula for the discriminant.
$D = b^2 - 4ac = 7^2 - 4(1)(12) = 49 - 48 = 1$

Step 3: The discriminant is 1. Looking at the chart above, we see that $1 > 0$, so there are two real roots of the quadratic equation $x^2 + 7x + 12 = 0$.

NOTE: $x^2 + 7x + 12 = 0$ factors to $(x + 3)(x + 4) = 0$

Solve for x: $x + 3 = 0$, $x = -3$; $x + 4 = 0$, $x = -4$

We see that the roots are -4 and -3. Therefore, there are two real roots for the quadratic equation $x^2 + 7x + 12 = 0$.

Find the discriminant of the quadratic equations.

1. $x^2 + 4x + 4 = 0$
2. $x^2 + 8x - 33 = 0$
3. $x^2 - 9 = 0$
4. $2x^2 + 3x - 14 = 0$
5. $x^2 - 11x + 30 = 0$
6. $2x^2 + 5x - 6 = 0$
7. $x^2 - 4x + 2 = 0$
8. $5x^2 - 6x + 21 = 0$
9. $x^2 + 9x +$ [illegible] $= 0$
10. $x^2 - 3x + 15 = 0$
11. $x^2 - 6x + 9 = 0$
12. $3x^2 + x + 6 = 0$

First, find the discriminant. Then, look at the chart above to determine how many roots the equations have.

13. $x^2 + 8x + 16 = 0$
14. $3x^2 - x + 2 = 0$
15. $x^2 - 7x + 12 = 0$
16. $x^2 + 8x + 15 = 0$
17. $2x^2 + 20x + 50 = 0$
18. $x^2 + 10x + 24 = 0$

9.6 Real-World Quadratic Equations

The most common real life situation that would use a quadratic equation is the motion of an object under the force of gravity. Two examples are a ball being kicked into the air or a rocket being shot into the air.

Example 9: A high school football player is practicing his field goal kicks. The equation below represents the height of the ball at a specific time.

$s = -9t^2 + 45t$

$t =$ amount of time in seconds

$s =$ height in feet

Question 1: Where will the ball be at 4 seconds?

Solution 1: Since there are only two variables, you will only need the value of one variable to solve the problem. Simply plug in the number 4 in place of the variable t and solve the equation as shown below.

$s = -9(4)^2 + 45(4)$

$s = -9(16) + 180$

$s = -144 + 180$

$s = 36$

At 4 seconds the ball will be 36 ft in the air.

Question 2: If the ball is 54 ft in the air, how much time has gone by?

Solution 2: This question is similar to the previous one, except that the given variable is different. This time you would be replacing s with 54 and then solve the equation.

$54 = -9t^2 + 45t$	Subtract 54 on both sides.
$0 = -9t^2 + 45t - 54$	Divide the entire equation by -9.
$0 = t^2 - 5t + 6$	Factor the equation.
$0 = (t - 3)(t - 2)$	Solve for t.
$t = 3 \qquad t = 2$	

For this question, we got 2 answers. The ball is 54 ft in the air when 2 and 3 seconds have gone by.

Example 10: John and Alex are kicking a soccer ball back and forth to each other. The equation below represents the height of the ball at a specific point in time. $s = -4t^2 + 24t$, where t = amount of time in seconds and s = height in feet

Question 1: How long does it take for the soccer ball to come back down to the ground?

Solution 1: Looking at this problem you can see that no value was given, but one was indirectly given. The question asks when will the ball come back down. This is just another way of asking "When will the height of the ball be zero?" The value 0 will be used for s. Substitute 0 back in for s and solve.

$0 = -4t^2 + 24t$ Factor out the greatest common factor.
$0 = -4t(t - 6)$ Set each factor to 0 and solve.
$t = 0$, $t = 6$

It is clear that the ball is on the ground at 0 seconds, so the value of $t = 0$ is not the answer and the second value of t is used instead. It takes the ball 6 seconds to go up into the air and then come back down to the ground.

Question 2: What is the highest point the ball will go?

Solution 2: This is asking what is the vertex of the equation. You will need to use the vertex formula. As a reminder, the quadratic equation is defined as $y = ax^2 + bx + c$, where $a \neq 0$. The quadratic equation can also be written as a function of x by substituting $f(x)$ for y, such as $f(x) = ax^2 + bx + c$. To find the point of the vertex of the graph, you must use the formula below.

$$\text{vertex} = \left(-\frac{b}{2a}, f\left(-\frac{b}{2a}\right)\right)$$

where $f\left(-\frac{b}{2a}\right)$ is the quadratic equation evaluated at the value $-\frac{b}{2a}$. To do this, plug $-\frac{b}{2a}$ in for x.

To use the vertex equation, put the original equation in quadratic form and find a and b.

$s = -4t^2 + 24t \Rightarrow -4t^2 + 24t + 0.$

Since a is the coefficient of t^2, $a = -4$. b is the coefficient of t, so $b = 24$.

Find the solution to $-\frac{b}{2a}$ by substituting the values of a and b from the equation into the expression.

$$-\frac{b}{2a} = -\left(\frac{24}{2 \times -4}\right) = -\left(\frac{24}{-8}\right) = -(-3) = 3$$

Find the solution to $f\left(-\frac{b}{2a}\right)$. We know that $-\frac{b}{2a} = 3$, so we need to find $f(3)$. To do this, we must substitute 3 into the quadratic equation for x.

$f(t) = -4t^2 + 24t$
$f(3) = -4(3)^2 + 24(3) = -4(9) + 72 = -36 + 72 = 36$

The vertex equals $(3, 36)$. This means at 3 seconds, the ball is 36 feet in the air. Therefore the highest the soccer ball will go is 36 ft.

Solve the following quadratic problems.

1. Eric is at the top of a cliff that is 500 ft from the ocean's surface. He is waiting for his friend to climb up and meet him. As he is waiting he decides to start casually tossing pebbles off the side of the cliff. The equation that represents the height of his pebbles tosses is $s = -t^2 + 5t + 500$, where s = distance in feet and t = time in seconds.

   (A) How long does it take the pebble to hit the water?

   (B) If fifteen seconds have gone by, what is the height of the pebble from the ocean?

   (C) What is the highest point the pebble will go?

2. Devin is practicing golf at the driving range. The equation that represents the height of his ball is $s = -0.5t^2 + 12t$, where s = distance in feet and t = time in seconds.

   (A) What is the highest his ball will ever go?

   (B) If the ball is at 31.5 ft in the air, how many seconds has gone by?

   (C) How long will it take for the ball to hit the ground?

3. Jack throws a ball up in the air to see how high he can get it to go. The equation that represents the height of the ball is $s = -2t^2 + 20t$, where s = distance in feet and t = time in seconds.

   (A) How high will the ball be at 7 seconds?

   (B) If the ball is 48 feet in the air, how many seconds have gone by?

   (C) How long does it take for the ball to go up and come back down to the ground?

4. Kali is jumping on her super trampoline, getting as high as she possibly can. The equation to represent her height is $s = -5t^2 + 20t$, where s = distance in feet and t = time in seconds.

   (A) What is the highest Kali can jump on her trampoline?

   (B) How high will Kali be at 4 seconds?

   (C) If Kali is 18.75 ft in the air, then how many seconds have gone by?

9.7 Solving Quadratic Inequalities

A **quadratic inequality** is a polynomial inequality of degree 2. The standard form of a quadratic inequality is similar to that of a quadratic equation, which has the standard form $ax^2 + bx + c = 0$, where $a \neq 0$. The only difference in the standard form of a quadratic inequality is that the equal sign in the standard form of a quadratic equation is replaced by either $>$, $\geq$, $<$, or $\leq$.

Example 11: Solve the inequality $-x(x-2) < -3$.

Step 1: First put all of the terms in the quadratic inequality on one side of the inequality sign.
$-x(x-2) < -3 \rightarrow -x^2 + 2x + 3 < 0$

Step 2: Now find the root(s) of the corresponding quadratic equation.
$(x-3)(-x-1) = 0$

$x - 3 = 0 \qquad -x - 1 = 0 \qquad$ Set each factor equal to zero.
$x = 3 \qquad x = -1$

Step 3: Graphing the two points -1 and 3 on a number line determines the three regions that could satisfy the inequality.

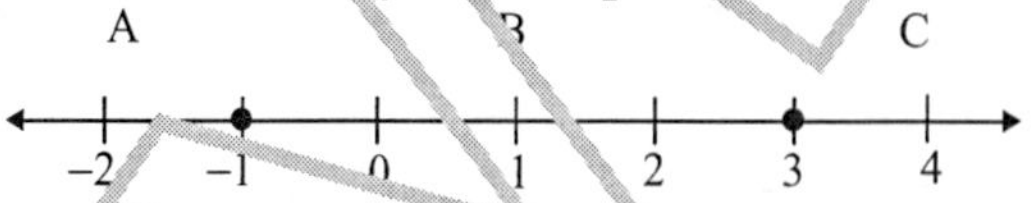

Step 4: Now pick a number from each of three regions in the graph above to determine which region satisfies the inequality.

Region	Number Chosen	Substitute into Equation	Satisfy Inequality?
A $(x < -1)$	-2	$-(-2)^2 + 2(-2) + 3 = -5 < 0$	Yes
B $(-1 < x < 3)$	0	$-(0)^2 + 2(0) + 3 = 3 > 0$	No
C $(x > 3)$	4	$-(4)^2 + 2(4) + 3 = -5 < 0$	Yes

Step 5: The numbers from region A and C satisfy the inequality. The solution to the quadratic inequality is $x < -1$ or $x > 3$. A graph of this solution is shown below.

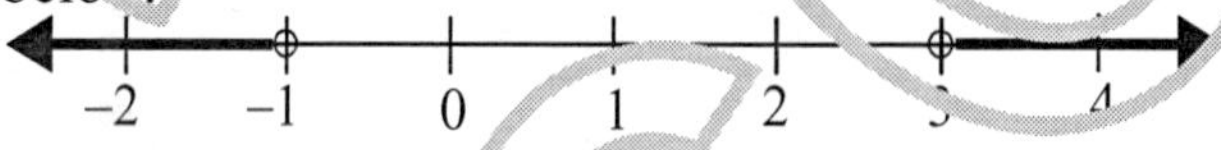

Solve each of the following quadratic inequalities.

1. $x^2 + 2x - 8 > 0$
2. $x(x+7) \geq -12$
3. $-x^2 - 5x + 14 < 0$
4. $5x^2 + 34x - 7 \leq 0$
5. $x^2 - 14x + 24 \geq 0$
6. $x(x+8) \leq 9$
7. $x^2 - 11x + 30 > 0$
8. $3x^2 + 8x < 16$
9. $-x^2 + x + 56 > 0$
10. $-x^2 + 4x - 9 \leq 0$
11. $x^2 - x + 7 < 0$
12. $x(x-4) > -5$
13. $4x^2 - x + 1 \geq 0$
14. $(x-3)^2 < 0$
15. $x^2 + 2x + 6 \leq 0$
16. $5x(x-1) > -2$
17. $8x^2 - 7x + 2 \geq 0$
18. $-x^2 + 3x - 11 > 0$

9.8 Complex Numbers

Complex numbers are usually written in the form $a + bi$, where a and b are real numbers. The number i is defined as $\sqrt{-1}$ and $i^2 = -1$. Because $\sqrt{-1}$ does not exist in the set of real numbers, i is referred to as the imaginary unit. Complex numbers have two parts, a real part and imaginary part. The number a is called the real part of the number, and the number bi is called the imaginary part of the number. Even though real numbers are not often thought of as complex numbers, every real number is a complex number with an imaginary part of 0.

Example 12: Simplify the expression $[(3+6i)+(2-5i)]^2 \div (4+7i)$.

Step 1: The first operation that needs to be performed is the addition of the complex numbers $3 + 6i$ and $2 - 5i$. To add two complex numbers together, the real parts need to be added to each other, and the imaginary parts need to be added to each other.
$(3+6i)+(2-5i) = (3+2)+(6i-5i) = 5+1i = 5+i$

Step 2: The next operation that needs to be performed is the raising of the complex number $5 + i$ to the power 2. To multiply two complex numbers together, the complex numbers should be treated the same as two binomials would, and the FOIL method used.
$(5+i)(5+i) = (5)(5)+(5)(i)+(5)(i)+(i)(i) = 25+5i+5i+i^2 = 25+10i+i^2$.

Step 3: It's possible to simplify $25 + 10i + i^2$ even further. Since i is defined as $\sqrt{-1}$, $i^2 = (\sqrt{-1})^2 = -1$.
$25 + 10i + i^2 = 25 + 10i + (-1) = 24 + 10i$.

Step 4: The final operation that needs to be performed is the division of $24 + 10i$ by $4 + 7i$. To divide one complex number by another, the division of the complex numbers should be written as a fraction.

Therefore, $(24+10i) \div (4+7i) = \dfrac{24+10i}{4+7i}$.

Both the numerator and the denominator of the fraction should be multiplied by the **complex conjugate** of the denominator.
(The complex conjugate of the denominator is obtained by changing the sign of the imaginary part.)

$$\frac{(24+10i)(4-7i)}{(4+7i)(4-7i)} = \frac{(24)(4)+(24)(-7i)+(4)(10i)+(10i)(-7i)}{(4)(4)+(4)(-7i)+(4)(7i)+(7i)(-7i)}$$

$$= \frac{96-168i+40i-70i^2}{16-28i+28i-49i^2} = \frac{96-128i-70(\sqrt{-1})^2}{16-49(\sqrt{-1})^2} = \frac{96-128i-70(-1)}{16-49(-1)}$$

$$= \frac{96-128i+70}{16+49} = \frac{166-128i}{65} = \frac{166}{65} - \frac{128}{65}i.$$

Thus, the simplified expression is $\dfrac{166}{65} - \dfrac{128}{65}i$.

Simplify each of the following expressions.

1. $(33 - 8i) - (14 + 5i)$
2. $(2 + 3i)(6 - 7i)$
3. $(12 + 4i) + (\frac{3}{2} - 9i)$
4. $(3 + i) \div (9 - 2i)$
5. $(-1[illegible] - 3i) + (7 - 5i)$
6. $(13 - 3i)^2$
7. $(20 - i) \div (20 + i)$
8. $(14 + 3i)(11 - i)$
9. $(17 - 6i) - (-3 - 6i)$

Example 13: Find the roots of the quadratic equation $7x^2 - 8x + 3 = 0$.

Step 1: The quadratic equation cannot be factored, so the quadratic formula must be used.

$$x = \frac{-b \pm \sqrt{b^2 - 4ac}}{2a} = \frac{-(-8) \pm \sqrt{(-8)^2 - 4(7)(3)}}{2(7)} = \frac{8 \pm \sqrt{64 - 84}}{14} = \frac{8 \pm \sqrt{-20}}{14}$$

Step 2: As stated earlier, i is defined as $\sqrt{-1}$, so if $\frac{8 \pm \sqrt{-20}}{14}$ is rewritten as $\frac{8 \pm \sqrt{20 \times (-1)}}{14}$, it can be simplified to $\frac{8 \pm i\sqrt{20}}{14}$.

This, in turn, can be simplified as follows:

$$\frac{8 \pm i\sqrt{20}}{14} = \frac{8 \pm i\sqrt{4 \times 5}}{14} = \frac{8 \pm 2i\sqrt{5}}{14} = \frac{4 \pm i\sqrt{5}}{7} = \frac{4}{7} \pm \frac{\sqrt{5}}{7}i.$$

Therefore, the roots of the equation are $x = \frac{4}{7} + \frac{\sqrt{5}}{7}i$ or $\frac{4}{7} - \frac{\sqrt{5}}{7}i$.

Find the roots of each of the following quadratic equations.

10. $9x^2 - 5x + 3 = 0$
11. $\frac{3}{4}x^2 - x + 12 = 0$
12. $-11x^2 + 10x - 3 = 0$
13. $14x^2 - 3x + \frac{1}{2} = 0$
14. $-x^2 - 3x - 16 = 0$
15. $8x^2 + 3x + 10 = 0$
16. $x(19x - 2) = -1$
17. $x(1 - 5x) = $ [illegible]
18. $-10x^2 +$ [illegible] $- 7 = 0$

Chapter 9 Review

Factor and solve each of the following quadratic equations.

1. $16b^2 - 25 = 0$
2. $a^2 - a - 30 = 0$
3. $x^2 - x = 6$
4. $100x^2 - 49 = 0$
5. $81y^2 = 9$
6. $y^2 = 21 - 4y$
7. $y^2 - 7y + 8 = 16$
8. $6x^2 + x - 2 = 0$
9. $3y^2 + y - 2 = 0$
10. $b^2 + 2b - 8 = 0$
11. $4x^2 + 19x - 5 = 0$
12. $8x^2 = 6x + 2$
13. $2y^2 - 6y - 20 = 0$
14. $-6x^2 + 7x - 2 = 0$
15. $y^2 + 3y - 18 = 0$

Using the quadratic formula, find both solutions for the variable.

16. $x^2 +$ [illegible] $x - 11 = 0$
17. $y^2 - 14y + 49 = 0$
18. $b^2 + 9b - 18 = 0$
19. $y^2 - 12y - 13 = 0$
20. $a^2 - 8a - 48 = 0$
21. $x^2 + 2x - 63 = 0$
22. [illegible] $3x^2 - 2x - 2 = 0$
23. $4x^2 + x + 5 = 0$
24. $2x^2 - 8x + 9 = 0$

Solve each of the following quadratic inequalities.

25. $2x^2 + x - 15 \geq 0$
26. $-2x^2 + 21x + 11 < 0$
27. $x(3x + 1) \leq 24$
28. $-5x^2$ [illegible] $3x - 12 > 0$
29. $x^2 + 8x +$ [illegible] ≥ 0
30. $6x^2 - 7x + 8 \leq 0$

Simplify each of the following expressions.

31. $(7 + 12i)(7 - 12i)$
32. $(4 + 3i) \div (2 - i)$
33. $5 + 4i + (6 - 5i)^2$

Chapter 9 Test

1. Solve: $4y^2 - 9y = -5$

A. $\left\{1, \frac{5}{4}\right\}$

B. $\left\{-\frac{3}{4}, -1\right\}$

C. $\left\{-1, \frac{4}{5}\right\}$

D. $\left\{\frac{5}{16}, 1\right\}$

E. $\left\{\frac{5}{4}, -1\right\}$

2. Solve for y: $2y^2 + 13y + 15 = 0$

F. $\left\{\frac{3}{2}, \frac{5}{2}\right\}$

G. $\left\{-5, -\frac{3}{2}\right\}$

H. $\left\{5, -\frac{3}{2}\right\}$

J. $\left\{-5, \frac{3}{2}\right\}$

K. $\left\{\frac{2}{3}, \frac{2}{5}\right\}$

3. Solve for x:

$x^2 - 3x = 18$

A. $\{-6, 3\}$
B. $\{-6, -3\}$
C. $\{-9, 2\}$
D. $\{9, -2\}$
E. $\{6, -3\}$

4. What are the values of x in the quadratic equation?

$x^2 + 2x - 15 = x - 3$

F. $\{-4, 3\}$
G. $\{-3, 4\}$
H. $\{-3, 5\}$
J. $\{-3, -4\}$
K. Cannot be determined

5. Solve the equation $(x + 9)^2 = 49$

A. $x = -9, 9$
B. $x = -9, 7$
C. $x = -16, -2$
D. $x = -7, 7$
E. $x = -2, 16$

6. Solve the equation $c^2 + 8c - 9 = 0$ by completing the square.

F. $c = \{1, -9\}$
G. $c = \{-1, 9\}$
H. $c = \{3, 3\}$
J. $c = \{-3, -3\}$
K. $c = \{3, -3\}$

7. Using the quadratic formula, solve the following equation:

$3x^2 = 9x$

A. $x = \{-3, -1\}$
B. $x = \{0, 1\}$
C. $x = \{0, 3\}$
D. $x = \{3,$ [illegible]$\}$
E. $x = \{3,$ [illegible]$\}$

8. Solve $6a^2 + 11a - 10 = 0$, using the quadratic formula.

F. $\left\{-\frac{2}{5}, \frac{3}{2}\right\}$

G. $\left\{\frac{2}{5}, \frac{2}{3}\right\}$

H. $\left\{-\frac{5}{2}, \frac{2}{3}\right\}$

J. $\left\{\frac{5}{2}, \frac{2}{3}\right\}$

K. $\left\{-\frac{5}{2}, -\frac{2}{3}\right\}$

9. Which of the following quadratic inequalities has no solution?

A. $3x^2 - 17x - 6 < 0$
B. $-4x^2 - 11x + 3 > 0$
C. $5x^2 - 7x - 6 \leq 0$
D. $-6x^2 - 3x - 8 \geq 0$
E. $7x^2 + 23x + 6 < 0$

10. $\frac{17 + 7i}{9 - 15i} = ?$

F. $\frac{8}{53} + \frac{51}{53}i$

G. $\frac{8}{51} - \frac{51}{53}i$

H. $\frac{8}{51} + \frac{51}{53}i$

J. $\frac{8}{51} - \frac{53}{51}i$

K. $\frac{8}{51} + \frac{53}{51}i$

11. Which of the following solutions is correct for the quadratic inequality $6x^2 - 41x - 7 \leq 0$?

A. $x \leq -6$ or $x \geq 7$

B. $x \leq -\frac{1}{6}$ or $x \geq 7$

C. $-6 \leq x \leq 7$

D. $-6 < x < 7$

E. $-\frac{1}{6} \leq x \leq 7$

12. Which of the following expressions is a root of the quadratic equation $-7x^2 - x - 3 = 0$?

F. $-\frac{1}{14} - \frac{\sqrt{83}}{14}$

G. $-\frac{1}{14} + \frac{\sqrt{83}}{14}$

H. $-\frac{1}{14} - \frac{\sqrt{83}}{14}i$

J. $1 - \sqrt{83}i$

K. $1 + \sqrt{83}i$

Chapter 10
Relations and Functions

10.1 Relations

A **relation** is a set of ordered pairs. The set of the first members of each ordered pair is called the **domain** of the relation. The set of the second members of each ordered pair is called the **range**.

Example 1: State the domain and range of the following relation:

$$\{(2,4),(3,7),(4,9),(6,11)\}$$

Solution: Domain: $\{2,3,4,6\}$ the first member of each ordered pair

Range: $\{4,7,9,11\}$ the second member of each ordered pair

State the domain and range for each relation.

1. $\{(2,5),(9,12),(3,8),(6,7)\}$

2. $\{(6,4),(3,4),(7,12),(26,19)\}$

3. $\{(4,3),(7,14),(16,54),(5,11)\}$

4. $\{(2,45),(33,43),(98,9),(43,61),(67,54)\}$

5. $\{(78,14),(29,67),(84,43),(16,18),(98,46)\}$

6. $\{(-8,16),(23,-7),(-4,-9),(16,-8),(-3,6)\}$

7. $\{(-7,-4),(-3,16),(-4,17),(-6,-8),(-8,12)\}$

8. $\{(-1,-2),(3,6),(-7,14),(-2,3),(-6,2)\}$

9. $\{(0,9),(-8,5),(3,12),(-8,-3),(7,18)\}$

10. $\{(58,14),(44,97),(74,32),(6,18),(63,44)\}$

When given an equation in two variables, the domain is the set of x values that satisfies the equation. The range is the set of y values that satisfies the equation.

Example 2: Find the range of the relation $3x = y + 2$ for the domain $\{-1, 0, 1, 2, 3\}$.
Solve the equation for each value of x given. The result, the y values, will be the range.

Given:

x	y
-1	
0	
1	
2	
3	

Solution:

x	y
-1	-5
0	-2
1	1
2	4
3	7

The range is $\{-5, -2, 1, 4, 7\}$.

Find the range of each relation for the given domain.

Relation	**Domain**	**Range**
1. $y = 5x$	$\{1, 2, 3, 4\}$	
2. $y = \|x\|$	$\{-3, -2, -1, 0, 1\}$	
3. $y = 3x + 2$	$\{0, 1, 3, 4\}$	
4. $y = -\|x\|$	$\{-2 - 1, 0, 1, 2\}$	
5. $y = -2x + 1$	$\{0, 1, 3, 4\}$	
6. $y = 10x - 2$	$\{-2 - 1, 0, 1, 2\}$	
7. $y = 3\|x\| + 1$	$\{-2 - 1, 0, 1, 2\}$	
8. $y - x = 0$	$\{1, 2, 3, 4\}$	
9. $y - 2x = 0$	$\{1, 2, 3, 4\}$	
10. $y = 3x - 1$	$\{0, 1, 3, 4\}$	
11. $y = 4x + 2$	$\{0, 1, 3, 4\}$	
12. $y = 2\|x\| - 1$	$\{-2 - 1, 0, 1, 2\}$	

10.2 Determining Domain and Range From Graphs

The domain is all of the x values that lie on the function in the graph from the lowest x value to the highest x value. The range is all of the y values that lie on the function in the graph from the lowest y to the highest y.

Example 3: Find the domain and range of the graph.

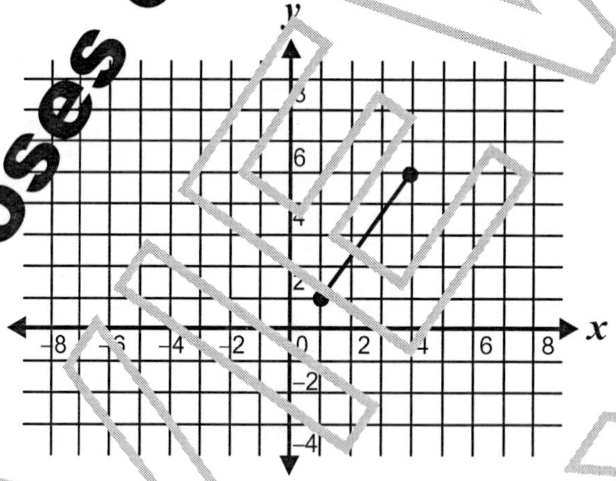

Step 1: First find the lowest x value depicted on the graph. In this case it is 1. Then find the highest x value depicted on the graph. The highest value of x on the graph is 4. The domain must contain all of the values between the lowest x value and the highest x value. The easiest way to write this is $1 \leq \text{Domain} \leq 4$ or $1 \leq x \leq 4$.

Step 2: Perform the same process for the range, but this time look at the lowest and highest y values. The answer is $1 \leq \text{Range} \leq 5$ or $1 \leq y \leq 5$.

Find the domain and range of each graph below. Write your answers on the line provided.

1.

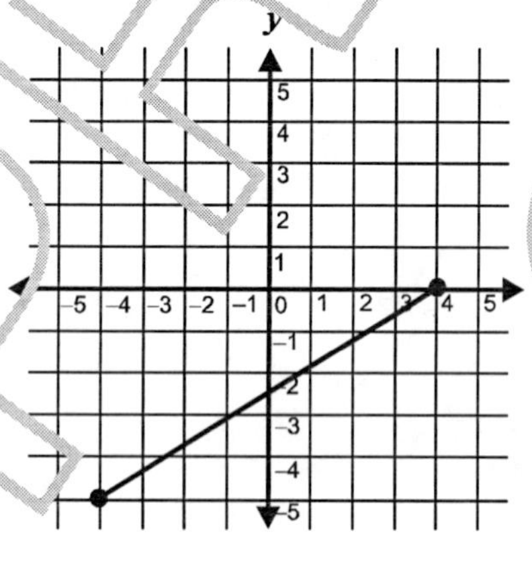

____

2.

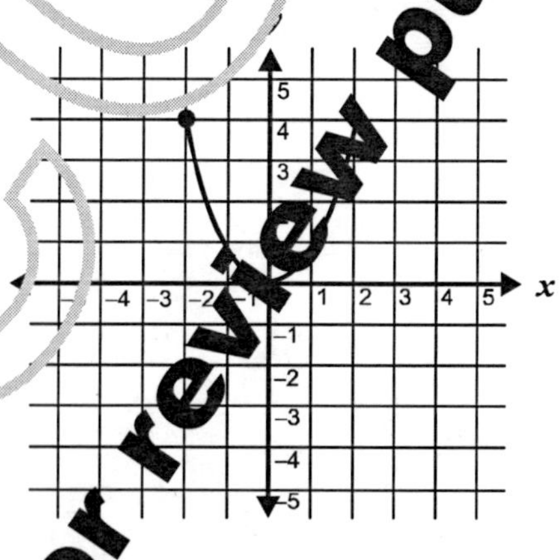

____

3.

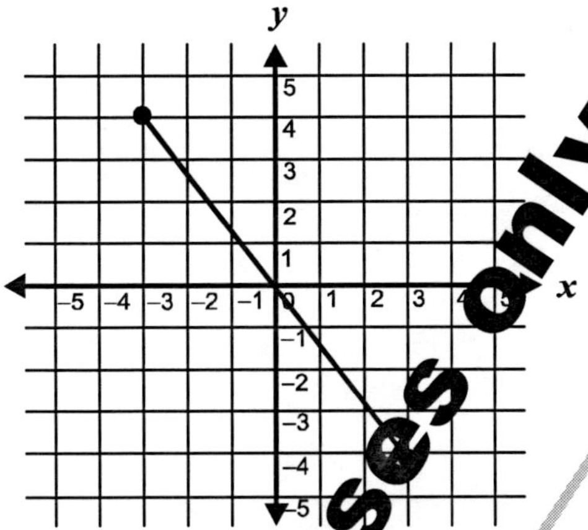
y
x
–5 –4 –3 –2 –1 0 1 2 3 4 5
5 4 3 2 1 –1 –2 –3 –4 –5

____

6.

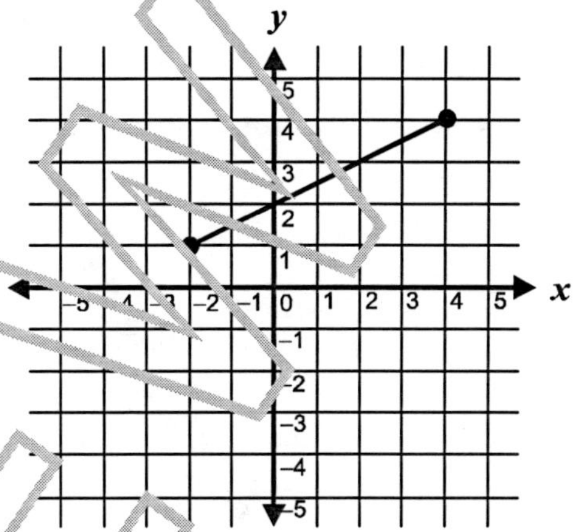
y
x
–5 –4 –3 –2 –1 0 1 2 3 4 5
5 4 3 2 1 –1 –2 –3 –4 –5

____

4.

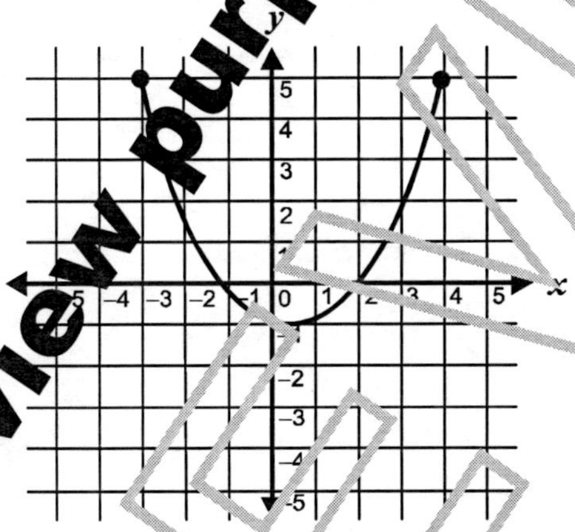
y
x

____

7.

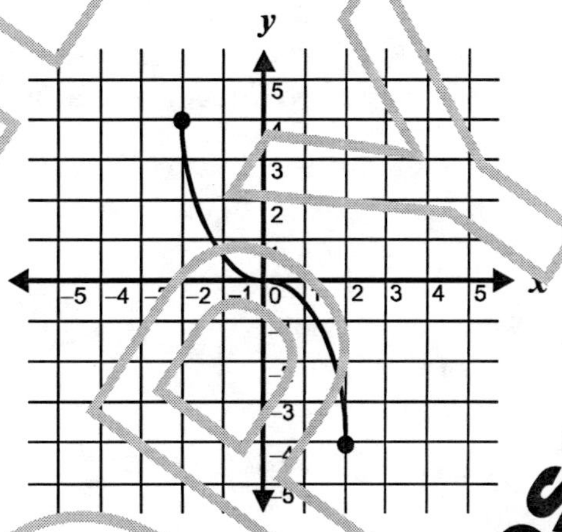
y
x

____

5.

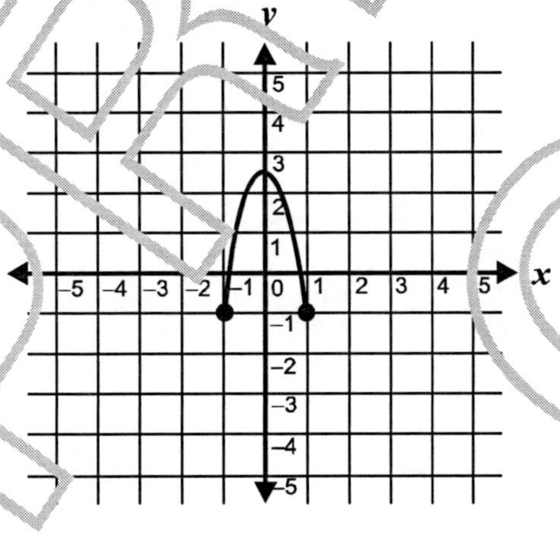
y
x
–5 –4 –3 –2 –1 0 1 2 3 4 5
5 4 3 2 1 –1 –2 –3 –4 –5

____

8.

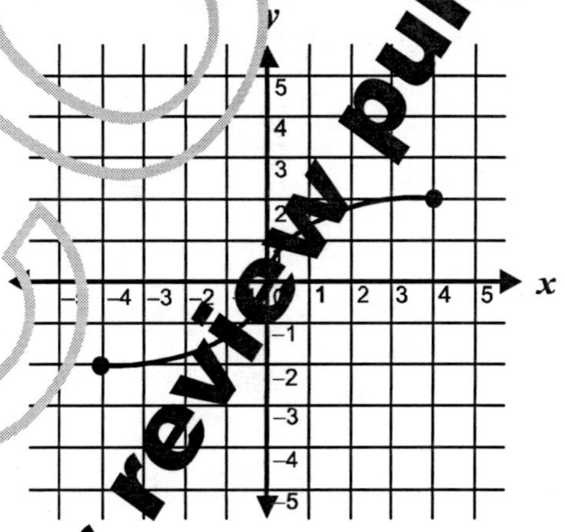
y
x

____

10.3 Functions

Some relations are also **functions**. A relation is a function if **for every element in the domain, there is exactly one element in the range.** In other words, for each value for x there is only one unique value for y.

Example 4: $\{(2,4), (2,5), (3,4)\}$ is **NOT** a function because in the first pair, 2 is paired with 4, and in the second pair, 2 is paired with 5. The 2 can be paired with only one number to be a function. In this example, the x value of 2 has more than one value for y: 4 and 5.

Example 5: $\{(1,2), (3,2), (5,6)\}$ **IS** a function. Each first number is paired with only one second number. The 2 is repeated as a second number, but the relation remains a function.

Determine whether the ordered pairs of numbers below represent a function. Write "F" if it is a function. Write "NF" if it is not a function.

1. $\{(-1, [illegible]), (-3,3), (0,0), (2,2)\}$ ______
2. $\{([illegible], -3), (-2, -3), (-1, -3), (2, -3)\}$ ______
3. $\{(0, -1), (2,0), (2,2), (5,3)\}$ ______
4. $\{(-3,3), (0,2), (1,1), (2,0)\}$ ______
5. $\{(-2,-5), (-2,-1), (-2,1), (-2,3)\}$ ______
6. $\{(0,2), (1,1), (2,2), (4,3)\}$ ______
7. $\{(4,2), (3,3), (2,2), (0,3)\}$ ______
8. $\{(-1,-1), (-2,-2), (3,-1), (3,2)\}$ ______
9. $\{(2,-2), (0,-2), (-2,0), (1,-3)\}$ ______
10. $\{(2,1), (3,2), (4,3), (5,-1)\}$ ______
11. $\{(-1,0), (2,1), (2,4), (-2,2)\}$ ______
12. $\{(1,4), (2,3), (0,2), (0,4)\}$ ______
13. $\{(0,0), (1,0), (2,0), (3,0)\}$ ______
14. $\{(-5,-1), (-3,-2), (-4,-9), (-7,-3)\}$ ______
15. $\{(8,-3), (-4,4), (8,0), (6,2)\}$ ______
16. $\{(7,-1), (4,3), (8,2), (2,8)\}$ ______
17. $\{(4,-3), (2,0), (5,3), (4,1)\}$ ______
18. $\{(2,-6), (7,3), (-3,4), (2,-3)\}$ ______
19. $\{(1,1), (3,-2), (4,16), (1,-5)\}$ ______
20. $\{(5,7), (3,8), (5,3), (6,9)\}$ ______

10.4 Function Notation

Function notation is used to represent relations which are functions. Some commonly used letters to represent functions include f, g, h, F, G, and H.

Example 6: $f(x) = 2x - 1$; find $f(-3)$

Step 1: Find $f(-3)$ means to replace x with -3 in the relation $2x - 1$.
$f(-3) = 2(-3) - 1$

Step 2: Solve $f(-3)$. $f(-3) = 2(-3) - 1 = -6 - 1 = -7$
$f(-3) = -7$

Example 7: $g(x) = 4 - 2x^2$, find $g(2)$

Step 1: Replace x with 2 in the relation $4 - 2x^2$.
$g(2) = 4 - 2(2)^2$

Step 2: Solve $g(2)$. $g(2) = 4 - 2(2)^2 = 4 - 2(4) = 4 - 8 = -4$
$g(2) = -4$

Find the solutions for each of the following.

1. $F(x) = 2 + 3x^2$; find $F(3)$
2. $f(x) = 4x + 6$; find $f(-4)$
3. $H(x) = 6 - 2x^2$; find $H(-1)$
4. $g(x) = -3x + 7$; find $g(-3)$
5. $f(x) = -5 + 4x$; find $F(7)$
6. $G(x) = 4x^2 + 4$; find $G(0)$
7. $f(x) = 7 - 6x$; find $f(-4)$
8. $h(x) = 2x^2 + 10$; find $h(5)$
9. $F(x) = 7 - 5x$; find $F(2)$
10. $f(x) = -4x^2 + 5$; find $f(-2)$

10.5 Using Function Notation to Solve Problems

Example 8: Given the function $f(x) = 4x - 1$. Find $f(x - 3)$.

Step 1: Substitute $x - 3$ into $f(x)$ for x.
$f(x-3) = 4(x-3) - 1$

Step 2: Simplify.
$f(x-3) = 4(x-3) - 1 = 4x - 12 - 1 = 4x - 13$
$f(x-3) = 4x - 13$

Example 9: Given the functions $f(x) = x^2 - 1$ and $g(x) = 2x + 3$. Find $f(g(x))$.

Step 1: Substitute $g(x)$ into $f(x)$ for x.
$f(g(x)) = f(2x+3) = (2x+3)^2 - 1$

Step 2: Simplify.
$f(g(x)) = (2x+3)^2 - 1 = 4x^2 + 6x + 6x + 9 - 1 = 4x^2 + 12x + 8$
$f(g(x)) = 4x^2 + 12x + 8$

Simplify.

1. For $f(x) = x + 3$ and $h(x) = 5 - x$; find $h(f(x))$
2. For $f(x) = x$; find $f(4x + 12)$
3. For $g(x) = 8x$ and $h(x) = x^3$; find $g(h(x))$
4. For $f(x) = x + 1$ and $g(x) = x^2$; find $g(f(x))$
5. For $f(x) = x^2 - 4$; find $f(x + a)$
6. For $h(x) = \frac{1}{2}x - 7$; find $h(6x)$
7. For $f(x) = 2x - 5$ and $g(x) = 5x$; find $f(g(x))$
8. For $f(x) = x^2 - 4$; find $f(x + 4)$
9. For $f(x) = 12x$ and $g(x) = -x$; find $f(g(x))$
10. For $f(x) = 2 - x$ and $g(x) = x - 2$; find $g(f(x))$
11. For $f(x) = 5$ and $h(x) = x^2 - 14$; find $f(h(x))$
12. For $g(x) = 5x - 17$; find $g(x - 6)$

10.6 Function Tables

Functions can also use a variable such as n to be the input of the function and $f(n)$, read "f of n," to represent the output of the function.

Example 10: Function rule: $3n + 4$

n	$f(n)$
-1	1
0	4
1	7
2	10

Fill in the tables for each function rule below.

1. rule: $2(n - 5)$

n	$f(n)$
0	
1	
2	
3	

2. rule: $3x(x - 4)$

x	$f(x)$
0	
1	
2	
3	

3. rule: $\frac{2 - n}{2}$

n	$f(n)$
0	
2	
4	
6	
8	

4. rule: $2x(x - 1)$

x	$f(x)$
1	
2	
3	
4	

5. rule: $\frac{1}{n + 3}$

n	$f(n)$
1	
2	
3	
4	

6. rule: $4x - x$

x	$f(x)$
-2	
-1	
0	
1	
2	

7. rule: $n(n + 2)$

n	$f(n)$
1	
2	
3	
4	

8. rule: $2x - 3$

x	$f(x)$
1	
2	
3	
4	

9. rule: $3 - 2n$

n	$f(n)$
-2	
-1	
0	
1	
2	

10.7 Recognizing Functions

Recall that a relation is a function with only one y value for every x value. We can depict functions in many ways including through graphs.

Example 11:

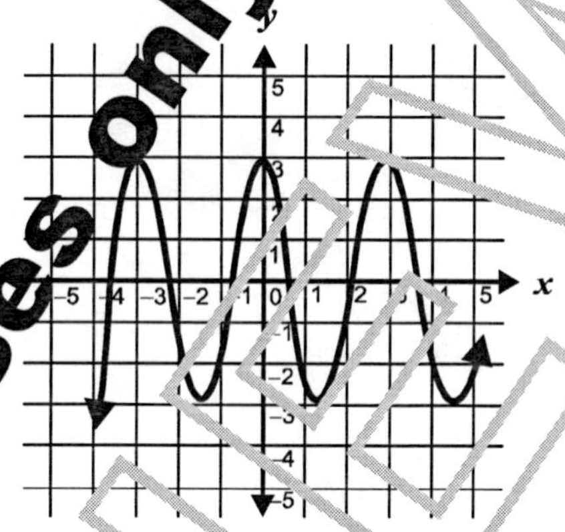

This graph **IS** a function because it has only one y value for each value of x.

Example 12:

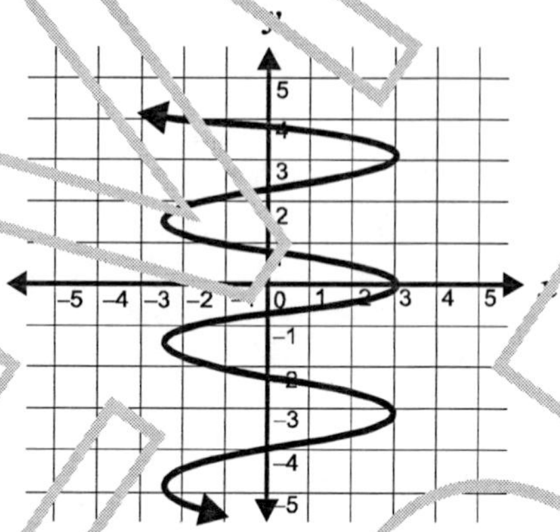

This graph is **NOT** a function because there is more than one y value for each value of x.

Hint: An easy way to determine a function from a graph is to do a vertical line test. First, draw a vertical line that crosses over the whole graph. If the line crosses the graph more than one time, then it is not a function. If it only crosses it once, it is a function. Take Example 9 above:

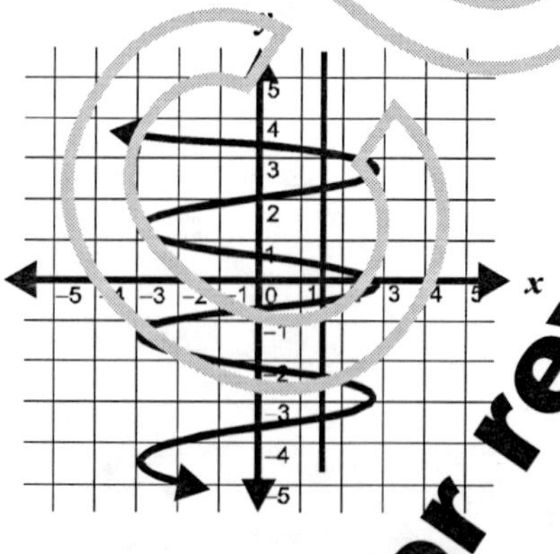

Since the vertical line passes over the graph six times, it is not a function.

Determine whether or not each of the following graphs is a function. If it is, write function on the line provided. If it is not a function, write NOT a function on the line provided.

1. 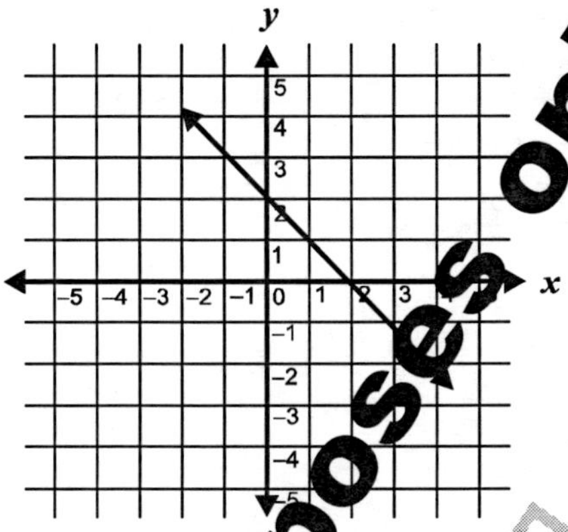

____

2. 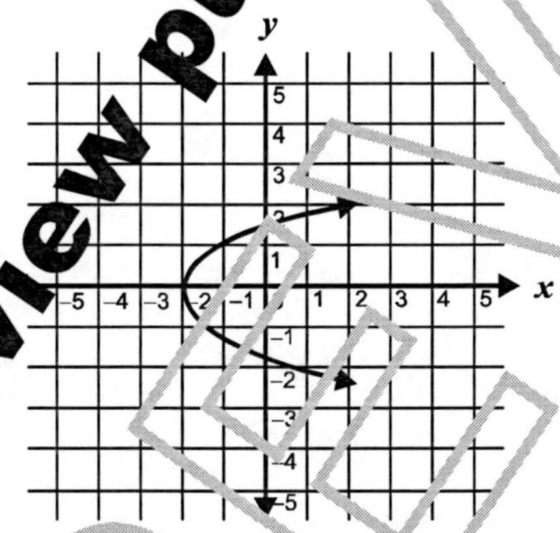

____

3. 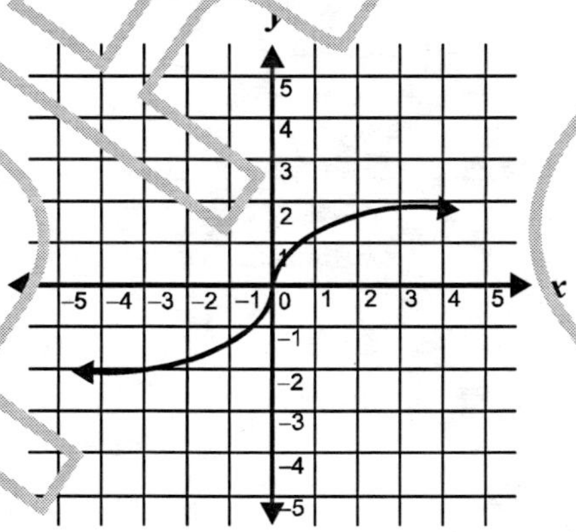

____

4. 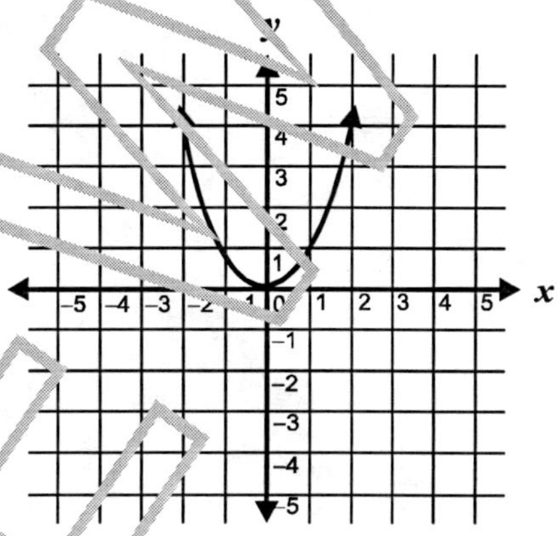

____

5. 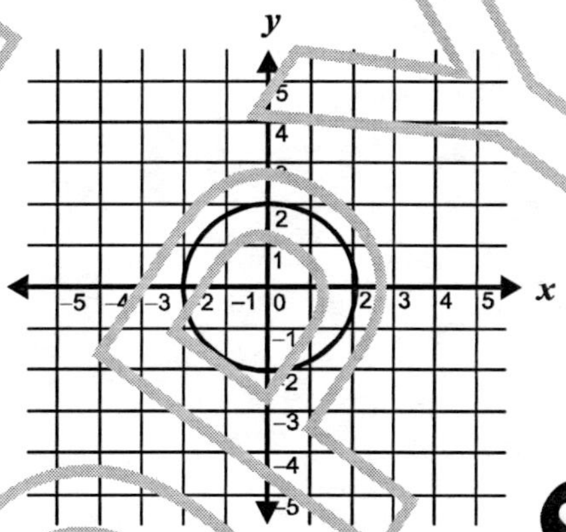

____

6. 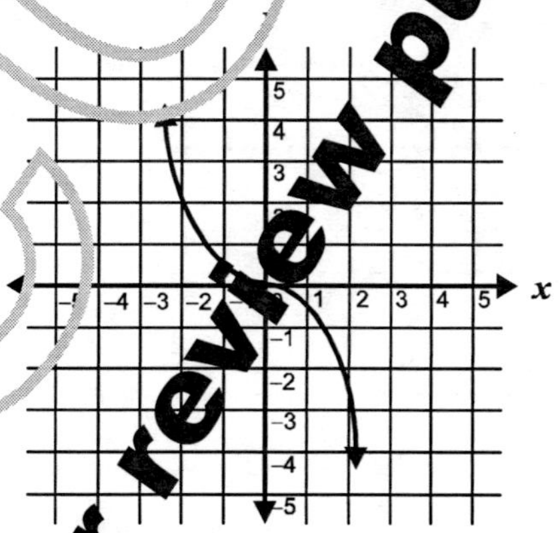

____

7.

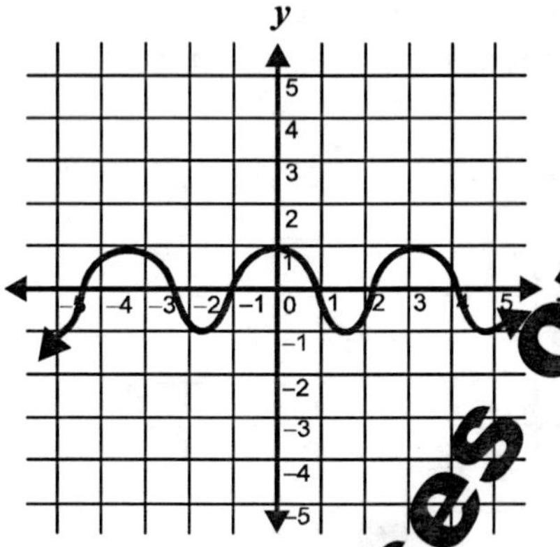

____

8.

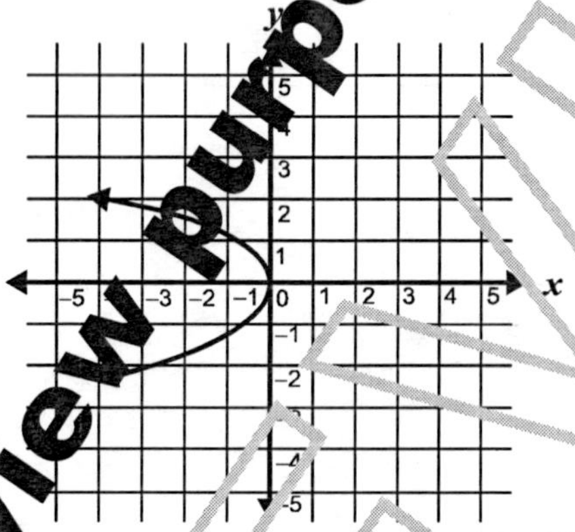

____

9.

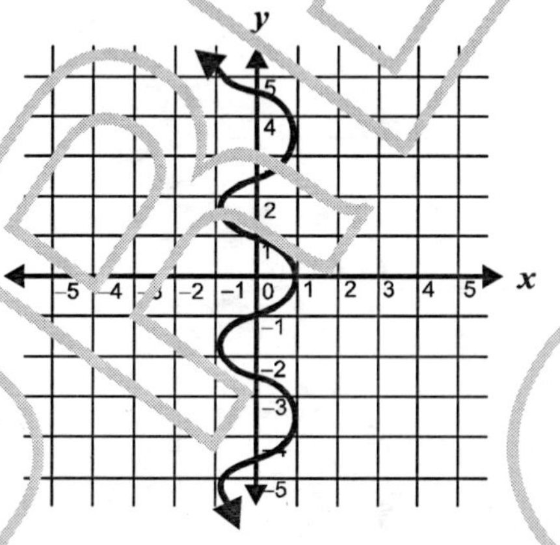

____

10.

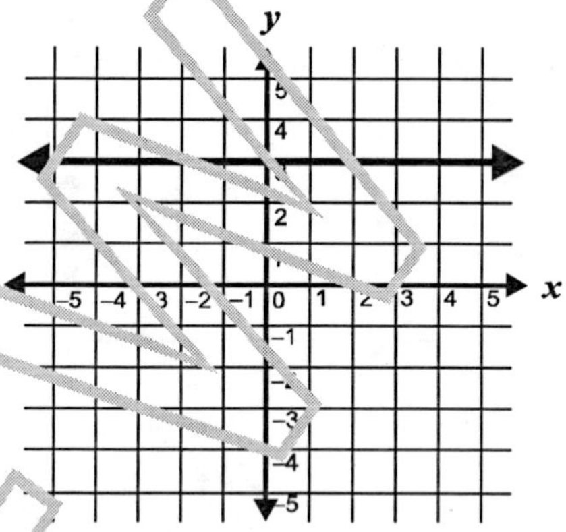

____

11.

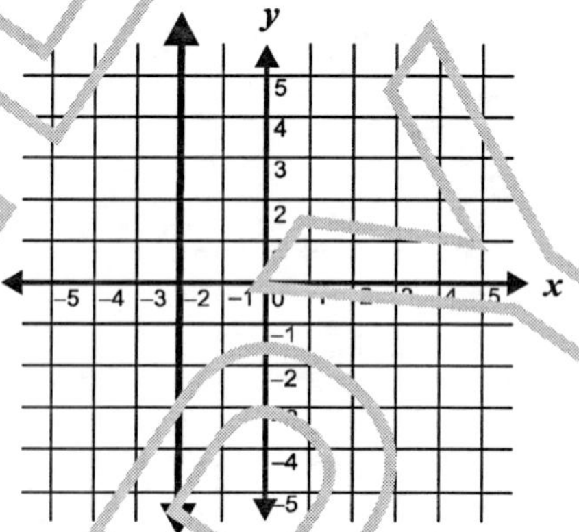

____

12.

____

10.8 Characteristics of Functions

There are many different types of functions. For our purposes, however, we will only look at the six basic functions and their characteristics.

The Linear Function: $f(x) = x$

Standard Form: $y = mx + b$, where m is the constant slope and b is the y-intercept

Characteristics: straight line

Domain: All Real Numbers

Range: All Real Numbers

Example 13: $f(x) = 2x + 7$; slope = 2, y-intercept = 7

x	-2	-1	0	1	2
$f(x)$	3	5	7	9	11

The Quadratic Function: $f(x) = x^2$

Standard Form: $f(x) = ax^2 + bx + c$, where $a \neq 0$, a, b, and c are real numbers, and c is the y-intercept

Characteristics: Has a vertex, parabola (U) shape

Domain: All Real Numbers

Range: $(0, \infty)$

Example 14: $f(x) = x^2 + 3x + 2$

x	-2	-1	0	1	2
$f(x)$	0	0	2	6	12

The Cubic Function: $f(x) = x^3$

Standard Form: $f(x) = ax^3 + bx^2 + cx + d$, where $a \neq 0$

Characteristics: N shape

Domain: All Real Numbers

Range: All Real Numbers

Example 15: $f(x) = x^3 + 3x^2 + 6x + 2$

x	-2	-1	0	1	2
$f(x)$	-6	-2	2	12	34

The Square Root Function: $f(x) = \sqrt{x}$

Characteristics: Never negative (neither x nor answer is negative), always contains a radical

Domain: $(0, \infty)$

Range: $(0, \infty)$

Example 16: $f(x) = \sqrt{x} + 2$

x	0	1	2	3	4
$f(x)$	2	3	$2 + \sqrt{2}$	$2 + \sqrt{3}$	4

The Absolute Value Function: $f(x) = |x|$

Characteristics: Answer usually positive unless outside value is being subtracted and is larger than inside value (i.e. $|-2| - 3 = -1$), V shape

Domain: All Real Numbers

Range: $(0, \infty)$

Example 17: $f(x) = |x| + 2$

x	-2	-1	0	1	2
$f(x)$	4	3	2	3	4

The Inverse Function: $f(x) = \dfrac{1}{x}$

Characteristics: Vertical asymptote at $x = 0$, undefined at $x = 0$

Domain: $(-\infty, 0) \cup (0, \infty)$

Range: $(-\infty, 0) \cup (0, \infty)$

Example 18: $f(x) = \dfrac{1}{x} + 2$

x	-2	-1	0	1	2
$f(x)$	$1\frac{1}{2}$	1	Undefined	3	$2\frac{1}{2}$

Determine the function described by the characteristics.

1. Its shape is a parabola.
2. It NEVER includes negative numbers.
3. It has an N shape.
4. It is undefined at $x = 0$.
5. The values of y are always positive, but x can be negative.
6. It is a straight line.
7. Of the 6 functions, how many have domains of all real numbers?
8. How many have limited ranges (not all real numbers)?

10.9 Function Symmetry

In Mathematics, functions can be defined as symmetrical with respect to the y-axis or the origin. To test equations for symmetry, it is helpful to remember the following:

$f(-x) = f(x)$ means the function is symmetrical with respect to the y-axis. Being symmetrical with the y-axis means the function is **even**.

$f(-x) = -f(x)$ means the function is symmetrical with respect to the origin. Being symmetrical with the origin means the function is **odd**.

$f(-x) \neq -f(x)$ or $f(x)$ then the function is not symmetrical.

Example 19: Test the following function for symmetry. $f(x) = x^4 + x^2 + 3$

Step 1: First, we need to substitute $-x$ in the function for x.

$f(-x) = (-x)^4 + (-x)^2 + 3$

Step 2: Carry out the operations.

$f(-x) = x^4 + x^2 + 3$

Step 3: Since $f(-x) = x^4 + x^2 + 3$ and $f(x) = x^4 + x^2 + 3$, then $f(-x) = f(x)$.

This means $f(x) = x^4 + x^2 + 3$ is symmetrical with respect to the y-axis.

The function $f(x) = x^4 + x^2 + 3$ is even.

Determine whether the function is even, odd, or neither.

1. $f(x) = x^3 + x^2 + x + 1$
2. $f(x) = 2x^3 - 4x$
3. $f(x) = 7x^2 - 11$
4. $f(x) = 8x^2 + x^4$
5. $f(x) = 4x^3 + x$
6. $f(x) = 6x^3 + 2$[illegible] $+ x$
7. $f(x) = x^5$ [illegible] $+ 11$
8. $f(x) = x^7 - x^4 + x^2 - 11$

10.10 Relations That Can Be Represented by Functions

Real-life examples can be represented by functions. The most common functions are exponential growth and decay and half-life.

Example 20: Atlanta, GA has a population of about 410,000 people. The U.S. Census Bureau estimates that the population will double in 26 years. If the population continues at the same rate, what will the population be in

a) 10 years?

b) 50 years?

Step 1: Use the double growth equation $P = P_0(2^{t/d})$, where $P =$ population at time t, $P_0 =$ population at time $t = 0$, and $d =$ double time.

Step 2: Determine the variable of each of the facts given in the problem. In this case, $P_0 = 410,000$ people, $d = 26$ years, and $t = 10$ years for part a and $t = 50$ years for part b.

Step 3: Plug all of the information into the given equation. Round to the nearest whole number.

a) $P = 410,000(2^{10/26}) = 410,000\,(1.3055) = 535,260$ people

b) $P = 410,000(2^{50/26}) = 410,000\,(3.7923) = 1,554,847$ people

Find the answers to the real-life problems by using the equations and variables given. Round your answers to the nearest whole numbers.

For questions 1 and 2 use the following half-life formula.

$A = A_0\left(\frac{1}{2}\right)^{t/h}$

$A =$ amount at time t

$A_0 =$ amount at time $t = 0$

h is the half-life

1. If you have 6,000 atoms of hydrogen (H), and hydrogen's half-life is 12.3 years, how many atoms will you have left after 7 years?

2. Chlorine (Cl) has a half-life of 55.5 minutes. If you start with 200 milligrams of chlorine, how many will be left after 5 hours?

For questions 3 and 4 use the double growth formula.

$P = P_0(2)^{t/d}$
P = amount at time t
P_0 = amount at time $t = 0$
d is the half-life

3. There are about 3,390,000 Girl Scouts in the United States. The Girl Scout Council says that there is a growth rate of [illegible] 10% per year, so they expect the Girl Scout population in the United States to double in 12 years. If the Girl Scout's organization expands as continuously as it has been, what will the population be
   (A) in 8 years?
   (B) next year?

4. Dr. Kellie [illegible]ed the bacteria growth in her laboratory. After observing the bacteria, she concluded that the double time of the bacteria is 40 minutes, and she started off with just 2,500 bacteria. Assuming this information is accurate and constant, how many bacteria will be in Dr. Kellie's lab
   (A) in [illegible] minutes?
   (B) after 3 hours?

For questions 5 and 6 use the compound interest formula.

$A = P\left(1 + \frac{r}{k}\right)^{kt}$
A = amount at time t
P = principle amount invested
k = how many times per year interest is compounded
r = rate

5. Lisa invested $1,000 into an account that pays 6% interest compounded monthly. If this account is for her newborn, how much will the account be worth on his 21st birthday, which is exactly 21 years from now?

6. Mr. Dumple wants to open up a savings account. He has looked at two different banks. Bank 1 is offering a rate of 5% compounded daily. Bank 2 is offering an account that has a rate of 8%, but is only compounded semi-yearly. Mr. Dumple puts $5,000 in an account and wants to take it out for his retirement in 10 years. Which bank will give him the most money back?

10.11 Exponential Growth and Decay

Many quantities experience exponential growth or decay under certain conditions. Examples include bacteria, populations, disease, money in a savings account that compounds interest, and radioisotopes. Exponential functions are those functions in which the independent variable is time, and time is an exponent (thus the name exponential function). For instance, the formula for growth of money in a savings account that compounds interest annually is:

$$A = P(1 + r)^t$$

where A is the value of the account after t years, P is the original amount of money in the account, and r is the annual interest rate.

Below are graphs of the general forms of exponential growth functions and exponential decay functions. Time is represented on the x-axis. Whatever is growing or decaying exponentially, such as population or money, is represented on the y-axis. Note that exponential function graphs are generally in Quadrant I since time and objects cannot be assigned negative values.

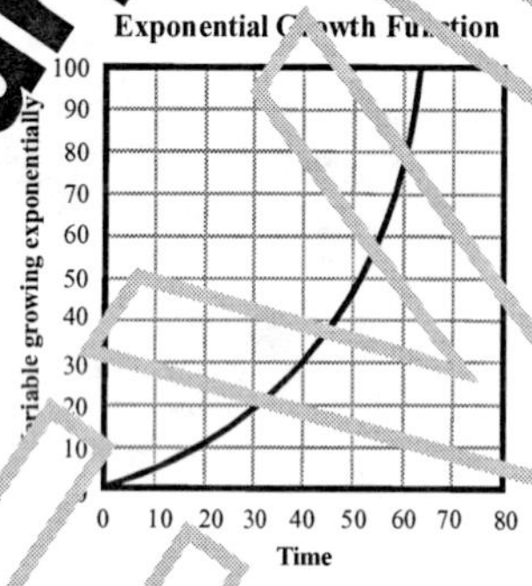

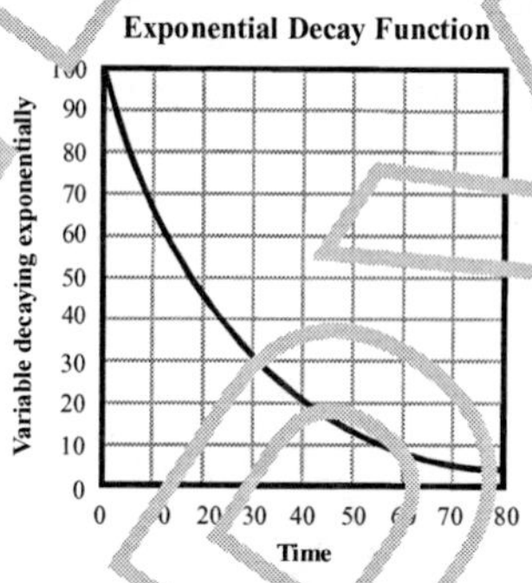

Example 21: Mason deposited \$2,000 into a savings account that pays an annual interest rate of 9% compounded annually. Using the formula $A = P(1 + r)^t$ determine the amount of money in the savings account after 1 year, 5 years, and 20 years. Using the calculated values, construct a graph.

Step 1: Consider the known values. $P = 2,000$, and $r = 0.09$. The problem will have to be worked three times where $t = 1$, $t = 5$, and $t = 20$. A is the amount being calculated.

Step 2:

$A = 2000\,(1 + 0.09)^1$	$A = 2000\,(1 + 0.09)^5$	$A = 2000\,(1 + 0.09)^{20}$
$A = 2000\,(1.09)^1$	$A = 2000\,(1.09)^5$	$A = 2000\,(1.09)^{20}$
$A = \$2,180$	$A = \$3,077.25$	$A = \$11,208.82$

Step 3: Use the calculated values to graph the function.

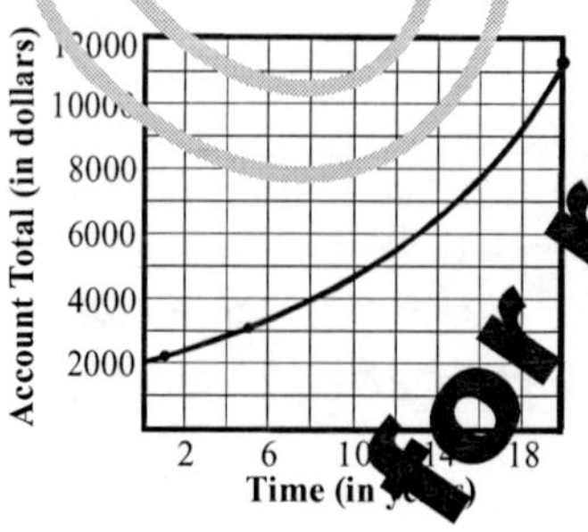

Fill in the tables for the following functions. On the line under each table, label the given function as an exponential growth function or an exponential decay function. Round your answers to two decimal places. For extra practice, graph the functions.

1. $F(t) = 15(1.01)^t$

t	$F(t)$
1	
2	
3	
4	

____

2. $S(t) = 350(0.[illegible]5)^t$

t	$S(t)$
1	
3	
5	
7	

____

3. $M(t) = 1000(1.04)^t$

t	$M(t)$
2	
4	
6	
8	

____

4. $B(t) = 2([illegible].50)^t$

t	$B(t)$
1	
2	
3	
4	

____

5. $C(t) = [illegible]300(0.5)^t$

t	$C(t)$
5	
10	
15	
20	

____

6. $R(t) = [illegible]0\left(\frac{[illegible]}{3}\right)^t$

t	$R(t)$
2	
4	
6	
8	

____

Refer to the graph at right to answer questions 7–10.

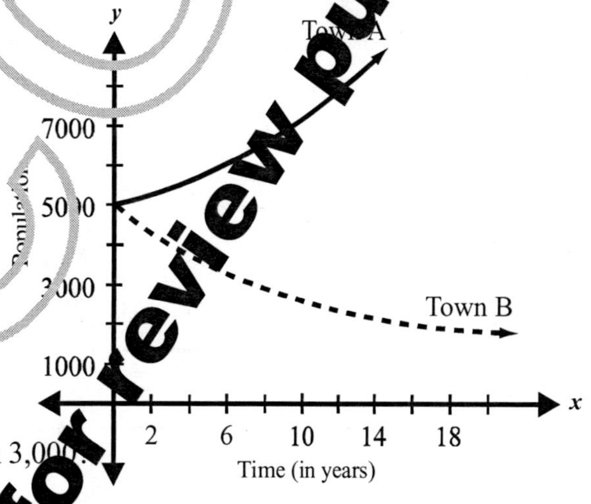

7. Which town is experiencing exponential decay? growth?

8. Considering both towns A and B, what is changing exponentially with time?

9. Why would it not make sense to draw the graph of town B below the x-axis?

10. In what year does the population of town B reach 3,000?

10.12 Piecewise Functions

A **piecewise function** is a function consisting of 2 or more formulas over a sequence of intervals. These **intervals** are defined by the possible values of x, also known as the domain of the function. The graph of a piecewise function consists of the graphs of each interval formula.

Example 22: $f(x) = \begin{cases} 3 & \text{if } 0 \leq x < 1 \\ 2 & \text{if } 1 \leq x < 2 \\ 1 & \text{if } 2 \leq x < 3 \end{cases}$

Graph $f(x)$.

Step 1: Graph each formula over the given interval.
For example, $f(x) = 3$ when the domain is $0 \leq x < 1$. This means that you would draw the graph $y = 3$ first. (Recall that this is a horizontal line that passes through the point $(0, 3)$.) After this, you would only draw $y = 3$ between the points $(0, 3)$ and $(1, 3)$ because of the domain. The graph cannot go outside of those points.
When $f(x) = 2$ and the domain is $1 \leq x < 2$, draw the graph $y = 2$ between the points $(1, 2)$ and $(2, 2)$.
When $f(x) = 3$ and the domain is $2 \leq x < 3$, draw the graph $y = 3$ between the points $(2, 3)$ and $(3, 3)$.

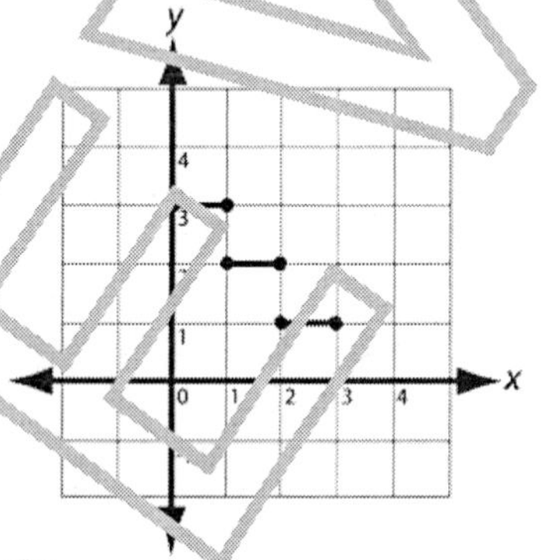

Step 2: Since the function cannot equal two y values for an x value (otherwise, it would not be a function), you must look at the inequalities in the domain. When the inequality is less than or equal to ($\leq$), you must draw the endpoint as a filled in circle. This shows that the function can equal to that point. For the strict inequalities ($<$), you must draw an endpoint with an open (not filled in) circle.

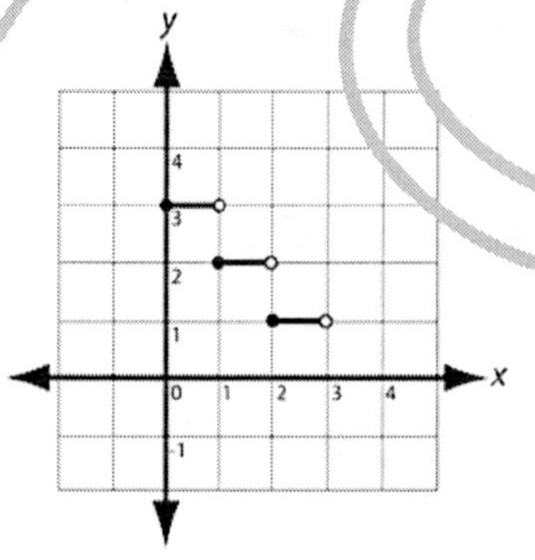

Example 23: $f(x) = \begin{cases} x^2 & \text{if } x \geq 2 \\ 3 - x & \text{if } x < 2 \end{cases}$

Find (A) $f(1)$, (B) $f(3)$, and (C) $f(2)$.

Step 1: Determine which interval of the domain includes the value of x.
(A) For $f(1)$, $x = 1$. Since 1 is less than 2, you would plug $x = 1$ into $3 - x$.
(B) For $f(3)$, $x = 3$. Since 3 is greater than 2, you would plug $x = 3$ into x^2.
(C) For $f(2)$, $x = 2$. Since 2 is equal to 2, you would plug $x = 2$ into x^2.

Step 2: Plug the value of x into the appropriate formula to solve for the value of $f(x)$.
(A) $f(x) = 3 - x$, so $f(1) = 3 - 1 = 2$
(B) $f(x) = x^2$, so $f(3) = (3)^2 = 9$
(C) $f(x) = x^2$, so $f(2) = (2)^2 = 4$

Graph each of the following functions.

1. $f(x) = \begin{cases} x & \text{if } x \geq 0 \\ -x & \text{if } x < 0 \end{cases}$

2. $f(x) = \begin{cases} 1 & \text{if } x < 1 \\ x^2 & \text{if } x \geq 1 \end{cases}$

3. $f(x) = \begin{cases} \sqrt{x} & \text{if } x \geq 2 \\ x^2 & \text{if } x < 2 \end{cases}$

4. $f(x) = \begin{cases} 2x + 3 & \text{if } x < 0 \\ 2x - 3 & \text{if } x \geq 0 \end{cases}$

5. $f(x) = \begin{cases} x^2 & \text{if } x < -1 \\ x & \text{if } -1 \leq x \leq 1 \\ -(x^2) & \text{if } x > 1 \end{cases}$

6. Phil's long distance phone service charges him 50 cents for the first 10 minutes and 10 cents for each minute afterwards. Graph the function that represents Phil's long distance phone service and find how much he would pay for
(A) a 5 minute call.
(B) a 10 minute call.
(C) a 15 minute call.

7. The tuition at State University is determined by the number of class hours a student takes. Tuition is $100 for the first three hours and doubles every 3 hours up to 12 hours. After 12 hours, tuition does not change. Graph the function that represents the tuition at State University and find the tuition for a student taking
(A) 6 class hours.
(B) 12 class hours.
(C) 15 class hours.

Chapter 10 Review

1. What is the domain of the following relation? $\{(-1, 2), (2, 5), (4, 9), (6, 11)\}$

2. What is the range of the following relation? $\{(0, -2), (-1, -4), (-2, 6), (-3, -8)\}$

3. Find the range of the relation $y = [illegible]x$ for the domain $\{0, 1, 2, 3, 4\}$.

4. Find the values of $M(y)$ of the relation $M(y) = 2(1.1)^y$ for the domain $\{2, 3, 4, 5, 6\}$.

5. Find the range of the following relation for the domain $\{0, 2, 6, 8, 10\}$. $B(t) = 600(0.75)^t$

6. Find the range of the relation $y = \frac{3(x-2)}{5}$ for the domain $\{-8, -3, 7, 12, 17\}$.

7. Find the range of the relation $y = 10 - 2x$ for the domain $\{-8, -4, 0, 4, 8\}$.

8. Find the range of the relation $y = \frac{4+x}{3}$ for the domain $\{-7, -1, 2, 5, 8\}$.

For each of the following relations given in questions 9–13, write F if it is a function and NF if it is not a function.

9. $\{(1, [illegible]), (2, 2), (3, 2)\}$

10. $\{(-1, 0), (0, 1), (1, 2), (2, 3)\}$

11. $\{(2, 1), (2, 2), (2, 3)\}$

12. $\{(1, 7), (2, 5), (3, 6), (2, 4)\}$

13. $\{(0, -1), (-1, -2), (-2, -3), (-3, -4)\}$

For questions 14–23, find the range of the following functions for the given value of the domain.

14. For $g(x) = 2x^2 - 4x$; find $g(-1)$

15. For $h(x) = 3x(x-4)$; find $h(3)$

16. For $f(n) = \frac{1}{n+3}$; find $f(4)$

17. For $G(n) = \frac{2-n}{2}$; find $G(8)$

18. For $H(x) = 2x(x-1)$; find $H(4)$

19. For $f(x) = [illegible]x^2 + 3x - [illegible]$; find $f(2)$

20. For $f(x) = 5x - 2$ and $g(x) = 2x^2$; find $f(g(x))$

21. For $f(x) = x + [illegible]$ and $g(x) = 1 - x$; find $f(g(x))$

22. For $f(x) = x^2 - x$; find $f(x+2)$

23. For $f(x) = 4x$; find $f(x+c)$

Fill in the following function tables.

24. Rule: $\frac{(4-2n)}{2}$

n	$f(n)$
0	
1	
2	
3	
4	

25. Rule: $2n(n+1)$

n	$f(n)$
0	
1	
2	
3	
4	

26. Rule: $6n - 3$

n	$f(n)$
2	
3	
4	
5	
6	

Answer the following questions about the six basic functions.

27. What is the domain of a linear function?

28. What is the range of $f(x) = \frac{1}{x}$?

29. What function has a constant rate of change?

30. What is the standard form of a quadratic function?

31. What is the range of the square root function?

Solve the following problems about function symmetry.

32. True or False. If for a function $f(x)$, $f(-x) = -f(x)$ is true, then the function is odd.

33. True or False. If for a function $f(x)$, $f(-x) = f(x)$ is true, then the function is even.

34. Fill in the blank. When all exponents in a function are ____, the function will be even.

35. Is the function $f(x) = x^6 + x^4 + 7$ even, odd, or neither?

36. Is the function $f(x) = x^5 + x^3 + 2$ even, odd, or neither?

37. Fill in the blank. When all exponents in a function are ____, the function will be odd.

38. Is the function $f(x) = x^4 - x + 2$ even, odd, or neither?

Chapter 10 Test

1. Which of the following graphs is a function?

A.

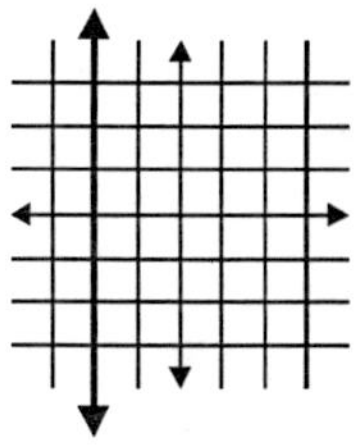

B.

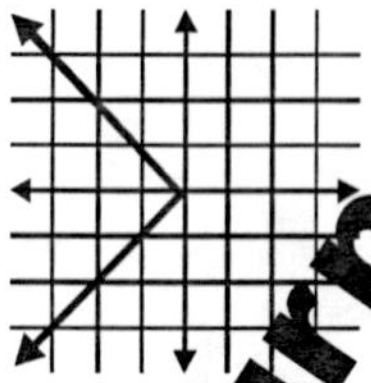

C.

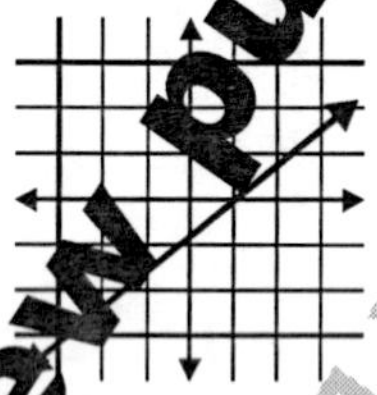

D.

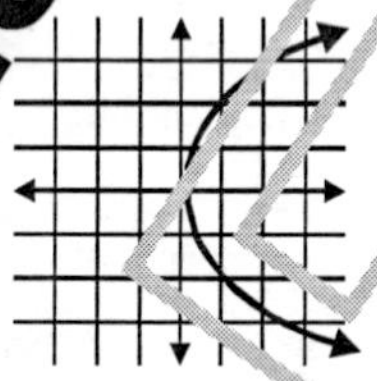

E.

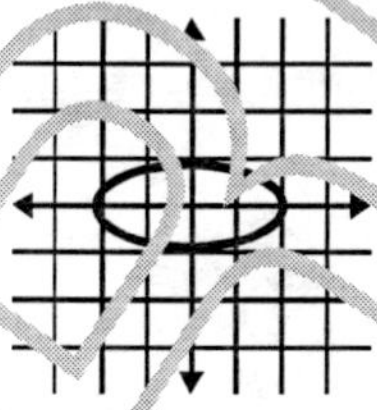

2. The function rule is $3x(x+5)$.

x	$f(x)$
-2	?

F. -18
G. 18
H. -42
J. 42
K. 9

3. Find the range of the following function for the domain $\{-2, -1, 0, 3\}$.

$$y = \frac{2+x}{4}$$

A. $\left\{0, \frac{3}{4}, 1, \frac{5}{4}\right\}$
B. $\left\{0, \frac{1}{4}, \frac{1}{2}, \frac{5}{4}\right\}$
C. $\left\{[illegible], -\frac{1}{4}, \frac{1}{2}, \frac{5}{4}\right\}$
D. $\left\{\frac{1}{4}, \frac{3}{4}, \frac{1}{2}, \frac{5}{4}\right\}$
E. $\{-2, -1, 0, 3\}$

4. Which function is undefined at $x = 0$?

F. the cubic function
G. the square root function
H. the absolute value function
J. $\frac{1}{x}$
K. the linear function

5. For $f(x) = 3x^2 - 5x$, find $f([illegible])$.

A. 12
B. -6
C. 42
D. [illegible]
E. 22

6. Which of the following relations is a function?

F. $\{(0, -[illegible])([illegible], -1)(0, -2)\}$
G. $\{(-1, 1)(-1, -1)(0, 0)\}$
H. $\{(2, 1)(1, 0)(0, -1)\}$
J. $\{([illegible]1, 1)(-1, 0)(-1, -1)\}$
K. $\{(-1, -1)(-1, -1)(-1, -1)\}$

7. What is the range of the following relation?
$\{(1,2)(4,9)(7,8)(10,13)\}$

A. $\{1,4,7,10\}$
B. $\{3,13,15,23\}$
C. $\{1,3,1,3\}$
D. $\{1,9,7,13\}$
E. $\{2,9,8,13\}$

8. Which function is not linear?

F. $f(x) = -3x - 7$
G. $f(x) = 8$
H. $f(x) = \frac{2}{3}x - 5$
J. $f(x) = 2x^2$
K. $f(x) = x +$ [illegible]

9. Which function does not have a zero?

A. $f(x) = x - 3$
B. $f(x) = -7$
C. $f(x) = 2x + 3$
D. $f(x) = -3x + 2$
E. $f(x) = x$

10. Which function has a V shape?

F. the linear function
G. the absolute value function
H. the cubic function
J. the square root function
K. $\frac{1}{x}$

11. Which equation is a function of x?

A. $f(b) = 3b + 2$
B. $f(x) = 3x + 2$
C. $f(a) = 3a + 2$
D. $f(z) = 3z + 2$
E. $f(y) = 3y + 2$

12. Which is the equation $y = 7x^2 + 2x + 3$ as a function of m?

F. $m = 7x^2 + 2x + 3$
G. $y = 7m^2 + 2m + 3$
H. $m(x) = 7m^2 + 2m + 3$
J. $f(m) = 7m^2 + 2m + 3$
K. $f(m) = 7x^2 + 2m + 3$

13. $f(x) = ax^3 + bx^2 + cx + d$ is the standard form of which function?

A. the cubic function
B. the square root function
C. the quadratic function
D. the linear function
E. the square root function

14. Is the following function even or odd?
$f(x) = x^{10} + x^6 + x^2 + 4$

F. even
G. odd
H. both even and odd
J. neither
K. not enough information

15. For $f(x) = 3x - 1$ and $g(x) = x^3 + 1$, find $f(g(x))$.

A. $3x^3$
B. $3x^3 + 1$
C. $3x$
D. $3x^3 + 3$
E. $3x^3 + 2$

16. For $f(x) = 2x$, find $f(x - 4)$.

F. $2x - 4$
G. $2x$
H. $2x -$ [illegible]
J. $x - 8$
K. [illegible] $- 6$

Chapter 11
Graphing and Writing Linear Equations and Inequalities

11.1 Graphing Linear Equations

In addition to graphing ordered pairs, the Cartesian plane can be used to graph the solution set for an equation. Any equation with two variables that are both to the first power is called a **linear equation.** The graph of a linear equation will always be a straight line.

Example 1: Graph the solution set for $x + y = 7$.

Step 1: Make a list of some pairs of numbers that will work in the equation.

$x + y = 7$		
$4 + 3 = 7$	$(4, 3)$	ordered pair solutions
$-1 + 8 = 7$	$(-1, 8)$	
$5 + 2 = 7$	$(5, 2)$	
$0 + 7 = 7$	$(0, 7)$	

Step 2: Plot these points on a Cartesian plane.

Step 3: By passing a line through these points, we graph the solution set for $x + y = 7$. This means that every point on the line is a solution to the equation $x + y = 7$. For example, $(1, 6)$ is a solution, so the line passes through the point $(1, 6)$.

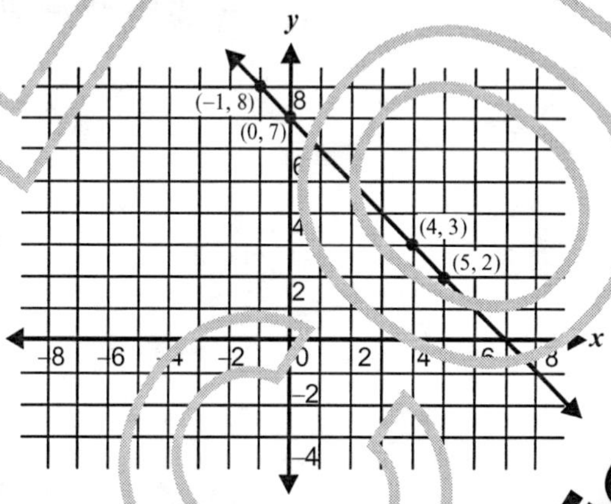

Make a table of solutions for each linear equation below. Then plot the ordered pair solutions on graph paper. Draw a line through the points. (If one of the points does not line up, you have made a mistake.)

1. $x + y = 6$
2. $y = x + 1$
3. $y = x - 2$
4. $x + 2 = y$
5. $x - 5 = y$
6. $x - y = 0$

Example 2: Graph the equation $y = 2x - 5$.

Step 1: This equation has 2 variables, both to the first power, so we know the graph will be a straight line. Substitute some numbers for x or y to find pairs of numbers that satisfy the equation. Record the values for x and y in a table.

	x	y
If x is 0, y would be -5	0	-5
If x is 1, y would be -3	1	-3
If x is 2, y would be -1	2	-1
If x is 3, y would be 1	3	1

Step 2: Plot the ordered pairs and draw your line.

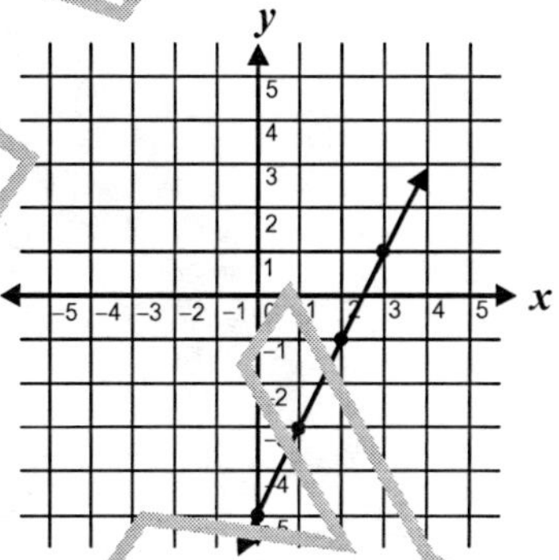

Find pairs of numbers that satisfy the equations below, and graph the line on graph paper.

1. $y = 2x + 2$
2. $2x - 2 = y$
3. $-x + 3 = y$
4. $y = x + 1$
5. $4x - 2 = y$
6. $y = 3x - 3$
7. $x = 4y - 3$
8. $2x = 3y + 1$

11.2 Finding the Distance Between Two Points

Notice that a subscript added to the x and y identifies each ordered pair uniquely in the plane. For example, point 1 is identified as (x_1, y_1), point 2 as (x_2, y_2), and so on. This unique subscript identification allows us to calculate slope, distance, and midpoints of line segments in the plane using standard formulas like the distance formula. To find the distance between two points on a Cartesian plane, use the following formula:

$$d = \sqrt{(y_2 - y_1)^2 + (x_2 - x_1)^2}$$

Example 3: Find the distance between $(-2, 1)$ and $(3, -4)$.
Plugging the values from the ordered pairs into the formula, we find:
$d = \sqrt{(-4 - 1)^2 + [3 - (-2)]^2} = \sqrt{(-5)^2 + (5)^2} = \sqrt{25 + 25} = \sqrt{50} = 5\sqrt{2}$

Find the distance between the following pairs of points using the distance formula above.

1. $(6, -1)\ (5, 2)$
2. $(-4, 3)\ (2, -1)$
3. $(10, 2)\ (6, -1)$
4. $(-2, 5)\ (-4, 3)$
5. $(8, -2)\ (3, -9)$
6. $(2, -2)\ (8, 1)$
7. $(3, 1)\ (5, 5)$
8. $(-2, -1)\ (3, 4)$
9. $(5, -3)\ (-1, -5)$
10. $(6, 5)\ (3, -4)$
11. $(-1, 0)\ (-9, -8)$
12. $(-2, 0)\ (-6, 6)$

11.3 Finding the Midpoint of a Line Segment

You can use the coordinates of the endpoints of a line segment to find the coordinates of the midpoint of the line segment. The formula to find the midpoint between two coordinates is:

$$\text{midpoint}, M = \left(\frac{x_1 + x_2}{2}, \frac{y_1 + y_2}{2}\right)$$

Example 4: Find the midpoint of the line segment having endpoints at $(-3, -1)$ and $(4, 3)$.

Use the formula for the midpoint. $M = \left(\frac{4 + (-3)}{2}, \frac{3 + (-1)}{2}\right)$

When we simplify each coordinate, we find the midpoint, M, is $\left(\frac{1}{2}, 1\right)$.

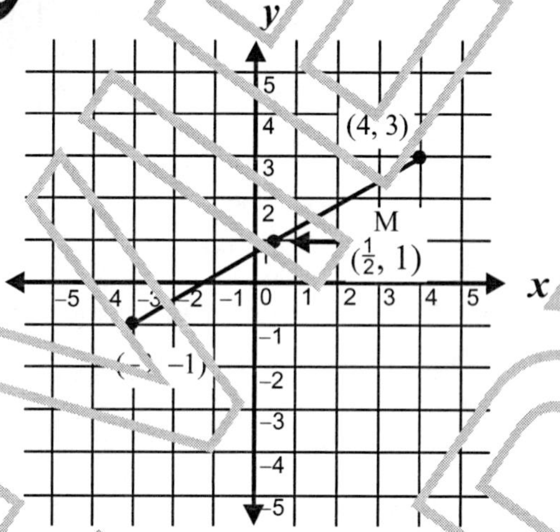

For each of the following pairs of points, find the coordinate of the midpoint, M, using the formula given above.

1. $(4, 5)\ (-6, 9)$
2. $(-3, 2)\ (-1, -2)$
3. $(3, 6)\ (9, 12)$
4. $(2, 5)\ (6, 9)$
5. $(8, 9)\ (6, 11)$
6. $(-4, 3)\ (8, 7)$
7. $(-1, -5)\ (-3, -11)$
8. $(4, 2)\ (-2, 8)$
9. $(4, 3)\ (-1, -5)$
10. $(-6, 2)\ (8, -8)$
11. $(-3, 9)\ (-9,$ [illegible]$)$
12. $(7, 8)$ [illegible]
13. $(12, 19)\ (2, 3)$
14. $(5, 4)\ (9, -2)$
15. $(-4, 6)\ (10, -2)$

11.4 Finding the Intercepts of a Line

The x-intercept is the point where the graph of a line crosses the x-axis. The y-intercept is the point where the graph of a line crosses the y-axis.

To find the x-intercept, set $y = 0$

To find the y-intercept, set $x = 0$

Example 5: Find the x- and y-intercepts of the line $6x + 2y = 18$

Step 1: To find the x-intercept, set $y = 0$.

$$\begin{aligned} 6x + 2(0) &= 18 \\ \frac{6x}{6} &= \frac{18}{6} \\ x &= 3 \end{aligned}$$

The x-intercept is at the point $(3, 0)$.
To find the y-intercept, set $x = 0$.

$$\begin{aligned} 6(0) + 2y &= 18 \\ \frac{2y}{2} &= \frac{18}{2} \\ y &= 9 \end{aligned}$$

The y-intercept is at the point $(0, 9)$.

You can now use the two intercepts to graph the line.

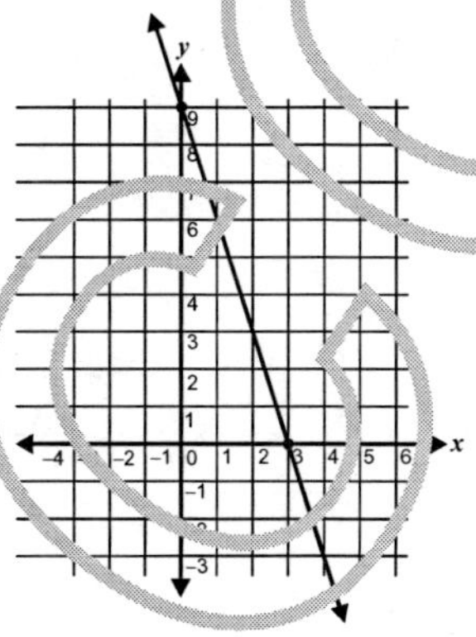

11.5 Understanding Slope

The slope of a line refers to how steep a line is. Slope is also defined as the rate of change. When we graph a line using ordered pairs, we can easily determine the slope. Slope is often represented by the letter m.

$$\text{The formula for slope of a line is: } m = \frac{y_2 - y_1}{x_2 - x_1} \text{ or } \frac{\text{rise}}{\text{run}}$$

Example 6: What is the slope of the following line that passes through the ordered pairs $(-4, -3)$ and $(1, 3)$?

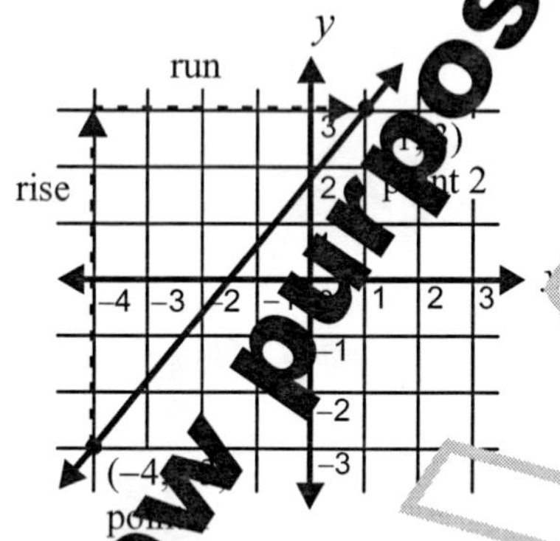

y_2 is 3, the y-coordinate of point 2.

y_1 is -3, the y-coordinate of point 1.

x_2 is 1, the x-coordinate of point 2.

x_1 is -4, the x-coordinate of point 1.

Use the formula for slope given above:

$$m = \frac{3 - (-3)}{1 - (-4)} = \frac{6}{5}$$

The slope is $\frac{6}{5}$. This shows us that we can go up 6 (rise) and over 5 to the right (run) to find another point on the line.

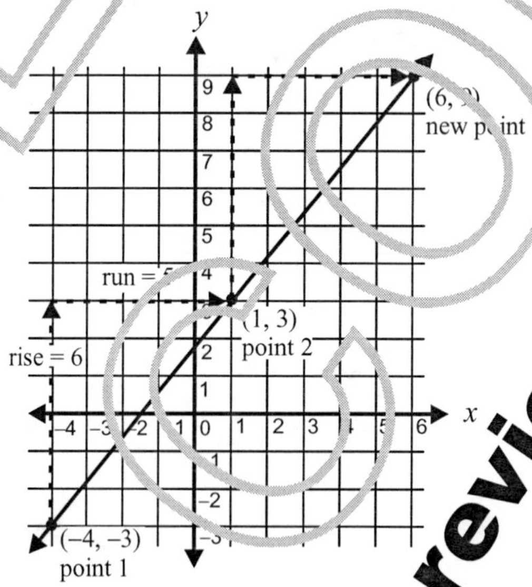

Example 7: What is the slope of a line that passes through $(1, 1)$ and $(3, 1)$?

$$\text{slope} = \frac{1-1}{3-1} = \frac{0}{2} = 0$$

When $y_2 - y_1 = 0$, the slope will equal 0, and the line will be horizontal.

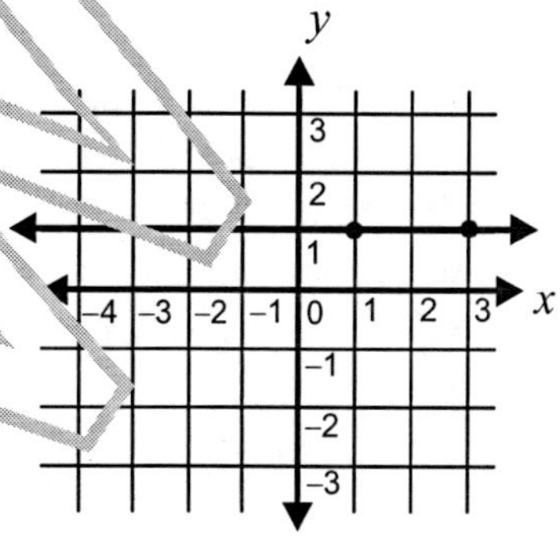

Example 8: What is the slope of a line that passes through $(2, 1)$ and $(2, -3)$?

$$\text{slope} = \frac{-3-1}{2-2} = \frac{-4}{0} = \text{undefined}$$

When $x_2 - x_1 = 0$, the slope is undefined, and the line will be vertical.

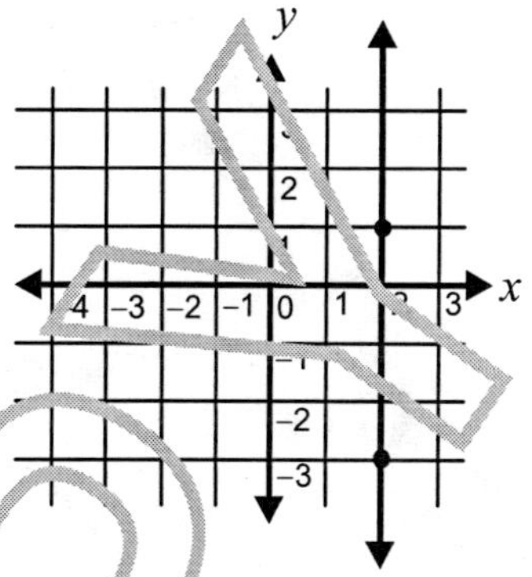

The following lines summarize what we know about slope.

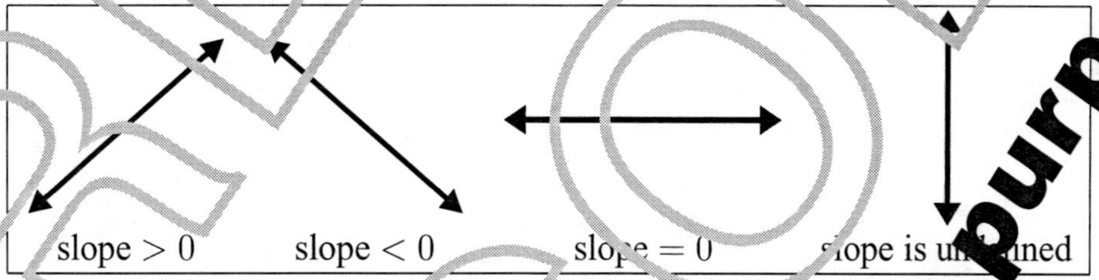

Find the slope of the line that goes through the following pairs of points. Then, using graph paper, graph the line through the two points, and label the rise and run. (See Examples 6–8).

1. $(2, 3)\ (4, 5)$
2. $(1, 3)\ (2, 5)$
3. $(-1, 2)\ (4, 1)$
4. $(1, -2)\ (4, -2)$
5. $(3, 0)\ (3, 4)$
6. $(3, 2)\ (-1, 8)$
7. $(4, 3)\ (2, 4)$
8. $(2, 2)\ (1, 5)$
9. $(3, 4)\ (1, 2)$
10. $(3, 2)\ (3, 6)$
11. $(6, -2)\ (3, -2)$
12. (1, [illegible]) $(3, 4)$
13. $(-2, 1)\ (-4, 3)$
14. $(5, 2)\ (4, -1)$
15. $(1, -3)\ (-2, 4)$
16. $(2, -1)\ (3, 5)$

11.6 Slope-Intercept Form of a Line

An equation that contains two variables, each to the first degree, is a **linear equation**. The graph for a linear equation is a straight line. To put a linear equation in slope-intercept form, solve the equation for y. This form of the equation shows the slope and the y-intercept. Slope-intercept form follows the pattern of $y = mx + b$. The "m" represents slope, and the "b" represents the y-intercept. The y-intercept is the point at which the line crosses the y-axis.

When the slope of a line is not 0, the graph of the equation shows a **direct variation** between y and x. When y increases, x increases in a certain proportion. The proportion stays constant. The constant is called the **slope** of the line.

Example 9: Put the equation $2x + 3y = 15$ in slope-intercept form. What is the slope of the line? What is the y-intercept? Graph the line.

Step 1: Solve for y:

$$\begin{array}{rcrcr} 2x & + & 3y & = & 15 \\ -2x & & & & -2x \\ \hline \frac{3y}{3} & = & -\frac{2x}{3} & + & \frac{15}{3} \end{array}$$

slope-intercept form: $y = -\frac{2}{3}x + 5$

The slope is $-\frac{2}{3}$ and the y-intercept is 5.

Step 2: Knowing the slope and the y-intercept, we can graph the line.

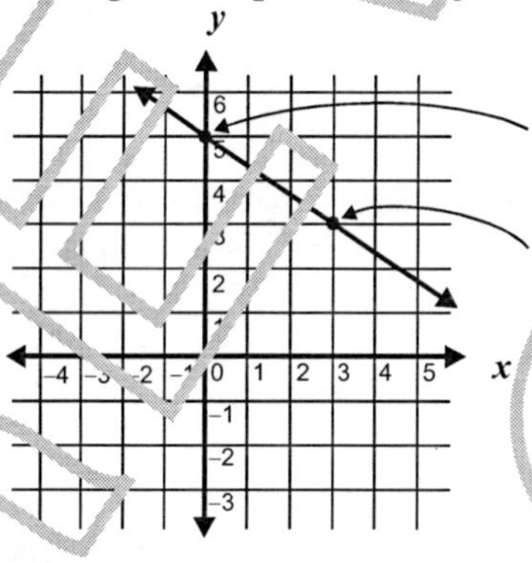

The y-intercept is 5, so the line passes through the point $(0, 5)$ on the y-axis.

The slope is $-\frac{2}{3}$, so go down 2 and over 3 to get a second point.

Put each of the following equations in slope-intercept form by solving for y. On your graph paper, graph the line using the slope and y-intercept.

1. $4x - 5y = 5$	6. $8x - 5y = 10$	11. $3x - 2y = -6$	16. $4x + 2y = 8$
2. $2x + 4y = 16$	7. $-2x + y = 4$	12. $3x + 4y = 2$	17. $6x - y = 4$
3. $3x - 2y = 10$	8. $-4x + 3y = 12$	13. $-x = 2 + 4y$	18. $-2x - 4y = 8$
4. $x + 3y = -12$	9. $-6x + 2y = 12$	14. $2x = 4y - 2$	19. $5x + 4y = 16$
5. $6x + 2y = 0$	10. $x - 5y = 5$	15. $6x - 3y = 9$	20. $6 = 2y - 3x$

11.7 Graphing a Line Knowing a Point and Slope

If you are given a point of a line and the slope of a line, the line can be graphed.

Example 10: Given that line l has a slope of $\frac{4}{3}$ and contains the point $(2, -1)$, graph the line.

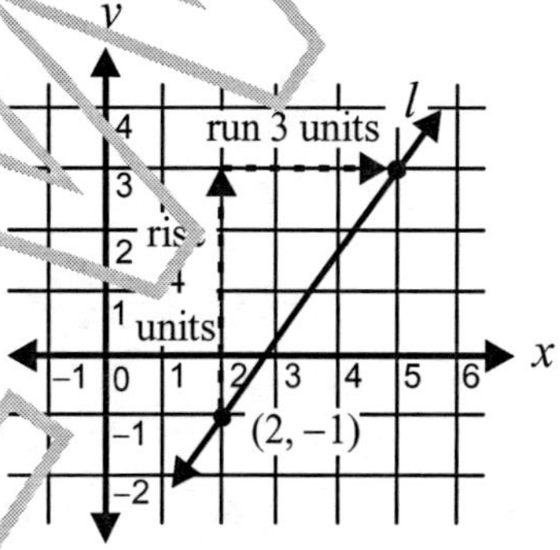

Plot and label the point $(2, -1)$ on a Cartesian plane.

The slope, m, is $\frac{4}{3}$, so the rise is 4, and the run is 3. From the point $(2, -1)$ count 4 units up and 3 units to the right.

Draw the line through the two points.

Example 11: Given a line that has a slope of $-\frac{1}{4}$ and passes through the point $(-3, 2)$, graph the line.

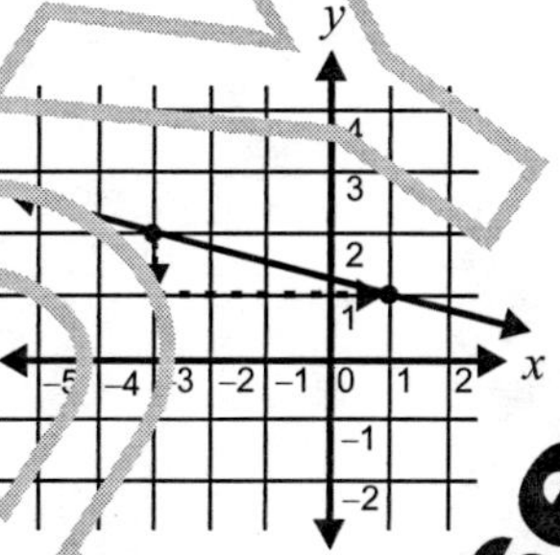

Plot the point $(-3, 2)$.

Since the slope is negative, go **down** 1 unit and over 4 units to get a second point.

Graph the line through the two points.

Graph a line on your own graph paper for each of the following problems. First plot the point. Then use the slope to find a second point. Draw the line formed from the point and the slope.

1. $(2, -2)$, $m = \frac{3}{4}$
2. $(3, -4)$, $m = \frac{1}{2}$
3. $(1, 3)$, $m = -\frac{1}{3}$
4. $(2, -4)$, $m = 1$
5. $(3, 0)$, $m = -\frac{1}{2}$
6. $(-2, 1)$, $m = \frac{4}{3}$
7. $(-4, -2)$, $m = \frac{1}{2}$
8. $(1, -4)$, $m = \frac{3}{4}$
9. $(2, -1)$, $m = -\frac{1}{2}$
10. $(5, -2)$, $m = \frac{1}{4}$
11. $(-2, -3)$, $m = \frac{2}{3}$
12. $(4, -1)$, $m = -\frac{1}{3}$
13. $(-1, 5)$, $m = \frac{2}{5}$
14. $(-2, 3)$, $m = \frac{3}{4}$
15. $(4, 4)$, $m = -\frac{1}{2}$
16. $(3, -3)$, $m = \frac{3}{4}$
17. $(-2, 5)$, $m = \frac{1}{3}$
18. $(-2, -3)$, $m = -\frac{3}{4}$
19. $(4, -3)$, $m = \frac{2}{3}$
20. ([illegible], 4), $m = -\frac{1}{2}$

11.8 Finding the Equation of a Line Using Two Points or a Point and Slope

If you can find the slope of a line and know the coordinates of one point, you can write the equation for the line. You know the formula for the slope of a line is:

$$m = \frac{y_2 - y_1}{x_2 - x_1} \text{ or } \frac{y_2 - y_1}{x_2 - x_1} = m$$

Using algebra, you can see that if you multiply both sides of the equation by $x_2 - x_1$, you get:

$$y - y_1 = m\,(x - x_1) \longleftarrow \text{point-slope form of an equation}$$

Example 12: Write the equation of the line passing through the points $(-2, 3)$ and $(1, 5)$.

Step 1: First, find the slope of the line using the two points given.

$$m = \frac{y_2 - y_1}{x_2 - x_1} = \frac{5 - 3}{1 - (-2)} = \frac{2}{3}$$

Step 2: Pick one of the two points to use in the point-slope equation. For point $(-2, 3)$, we know $x_1 = -2$ and $y_1 = 3$, and we know $m = \frac{2}{3}$. Substitute these values into the point-slope form of the equation.

$$y - y_1 = m\,(x - x_1)$$

$$y - 3 = \frac{2}{3}[x - (-2)]$$

$$y - 3 = \frac{2}{3}x + \frac{4}{3}$$

$$y = \frac{2}{3}x + \frac{13}{3}$$

Use the point-slope formula to write an equation for each of the following lines.

1. $(1, -2)$, $m = 2$
2. $(-3, 3)$, $m = \frac{1}{3}$
3. $(4, 2)$, $m = \frac{1}{4}$
4. $(5, 0)$, $m = 1$
5. $(3, -4)$, $m = \frac{1}{2}$
6. $(-1, -4)$ $(2, -1)$
7. $(2, 1)$ $(-1, -3)$
8. $(-2, 5)$ $(-4, 3)$
9. $(-4, 3)$ $(2, -1)$
10. $(3, 1)$ $(5, 5)$
11. $(-3, 1)$, $m = 2$
12. $(-1, 2)$, $m = \frac{4}{3}$
13. $(2, -5)$, $m = -2$
14. $(-1, 3)$, $m = \frac{1}{3}$
15. $(0, -2)$, $m = -\frac{3}{2}$

11.9 Graphing Inequalities

In the previous section, you would graph the equation $x = 3$ as:

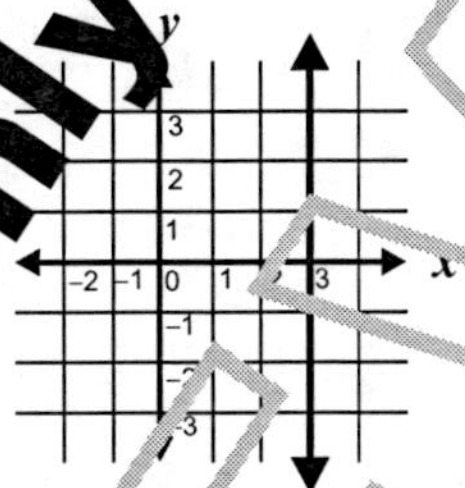

In this section, we graph inequalities such as $x > 3$ (read x is greater than 3). To show this, we use a broken line since the points on the line $x = 3$ are not included in the solution. We shade all points greater than 3.

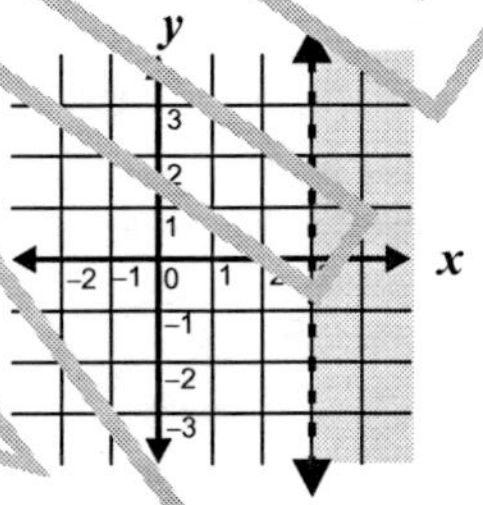

When we graph $x \geq 3$ (read x is greater than or equal to 3), we use a solid line because the points on the line $x = 3$ are included in the graph.

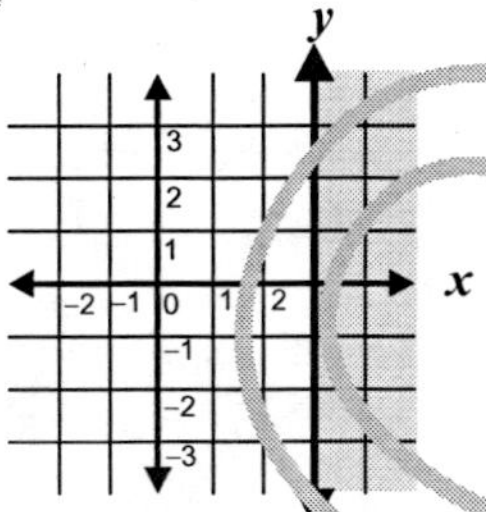

Graph the following inequalities on your own graph paper.

1. $y < 2$
2. [illegible] ≥ 4
3. $y \geq 1$
4. $x <$ [illegible] -1
5. $y \geq -2$
6. $x \leq -4$
7. $x > -3$
8. $y \leq 3$
9. $x \leq 5$
10. $y > -5$
11. $x \geq 3$
12. $y < -1$
13. $x \leq$ [illegible]
14. $y > -1$
15. $y \leq 4$
16. $x \geq 0$
17. $y \geq$ [illegible]
18. x [illegible]
19. $x \leq -2$
20. $y < -2$
21. $y \geq -4$
22. $x \geq -1$
23. $y \leq 5$
24. $x < -3$

For more complex inequalities, it is easier to graph by first changing the inequality to an equality and then put the equation in slop-intercept form.

Example 13: Graph the inequality $2x + 4y \leq 8$.

Step 1: Change the inequality to an equality.
$2x + 4y = 8$

Step 2: Put the equation in slop-intercept form by solving the equation for y.

$$2x + 4y = 8$$

$$2x - 2x + 4y = -2x + 8 \quad \text{Subtract } 2x \text{ from both sides of the equation.}$$

$$4y = -2x + 8 \quad \text{Simplify.}$$

$$\frac{4y}{4} = \frac{-2x + 8}{4} \quad \text{Divide both sides by 4.}$$

$$y = \frac{-2x}{4} + \frac{8}{4} \quad \text{Find the lowest terms of the fractions.}$$

$$y = -\tfrac{1}{2}x + 2$$

Step 3: Graph the line. If the inequality is $<$ or $>$, use a dotted line. If the inequality is $\leq$ or $\geq$, use a solid line. For this example, we should use a solid line.

Step 4: Determine which side of the line to shade. Pick a point such as $(0, 0)$ to see if it is true in the inequality.

$2x + 4y \leq 8$, so substitute $(0, 0)$.
Is $0 + 0 \leq 8$? Yes, $0 \leq 8$, so shade the side of the line that includes the point $(0, 0)$.

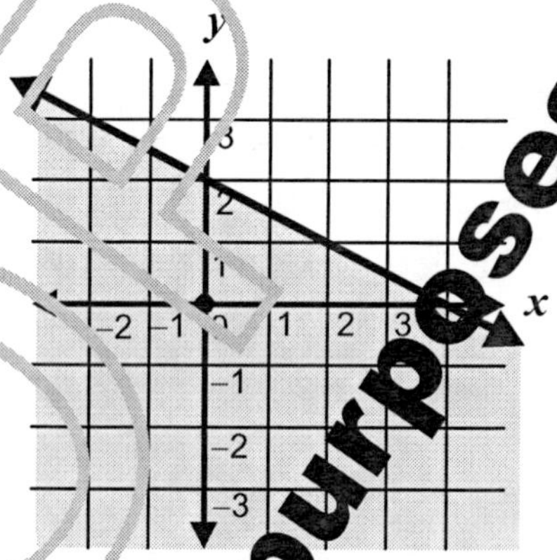

Graph the following inequalities on your own graph paper.

1. $2x + y \geq 1$
2. $3x - y \leq 3$
3. $x + 3y > 12$
4. $4x - 3y < 12$
5. $y \geq 3x + 1$
6. $x - 2y > -2$
7. $x \leq y + 4$
8. $x + y < -1$
9. $-4y \geq 2x + 1$
10. $x \leq 4y - 2$
11. $3x - y \geq 4$
12. $y \geq 2x - 5$

Chapter 11 Review

Answer the following questions.

1. In which quadrant does the point $(2, 5)$ lie?

2. In which quadrant does the point $(-5, -2)$ lie?

3. Graph the solution set for the linear equation: $x - 3 = y$.

4. Graph the equation $2x - 4 = 0$.

5. What is the slope of the line that passes through the points ([illegible], 3) and $(6, 1)$?

6. What is the slope of the line that passes through the points $(-1, 4)$ and $(-6, -2)$?

7. What is the x-intercept for the following equation? $6x - y = 30$

8. What is the y-intercept for the following equation? $4x + 2y = 28$

9. Graph the equation $3y = 9$.

10. Write the following equation in slope-intercept form.
$$2x = -2y + 4$$

11. What is the slope of the line $y = -\frac{1}{2}x + 3$?

12. What is the x-intercept of the line $y = 5x + 6$?

13. What is the y-intercept of the line $y - \frac{2}{3}x + 3 = 0$?

14. Graph the line which has a slope of -2 and a y-intercept of -3.

15. Find the equation of the line which contains the point $(0, 2)$ and has a slope of $\frac{3}{4}$.

Graph the following inequalities on a Cartesian plane using your graph paper.

16. $x \geq 4$

17. $x \leq -2$

18. $5y > -10x + 5$

19. $y < 2$

20. $2x + y < 5$

21. $y - 2x \leq 3$

22. $y \geq x + 2$

23. $3 + y > x$

24. What is the distance between the points $(3, 2)$ and $(6, -1)$?

25. What is the distance between the two points $(-3, 0)$ and $(2, 5)$?

For questions 26 and 27, use the following formula to find the coordinates of the midpoint of the line segments with the given endpoints.

$$\text{midpoint} = \left(\frac{x_1 + x_2}{2}, \frac{y_1 + y_2}{2}\right)$$

26. $(6, 10)$ $(-4, 4)$

27. $(-1, -7)$ $(5, 3)$

Chapter 11 Test

1. Which is the graph of $x - 3y = 6$?

A.
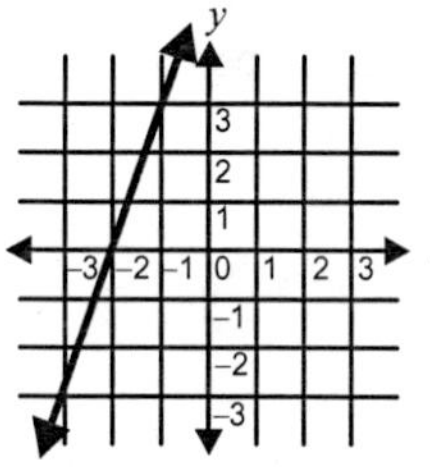

B.
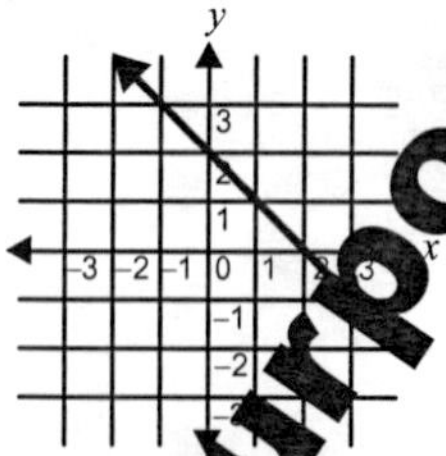

C.
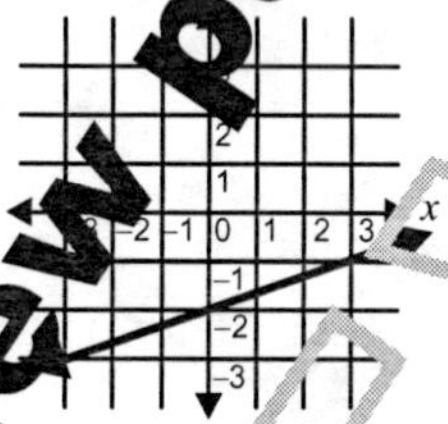

D.
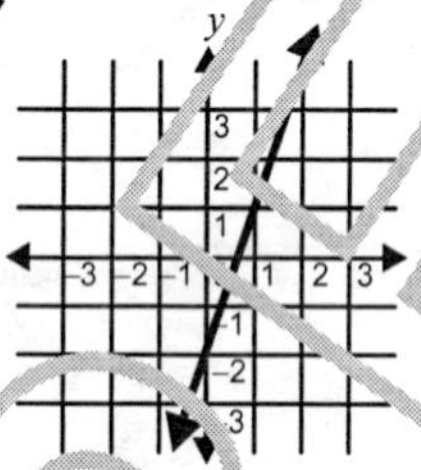

E.
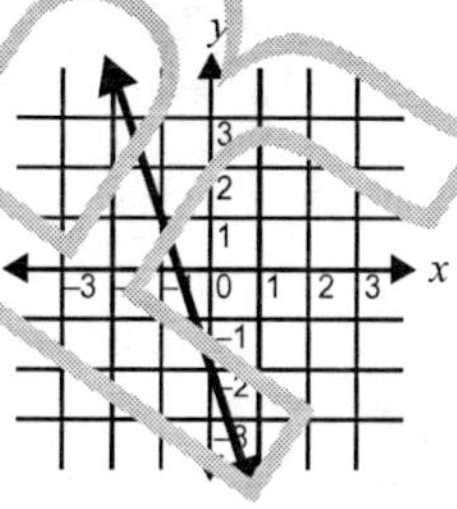

2. $(-2, 1)$ is a solution for which of the following equations?

F. $y + 2x = 4$
G. $-2x - y = 5$
H. $x + 2y = -4$
J. $x - y = -5$
K. $2x - y = -5$

3. Which of the following is the graph of the equation $y = x - 3$?

A.
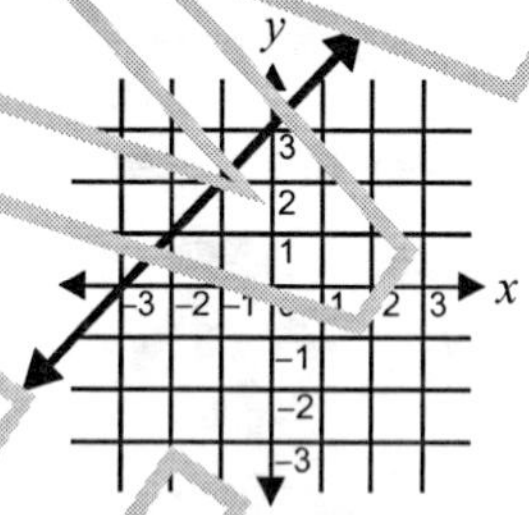

B.
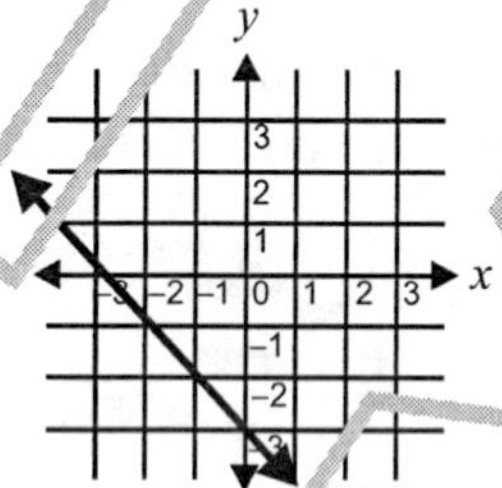

C.
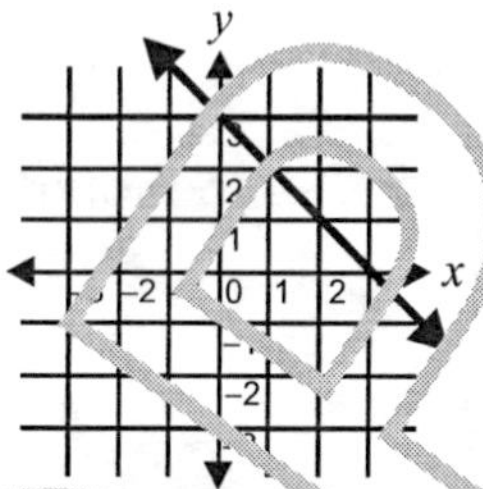

D.
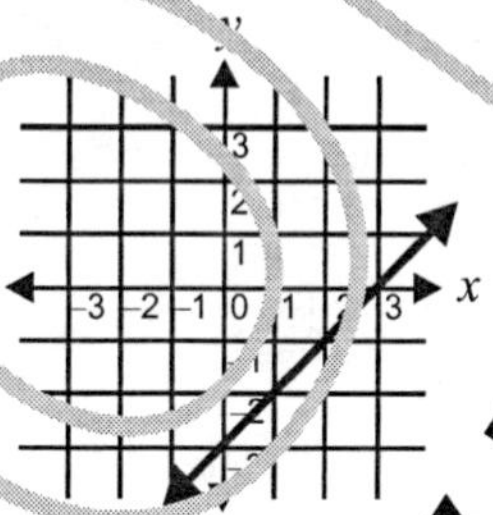

E.
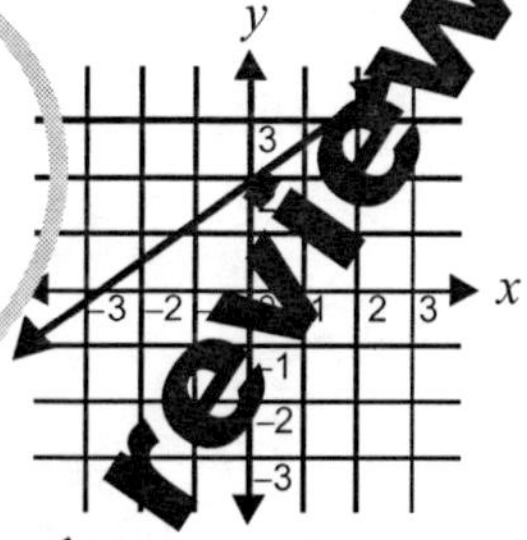

4. Which of the following points does **not** lie on the line $y = 3x - 2$?

F. $(0, -2)$
G. $(1, 1)$
H. $(-1, -5)$
J. $(2, 4)$
K. $(0, 3)$

5. Which of the following is not a solution of $3x = 5y - 1$?

A. $(3, 2)$
B. $(7, 4)$
C. $(-\frac{1}{3}, 0)$
D. $(-2, -1)$
E. $(0, \frac{1}{5})$

6. What is the x-intercept of the following linear equation? $3x + 4y = 12$

F. $(0, 3)$
G. $(3, 0)$
H. $(0, 4)$
J. $(4, 0)$
K. $(3, 4)$

7. Which of the following equations is represented by the graph?

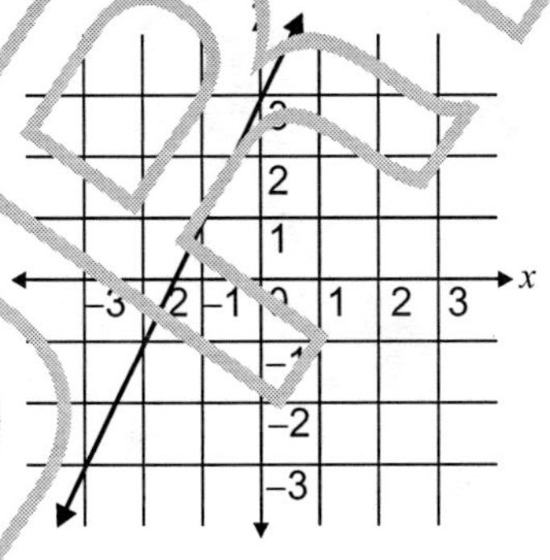

A. $y = -3x + 3$
B. $y = -\frac{1}{3}x + 3$
C. $y = 3x - 3$
D. $y = x + 3$
E. $y = 2x + 3$

8. What is the equation of the line that includes the point $(4, -3)$ and has a slope of -2?

F. $y = -2x - 5$
G. $y = -2x - 2$
H. $y = -2x + 5$
J. $y = 2x - 5$
K. $y = 2x + 5$

9. What is the x-intercept and y-intercept for the equation $x + 2y = 6$?

A. x-intercept = $(0, 6)$
y-intercept = $(3, 0)$

B. x-intercept = $(4, 1)$
y-intercept = $(2, 2)$

C. x-intercept = $(0, 6)$
y-intercept = $(0, 3)$

D. x-intercept = $(6, 0)$
y-intercept = $(0, 3)$

E. x-intercept = $(1, 2)$
y-intercept = $(0, 6)$

10. Put the following equation in slope-intercept form.

$2x - 3y = 6$

F. $y = \frac{2}{3}x - 2$
G. $y = 2x - 2$
H. $y = -\frac{2}{3}x + 2$
J. $y = 2x + 2$
K. $y = \frac{2}{3}x + 2$

11. What is the distance between $(0, 0)$ and $(3, 4)$?

A. 5
B. 4
C. 3
D. 2
E. 1

12. Which of the following graphs shows a line with a slope of 0 that passes through the point $(3, 2)$?

F.

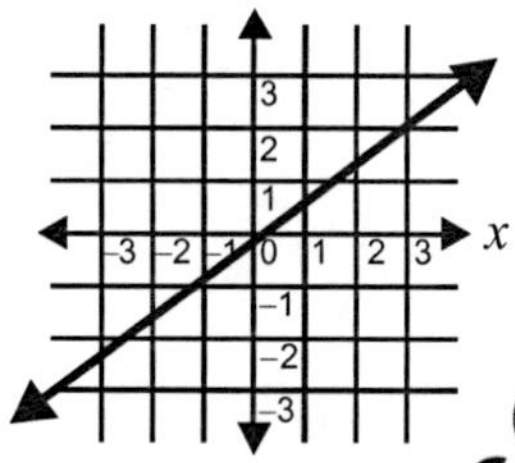

G.

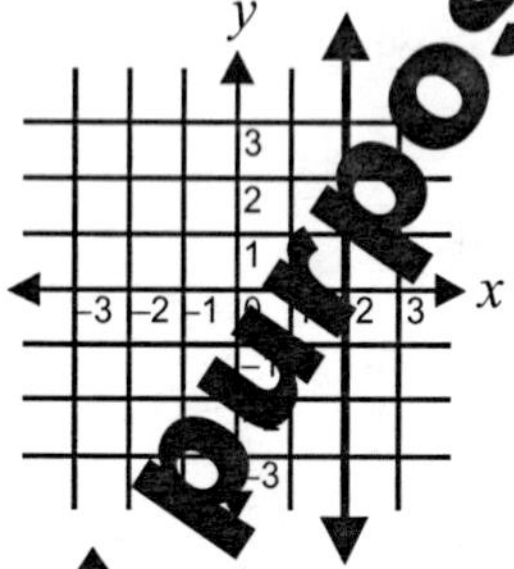

H.

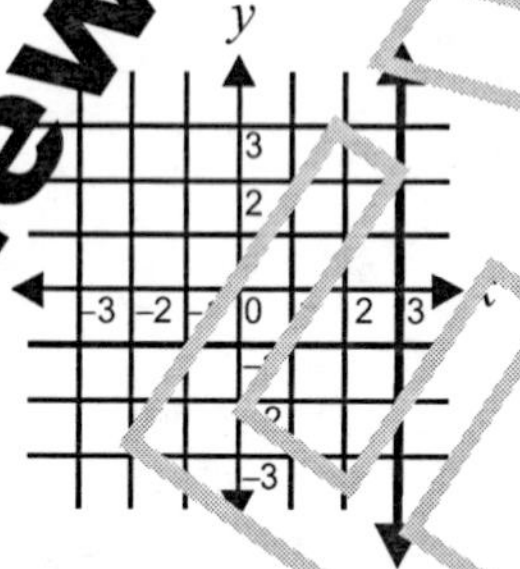

J.

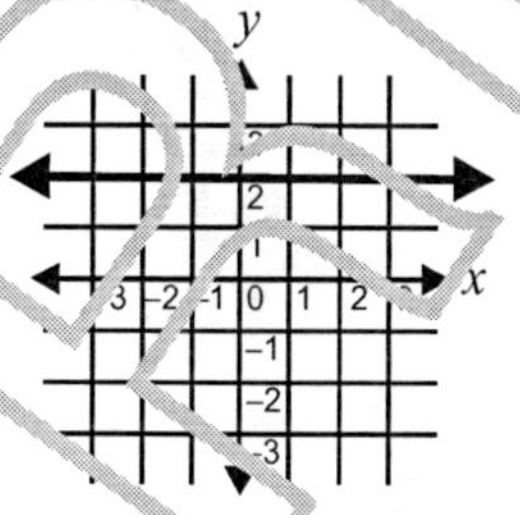

K.

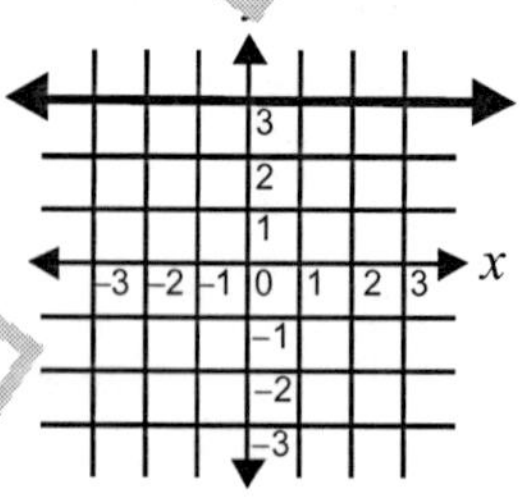

13. Which of the following is a graph of the inequality $y \leq x - 3$?

A.

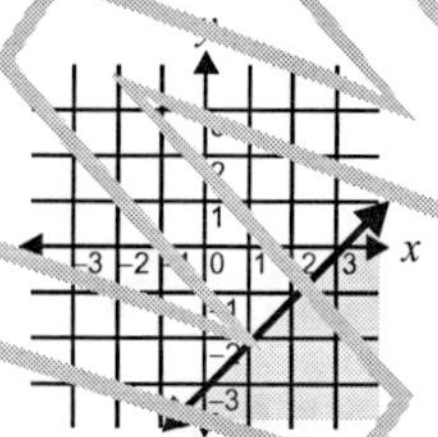

B.

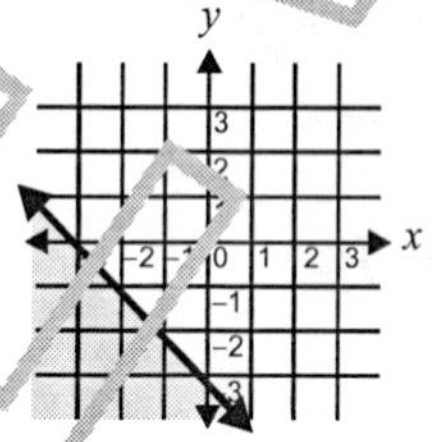

C.

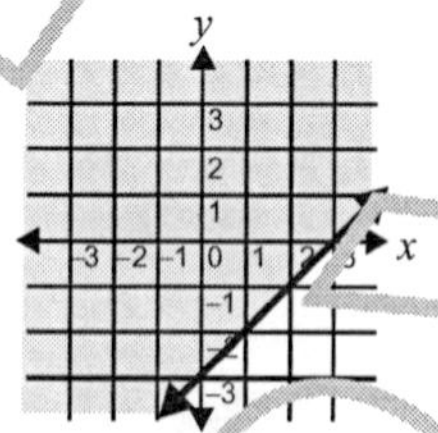

D.

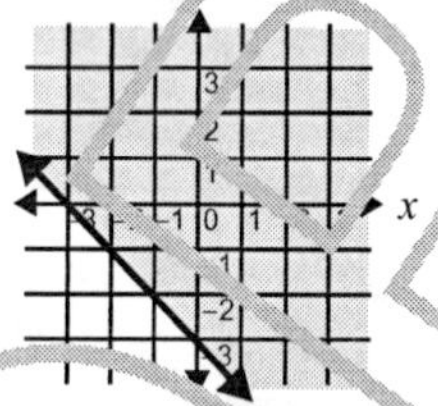

E.

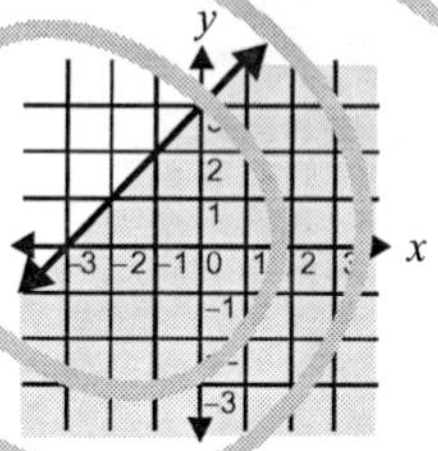

14. The coordinates of a line segment are $(1, 6)$ and $(11, -4)$. What are the coordinates for the midpoint?

F. $(6, 1)$
G. $(10, 2)$
H. $(5, 1)$
J. ([illegible], 2)
K. ([illegible]5, 5)

15. The coordinates of a line segment are $(-5, 3)$ and $(3, -7)$. What are the coordinates for the midpoint?

A. $(4, -2)$
B. $(-1, -2)$
C. $(4, 5)$
D. $(-4, -5)$
E. $(-4, 5)$

16. Look at the graphs below. Which of the following statements is false?

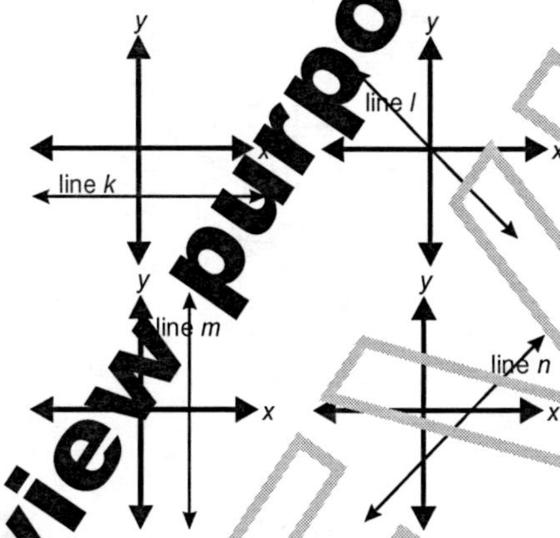

F. The slope of line k is undefined.
G. The slope of line l is negative.
H. The slope of line m is undefined.
J. The slope of line n is positive.
K. The slope of line k is zero.

17. What is the slope of the line that passes through the points $(7, 4)$ and $(-1, -2)$?

A. $\frac{1}{2}$
B. $-\frac{3}{4}$
C. 1
D. $\frac{5}{3}$
E. $\frac{3}{4}$

18. Which of the following is a graph of the inequality $-y \geq 2$?

F.
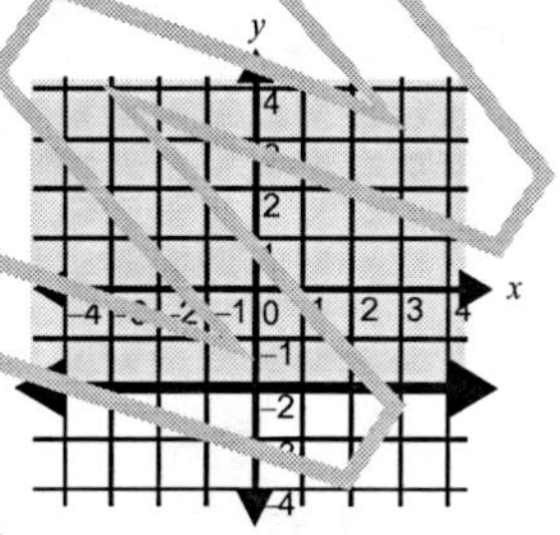

G.
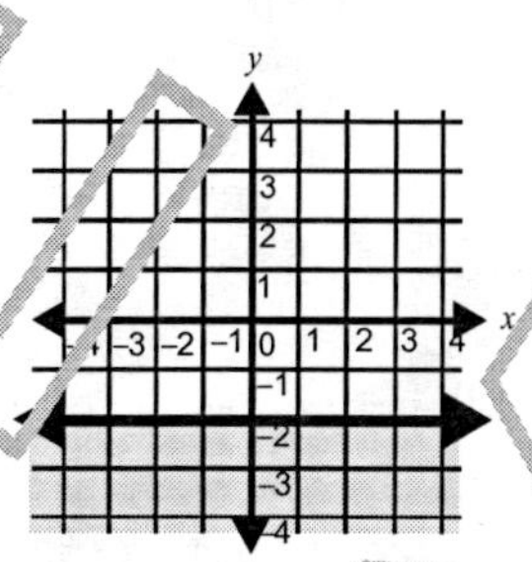

H.
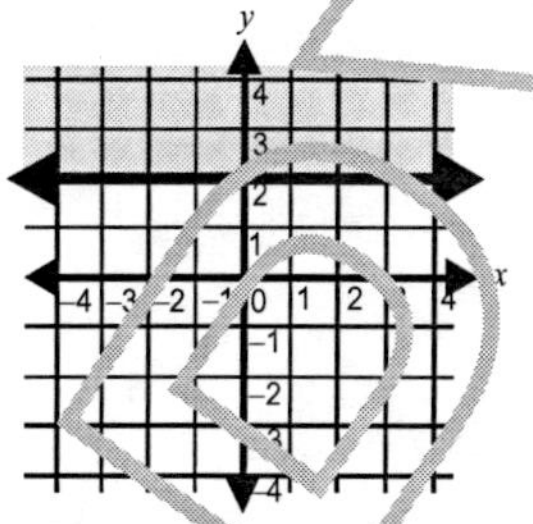

J.
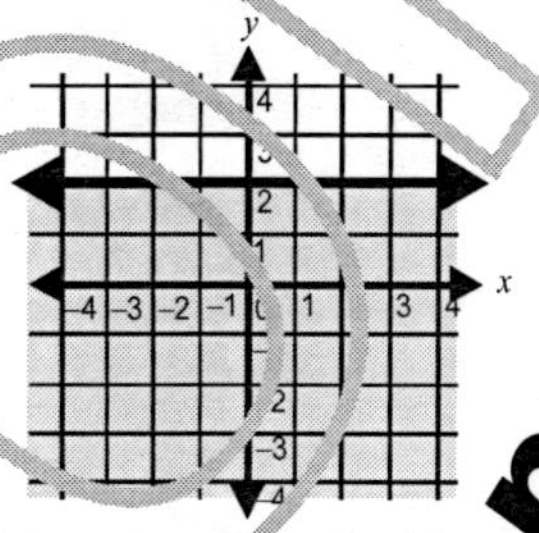

K.
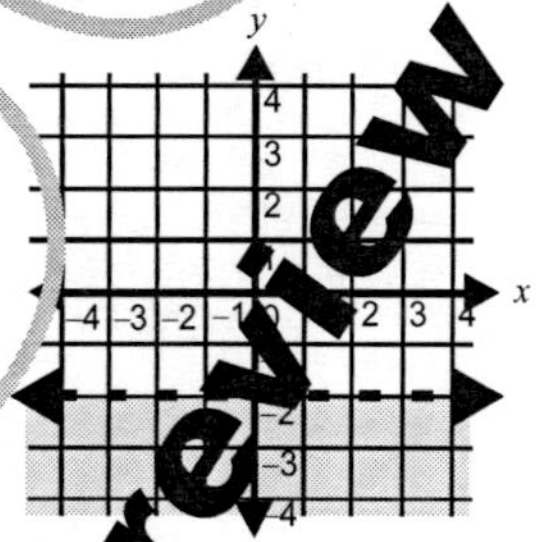

Chapter 12
Applications of Linear Graphs

12.1 Changing the Slope or Y-Intercept of a Line

When the slope and/or the y-intercept of a linear equation changes, the graph of the line will also change.

Example 1: Consider line l shown in Figure 1 at right. What happens to the graph of the line if the slope is changed to $\frac{4}{5}$?

Determine the y-intercept of the line. For line l, it can easily be seen from the graph that the y-intercept is at the point $(0, -1)$.

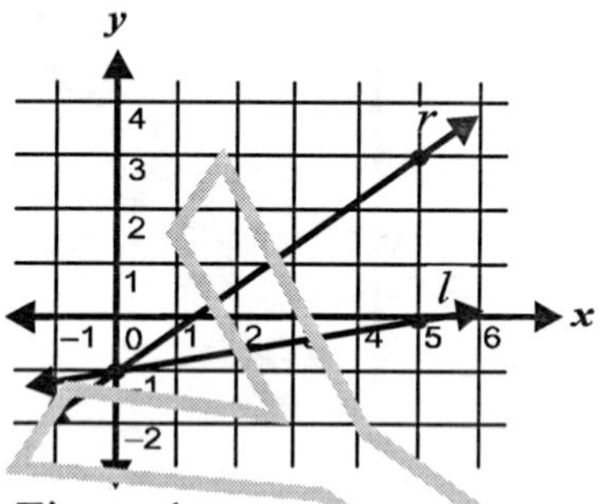

Figure 1

Find the slope of the line using two points that the line goes through: $(0, -1)$ and $(5, 0)$.

$$m = \frac{y_2 - y_1}{x_2 - x_1} = \frac{0 - (-1)}{5 - 0} = \frac{1}{5}$$

Write the equation of line l in slope-intercept form:
$y = mx + b \quad \Longrightarrow \quad y = \frac{1}{5}x - 1$

Rewrite the equation of the line using a slope of $\frac{4}{5}$, and then graph the line. The equation of the new line is $y = \frac{4}{5}x - 1$.

The graph of the new line is labeled line r and is shown in Figure 1. A line with a slope of $\frac{4}{5}$ is steeper than a line with a slope of $\frac{1}{5}$.

Note: The greater the numerator, or "rise," of the slope, the steeper the line will be. The greater the denominator, or "run," of the slope, the flatter the line will be.

Consider the line (l) shown on each of the following graphs, and write the equation of the line in the space provided. Then, on the same graph, graph the line (r) for which the equation is given. Write how the slope and y-intercept of line l compare to the slope and y-intercept of line r for each graph.

1.

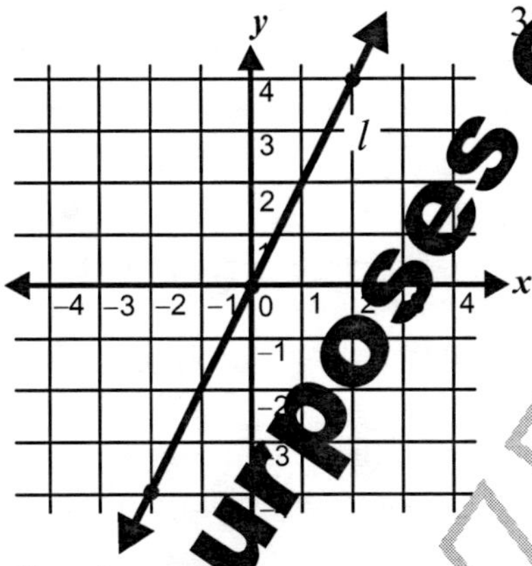

line l: ______________

line r: $y = -2x$

slopes: ______________

y-intercepts: ______________

2.

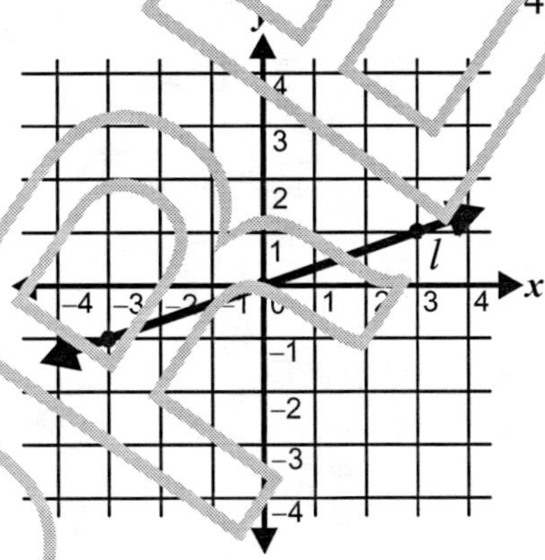

line l: ______________

line r: $y = \frac{1}{3}x + 2$

slopes: ______________

y-intercepts: ______________

3.

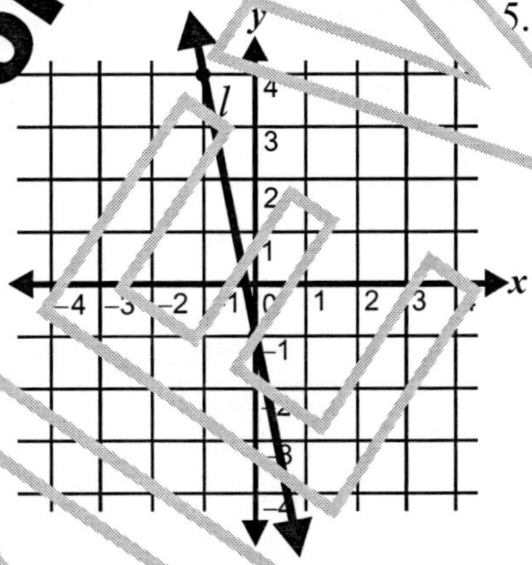

line l: ______________

line r: $y = -3x - 1$

slopes: ______________

y-intercepts: ______________

4.

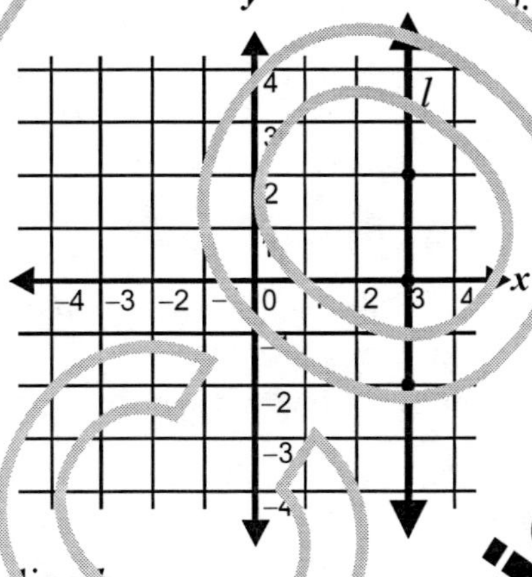

line l: ______________

line r: $y = -3$

slopes: ______________

y-intercepts: ______________

5.

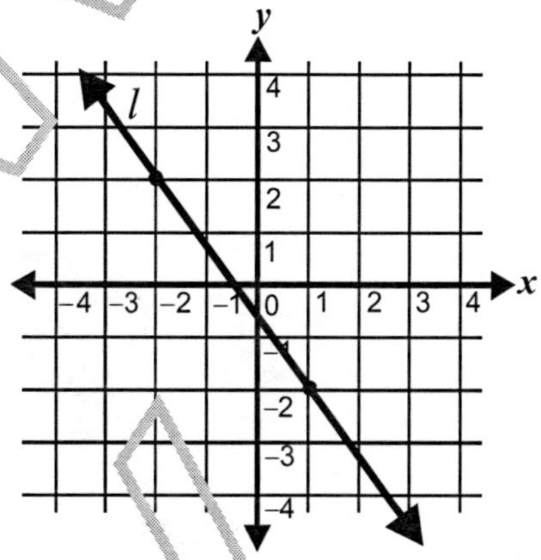

line l: ______________

line r: $y = \frac{1}{4}x - 2$

slopes: ______________

y-intercepts: ______________

6.

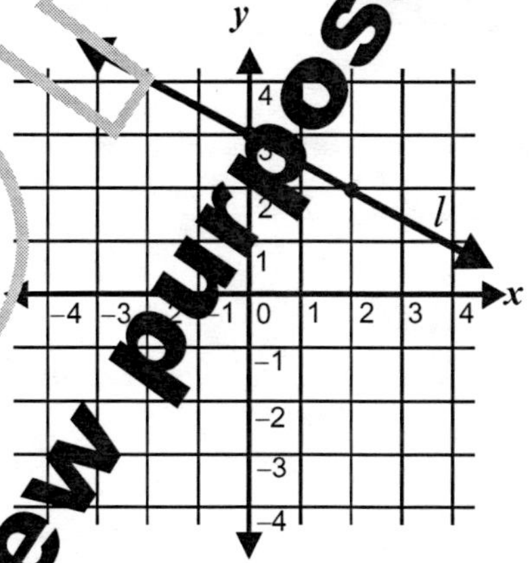

line l: ______________

line r: $y = -\frac{1}{2}x - 3$

slopes: ______________

y-intercepts: ______________

12.2 Equations of Parallel Lines

If two linear equations have the same slope but different y-intercepts, they are **parallel** lines. Parallel lines never touch each other, so they have no points in common.

Example 2: Consider line l shown in Figure 2 at right. The equation of the line is $y = -\frac{1}{2}x + 3$. What happens to the graph of the line if the y-intercept is changed to -1?

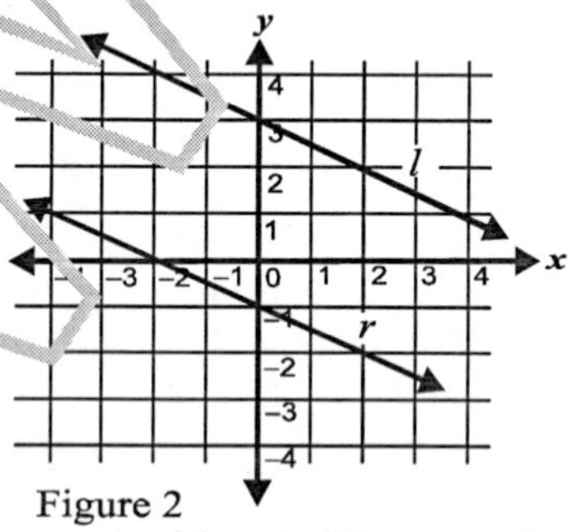

Figure 2

Rewrite the equation of the line replacing the y-intercept with -1. The equation of the new line is $y = -\frac{1}{2}x - 1$.

Graph the new line. Line r in Figure 2 is the graph of the equation $y = -\frac{1}{2}x - 1$. Since both lines l and r have the same slope, they are parallel. Line r, with a y-intercept of -1 sits below line l, with a y-intercept of 3.

Put each pair of the following equations in slope-intercept form. Write P if the lines are parallel and NP if the lines are not parallel.

1. $y = x + 1$ _____
   $2y - 2x = 6$
2. $2x + y = 6$ _____
   $2x = 8 - y$
3. $x + 5y = 0$ _____
   $5y + 5 = x$
4. $y = 3 - \frac{1}{2}x$ _____
   $2y + x = -6$
5. $x = 2y$ _____
   $-x = -2y + 14$
6. $y = x + 2$ _____
   $-y = x + 4$
7. $y = 4 - \frac{1}{4}x$ _____
   $3x + 4y = 4$
8. $x + y = 5$ _____
   $5 + y = 2x$
9. $x - 4y = 0$ _____
   $4y = x - 8$

12.3 Equations of Perpendicular Lines

Now that we know how to calculate the slope of lines using two points, we are going to learn how to calculate the slope of a line perpendicular to a given line, then find the equation of that perpendicular line. To find the slope of a line perpendicular to any given line, take the slope of the first line, m:

1. multiply the slope by -1
2. invert (or flip over) the slope

You now have the slope of a perpendicular line. Writing the equation for a line perpendicular to another line involves three steps:

1. Find the slope of the perpendicular line.
2. Choose one point on the first line.
3. Use the point-slope form to write the equation.

Example 3: The solid line on the graph below has a slope of $\frac{2}{3}$. Write the equation of a line perpendicular to the solid line.

Step 1: Find the slope of the solid line. Multiply the slope by -1 and then find the inverse (flip it over).

$$\frac{2}{3} \times -1 = -\frac{2}{3} \curvearrowright -\frac{3}{2}$$

The slope of the perpendicular line, shown as a dotted line on the graph below, is $-\frac{3}{2}$.

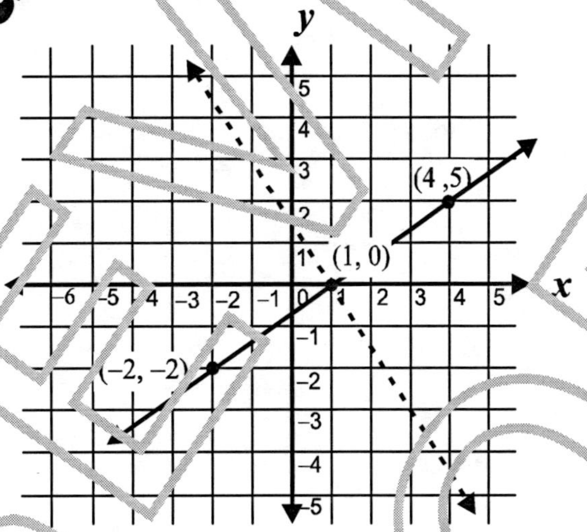

Step 2: Choose one point on the first line. We will use $(1, 0)$ in this example. The point $(-2, -2)$ or $(4, 5)$ could also be used.

Step 3: Use the point-slope formula, $(y - y_1) = m(x - x_1)$ to write the equation of the perpendicular line. Remember, we chose $(1, 0)$ as our point. So, $(y - 0) = -\frac{3}{2}(x - 1)$. Simplified, $y = -\frac{3}{2}x + \frac{3}{2}$.

Solve the following problems involving perpendicular lines.

1. Find the slope of the line perpendicular to the solid line shown at right, and draw the perpendicular as a dotted line. Use the point $(-1, 0)$ on the solid line and the calculated slope to find the equation of the perpendicular line.

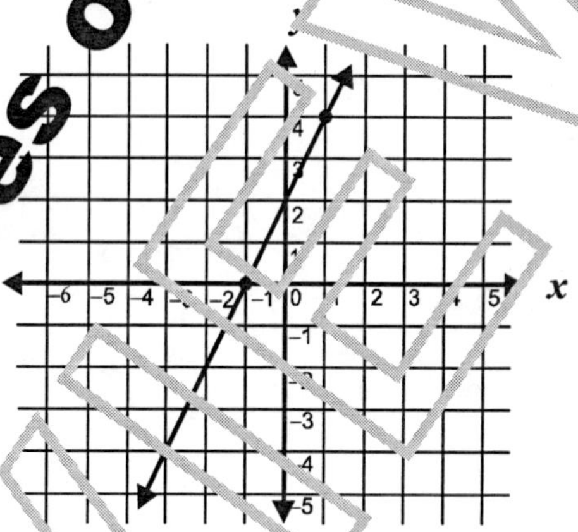

Find the equation of the perpendicular line using the point and slope given and the formula $(y - y_1) = m(x - x_1)$.

2. $(2, 1), 5$

3. $(3, 2), 2$

4. $(-2, 1), -3$

5. $(-4, 2), -\frac{1}{2}$

6. $(-1, 4), 1$

7. $(3, 3), \frac{2}{3}$

8. $(5, -1), -1$

9. $\left(\frac{1}{2}, \frac{3}{4}\right), 4$

10. $\left(\frac{2}{3}, \frac{3}{4}\right), -\frac{1}{6}$

11. $(7, -2), -\frac{1}{8}$

12. $(5, 0), \frac{4}{5}$

13. $(-3, -3), -\frac{7}{3}$

14. $\left(\frac{1}{4}, 4\right), \frac{1}{2}$

15. $(0, 6), -\frac{1}{9}$

12.4 Writing an Equation From Data

Data is often written in a two-column format. If the increases or decreases in the ordered pairs are at a constant rate, then a linear equation for the data can be found.

Example 4: Write an equation for the following set of data.

Dan set his car on cruise control and noted the distance he went every 5 minutes.

Minutes in operation (x)	Odometer reading (y)
5	28,490 miles
10	28,494 miles

Step 1: Write two order pairs in the form (minutes, distance) for Dan's driving, (5, 28490) and (10, 28494), and find the slope.

$$m = \frac{28494 - 28490}{10 - 5} = \frac{4}{5}$$

Step 2: Use the ordered pairs to write the equation in the form $y = mx + b$. Place the slope, m, that you found and one of the pairs of points as x_1 and y_1 in the following formula, $y - y_1 = m(x - x_1)$.

$$y - 28490 = \tfrac{4}{5}(x - 5)$$
$$y - 28490 = \tfrac{4}{5}x - 4$$
$$y - 28490 + 28490 = \tfrac{4}{5}x - 4 + 28490$$
$$y + 0 = \tfrac{4}{5}x + 28486$$
$$y = \tfrac{4}{5}x + 28486$$

Write an equation for each of the following sets of data, assuming the relationship is linear.

1. **Doug's Doughnut Shop**

Year in Business	Total Sales
1	$55,000
4	$85,000

2. **Gwen's Green Beans**

Days Growing	Height in Inches
2	5
6	12

3. **Jim's Depreciation on His Jet Ski**

Years	Value
1	$4,500
6	$2,500

4. **Stepping on the Brakes**

Seconds	MPH
2	51
5	18

12.5 Graphing Linear Data

Many types of data are related by a constant ratio. As you learned on the previous page, this type of data is linear. The slope of the line described by linear data is the ratio between the data. Plotting linear data with a constant ratio can be helpful in finding additional values.

Example 5: A department store prices socks per pair. Each pair of socks costs $0.75. Plot pairs of socks versus price on a Cartesian plane.

Step 1: Since the price of the socks is constant, you know that one pair of socks costs $0.75, 2 pairs of socks cost $1.50, 3 pairs of socks cost $2.25, and so on. Make a list of a few points.

Pair(s) x	Price y
1	0.75
2	1.50
3	2.25

Step 2: Plot these points on a Cartesian plane, and draw a straight line through the points.

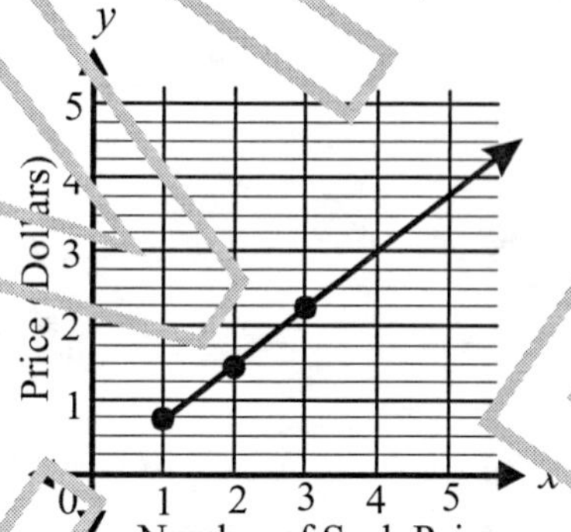

Example 6: What is the slope of the data in the example above? What does the slope describe?

Solution: You can determine the slope either by the graph or by the data points. For this data, the slope is .75. Remember, slope is rise/run. For every $0.75 going up the y-axis, you go across one pair of socks on the x-axis. The slope describes the price per pair of socks.

Example 7: Use the graph created in the above example to answer the following questions. How much would 5 pairs of socks cost? How many pairs of socks could you purchase for $3.00? Extending the line gives useful information about the price of additional pairs of socks.

Solution 1: The line that represents 5 pairs of socks intersects the data line at $3.75 on the y-axis. Therefore, 5 pairs of socks would cost $3.75.

Solution 2: The line representing the value of $3.00 on the y-axis intersects the data line at 4 on the x-axis. Therefore, $3.00 will buy exactly 4 pairs of socks.

Use the information given to make a line graph for each set of data, and answer the questions related to each graph.

1. The diameter of a circle versus the circumference of a circle is a constant ratio. Use the data given below to graph a line to fit the data. Extend the line, and use the graph to answer the next question.

Circle

Diameter	Circumference
4	12.56
5	15.70

2. Using the graph of the data in question 1, estimate the circumference of a circle that has a diameter of 3 inches.

3. If the circumference of a circle is 3 inches, about how long is the diameter?

4. What is the slope of the line you graphed in question 1?

5. What does the slope of the line in question 4 describe?

6. The length of a side on a square and the perimeter of a square are constant ratios to each other. Use the data below to graph this relationship.

Square

Length of side	Perimeter
2	8
3	12

7. Using the graph from question 6, what is the perimeter of a square with a side that measure 4 inches?

8. What is the slope of the line graphed in question 6?

9. Conversions are often constant ratios. For example, converting from pounds to ounces follows a constant ratio. Use the data below to graph a line that can be used to convert pounds to ounces.

Measurement Conversion

Pounds	Ounces
2	32
4	64

10. Use the graph from question 9 to convert [illegible]0 ounces to pounds.

11. What does the slope of the line graphs for question 9 represent?

12. Graph the data below, and create a line that shows the conversion from weeks to days.

Time

Weeks	Days
[illegible]	7
[illegible]	14

13. About how many days are in $2\frac{1}{2}$ weeks?

Chapter 12 Review

1. The graph of the line $y = 3x - 1$ is shown below. On the same graph, draw the line $y = -\frac{1}{3}x - 1$.

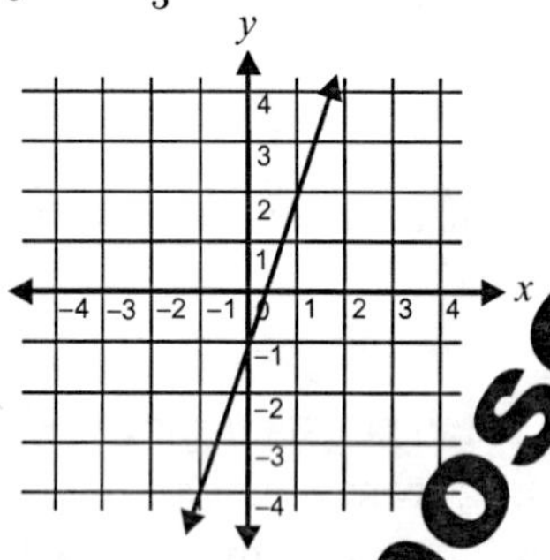

2. What is the equation of a line that is perpendicular to the line $3x + 2y = 6$ and passes through the point $(12, -15)$?

3. What is the equation of a line that is parallel to the line $-5x + y = -4$ and passes through the point $(-1, 7)$?

4. If you change the slope of the line $2x - y = 4$ to -1, how will the graph of the line be affected?

5. Paulo turned on the oven to preheat it. After one minute, the oven temperature was 200°. After 2 minutes, the oven temperature was 325°.

Oven Temperature

Minutes	Temperature
1	200°
2	325°

Assuming the oven temperature rose at a constant rate, write an equation that fits the data.

6. Write an equation that fits the data given below. Assume the data is linear.

Plumber Charges/Hour

Hour	Charge
1	$170
2	$220

7. The data given below show conversions between miles per hour and kilometers per hour. Based on this data, graph a conversion line on the Cartesian plane below.

Speed

MPH	KPH
5	8
10	16

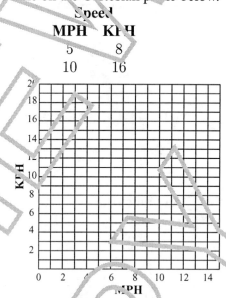

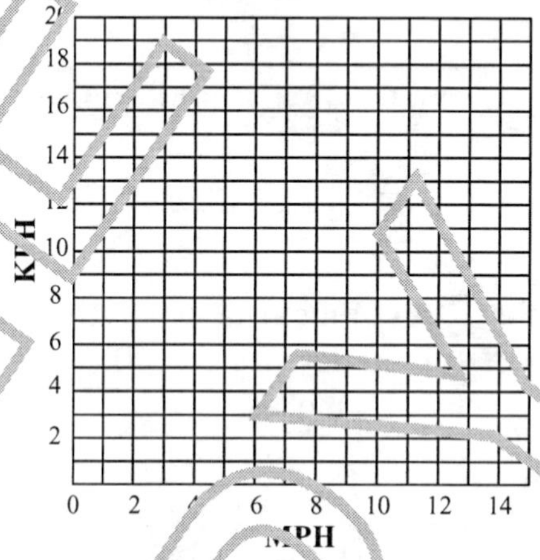

8. What would be the approximate conversion of 9 mph to kph?

9. What would be the approximate conversion of 13 kph to mph?

10. A bicyclist travels 12 mph downhill. Approximately how many kph is the bicyclist traveling?

11. Use the data given below to graph the interest rate versus the interest rate on $80.00 in one year.

$80.00 Principal

Interest Rate	Interest - 1 Year
5%	$4.00
10%	$8.00

12. About how much interest would accrue in one year at an 8% interest rate?

13. What is the slope of the line describing interest versus interest rate?

14. What information does the slope give in problem 13?

Chapter 12 Test

1. Which of the following is an equation of a line that is perpendicular to the line l in the graph?

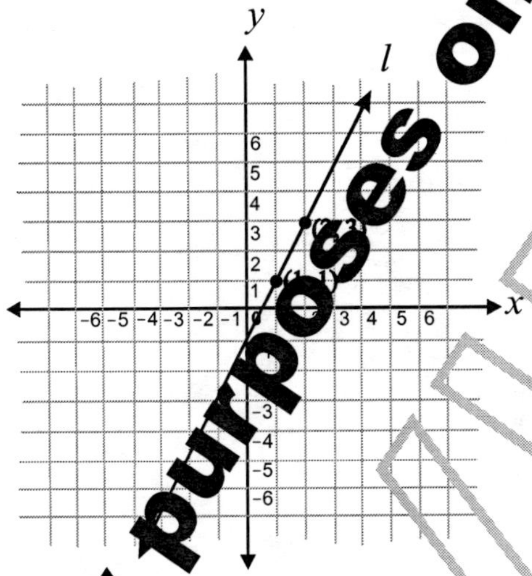

A. $x - 2y = -4$
B. $x - 2y = 4$
C. $x + 2y = 4$
D. $2x + y = 4$
E. $2x + 2y = 4$

2. The graph of which pair of equations below will be parallel?

F. $x + 4y = 3$
$3x + 4y = 3$

G. $x - 4y = 3$
$4y - x = -3$

H. $2x - 8 = 2y$
$2x + 8 = 2y$

J. $6x + 6 = 6y$
$11x - 12 = 7y$

K. $2x + 2 = 2y$
$x - 2 = 2y$

3. What happens to a graph of the line if the slope changes from 2 to -2?

A. The graph will move down 4 spaces.

B. The graph will flatten out to be more vertical.

C. The graph will slant towards the right instead of the left.

D. The graph will flatten out to be more horizontal.

E. The graph will slant towards the left instead of the right.

4. What happens to a graph if the y-intercept changes from 4 to -2?

F. The graph will move down 2 spaces.

G. The graph will slant towards the left instead of the right.

H. The graph will move down 6 spaces.

J. The graph will move up 6 spaces.

K. The graph will move up 2 spaces.

5. Which of the following statements is an accurate comparison of the lines $y = 3x - 1$ and $y = -\frac{1}{3}x - 1$?

A. Only their y-intercepts are different.

B. Only their slopes are different.

C. Both their y-intercepts and their slopes are different.

D. The lines are parallel.

E. There is no difference between these two lines.

6. Which of the following Cartesian planes is an accurate graph of the point values below?

Cups	Ounces
1	8
2	16
3	24

F.

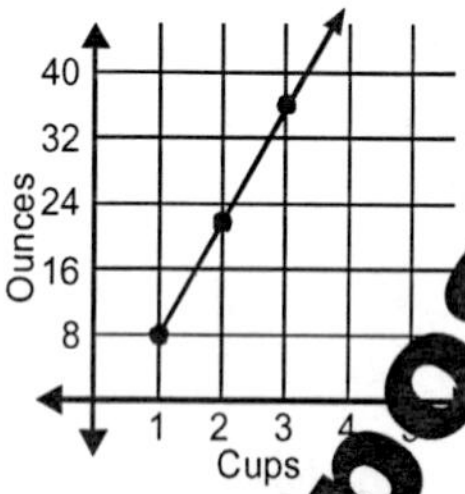

G.

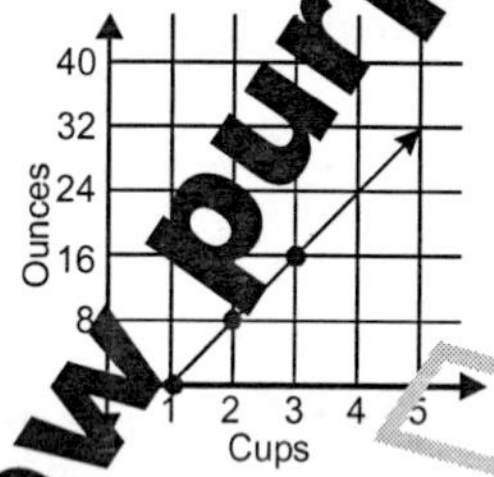

H.

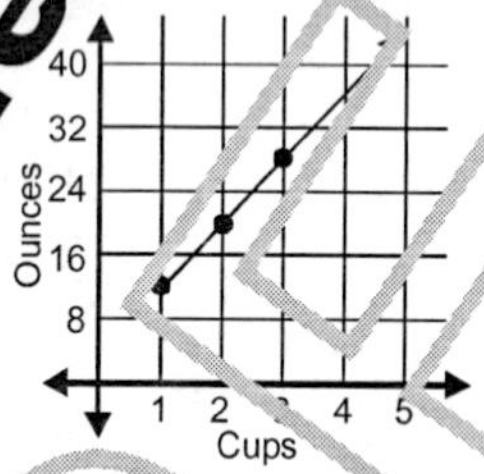

J.

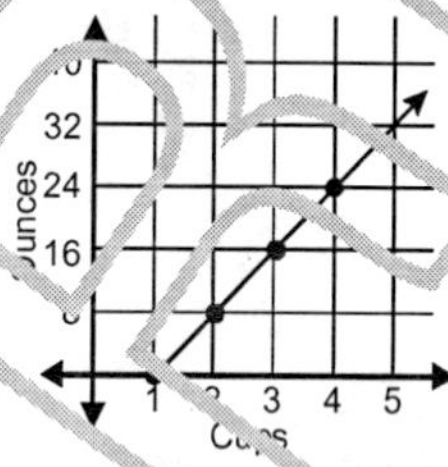

K.

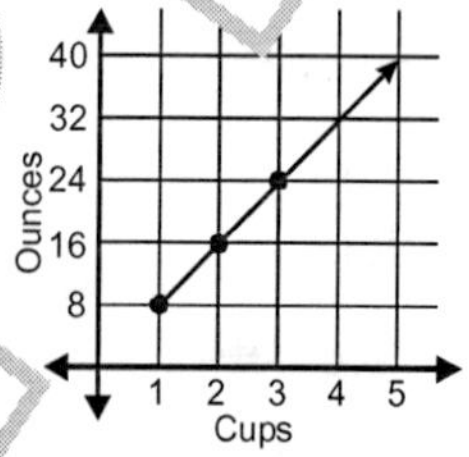

7. Florence follows Great Aunt Emma's instructions for making coffee in various size coffee urns.

Capacity of the Coffee Urn	Number of Scoops of Coffee
4 quarts	15 scoops
6 quarts	25 scoops
10 quarts	40 scoops

Which of these graphs correctly plots the number of scoops as a function of the capacity of the urn?

A.

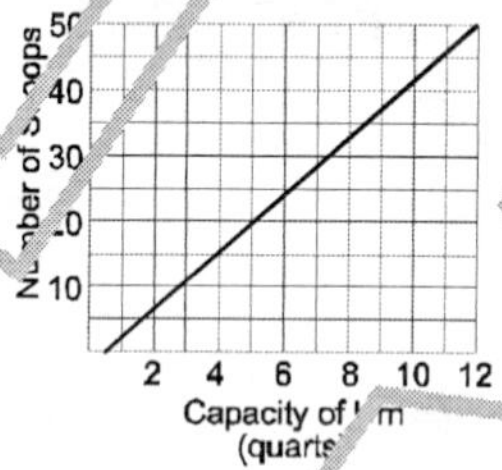

B.

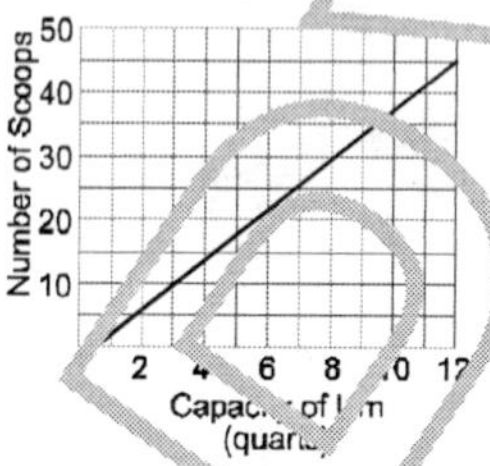

C.

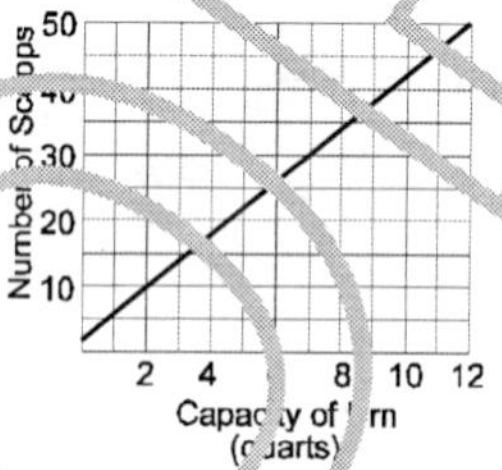

D.

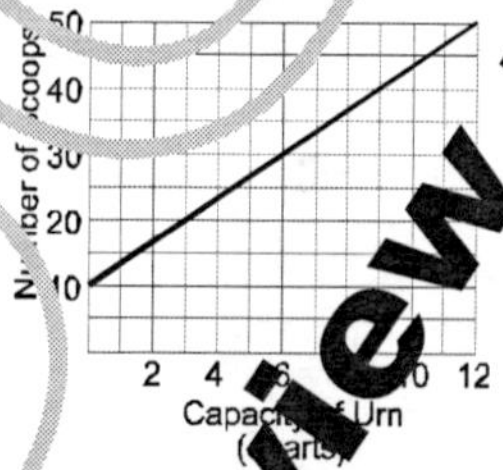

E.

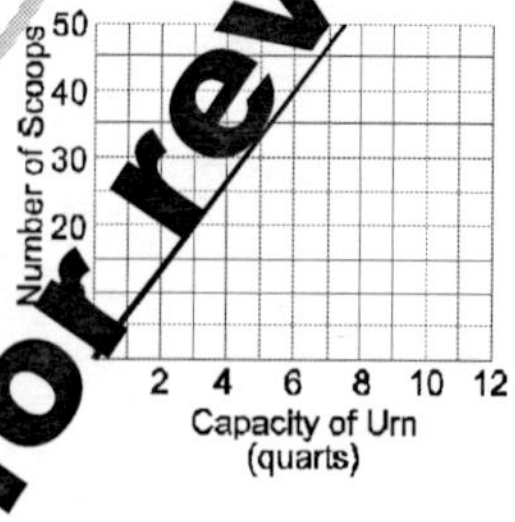

Chapter 13
Graphing Non-Linear Equations

13.1 Graphing Quadratic Equations

Equations that you may encounter on the math portion on the ACT will possibly involve variables which are squared (raised to the second power). The best way to find values for the x and y variables in an equation is to plug one number into x, and then find the corresponding value for y just as you did at the beginning of this chapter. Then, plot the points and draw a line through the points.

Example 1: Graph $y = x^2$.

Step 1: Make a table and find several values for x and y.

x	y
−2	4
−1	1
0	0
1	2
2	4

Step 2: Plot the points, and draw a curve through the points. Notice the shape of the curve. This type of curve is called a **parabola**. Equations with one squared term will be parabolas.

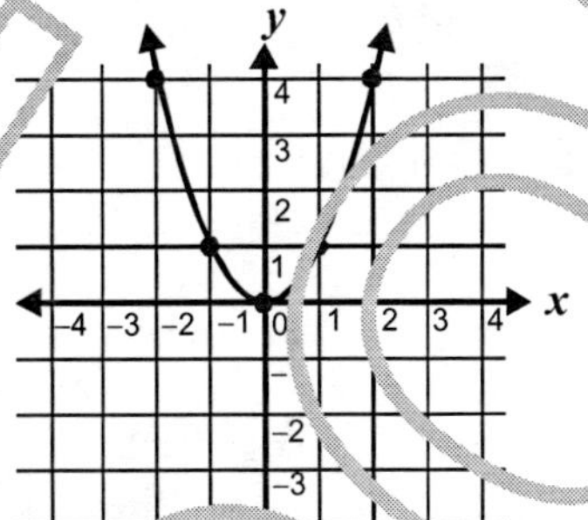

Note: In the equation $y = ax^2 + c$, changing the value of a will widen or narrow the parabola around the y-axis. If the value of a is a negative number, the parabola will be reflected across the x axis (the vertex will be at the top of the parabola instead of at the bottom.) If $a = 0$, the graph will be a straight line, not a parabola. Changing the value of c will move the vertex of the parabola from the origin to a different point on the y-axis.

Graph the equations below on a Cartesian plane.

1. $y = 2x^2$
2. $y = 3 - x^2$
3. $y = x^2 - 2$
4. $y = -2x^2$
5. $y = x^2 + 3$
6. $y = -3x^2 + 2$
7. $y = 3x^2 - 5$
8. $y = x^2 + 1$
9. $y = -x^2 - 6$
10. $y = -x^2$
11. $y = 2x^2 - 1$
12. $y = 2 - 2x^2$

13.2 Finding the Vertex of a Quadratic Equation

The vertex of a quadratic equation is the point on the parabola where the graph changes directions from increasing to decreasing or decreasing to increasing.

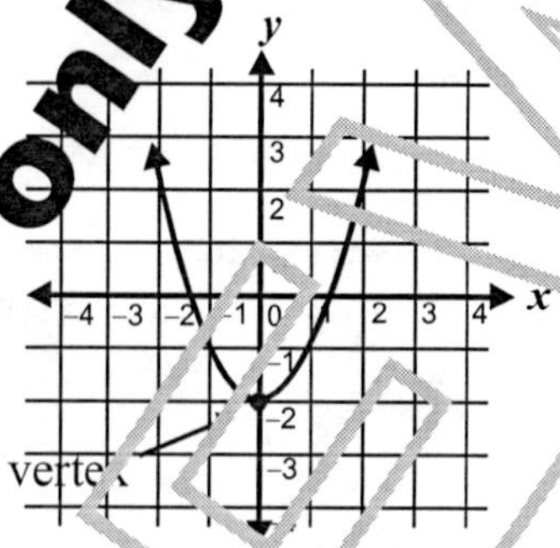

As a reminder, the quadratic equation is defined as $y = ax^2 + bx + c$, in which the coefficient a can never equal zero. If $a = 0$, then the equation will not have a x^2 term, which is what makes it a quadratic equation. The quadratic equation can also be written as a function of x by substituting $f(x)$ for y, such as $f(x) = ax^2 + bx + c$. To find the point of the vertex of the graph, you must use the formula below.

$$\text{vertex} = \left(-\frac{b}{2a}, f\left(-\frac{b}{2a}\right)\right)$$

where $f\left(-\frac{b}{2a}\right)$ is the quadratic equation evaluated at the value $-\frac{b}{2a}$. To do this, plug $-\frac{b}{2a}$ in for x.

Example 2: Find the point of the vertex of $f(x) = 2x^2 - 12x + 10$.

Step 1: First, find out what a and b equal. Since a is the coefficient of x^2, $a = 2$. b is the coefficient of x, so $b = -12$.

Step 2: Find the solution to $-\frac{b}{2a}$ by substituting the values of a and b from the equation into the expression.

$$-\frac{b}{2a} = -\left(\frac{-12}{2 \times 2}\right) = -\left(\frac{-12}{4}\right) = -(-3) = 3$$

Step 3: Find the solution to $f\left(-\frac{b}{2a}\right)$. We know that $-\frac{b}{2a} = 3$, so we need to find $f(3)$. To do this, we must substitute 3 into the quadratic equation for x.

$f(x) = 2x^2 - 12x + 10$

$f(3) = 2(3)^2 - 12(3) + 10 = 2(9) - 36 + 10 = 18 - 36 + 10 = -8$

The vertex equals $(3, -8)$.

Find the point of the vertex for the following equations.

1. $f(x) = x^2 + 6$
2. $f(x) = 2x^2 - 8$
3. $f(x) = x^2 + 10x - 4$
4. $f(x) = 2x^2 - 16x - 8$
5. $f(x) = x^2 + 4x - 5$
6. $f(x) = 3x^2 - 12x + 16$
7. $f(x) = x^2 - 25$
8. $f(x) = -x^2 + 6x - 12$
9. $f(x) = 4x^2 - 64x + 200$

13.3 Graphing Basic Functions

A graph is an image that shows the relationship between two or more variables. In this section, we will learn how to graph six basic functions.

Example 3: $f(x) = x$

The notation $f(x)$ is the same as y, it just means f as a function of x

The easiest way to begin graphing this is to draw a table of values. To create an accurate graph, you should choose at least 5 values for your table. These values are now your (x, y) ordered pair and they are ready to be plotted.

x	$f(x)$
-2	-2
-1	-1
0	0
1	1
2	2

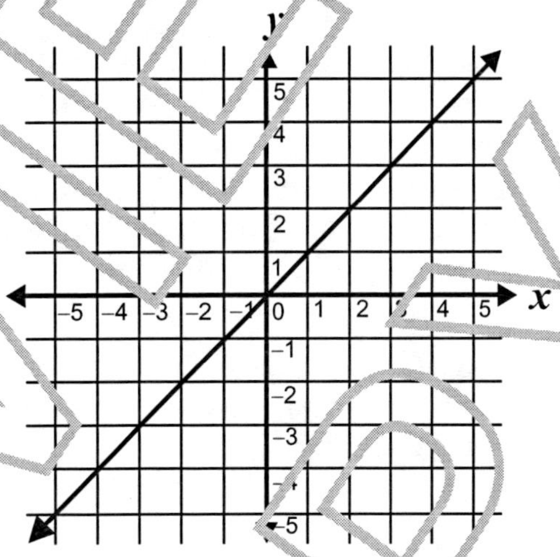

This is called the graph of a **linear function**.

Example 4: $f(x) = x^2$

Exponential functions can be graphed the same way as linear functions.

x	$f(x)$
-2	4
-1	1
0	0
1	1
2	4

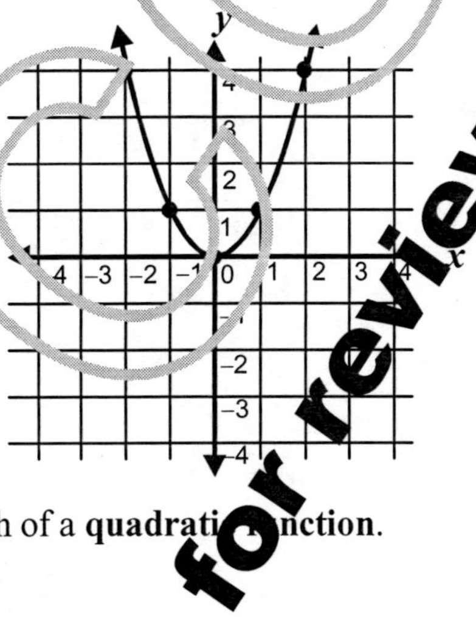

This is called the graph of a **quadratic function**.

Example 5: $f(x) = x^3$

x	$f(x)$
-2	-8
-1	-1
0	0
1	1
2	8

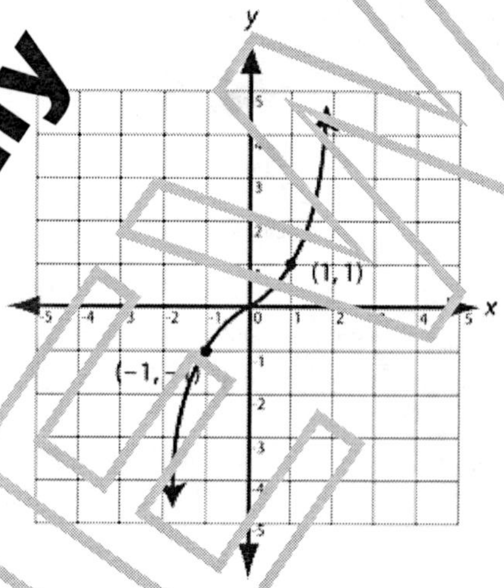

This is called the graph of a **cubed function**.

Example 6: $f(x) = \sqrt{x}$

An equation like this will be easier to graph if you choose values of x that are perfect squares and because you can't take the square root of a negative, there is no need to select negative values.

x	$f(x)$
0	0
1	1
4	2
9	3

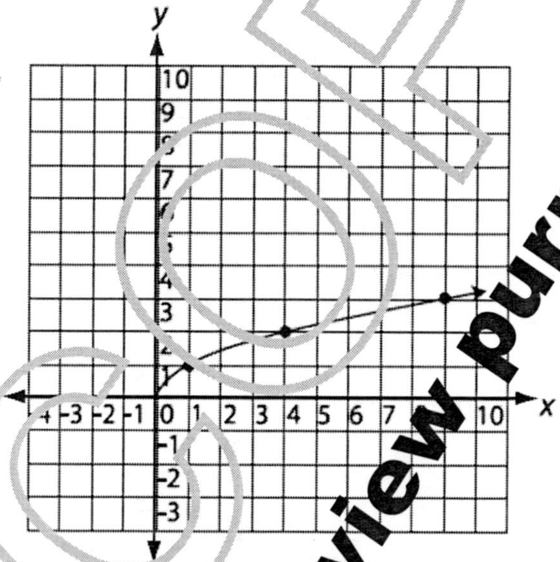

This is called the graph of a **square root function**.

Example 7: $f(x) = |x|$

Don't forget, when you take the absolute value of a negative number, it becomes positive!

x	$f(x)$
-2	2
-1	1
0	0
1	[illegible]
2	[illegible]

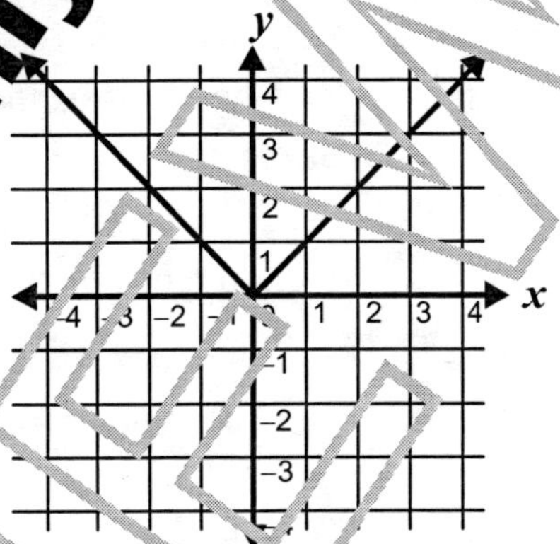

This is called the graph of an **absolute value function**.

Example 8: $f(x) = \dfrac{1}{x}$

Don't forget, anything over zero is undefined and therefore does not exist!

x	$f(x)$
-2	$-\frac{1}{2}$
-1	-1
$-\frac{1}{2}$	-2
0	Does not exist
$\frac{1}{2}$	2
1	1
2	$\frac{1}{2}$

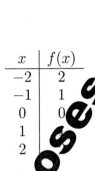

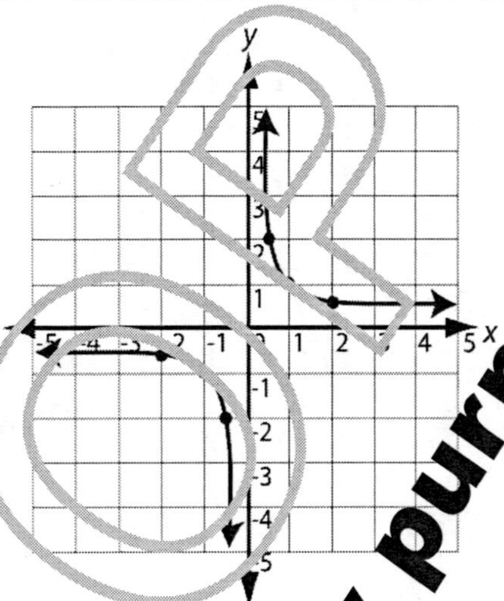

Graph the following.

1. $f(x) = 2x$
2. $f(x) = 3x^3$
3. $f(x) = -\left|\frac{1}{2}x\right|$
4. $f(x) = |4x|$
5. $f(x) = \sqrt{2x}$
6. $f(x) = \dfrac{6}{x}$
7. $f(x) = \frac{1}{3}x^2$
8. $f(x) = -4x^2$
9. $f(x) = -\dfrac{2}{x}$
10. $f(x) = -\sqrt{x}$

13.4 Reading Non-Linear Graphs

In addition to continuity, there are a number of features that you can identify from the graph of a non-linear function.

Zeroes are the points where $y = 0$. The zeros are the function's x intercepts.
The **maximum** (plural: maxima) is the highest y value that a function reaches.
The **minimum** (plural: minima) is the lowest y value that a function reaches.
The **range** is all of the y values that are defined by the function.
Similarly, the **domain** is all of the x values defined by the function.
Finally, you can determine the **rate of increase or decrease** between two points by finding the rise over the run (slope).

Example 9: What are the zeroes, maximum, minimum, range, and domain of the function below? At what point is the function discontinuous? Also, what is the rate of increase between $x = 0$ and $x = 2$.

$$y = \begin{cases} 2x & \text{where } 0 \leq x \leq 2 \\ \dfrac{x}{2} & \text{where } 2 < x \leq 4 \end{cases}$$

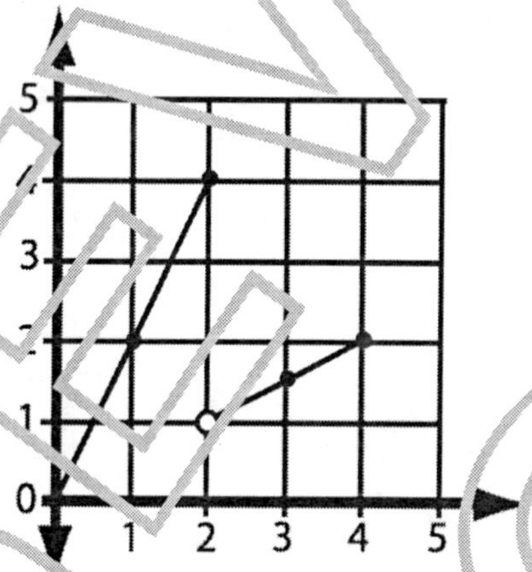

If the graph contains a point, it is shown with a closed circle.

If the graph does not contain a point, like point (2, 1), you must use an open circle.

Zeroes: Where does $y = 0$? Where does the graph intersect the x-intercept? Only at $x = 0$.
Maximum: Highest point is $(2, 4)$. Since the maximum point of the graph is always the largest y value that the graph reaches, 4 is the maximum.
Minimum: Lowest point is $(0, 0)$. Since the minimum point of the graph is always the smallest y value that the graph reaches, 0 is the minimum.
Range: Maximum − Minimum $= 4 - 0 = 4$
Domain: Highest x − Lowest x $= 4 - 0 = 4$
The function is discontinuous at $x = 2$ because this is the point where the graph is not connected.
Rate of increase between $x = 0$ and $x = 2$: At $x = 0$, $y = 0$. At $x = 2$, $y = 4$. Therefore, the rise is $4 - 0 = 4$, and the run is $2 - 0 = 2$.
Slope = rise over run $= \frac{4}{2} = 2$.

Use the following graph of the absolute value function $y = |x - 2|$ for questions 1 and 2.

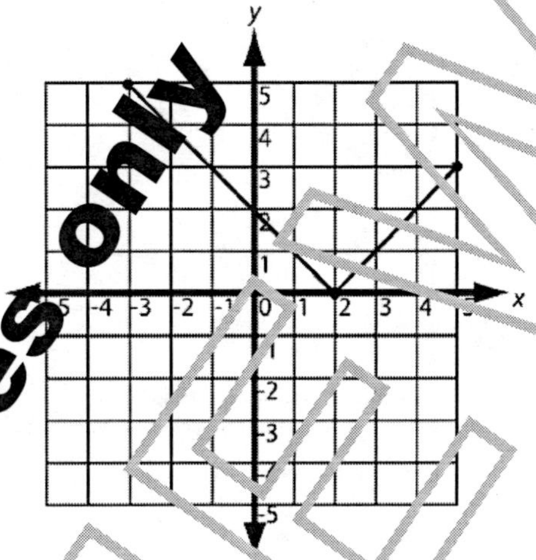

1. According to the graph, what is the minimum value of the function?
   (A) -3
   (B) 0
   (C) 2
   (D)

2. At what point is this graph discontinuous?
   (A) $(-3, 5)$
   (B) $(0, 2)$
   (C) $(2, 0)$
   (D) None of the above. The graph is continuous.

The following graph shows a piecewise function.

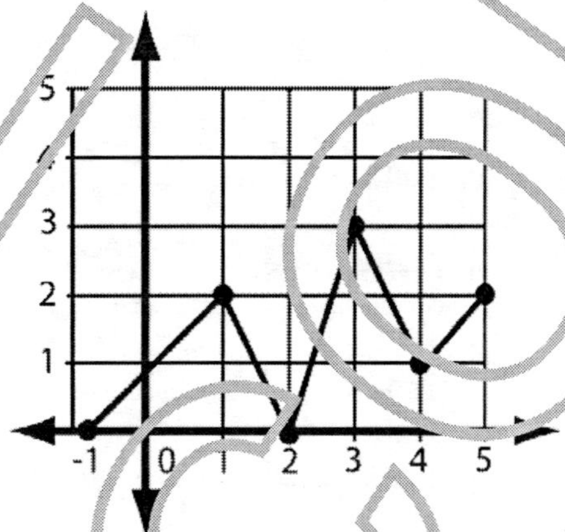

3. How many zeroes does this function have?
   (A) -1
   (B) 0
   (C) 1
   (D) 2

4. What are the range and domain of the function?
   (A) range: $0 \le y \le 3$, domain: $-3 \le x \le 5$
   (B) range: $-3 \le x \le 3$, domain: $0 \le y \le 5$
   (C) range: $-1 \le x \le 5$, domain: $0 \le y \le 3$
   (D) range: $0 \le y \le 3$, domain: $-1 \le x \le 5$

Use the following graph of a step function for questions 5 and 6.

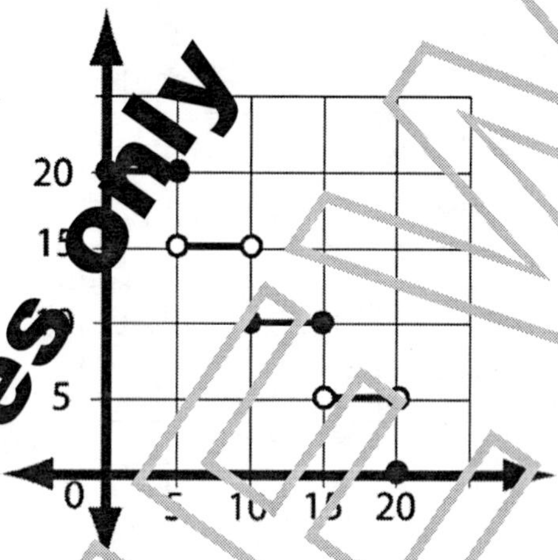

5. At how many points is this graph discontinuous?
   (A) 4
   (B) 8
   (C) 6
   (D) [illegible]

6. What is the rate of increase of the function between 10 and 15?
   (A) -5
   (B) 0
   (C) 1
   (D) 5

Use the following graph of a non-linear function for questions 7 and 8.

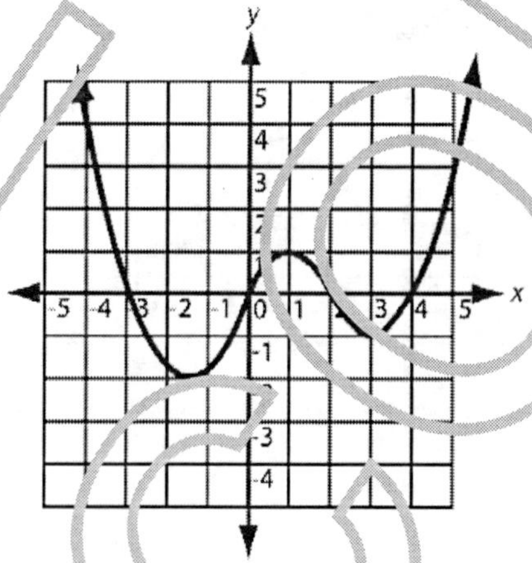

7. What are the zeroes of this function?
   (A) 0
   (B) $-3, 0, 2, 4$
   (C) $-3, -1, 1, 3$
   (D) $0, 2, 4$

8. Which of the following is true of this function?
   (A) The minimum value is -2.
   (B) The graph is discontinuous at $x = 0$.
   (C) The maximum value is 5.
   (D) The graph has only 2 zeroes.

13.5 Identifying Graphs of Real-World Situations

Real-world situations are sometimes modeled by graphs. Although an equation cannot be written for most of these graphs, interpreting these graphs provides valuable information. Situations may be represented on a graph as a function of time, length, temperature, etc.

The graph below depicts the temperature of a pond at different times of the day. Refer to the graph as you read through examples 1 and 2.

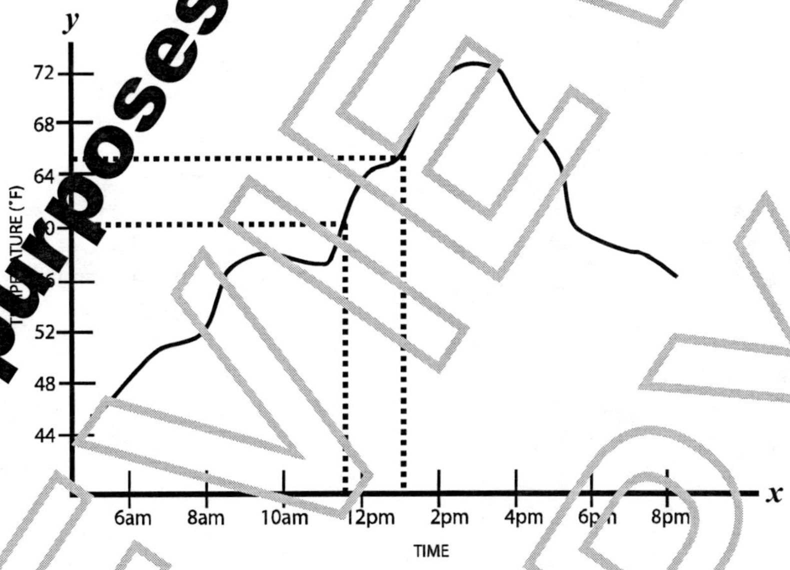

Example 10: If it is known that a specific breed of fish is most active in waters between 60°F and 65°F, what time of the day would this fish be the most active in this particular pond?

To find the answer, draw lines from the 60°F and 65°F points on the y-axis to the graph. Then, draw vertical lines from the graph to the x-axis. The time range between the two vertical lines on the x-axis indicates the time that the fish are most active. It can be determined from the graph that the fish are most active between 11:30 am and 1:00 PM.

Example 11: Describe the way the temperature of the pond acts as a function of time.

At 6:00 AM, the temperature of the pond is about 47°F. The temperature increases relatively steadily throughout the morning and early afternoon. The temperature peaks at 72°F, which is around 2:30 PM during the day. Afterwards, the temperature of the pond starts to decrease. The later it gets in the evening, the more the temperature of the water decreases. The graph shows that at 8 PM the temperature of the pond is about 57°F.

Use the graphs to answer the questions. Circle your answers.

The following graph depicts the number of articles of clothing as a function of time throughout the year. Use this graph for questions 1 and 2.

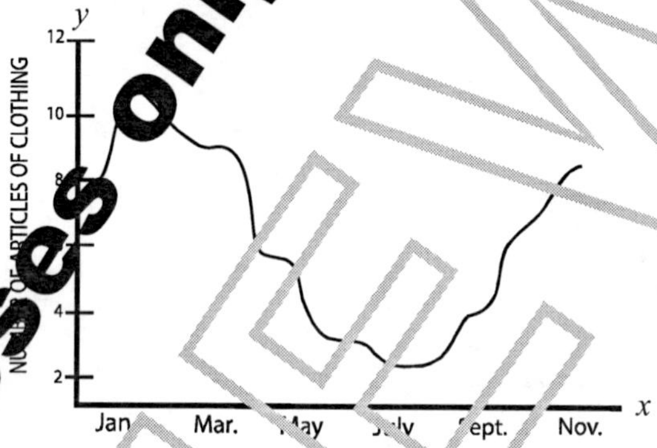

1. According to the graph, in what month are the most articles of clothing worn?
   (A) January
   (B) March
   (C) May
   (D) November

2. What is the average number of clothing a person wears in June?
   (A) 6
   (B) 3
   (C) 2
   (D) 5

The graph below depicts the efficiency of energy transfer as a function of distance in a certain element. Use the graph to answer question 3 and 4.

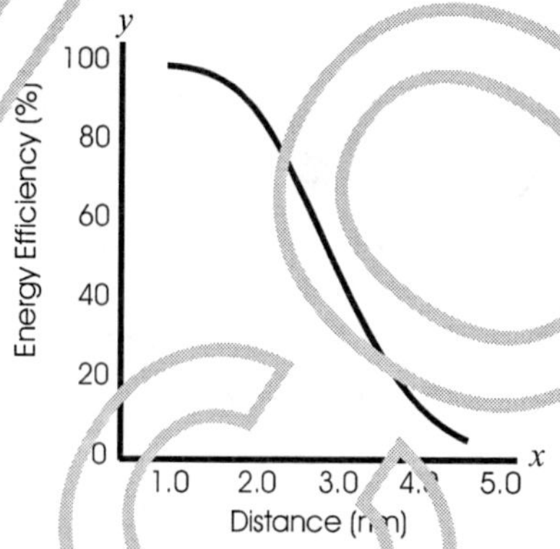

3. At what distance is the energy efficiency at 50%?
   (A) 1.0 nm
   (B) 2.0 nm
   (C) 3.5 nm
   (D) 3.0 nm

4. What is the energy efficiency at distance 2.5 nm?
   (A) 100%
   (B) 90%
   (C) 80%
   (D) 70%

Find the best non-linear graph to match each scenario.

1. Cathy begins her two-hour drive to her mother's house in her new sedan. She drives slowly through her city for thirty minutes to reach Interstate 95. After she gets on the highway, she travels a constant 70 miles per hour for the next hour until she reaches her mother's exit. She then drives slowly down back roads to arrive at her mother's house.

2. Phillip is flying to Texas for a business meeting. When his flight leaves, the airplane increases its speed a great deal until it reaches about 550 miles per hour. After 20 minutes, the plane levels off for the last 45 minutes at 500 miles per hour. As the airplane nears the airport in Fort Worth, TX, it decreases its speed until it lands and reaches zero miles per hour.

3. Erica and her father like to build rockets for fun, and every Saturday they go to the park by their house to launch the rockets. Almost immediately after takeoff, the rocket reaches its greatest speed. Affected by gravity, it slows down until it reaches its peak height. It again speeds up as it descends to the ground.

4. Molly and her mother ride the train each time they go to the zoo. Molly knows that the train slows down twice so that the passengers can view the animals. Her favorite part of the ride, though, is when the train moves very quickly before it slows down to approach the station and come to a stop.

(A)

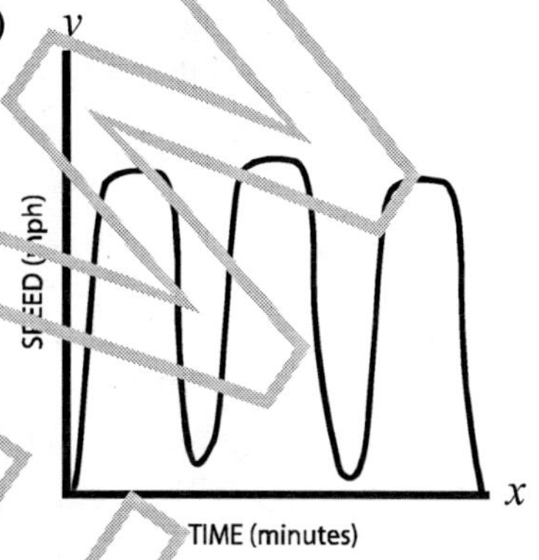

(B)

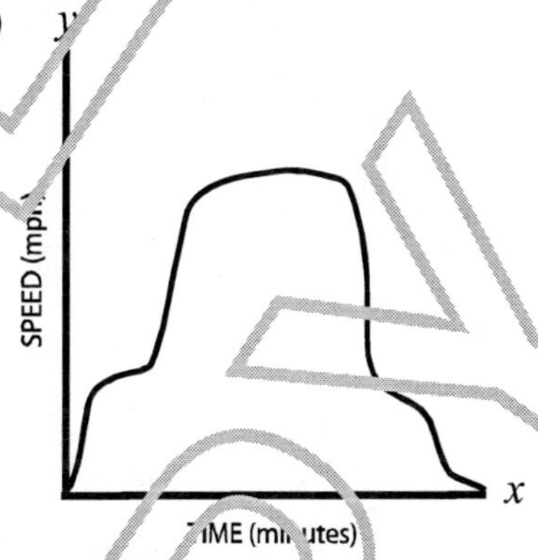

(C)

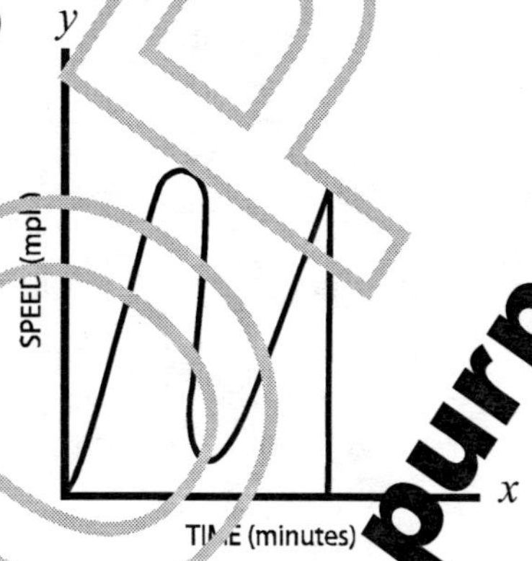

(D)

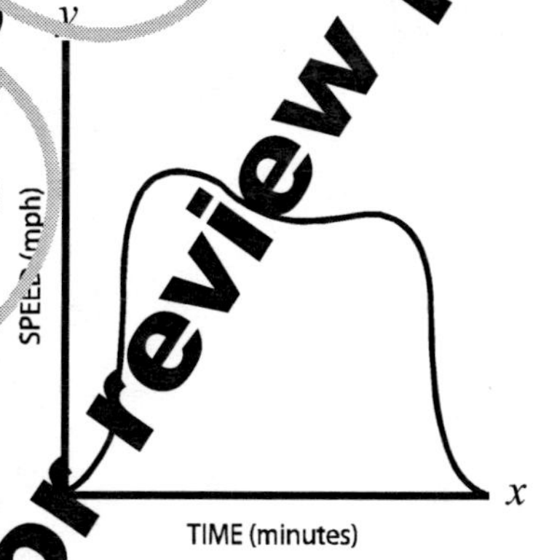

13.6 Graphs and Equations of Circles

A circle can be described as the set of all points (x, y) in a plane that are a distance r from point (a, b). The distance r is called the **radius** of the circle, while the point (a, b) is called the **center** of the circle.

A circle with a radius of r and a center of (a, b) that is graphed on a coordinate grid can be defined by the equation $(x-a)^2+(y-b)^2 = r^2$. From this equation it is clear that if the center of the circle is at the origin of the coordinate grid (i.e. at the point $(0, 0)$), then the equation can be simplified to $x^2 + y^2 = r^2$.

Example 12: A circle has a diameter with endpoints at $(-3, -2)$ and $(45, 12)$. Write the equation for the circle, and sketch its graph.

Step 1: Since a diameter of a circle is a line segment passing through the center of the circle with endpoints on the circle, the center of the circle must be at the midpoint of the diameter.

The x-coordinate of the circle's center must be $\frac{x_1+x_2}{2} = \frac{-3+45}{2} = \frac{42}{2} = 21$.

The y-coordinate of the circle's center must be $\frac{y_1+y_2}{2} = \frac{-2+12}{2} = \frac{10}{2} = 5$.

The center of the circle is at the point $(21, 5)$.

Step 2: A diameter of a circle is twice the length of its radius. The length of the diameter with endpoints at $(-3, -2)$ and $(45, 12)$ can be found by using the distance formula as follows:

$d = \sqrt{(x_2 - x_1)^2 + (y_2 - y_1)^2} = \sqrt{(45 - (-3))^2 + (12 - (-2))^2}$
$= \sqrt{48^2 + 14^2} = \sqrt{2304 + 196} = \sqrt{2500} = 50$.

Because the length of the diameter is 50, the length of the radius must be 25.

Step 3: The center of the circle is at the point $(21, 5)$, and the radius is 25.
The equation of the circle must be $(x - 21)^2 + (y - 5)^2 = 25^2$ or
$(x - 21)^2 + (y - 5)^2 = 625$.
The graph of the circle with its center and diameter shown would look as follows:

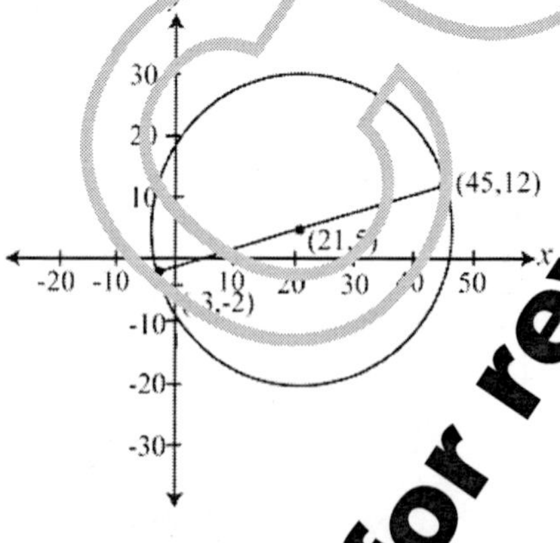

Find the equations of the circles with each of the following centers and radii.

1. Center: $(-2, 10)$; Radius: 13

2. Center: $(12, -1)$; Radius: 21

3. Center: $(-8, -9)$; Radius: [illegible]

4. Center: $(17, 3)$; Radius: 11

5. Center: $(2, -4)$; Radius: 3

6. Center: $(20, -5)$; Radius: 15

7. Determine the equation of the circle shown below.

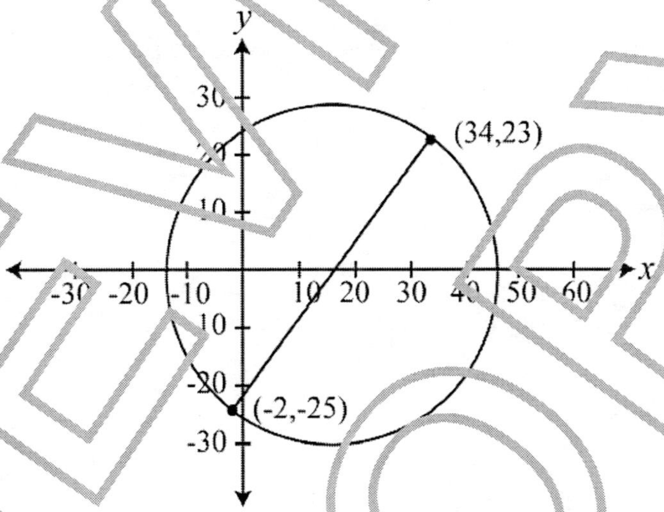

8. A circle has a center at the point $(-6, -7)$ and a circumference of 98π units. Determine the equation of the circle.

9. A circle has a center at the point $(15, -8)$ and an area of 361π units. Determine the equation of the circle.

10. The origin of a coordinate grid lies on a circle with a center at the point $(8, 6)$. Determine the equation of the circle.

13.7 Conics

A **conic** (or conic section) is defined as a curve that is formed when a plane intersects a right circular cone. Conics can be divided into three general categories: ellipses, parabolas, and hyperbolas.

An **ellipse** is an oval-shaped closed curve that has two axes, a major axis and a minor axis. (When the major axis and the minor axis are the same length, the result is a circle.) An ellipse with a semi-major axis of a, a semi-minor axis of b, and a center of (h, k) can be defined by the equation $\dfrac{(x-h)^2}{a^2} + \dfrac{(y-k)^2}{b^2} = 1$.

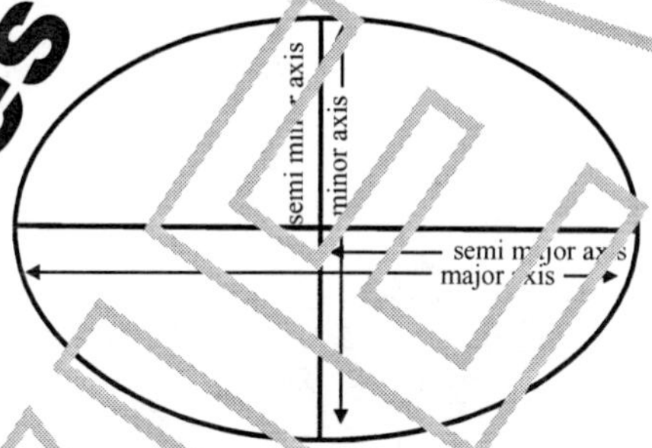

A **parabola** is an open curve that is the graph of a two-variable quadratic equation in the form $y = ax^2 + bx + c$, where a, b, and c are constants. The quadratic equation can also be written in the form $y = a(x-h)^2 + k$. In this case, the point (h, k) is the vertex of the parabola.

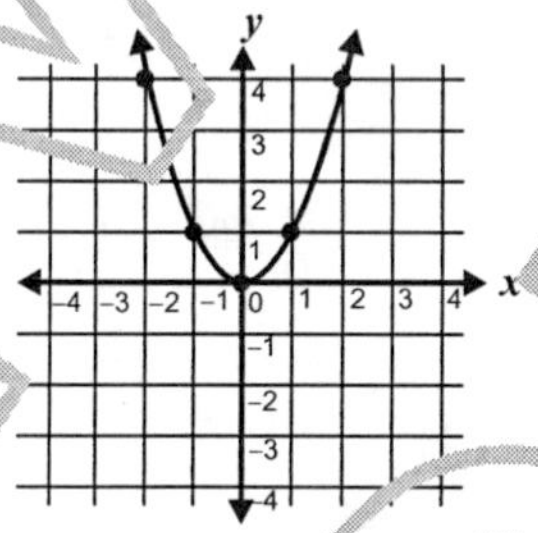

A **hyperbola** is two open curves separated by twice the distance of the semi-major axis. These two open curves have asymptotes. A hyperbola with a semi-major axis of a, a semi-minor axis of b, and a center of (h, k) can be defined by the equation $\dfrac{(x-h)^2}{a^2} - \dfrac{(y-k)^2}{b^2} = 1$.

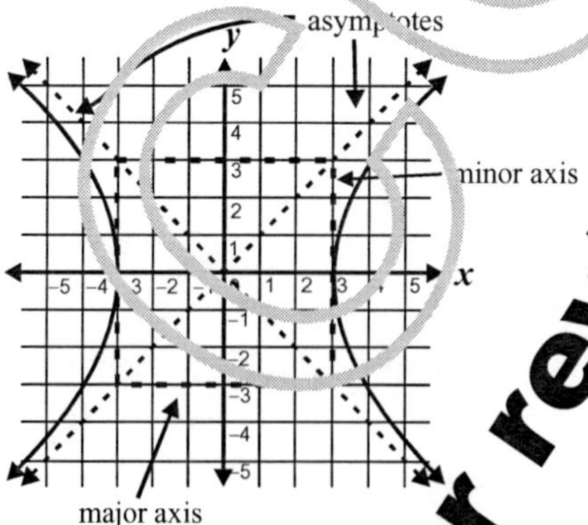

Example 13: The ellipse shown below has its center at the point $(3, 7)$. Determine its equation.

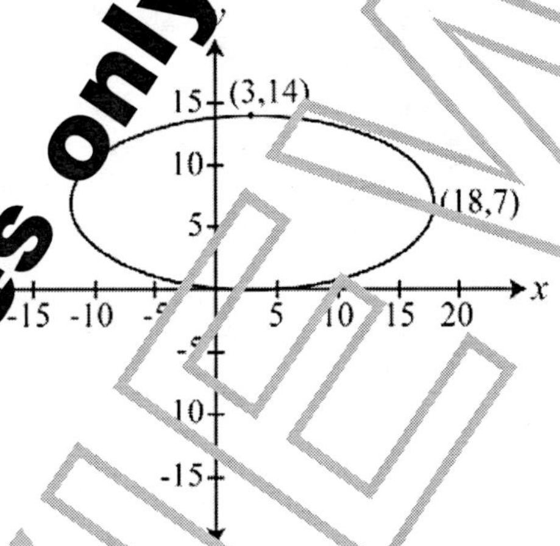

Step 1: The center of the ellipse is at the midpoint of the major axis and also at the midpoint of the minor axis. The center is at the point $(3, 7)$. It is given that the point $(18, 7)$ is on the major axis, and that the point $(3, 14)$ is on the minor axis.

Step 2: Because the center is at the midpoint of these axes, the distance from the center, or point $(3, 7)$, to point $(18, 7)$ is the length of the semi-major axis, while the distance from point $(3, 7)$ to point $(3, 14)$ is the length of the semi-minor axis.

Step 3: Therefore the length of the semi-major axis is 15 units, and the length of the semi-minor axis is 7 units, so the equation of the ellipse is $\dfrac{(x-3)^2}{225} + \dfrac{(y-7)^2}{49} = 1.$

Find the equation of the ellipse that contains the following center and points.

1. Center: $(5, 11)$; Points: $(5, 12)$, $(3, 11)$
2. Center $(-3, 4)$; Points: $(1, 4)$, $(-3, 10)$
3. Center $(19, 2)$; Points: $(19, -6)$, $(2, 2)$
4. Center: $(-1, -8)$; Points: $(-1, 9)$, $(12, -8)$
5. Center: $(20, 6)$; Points: $(10, 6)$, $(20, -2)$
6. Center: $(5, -5)$; Points: $(5, -9)$, $(-9, -5)$

for review purposes only

Example 14: The parabola shown below has its vertex at the point $(15, 8)$. Write its equation in the form $y = ax^2 + bx + c$, where a, b, and c are constants.

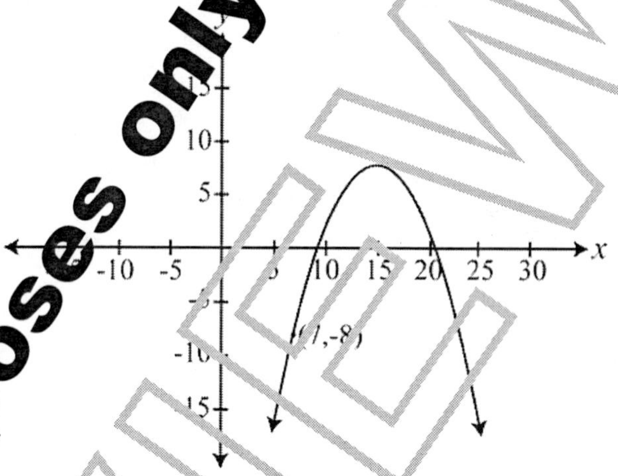

Step 1: Since the parabola's vertex is at the point $(15, 8)$, its equation can be written as $y = a(x - 15)^2 + 8$. However, it's still necessary to solve for a. To do this, the point $(7, -8)$ should be substituted into the equation, and a should be solved for as follows:

$$y = a(x - 15)^2 + 8$$
$$-8 = a(7 - 15)^2 + 8 = a(-8)^2 + 8 = 64a + 8$$
$$-8 - 8 = 64a + 8 - 8$$
$$-16 = 64a \rightarrow a = -\frac{1}{4}$$

Step 2: Because the value of a is $-\frac{1}{4}$, the equation of the parabola becomes $y = -\frac{1}{4}(x - 15)^2 + 8$. Now it's necessary to transform the equation into the form $y = ax^2 + bx + c$.

$$y = -\frac{1}{4}(x - 15)^2 + 8 = -\frac{1}{4}(x^2 - 30x + 225) + 8 = -\frac{1}{4}x^2 + \frac{15}{2}x - \frac{225}{4} + 8$$
$$y = -\frac{1}{4}x^2 + \frac{15}{2}x - \frac{193}{4}$$

Determine the equation of the parabola in the form $y = ax^2 + bx + c$ given the vertex and a point.

7. Vertex: $(-7, 1)$; Point: $(1, 129)$
8. Vertex: $(5, 2)$; Point: $(0, 17)$
9. Vertex: $(3, -3)$; Point: $(2, 3)$
10. Vertex: ([illegible], $-2)$; Point: $(-2, 3)$
11. Vertex: $(4, -1)$; Point: $(3, -3)$
12. Vertex: $(-2, 6)$; Point: $(2, 2)$

Example 15: The hyperbola shown below has its center at the point $(-2, 6)$. Determine its equation.

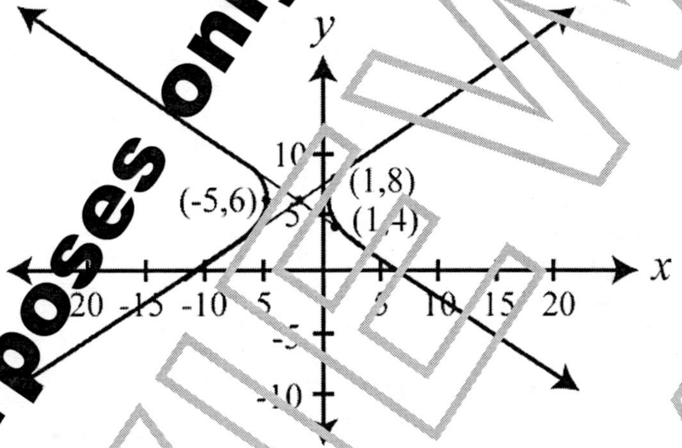

Step 1: The center of the hyperbola is half the distance between the two curves, so the length of the semi-major axis is the distance between the center and one of the curves. For this reason, the length of the semi-major axis is $-2-(-5)=3$. Therefore, $a=3$.

Step 2: The length of the semi-minor axis is half the distance between the points where the line tangent to the vertex of one of the curves intersects the asymptotes. It's clear from the graph that the distance between the points where the line $x=1$ intersects the asymptotes is $8-4$ or 4, so half this distance is 2. Therefore, the length of the semi-minor axis is 2 and $b=2$.

The equation of the hyperbola is $\frac{(x-h)^2}{a^2}-\frac{(y-k)^2}{b^2}=1$.

Substitute known values into the equation.

$$\frac{(x+2)^2}{9}-\frac{(y-6)^2}{4}=1$$

Determine the equation of the hyperbola that satisfies each of the following sets of conditions.

13. Center: $(11,-4)$; Point on Curve: $(7,-4)$; Points on Asymptotes: $(15,1)$, $(15,-9)$

14. Center: $(-5,3)$; Point on Curve: $(1,3)$; Points on Asymptotes: $(-11,6)$, $(-11,0)$

15. Center: $(2,9)$; Point on Curve: $(9,9)$; Points on Asymptotes: $(9,0)$, $(9,18)$

Chapter 13 Review

1. Graph the equation $y = -\frac{1}{2}x^2 + 1$.

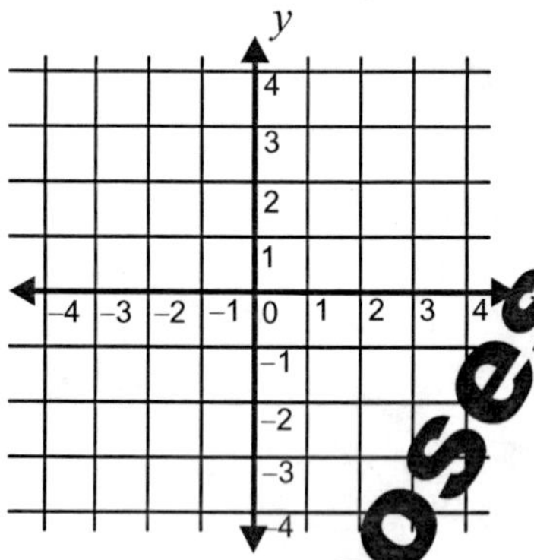

2. What is the name of the curve described by the equation $y = 2x^2 - 1$?

3. Find the point of the vertex of $f(x) = 2x^2 - 8x + 5$.

Graph the equations below on a Cartesian plane.

4. $y = -x^2 + 4$
5. $y = 3x^2 - 1$
6. $y = 4 - x^2$
7. $y = 3x^2 + 6$

Graph each function.

8. $f(x) = -|2x|$
9. $f(x) = \frac{1}{2}x^2$
10. $f(x) = |-6x|$
11. $f(x) = $ [illegible]
12. $f(x) = |4x|$
13. $f(x) = -3\sqrt{x}$
14. $f(x) = \frac{1}{4}x^3$
15. $f(x) = -\frac{1}{8}\sqrt{x}$

16. Draw the graph of the following situation on the Cartesian plane provided. A girl rode her bicycle up a hill, then coasted down the other side of the hill on her bike. At the bottom she stopped.

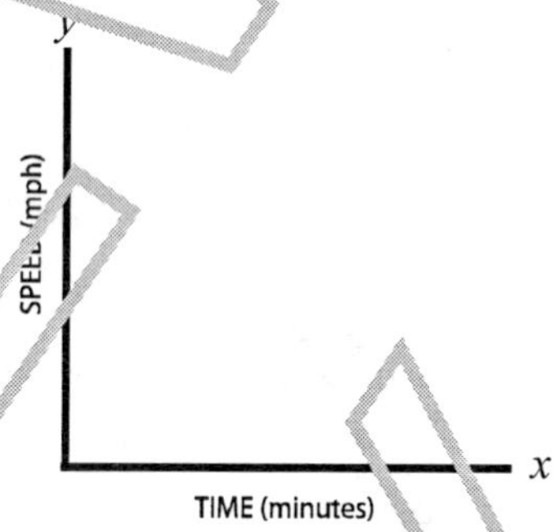

Find the equation of the circle given the center and radius.

17. Center: $(12, -17)$; Radius: 24
18. Center: $(-3, 22)$; Radius: $\frac{1}{9}$

Find the equation of the ellipse given the following center and points.

19. Center: $(9, 8)$; Points: $(-10, 8)$, (9, [illegible])
20. Center: $(-2, 17)$; Points: (−2, [illegible]), $(2, 17)$

Find the equation of the parabola in the form $y = ax^2 + bx + c$ given the vertex and a point on the parabola.

21. Vertex: $(-9, 3)$; Point: $(-8, 1)$
22. Vertex: $(4, 32)$; Point: $(3, 29)$

Determine the equation of the hyperbola that satisfies each of the following sets of conditions.

23. Center: ([illegible], -5); Point on Curve: $(-1, -5)$; Points on Asymptotes: $(11, -12)$, $(11, 2)$
24. Center: $(-3, 2)$; Point on Curve: $(20, 2)$; Points on Asymptotes: $(20, -18)$, $(20, 22)$

Chapter 13 Test

1. Which of the following graphs represents $y = 2x^2$?

A.

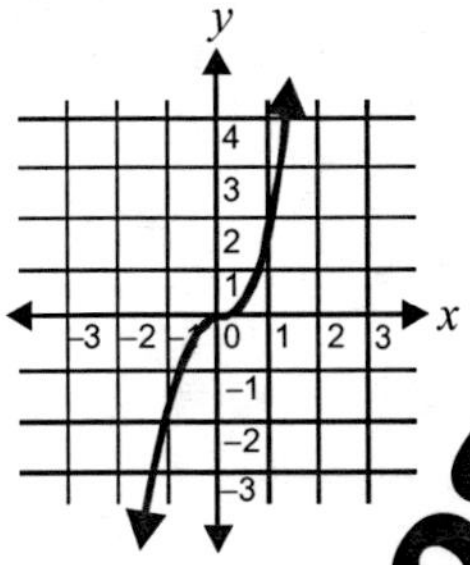

B.

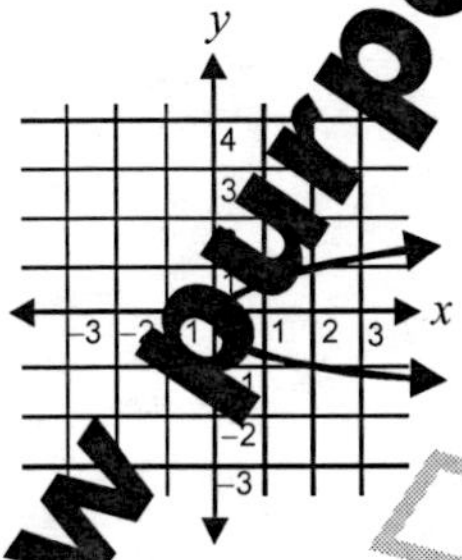

C.

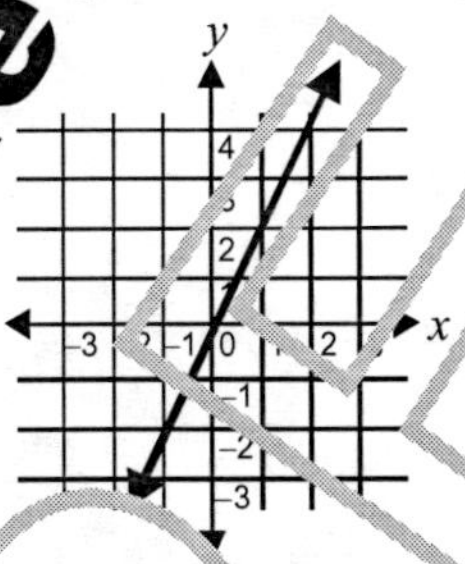

D.

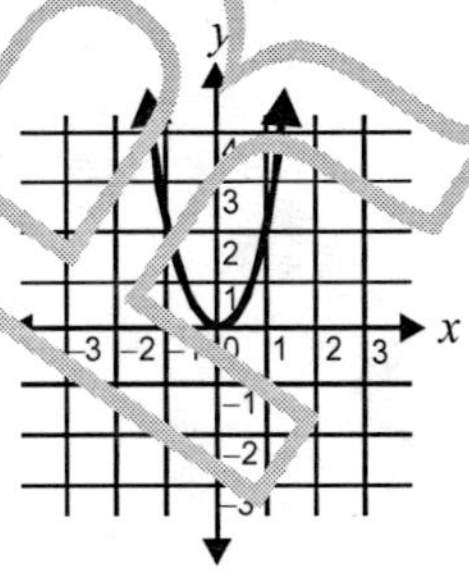

E.

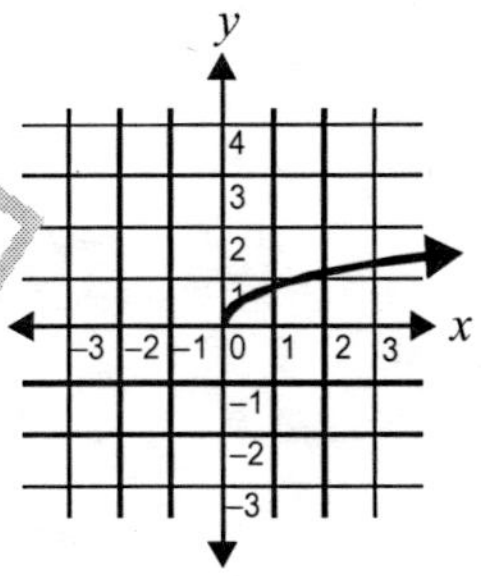

2. Which is the graph of $f(x) = \frac{1}{x}$?

F.

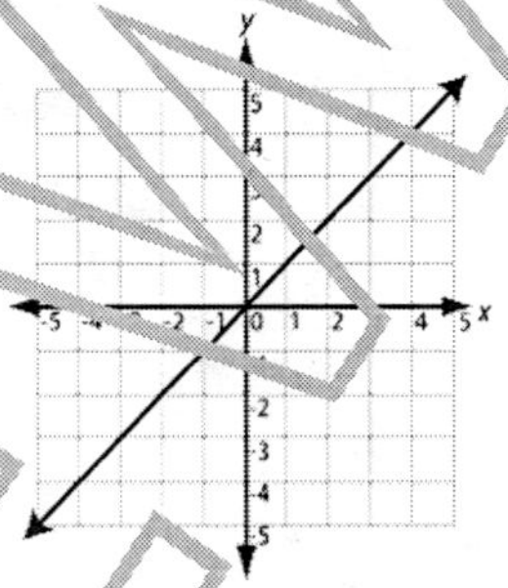

G.

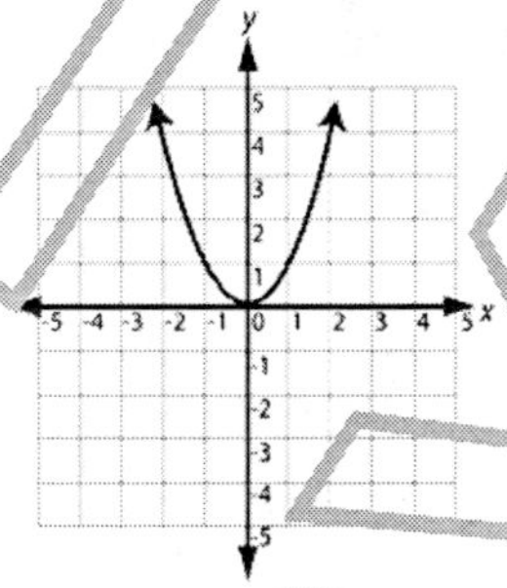

H.

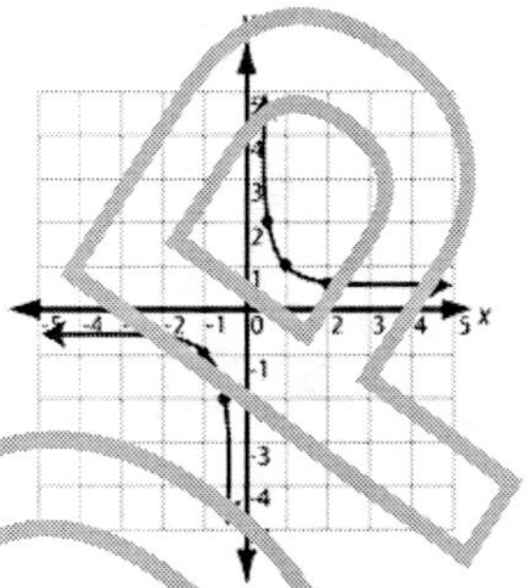

J.

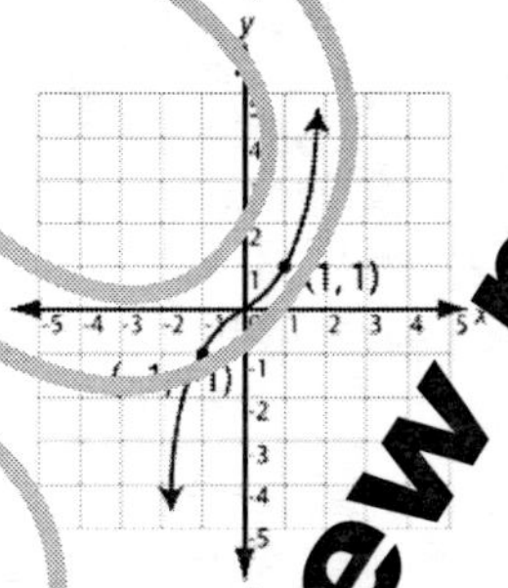

K.

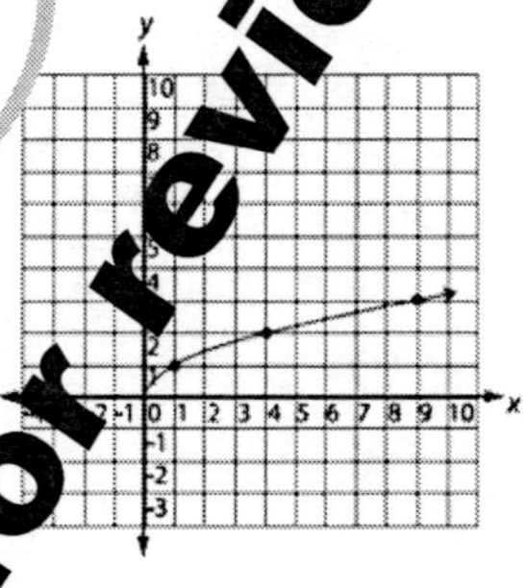

3. $f(x) = \dfrac{1}{x}$ does not exist at what point?

A. $x = 1$
B. $x = -1$
C. x exists everywhere
D. $y = 0$
E. $x = 0$

4. The equation of a hyperbola is $\dfrac{(x+12)^2}{121} - \dfrac{(y-10)^2}{144} = 1$.
Which of the following points does not lie on one of its asymptotes?

F. $(-23, -22)$
G. $(-23, -2)$
H. $(-23, 22)$
J. $(-1, -2)$
K. $(-1, 22)$

5. The origin of a coordinate grid lies on a circle with a center at the point $(-5, 12)$. What is the equation of the circle?

A. $(x-5)^2 + (y+12)^2 = 13$
B. $(x+5)^2 + (y-12)^2 = 13$
C. $(x-5)^2 + (y-12)^2 = 169$
D. $(x-5)^2 + (y+12)^2 = 169$
E. $(x+5)^2 + (y-12)^2 = 169$

6. A circle has a center at the point $(11, -16)$ and a circumference of 78π units. What is the equation of the circle?

F. $(x-11)^2 + (y+16)^2 = 1521$
G. $(x+11)^2 + (y-16)^2 = 1521$
H. $(x-11)^2 + (y-16)^2 = 1521$
J. $(x-11)^2 + (y+16)^2 = 6084$
K. $(x+11)^2 + (y-16)^2 = 6084$

7. Which of the following equations is that of a parabola with a vertex at $(-10, -3)$ and a point on the parabola is $(-8, 45)$?

A. $y = x^2 + 20x + 97$
B. $y = x^2 + 20x + 100$
C. $y = 12x^2 + 240x + 1197$
D. $y = 12x^2 + 240x + 1200$
E. $y = 12x^2 + 240x + 1203$

8. Elisha set out walking to the bus stop. Suddenly, she realized she had forgotten her lunch box. She ran back home, found her lunch box, and ran to the bus stop so as not to miss her bus. Which of the following graphs best models this situation?

F.

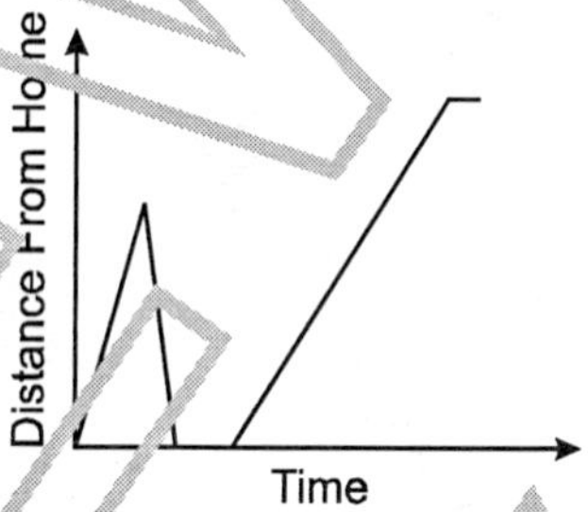

G.

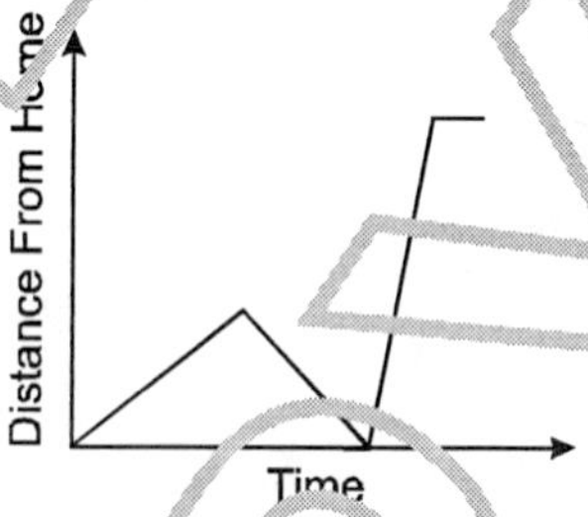

H.

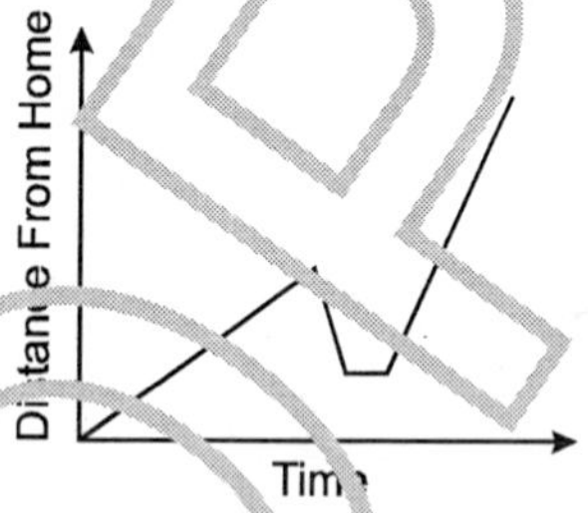

J.

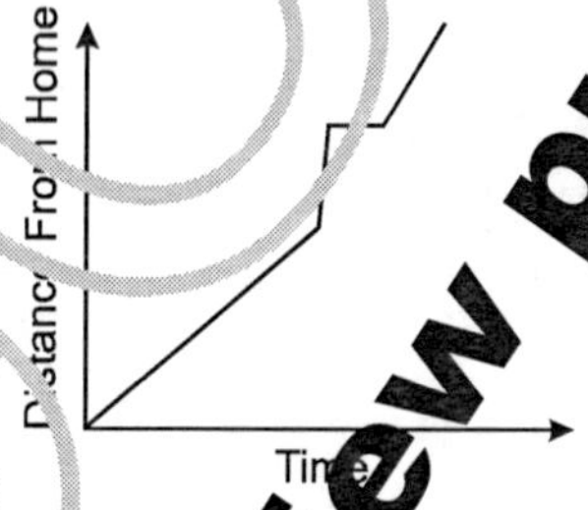

K.

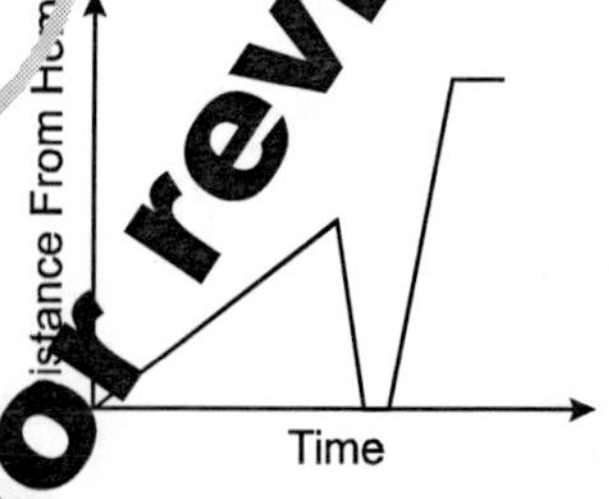

Chapter 14
Systems of Equations and Systems of Inequalities

Two linear equations considered at the same time are called a **system** of linear equations. The graph of a linear equation is a straight line. The graphs of two linear equations can show that the lines are **parallel**, **intersecting** or **collinear**. Two lines that are **parallel** will never intersect and have no ordered pairs in common. If two lines are **intersecting**, they have one point in common, and in this chapter, you will learn to find the ordered pair for that point. If the graph of two linear equations is the same line, the lines are said to be **collinear**.

If you are given a system of two linear equations, and you put both equations in slope-intercept form, you can immediately tell if the graph of the lines will be **parallel**, **intersecting**, or **collinear**.

If two linear equations have the same slope and the same y-intercept, then they are both equations for the same line. They are called **collinear** or **coinciding** lines. A line is made up of an infinite number of points extending infinitely far in two directions. Therefore, collinear lines have an infinite number of points in common.

Example 1: $2x + 3y = -3$ **In slope intercept form:** $y = -\frac{2}{3}x - 1$

$4x + 6y = -6$ **In slope intercept form:** $y = -\frac{2}{3}x - 1$

The slope and y-intercept of both lines are the same. These are collinear lines.

If two linear equations have the same slope but different y-intercepts, they are **parallel** lines. Parallel lines never touch each other, so they have no points in common.

If two linear equations have different slopes, then they are intersecting lines and share exactly one point in common.

The chart below summarizes what we know about the graphs of two equations in slope-intercept form.

y-Intercepts	Slopes	Graphs	Number of Solutions
same	same	collinear	infinite
different	same	distinct parallel lines	none (they never touch)
same or different	different	intersecting lines	exactly one

For the pairs of equations below, put each equation in slope-intercept form, and tell whether the graphs of the lines will be collinear, parallel, or intersecting.

1. $x - y = -1$
   $-x + y = -1$

2. $x - 2y = 4$
   $-x + 2y = 6$

3. $y - 2 = x$
   $x + 2 = y$

4. $x = y - 1$
   $-x = y$

5. $2x + 5y = 10$
   $4x + 10y = 20$

6. $x + y = 3$
   $x - y = 1$

7. $2y = 4y - 6$
   $-6x + y = 3$

8. $x + y = 5$
   $2x + 2y = 10$

9. $2x = 3y - 6$
   $4x = 6y - 6$

10. $2x - 2 = 2$
    $3y = -x + 5$

11. $x = -y$
    $x = 4 - y$

12. $2x = y$
    $x + y = 3$

13. $x = y + 1$
    $y = x + 1$

14. $x - 2y = 4$
    $-2x + 4y = -8$

15. $2x + 3y = 4$
    $-2x + 3y = -8$

16. $2x - 4y = 1$
    $-6x + 12y = 3$

17. $-3x + 4y = 1$
    $6x + 8y = 2$

18. $x + y = 2$
    $5x + 5y = 10$

19. $x + y = 4$
    $x - y = 4$

20. $y = -x + 3$
    $x - y = 1$

14.1 Finding Common Solutions for Intersecting Lines

When two lines intersect, they share exactly one point in common.

Example 2: $3x + 4y = 20$ and $4x + 2y = 12$

Put each equation in slope-intercept form.

$$\begin{aligned} 3x + 4y &= 20 \\ 4y &= -3x + 20 \\ y &= -\tfrac{3}{4}x + 5 \end{aligned} \qquad \begin{aligned} 2y - 4x &= 12 \\ 2y &= 4x + 12 \\ y &= 2x + 6 \end{aligned}$$

slope-intercept form

Straight lines with different slopes are **intersecting lines**. Look at the graphs of the lines on the same Cartesian plane.

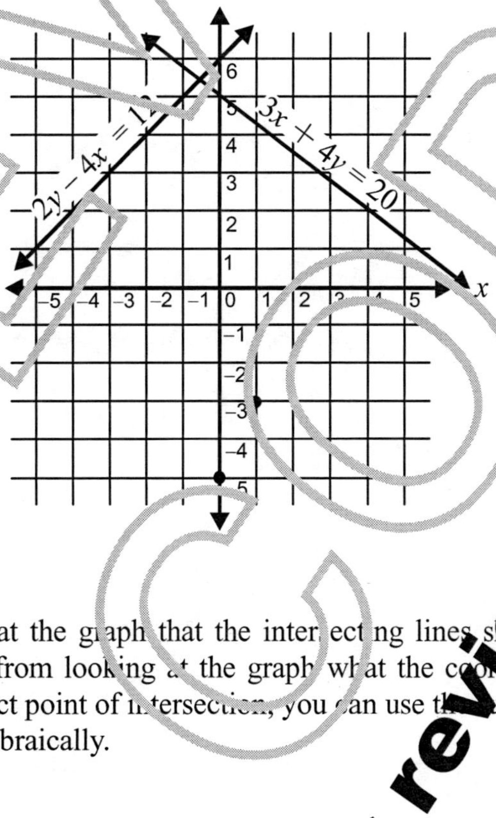

You can see from looking at the graph that the intersecting lines share one point in common. However, it is hard to tell from looking at the graph what the coordinates are for the point of intersection. To find the exact point of intersection, you can use the **substitution method** to solve the system of equations algebraically.

14.2 Solving Systems of Equations by Substitution

You can solve systems of equations by using the substitution method.

Example 3: Find the point of intersection of the following two equations:

Equation 1: $x - y = 3$
Equation 2: $2x + y = 9$

Step 1: Solve one of the equations for x or y. Let's choose to solve equation 1 for x.
Equation 1: $x - y = 3$
$x = y + 3$

Step 2: Substitute the value of x from equation 1 in place of x in equation 2.
Equation 2: $2x + y = 9$
$2(y + 3) + y = 9$
$2y + 6 + y = 9$
$3y + 6 = 9$
$3y = 3$
$y = 1$

Step 3: Substitute the solution for y back in equation 1 and solve for x.
Equation 1: $x - y = 3$
$x - 1 = 3$
$x = 4$

Step 4: The solution set is $(4, 1)$. Substitute in one or both of the equations to check.

Equation 1: $x - y = 3$
$4 - 1 = 3$
$3 = 3$

Equation 2: $2x + y = 9$
$2(4) + 1 = 9$
$8 + 1 = 9$
$9 = 9$

The point $(4, 1)$ is common for both equations. This is the **point of intersection**.

For each of the following pairs of equations, find the point of intersection, the common solution, using the substitution method.

1. $x + 2y = 8$
   $2x - 3y = 2$
2. $x - y = -5$
   $x + y = 1$
3. $x - y = 4$
   $x + y = 2$
4. $x - y = -1$
   $x + y = 9$
5. $-x + y = 2$
   $x + y = 8$
6. $x + 4y = 10$
   $x + 5y = 12$
7. $2x + 3y = 2$
   $4x - 9y = -1$
8. $x + 3y = 5$
   $x - y = 1$
9. $-x = y - 1$
   $x = y - 1$
10. $x - 2y = 2$
    $2y + x = -2$
11. $3x + 2y = 1$
    $2x + 4y = 10$
12. $3x - y = 2$
    $5x + y = 6$
13. $2x + 3y = 3$
    $4x + 5y = 5$
14. $x - y = 1$
    $-x - y = 1$
15. $x = y + 3$
    $y = 3 - x$

14.3 Solving Systems of Equations by Adding or Subtracting

You can solve systems of equations algebraically by adding or subtracting an equation from another equation or system of equations.

Example 4: Find the point of intersection of the following two equations.
Equation 1: $x + y = 10$
Equation 2: $-x + 4y = 5$

Step 1: Eliminate one of the variables by adding the two equations together. Since the x has the same coefficient in each equation, but opposite signs, it will cancel nicely by adding.

$$\begin{aligned} x + y &= 10 \\ +(-x + 4y &= 5) & \text{Add each like term together.} \\ \hline 0 + 5y &= 15 & \text{Simplify.} \\ 5y &= 15 & \text{Divide both sides by 5.} \\ y &= 3 \end{aligned}$$

Step 2: Substitute the solution for y back into an equation, and solve for x.

$$\begin{aligned} \text{Equation 1:} \quad x + y &= 10 & \text{Substitute 3 for } y. \\ x + 3 &= 10 & \text{Subtract 3 from both sides.} \\ x &= 7 \end{aligned}$$

Step 3: The solution set is $(7, 3)$. To check, substitute the solution into both of the original equations.

Equation 1:
$$\begin{aligned} x + y &= 10 \\ 7 + 3 &= 10 \\ 10 &= 10 \end{aligned}$$

Equation 2:
$$\begin{aligned} -x + 4y &= 5 \\ -(7) + 4(3) &= 5 \\ -7 + 12 &= 5 \\ 5 &= 5 \end{aligned}$$

The point $(7, 3)$ is the point of intersection.

Example 5: Find the point of intersection of the following two equations:
Equation 1: $3x - 2y = -1$
Equation 2: $-4y = -x - 7$

Step 1: Put the variables on the same side of each equation. Take equation 2 out of y-intercept form.

$$\begin{aligned} -4y &= -x - 7 & \text{Add } x \text{ to both sides.} \\ x - 4y &= -x + x - 7 & \text{Simplify.} \\ x - 4y &= -7 \end{aligned}$$

Step 2: Add the two equations together to cancel one variable. Since each variable has the same sign and different coefficients, we have to multiply one equation by a negative number so one of the variables will cancel. Equation 1's y variable has a coefficient of 2, and if multiplied by -2, the y will have the same variable as the y in equation 2, but a different sign. This will cancel nicely when added.

$$\begin{aligned} -2\,(3x - 2y &= -1) & \text{Multiply by } -2. \\ -6x + 4y &= 2 \end{aligned}$$

Step 3: Add the two equations.

$$\begin{aligned} -6x + 4y &= 2 \\ +(x - 4y &= -7) \\ \hline -5x + 0 &= -5 \\ -5x &= -5 \\ x &= 1 \end{aligned}$$

Add equation 2 to equation 1.
Simplify.
Divide both sides by −5.

Step 4: Substitute the solution for x back into an equation and solve for y.

Equation 1:

$3x - 2y = -1$	Substitute 1 for x.
$3(1) - 2y = -1$	Simplify.
$3 - 2y = -1$	Subtract 3 from both sides.
$3 - 3 - 2y = -1 - 3$	Simplify.
$-2y = -4$	Divide both sides by −2.
$y = 2$	

Step 5: The solution set is $(1, 2)$. To check, substitute the solution into both of the original equations.

Equation 1:
$$\begin{aligned} 3x - 2y &= -1 \\ 3(1) - 2(2) &= -1 \\ 3 - 4 &= -1 \\ -1 &= -1 \end{aligned}$$

Equation 2:
$$\begin{aligned} -4y &= -x - 7 \\ -4(2) &= -1 - 7 \\ -8 &= -8 \end{aligned}$$

The point $(1, 2)$ is the point of intersection.

For each of the following pairs of equations, find the point of intersection by adding the 2 equations together. Remember you might need to change the coefficients and/or signs of the variables before adding.

1. $x + 2y = 8$
   $-x - 3y = 2$

2. $x - y = 5$
   $2x + y = 1$

3. $x - y = -1$
   $x + y = 9$

4. $3x - y = -1$
   $x + y = 13$

5. $-x + 4y = 2$
   $x + y = 8$

6. $x + 4y = 10$
   $x + 7y = 16$

7. $2x - y = 2$
   $4x - 3y = -3$

8. $x + 3y = 13$
   $5x - y = 1$

9. $-x = y - 1$
   $x = y - 1$

10. $x - y = 2$
    $2y + x = 5$

11. $5x + 2y =$ [illegible]
    $4x + 8y = 20$

12. $3x -$ [illegible] $= 14$
    $x - y = 6$

13. [illegible] $+ 3y = 3$
    $3x + 5y = 5$

14. $x - 4y = 6$
    $-x - y = -1$

15. $x = 2y + 3$
    $y = 3 - x$

14.4 Graphing Systems of Inequalities

Systems of inequalities are best solved graphically. Look at the following example.

Example 6: Sketch the solution set of the following systems of inequalities:

$y > -2x - 1$ and $y \leq 3x$

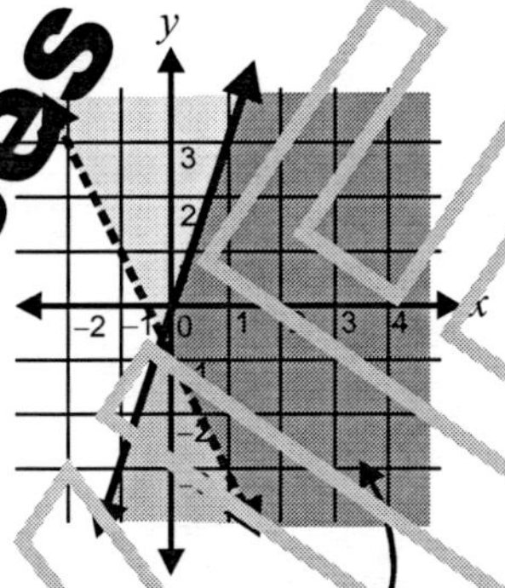

solution set

Step 1: Graph both inequalities on a Cartesian plane. Study the chapter on graphing inequalities if you need to review.

Step 2: Shade the portion of the graph that represents the solution set to each inequality just as you did in the chapter on graphing inequalities.

Step 3: Any shaded region that overlaps is the solution set of both inequalities.

Graph the following systems of inequalities on your own graph paper. Shade and identify the solution set for both inequalities.

1. $2x + 2y \geq -4$
   $3y < 2x + 6$
2. $7x + 7y \leq 21$
   $3x < 6y - 24$
3. $9x + 12y < 36$
   $34x - 17y > 34$
4. $-11x - 22y \geq 44$
   $-4x + 2y \leq 8$
5. $24x < 72 + 36y$
   $11x + 22y \leq -33$
6. $15x - 60 < 30y$
   $20x + 10y < 40$
7. $-12x + 24y > -24$
   $10x < -5y + 15$
8. $y \geq 2x + 2$
   $y < -x - 3$
9. [illegible] $+ 4y \geq 12$
   $y > -3x + 2$
10. $-3x \leq 6 + 2y$
    $y \geq -x - 2$
11. $2x - 2y \leq 4$
    $3x + 3y \leq -9$
12. $-x \geq -2y - 2$
    $-2x - 2y > 4$

14.5 Solving Word Problems with Systems of Equations

Certain word problems can be solved using systems of equations.

Example 7: In a game show, Andre earns 6 points for every right answer and loses 12 points for every wrong answer. He has answered correctly 12 times as many as he has missed. His final score was 120. How many times did he answer correctly?

Step 1: Let r = number of right answers.
Let w = number of wrong answers.

We know 2 facts of information that can be made into equations with 2 variables.

He earns +6 points for right answers and loses 12 points for wrong answers.

His wins and losses = 120

$$\begin{aligned} 6r - 12w &= 120 \\ 12w &= r \end{aligned}$$

12 times the number of wrong answers = the number of right answers.

Step 2: Substitute the value for r $(12w)$ in the first equation.

$$\begin{aligned} 6(12w) - 12w &= 120 \\ 72w - 12w &= 120 \\ 60w &= 120 \\ w &= 2 \end{aligned}$$

Step 3: Substitute the value for w back in the equation.

$$\begin{aligned} 6r - 12(2) &= 120 \\ 6r - 24 &= 120 \\ 6r &= 144 \\ r &= 24 \end{aligned}$$

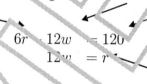

Use systems of equations to solve the following word problems.

1. The sum of two numbers is 210 and their difference is 30. What are the two numbers?

2. The sum of two numbers is 126 and their difference is 42. What are the two numbers?

3. Kayla gets paid \$6.00 for raking leaves and \$8.00 for mowing the lawn for the neighbors around her subdivision. This year she mowed the lawns 12 times more than she raked leaves. In total, she made \$918.00 for doing both. How many times did she rake the leaves?

4. Prices for the movie were \$4.00 for children and \$8.00 for adults. The total amount of ticket sales was \$1,176. There were 172 tickets sold. How many adults and children bought tickets?

5. A farmer sells a dozen eggs at the market for \$2.00 and one of his bags of grain for \$5.00. He has sold 5 times as many bags of grain as he has dozens of eggs. By the end of the day, he has made \$243.00 worth of sales. How many bags of grain did he sell?

6. Every time Lauren does one of her chores, she gets 15 minutes to talk on the phone. When she does not perform one of her chores, she gets 20 minutes of phone time taken away. This week she has done her chores 5 times more than she has not performed her chores. In total, she has accumulated 165 minutes. How many times has Lauren not performed her chores?

7. The choir sold boxes of candy and teddy bears near Valentine's Day to raise money. They sold twice as many boxes of candy as they did teddy bears. Bears sold for \$8.00 each and candy sold for \$6.00. They collected \$360. How much of each item did they sell?

8. Mr. Marlow keeps ten and twenty dollar bills in his dresser drawer. He has 1 less than twice as many 10's as 20's. He has \$550 altogether. How many tens does he have?

9. Kosta was a contestant on a math quiz show. For every correct answer, Kosta received \$18.00. For every incorrect answer, Kosta lost \$24.00. Kosta answered the questions correctly twice as often as he answered the questions incorrectly. In total, Kosta won \$72.00. How many questions did Kosta answer incorrectly?

10. John Vasilovik works in landscaping. He gets paid \$50 for each house he pressure washes and \$20 for each lawn he mows. He gets 4 times more jobs for mowing lawns than for pressure washing houses. During a given month John earned \$2,600. How many houses did John pressure wash?

14.6 Interpreting and Graphing Real-World Systems of Equations

On the ACT, you will be asked to set up systems of two linear equations from word problems, and evaluate real-world graphs with intersecting lines.

Example 8: Felipe is choosing between kayak rental companies on the river. WhiteWater Xtreme offers kayaks for \$50 up-front plus \$5 per hour, while Down The River offers kayaks for \$20 up-front plus \$10 per hour. Write a system of equations that depicts this situation. How many hours would it take for the total cost to be the same for each company? What is that total cost for that number of hours? If Felipe plans to spend 4 hours out on the river, which company should he choose to pay the least amount of money?

Step 1: Set up a system of equations that represents this situation. Identify your variables. In this case, x is the number of hours that Felipe rents the kayak, and y is the total cost (in dollars). Translate each phrase into its own equation:

WhiteWater Xtreme's total cost, y, is \$50 plus \$5 times the number of hours x of the rental.

$y = 50 + 5x$

Down the River's total cost, y, is \$20 plus \$10 times the number of hours x of the rental.

$y = 20 + 10x$

Step 2: How many hours would it take for the total cost to be the same for each company? What is that total cost for that number of hours?

Substitute for y into one of the equations:

$y = 20 + 10x \Longrightarrow (50 + 5x) = 20 + 10x$

Step 3: Solve for x.

$50 - 20 + 5x - 5x = 20 - 20 + 10x - 5x$

$30 = 5x$

$x = 6$

Step 4: Plug x back into either equation to solve for y.

$y = 50 + 5(6) = 50 + 30 = 80$

At 6 hours, the total cost is the same, \$80.

Step 5: Felipe plans to spend 4 hours out on the river. Which company should he choose to pay the least amount of money?

Plug 4 into both equations for x.

WhiteWater Xtreme: $y = 50 + 5(4) = 50 + 20 =$ \$70 total cost

Down the River: $y = 20 + 10(4) = 20 + 40 =$ \$60 total cost.

Down the River is cheaper by \$10.

Example 9: Norman works for the Maryland Forest Service. He is in charge of planting trees in the "buffer zones" within 100 ft of two streams. The graph below shows the number of new trees planted along each stream by month:

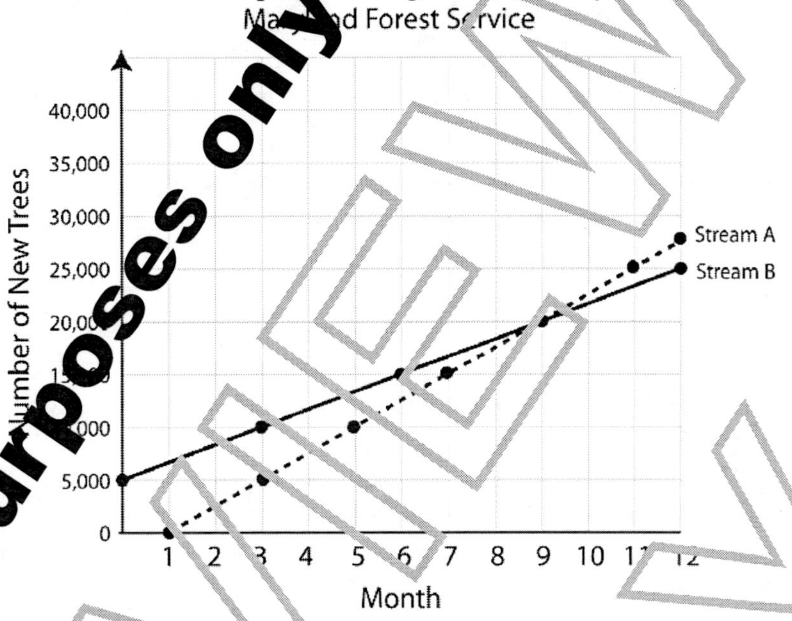

At what point did the two streams have the same number of new trees? Up to that point, which stream had fewer new trees? After that point, which stream had fewer new trees?

Answer: The streams had the same number of new trees in month 9 (20,000 new trees). Up to that point, Stream A had fewer new trees, and Stream B had more. After that point, Stream B had fewer new trees, and Stream A had more.

Answer the following questions about the graph of system of equations.

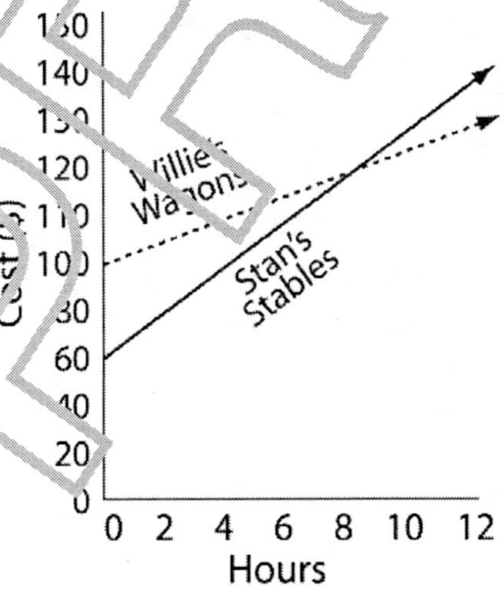

1. Find the system of equations that represents the graph to the left.
2. Willie's Wagons and Stan's stables have different prices when it comes to horseback riding lessons, but the price is the same at one point. How many hours would you sign up for horseback riding lessons for it to be the same price at Willie's Wagons and Stan's Stables?
3. How much does it cost for four hours of horseback riding lessons at Willie's Wagons?
4. Which place is more expensive for twelve or more hours of horseback riding lessons?

14.7 Comparing the Graphs of Linear and Quadratic Equations

If the graph of the quadratic equation $y = ax^2 + bx + c$ intersects a line segment at its endpoints (x_1, y_1) and (x_2, y_2), the portion of the graph of the quadratic equation in the interval from $x = x_1$ to $x = x_2$ will always be longer than the line segment.

If $a > 0$, the portion of the graph of the quadratic equation in the interval from $x = x_1$ to $x = x_2$ will be below the line segment, and if $a < 0$, it will be above the line segment.

The line segment can be used to approximate the area under the graph of the quadratic equation in the interval from $x = x_1$ to $x = x_2$.

Example 10: The graph of the quadratic equation $y = ax^2 - 5x + c$ in the interval from $x = -4$ to $x = 0$ intersects the line segment $\overline{FG}$ at its endpoints $(-4, 13)$ and $(0, 1)$ as shown below. Find the values of a and c, and determine the y-coordinate of the point on the curve with an x-coordinate of -3.

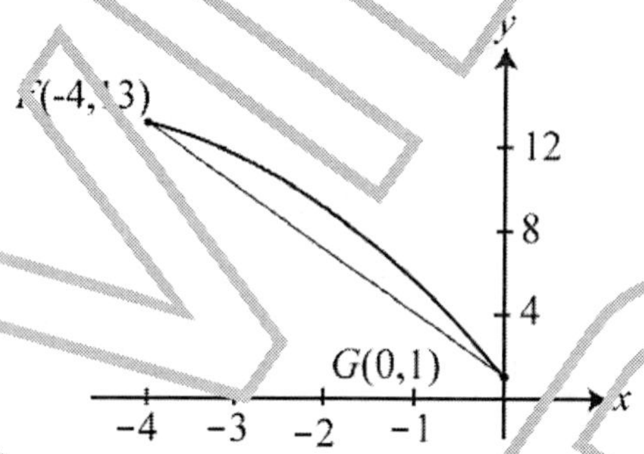

Step 1: To find the values of a and c, the points $(-4, 13)$ and $(0, 1)$ should be substituted into the quadratic equation $y = ax^2 - 5x + c$ as follows:

$13 = a(-4)^2 - 5(-4) + c$

$13 = 16a + 20 + c$

$13 - 20 = 16a + 20 + c - 20$

$16a + c = -7$

$1 = a(0)^2 - 5(0) + c = 0a - 0 + c = 0 - 0 + c$

$c = 1$

Step 2: The value of c can now be substituted back into the equation $16a + c = -7$ as follows to solve for a:

$16a + 1 = -7$

$16a + 1 - 1 = -7 - 1$

$16a = -8$

$a = -\frac{8}{16} = -\frac{1}{2}$

Step 3: Because the value of a is $-\frac{1}{2}$ and the value of c is 1, the quadratic equation is $y = -\frac{1}{2}x^2 - 5x + 1$.

Therefore, the y-coordinate of the point on the curve with an x-coordinate of -3 is $y = -\frac{1}{2}(-3)^2 - 5(-3) + 1 = -\frac{1}{2}(9) + 15 + 1 = -\frac{9}{2} + 15 + 1 = \frac{23}{2}$.

The graph of the quadratic equation $y = ax^2 - 8x + c$ in the interval from $x = -3$ to $x = 0$ intersects the line segment $\overline{FG}$ at its endpoints $(-3, 53)$ and $(0, 2)$ as shown below. Use this information to answer the following questions.

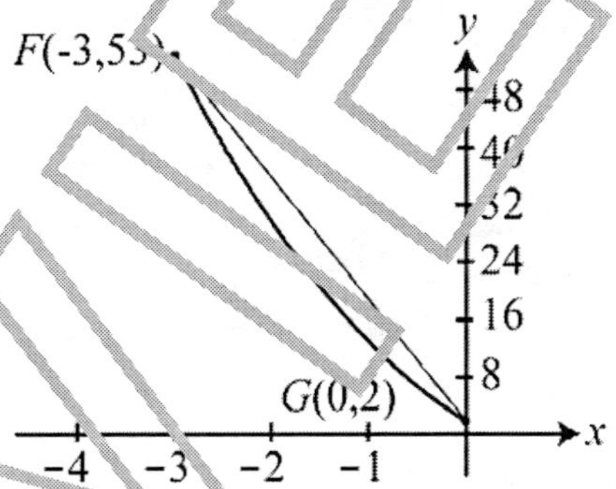

1. What is the value of a?

2. What is the value of c?

3. What is the y-coordinate of the point on the curve with an x-coordinate of -2?

4. What is the length of $\overline{FG}$?

5. Is the length of the graph of the quadratic equation from $x = -3$ to $x = 0$ greater than equal to, or less than the length of $\overline{FG}$?

6. If the value of a had not already been found, how could it be determined if a is positive or negative?

Example 11: Approximate the area under the graph of the quadratic equation $y = 4x^2 - 7x - 2$ shown below in the interval from $x = 2$ to $x = 5$ by using line segment $\overline{AB}$.

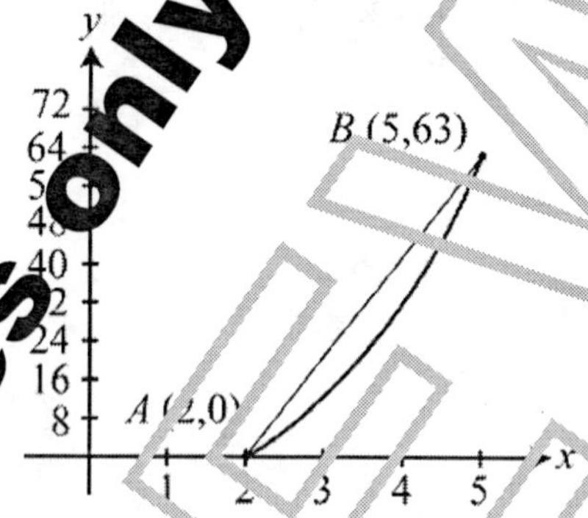

Step 1: To approximate the area under the graph of the quadratic equation $y = 4x^2 - 7x - 2$ in the interval from $x = 2$ to $x = 5$, the area under the line segment $\overline{AB}$ can be found. Finding the area under $\overline{AB}$ would be the same as finding the area of a triangle with a base of length $5 - 2$, or 3, and height $63 - 0$, or 63.

Step 2: Since the formula for the area of a triangle is $A = \left(\frac{\text{base} \times \text{height}}{2}\right)$, the area under line segment $\overline{AB}$ is $\left(\frac{3 \times 63}{2}\right) = \left(\frac{189}{2}\right) = 94.5$.

Therefore, the approximate area under the graph of the quadratic equation $y = 4x^2 - 7x - 2$ is 94.5.

NOTE: The actual area under the curve is less than 94.5.

Approximate the area under each of the following quadratic equations in the given interval by using the line segment with the given endpoints.

7. Quadratic equation: $y = 9x^2 - x - 8$; Interval: $1 \le x \le 4$; Endpoints: $(1, 0), (4, 132)$
8. Quadratic equation: $y = -2x^2 + 2x + 4$; Interval: $0 \le x \le 2$; Endpoints: $(0, 4), (2, 0)$
9. Quadratic equation: $y = x^2 - 7x + 12$; Interval: $4 \le x \le 7$; Endpoints: $(4, 0), (7, 12)$
10. Quadratic equation: $y = 3x^2 - 10x$; Interval: $-3 \le x \le 0$; Endpoints: $(-3, 57), (0, 0)$
11. Quadratic equation: $y = -x^2 + 8x + 20$; Interval: $-2 \le x \le 2$; Endpoints: $(-2, 0), (2, 32)$
12. Quadratic equation: $y = 5x^2 - 11x + 2$; Interval: $2 \le x \le 5$; Endpoints: $(2, 0), (5, 72)$
13. Quadratic equation: $y = -4x^2 + x + 5$; Interval: $-1 \le x \le 0$; Endpoints: $(-1, 0), (0, 5)$
14. Quadratic equation: $y = x^2 - 15x + 54$; Interval: $9 \le x \le 12$; Endpoints: $(9, 0), (12, 18)$
15. Quadratic equation: $y = 6x^2 - 3x$; Interval: $0 \le x \le 4$; Endpoints: $(0, 0), (4, 84)$

If the a in the equation is negative, the curve is greater than the line segment formed by the endpoints.

Chapter 14 Review

For each pair of equations below, tell whether the graphs of the lines will be collinear, parallel, or intersecting.

1. $y = 4x + 1$
   $y = 4x - 3$
2. $y - 4 = x$
   $2x + 8 = 2y$
3. $x + y = 5$
   $x - y = -1$
4. $2y - 3x = 6$
   $4y = 6x + 8$
5. $5y = 3x - 7$
   $4x - 3y = -7$
6. $2x - 2y = 2$
   $y - x = -1$

Find the common solution for each of the following pairs of equations.

7. $x - y = 2$
   $x + 4y = -3$
8. $x + y = 1$
   $x + 3y = 1$
9. $-4y = -2x + 4$
   $x = -2y - 2$
10. $2x + 3y = 20$
    $5y = 12 - x$
11. $x = y - 3$
    $-x = y + 3$
12. $-2x + y = -3$
    $x - y = 9$

Find the point of intersection for each pair of equations by adding and/or subtracting the two equations.

13. $2x + y = 4$
    $3x - y = 6$
14. $x + 2y = 3$
    $x + 5y = 0$
15. $x + y = 1$
    $y = x + 7$
16. $2x + 4y = 5$
    $3x + 8y = 9$
17. $2x - 2y = 7$
    $3x - 5y = \frac{5}{2}$
18. $x - 3y = -2$
    $y = -\frac{1}{3}x + 4$

Graph the following systems of inequalities on your own graph paper. Identify the solution set to both inequalities.

19. $x + 2y \geq 2$
    $2x - y \leq 4$
20. $20x + 10y \leq 40$
    $3x + 2y \geq 6$
21. $6x + 8y \leq -24$
    $-4x + 8y \geq 16$
22. $14x - 7y \geq -28$
    $3x + 4y \leq -12$
23. $2y \geq 6x + 6$
    $2x - 4y \geq -4$
24. $9x - 6y \geq$ [illegible]
    $3y \geq 6x - 2$

Use systems of equations to solve the following word problems.

25. Chelsea Johnson is a bank teller. At the end of the day, she had 85 $5 and $10 bills. They should total $785. How many $5's and $10's should she have in her drawer?

26. Hargrove High School sold 227 tickets for their last basketball game. Adult tickets sold for $5 and student tickets were $2. How many adult tickets were sold if the ticket sales totalled $574?

27. Every time Stephen walks the dog, he gets 30 minutes to play video or computer games. When he does not take out the dog on time, he gets a mess to clean up and loses 1 hour of video/computer game time. This week he has walked the dog on time 8 times more than he did not walk the dog on time. In total, he has accumulated 3 hours of video/computer time. How many times has Stephen not walked the dog on time?

28. On Friday, Rosa bought party hats and kazoos for her friend's birthday party. On Saturday she decided to purchase more when she found out more people were coming. How much did she pay for each party hat?

	Hats	Kazoos	Total Cost
Friday	15	20	\$15.00
Saturday	10	5	\$8.75

29. Timothy and Jesse went to purchase sports clothing they needed as soccer players. The table below shows what they bought and the amount they paid. What is the price of 1 soccer jersey?

	Soccer Jerseys	Tube Socks	Total Cost
Timothy	4	7	\$78.30
Jesse	3	5	\$57.60

The graph of the quadratic equation $y = ax^2 + 25x + c$ in the interval from $x = 0$ to $x = 3$ intersects the line segment $\overline{FG}$ at its endpoints $(0, 0)$ and $(3, 111)$ as shown below. Use this information to answer the following questions.

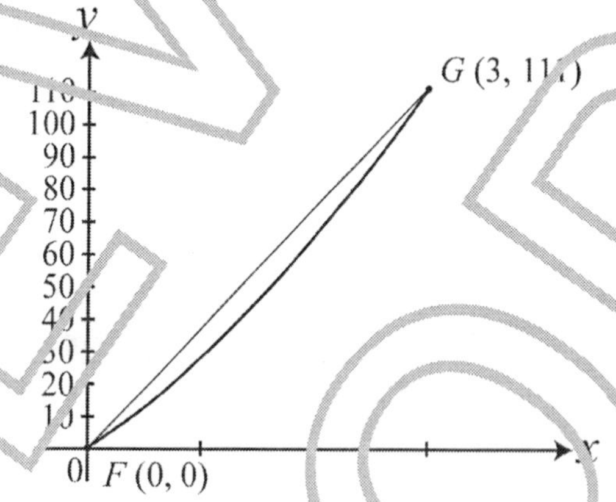

30. What is the value of a?

31. What is the value of c?

32. What is the y-coordinate of the point on the curve with an x-coordinate of 2?

33. Is the length of the graph of the quadratic equation from $x = 0$ to $x = 3$ greater than, equal to, or less than the length of $\overline{FG}$?

Approximate the area under each of the following quadratic equations in the given interval by using the line segment with the given endpoints.

34. Quadratic equation: $y = 12x^2 + 2x + 5$; Interval: $1 \leq x \leq 3$; Endpoints: $(1, 0)$, $(3, 119)$

35. Quadratic equation: $y = -3x^2 + 4x + 70$; Interval: $-4 \leq x \leq 0$; Endpoints: $(-4, 0)$, $(0, 70)$

Chapter 14 Test

1. Consider the following equations:

   $f(x) = 6x + 2$ and $f(x) = 3x + 2$

   Which of the following statements is true concerning the graphs of these equations?

   A. The lines are collinear.
   B. The lines intersect at exactly one point.
   C. The lines are parallel to each other.
   D. The graphs of the lines intersect each other at the point $(0, 2)$.
   E. The graphs of the lines intersect each other at the point $(2, 0)$.

2. What is the solution to the following system of equations?

   $y = 4x - 8$
   $y = 2x$

   F. $(-4, -8)$
   G. $(4, 4)$
   H. $(-1, -2)$
   J. $(1, 2)$
   K. $(4, 8)$

3. The graph of which pair of equations below is parallel?

   A. $x + 3y = 3$
   $3x + y = 3$

   B. $2x + 3y = 6$
   $9x - 3y = 6$

   C. $x - 3y = 6$
   $3y - x = -3$

   D. $x + 3 = y$
   $x - 3 = 2y$

   E. $x - 3 = 2y$
   $x - 3 = 2y$

4. Two lines are shown on the grid. One line passes through the origin and the other passes through $(-1, -1)$ with a y-intercept of 2. Which pair of equations below the grid identifies these lines?

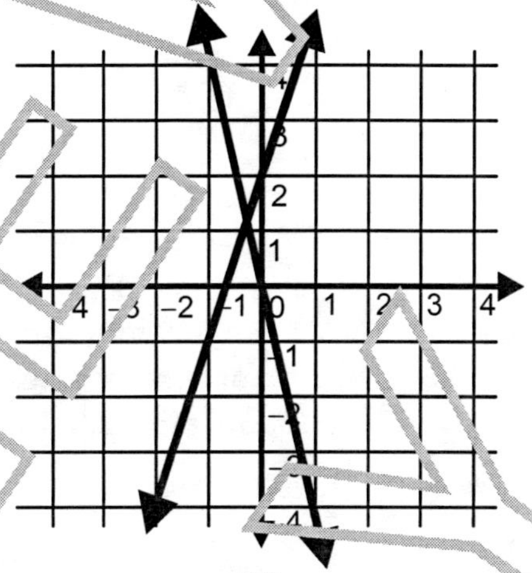

   F. $y = \frac{1}{4}x$ and $y = \frac{1}{3}x + 2$
   G. $x - 2y = 6$ and $2x + y = 4$
   H. $y = 4x$ and $y = \frac{1}{2}x$
   J. $y = 3x + 2$ and $y = -4x$
   K. $y = 2x + 2$ and $y = -3x$

5. Which ordered pair is a solution for the following system of equations?

   $-3x + 7y = 25$
   $3x + 3y = -15$

   A. $(-13, -2)$
   B. $(-6, 1)$
   C. $(-3, -2)$
   D. $(6, 2)$
   E. $(-20, -5)$

6. A coin bank contains dimes and quarters. The number of dimes is three less than four times the number of quarters. The total amount in the bank is \$8.15. How many dimes are in the bank?

F. 13

G. 41

H. 49

J. 51

K. 65

7. Last year, the Blossom Antique Fair required its vendors to pay \$75 to rent a booth and then give 20% of their earnings to a local charity. The cost of participating in the fair is represented in the graph below.

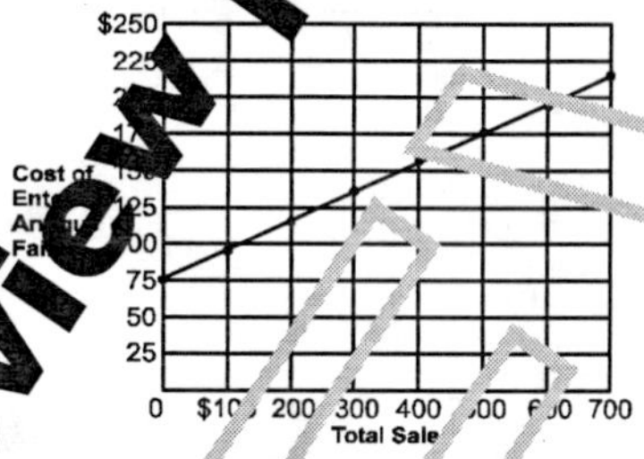

This year, the Blossom Antique Fair is charging only \$50 to rent a booth, but is requiring its vendors to give 25% of their earnings to a local charity. How will the graph of the cost of participating in the fair this year compare to the graph of last year's cost?

A. The graph for this year's cost will have a greater y-intercept and a steeper slope.

B. The graph for this year's cost will have a greater y-intercept, but there will be no change in the slope.

C. The graph for this year's cost will have a smaller y-intercept and a steeper slope.

D. The graph for this year's cost will have a smaller y-intercept, but there will be no change in the slope.

E. The graph for this year's cost will be the same.

8. For the following pair of equations, find the point of intersection (common solution) using the substitution method.

$$-3x - y = -2, 5x + 2y = 20$$

F. $(2, -4)$

G. $(2, 5)$

H. $(-16, 50)$

J. $\left(\frac{1}{5}, \frac{1}{2}\right)$

K. $(5, 2)$

9. The sum of two numbers is fourteen. The sum of six times the smaller number and two equals four less than the product of three and the larger number. Find the two numbers.

A. 6 and 8

B. 5 and 9

C. 3 and 11

D. 4 and 10

E. 14 and 0

10. The graph of the quadratic equation $y = ax^2 - 14x + c$ in the interval from $x = -4$ to $x = 0$ intersects the line segment FG at its endpoints $(-4, 120)$ and $(0, 8)$. What is the y-coordinate of the point on the graph of the quadratic equation that has an x-coordinate of -2?

F. 12

G. 16

H. 28

J. 48

K. 56

11. The graph of $f(x) = x^2$ intersects the graph of $g(x) = x$ at two points. Which of the following statements must be true?

A. $f(x) > g(x)$ between the two points

B. $f(x) < g(x)$ between the two points

C. $f(x) = g(x)$ between the two points

D. $f(x) - g(x) > 0$ between the two points

E. $f(x) - g(x) = 0$ between the two points

Chapter 15
Statistics

15.1 Mean

In statistics, the arithmetic mean is the same as the average. To find the arithmetic mean of a list of numbers, first add together all of the numbers in the list, and then divide by the number of items in the list.

Example 1: Find the mean of 38, 72, 110, 548.

Step 1: First add: $38 + 72 + 110 + 548 = 768$

Step 2: There are 4 numbers in the list so divide the total by 4. $768 \div 4 = 192$
The mean is 192.

Find the mean (average) of the following word problems.

1. Val's science grades are 95, 87, 65, 94, 78, and 97. What is her average?
2. Ann runs a business from her home. The number of orders for the last 7 business days are 17, 24, [illegible], 8, 11, 15, and 9. What is the average number of orders per day?
3. Melissa tracks the number of phone calls she has per day: 8, 2, 5, 4, 7, 3, 6, 1. What is the average number of calls she receives?
4. The Cheese Shop tracks the number of lunches they serve this week: 42, 55, 36, 41, 38, [illegible], and 46. What is the average number of lunches served?
5. Leah drives 364 miles in 7 hours. What is her average miles per hour?

Find the data missing from the following problems.

6. Gabriel earns 87% on his first geography test. He wants to keep a 92% average. What does he need to get on his next test to bring his average up?
7. Rian earned $68.00 on Monday. How much money must she earn on Tuesday to have an average of $80 earned for the two days?
8. Haley, Chuck, Dana, and Chris enter a contest to see who could bake the most chocolate chip cookies in an hour. They bake an average of 75 cookies. Haley bakes 65, Chuck bakes 70, and Dana bakes 90. How many does Chris bake?
9. Four wrestlers make a pact to lose some weight before the competition. They lose an average of 7 pounds each over the course of 3 weeks. Carlos loses 6 pounds, Steve loses 5 pounds, and Greg loses 9 pounds. How many pounds does Wes lose?
10. Three boxes are ready for shipment. The boxes average 26 pounds each. The first box weighs 30 pounds; the second box weighs 25 pounds. How much does the third box weigh?

15.2 Median

In a list of numbers ordered from lowest to highest, the **median** is the middle number. To find the **median**, first arrange the numbers in numerical order. If there is an odd number of items in the list, the **median** is the middle number. If there is an even number of items in the list, the **median** is the **average of the two middle numbers.**

Example 2: Find the median of 42, 35, 45, 37, and 41.

Step 1: Arrange the numbers in numerical order. 35 37 [41] 42 45

Step 2: Find the middle number. The median is 41.

Example 3: Find the median of 14, 53, 42, 6, 14, and 46.

Step 1: Arrange the numbers in numerical order: 6 14 [14 42] 46 53.

Step 2: Find the average of the two middle numbers.
$(14 + 42) \div 2 = 28$. The median is 28.

Find the median in each list of numbers.

1. 35, 55, 40, 30, 45
2. 7, 2, [illegible], 5, 1, 8
3. 65, 42, 60, 46, 90
4. 15, 16, 19, 25, 20
5. 10, 8, 21, 14, 9, 12
6. 43, 36, 20, 40
7. 5, 24, 9, 18, 12, 3
8. 48, 8, 54, 82, 90, 7

15.3 Mode

In statistics, the mode is the number that occurs most frequently in a list of numbers.

Example 4: Exam grades for a math class were as follows:
70 88 92 85 99 85 70 85 99 100 88 70 99 88 88 99 88 92 85 88

Step 1: Count the number of times each number occurs in the list.

70 - 3 times
88 - 6 times
92 - 2 times
85 - 4 times
99 - 4 times
100 - 1 times

Step 2: Find the number that occurs most often.
The mode is 88 because it is listed 6 times. No other number is listed as often.

Find the mode in each of the following lists of numbers.

1. 48, 32, 56, 32, 56, 48, 56
2. 12, 16, 54, 78, 16, 25, 20
3. 5, 4, 8, 3, 4, 2, 7, 8, 4, 2
4. 11, 9, 7, 11, 7, 5, 7, 7, 5
5. 84, 22, 79, 22, 87, 22, 22
6. 95, 87, 65, 94, 78, 95

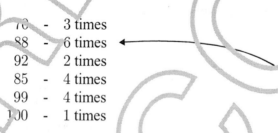

15.4 Applying Measures of Central Tendency

On the ACT, you may be asked to solve real-world problems involving measures of central tendency.

Example 5: Aida is shopping around for the best price on a 17" computer monitor. She travels to seven stores and finds the following prices: \$199, \$159, \$249, \$329, \$199, \$209, and \$189. When Aida goes to the eighth and final store, she finds the price for the 17" monitor is \$549. Which of the measures of central tendency, mean, median, or mode, changes the most as a result of the last price Aida finds?

Step 1: **Solve for all three measures of the seven values.**

Mean: $\frac{\$199 + \$159 + \$249 + \$329 + \$199 + \$209 + \$189}{7} = \$219$

Median: From least to greatest: \$159, \$189, \$199, \$199, \$209, \$249, \$329. The 4th value = \$199

Mode: The number repeated the most is \$199.

Step 2: **Find the mean, median, and mode with the eighth value included.**

Mean: $\frac{\$199 + \$159 + \$249 + \$329 + \$199 + \$209 + \$189 + \$549}{8} = \$260.25$

Median: \$159, \$189, \$199, \$199, \$209, \$249, \$329, \$549. The avg. of 4th and 5th number = \$204

Mode: The number still repeated most is \$199.

Answer: The measure which changed the most by adding the 8th value is the **mean**.

1. The Realty Company has the selling prices for 10 houses sold during the month of July. The following prices are given in thousands of dollars:
   176 89 325 125 107 100 525 61 75 114
   Find the mean, median, and mode of the selling prices. Which measure is most representative for the selling price of such homes? Explain.

2. A soap manufacturing company wants to know if the weight of its product is on target, meaning 4.75 oz. With that purpose in mind, a quality control technician selects 15 bars of soap from production, 5 from each shift, and finds the following weights in oz.

   1st shift: 4.76, 4.75, 4.77, 4.77, 4.74
   2nd shift: 4.72, 4.72, 4.75, 4.76, 4.73
   3rd shift: 4.76, 4.76, 4.77, 4.76, 4.76

   (A) What are the values for the measures of central tendency for the sample from each shift?
   (B) Find the mean, median, and mode for the 24 hour production sample.
   (C) Which measure is the most accurate measure of central tendency for the 24 hour production?
   (D) Find the range of values for each shift. Is the range an effective tool for drawing a conclusion in this case? Why or why not?

Chapter 15 Review

Find the mean, median, mode, and range for each of the following sets of data. Fill in the table below.

❶ Miles Run by Track Team Members

Jeff	24
Eric	20
Craig	19
Simon	20
Elijah	25
Rich	[illegible]
Marcus	[illegible]

❷ 199[illegible] SUMMER OLYMPIC GAMES
Gold Medals Won

Unified Team	45	Hungary	11
United States	37	South Korea	12
Germany	33	France	8
China	16	Australia	7
Cuba	14	Japan	3
Spain	13		

❸ Hardware Store Payroll June Week 2

Erica	$280
Dane	$206
Sam	$240
Nancy	$404
Elsie	$210
Gail	$305
David	$280

Data Set Number	Mean	Median	Mode	Range
❶				
❷			(shaded)	
❸				

4. Jenica bowls three games and scores an average of 116 points per game. She scores 105 on her first game and 128 on her second game. What does she score on her third game?

5. Concession stand sales for each game in season are $320, $540, $230, $450, $280, and $[illegible]0. What is the mean sales per game?

6. Cendrick D'Amitrano works Friday and Saturday delivering pizza. He delivers 8 pizzas on Friday. How many pizzas must he deliver on Saturday to average 11 pizzas per day?

7. Long cooks three Vietnamese dinners that weigh a total of 40 ounces. What is the average weight for each dinner?

8. The Swamp Foxes scored an average of 7 points per soccer game. They scored 9 points in the first game, 4 points in the second game, and 5 points in the third game. What was their score for their fourth game?

9. Shondra is 66 inches tall, and DeWayne is 72 inches tall. How tall is Michael if the average height of these three students is 67 inches?

Nine cooks are asked, "If you use a thermometer, what is the actual temperature inside your oven when it is set at 350°F?" The responses are in the chart below.

Temperature (°F)	104	347	348	349	350	351	352
Number of Cooks	1	1	1	2	[illegible]	2	1

10. Find the mean of the data above.

11. Find the median of the data above.

Use the data given to answer the questions that follow.

The 6th grade did a survey on the number of pets each student had at home. The following give the data produced by the survey.

NUMBER OF PETS PER STUDENT																									
0	2	6	2	1	0	4	2	3	3	[illegible]	2	3	5	1	4	2	0	5	2	3	3	4	3	6	2
5	1	2	3	5	6	3	2	2	[illegible]	2	3	4	3	0	1	4	1	2	4	5	7	6	1	4	7

12. Fill in the frequency table.

Number of Pets	Frequency

13. Fill in the histogram.

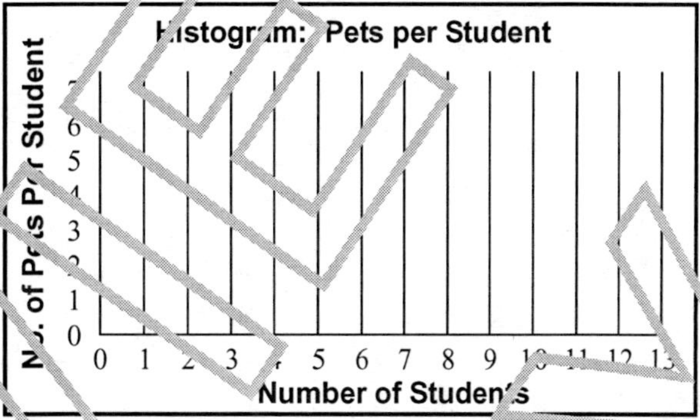

KNIGHTS BASKETBALL Points Scored				
Player	game 1	game 2	game 3	game 4
[illegible]	[illegible]	[illegible]	4	8
Jason	10	8	10	12
Brandon	2	6	[illegible]	6
Ned	1	3	6	2
Austin	0	4	7	8
David	7	2	9	4
Zac	8	6	7	4

14. How many points did the Knights basketball team score in game 1?

15. How many more points does David score in game 3 than in game 1?

16. How many points does Jason score in the first 4 games?

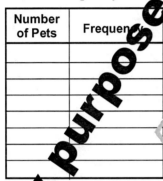

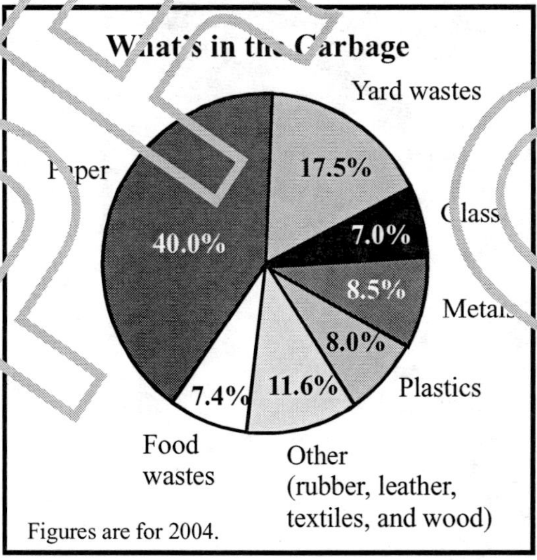

17. In 2004, the United States produced 160 million metric tons of garbage. According to the pie chart, how much glass was in the garbage?

18. Out of the 160 million metric tons of garbage, how much was glass, plastic, and metal?

19. If in 2006, the garbage reaches 200 million metric tons, and the percentage of wastes remains the same as in 2004, how much food in metric tons will be in the 2006 garbage?

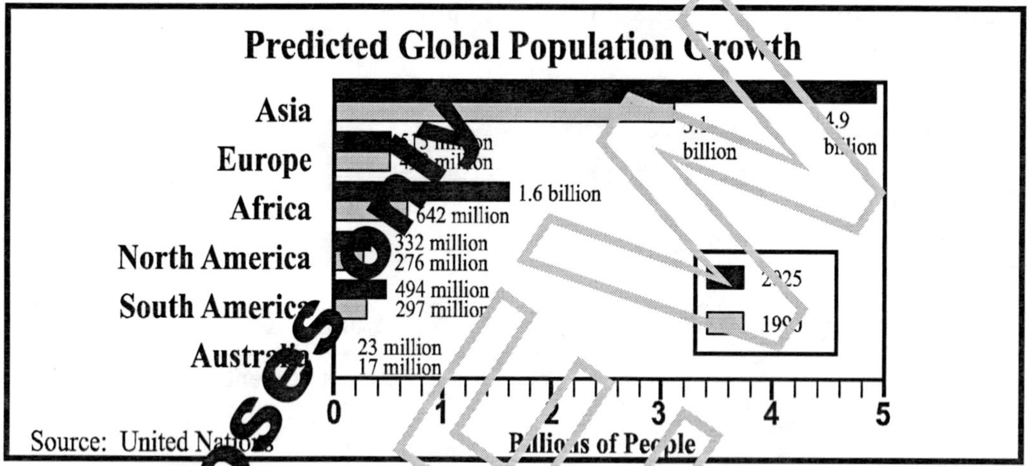

20. By how many people is Asia's population predicted to increase between 1990 and 2025?

21. In 1990, how much larger was Africa's population than Europe's?

22. Where is the population expected to more than double between 1990 and 2025?

Use the pictograph below to answer the following questions.

Number of Military Officers by Branch of Service

U.S. Bureau of the Census, 1994

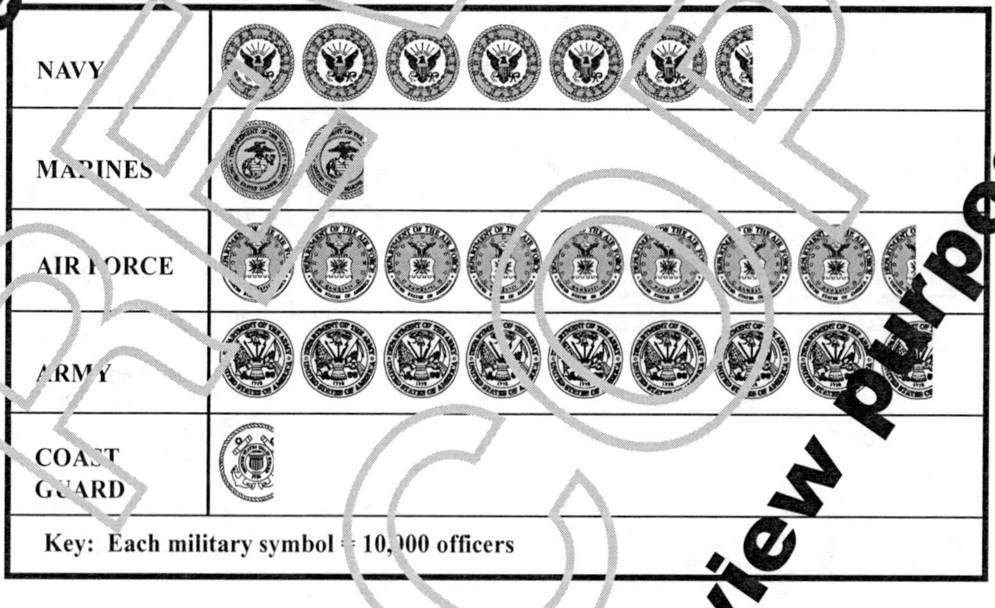

23. How many military officers are in the Marines?

24. Which branch of the service has the fewest number of officers?

25. Are there more Air Force officers or Army officers?

26. How many military officers are there in all?

27. How many officers do the Navy and Marines have altogether?

Chapter 15 Test

1. What is the mean of 36, 54, 66, 45, 36, 36, and 63?

A. 36
B. 45
C. 48
D. 63
E. 27

2. A neighborhood surveyed the times of day people water their lawns and tallied the data below.

Time	Tally
midnight - 3:59 a.m.	||
4:00 a.m. - 7:59 a.m.	𝍸 |
8:00 a.m. - 11:59 a.m.	𝍸 ||||
noon - 3:59 p.m.	𝍸
4:00 p.m. - 7:59 p.m.	𝍸 𝍸
8:00 p.m. - 11:59 p.m.	𝍸 |||

If you wanted to find which was the most popular time of day to water the lawn, it would be best to find the ____________ of data.

F. mean
G. median
H. range
J. mode
K. none of the above

3. Examine the following two data sets:

Set #1: 4[illegible], 55, [illegible]8, 72, 98
Set #2: 20, 3[illegible], 47, 68, 75, 82, 89

Which of the following statements is true?

A. They have the same mode
B. They have the same median.
C. They have the same mean.
D. They have the same mean, median, and mode.
E. None of the above.

4. What is the median of the following set of data?

33, 31, 35, [illegible]4, 3[illegible], 30

F. 32
G. 31
H. 30
J. 29
K. 28

5. Concession stand sales for the first 6 games of the season averaged $400.00. If the total sales of the first 5 games were $320, $540, $230, $450, and $280, what were the total sales for the sixth game?

A. $230
B. $364
C. $580
D. $280
E. $350

6. What is the mean of 12, 23, 8, 26, 3[illegible], [illegible]1, and 9?

F. 29
G. 18
H. 19
J. 24
K. 12

7. Which of the following sets of numbers has a median of 42?

A. {60, 42, 3[illegible], 22, 19}
B. {16, 28, [illegible]2, 48}
C. {42, [illegible], [illegible]0}
D. {12, 4[illegible], 40, 50}
E. {[illegible]6, 18, 42, 42}

8. The student council surveyed the student body on favorite lunch items. The frequency chart below shows the results of the survey.

Favorite Lunch Item	Frequency
corndog	140
hamburger	245
hotdog	210
pizza	235
spaghetti	90
other	65

Which lunch item indicates the mode of the data?

F. other
G. hotdog
H. hamburger
J. corndog
K. spaghetti

Read the table below, and answer questions 9 and 10.

Name	Total CDs owned
Maggie	97
Erica	164
John	81
Philip	151
Tanya	122

9. Which person has about twice as many CDs as John?

A. Philip
B. Tanya
C. Erica
D. Maggie
E. none of the above

10. Which person owns about 20% less than Philip?

F. Maggie
G. Tanya
H. John
J. Erica
K. none of the above

Use the line graph below, and answer questions 11 and 12.

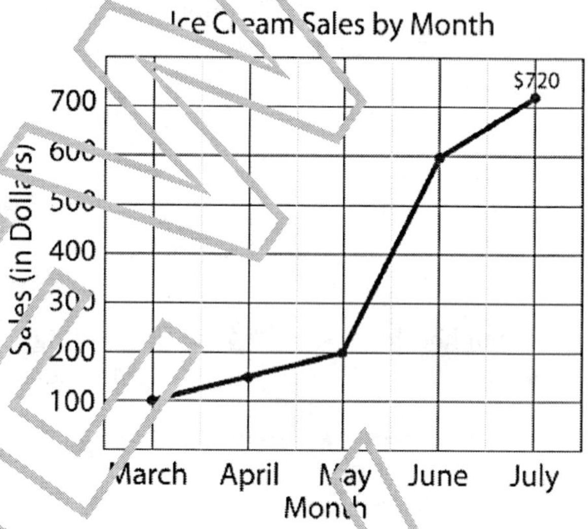

11. Which two months marked the greatest increase in sales?

A. May – June
B. June – July
C. March – April
D. April – May
E. none of the above

12. If the owner expects sales in August to be 10% higher than July, how much should sales be in August?

F. \$902
G. \$750
H. \$792
J. \$800
K. \$700

Use the circle graph below, and answer questions 13 and 14.

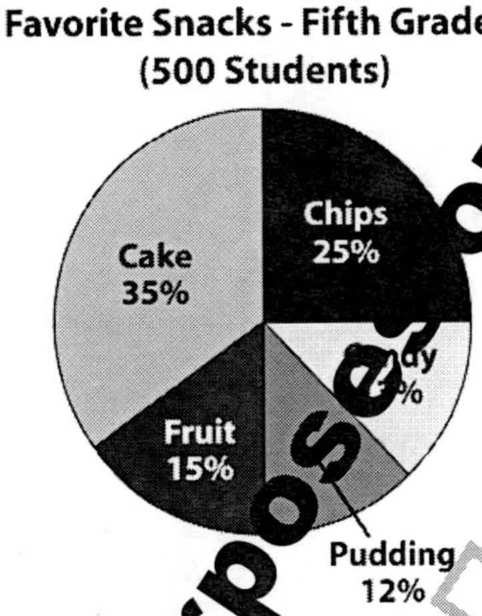

13. If 500 students were surveyed, how many students prefer cake as a favorite snack?

    A. 450 students
    B. 120 students
    C. 150 students
    D. 300 students
    E. 175 students

14. How many students prefer candy and pudding?

    F. 65 students
    G. 60 students
    H. 125 students
    J. 100 students
    K. 250 students

Use the bar graph below, and answer questions 15 and 16.

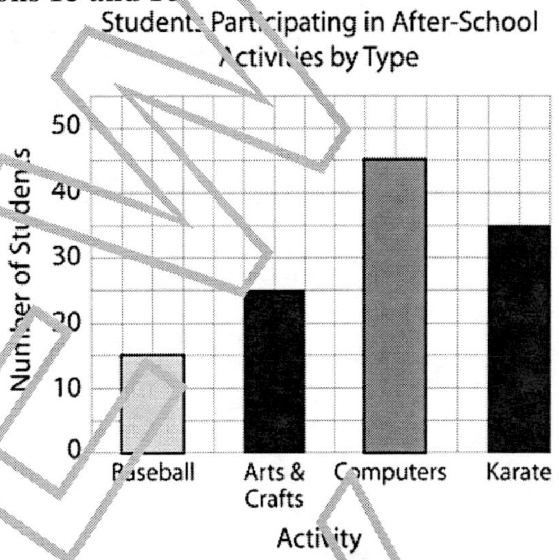

15. Which after school activity was the most popular?

    A. Basketball
    B. Arts & Crafts
    C. Computers
    D. Karate
    E. Football

16. The After-School Coordinator anticipates twice as many participants in karate next year. Each class has a maximum of 20 students per class. If the coordinator is correct, how many classes will she need?

    F. 3
    G. 1
    H. 4
    J. 5
    K. 2

Chapter 16
Probability and Counting

16.1 Principles of Counting

Principles of counting provide us with counting techniques that can be used to handle large amounts of data. There are two types of principles of counting, the addition rule and the multiplication rule.

Addition Rule: Let X_1 and X_2 be mutually exclusive events (there are no common outcomes). Let X describe the situation where either event X_1 or X_2 will occur. The number of times X may occur is given by:

$$n(X) = n(X_1) + n(X_2)$$

$n(X)$ = number of outcomes of event X
$n(X_1)$ = number of outcomes of event X_1
$n(X_2)$ = number of outcomes of event X_2

Example 1: Consider the set $C = \{-7, -4, -1, 3, 5, 7, 9, 11\}$. How many different ways could you choose a number that is positive or even? Find $n(X)$.

Step 1: Define your variables.
X = choosing a positive or even number from C
X_1 = pick a positive number from C
X_2 = pick an even number from C

Step 2: Find X_1 and X_2.
X_1 = the positive integers in the set $= \{3, 5, 7, 9, 11\} \rightarrow n(X_1) = 5$
X_2 = the even integers in the set $= \{-4\} \rightarrow n(X_2) = 1$

Step 3: Substitute the values of X_1 and X_2 into the equation $n(X) = n(X_1) + n(X_2)$.
$n(X) = 5 + 1 = 6$

Example 2: How many different ways could you choose a number from 1 to 25 so that it is a multiple of 4 or 7?

Step 1: Define your variables.
X = choosing a number from 1 to 25 that is either a multiple of 4 or 7
X_1 = the numbers from 1 to 25 that are multiples of 4
X_2 = the numbers from 1 to 25 that are multiples of 7

Step 2: Find X_1 and X_2.
X_1 = multiples of 4 $= \{4, 8, 12, 16, 20, 24\} \rightarrow n(X_1) = 6$
X_2 = multiples of 7 $= \{7, 14, 21\} \rightarrow n(X_2) = 3$

Step 3: Substitute the values of X_1 and X_2 into the equation $n(X) = n(X_1) + n(X_2)$.
$n(X) = 6 + 3 = 9$
There are nine ways to choose a number from 1 to 25 that is either a multiple of 4 or 7.

Example 3: How many different ways could you choose a number from 1 to 10 so that it is a multiple of 2 or 6?

Step 1: Find X_1 and X_2.
$X_1 =$ multiples of $2 = \{2, 4, 6, 8, 10\} \rightarrow n(X_1) = 5$
$X_2 =$ multiples of $6 = \{6\} \rightarrow n(X_2) = 1$
As you can see from the listed multiples, one of the values is the same, 6. Therefore, this problem is not mutually exclusive, so you cannot use the equation for the addition rule. You must use the equation $n(X) = n(X_1) + n(X_2) - n(X_1 \cap X_2)$.

Step 2: Substitute the values of X_1 and X_2 into the equation $n(X) = n(X_1) + n(X_2) - n(X_1 \cap X_2)$.
$X_1 \cap X_2 =$ the values that are multiples of 2 and of $6 = \{6\} \rightarrow n(X_1 \cap X_2) = 1$
$n(X) = 5 + 1 - 1 = 5$
There are five ways to choose a number from 1 to 10 that is either a multiple of 2 or 6.

Multiplication Rule: Let X_1 and X_2 be independent events (neither will affect the other's outcome) given by: $n(X) = n(X_1) \times n(X_2)$

Example 4: Samuel goes to a fast food restaurant for lunch. There are 5 sandwiches and 4 sides to choose from. He wants to pick one sandwich and one side. How many different meals can he order?

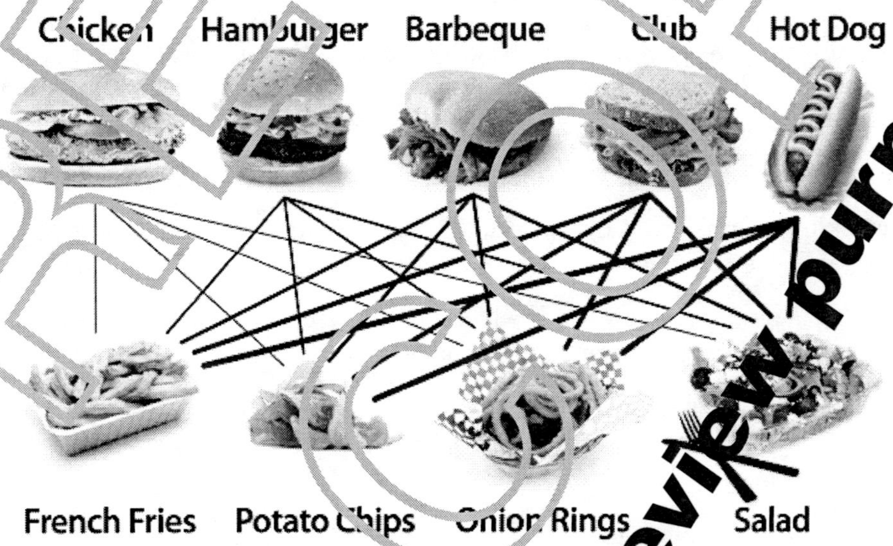

Solution: There are 5 sandwiches and 4 sides to choose from. To find the number of different meals he can get, you must multiply the choices together.
$5 \times 4 = 20$
There 20 different choices Samuel has for lunch.

Example 5: Stephany needs to choose a password for her e-mail account. It must be a eight characters long. Four of the characters must be numbers and four of the characters must be letters. How many different password choices does she have?

Step 1: There are 10 numbers, so there are 10 choices for the first four characters of the password. There are 26 letters, so there are 26 choices for the next four characters of the password.

Step 2: Now, multiply all the possible choices together to get the total number of choices for the password.
$10 \times 10 \times 10 \times 10 \times 26 \times 26 \times 26 \times 26 = 4,569,760,000$
There are $4,569,760,000$ different possibilities for an eight character password with four numbers and four letters.

Answer the following counting problems.

1. Consider the set $A = \{-7, -6, 1, 3, 5, 7\}$. How many different ways can you pick a positive or even number?
2. Consider the set $A = \{-7, -5, 1, 3, 4, 6, 8\}$. How many different ways can you pick a negative or even number?
3. How many different ways could you choose a number from 1 to 30 so that it is a multiple of [illegible] or 8?
4. How many different ways could you choose a number from 1 to 10 so that it is a multiple of 4 or 7?
5. Raymond has 7 baseball caps, 2 jackets, 10 pairs of jeans, and 2 pairs of sneakers. How many combinations of the 4 items can he make?
6. Claire has 6 kinds of lipstick, 4 eye shadows, 2 kinds of lip liner, and 2 mascaras. How many combinations can she use to make up her face?
7. Clarence's dad is ordering a new truck. He has a choice of 5 exterior colors, [illegible] interior colors, 2 kinds of seats, and 3 sound systems. How many combinations does he have to pick from?
8. A fast food restaurant has 8 kinds of sandwiches, [illegible] kinds of French fries, and 5 kinds of soft drinks. How many combinations of meals could you order if you ordered a sandwich, fries, and a drink?
9. In summer camp, Tyrone can choose from 4 outdoor activities, [illegible] indoor activities, and 3 water sports. He has to choose one of each. How many combinations of activities can he choose?
10. Jackie won a contest at school and gets to choose one pencil and one pen from the school store and an ice cream from the lunch room. There are 5 colors of pencils, 3 colors of pens, and 4 kinds of ice cream. How many combinations of prize packages can she choose?

16.2 Probability

Probability is the chance something will happen. Probability is most often expressed as a fraction, a decimal, a percent, or can also be written out in words.

Example 6: Billy has 3 red marbles, 5 white marbles, and 4 blue marbles on the floor. His cat comes along and eats one marble under the chair. What is the **probability** it is a red marble?

Step 1: The number of red marbles will be the top number of the fraction. → $\mathbf{\dfrac{3}{12}}$

Step 2: The total number of marbles is the bottom number of the fraction.

The answer may be expressed in lowest terms. $\dfrac{3}{12} = \dfrac{1}{4}$.

Expressed as a decimal, $\frac{1}{4} = 0.25$, as a percent, $\frac{1}{4} = 25\%$, and written out in words $\frac{1}{4}$ is one out of four.

Example 7: Determine the probability that the pointer will stop on a shaded wedge or the number 1.

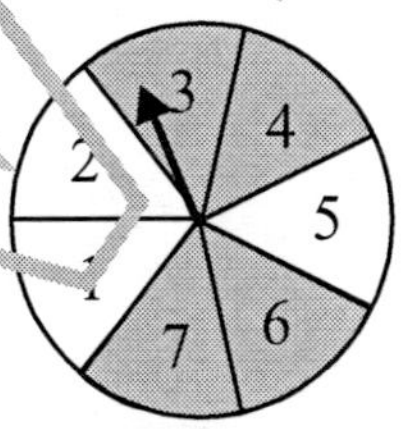

Step 1: Count the number of possible wedges that the spinner can stop on to satisfy the above problem. There are 5 wedges that satisfy it (4 shaded wedges and one number 1). The top number of the fraction is 5.

Step 2: Count the total number of wedges, 7. The bottom number of the fraction is 7. The answer is $\frac{5}{7}$ or **five out of seven.**

Example 8: Refer to the spinner above. If the pointer stops on the number 7, what is the probability that it will **not** stop on 7 the next time?

Step 1: Ignore the information that the pointer stopped on 7 the previous spin. The probability of the next spin does not depend on the outcome of the previous spin. Simply find the probability that the spinner will **not** stop on 7. Remember, if P is the probability of an event occurring, $1 - P$ is the probability of an event **not** occurring. In this example, the probability of the spinner landing on 7 is $\frac{1}{7}$.

Step 2: The probability that the spinner will not stop on 7 is $1 - 7$ which equals $\frac{6}{7}$. The answer is $\frac{6}{7}$ or **six out of seven**.

Find the probability of the following problems. Express the answer as a percent.

1. A computer chooses a random number between 1 and 50. What is the probability that you will guess the same number that the computer chose in 1 try?

2. There are 24 candy-coated chocolate pieces in a bag. Eight have defects in the coating that can be seen only with close inspection. What is the probability of pulling out a defective piece without looking?

3. Seven sisters have to choose which day each will wash the dishes. They put equal-sized pieces of paper in a hat, each labeled with a day of the week. What is the probability that the first sister who draws will choose a weekend day?

4. For his garden, Clay has a mixture of 12 white corn seeds, 24 yellow corn seeds, and 16 bicolor corn seeds. If he reaches for a seed without looking, what is the probability that Clay will plant a bicolor corn seed first?

5. Mom just got a new department store credit card in the mail. What is the probability that the last digit is an odd number?

6. Alex has a paper bag of cookies that holds 8 chocolate chip, 4 peanut butter, 6 butterscotch chip, and 12 ginger. Without looking, his friend John reaches in the bag for a cookie. What is the probability that the cookie is peanut butter?

7. An umpire at a little league baseball game has 14 balls in his pockets. Five of the balls are brand A, 6 are brand B, and 3 are brand C. What is the probability that the next ball he throws to the pitcher is a brand C ball?

8. What is the probability that the spinner's arrow will land on an even number?

9. The spinner in the problem above stopped on a shaded wedge on the first spin and stopped on the number 2 on the second spin. What is the probability that it will not stop on a shaded wedge or on the 2 on the third spin?

10. A company is offering 1 grand prize, 3 second place prizes, and 25 third place prizes based on a random drawing of contest entries. If your entry is one of the 500 total entries, what is the probability you will win a third place prize?

11. In the contest problem above, what is the probability that you will win the grand prize or a second place prize?

12. A box of a dozen doughnuts has 3 lemon cream-filled, 5 chocolate cream-filled, and 4 vanilla cream-filled. If the doughnuts look identical, what is the probability of picking a lemon cream-filled?

16.3 Independent and Dependent Events

In mathematics, the outcome of an event may or may not influence the outcome of a second event. If the outcome of one event does not influence the outcome of the second event, these events are **independent.** However, if one event has an influence on the second event, the events are **dependent**. When someone needs to determine the probability of two events occurring, he or she will need to use an equation. These equations will change depending on whether the events are independent or dependent in relation to each other. When finding the probability of two **independent** events, multiply the probability of each favorable outcome together.

Example 9: One bag of marbles contains 1 white, 1 yellow, 2 blue, and 3 orange marbles. A second bag of marbles contains 2 white, 3 yellow, 1 blue, and 2 orange marbles. What is the probability of drawing a blue marble from each bag?

Solution: Probability of favorable outcome

Bag 1: $\frac{2}{7}$

Bag 2: $\frac{1}{8}$

Probability of a blue marble from each bag: $\frac{2}{7} \times \frac{1}{8} = \frac{2}{56} = \frac{1}{28}$

In order to find the probability of two **dependent** events, you will need to use a different set of rules. For the first event, you must divide the number of favorable outcomes by the number of possible outcomes. For the second event, you must subtract one from the number of favorable outcomes **only if** the favorable outcome is the **same**. However, you must subtract one from the number of total possible outcomes. Finally, you must multiply the probability for event one by the probability for event two.

Example 10: One bag of marbles contains 3 red, 4 green, 7 black, and 2 yellow marbles. What is the probability of drawing a green marble, removing it from the bag, and then drawing another green marble?

	Favorable Outcomes	Total Possible Outcomes
Draw 1	4	16
Draw 2	3	15
Draw 1 × Draw 2	12	240

Answer: $\frac{12}{240}$ or $\frac{1}{20}$

Example 11: Using the same bag of marbles, what is the probability of drawing a red marble and then drawing a black marble?

	Favorable Outcomes	Total Possible Outcomes
Draw 1	3	16
Draw 2	7	15
Draw 1 × Draw 2	21	240

Answer $\frac{21}{240}$ or $\frac{7}{80}$

Find the probability of the following problems. Express the answer as a fraction.

1. Prithi has two boxes. Box 1 contains 3 red, 2 silver, 4 gold, and 2 blue combs. She also has a second box containing 1 black and 1 [illegible] brush. What is the probability that Prithi selects a red brush from box 1 and a black brush from box 2?

2. Steve Marduke has two spinners in front of him. The first one is numbered 1 – 6, and the second is numbered 1 – 3. If Steve spins each spinner once, what is the probability that the first spinner will show an odd number and the second spinner will show a "1"?

3. Carrie McCallister flips a coin twice and gets heads both times. What is the probability that Carrie will get tails the third time she flips the coin?

4. Artie Drake turns a spinner which is evenly divided into 11 sections numbered 1 – 11. On the first spin, Artie's pointer lands on "8". What is the probability that the spinner lands on an even number the second time he turns the spinner?

5. Leanne Bass plays a game with a street entertainer. In this game, a ball is placed under one of three coconut halves. The vendor shifts the coconut halves so quickly that Leanne can no longer tell which coconut half contains the ball. She selects one and misses. The entertainer then shifts all three around once more and asks Leanne to pick again. What is the probability that Leanne will select the coconut half containing the ball?

6. What is the probability that Jane Robelot reaches into a bag containing 1 daffodil and 2 gladiola bulbs and pulls out a daffodil bulb, and then reaches into a second bag containing 6 tulip, 3 lily, and 2 gladiola bulbs and pulls out a lily bulb?

7. Terrell casts his line into a pond containing 7 catfish, 8 bream, 3 trout, and 6 northern pike. He immediately catches a bream. What are the chances that Terrell will catch a second bream the next time he casts his line?

8. Gloria Quintero enters a contest in which the person who draws his or her initials out of a box containing all 26 letters of the alphabet wins the grand prize. Gloria reaches in, draws a "G", keeps it, then draws another letter. What is the probability that Gloria will next draw a "Q"?

9. Vince Macaluso is pulling two socks out of a washing machine in the dark. The washing machine contains three tan, one white, and two black socks. If Vince reaches in and pulls out the socks one at a time, what is the probability that he will pull out two tan socks on his first two tries?

10. John Salome has a bag containing 2 yellow plums, 2 red plums, and 3 purple plums. What is the probability that he reaches in without looking and pulls out a yellow plum and eats it, then reaches in again without looking and pulls out a red plum to eat?

16.4 More Probability

Example 12: You have a cube with one number, 1, 2, 3, 4, 5 and 6 painted on each face of the cube. What is the probability that if you throw the cube 3 times, you will get the number 2 each time?

If you roll the cube once, you have a 1 in 6 chance of getting the number 2. If you roll the cube a second time, you again have a 1 in 6 chance of getting the number 2. If you roll the cube a third time, you again have a 1 in 6 chance of getting the number 2. The probability of rolling the number 2 three times in a row is:

$$\frac{1}{6} \times \frac{1}{6} \times \frac{1}{6} = \frac{1}{216}$$

Find the probability that each of the following events will occur.

There are 10 balls in a box, each with a different digit on it: 0, 1, 2, 3, 4, 5, 6, 7, 8, & 9. A ball is chosen at random and then put back in the box.

1. What is the probability that if you pick out a ball 3 times, you will get number 7 each time?

2. What is the probability you will pick a ball with 5, then 9, and then 3?

3. What is the probability that if you pick out a ball 4 times, you will always get an odd number?

4. A couple has 4 children ages 9, 6, 4, and 1. What is the probability that they are all girls?

There are 26 letters in the alphabet, allowing a different letter to be on each of 26 cards. The cards are shuffled. After each card is chosen at random, it is put back in the stack of cards and the cards are shuffled again.

5. What is the probability that when you pick 3 cards, you would draw first a "[illegible]", then and "e", and then an "s"?

6. What is the probability that you would draw 4 cards and get the letter "z" each time?

7. What is the probability that you draw twice and get a letter in the word "random" both times?

8. If you flip a coin 3 times, what is the probability you will get heads every time?

9. Marie is clueless about 4 of her multiple-choice answers. The possible answers are A, B, C, D, E, or F. What is the probability that she will guess all four answers correctly?

Chapter 16 Review

1. There are 50 students in the school orchestra in the following sections:

   25 string section
   15 woodwind
   5 percussion
   5 brass

   One student will be chosen at random to present the orchestra director with an award. What is the probability the student will be from the woodwind section?

2. Fluffy's cat treat box contains 6 chicken-flavored treats, 5 beef-flavored treats, and 7 fish-flavored treats. If Fluffy's owner reaches in the box without looking, and chooses one treat, what is the probability that Fluffy will get a chicken-flavored treat?

3. The spinner in figure A stopped on the number 5 on the first spin. What is the probability that it will not stop on 5 on the second spin?

Fig. A

Fig. B

4. Sherri turns the spinner in figure B above 3 times. What is the probability that the pointer always lands on a shaded number?

5. Three cakes are sliced into 20 pieces each. Each cake contains 1 gold ring. What is the probability that one person who eats one piece of cake from each of the 3 cakes will find 3 gold rings?

6. Brianna tosses a coin 4 times. What is the probability she gets all tails?

Read the following, and answer questions 7–11.

There are 9 slips of paper in a hat, each with a number from 1 to 9. The numbers correspond to a group of students who must answer a question when the number for their group is drawn. Each time a number is drawn, the number is put back in the hat.

7. What is the probability that the number 6 will be drawn twice in a row?

8. What is the probability that the first 5 numbers drawn will be odd numbers?

9. What is the probability that the second, third, and fourth numbers drawn will be even numbers?

10. What is the probability that the first five times a number is drawn it will be the number 5?

11. What is the probability that the first five numbers drawn will be 1, 2, 3, 4, 5 in that order?

Solve the following word problems. For questions 12–14, write whether the problem is "dependent" or "independent."

12. Felix Perez reaches into a 10-piece puzzle and pulls out one piece at random. This piece has two places where it could connect to other pieces. What is the probability that he will select another piece which fits the first one if he selects the next piece at random?

13. Barbara Stein is desperate for a piece of chocolate candy. She reaches into a bag which contains 8 peppermint, 5 butterscotch, 7 toffee, 3 mint, and 6 chocolate pieces and pulls out a toffee piece. Disappointed, she throws it back into the bag and then reaches back in and pulls out one piece of candy. What is the probability that Barbara pulls out a chocolate piece on the second try?

14. Christen Solis goes to a pet shop and immediately decides to purchase a guppy she saw swimming in an aquarium. She reaches into the tank containing 5 goldfish, 6 guppies, 4 miniature catfish, and 3 minnows and accidently pulls up a goldfish. Breathing a sigh, Christen places the goldfish back in the water. The fish are swimming so fast, it is impossible to tell what fish Christen would catch. What is the probability that Christen will catch a guppy on her second try?

Answer the following counting problems.

15. Consider the set $B = \{-100, -56, -32, 1, 39, 85, 213\}$. How many ways are there to choose a negative or odd number?

16. Consider the set $B = \{-100, -56, -32, 1, 39, 85, 213\}$. How many ways are there to choose a positive or even number?

17. How many different ways could you choose a number from 1 to 30 so that it is a multiple of 4 or 9?

18. How many different ways could you choose a number from 1 to 50 so that it is a multiple of 4 or 6?

19. How many different outfits can Joe make if he has 10 shirts, 6 pairs of pants, and two pairs of shoes?

20. How many different outfits cam you make if you have 8 shirts, 4 pairs of pants, and two pairs of shoes?

21. The buffet line offers 5 kinds of meat, 3 different salads, a choice of 4 desserts, and 5 different drinks. If you choose one food from each category, from how many combinations would you have to choose?

22. In the lunch line, students can choose 1 out of 3 meats, 1 out of 4 vegetables, 1 out of 3 desserts, and 1 out of 5 drinks. How many lunch combinations are there?

23. Adrianna has 4 hats, 8 shirts, and 9 pairs of pants. Choosing one of each, how many different clothes combinations can she make?

Chapter 16 Test

Use the spinner below for questions 1–3.

1. What is the probability that the spinner will stop on a shaded wedge or the number 2?

   A. $\frac{3}{8}$

   B. $\frac{1}{3}$

   C. $\frac{1}{4}$

   D. $\frac{1}{2}$

   E. $\frac{3}{4}$

2. What is the probability of the spinner stopping on a shaded wedge?

   F. 0.25
   G. 0.5
   H. 0.429
   J. 3
   K. 0.375

3. What is the probability of the spinner stopping on the number three or a shaded wedge?

   A. 25%
   B. 50%
   C. 37.5%
   D. 33.3%
   E. 42.9%

4. Joseph has two bags of marbles with the following distributions:

Bag 1	4 Blue	3 Yellow	2 Red	1 Green
Bag 2	1 Blue	5 Yellow	2 Red	2 Green

   What is the probability of drawing a yellow marble from each bag?

   F. 8

   G. $\frac{3}{20}$

   H. $\frac{1}{4}$

   J. $\frac{1}{5}$

   K. $\frac{2}{5}$

5. Lindsey is selling cookies. She has two boxes with several different kinds of cookies. Each box has three chocolate chip, four sugar, two snickerdoodle, and one peanut butter. What is the probability of her pulling a sugar cookie out of each box?

   A. 16%
   B. 15%
   C. 40%
   D. 4%
   E. 80%

6. Ally has two spinners. One is numbered 1–6 and the other is numbered 1–3. If she spins both spinners, what is the probability that both spinners will show the number 2?

   F. $\frac{1}{3}$

   G. $\frac{1}{6}$

   H. $\frac{1}{9}$

   J. $\frac{1}{18}$

   K. $\frac{2}{9}$

7. Samantha just got a new ceramic archway for her fish tank. She has 3 African butterfly fish, 5 angelfish, 6 neon tetra, and 1 rainbow shark. What is the probability that a neon tetra fish will be the first to pass through the new archway?

A. 0.33
B. 0.20
C. 0.4
D. 0.43
E. 0.6

8. Adam has a spinner divided into eight equal segments numbered 1–8. What is the probability that if Adam spins the spinner twice the numbers added together will equal 12?

F. 20%
G. 6.25%
H. 7.[illegible]%
J. [illegible]%
K. [illegible].5%

9. If Alex rolls two six-sided dice, what is the probability that the two numbers will add up to 9?

A. $\frac{5}{36}$
B. $\frac{[illegible]}{30}$
C. $\frac{2}{[illegible]}$
D. $\frac{8}{36}$
E. $\frac{1}{9}$

10. Savannah is going to the school dance. She has three dresses, six necklaces, and eight pairs of earrings. How many different outfits does she have to chose from if she chooses only one dress, one necklace, and one pair of earrings?

F. 17
G. 144
H. 48
J. 12
K. 18

Use number set A to answer questions 11–13.

$A = \{-11, -7, -3, -1, 0, 2, 4, 8, 10, 16\}$

11. How many ways can you choose a negative or even number from A?

A. 11
B. 10
C. 9
D. 7
E. 6

12. How many ways can you choose a negative or a multiple of 8 number from A?

F. 6
G. 2
H. 4
J. 8
K. 10

13. How many ways can you choose a multiple of 16 or an odd number from A?

A. 4
B. 1
C. 9
D. 6
E. 5

14. How many different ways could you choose a number from 1 to 40 so that it is a multiple of 15 or 10?

F. 3
G. 6
H. 5
J. 4
K. 3

Chapter 17
Angles

17.1 Complementary and Supplementary Angles

Two angles are **complementary** if the sum of the measures of the angles is 90°.
Two angles are **supplementary** if the sum of the measures of the angles is 180°.
The angles may be adjacent but do not need to be.

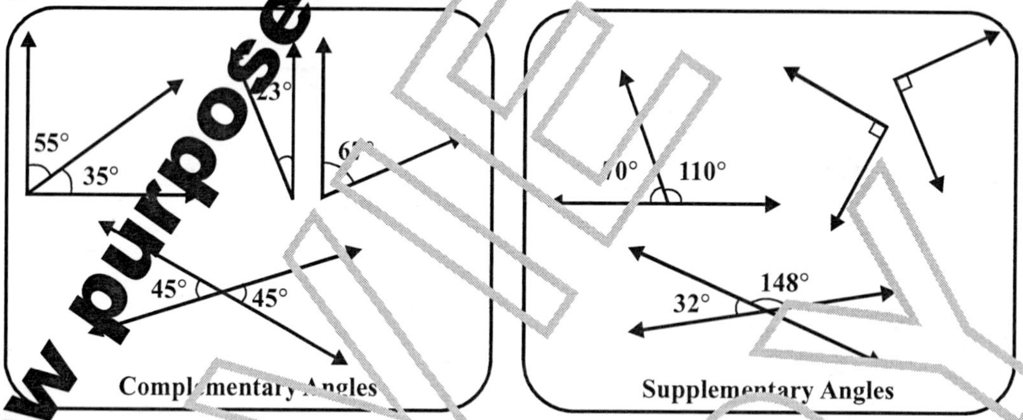

Calculate the measure of each unknown angle.

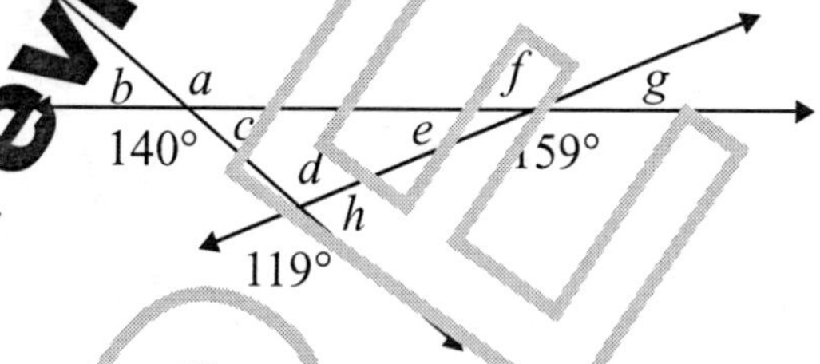

1. $\angle a =$ ______
2. $\angle b =$ ______
3. $\angle c =$ ______
4. $\angle d =$ ______
5. $\angle e =$ ______
6. $\angle f =$ ______
7. $\angle g =$ ______
8. $\angle h =$ ______

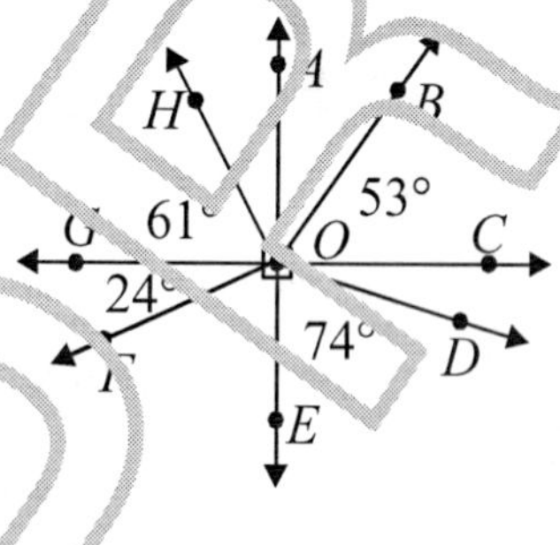

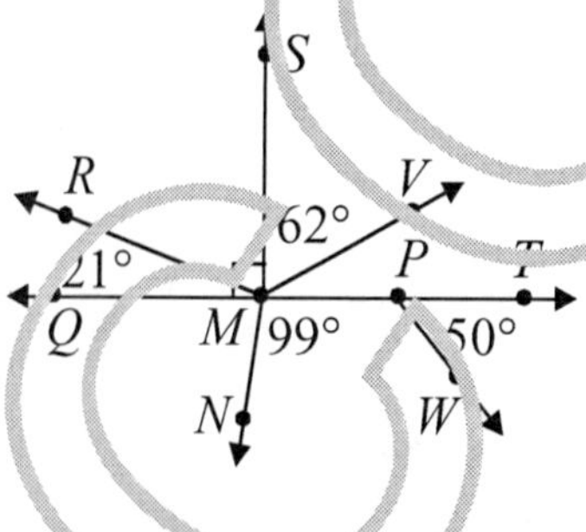

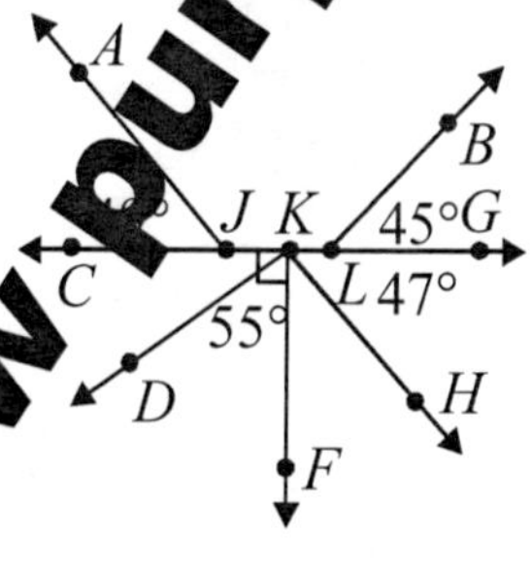

9. $\angle AOB =$ ______
10. $\angle COD =$ ______
11. $\angle EOF =$ ______
12. $\angle AOH =$ ______
13. $\angle RMS =$ ______
14. $\angle VMT =$ ______
15. $\angle QMN =$ ______
16. $\angle WPQ =$ ______
17. $\angle AJK =$ ______
18. $\angle CKD =$ ______
19. $\angle FKH =$ ______
20. $\angle BLC =$ ______

17.2 Corresponding, Alternate Interior, and Alternate Exterior Angles

If two parallel lines are intersected by a **transversal**, a line passing through both parallel lines, the **corresponding angles** are congruent.

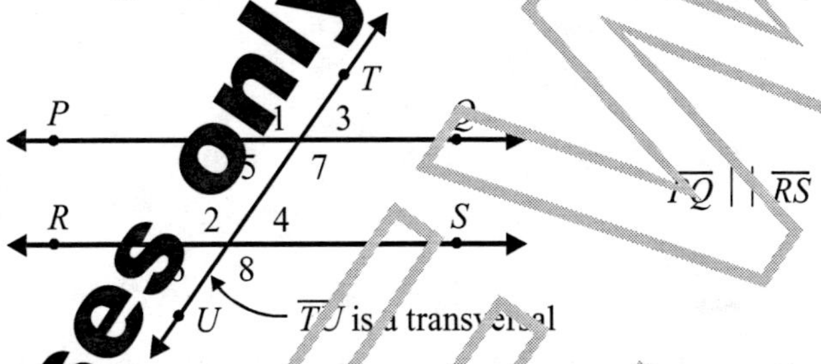

∠1 and ∠2 are congruent.	They are corresponding angles.
∠3 and ∠4 are congruent.	They are corresponding angles.
∠5 and ∠6 are congruent.	They are corresponding angles.
∠7 and ∠8 are congruent.	They are corresponding angles.

Alternate interior angles are also congruent. They are on the opposite sides of the transversal and inside the parallel lines.

∠5 and ∠4 are congruent.	They are alternate interior angles.
∠7 and ∠2 are congruent.	They are alternate interior angles.

Alternate exterior angles are also congruent. They are on the opposite sides of the transversal and above and below the parallel lines.

∠1 and ∠8 are congruent.	They are alternate exterior angles.
∠3 and ∠6 are congruent.	They are alternate exterior angles.

Look at the diagram below. For each pair of angles, state whether they are corresponding (C), alternate interior (I), alternate exterior (E), vertical (V), or supplementary angles (S).

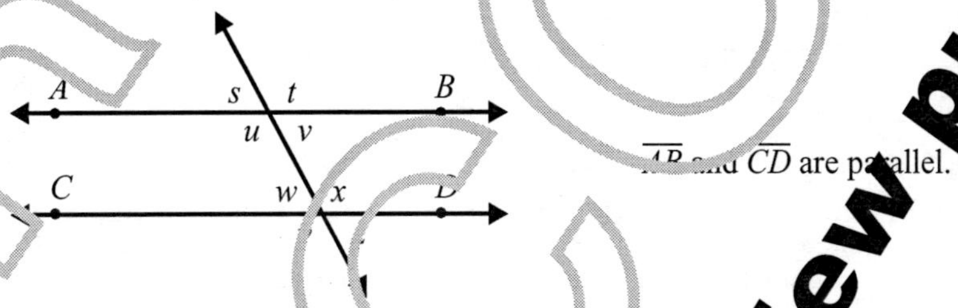

1. $\angle u$, $\angle x$
2. $\angle w$, $\angle s$
3. $\angle t$, $\angle y$
4. $\angle s$, $\angle t$
5. $\angle w$, $\angle y$
6. [illegible], $\angle x$
7. $\angle w$, $\angle z$
8. $\angle v$, $\angle w$
9. $\angle v$, $\angle z$
10. $\angle s$, $\angle z$
11. $\angle t$, $\angle u$
12. $\angle w$, $\angle x$
13. $\angle w$, $\angle s$
14. $\angle s$, $\angle v$
15. $\angle x$, $\angle z$

17.3 Angle Relationships

When two lines meet at a point, they form an angle. On the ACT, you will be asked to apply knowledge of angle relationships to real-world situations. You will also apply these skills in later classes in mathematics.

Example 1: Make a graphic relationship between a clock and a Cartesian plane. Draw and explain two congruent triangles using the digits on the clock.

1. Use the center of a clock as the origin of the Cartesian plane.
2. The x-axis aligns with the hours 3 and 9. The y-axis aligns with the hours 12 and 6.
3. The clock can be divided into four quadrants, each of 90 degrees on the Cartesian plane.

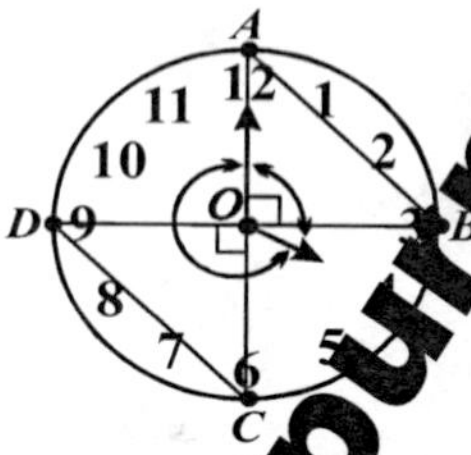

Point $A = 12$. Point $B = 3$. Point $C = 6$. Point $D = 9$.
O is the center.

1. $\overline{OA} = \overline{OB} = \overline{OC} = \overline{OD}$. Points on the circumference are equal distance from the center.
2. $\angle AOB \cong \angle COD$. First and third quadrants of the Cartesian plane.
3. $\triangle AOB \cong \triangle COD$

Answer the questions below.

1. Find the measure of the two angles formed by the hands of the clock, a) at 7:00 AM and b) at 2:00 PM.
2. A grandfather clock that is supposed to strike a bell at every hour, does not work properly when the hands of the clock form angles in which one angle formed is twice the measure of the opposite angle. Is there a time when this event would happen? If so, find it.
3. Given: $\overline{PQ} \parallel \overline{MN}$; $\overline{AB}$ intersects $\overline{PQ}$ at R, and $\overline{MN}$ at S; $\angle ARP = 5x$ and $\angle ASN = 13x$. Find all the measures of all the angles in degrees.

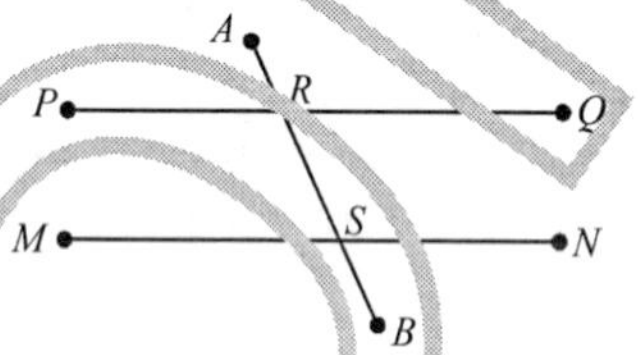

4. If two parallel lines are cut by a transversal, find the measures of:
   A Two alternate exterior angles represented by $x + 14$ and $2x - 55$.
   B Two corresponding angles represented by $4x + 10$ and $5x - 5$.
   C Two exterior angles on the same side of the transversal whose values are $3x$ and $7x$.
5. Given $\overline{MN}$ and measures of angles as shown in the figures, find the value of the remaining angles.
   (A) $\angle B = 62°$ and $\angle G = 103°$ (B) $\angle C = 76°$ and $\angle F = 34°$

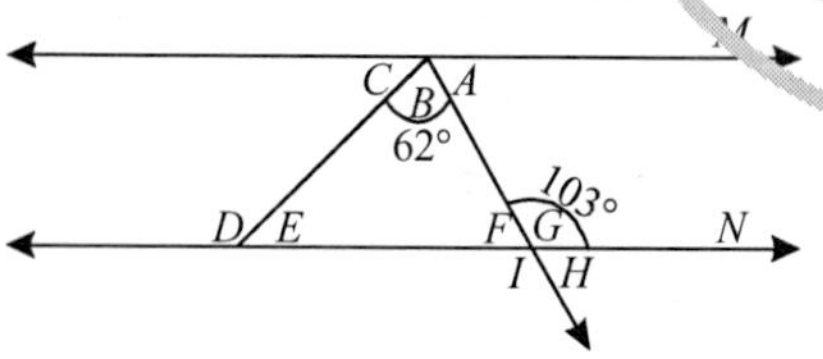

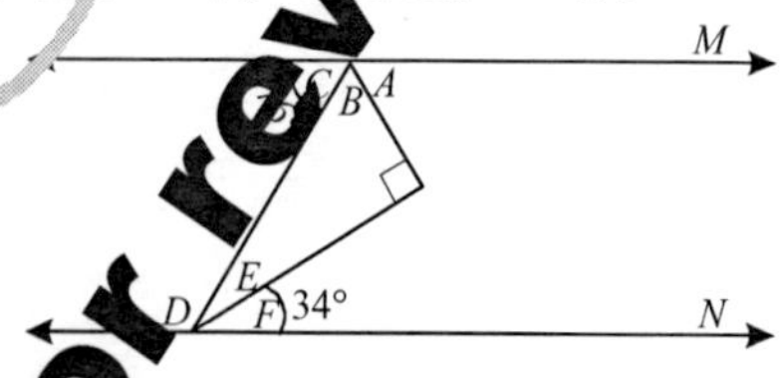

17.4 Congruent Figures

Two figures are **congruent** when they are exactly the same size and shape. If the corresponding sides and angles of two figures are congruent, then the figures themselves are congruent. For example, look at the two triangles below.

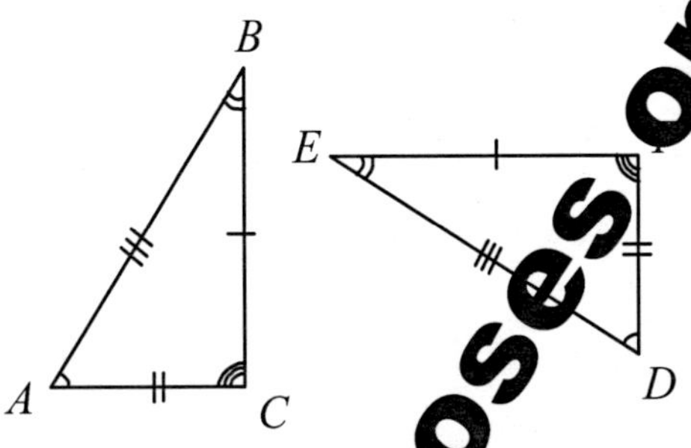

Compare the lengths of the sides of the triangles. The slash marks indicate that $\overline{AB}$ and $\overline{ED}$ have the same length. Therefore, they are congruent, which can be expressed as $\overline{AB} \cong \overline{ED}$. We can also see that $\overline{BC} \cong \overline{EF}$ and $\overline{AC} \cong \overline{FD}$. In other words, the corresponding sides are congruent. Now, compare the corresponding angles. The arc markings show that the corresponding angles have the same measure and are, therefore, congruent: $\angle A \cong \angle D$, $\angle B \cong \angle E$, and $\angle C \cong \angle F$. Because the corresponding sides and angles of the triangles are congruent, we say that the triangles are congruent: $\triangle ABC \cong \triangle DEF$.

Example 2: Decide whether the figures in each pair below are congruent or not.

PAIR 1

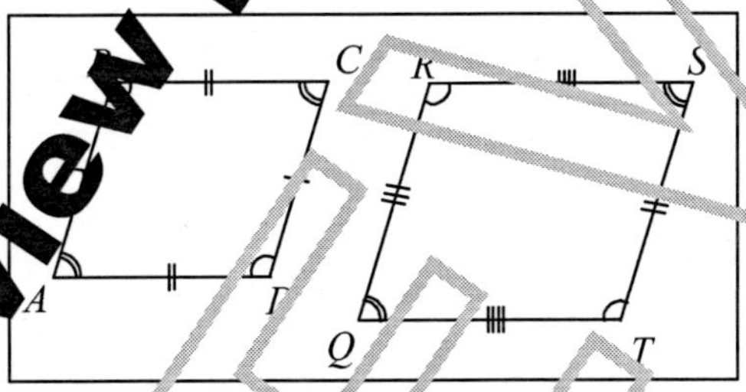

In Pair 1, the two parallelograms have congruent corresponding angles. However, because the corresponding sides of the parallelogram are not the same size, the figures are not congruent.

PAIR 2

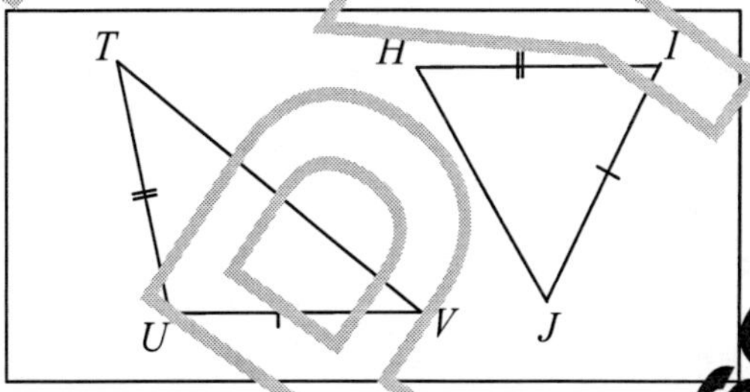

In Pair 2, the two triangles have two corresponding sides which are congruent. However, the hypotenuse of these triangles are not congruent (indicated by the lack of a triple hash mark).

PAIR 3

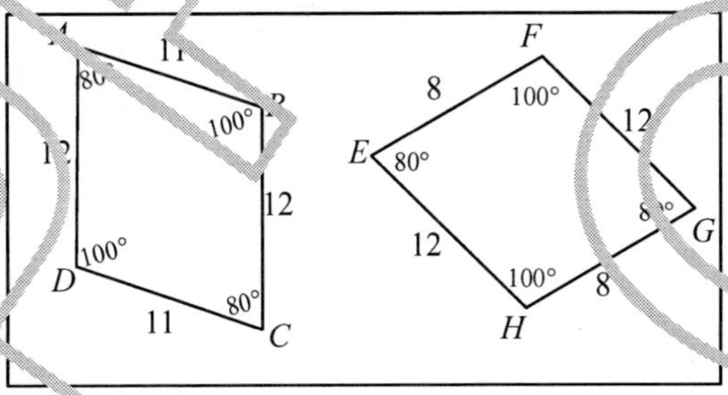

In Pair 3, all of the corresponding angles of these parallelograms are congruent; however, the corresponding sides are not congruent. Therefore, these figures are not congruent.

PAIR 4

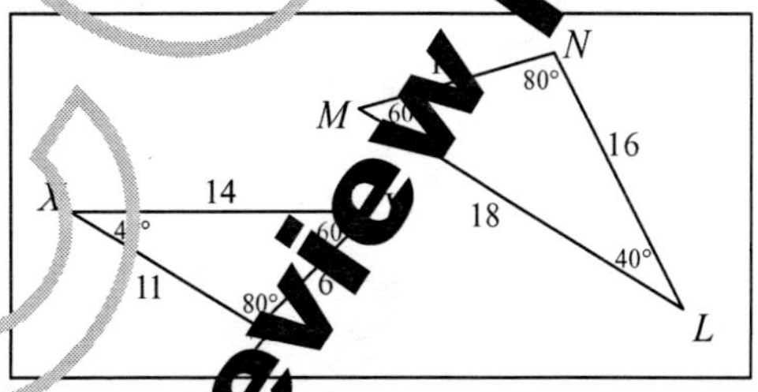

In Pair 4, the triangles share congruent corresponding angles, but the measures for all three corresponding sides of the triangles are not congruent. Therefore, the triangles are not congruent.

Examine the pairs of corresponding figures below. On the first line below the figures, write whether the figures are congruent or not congruent. On the second line, write a brief explanation of how you chose your answer.

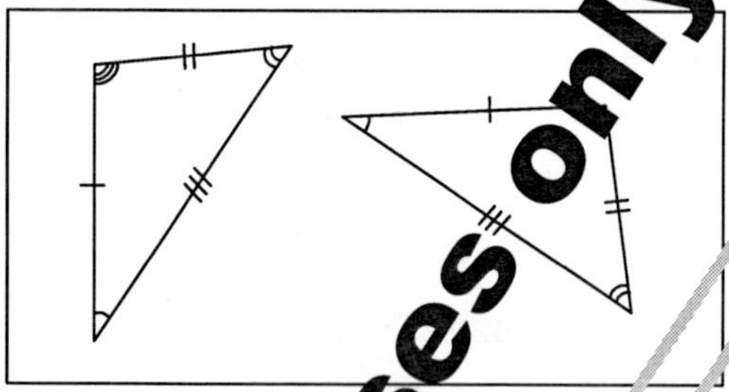

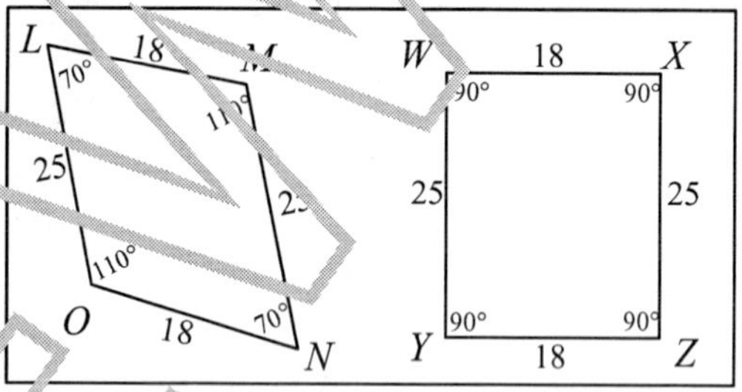

1. ______________________________
____

4. ______________________________
____

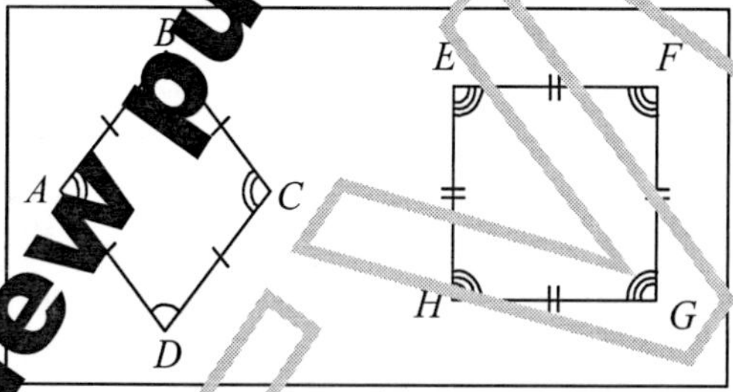

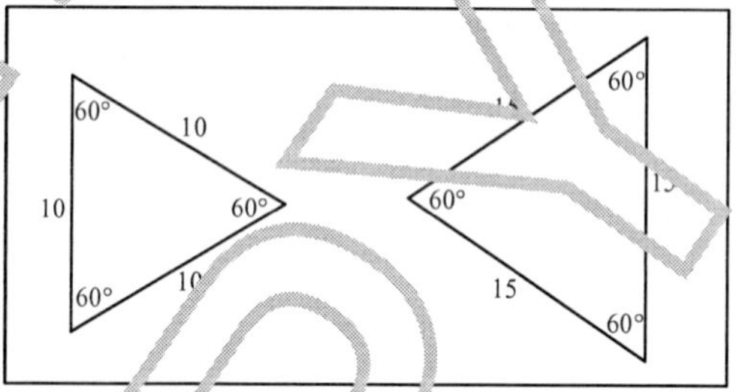

2. ______________________________
____

5. ______________________________
____

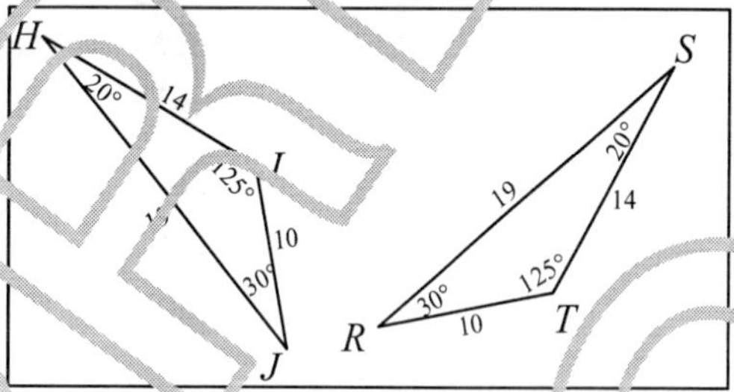

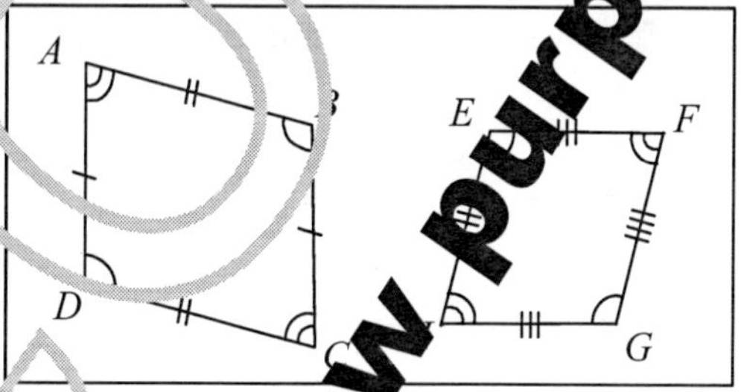

3. ______________________________
____

6. ______________________________
____

Chapter 17 Review

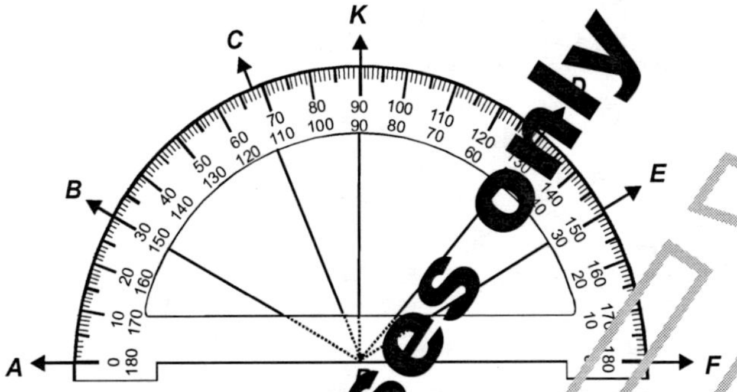

1. What is the measure of $\angle DRA$?

2. What is the measure of $\angle CRF$?

3. What is the measure of $\angle ARB$?

True or False.

4. Points are defined as small black dots that make up a line.

5. Points that are collinear are also coplanar.

6. Points that are coplanar are also collinear.

Use the following diagram for questions 7-17.

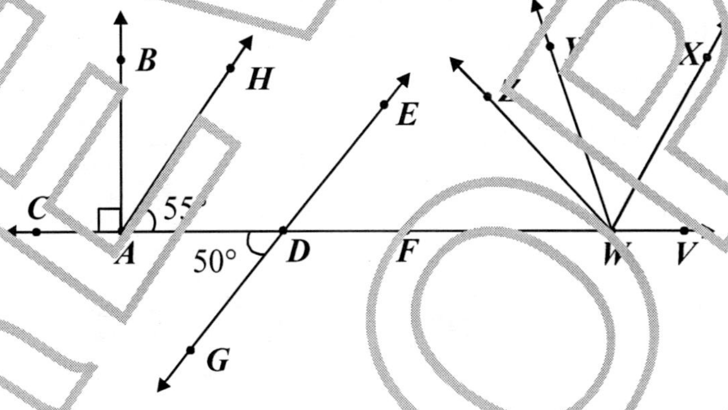

7. Which angle is a supplementary angle to $\angle EDF$?

8. What is the measure of $\angle GDF$?

9. Which two angles are right angles?

10. What is the measure of $\angle EDF$?

11. Which angle is adjacent to $\angle BAD$?

12. Which angle is a complementary angle to $\angle HAD$?

13. What is the measure of $\angle HAB$?

14. What is the measure of $\angle CAD$?

15. What kind of angle is $\angle FDA$?

16. What kind of angle is $\angle GDA$?

17. Which angles are adjacent to $\angle EDA$?

Look at the diagram below. For each pair of angles, state whether they are corresponding (C), alternate interior (I), alternate exterior (E), vertical (V), or supplementary (S) angles.

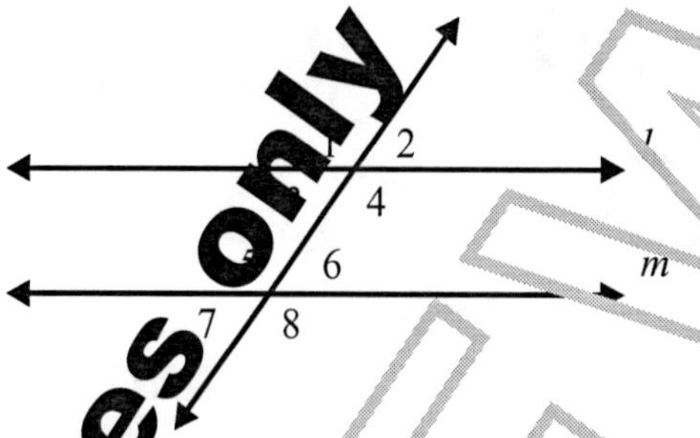

18. $\angle 1$ and $\angle 4$
19. $\angle 2$ and $\angle 6$
20. $\angle 1$ and $\angle 3$
21. $\angle 5$ and $\angle 8$
22. $\angle 5$ and $\angle 7$
23. $\angle 6$ and $\angle 5$
24. $\angle 2$ and $\angle 7$
25. $\angle 1$ and $\angle 2$
26. $\angle 4$ and $\angle 5$
27. $\angle 6$ and $\angle 8$
28. $\angle 3$ and $\angle 6$
29. $\angle 4$ and $\angle 8$

Examine the problems below. Use the rules you have learned in this chapter to answer the questions.

30. Mr. Ramirez was installing a new slide at the city park. In order to be certain the slide is welded properly, he will need to know the angle where the supporting beams meet the slide. Knowing the sum of the angle measures of a triangle, which of the following statements is true?

(A) The right angle plus $m\angle x = 135°$
(B) The right angle minus $m\angle x = 30°$
(C) $30° + m\angle x = 45°$
(D) $30°+$ the right angle $= 110°$

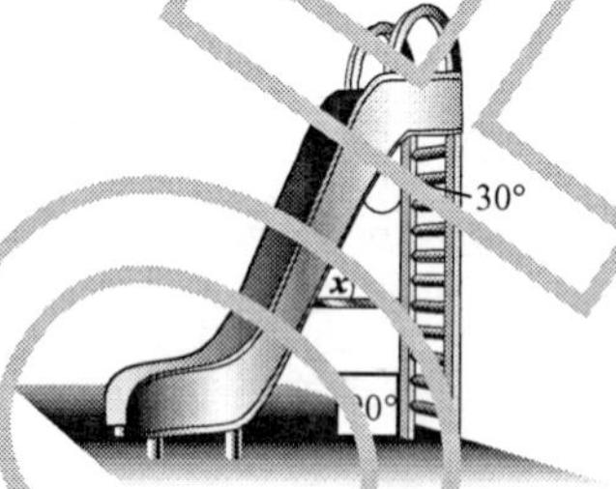

31. Danny and Eddie were trying to come up with the ideal model for a High-flying kite. Knowing the sum of the angle measures of a triangle and the laws of congruent shapes, which of the following statements is correct?

(A) $\angle d = \angle b$
(B) $\angle a + \angle c = 90°$
(C) $\angle c = 45°$
(D) $\angle d - \angle a = 15°$

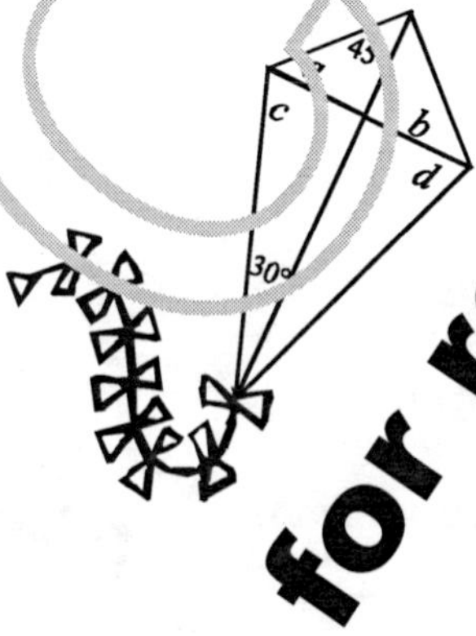

Chapter 17 Test

1. What is the definition of a point?

   A. A location in space that has length, but doesn't have width.
   B. A location in space that doesn't have length, but has width.
   C. A location in space that has height and length, but doesn't have width.
   D. A location in space that has neither length nor width.
   E. A location in space that has length and width.

2. What is the measure of an angle that is supplementary to 87°?

   F. −42°
   G. 3°
   H. 27°
   J. 93°
   K. 87°

3. What is the sum of two complementary angles?

   A. 180°
   B. 45°
   C. 90°
   D. 360°
   E. 100°

4. What type of angle is shown below?

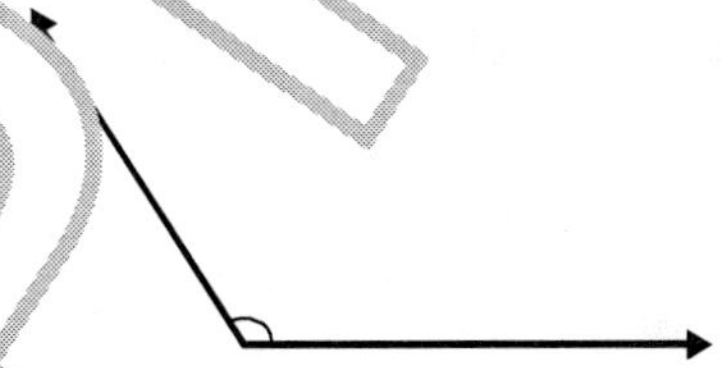

   F. right
   G. acute
   H. left
   J. straight
   K. obtuse

Use the following diagram to answer questions 5–7.

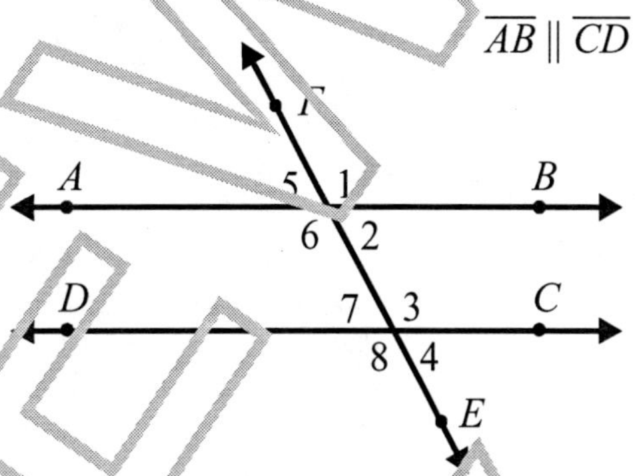

5. Which angles are alternate exterior angles?

   A. ∠2 and ∠7
   B. ∠3 and ∠8
   C. ∠1 and ∠8
   D. ∠5 and ∠3
   E. ∠1 and ∠4

6. Which angles are vertical angles?

   F. ∠1 and ∠2
   G. ∠1 and ∠3
   H. ∠1 and ∠4
   J. ∠1 and ∠5
   K. ∠1 and ∠6

7. Which angles are corresponding angles?

   A. ∠1 and ∠4
   B. ∠7 and ∠6
   C. ∠1 and ∠8
   D. ∠1 and ∠5
   E. ∠1 and ∠3

Chapter 18
Triangles

18.1 Exterior Angles

The **exterior angle** of a triangle is always equal to the sum of the opposite interior angles.

Example 1: Find the measure of $\angle x$ and $\angle y$.

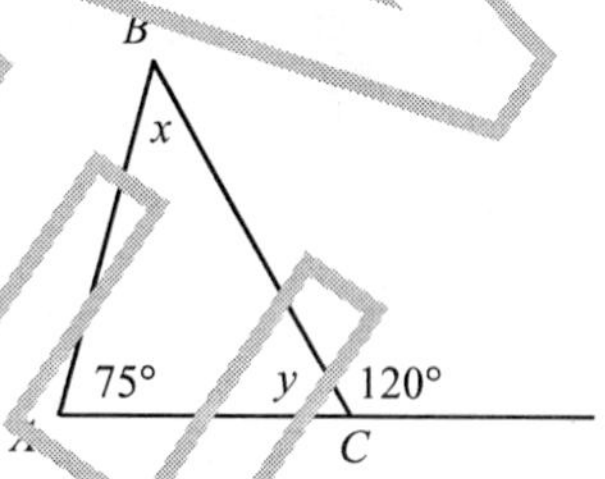

Step 1: Using the rule for exterior angles,
$120° = \angle A + \angle B$
$120° = 75° + x \rightarrow 45° = x$

Step 2: The sum of the interior angles of a triangle equals 180°, so
$180° = 75° + 45° + y \rightarrow 60° = y$

Find the measures of x and y.

1.
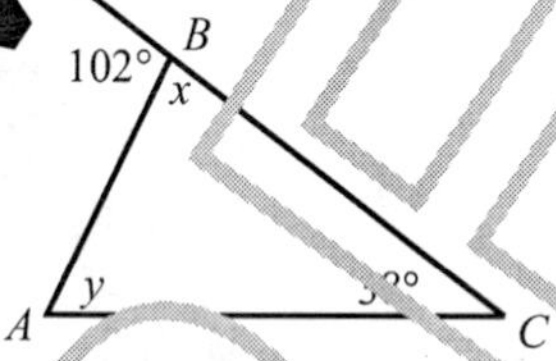

3.
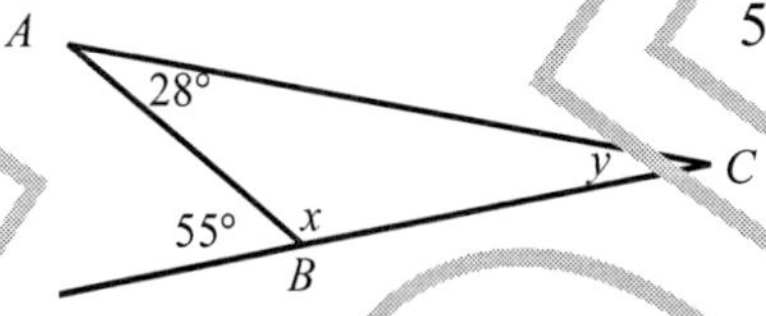

5.
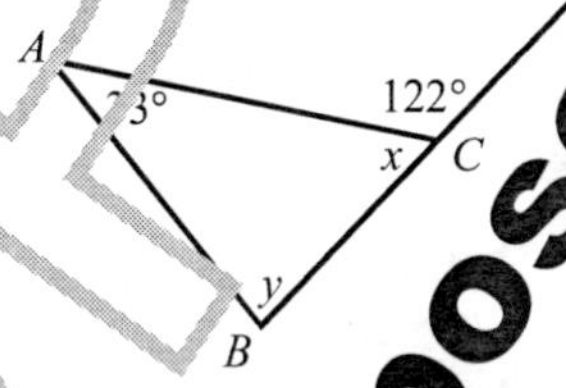

2.
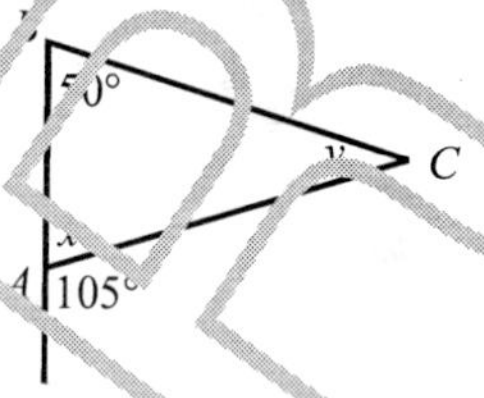

4.
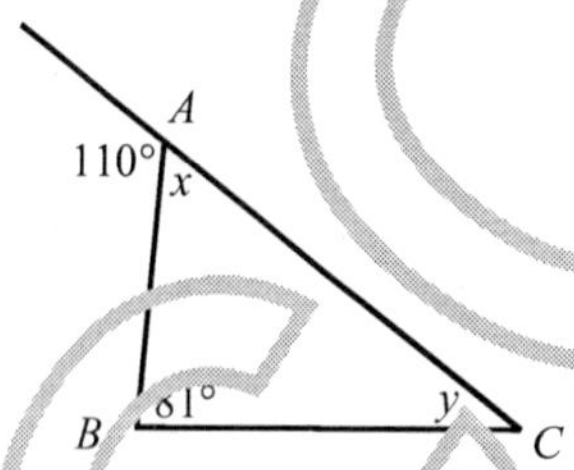

6.
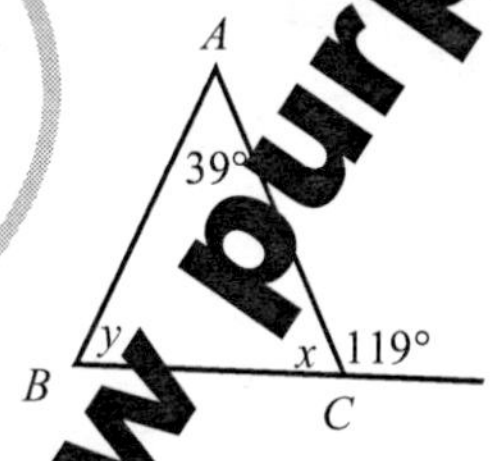

Find the measures of the angles.

7.
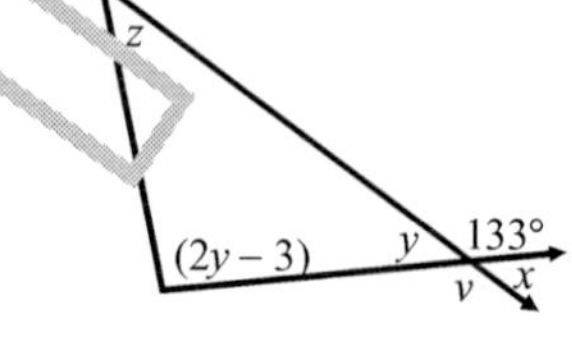

8.
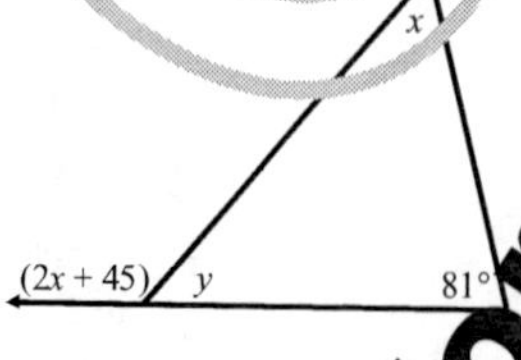

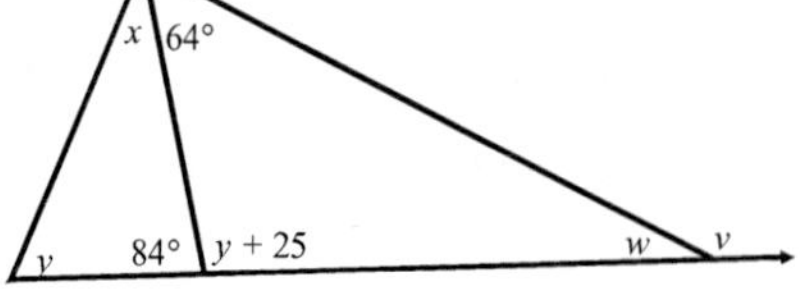

18.2 Similar Triangles

Two triangles are similar if the measurements of the three angles in both triangles are the same. If the three angles are the same, then their corresponding sides are proportional.

Corresponding Sides - The triangles below are similar. Therefore, the two shortest sides from each triangle, c and f, are corresponding. The two longest sides from each triangle, a and d, are corresponding. The two medium length sides, b and e, are corresponding.

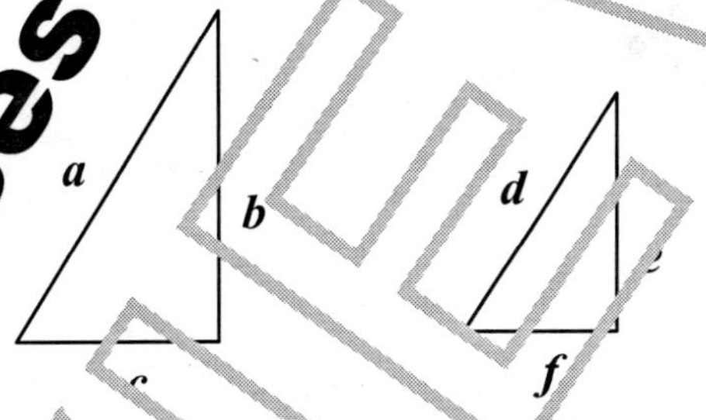

Proportional - The corresponding sides of similar triangles are proportional to each other. This means if we know all the measurements of one triangle, and we only know one measurement of the other triangle, we can figure out the measurements of the two other sides with proportion problems. The two triangles below are similar.

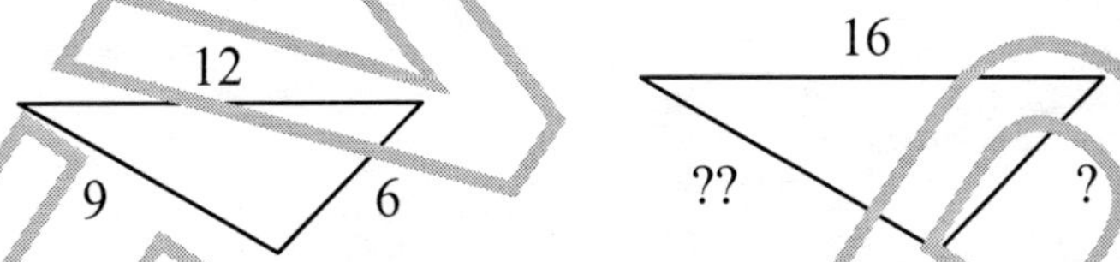

Note: To set up the proportion correctly, it is important to keep the measurements of each triangle on opposite sides of the equal sign.

To find the short side:
Step 1: Set up the proportion

$$\frac{\text{long side}}{\text{short side}} \quad \frac{12}{6} = \frac{16}{?}$$

Step 2: Solve the proportion. Multiply the two numbers diagonal to each other and then divide by the other number.

$16 \times 6 = 96$
$96 \div 12 = 8$

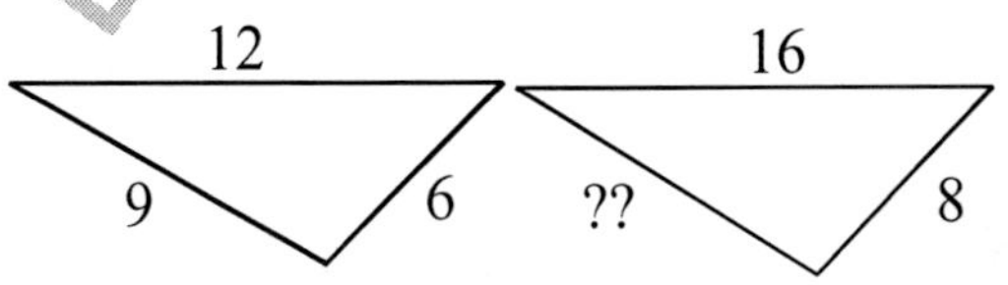

To find the medium length side:
Step 1: Set up the proportion

$$\frac{\text{long side}}{\text{medium}} \quad \frac{12}{9} = \frac{16}{??}$$

Step 2: Solve the proportion. Multiply the two numbers diagonal to each other and then divide by the other number.

$16 \times 9 = 144$
$144 \div 12 = 12$

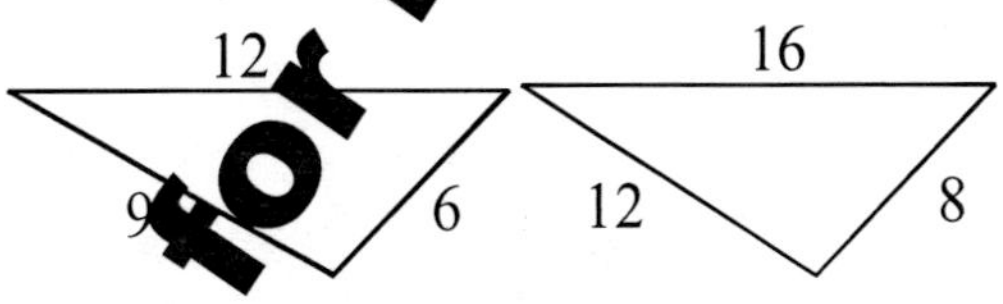

Find the missing side from the following similar triangles.

1.

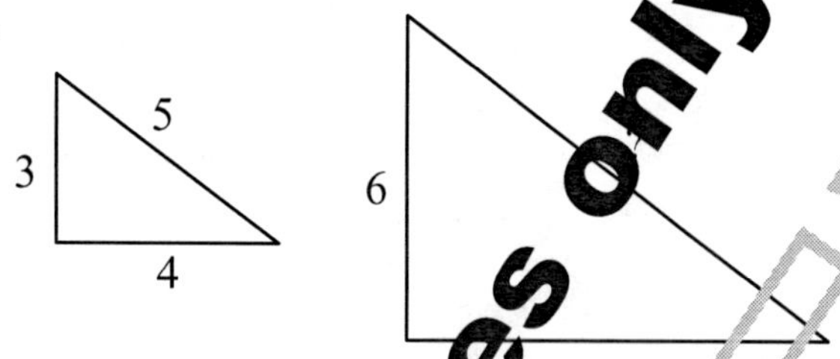

2.

3.

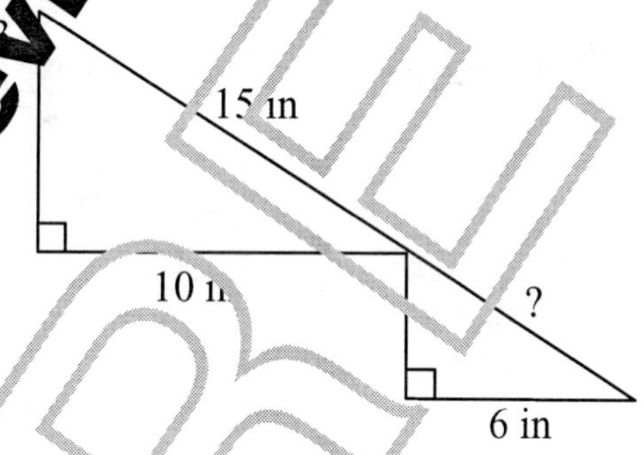

4.

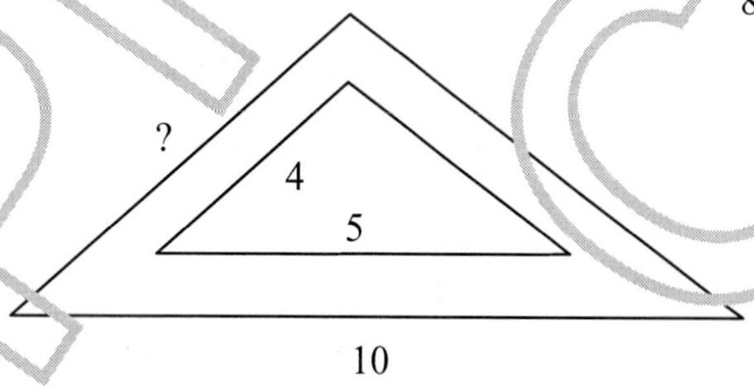

5.

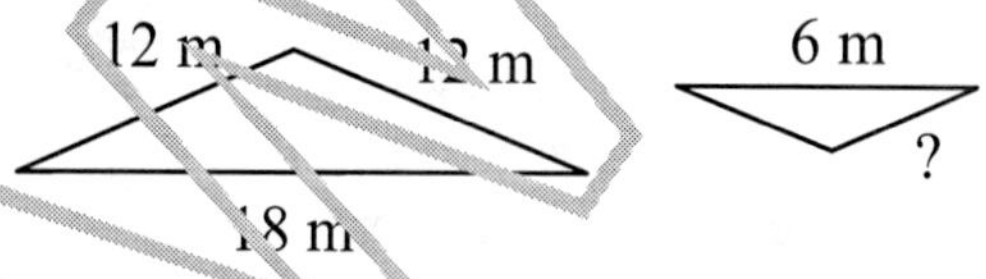

6.

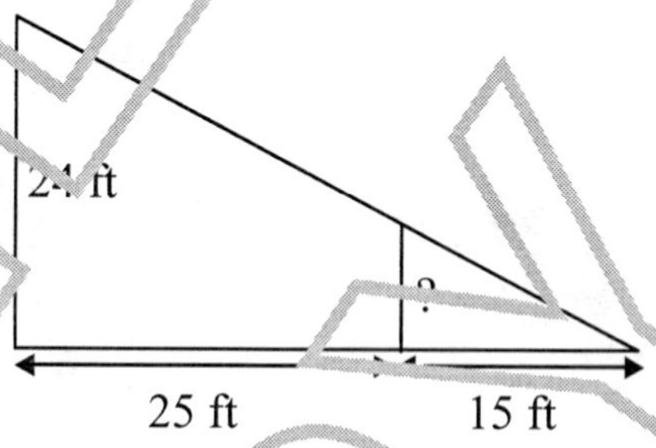

7.

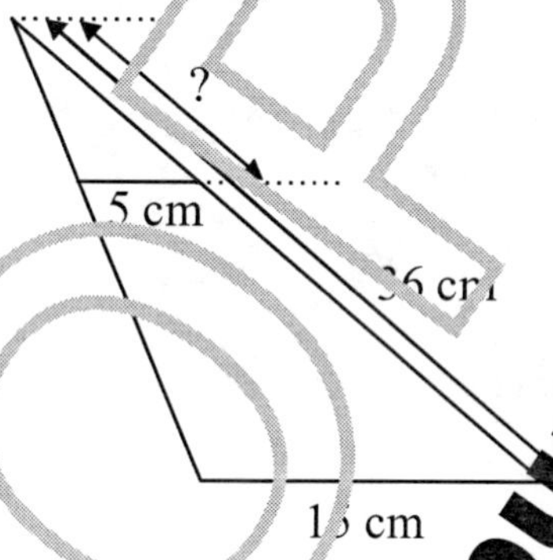

8.

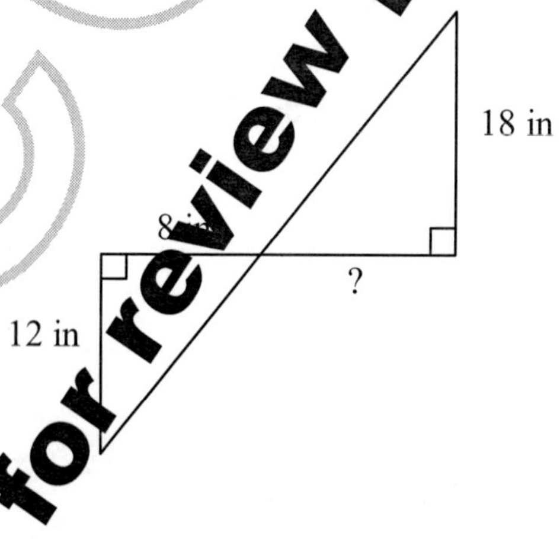

18.3 Pythagorean Theorem

Pythagoras was a Greek mathematician and philosopher who lived around 600 B.C. He started a math club among Greek aristocrats called the Pythagoreans. Pythagoras formulated the **Pythagorean Theorem** which states that in a **right triangle**, the sum of the squares of the legs of the triangle are equal to the square of the hypotenuse. Most often you will see this formula written as $a^2 + b^2 = c^2$. **This relationship is only true for right triangles.**

Example 2: Find the length of side c.

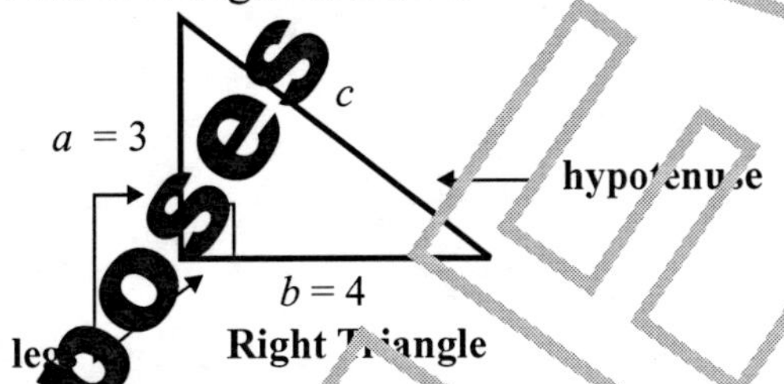

Formula:
$$a^2 + b^2 = c^2$$
$$3^2 + 4^2 = c^2$$
$$9 + 16 = c^2$$
$$25 = c^2$$
$$\sqrt{25} = \sqrt{c^2}$$
$$5 = c$$

Find the hypotenuse of the following triangles. Round the answers to two decimal places.

1.
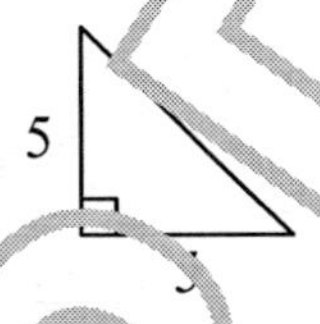

$c =$ ______

4.
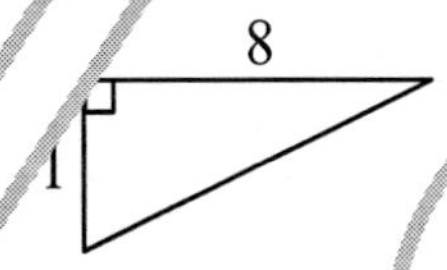

$c =$ ______

7.
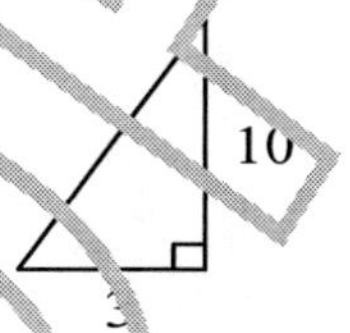

$c =$ ______

2.
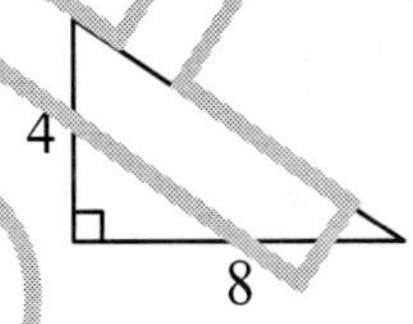

$c =$ ______

5.
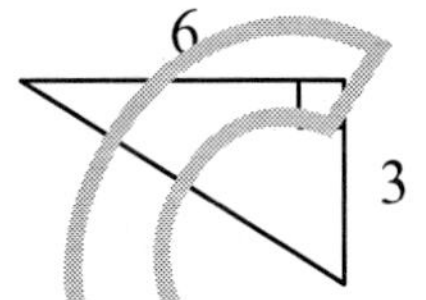

$c =$ ______

8.

$c =$ ______

3.
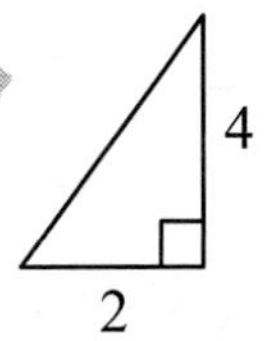

$c =$ ______

6.
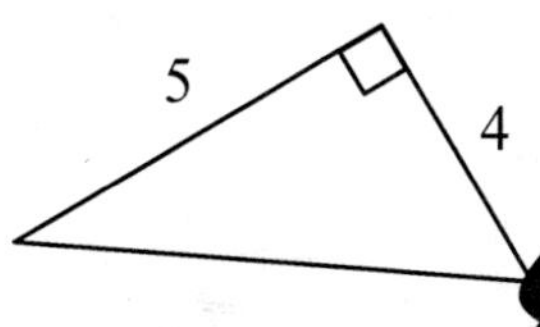

$c =$ ______

9.
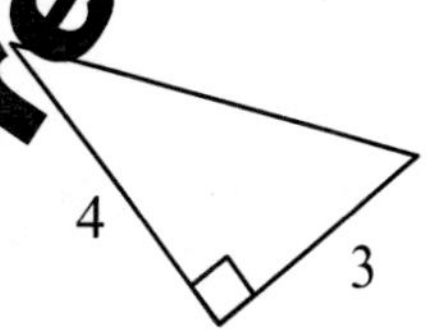

$c =$ ______

18.4 Finding the Missing Leg of a Right Triangle

In some triangles, we know the measurement of the hypotenuse as well as one of the legs. To find the measurement of the other leg, use the Pythagorean theorem by filling in the known measurements, and then solve for the unknown side.

Example 3: Find the measure of b.

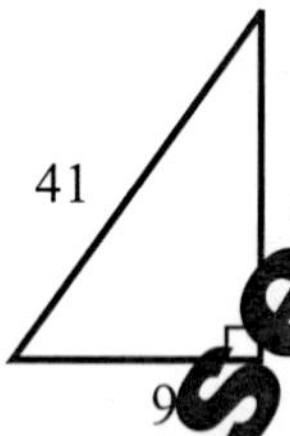

In the formula, $a^2 + b^2 = c^2$, a and b are the legs and c is always the hypotenuse.

$9^2 + b^2 = 41^2$
$81 + b^2 = 1681$
$b^2 = 1681 - 81$
$b^2 = 1600$
$\sqrt{b^2} = \sqrt{1600}$
$b = 40$

Practice finding the measure of the missing leg in each right triangle below. Simplify square roots.

1.
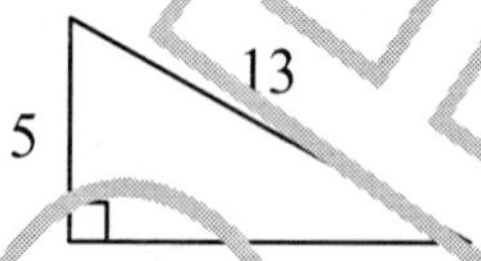

4.
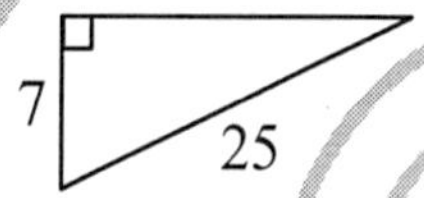

7.
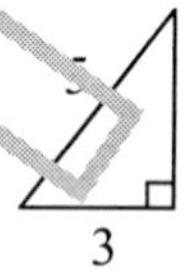

2.
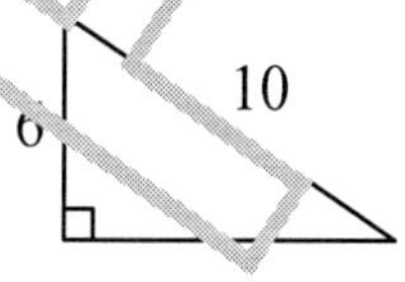

5.
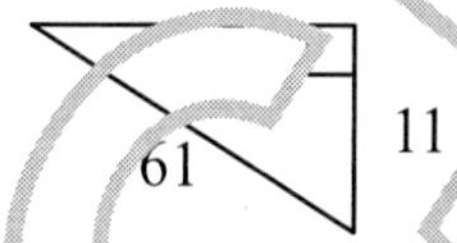

8.
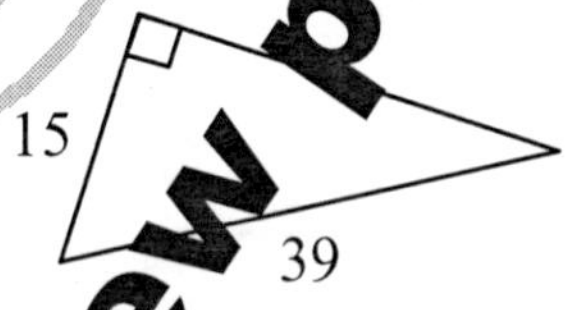

3.
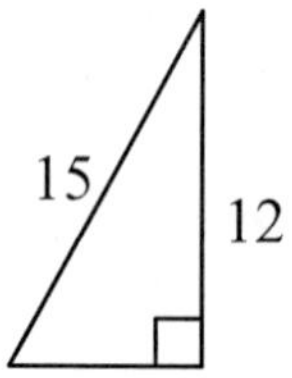

6.
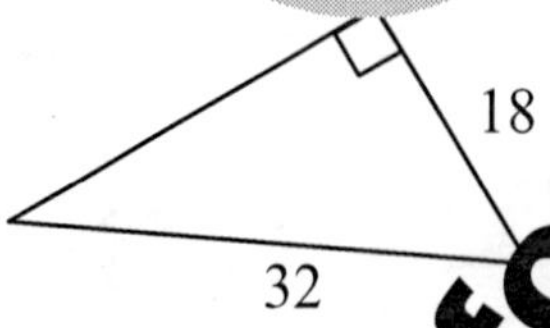

9.
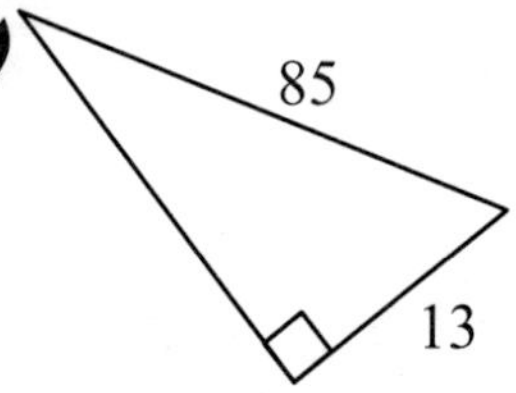

18.5 Applications of the Pythagorean Theorem

The Pythagorean Theorem can be used to determine the distance between two points in some situations. Recall that the formula is written $a^2 + b^2 = c^2$.

Example 4: Find the distance between point B and point A given that the length of each square is 1 inch long and 1 inch wide.

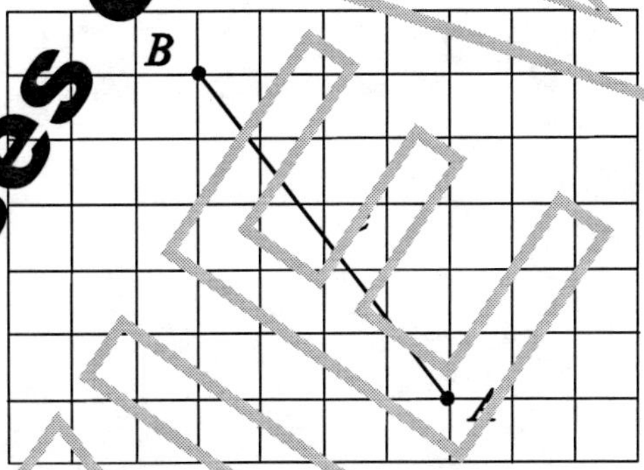

Step 1: Draw a straight line between the two points. We will call this side c.

Step 2: Draw two more lines, one from point B and one from point A. These lines should make a 90° angle. The two new lines will be labeled a and b. Now we can use the Pythagorean Theorem to find the distance from Point B to Point A.

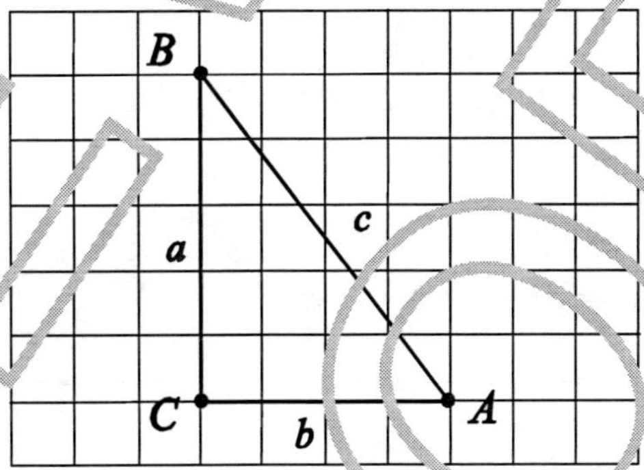

Step 3: Find the length of a and b by counting the number of squares each line has. We find that $a = 5$ inches and $b = 4$ inches. Now, substitute the values found into the Pythagorean Theorem.

$$
\begin{aligned}
a^2 + b^2 &= c^2 \\
5^2 + 4^2 &= c^2 \\
25 + 16 &= c^2 \\
41 &= c^2 \\
\sqrt{41} &= \sqrt{c^2} \\
\sqrt{41} &= c
\end{aligned}
$$

Use the Pythagorean Theorem to find the distances asked. Round your answers to two decimal points.

Below is a diagram of the mall. Use the grid to help answer questions 1 and 2. Each square is 25 feet × 25 feet.

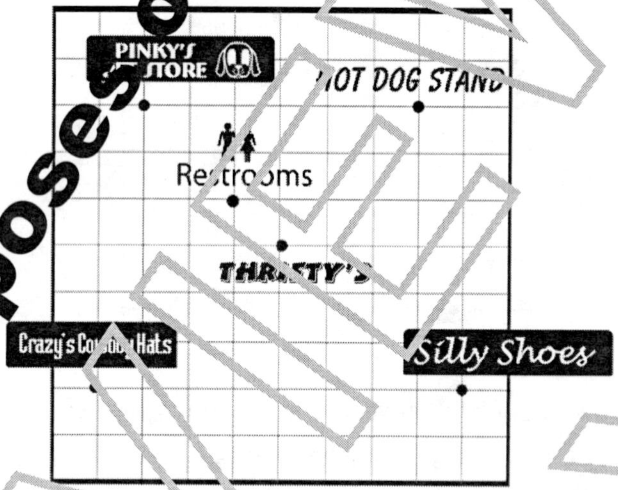

1. Marty walks from Pinky's Pet Store to the restroom to wash his hands. How far did he walk?
2. Betty needs to meet her friend at Silly Shoes, but she wants to get a hot dog first. If Betty is at Thrifty's, how far will she walk to meet her friend?

Below is a diagram of a football field. Use the grid on the football field to help find the answers to questions 3 and 4. Each square is 10 yards × 10 yards.

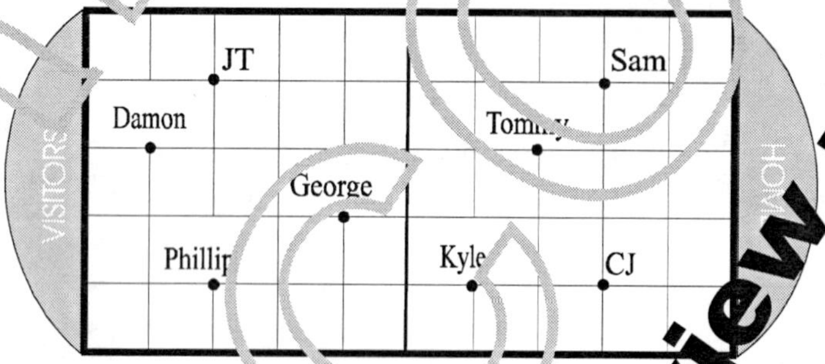

3. George must throw the football to a teammate before he is tackled. If CJ is the only person open, how far must George be able to throw the ball?
4. Damon has the football and is about to make a touchdown. Phillip wants to try to stop him. How far is Phillip from Damon?

18.6 Special Right Triangles

Two right triangles are special right triangles if they have fixed ratios among their sides.

45-45-90 Triangles

In a 45-45-90 triangle, the two sides opposite the 45° angles will always be equal. The length of the hypotenuse is $\sqrt{2}$ times the length of one of the sides opposite a 45° angle.

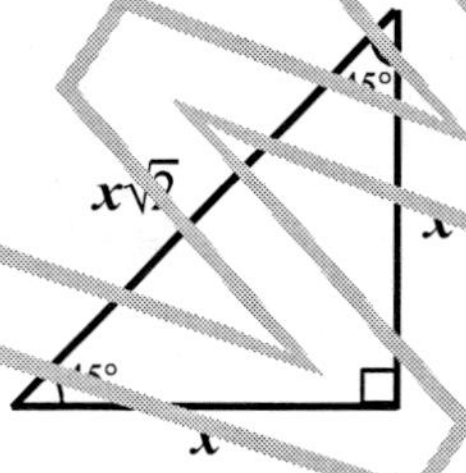

Example 5: What are the lengths of sides a and b?

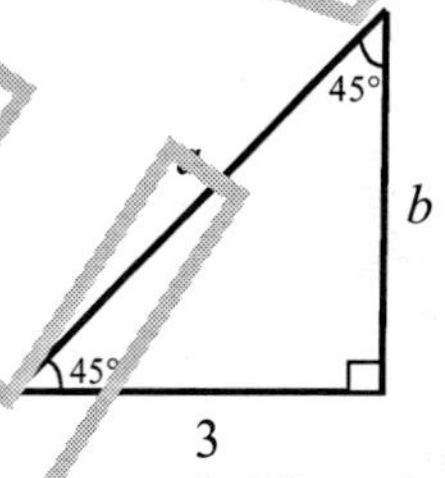

Step 1: The two sides opposite the 45° angles are equal. Therefore, side $b = 3$.

Step 2: The hypotenuse is $\sqrt{2}$ times the length of a side opposite a 45° angle.
Therefore, $a = 3 \times \sqrt{2}$
Simplify: $a = 3\sqrt{2}$

30-60-90 Triangles

In a 30-60-90 triangle, the side opposite the 30° angle is the shortest leg. The side opposite the 60° angle is $\sqrt{3}$ times as long as the shortest leg, and the hypotenuse is twice as long as the shortest leg.

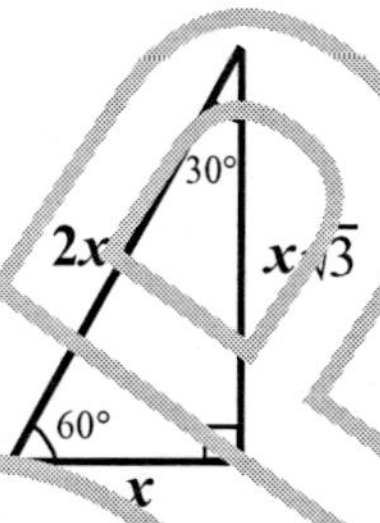

Example 6: What are the lengths of sides a and b?

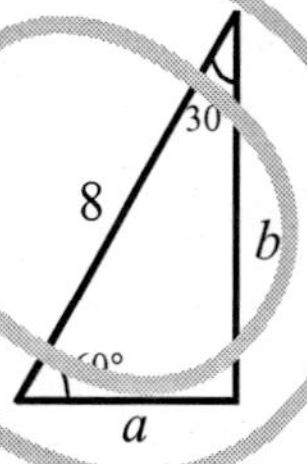

Step 1: The hypotenuse is 2 times the side opposite the 30° angle.
Write the above statement using algebra and then solve.
$8 = 2a$
$\frac{8}{2} = \frac{\not{2}a}{\not{2}}$
$4 = a$

Step 2: Now that it is known that the shortest leg has a length of 4, the side opposite the 60° angle can be calculated.
$b = a \times \sqrt{3}$
$b = 4 \times \sqrt{3}$
$b = 4\sqrt{3}$

Find the missing leg of each of the special right triangles. Simplify your answers.

1.
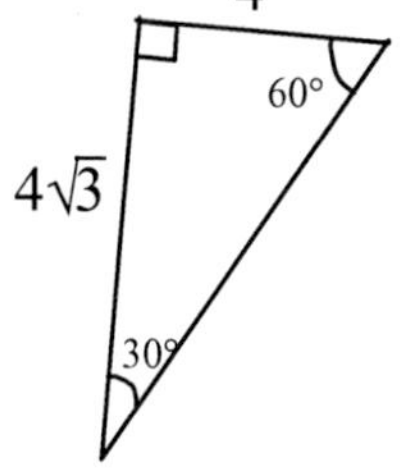
4
60°
$4\sqrt{3}$
30°

2.
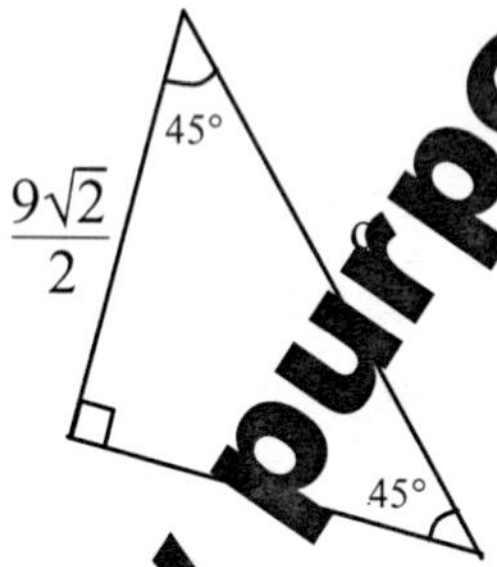
45°
$\frac{9\sqrt{2}}{2}$
45°

3.
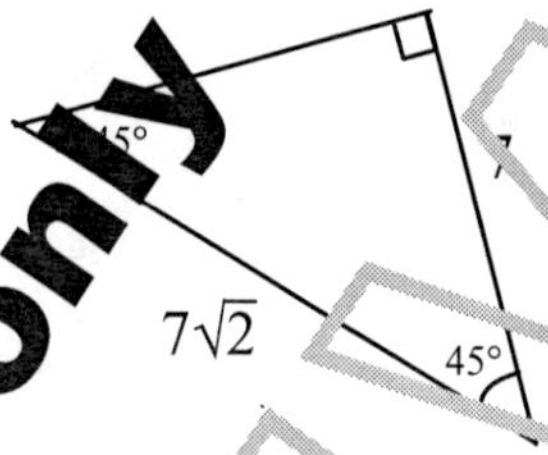
45°
7
$7\sqrt{2}$
45°

4.
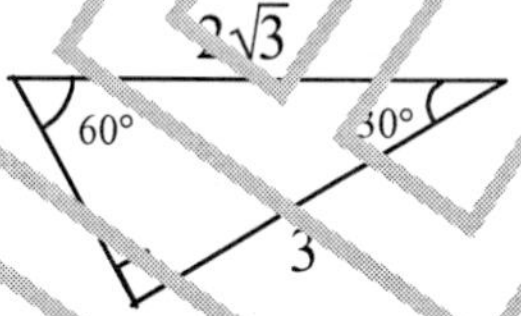
$2\sqrt{3}$
60°
30°
3

5.
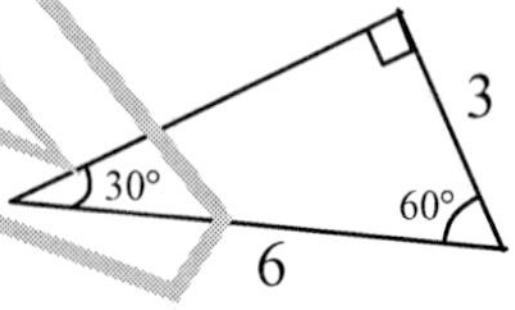
3
30°
60°
6

6.
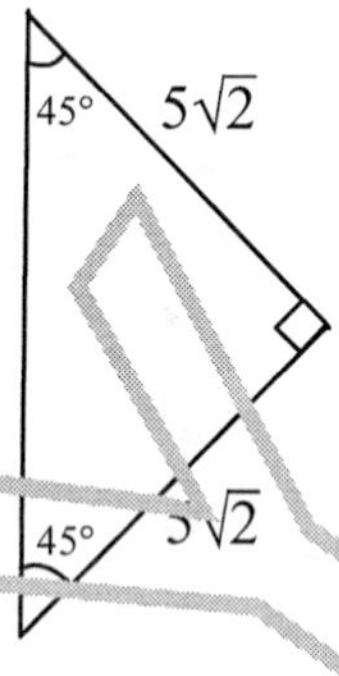
45°
$5\sqrt{2}$
45°
$5\sqrt{2}$

Find the lengths of sides *a* and *b* in each of the special right triangles.

7.
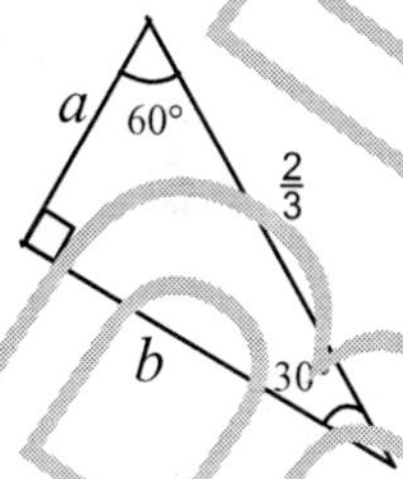
a
60°
$\frac{2}{3}$
b
30°

8.

a
45°
45°
b

9.
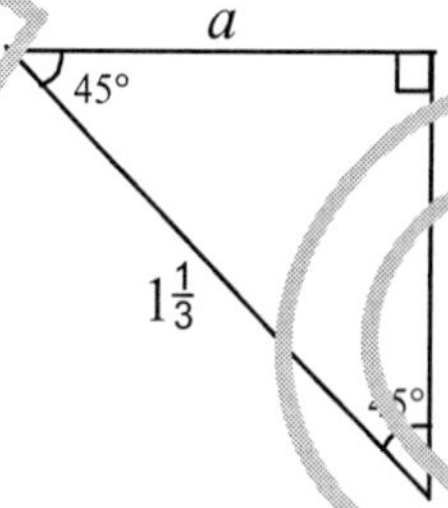
a
45°
$1\frac{1}{3}$
b
45°

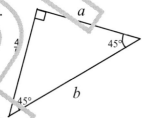

10.
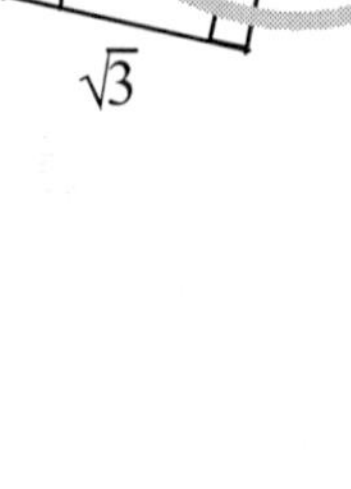
30°
a
b
60°
$\sqrt{3}$

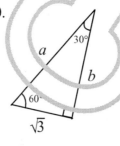

11.
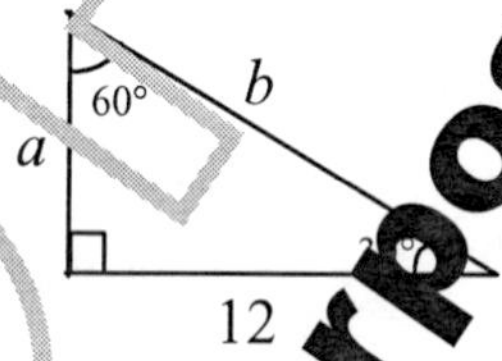
b
60°
a
12

12.
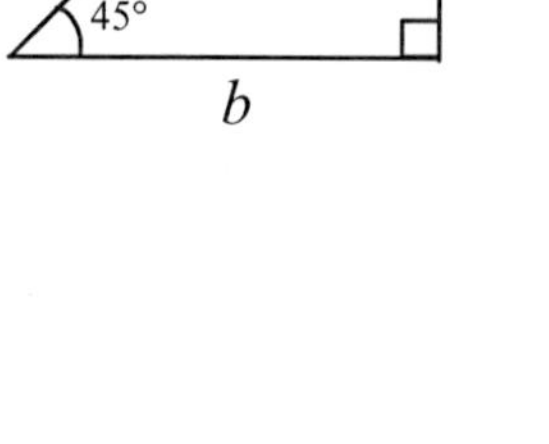
45°
a
$8\sqrt{2}$
45°
b

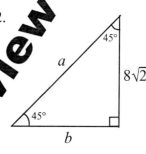

Chapter 18 Review

1. Find the missing angle.

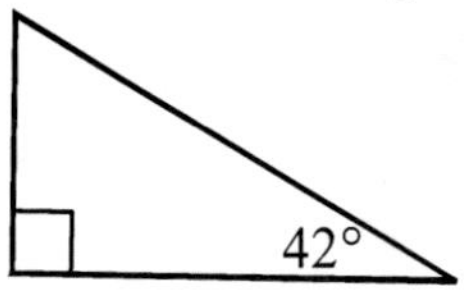

2. What is the length of line segment $\overline{WY}$?

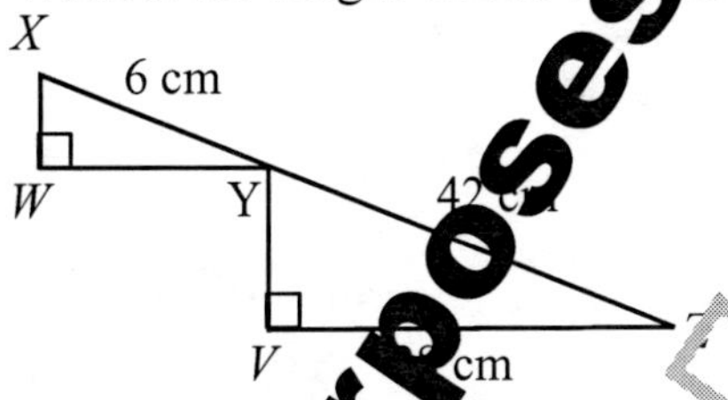

3. Find the missing side.

4. Find the measure of the missing leg of the right triangle below.

5. The following two triangles are similar. Find the length of the missing side.

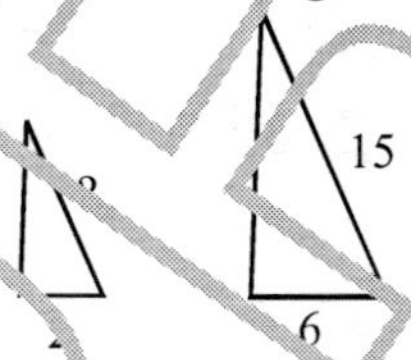

6. Chris walked east from his house to the gas station, which was 1.2 miles away. Then, he walked south from the gas station to his piano teacher's house. His piano teacher lives 2,112 feet from the gas station. Use the Pythagorean theorem to find the direct distance in miles from Chris's house to his piano teacher's house.

7.

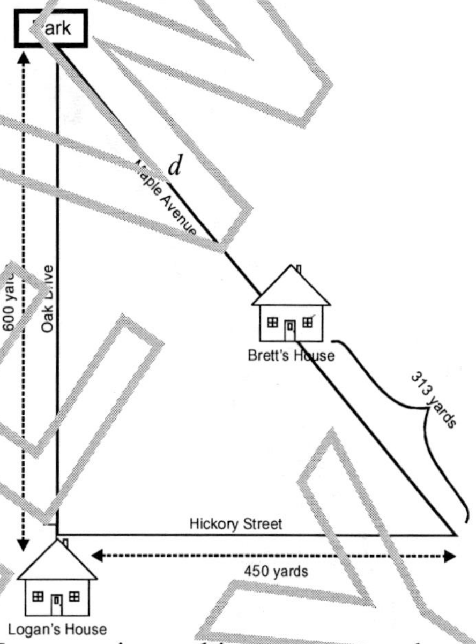

Logan enjoys taking his dog to the park. Some days he leaves his house, located on the corner of Hickory St. and Oak Dr., and walks directly to the park. Sometimes, though, he walks down Hickory St., turns onto Maple Ave. to meet his friend, Brett, and then continues on Maple Ave. to the park. What is the approximate distance (d) from Brett's house to the park?

For questions 8 and 9, find the missing angles.

8.

9.

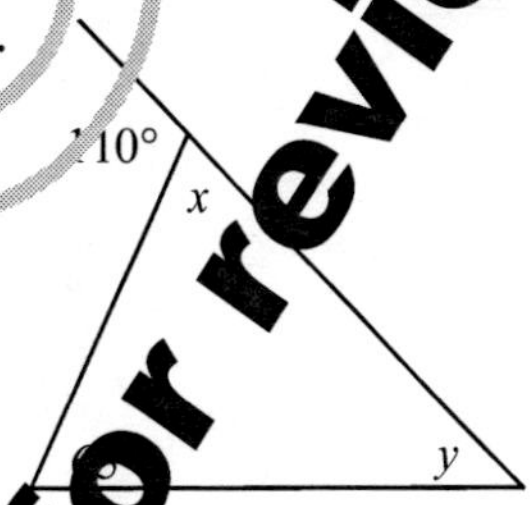

Chapter 18 Test

1. What is the measure of missing angle?

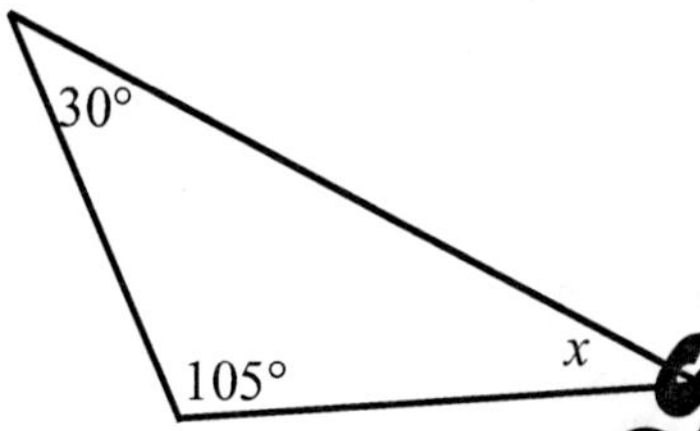

A. 225°
B. 45°
C. 75°
D. 30°
E. 55°

2. What is the measure of y?

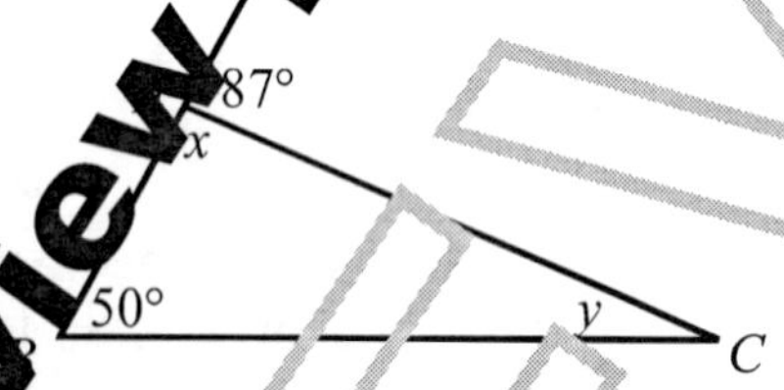

F. 93°
G. 87°
H. 37°
J. 47°
K. Cannot be determined

3. What is the measure of the two missing angles?

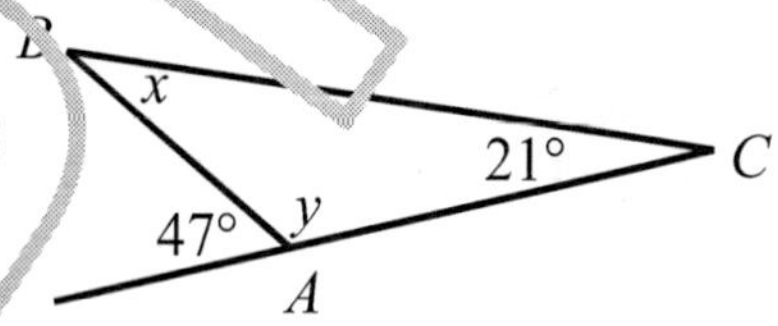

A. $x = 26°, y = 133°$
B. $x = 47°, y = 112°$
C. $x = 112°, y = 47°$
D. $x = 133°, y = 26°$
E. $x = 143°, y = 16°$

4. Given the measures of sides below, which cannot form a triangle?

F. 5, 7, 10
G. 2, 3, 4
H. 15, 6, 9
J. 19, 20, 30
K. 15, 17, 21

5. What type of triangle is illustrated?

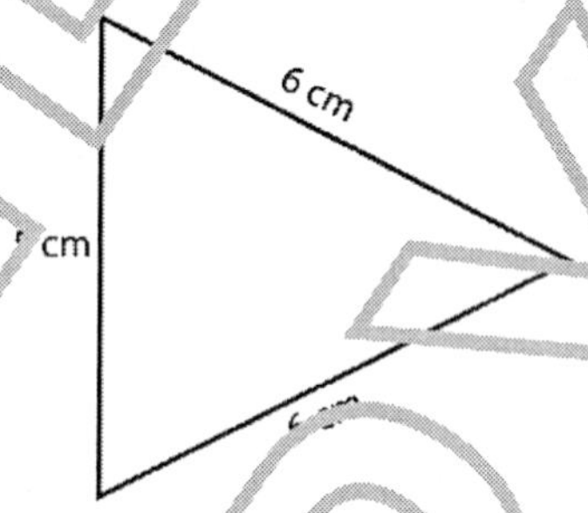

A. right
B. isosceles
C. equilateral
D. obtuse
E. normal

6. Which side in $\triangle ABC$ is the longest side?

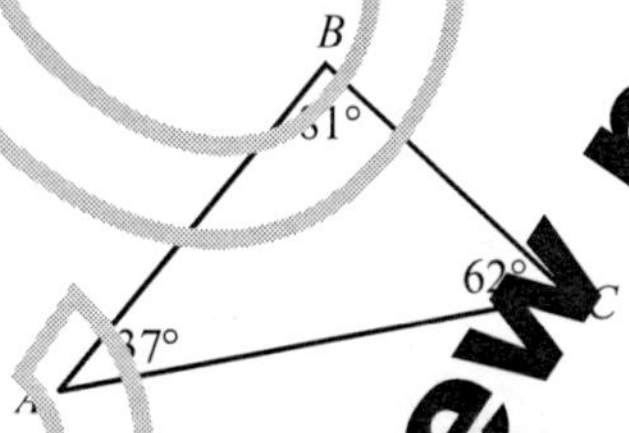

F. $\overline{AB}$
G. $\overline{AC}$
H. $\overline{BC}$
J. $\overline{ABC}$
K. Cannot be determined

7. Approximately what is the measure of the hypotenuse of the triangle?

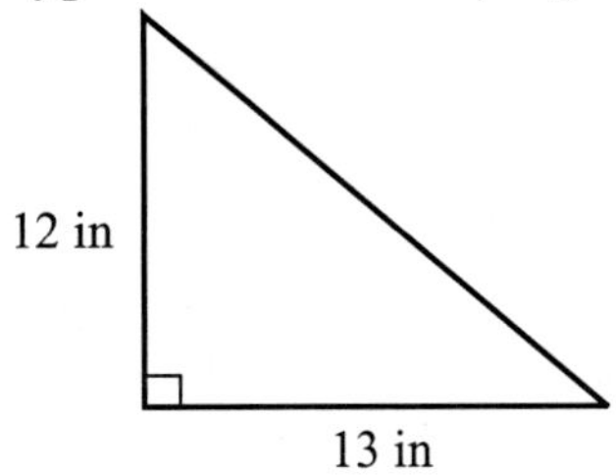

A. 14 in
B. 157 in
C. 313 in
D. 25 in
E. 18 in

8. What is the measure of the missing side in the triangle?

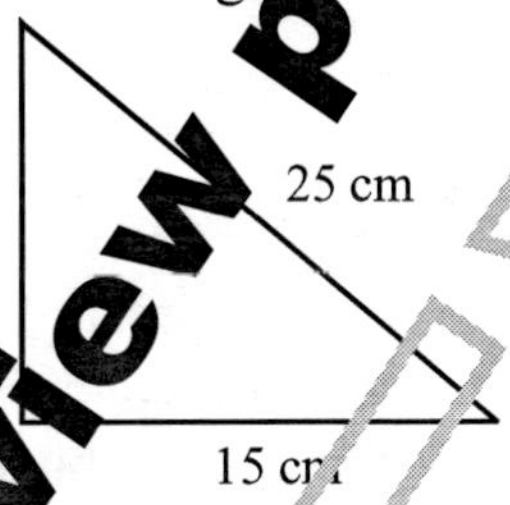

F. 5 cm
G. 29 cm
H. 10 cm
J. 20 cm
K. 11 cm

9. What is the measure of $\overline{AB}$?

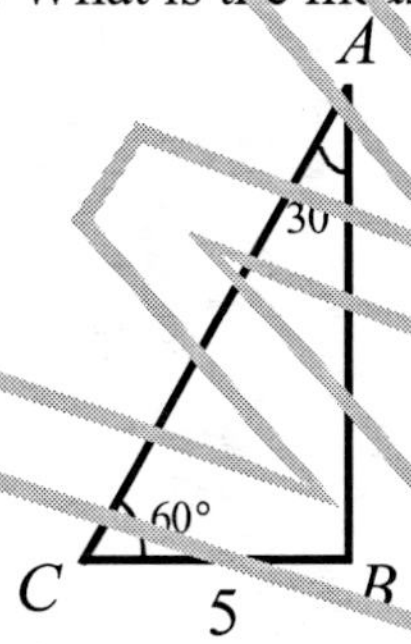

A. $5\sqrt{3}$
B. 10
C. 5
D. 2.5
E. $5\sqrt{2}$

Chapter 19
Plane Geometry

19.1 Quadrilaterals and Their Properties

A **quadrilateral** is a polygon with four sides. A **parallelogram** is a quadrilateral in which both pairs of opposite sides are parallel. The following properties of parallelograms are given without proof:

1. **Both pairs of opposite sides are parallel.**
2. **The opposite sides are congruent.**
3. **The opposite angles are congruent**
4. **Consecutive angles are supplementary.**
5. **The diagonals bisect each other**

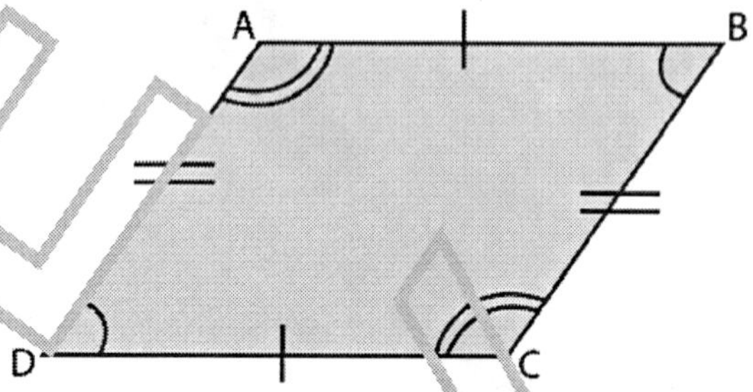

A **rectangle** is a parallelogram with four right angles. It follows that a rectangle has all of the properties listed above, plus all four angles are 90°. In addition, the diagonals of a rectangle are congruent. A **rhombus** is a parallelogram with four congruent sides. A rhombus has all the properties of a parallelogram, but both pairs of opposite sides are congruent as well as parallel. A **square** is a rhombus with four right angles. Therefore, a square has four congruent sides and four congruent angles (each 90°). As you can see, a square is also a quadrilateral, a parallelogram, rectangle, and a rhombus.

A **trapezoid** is a quadrilateral with only one pair of parallel sides. The parallel sides are called bases, and the other two sides are called legs.

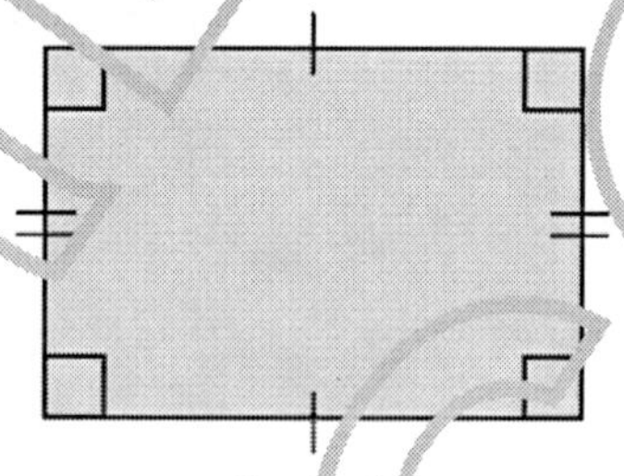

Rectangle

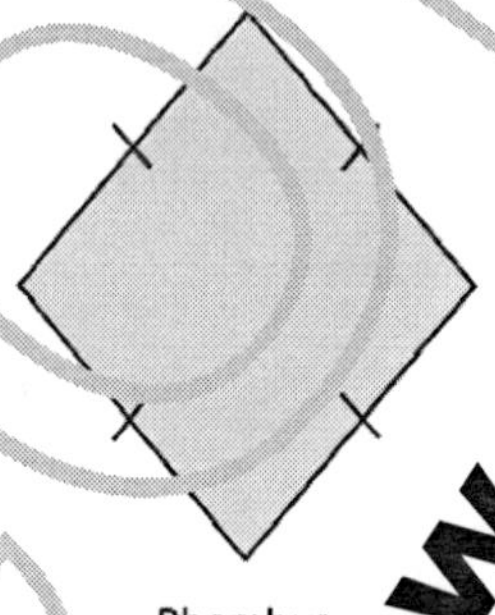

Rhombus

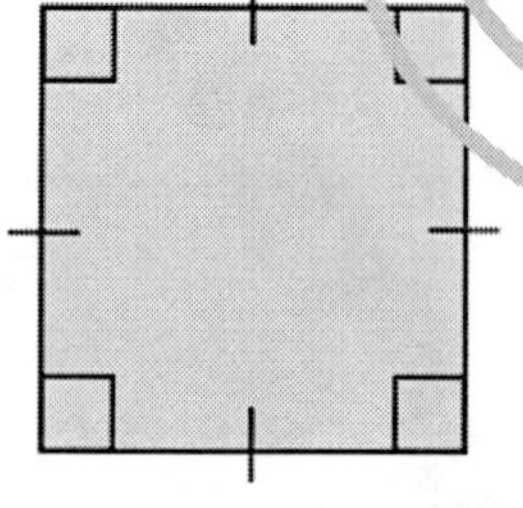

Square

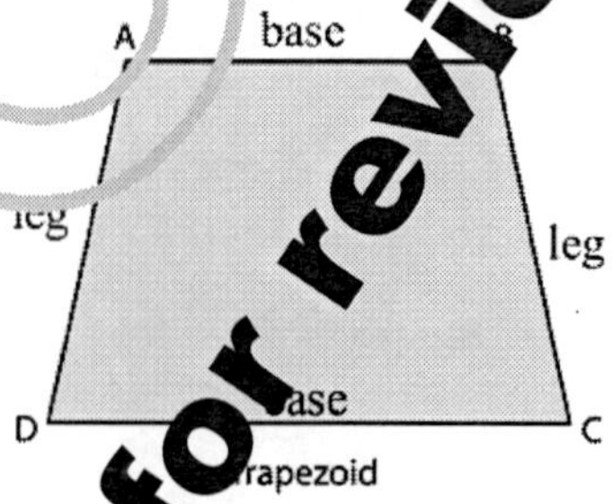

Trapezoid

19.2 Sum of Interior Angles of a Polygon

Given a polygon, you can find the sum of the measures of the interior angles using the following formula: Sum of the measures of the interior angles $= 180°(n-2)$, where n is the number of sides of the polygon.

Example 1: Find the sum of the measures of the interior angles of the following polygon:

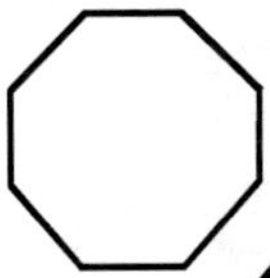

Solution: The figure has 8 sides. Using the formula we have $180°(8-2) = 180°(6) = 1080°$

Using the formula, $180°(n-2)$, find the sum of the interior angles of the following figures.

1. 

4. 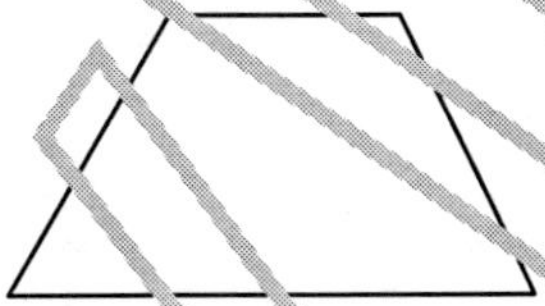

7. 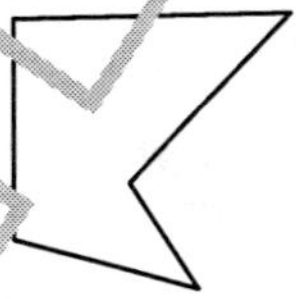

10. 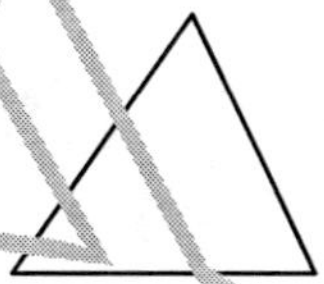

2. 

5. 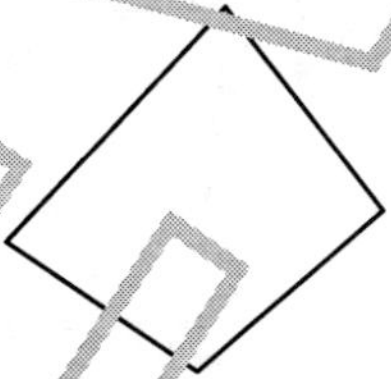

8. 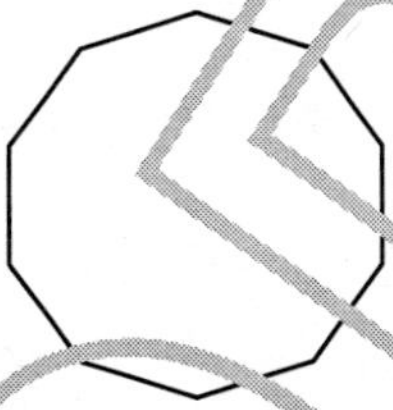

11. 

3. 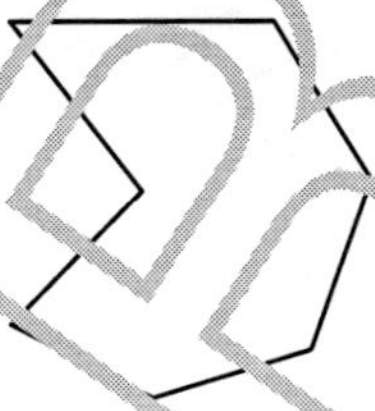

6. 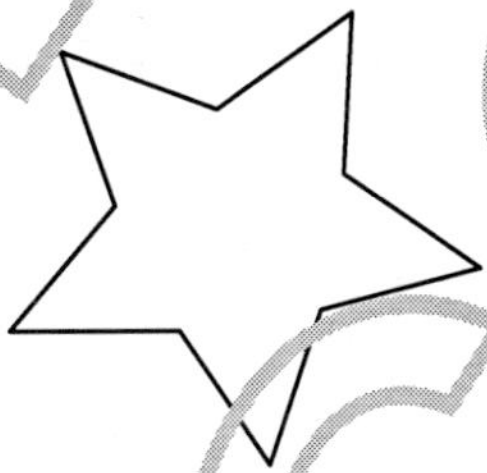

9. 

12. 

Find the measure of $\angle G$ in the regular polygons shown below. Remember that the sides of a regular polygon are equal.

13. 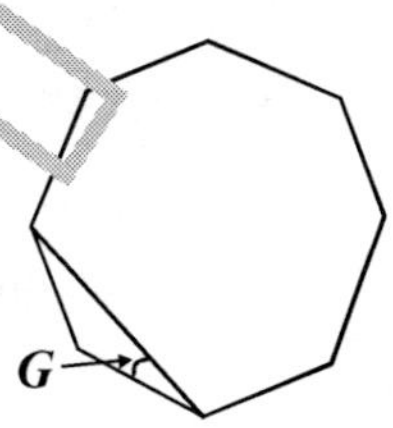

14. 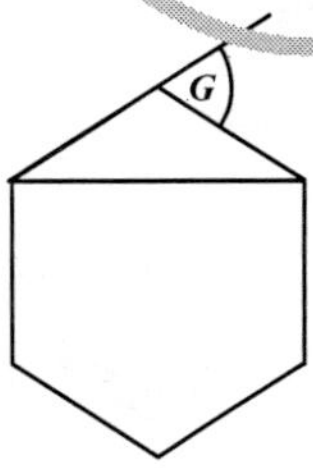

15. 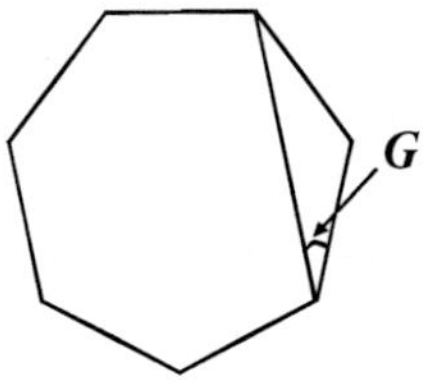

19.3 Exterior Angles of Polygons

The sum of the measures of the exterior angles of a convex polygon, one at each vertex, is 360°.

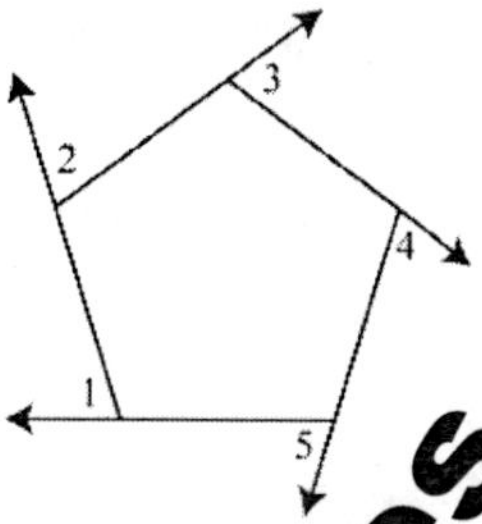

$$m\angle 1 + m\angle 2 + m\angle 3 + m\angle 4 + m\angle 5 = 360°.$$

In addition, for a regular n-gon, in which all angle measures are the same, the measure of each exterior angle is $\frac{1}{n} \times 360°$ or $\frac{360°}{n}$ where n is the number of sides.

Example 2: Find the value of x.

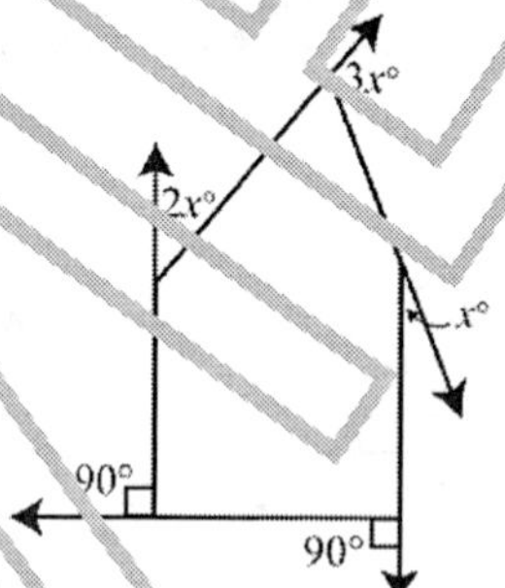

Solution: The sum of the measures of the exterior angles is 360°, so

$$\begin{aligned} 90° + 90° + x + 2x + 3x &= 360° \\ 180° + 6x &= 360° \\ 6x &= 180° \\ x &= 30° \end{aligned}$$

Example 3: One exterior angle of a regular convex n-gon measures 22.5°. How many sides does it have?

Solution: The measure of each exterior angle of a convex n-gon is $\frac{360°}{n}$, where n is the number of sides. Therefore,

$$22.5° = \frac{360°}{n} \quad \text{so} \quad n = \frac{360°}{22.5°} = 16$$

The polygon has 16 sides.

Solve the following problems.

1. Find the measure of each exterior angle of a regular dodecagon (12 sides).
2. Find the measure of each exterior angle of a regular octagon.
3. Each exterior angle of a regular polygon equals 40°. How many sides does the polygon have?
4. The exterior angles of a given polygon measure 45°, 125°, $2x°$, $3x°$, and $5x°$. Find the value of x and list the five angle measures.
5. If the measure of the exterior angles of a polygon are $x°$, $3x°$, $(x + 2)°$, $(5x - 4)°$, 30°, and 42°, find the value of x.

19.4 Area of Trapezoids and Parallelograms

Example 4: Find the area of the following parallelogram.

The formula for the area of a parallelogram is $A = bh$.
A = area
b = base
h = height

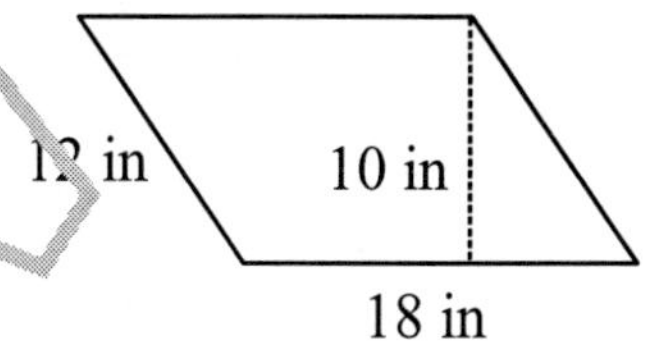

Step 1: Insert measurements from the parallelogram into the formula: $A = 18 \times 10$.

Step 2: Multiply. $18 \times 10 = 180$ in^2

Example 5: Find the area of the following trapezoid.
The formula for the area of a trapezoid is $A = \frac{1}{2}h(b_1 + b_2)$. A trapezoid has two bases that are parallel to each other. When you add the length of the two bases together and then multiply by $\frac{1}{2}$, you find their average length.

A = area
b = base
h = height

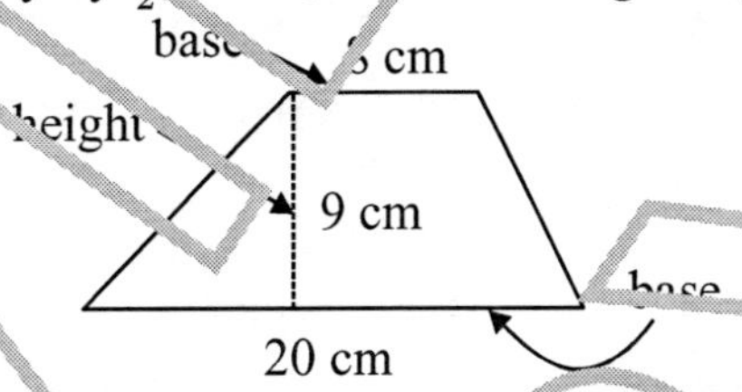

Insert the measurements from the trapezoid into the formula and solve:
$\frac{1}{2} \times 9\,(8 + 20) = 126$ cm^2

Find the area of the following parallelograms and trapezoids.

1.
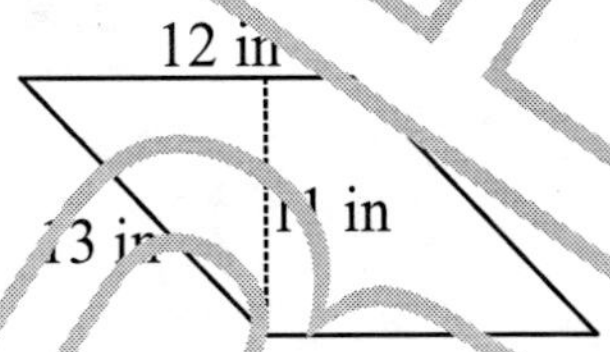

4.
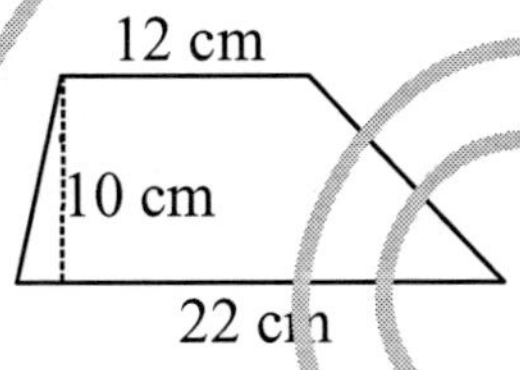

7.
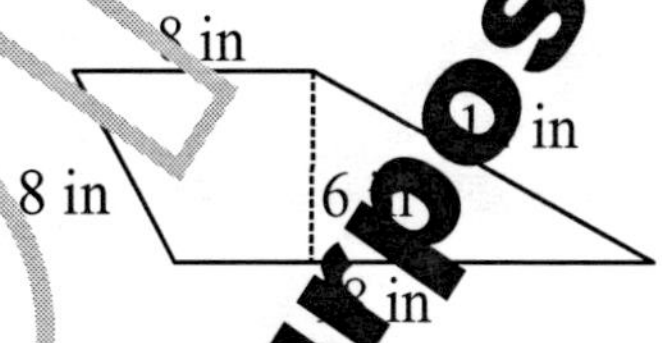

2.
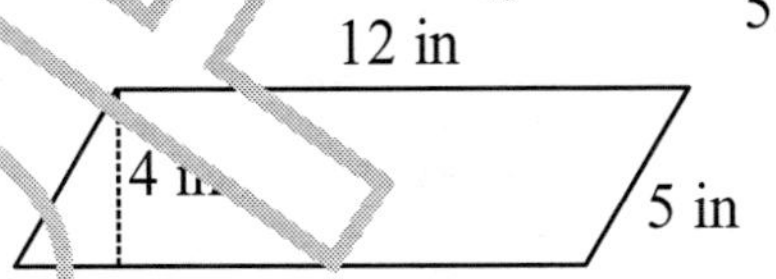

5.
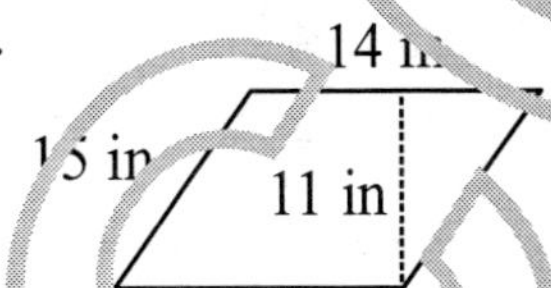

8.
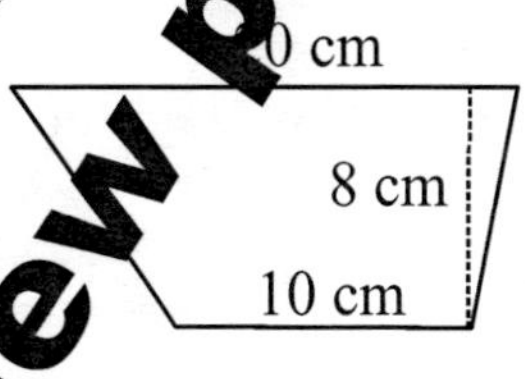

3.
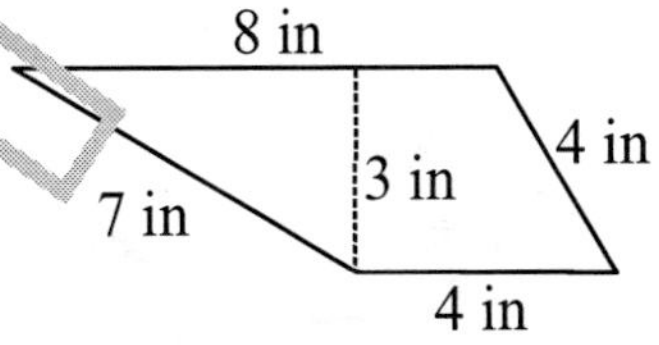

6.
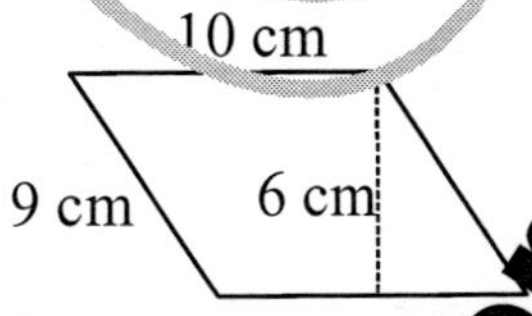

9.
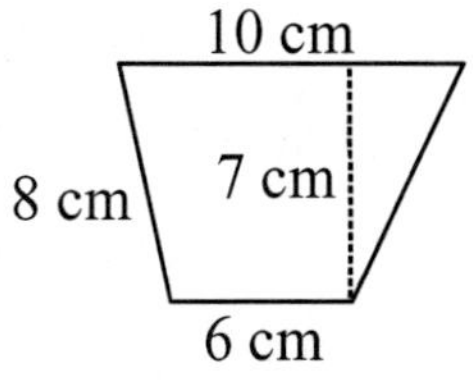

19.5 Parts of a Circle

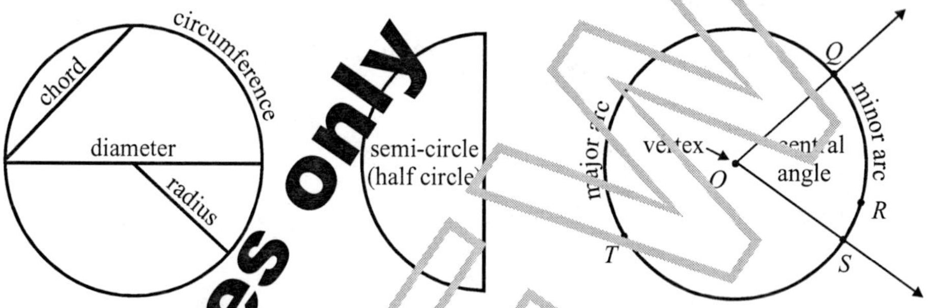

A **central angle** of a circle has the center of the circle as its vertex. The rays of a central angle each contain a radius of the circle. $\angle QOS$ is a central angle.

The points Q and S separate the circle into **arcs**. The arc lies on the circle itself. It does not include any points inside or outside the circle. $\widehat{QRS}$ or $\widehat{QS}$ is a **minor arc** because it is less than a semicircle. A minor arc can be named by 2 or 3 points. $\widehat{QTS}$ is a **major arc** because it is more than a semicircle. A major arc must be named by 3 points. The measure of a minor arc is the measure of its central angle. If an angle is inscribed in a circle, then the measure of the minor arc is two times the measure of the inscribed angle.

An **inscribed angle** is an angle whose vertex lies on the circle and whose sides contain **chords** of the circle. $\angle ABC$ in Figure 1 is an inscribed angle. A line is **tangent** to a circle if it only touches the circle at one point, which is called the point of tangency. See Figure 2 for an example. A **secant**, shown in figure 3, is a line that intersects with a circle at two points. Every secant forms a chord. In Figure 3, secant $\overleftrightarrow{AB}$ forms chord $\overline{AB}$.

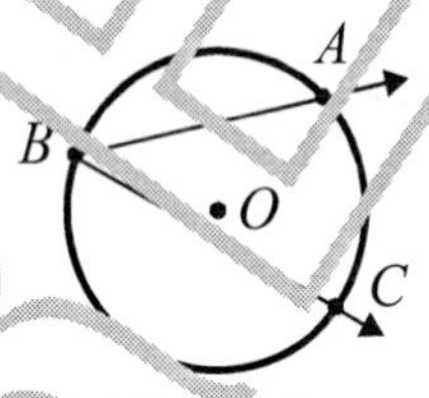

Figure 1

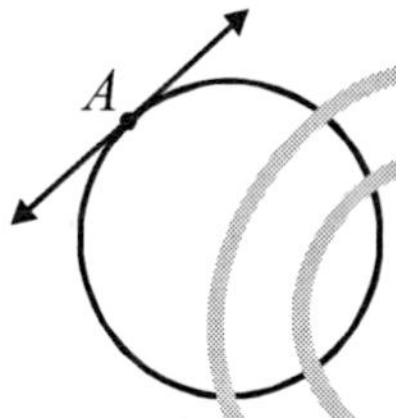

Figure 2

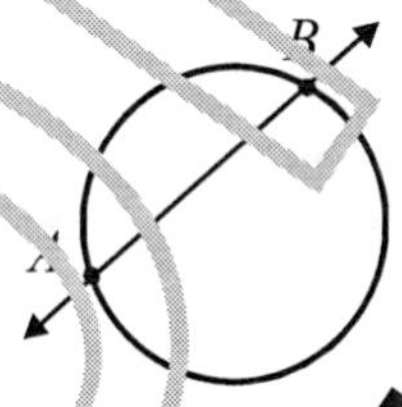

Figure 3

Refer to the figure on the right, and answer the following questions.

1. Identify the 2 line segments that are chords of the circle but not diameters.
2. Identify the largest major arc of the circle that contains point S.
3. Identify the vertex of the circle.
4. Identify the inscribed angle.
5. Identify the central angle.

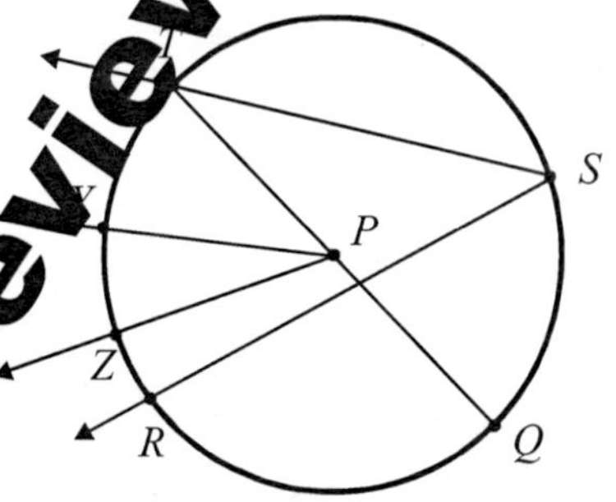

19.6 Two-Step Area Problems

Solving the problems below will require two steps. You will need to find the area of two figures, and then either add or subtract the two areas to find the answer. **Carefully read the examples.**

Example 6:
Find the area of the living room below.
Figure 1

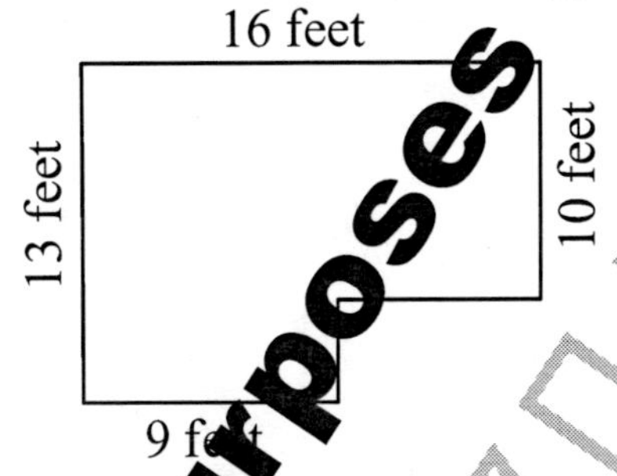

Step 1: Complete the rectangle as in Figure 2, and compute the area as if it were a complete rectangle.

Figure 2

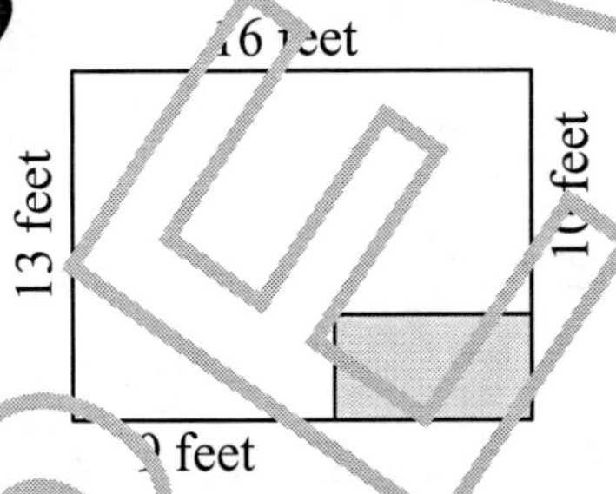

$A = \text{length} \times \text{width}$
$A = 16 \times 13$
$A = 208 \text{ ft}^2$

Step 2: Figure the area of the shaded part.

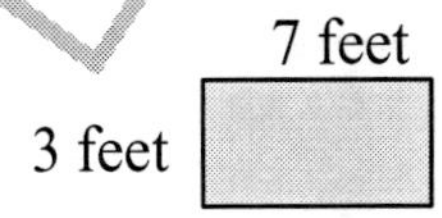

$7 \times 3 = 21 \text{ ft}^2$

Step 3: Subtract the area of the shaded part from the area of the complete rectangle

$208 - 21 = 187 \text{ ft}^2$

Example 7:
Find the area of the shaded sidewalk.

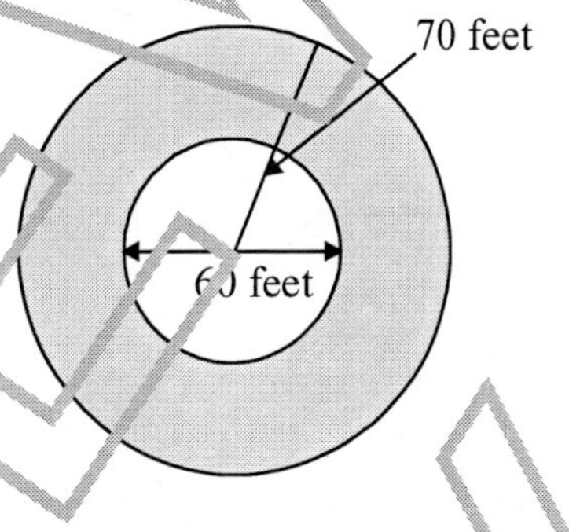

Step 1: Find the area of the outside circle.
$\pi = 3.14$
$A = \pi r^2$
$A = 3.14 \times 70 \times 70$
$A = 15,386 \text{ ft}^2$

Step 2: Find the area of the inside circle.
$\pi = 3.14$
$A = \pi r^2$
$A = 3.14 \times 30 \times 30$
$A = 2826 \text{ ft}^2$

Step 3: Subtract the area of the inside circle from the area of the outside circle.
$15,386 - 2826 = 12,560 \text{ ft}^2$

Find the area of the following figures.

1.

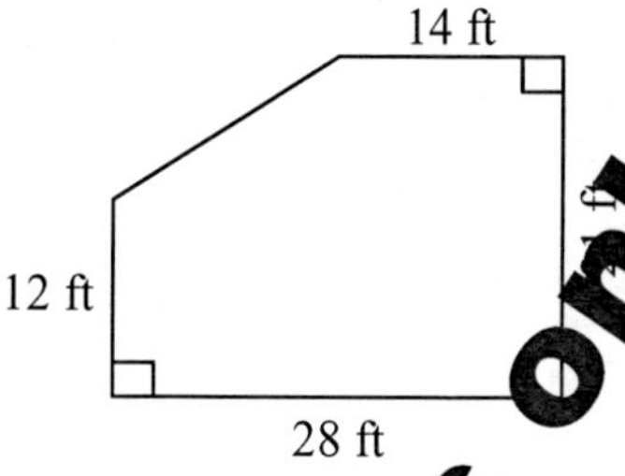

2.

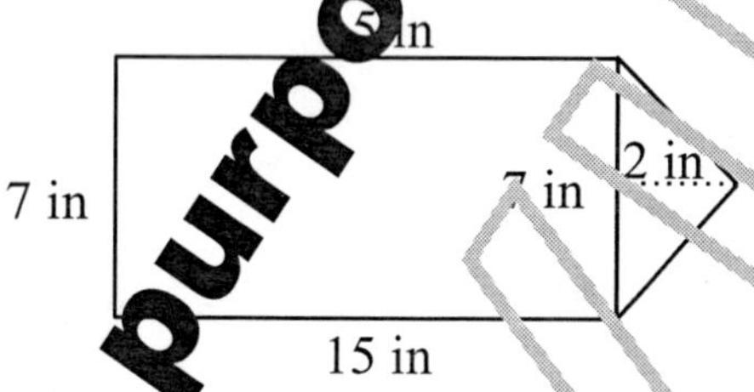

3. What is the area of the shaded circle? Use $\pi = 3.14$, and round the answer to the nearest whole number.

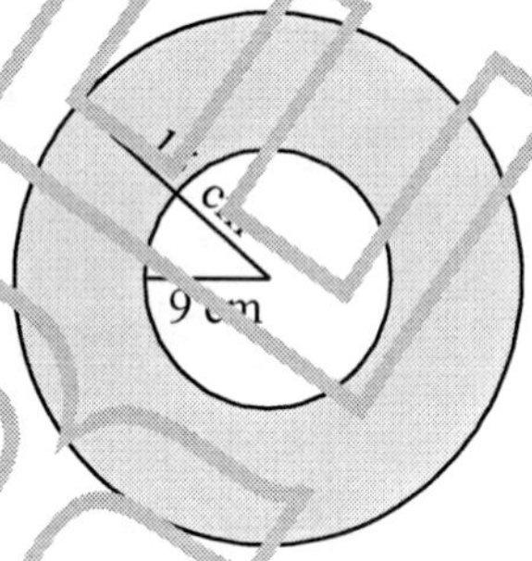

4.

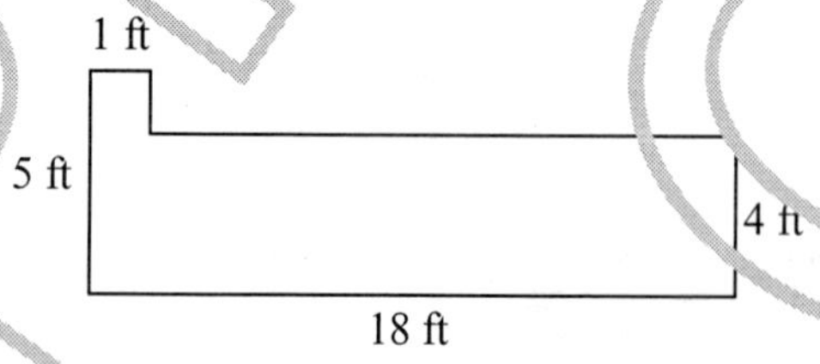

5. What is the area of the shaded part?

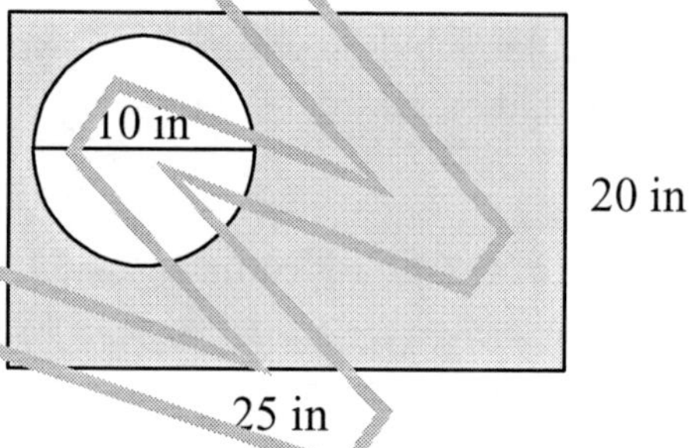

6. What is the area of the shaded part?

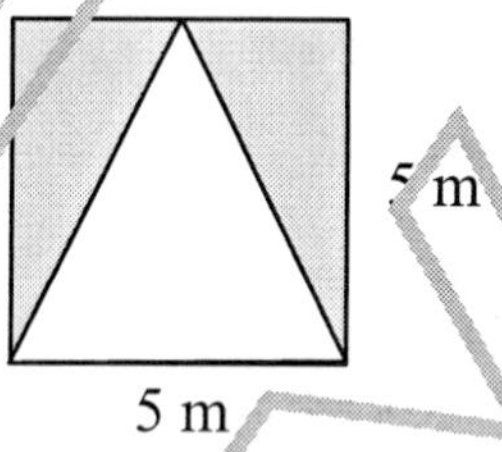

7. What is the area of the shaded part?

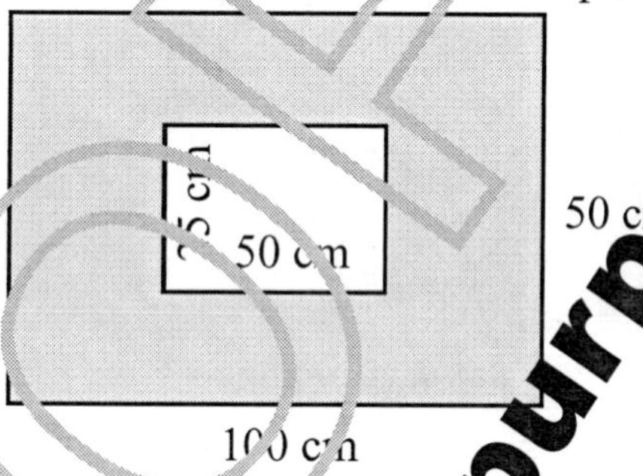

8.

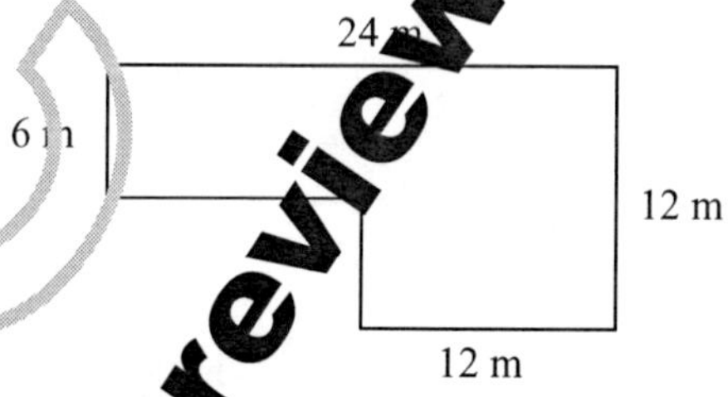

for review purposes only

19.7 Finding the Distances Between Points on Shapes

Sometimes it is necessary to find the distance between points on a shape. This often arises when you have to calculate the perimeter of the shape. Since the perimeter of a shape is the distance around it, to calculate its perimeter, one must know the distance between each of its adjacent vertices. The distance between a shape's adjacent vertices can be found by using the information given and the properties of the shape to deduce even more information about the shape. Likewise, if the shape is circumscribed around or inscribed within another shape, you can use the relationship between the two shapes to help determine the distance between the shape's adjacent vertices, and thus, its perimeter.

Example 8: A right triangle has a hypotenuse of 42 cm and one external angle measuring 120°. What is the perimeter of the triangle?

Step 1: To find the perimeter of the triangle, it's necessary to find the length of each of its sides, or in other words, the distance between each of its vertices.

Step 2: First of all, for any polygon, the sum of the measure of an external angle and the measure of the adjacent internal angle always equals 180°.
The right triangle has an external angle measuring 120°, it has an internal angle measuring $180° - 120° = 60°$.

Step 3: Because any triangle has three internal angles, the sum of which is 180°, and because a right triangle by definition has one internal angle measuring 90°, the third internal angle of the right triangle must measure $180° - 60° - 90° = 30°$.

Step 4: Since the three internal angles of the right triangle measure 30°, 60°, and 90°, it is a special type of right triangle known to have one leg with a length of $\frac{1}{2}$ the hypotenuse and another leg with a length of $\frac{\sqrt{3}}{2}$ the hypotenuse.
Therefore, the length of one of the legs of the right triangle is $(42\text{ cm})\left(\frac{1}{2}\right)$, or 21 cm, while the length of the other leg is $(42\text{ cm})\left(\frac{\sqrt{3}}{2}\right)$, or $21\sqrt{3}$ cm. By adding the lengths of the three sides of the right triangle together, one arrives at a perimeter of $42\text{ cm} + 21\text{ cm} + 21\sqrt{3}\text{ cm}$, or $63 + 21\sqrt{3}$ cm.
This can be simplified to $21\left(3 + \sqrt{3}\right)$ cm.

Calculate the perimeters of each of the following triangles.

1. A right triangle with a leg measuring 14 in and an external angle measuring 135°
2. A triangle with a side measuring 7 ft and two external angles, each measuring 120°
3. A right triangle with a hypotenuse measuring 50 cm and a leg measuring 3 cm
4. An equilateral triangle with a side measuring 19 in
5. An isosceles triangle with one side measuring 75 ft and another side measuring 3 ft
6. A triangle with two sides measuring 15 cm each and two angles measuring 30° each

Example 9: The figure below is a square with a circumscribed circle. If the area of the circle is 676π m^2, what is the perimeter of the square?

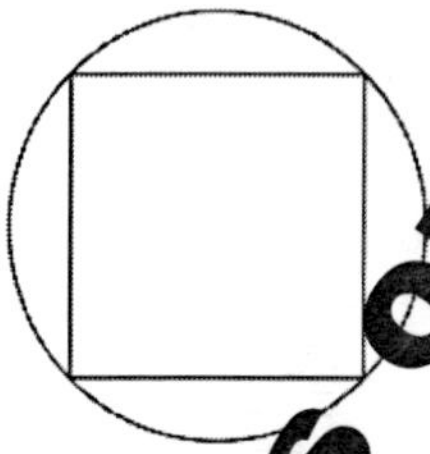

Step 1: The formula for the area of a circle is $A = \pi r^2$, so for the circle above, $\pi r^2 = 676\pi$ m^2. If both sides of the equation are divided by π, the equation becomes $r^2 = 676$ m^2, so the radius of the circle must be $\sqrt{676 \text{ m}^2}$, or 26 m.

Step 2: Since the radius of the circle is 26 m, the diameter of the circle must be (2)(26 m), or 52 m. If a diagonal of the square is drawn, it divides the square into two right triangles that both have the diagonal of the square as a hypotenuse, and a right triangle with a circumscribed circle always has a hypotenuse on which the center of the circle lies. For this reason, the diagonal of the square is the diameter of the circle, and its length is 52 m.

Step 3: The diagonal of a square always has a length equal to $\sqrt{2}$ times the length of one of the square's sides, so for the square above, the length of one of the sides, or the distance between two of the adjacent vertices, is $\frac{52}{\sqrt{2}}$ m $= \frac{52\sqrt{2}}{2}$ m $= 26\sqrt{2}$ m. Therefore, the perimeter of the square is $(4)(26\sqrt{2}$ m$)$, or $104\sqrt{2}$ m.

Calculate perimeter of a square with a circumscribed circle that has each of the following areas.

1. 81π in^2
2. 121π m^2
3. 625π ft^2
4. 441π in^2
5. 961π cm^2
6. 729π ft^2
7. A square with an area of 64 m^2 has a circumscribed circle. What is the circle's area?
8. The midpoints of the sides of square A are the vertices of square B. If square A has a perimeter of 76 ft, what is the perimeter of square B?
9. The midpoints of the sides of square C are the vertices of square D. If square D has a perimeter of 102 cm, what is the perimeter of square C?

19.8 Perimeter and Area with Algebraic Expressions

You have already calculated the perimeter and area of various shapes with given measurements. You must also understand how to find the perimeter of shapes that are described by algebraic expressions. Study the examples below.

Example 10: Use the equation $P = 2l + 2w$ to find the perimeter of the following rectangle.

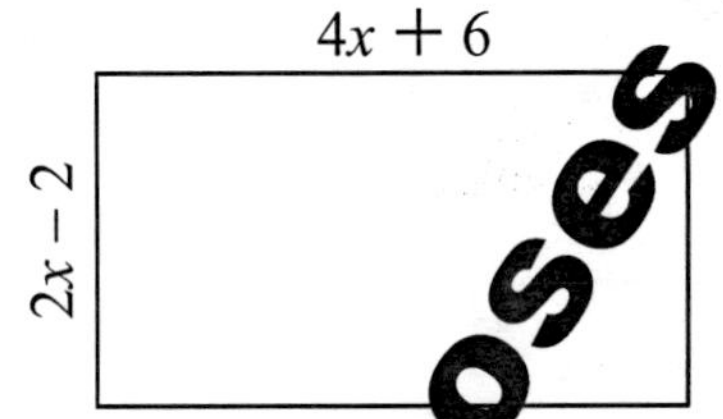

Step 1: Find $2l$. $2(4x+6) = 8x + 12$
Step 2: Find $2w$. $2(2x-2) = 4x - 4$
Step 3: Find $2l + 2w$. $12x + 8$

Perimeter $= 12x + 8$

Example 11: Using the formula $A = lw$, find the area of the rectangle below.

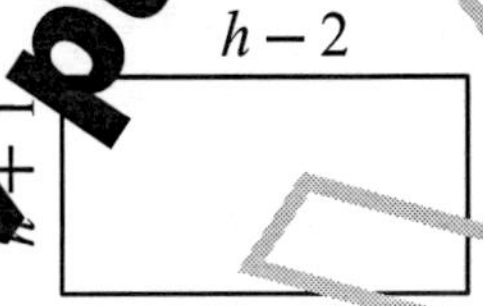

Step 1: $A = (h-2)(h+1)$
Step 2: $A = h^2 - 2h + h - 2$
Step 3: $A = h^2 - h - 2$

Area $= h^2 - h - 2$

Example 12: Find the area of the shaded part in the following figure.

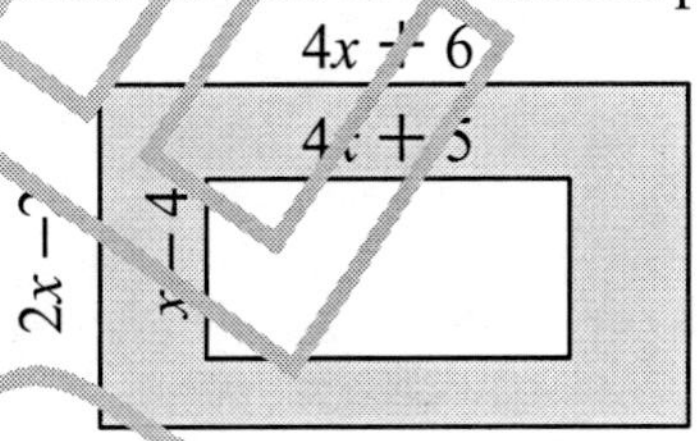

Step 1: Find the area of the larger rectangle.
$(4x+6)(2x-2) = 8x^2 - 8x + 12x - 12 = 8x^2 + 4x - 12$

Step 2: Find the area of the smaller rectangle.
$(4x+5)(x-4) = 4x^2 - 16x + 5x - 20 = 4x^2 - 11x - 20$

Step 3: Subtract the area of the smaller rectangle from the area of the larger rectangle.

$$\begin{array}{r} 8x^2 + 4x - 12 \\ -\,(4x^2 - 11x - 20) \\ \hline \end{array} \qquad \begin{array}{r} 8x^2 + 4x - 12 \\ -4x^2 + 11x + 20 \\ \hline 4x^2 + 15x + 8 \end{array}$$

← Changing signs
← Area of shaded section

Find the perimeter of each of the following rectangles.

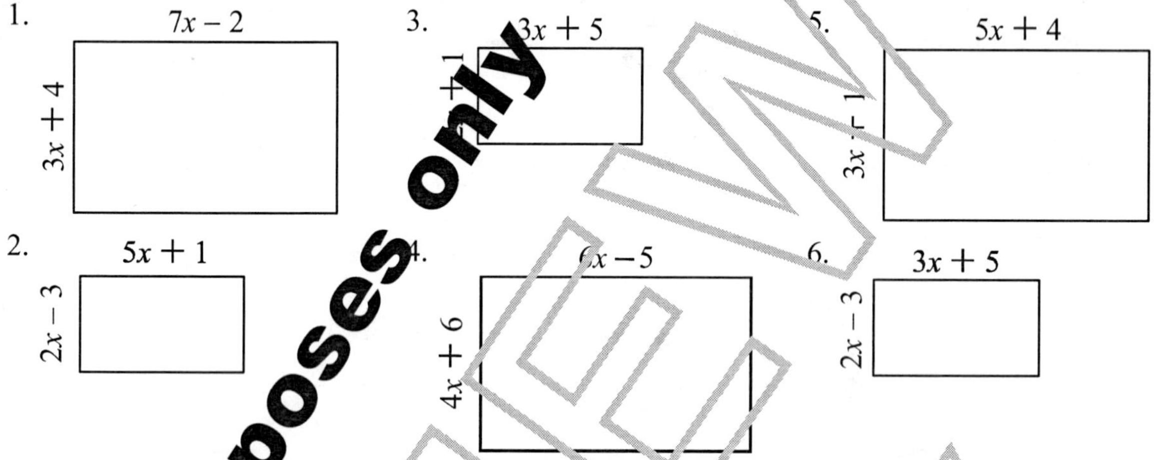

Find the area of each of the following rectangles.

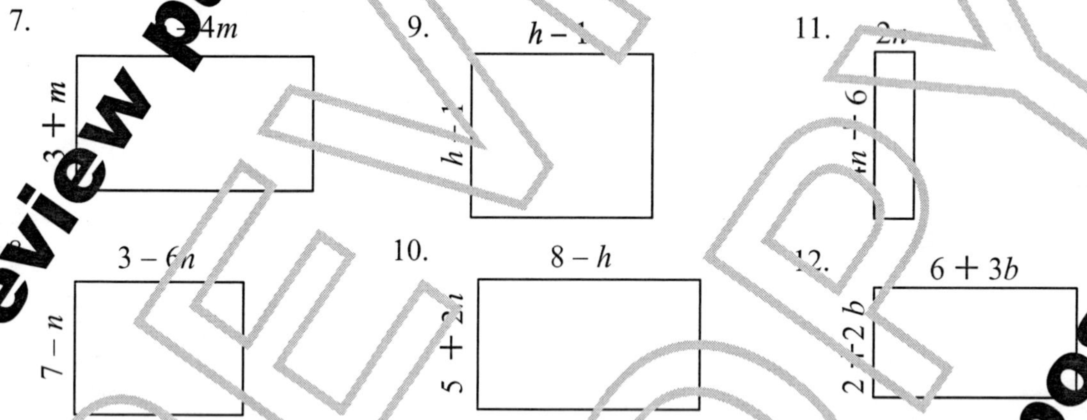

Find the area of the shaded portion of each figure below.

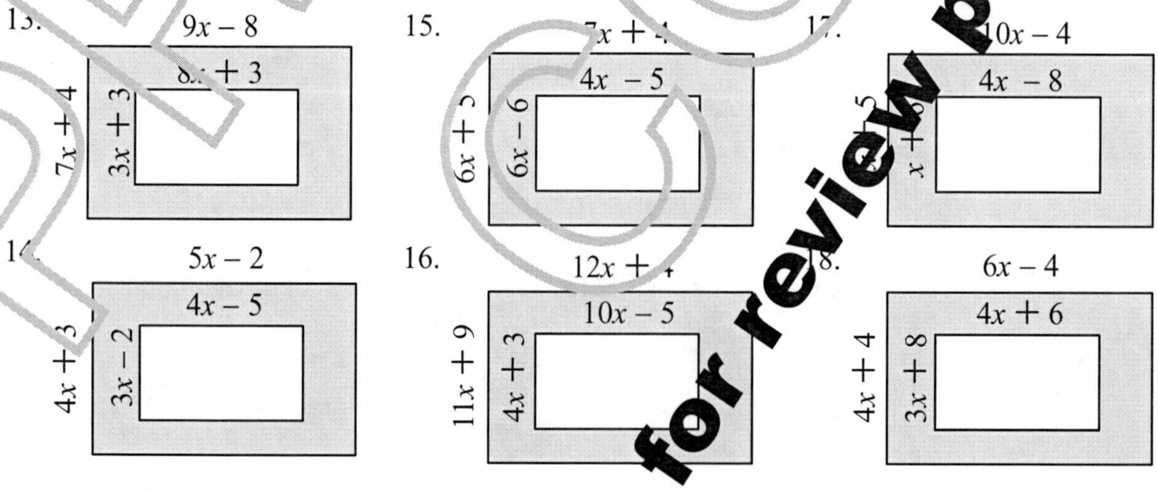

19.9 Geometry Word Problems

The perimeter of a geometric figure is the distance around the outside of the figure.

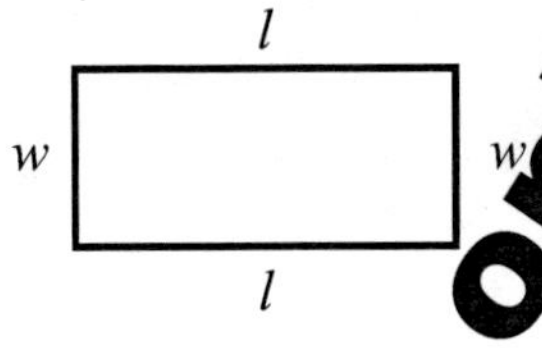

perimeter = $2l + 2w$

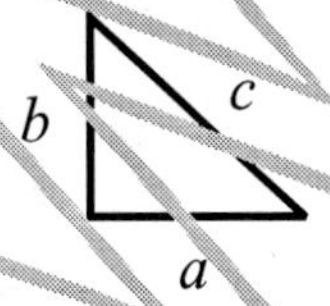

perimeter = $a + b + c$

Example 13: The perimeter of a rectangle is 44 feet. The length of the rectangle is 6 feet more than the width. What is the measure of the width?

Step 1: Let the variable be the length of the unknown side.
width = w length = $6 + w$

Step 2: Use the equation for the perimeter of a rectangle as follows:
$2l + 2w$ = perimeter of a rectangle
$2(w + 6) + 2w = 44$

Step 3: Solve for w.

Solution: width = 8 feet

Example 14: The perimeter of a triangle is 26 feet. The second side is twice as long as the first. The third side is 1 foot longer than the second side. What is the length of the 3 sides?

Step 1: Let x = first side $2x$ = second side $2x + 1$ = third side

Step 2: Use the equation for perimeter of a triangle as follows.
sum of the length of the sides = perimeter of a triangle.
$x + 2x + 2x + 1 = 26$

Step 3: Solve for x. $5x + 1 = 26$ so $x = 5$

Solution: first side $x = 5$ second side $2x = 10$ third side $2x + 1 = 11$

Solve the following word problems.

1. The length of a rectangle is 4 times longer than the width. The perimeter is 30. What is the width?
2. The length of a rectangle is 3 more than twice the width. The perimeter is 36. What is the length?
3. The perimeter of a triangle is 18 feet. The second side is two feet longer than the first. The third side is two feet longer then the second. What are the lengths of the sides?
4. In an isosceles triangle, two sides are equal. The third side is two less than twice the length of the sum of the two sides. The perimeter is 40. What are the lengths of the three sides?

Chapter 19 Review

1. Calculate the perimeter of the following figure.

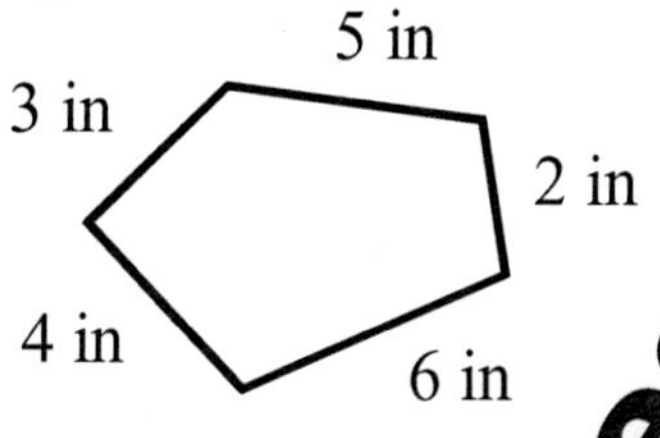

2. Find the area of the shaded region of the figure below.

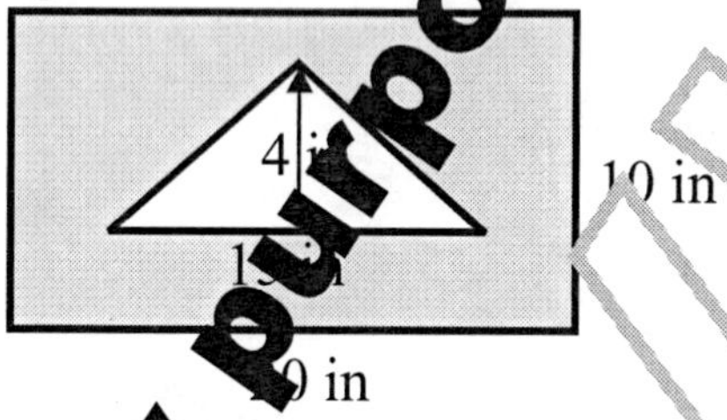

3. Calculate the perimeter and area.

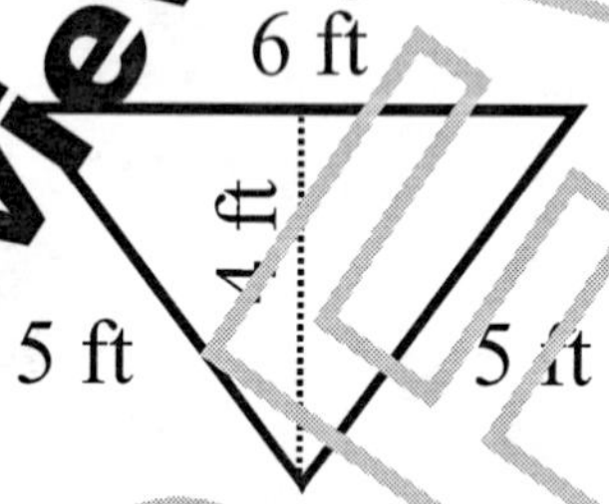

4. Calculate the perimeter and area.

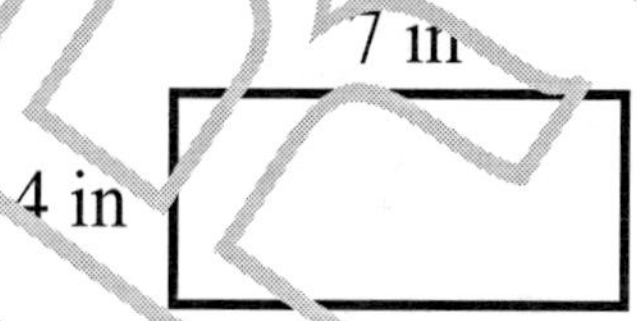

5. Find the area.

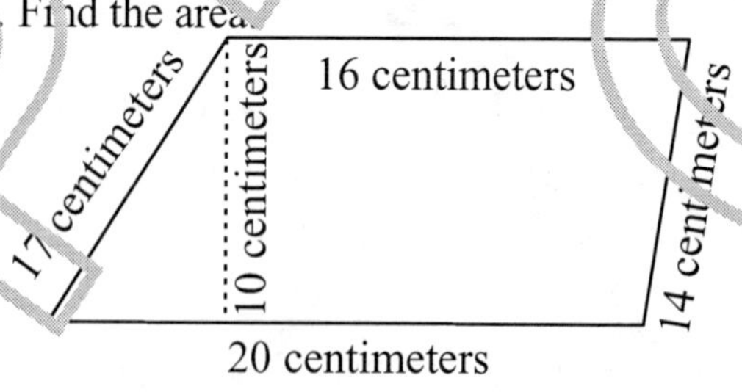

6. Find the area.

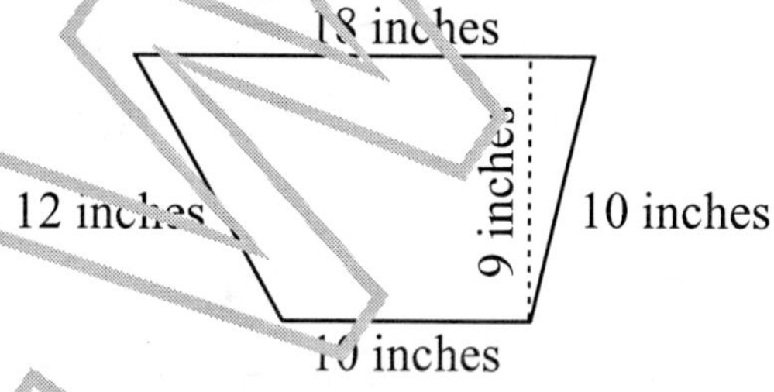

7. What fractional part of the total figure is shaded?

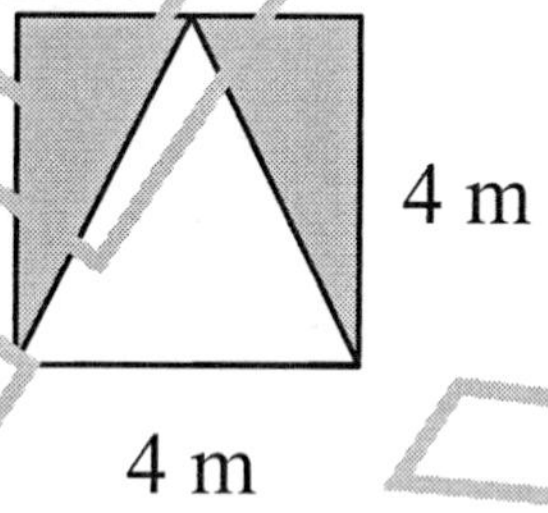

8. If you double the width of a square, how much does the area of the square increase?

9. Calculate the circumference and the area of the following circle. Use $\pi = 3.14$.

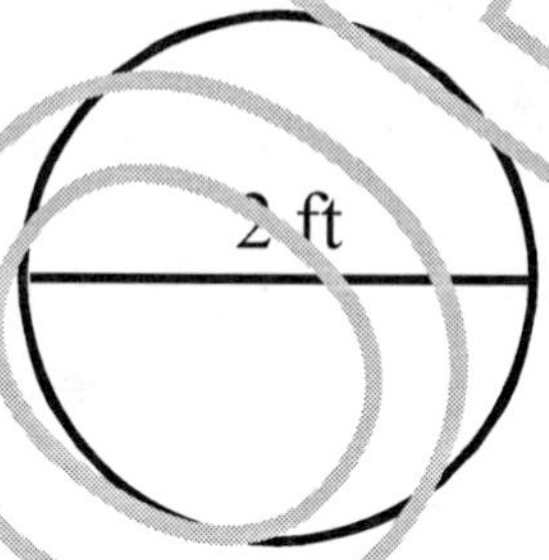

10. Find the area of the shaded part.

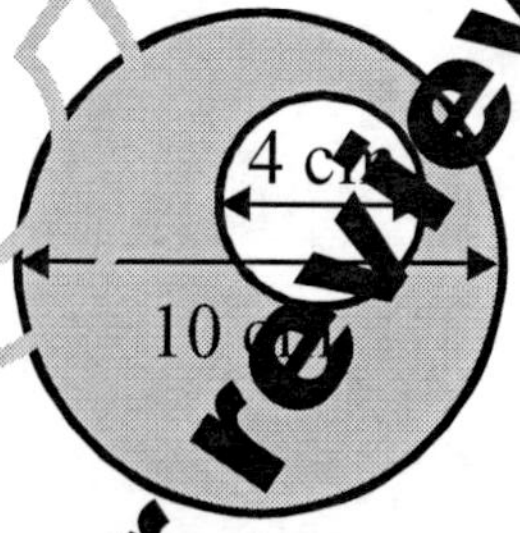

11. Find the area of the parallelogram.

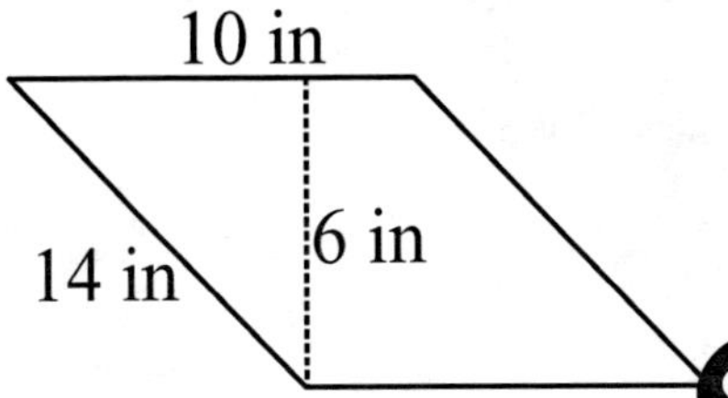

12. What is the area of a square which measures 8 inches on each side?

13. In the circle below, $\overline{AE}$ is a diameter, $\angle DAE$ measures 30° and $m\widehat{BC} = 45$. What is the measure of $\widehat{DE}$ and $\angle BOC$?

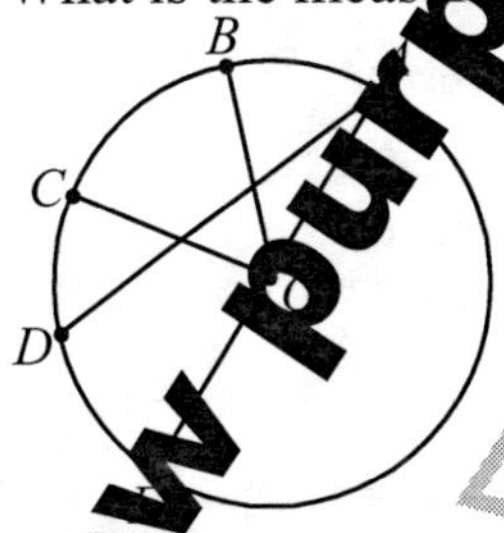

14. Calculate the circumference and the area of the following circle. Use $\pi = \frac{22}{7}$.

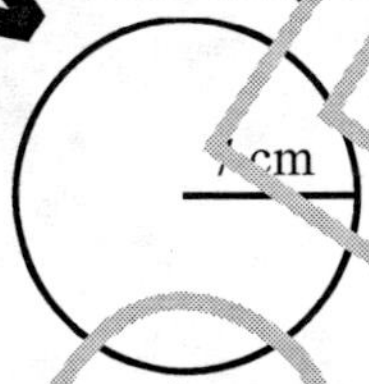

15. Which line represents a tangent of the circle?

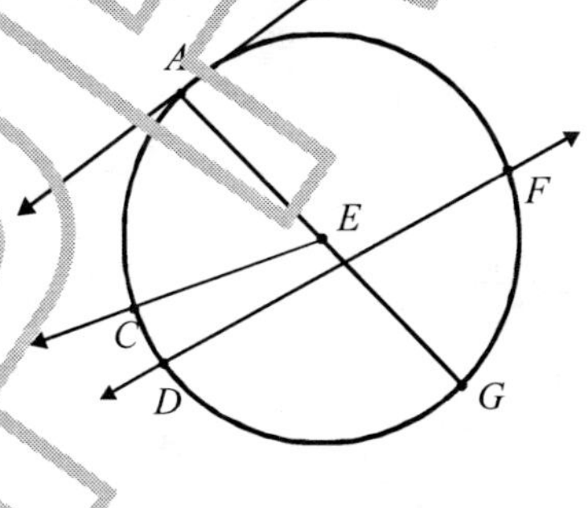

16. What is the sum of the measures of the interior angles in the figure below?

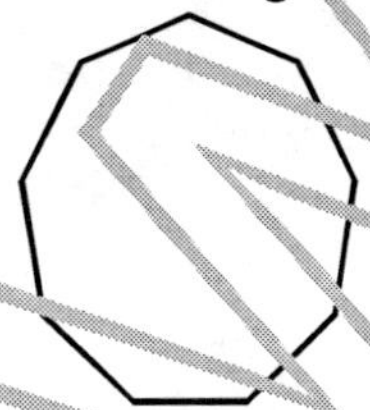

Calculate the perimeters of each of the following triangles.

17. A right triangle with a hypotenuse measuring 9 m and an external angle measuring 150°.

18. A right triangle with a hypotenuse measuring 19 cm and a leg measuring 18 cm.

19. An isosceles triangle with one side measuring 44 ft and another side measuring 15 ft.

Calculate the perimeter of a square with a circumscribed circle that has each of the following areas.

20. 484π in^2

21. 324π m^2

22. 256π cm^2

Chapter 19 Test

1. What is the area of a circle with a radius of 7 cm? (Round to the nearest whole number)
   - **A.** 196 square cm
   - **B.** 347 square cm
   - **C.** 616 square cm
   - **D.** 22 square cm
   - **E.** 154 square cm

2. What is the sum of the measures of the interior angles of a polygon with 7 sides?
   - **F.** 180°
   - **G.** 360°
   - **H.** 540°
   - **J.** 900°
   - **K.** 1260°

3. Which of the following figures is a parallelogram?
   - **A.** 
   - **B.** 
   - **C.** 
   - **D.** 
   - **E.** 

4. Which item below is not a polygon?
   - **F.** triangle
   - **G.** heptagon
   - **H.** octagon
   - **J.** rectangle
   - **K.** circle

5. Find the area. Use $\pi = 3.14$.

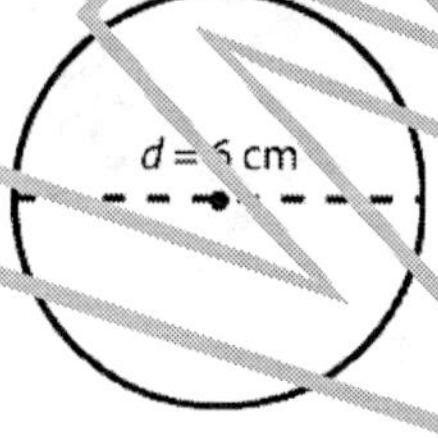

   - **A.** 113.04 cm^2
   - **B.** 28.26 cm^2
   - **C.** 18.84 cm^2
   - **D.** 1[illegible]8.4 cm^2
   - **E.** 9.42 cm^2

6. Find the circumference. Use $\pi = 3.14$.

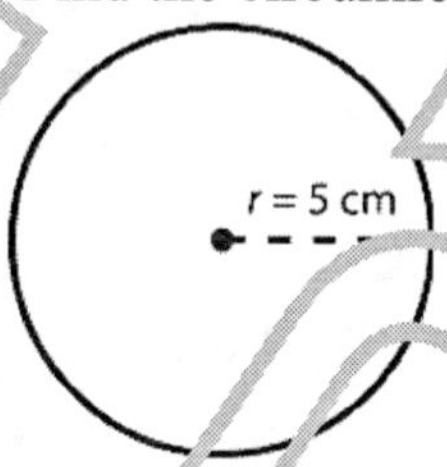

   - **F.** 15.7 cm
   - **G.** 62.8 cm
   - **H.** 31.4 cm
   - **J.** 0.314 cm
   - **K.** 57.2 cm

7. Find the values of x and y in the figure.

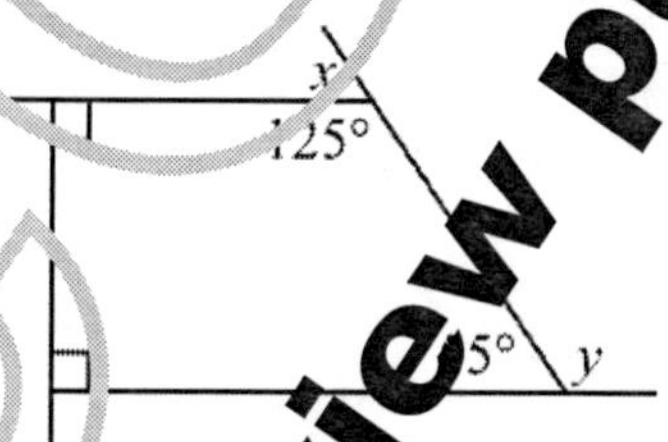

   - **A.** 55°, 125°
   - **B.** 90°, [illegible]0°
   - **C.** 55°, 90°
   - **D.** 90°, 125°
   - **E.** 5[illegible]°, 35°

8. If a regular octagon has eight sides, what is the measure of each exterior angle?

F. 15°
G. 30°
H. 45°
J. 360°
K. 1080°

9. What is the name of the polygon below?

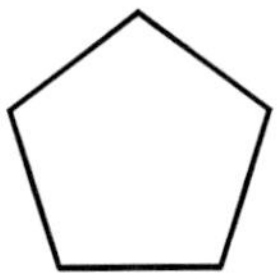

A. quadrilateral
B. pentagon
C. hexagon
D. octagon
E. heptagon

10. A square is

F. a quadrilateral.
G. parallelogram
H. rectangle.
J. all of the above.
K. none of the above

11. A parallelogram with four congruent sides is

A. a rhombus.
B. a rectangle.
C. a square.
D. both A and C.
E. both A and B.

12. Which is an angle whose vertex lies on a circle and whose sides contain chords of the circle?

F. central angle
G. tangent
H. inscribed angle
J. secant
K. circumscribed angle

13. A line that touches a circle only at one point is called a

A. chord.
B. secant.
C. inscribed line.
D. circumscribed line.
E. tangent.

14. What does the measure of $\widehat{ABC}$ equal?

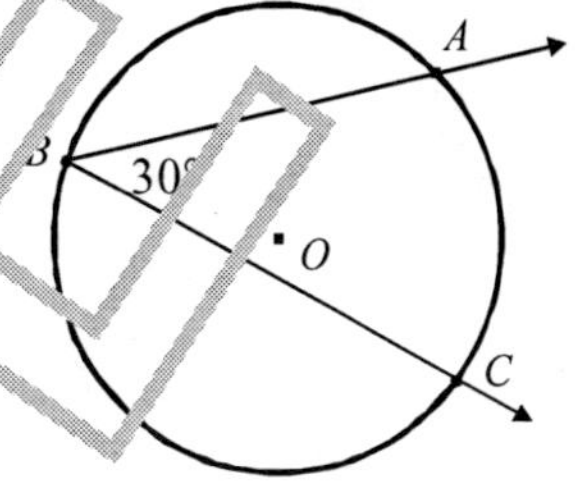

F. 30
G. 60
H. 330
J. 300
K. 210

15. What is the measure of angle B?

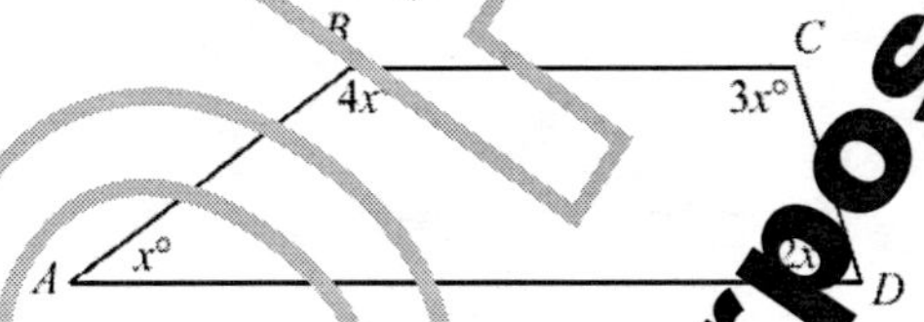

A. 36°
B. 90°
C. 108°
D. 144°
E. 156°

16. If you decide to divide a pie that has a diameter of 8 in into 6 equal slices, what is the area of each slice?

F. 8.37 in²
G. 4.19 in²
H. 33.49 in²
J. 50.24 in²
K. 18.9 in²

17. Find the area of the shaded region.

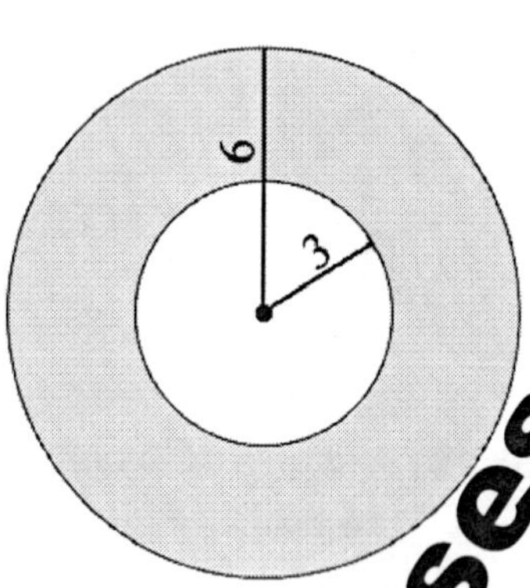

A. 24π
B. 3π
C. 27π
D. 15π
E. 9π

18. Find the value of x in the figure.

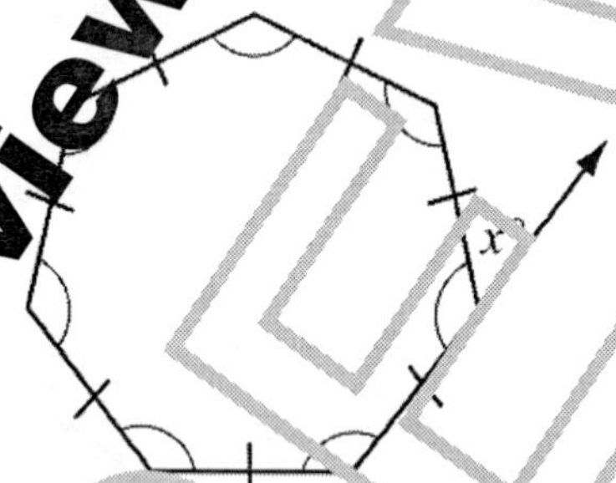

F. 45°
G. 51.4°
H. 90°
J. 180°
K. 360°

19. How many square feet of sod are needed to cover a 9-foot by 60-foot lawn?

A. 69 square feet
B. 138 square feet
C. 270 square feet
D. 320 square feet
E. 540 square feet

20. Lem wanted to cut a rusted stop sign into quarters in his shop class. Which of the following statements is factual?

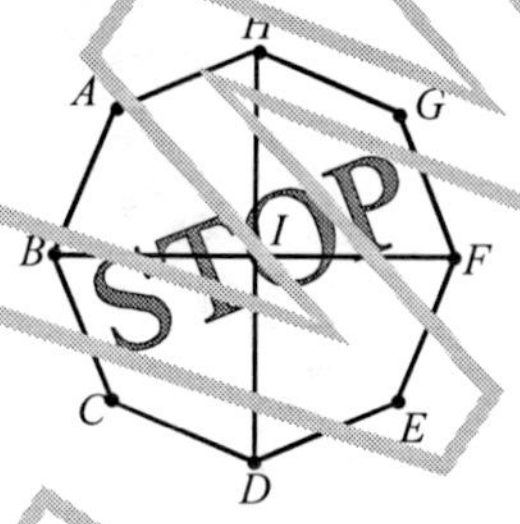

F. $m\angle ABF = 67.5°$
G. $m\angle CBF + m\angle BAH = 135°$
H. $m\angle HGF = 67.5°$
J. $m\angle BAH - m\angle HIF = 35°$
K. $m\angle GFB = 135°$

21. The figure below is a circle inscribed in a square. What is the area of the shaded region?

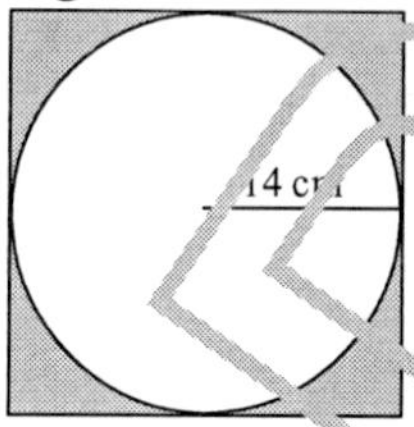

A. 44 square centimeters
B. 168 square centimeters
C. 196 square centimeters
D. 616 square centimeters
E. 482 square centimeters

22. What is the area of the figure below?

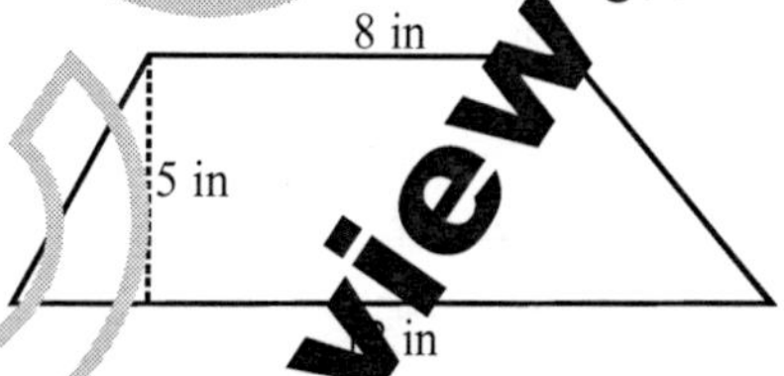

F. 25 in²
G. 50 in²
H. 100 in²
J. 480 in²
K. 720 in²

23. Using the formula $A = \frac{1}{2}bh$ for the area of a triangle, find the area of the triangle below.

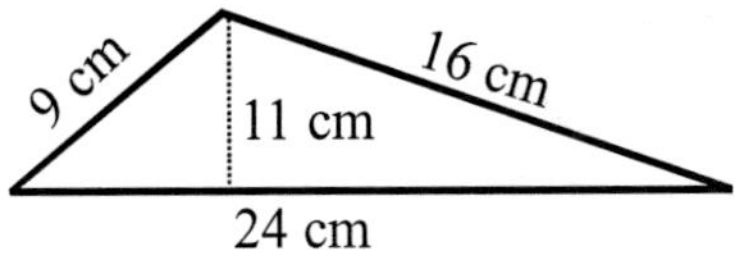

A. 49 cm^2
B. 132 cm^2
C. 264 cm^2
D. 3,456 cm^2
E. 847 cm^2

24. Find the area.

F. [illegible]8 $inches^2$
G. 24 $inches^2$
H. 132 $inches^2$
J. 12 $inches^2$
K. 144 $inches^2$

25. Find the area.

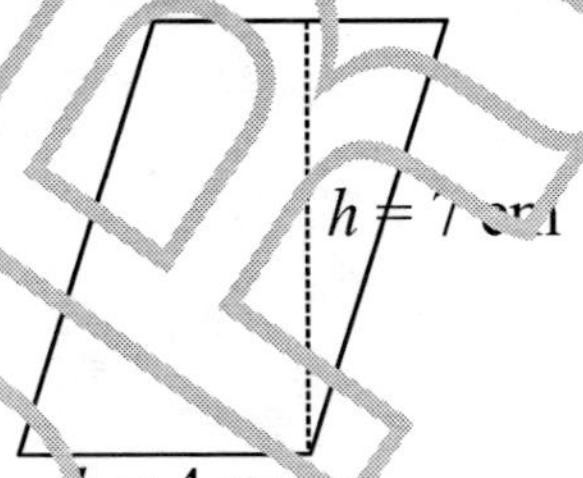

A. 28 cm
B. 28 cm^2
C. 22 cm
D. [illegible]2 cm^2
E. 11 cm^2

26. Find the area of the shaded region.

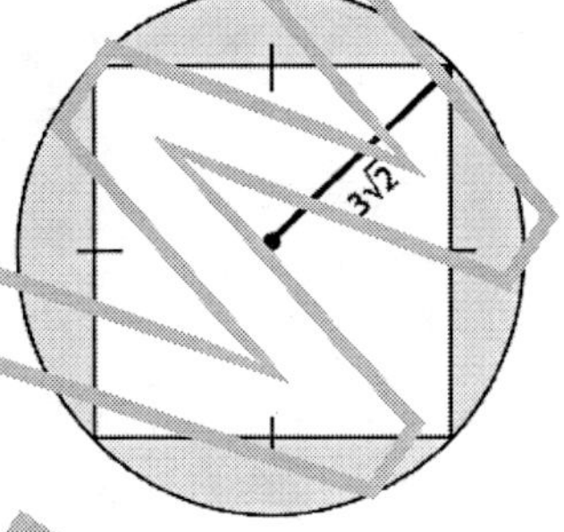

F. $3\sqrt{2}\pi - 36$
G. $18\pi - 36$
H. $18\pi - 18$
J. $3\sqrt{2}\pi - 18$
K. $3\sqrt{2}\pi - 12$

27. The midpoints of the sides of square A are the vertices of square B. If square B has a perimeter of 236 in, what is the perimeter of square A?

A. $59\sqrt{2}$ in
B. $118\sqrt{2}$ in
C. $177\sqrt{2}$ in
D. $236\sqrt{2}$ in
E. $472\sqrt{2}$ in

28. Find the perimeter.

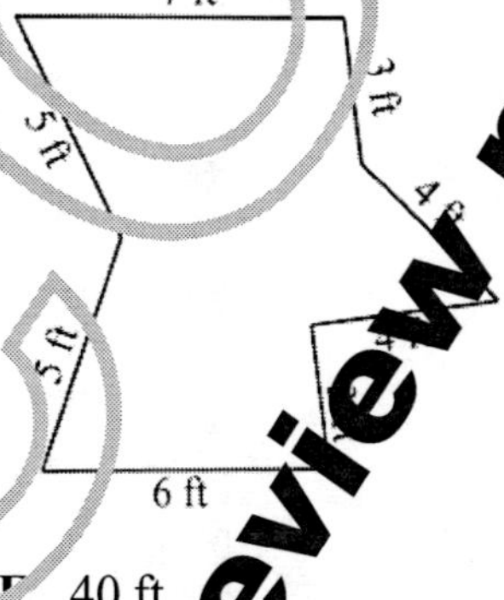

F. 40 ft
G. 39 ft
H. 38 ft
J. 3[illegible] ft
K. 3[illegible] ft

Chapter 20
Solid Geometry

20.1 Understanding Volume

Measurement of **volume** is expressed in cubic units such as in^3, ft^3, m^3, cm^3, or mm^3. The volume of a solid is the number of cubic units that can be contained in the solid.

First, let's look at rectangular solids.

Example 1: How many 1 cubic centimeter cubes will it take to fill up the figure below?

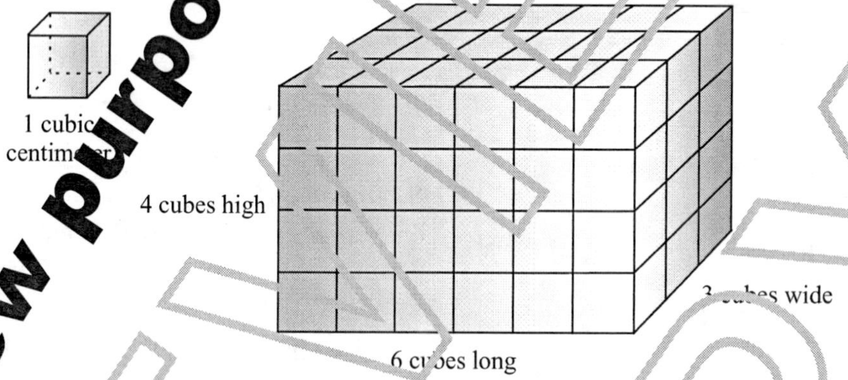

To find the volume, you need to multiply the length times the width times the height.
Volume of a rectangular solid = length × width × height ($V = lwh$). $V = 6 \times 3 \times 4 = 72 \text{ cm}^3$

Find the volume of the following rectangular solids.

1.

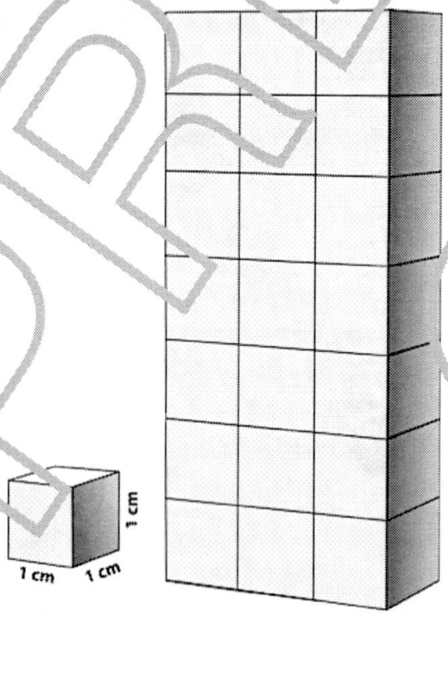

2.

20.2 Volume of Rectangular Prisms

You can calculate the volume (V) of a rectangular prism (box) by multiplying the length (l) by the width (w) by the height (h), as expressed in the formula $V = (lwh)$.

Example 2: Find the volume of the box pictured here:

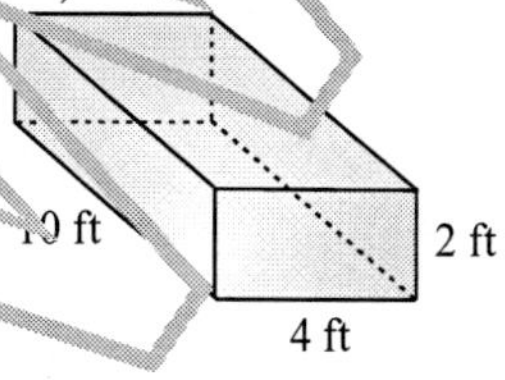

Step 1: Insert measurements from the figure into the formula.

Step 2: Multiply to solve. $10 \times 4 \times 2 = 80\ \text{ft}^3$

Note: **Volume is always expressed in cubic units such as in^3, ft^3, m^3, cm^3, or mm^3.**

Find the volume of the following rectangular prisms (boxes).

1. 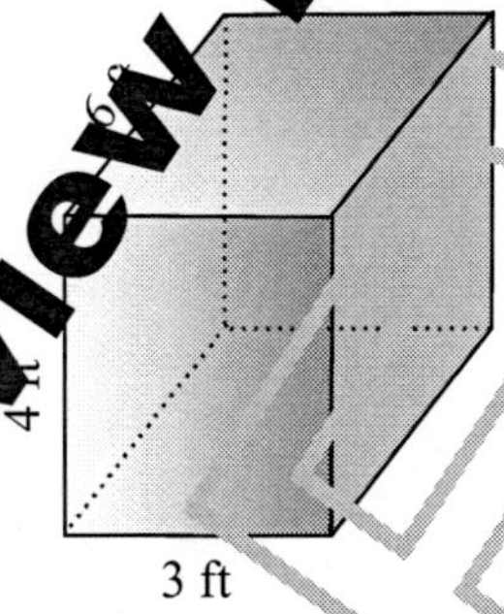

4. 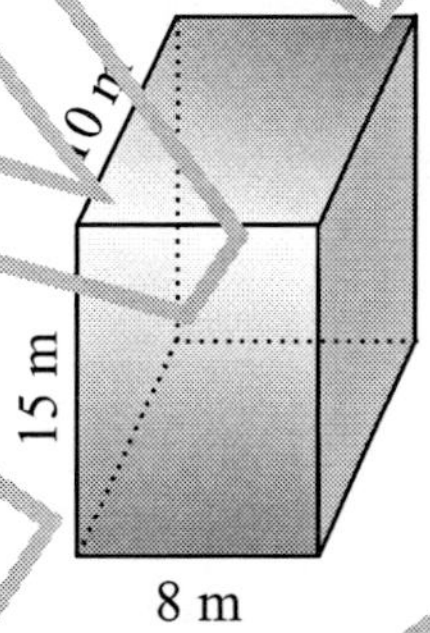

7. 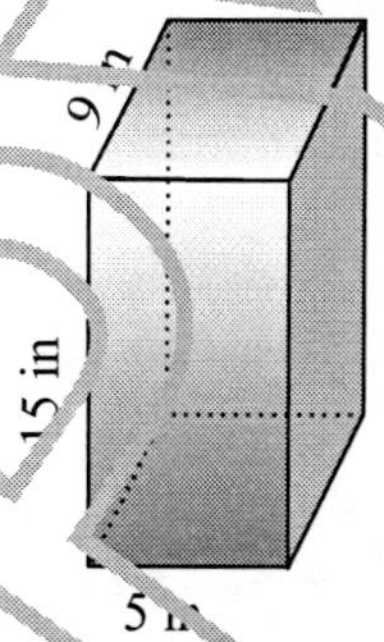

2. 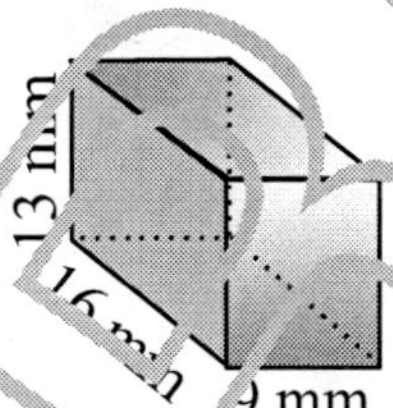

5. 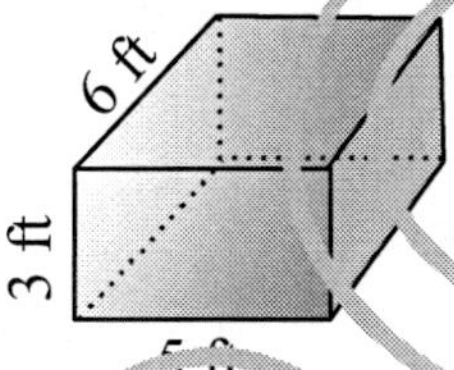

8. 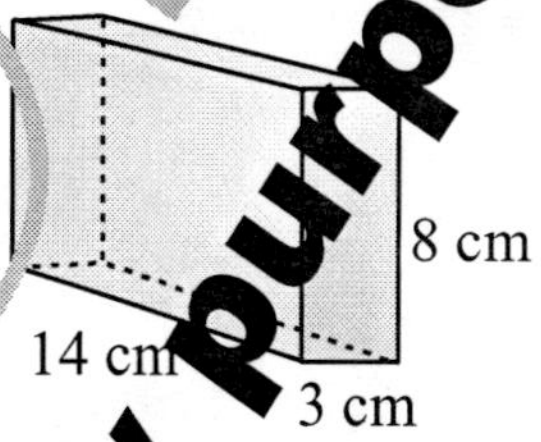

3. 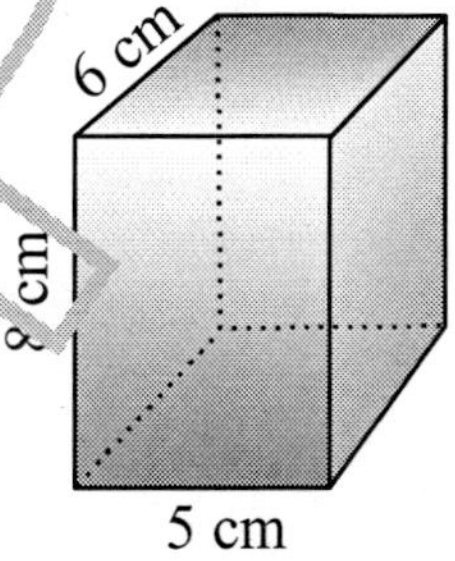

6. 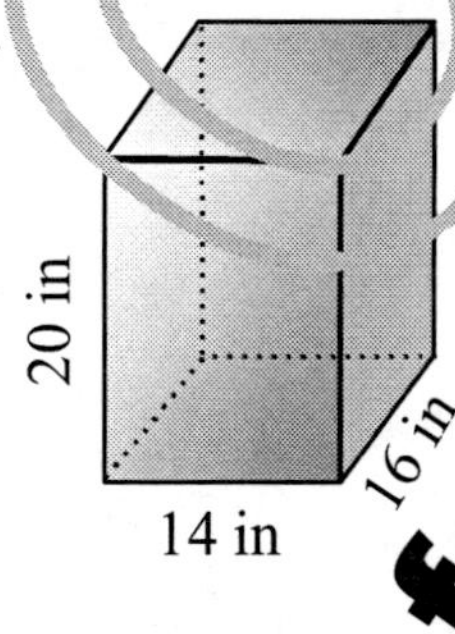

9. 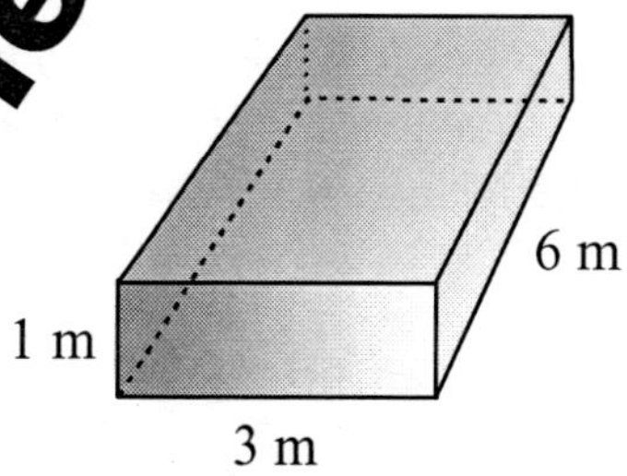

20.3 Volume of Cubes

A **cube** is a special kind of rectangular prism (box). Each side of a cube has the same measure. So, the formula for the volume of a cube is $V = s \times s \times s = s^3$.

Example 3: Find the volume of the cube at right:

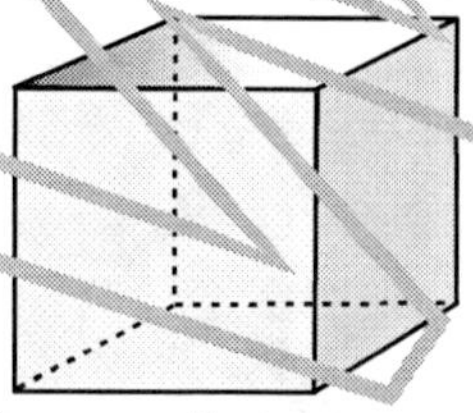

$s = 5$ cm

Step 1: Insert measurements from the figure into the formula.

Step 2: Multiply to solve. $5 \times 5 \times 5 = 125$ cm^3

Note: Volume is always expressed in cubic units such as in^3, ft^3, m^3, cm^3, or mm^3.

Answer each of the following questions about cubes.

1. If a cube is 3 centimeters on each edge, what is the volume of the cube?

2. If the measure of the edge is doubled to 6 centimeters on each edge, what is the volume of the cube?

3. If the edge of a 3-centimeter cube is tripled to become 9 centimeters on each edge, what will the volume be?

4. How many cubes with edges measuring 3 centimeters would you need to stack together to make a solid 12-centimeter cube?

5. What is the volume of a 2-centimeter cube?

6. Jerry built a 2-inch cube to hold his marble collection. He wants to build a cube with a volume 8-times larger. How much will each edge measure?

Find the volume of the following cubes.

7.

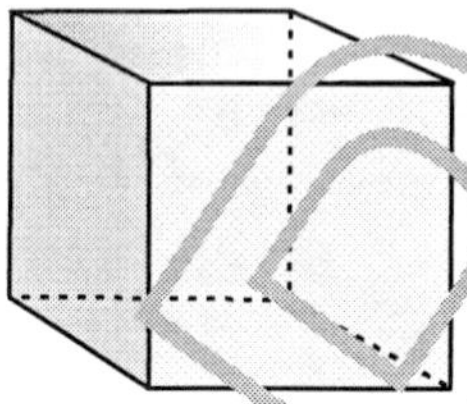

$s = 7$ in.

8.

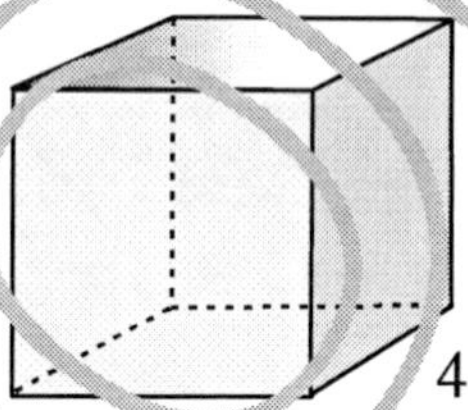

9. 12 inches = 1 foot

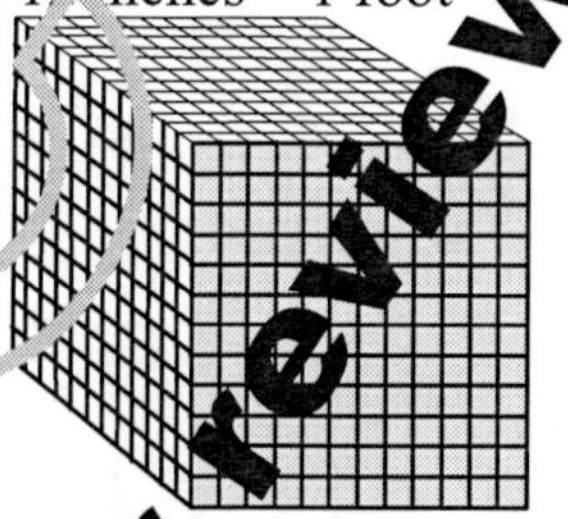

$s = 1$ foot

How many cubic inches are in a cubic foot?

20.4 Volume of Spheres, Cones, Cylinders, and Pyramids

To find the volume of a solid, insert the measurements given for the solid into the correct formula and solve. Remember, volumes are expressed in cubic units such as in^3, ft^3, m^3, cm^3, or mm^3.

Sphere

$V = \frac{4}{3}\pi r^3$

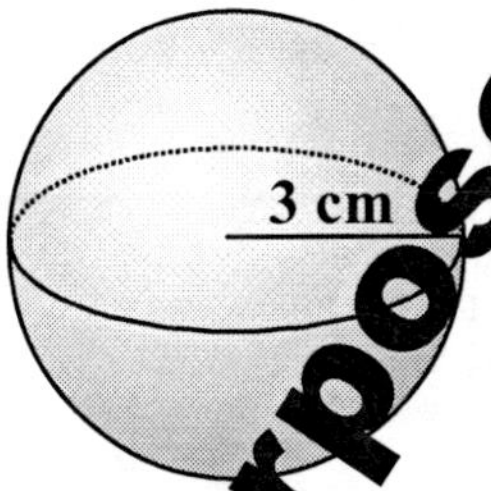

$V = \frac{4}{3}\pi r^3 \quad \pi = 3.14$

$V = \frac{4}{3} \times 3.14 \times 27$

$V = 113.04 \text{ cm}^3$

Cone

$V = \frac{1}{3}\pi r^2 h$

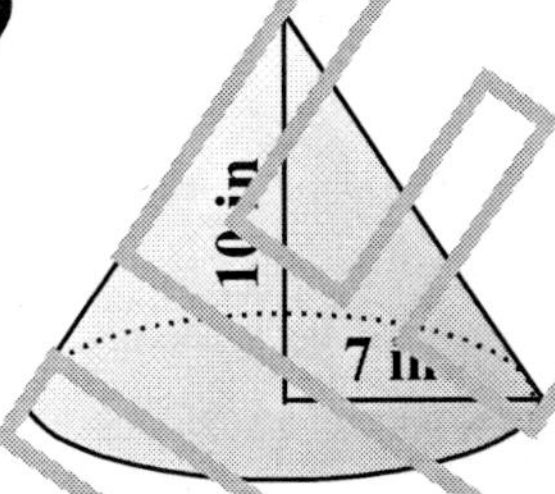

$V = \frac{1}{3}\pi r^2 h \quad \pi = 3.14$

$V = \frac{1}{3} \times 3.14 \times 49 \times 10$

$V = 512.87 \text{ in}^3$

Cylinder

$V = \pi r^2 h$

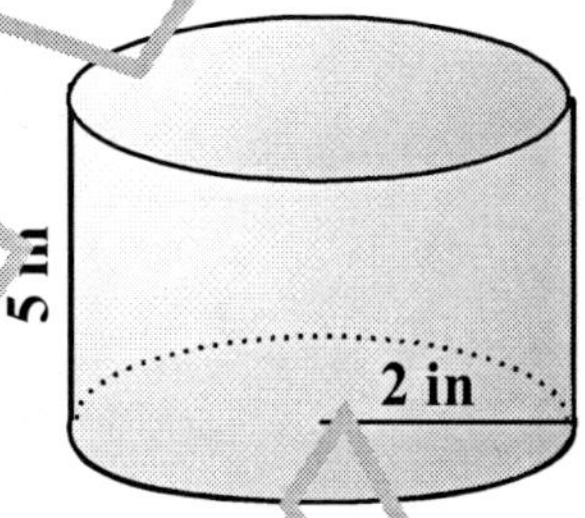

$V = \pi r^2 h \quad \pi = \frac{22}{7}$

$V = \frac{22}{7} \times 4 \times 5$

$V = 62\frac{6}{7} \text{ in}^3$

Pyramids

$V = \frac{1}{3}Bh \quad B =$ area of rectangular base

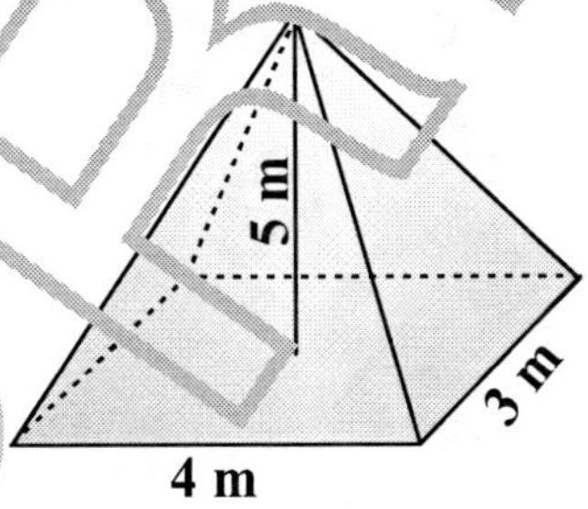

$V = \frac{1}{3}Bh \quad B = l \times w$

$V = \frac{1}{3} \times 4 \times 3 \times 5$

$V = 20 \text{ m}^3$

$V = \frac{1}{3}Bh \quad B =$ area of triangular base

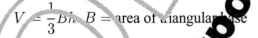

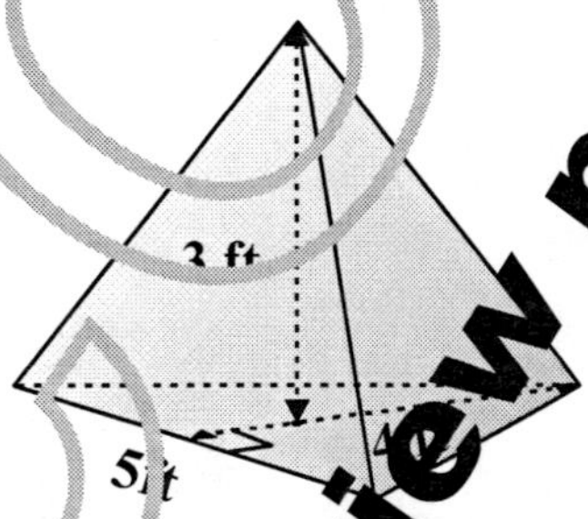

$V = \frac{1}{3}Bh \quad B = \frac{1}{2} \times b \times h$

$B = \frac{1}{2} \times 5 \times 4 = 10 \text{ ft}^2$

$V = \frac{1}{3} \times 10 \times 3$

$V = 10 \text{ ft}^3$

Find the volume of the following shapes. Use $\pi = 3.14$.

1.
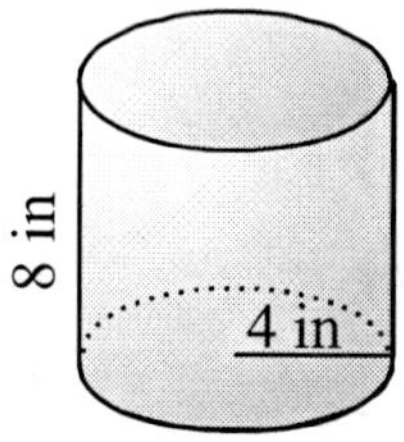

2.
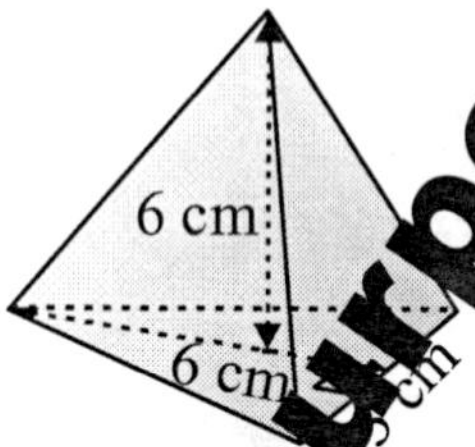

3.

4.
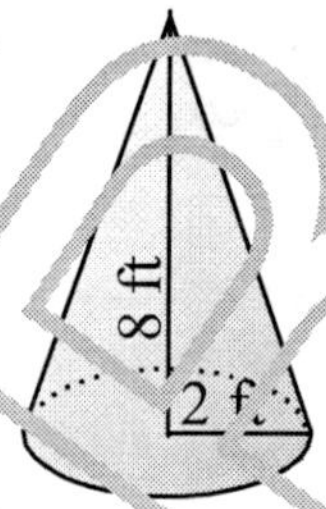

5.
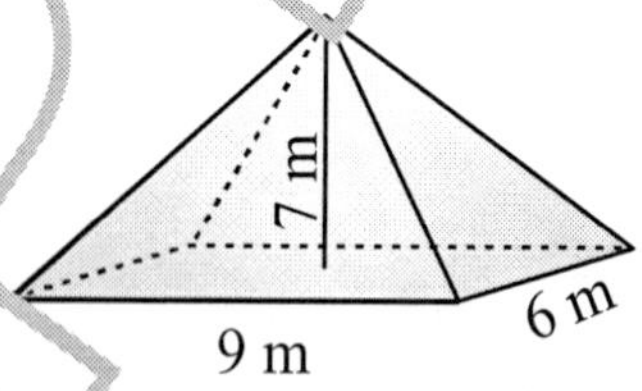

6.
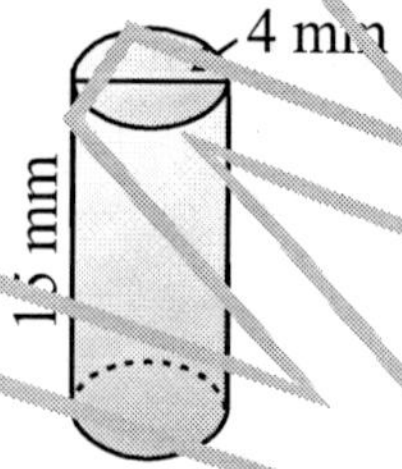

7.
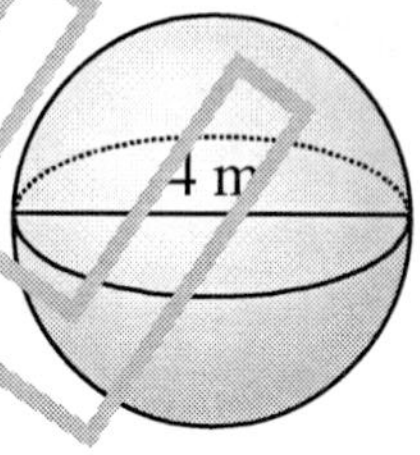

8.
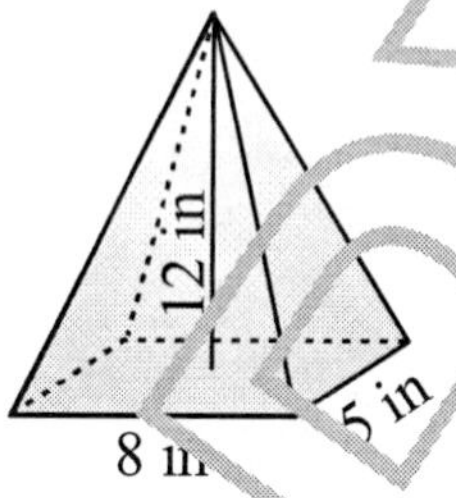

9.
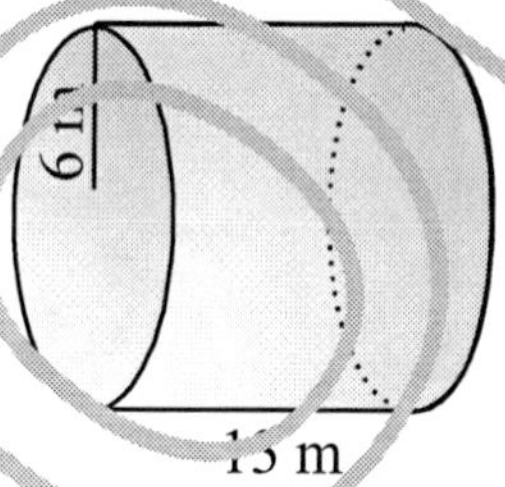

10.

20.5 Two-Step Volume Problems

Some objects are made from two geometric figures. For example, the tower below is made up of two geometric objects, a rectangular prism and a pyramid.

Example 4: Find the maximum volume of the tower.

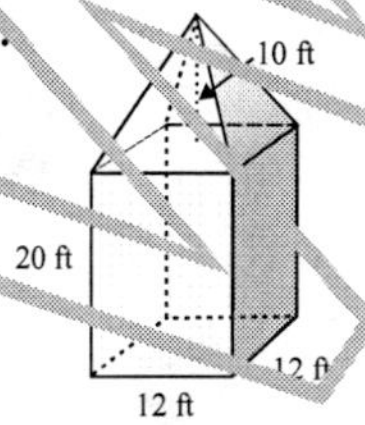

Step 1: Determine which formulas you will need. The tower is made from a pyramid and a rectangular prism, so you will need the formulas for the volume of these two figures.

Step 2: Find the volume of each part of the tower. The bottom of the tower is a rectangular prism $V = lwh$
$V = 12 \times 12 \times 20 = 2,880$ ft^3
The top of the tower is a rectangular pyramid. $V = \frac{1}{3}Bh$
$V = \frac{1}{3} \times 12 \times 12 \times 10 = 480$ ft^3

Step 3: Add the two volumes together. 2880 ft$^3 + 480$ ft$^3 = 3,360$ ft^3

Find the volume of the geometric figures below. Hint: If part of a solid has been removed, find the volume of the hole, and subtract it from the volume of the total object.

1.

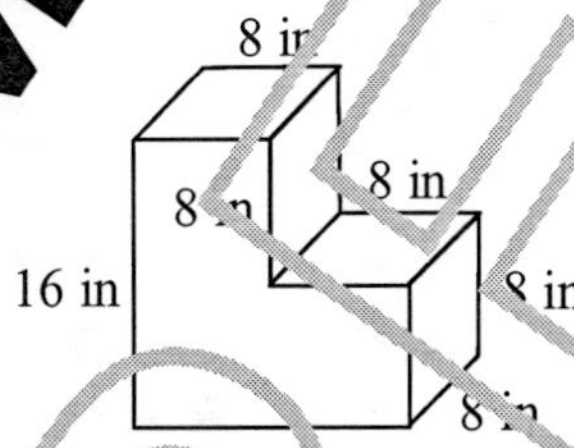

2. Each side measures 3 inches.

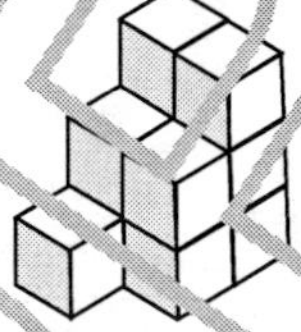

3. A rectangular hole passes through the middle of the figure below. The hole measures 1 cm on each side.

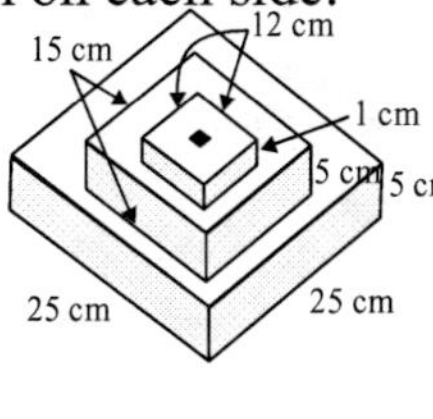

4. In the figure below, 3 cylinders are stacked on top of each other. The radii of the cylinders are 2 inches, 4 inches, and 6 inches. The height of each cylinder is 1 inch.

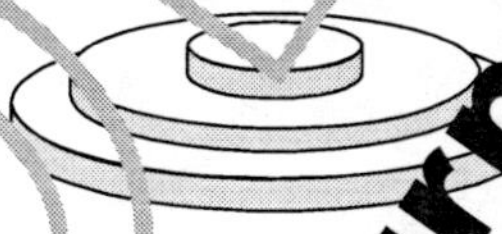

5.

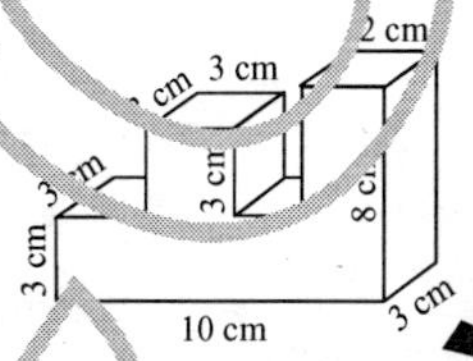

6. A hole, 1 meter in diameter, has been cut through the cylinder below.

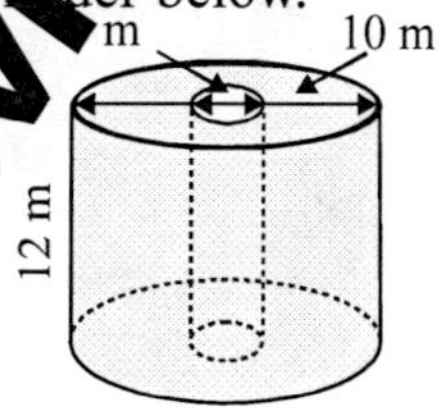

20.6 Surface Area

The **surface area of a solid** is the total area of all the sides of a solid.

20.7 Cube

There are six sides on a cube. To find the surface area of a cube, find the area of one side and multiply by 6.

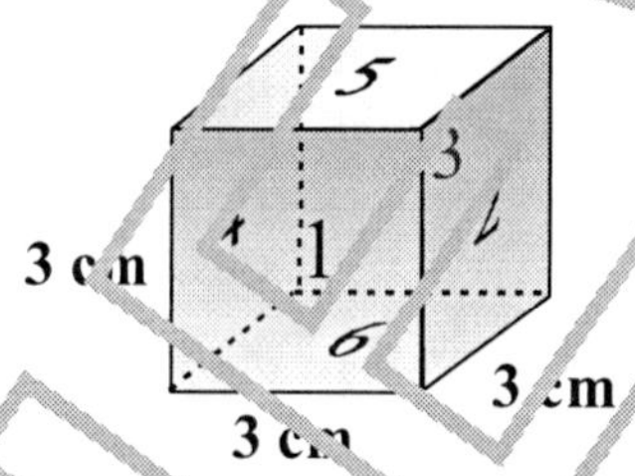

Area of each side of the cube: $3 \times 3 = 9$ cm^2

Total surface area: $9 \times 6 = 54$ cm^2

20.8 Rectangular Prisms

There are 6 sides on a rectangular prism. To find the surface area, add the areas of the six rectangular sides.

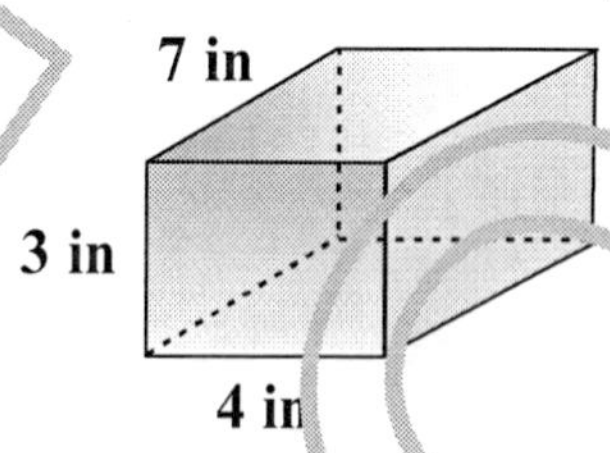

Top and Bottom

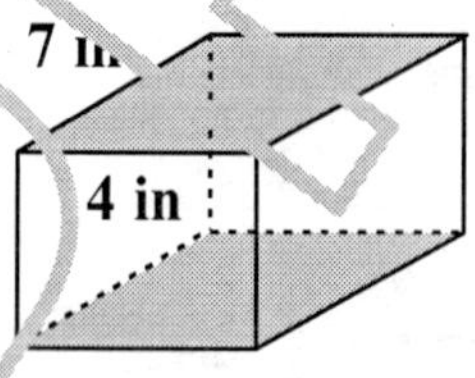

Area of top side:
$7 \text{ in} \times 4 \text{ in} = 28 \text{ in}^2$
Area of top and bottom:
$28 \text{ in} \times 2 = 56 \text{ in}^2$

Front and Back

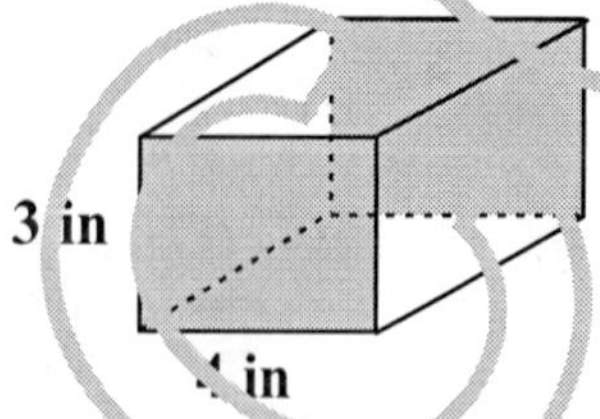

Area of front:
$3 \text{ in} \times 4 \text{ in} = 12 \text{ in}^2$
Area of front and back:
$12 \text{ in} \times 2 = 24 \text{ in}^2$

Left and Right

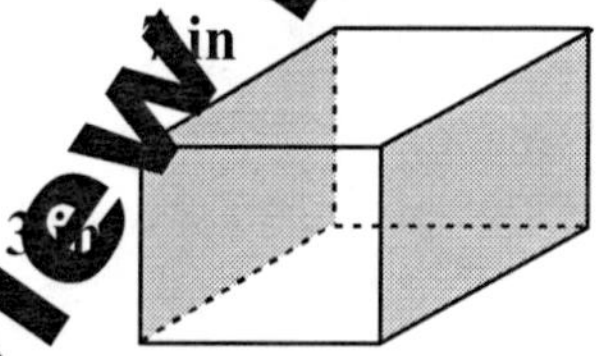

Area of left side:
$3 \text{ in} \times 7 \text{ in} = 21 \text{ in}^2$
Area of left and right:
$21 \text{ in} \times 2 = 42 \text{ in}^2$

Total surface area: $56 \text{ in}^2 + 24 \text{ in}^2 + 42 \text{ in}^2 = 122 \text{ in}^2$

Find the surface area of the following cubes and prisms.

1.
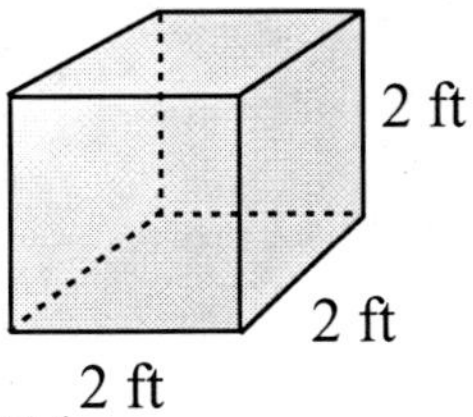

$SA =$ ____________

2.
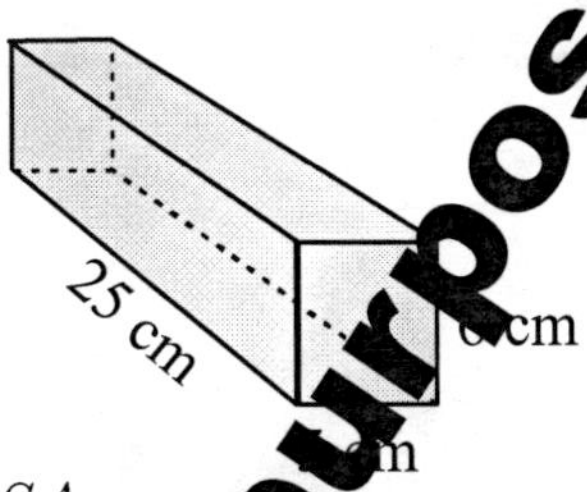

$SA =$ ____________

3.
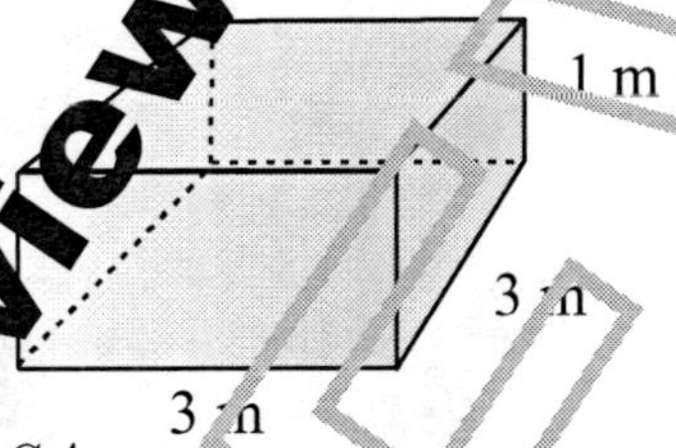

$SA =$ ____________

4.
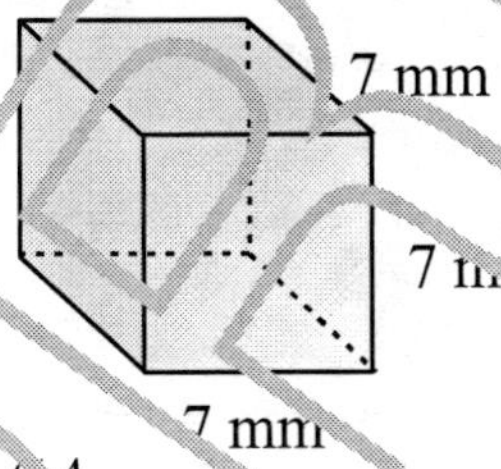

$SA =$ ____________

5.
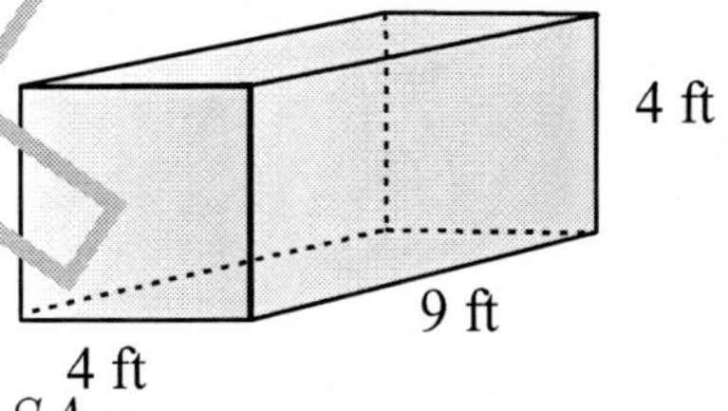

$SA =$ ____________

6.
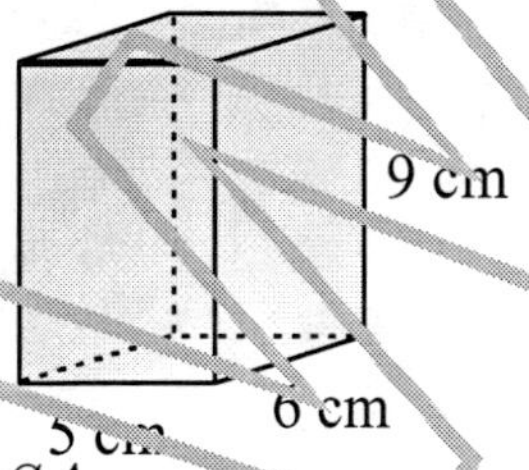

$SA =$ ____________

7.
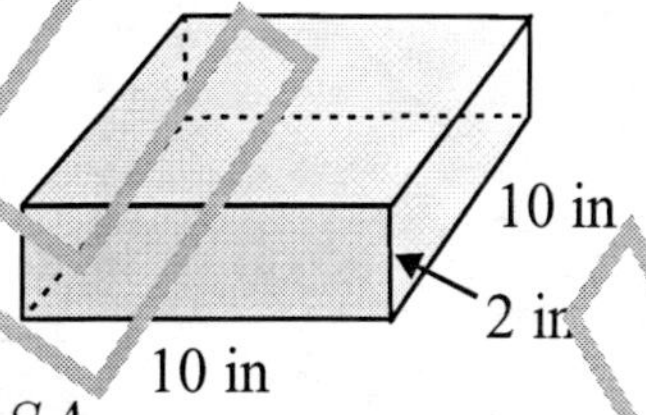

$SA =$ ____________

8.
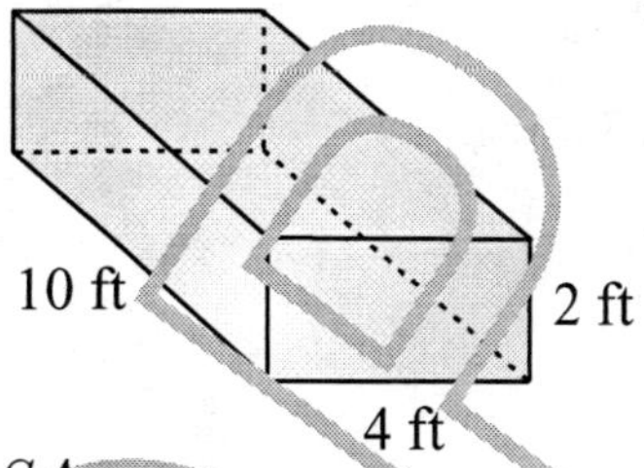

$SA =$ ____________

9.
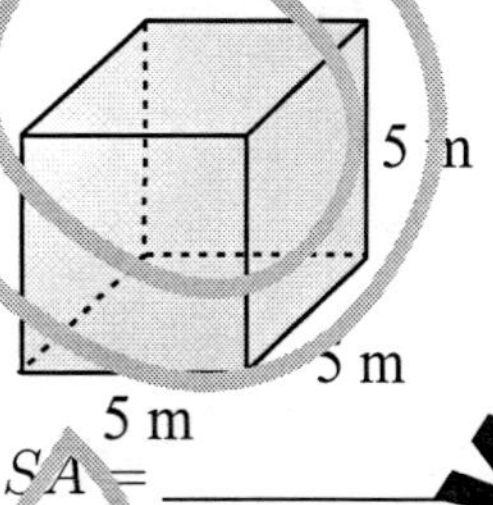

$SA =$ ____________

10.
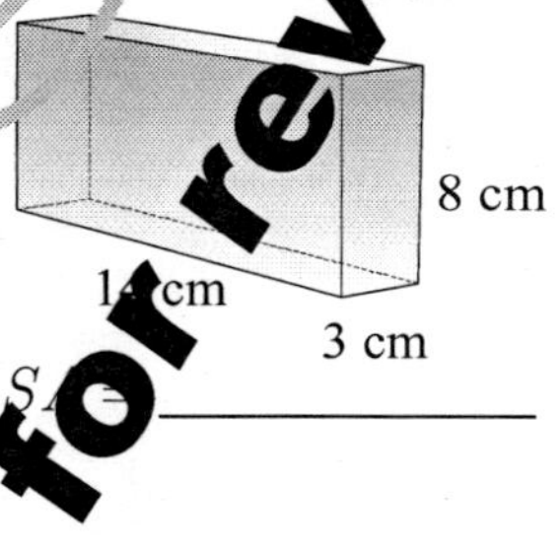

$SA =$ ____________

20.9 Pyramid

The pyramid below is made of a square base with 4 triangles on the sides.

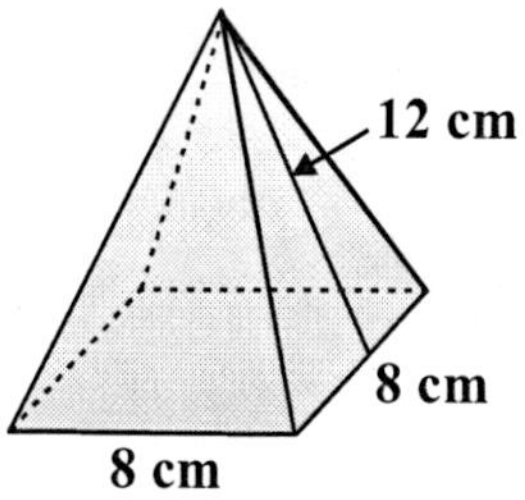

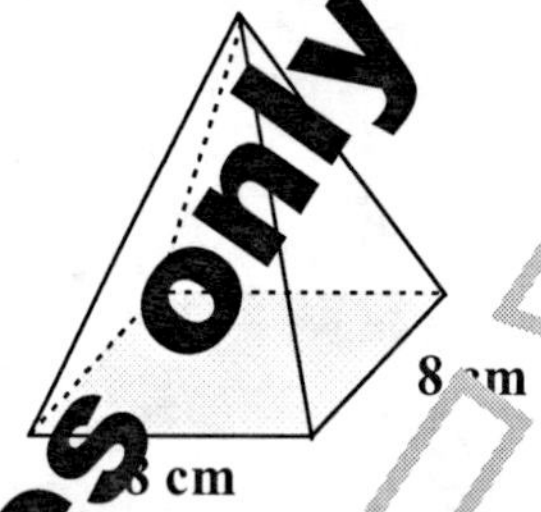

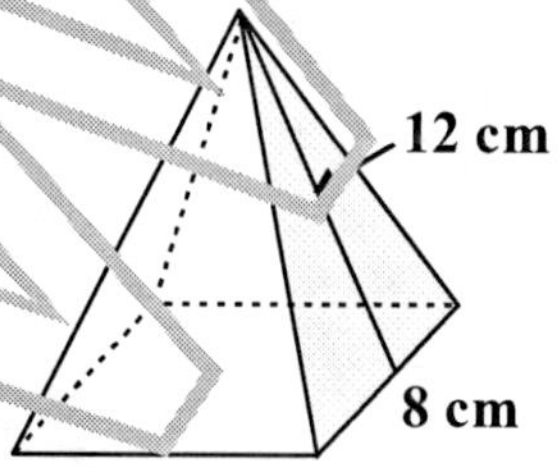

Area of square base:
$A = l \times w$
$A = 8 \times 8 = 64\ \text{cm}^2$

Area of sides:
Area of 1 side $= \frac{1}{2}bh$
$A = \frac{1}{2} \times 8 \times 12 = 48\ \text{cm}^2$
Area of 4 sides $= 48 \times 4 = 192\ \text{cm}^2$

Total surface area: $64 + 192 = 256\ \text{cm}^2$

Find the total surface of the following pyramids.

1.

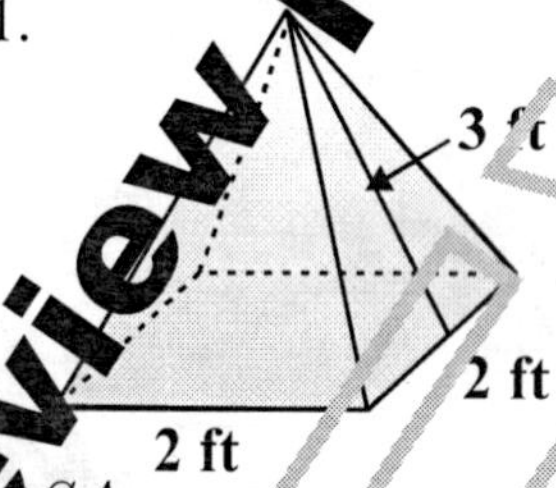

$SA =$ ____________

4.

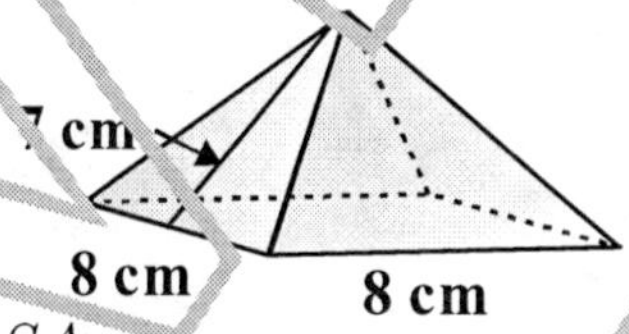

$SA =$ ____________

7.

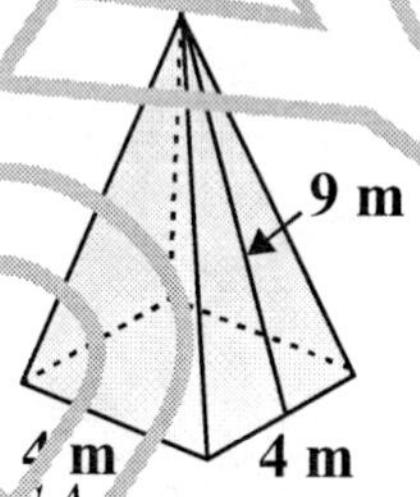

$SA =$ ____________

2.

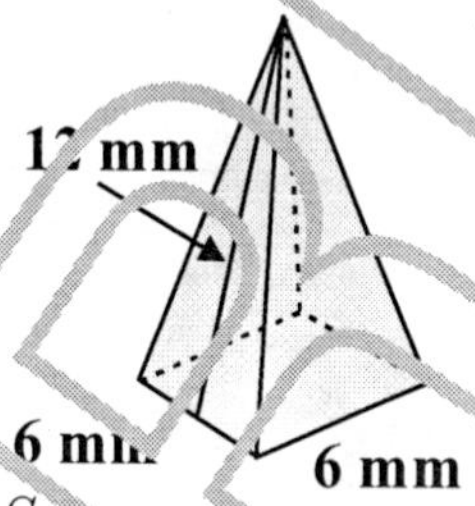

$SA =$ ____________

5.

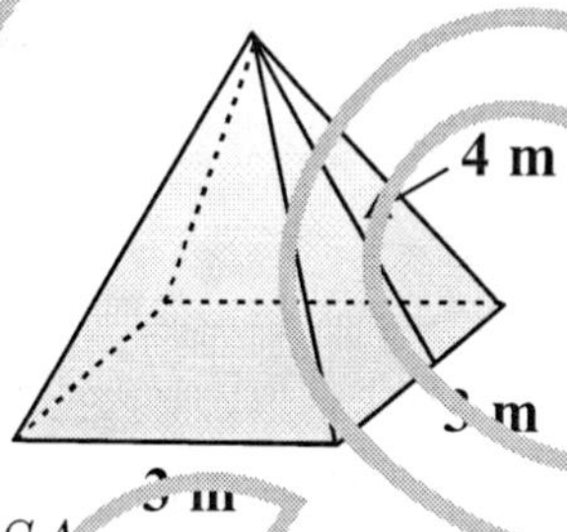

$SA =$ ____________

8.

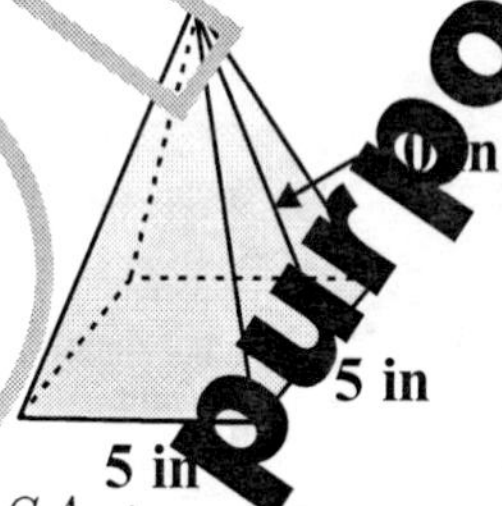

$SA =$ ____________

3.

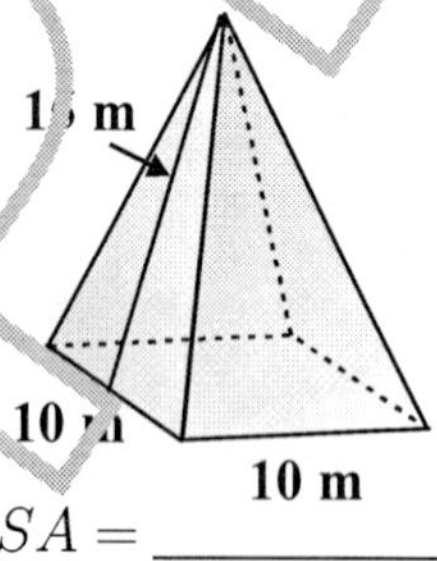

$SA =$ ____________

6.

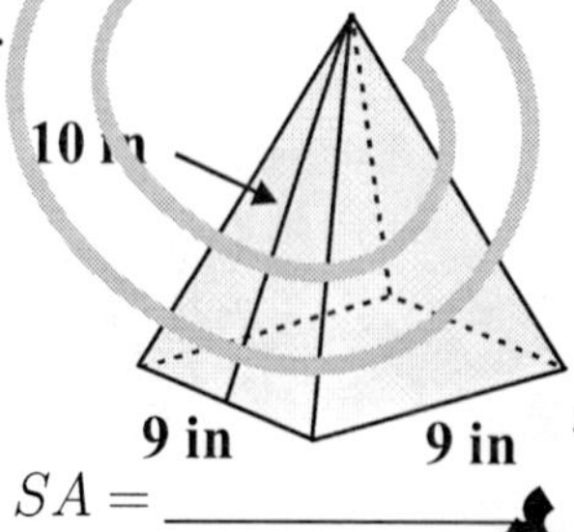

$SA =$ ____________

9.

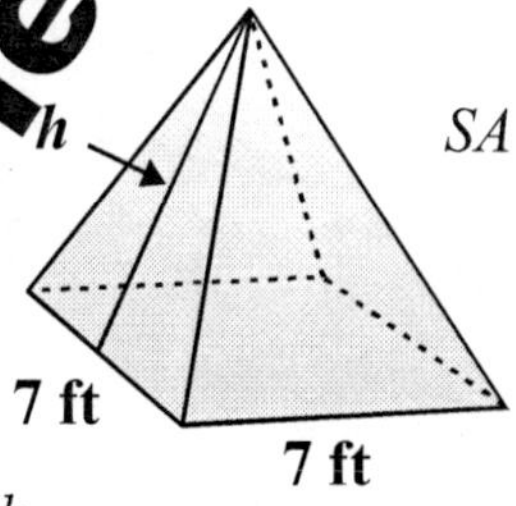

$SA = 171.5\ \text{ft}^2$

$h =$ ____________

20.10 Cylinder

If the side of a cylinder was slit from top to bottom and laid flat, its shape would be a rectangle. The length of the rectangle is the same as the circumference of the circle that is the base of the cylinder. The width of the rectangle is the height of the cylinder.

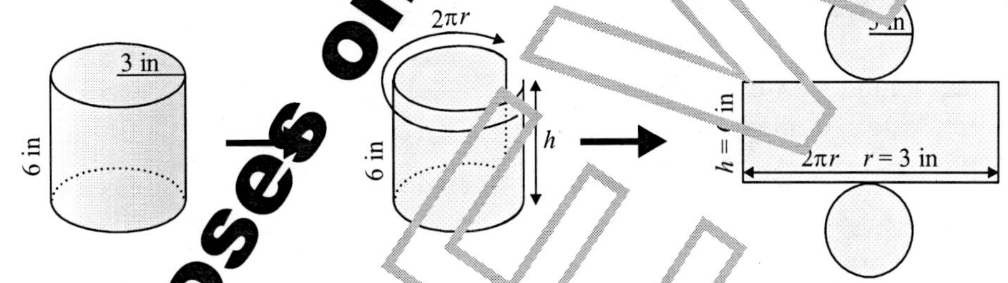

Total Surface Area of a Cylinder $= 2\pi r^2 + 2\pi rh$

Area of top and bottom:
Area of a circle $= \pi r^2$
Area of top $= 3.14 \times 3^2 = 28.26$ in^2
Area of top and bottom $= 2 \times 28.26 = 56.52$ in^2

Area of side:
Area of rectangle $= l \times h$
$l = 2\pi r = 2 \times 3.14 \times 3 = 18.84$ in
Area of rectangle $= 18.84 \times 6 = 113.04$ in^2

Total surface area $= 56.52 + 113.04 = 169.56$ in^2

Find the total surface area of the following cylinders. Use $\pi = 3.14$

1. 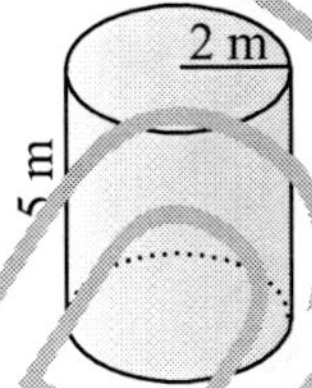

2. 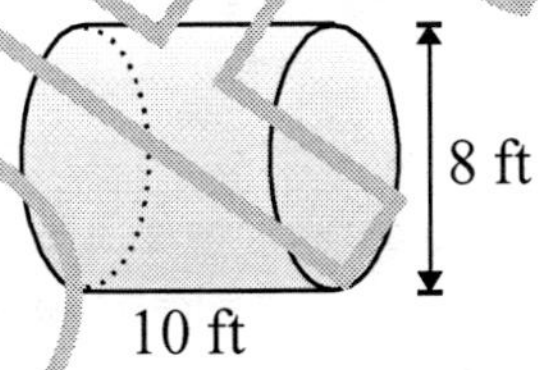

3. 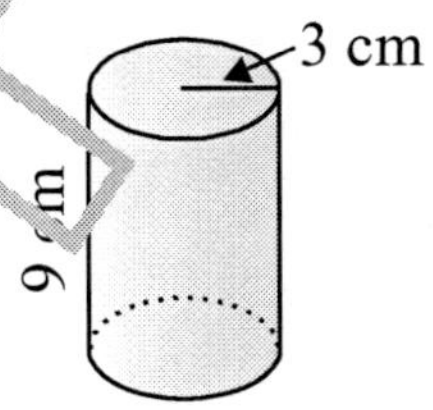

4. 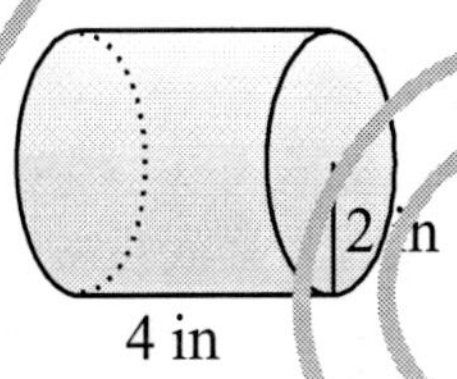

5. 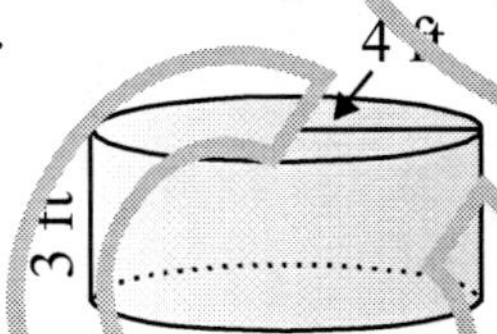

6. 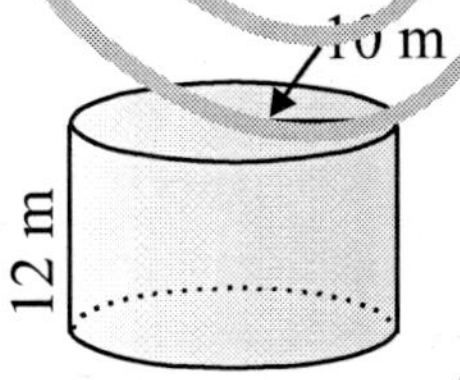

7. 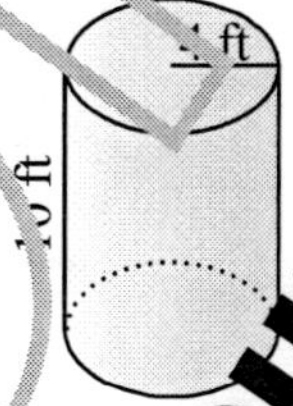

8. 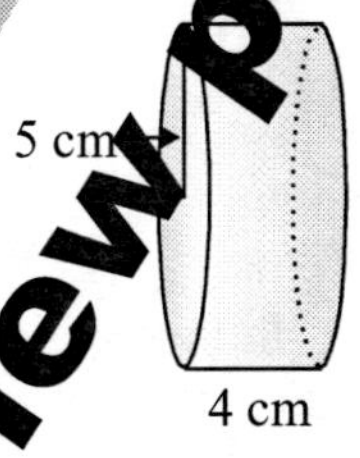

9. 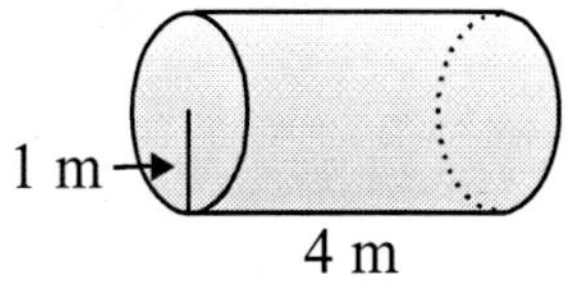

20.11 Solid Geometry Word Problems

1. If an Egyptian pyramid has a square base that measures 500 yards by 500 yards, and the pyramid stands 300 yards tall, what would be the volume of the pyramid? Use the formula for volume of a pyramid, $V = \frac{1}{3}Bh$ where B is the area of the base.

2. Robert is using a cylindrical barrel filled with water to flatten the sod in his yard. The circular ends have a radius of 1 foot. The barrel is 3 feet wide. How much water will the barrel hold? The formula for volume of a cylinder is $V = \pi r^2 h$. Use $\pi = 3.14$.

3. If a basketball measures 24 centimeters in diameter, what volume of air will it hold? The formula for volume of a sphere is $V = \frac{4}{3}\pi r^3$. Use $\pi = 3.14$.

4. What is the volume of a cone that is 2 inches in diameter and 5 inches tall? The formula for volume of a cone is $V = \frac{1}{3}\pi r^2 h$. Use $\pi = 3.14$.

5. Kelly has a rectangular fish aquarium that measures 24 inches wide, 12 inches deep, and 18 inches tall. What is the maximum amount of water that the aquarium will hold?

6. Jenny has a rectangular box that she wants to cover in decorative contact paper. The box is 10 cm long, 5 cm wide, and 5 cm high. How much paper will she need to cover all 6 sides?

7. Gasco needs to construct a cylindrical, steel gas tank that measures 6 feet in diameter and is 8 feet long. How many square feet of steel will be needed to construct the tank? Use the following formulas as needed: $A = l \times w$, $A = \pi r^2$, $C = 2\pi r$. Use $\pi = 3.14$.

8. Craig wants to build a miniature replica of San Francisco's Transamerica Pyramid out of glass. His replica will have a square base that measures 6 cm by 6 cm. The triangular sides will be 6 cm wide and 60 cm tall. How many square centimeters of glass will he need to build his replica? Use the following formulas as needed: $A = l \times w$ and $A = \frac{1}{2}bh$.

9. Jeff built a wooden, cubic toy box for his son. Each side of the box measures 2 feet. How many square feet of wood did he use to build the toy box? How many cubic feet of toys will the box hold?

Chapter 20 Review

Solve the following solid geometry problems.

1.

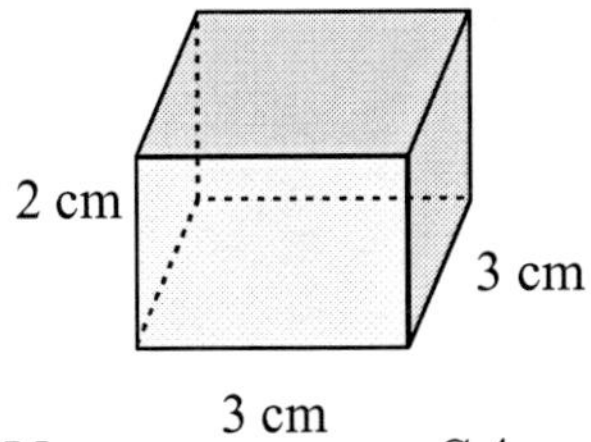

$V =$ ________ $SA =$ ________

2.

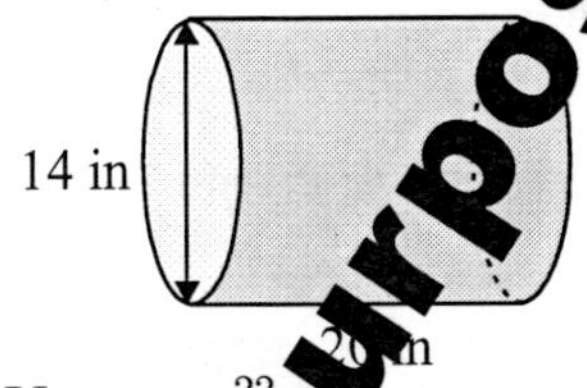

Use $\pi = \frac{22}{7}$.
$V =$ ________ $SA =$ ________

3.

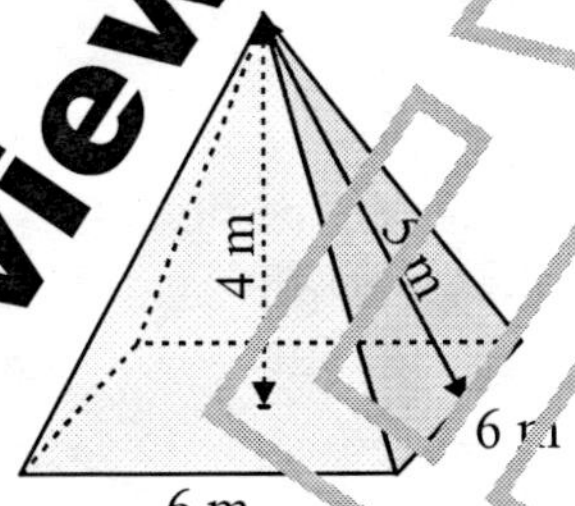

$V =$ ________ $SA =$ ________

4.

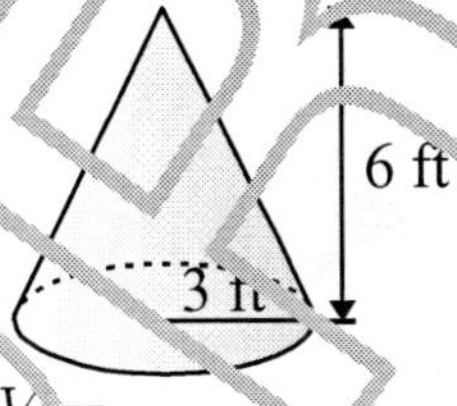

$V =$ ________

5.

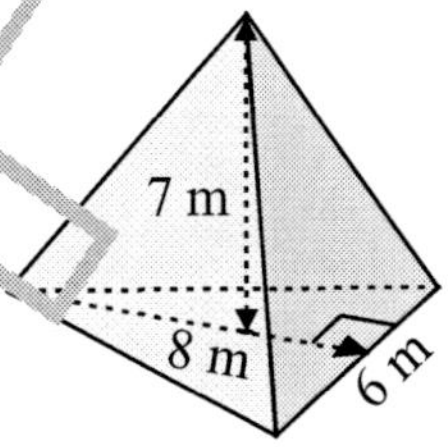

$V =$ ________

6. Use $\pi = \frac{22}{7}$.

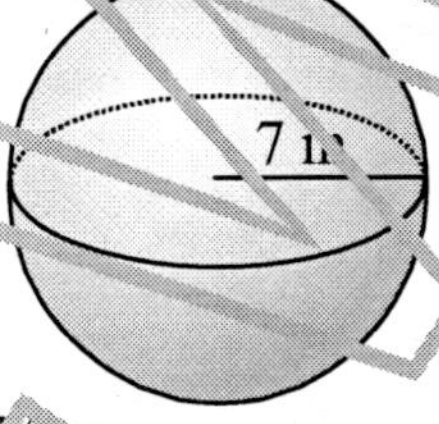

$V =$ ________

7. The sandbox at the local elementary school is 60 inches wide and 100 inches long. The sand in the box is 6 inches deep. How many cubic inches of sand are in the sandbox?

8. If you have cubes that are two inches on each edge, how many would fit in a cube that was 16 inches on each edge?

9. If you double each edge of a cube, how many times larger is the volume?

10. It takes 8 cubic inches of water to fill a cube. If each side of the cube is doubled, how much water is needed to fill the new cube?

11. If a ball is 4 inches in diameter, what is its volume? Use $\pi = 3.14$.

12. A grain silo is in the shape of a cylinder. If the silo has an inside diameter of 10 feet and a height of 35 feet, what is the maximum volume inside the silo? Use $\pi = \frac{22}{7}$.

13. A closed cardboard box is 30 centimeters long, 10 centimeters wide, and 20 centimeters high. What is the total surface area of the box?

14. Siena wants to build a wooden toy box with a lid. The dimensions of the toy box are 3 feet long, 4 feet wide, and 2 feet tall. How many square feet of wood will she need to construct the box?

15. How many 1-inch cubes will fit inside a larger 1 foot cube? (Figures are not drawn to scale.)

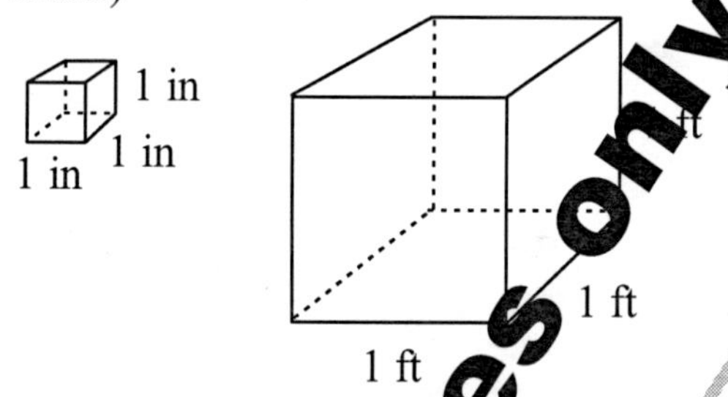

16. The cylinder below has a volume of 240 cubic inches. The cone below has the same radius and the same height as the cylinder. What is the volume of the cone?

17. Estimate the volume of the figure below.

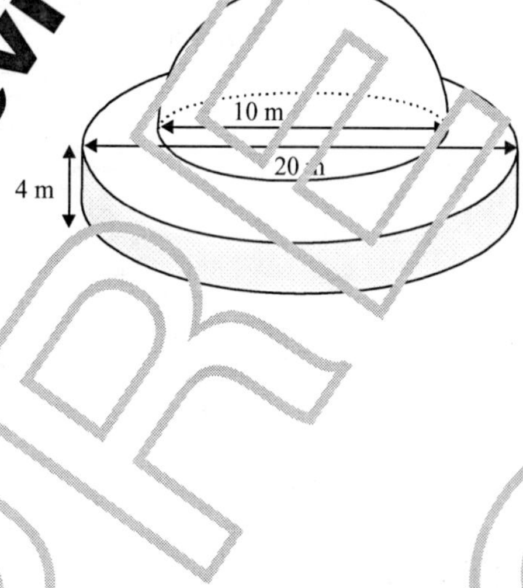

18. Find the volume of the figure below.

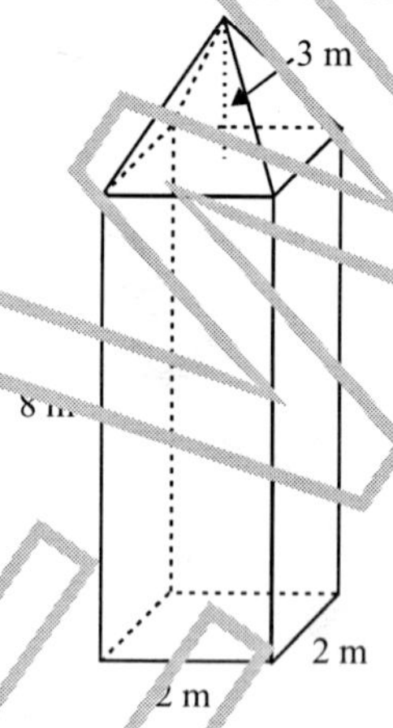

19. Find the volume of the figure below. Each side of each cube measures 4 feet.

20. A gigantic bronze sphere is being added to the top of a tall building downtown. The sphere will be 24 ft in diameter. What will be the volume of the globe?

Chapter 20 Test

1. What is the volume, in cubic feet, of the square pyramid below?

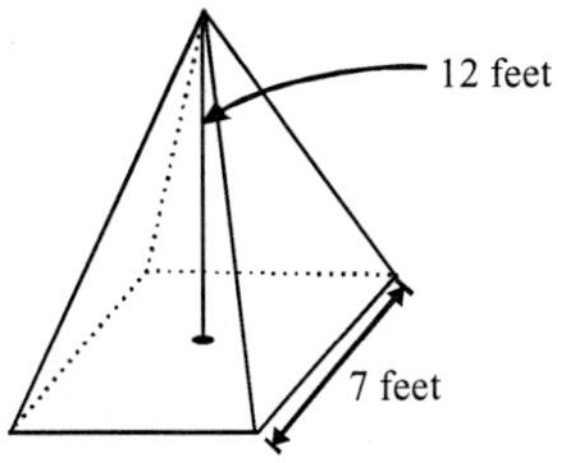

A. 168 cubic feet
B. 196 cubic feet
C. 294 cubic feet
D. 588 cubic feet
E. 84 cubic feet

2. What is the volume of the following oil tank? Round your answer to the nearest hundredth. Use $\pi = 3.14$.

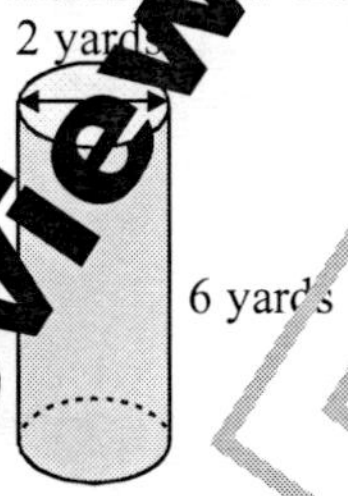

F. 18.84 yd^3
G. 37.68 yd^3
H. 44.48 yd^3
J. 75.36 yd^3
K. 6.28 yd^3

3. Find the volume of the cone. Use the formula $V = \frac{1}{3}\pi r^2 h$, $\pi = \frac{22}{7}$.

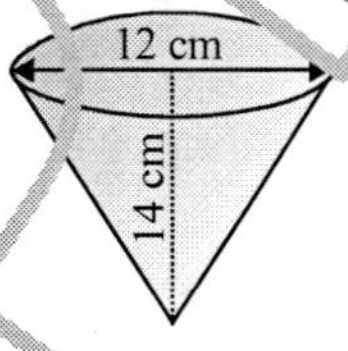

A. 88 cm^3
B. 176 cm^3
C. 254 cm^3
D. 528 cm^3
E. 2,112 cm^3

4. What is volume of the box shown below?

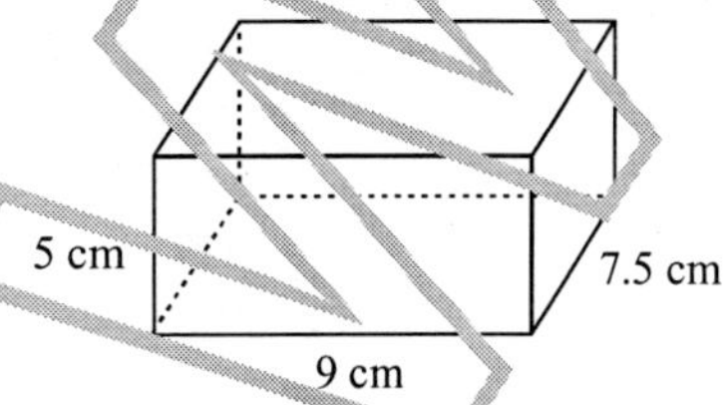

F. 22.5 cm^3
G. 1875 cm^3
H. 2250 cm^3
J. 230 cm^3
K. 337.5 cm^3

5. Find the volume of the figure below.

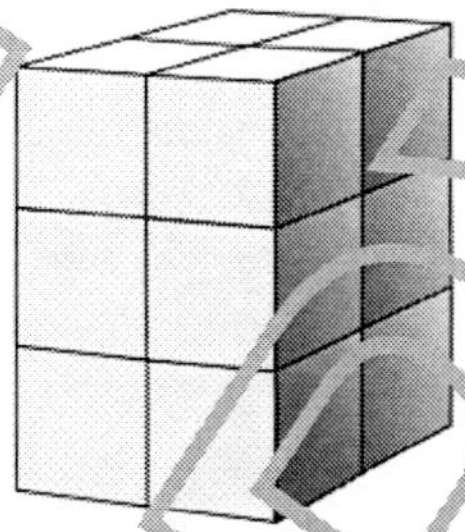

A. 6 units^3
B. 12 units^3
C. 36 units^3
D. 72 units^3
E. 32 units^3

6. If a sphere with a 6 m radius is cut out of a cube like the one shown below, what would the new volume be?

F. 823.22 m^3
G. 1728 m^3
H. 904.78 m^3
J. 14[illegible]1 m^3
K. 1[illegible]59 m^3

7. If the volume of a cylinder is 81π in^3 and has a height of 9 in, what is its total surface area?

A. 108π in^2
B. 72π in^2
C. 120π in^2
D. 36π in^2
E. 144π in^2

8. If a hole with a 3 inch diameter is cut through a cylinder, what is the volume afterwards?

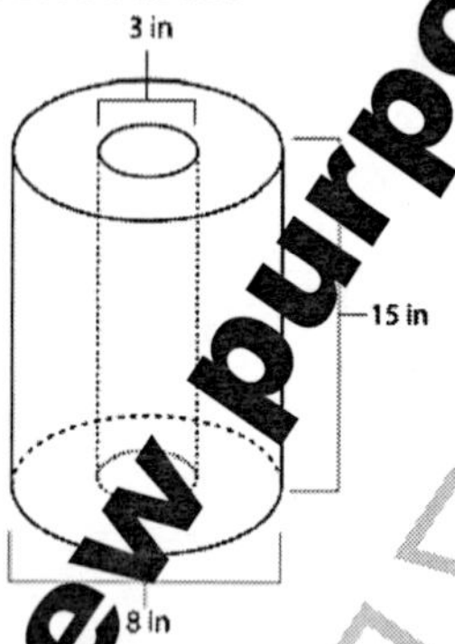

F. 375π in^3
G. 206.25π in^3
H. 240π in^3
J. 273.75π in^3
K. 281π in^3

9. What is the surface area of a cube whose sides measure 8 cm?

A. 512 cm^2
B. 64 cm^2
C. 384 cm^2
D. 448 cm^2
E. 96 cm^2

10. The length of a cube's edge is 3 cm. Find the volume of the cube.

F. 36 cm^3
G. 9 cm^3
H. 27 cm^3
J. 12 cm^3
K. 54 cm^3

11. If the radius of a sphere is tripled, how much larger will the volume be?

A. 81 times larger
B. 6 times larger
C. 9 times larger
D. 3 times larger
E. 27 times larger

12. If the radius of a cylinder is doubled, how much larger will the volume be?

F. 12 times larger
G. 8 times larger
H. 4 times larger
J. 2 times larger
K. It would be the same.

13. If the volume of a cube is 2197 mm^3, what is its total surface area?

A. 864 mm^2
B. 1183 mm^2
C. 169 mm^2
D. 1014 mm^2
E. 1352 mm^2

14. What is the surface area of a square pyramid that measures 7 feet on each side of its base and has a slant height of 8 feet?

F. 184 ft^2
G. 152 ft^2
H. 176 ft^2
J. 168 ft^2
K. 161 ft^2

15. What is the surface area of a cylinder whose radius is 6 m and its height is 12 m?

A. 180π m^2
B. 144π m^2
C. 216π m^2
D. 252π m^2
E. [illegible]π m^2

Chapter 21
Logic and Geometric Proofs

21.1 Mathematical Reasoning/Logic

The ACT curriculum calls for skill development in mathematical **reasoning** or **logic**. The ability to use logic is an important skill for solving math problems, but it can also be helpful in real-life situations. For example, if you need to get to Park Street, and the Park Street bus always comes to the bus stop at 3 PM, then you know that you need to get to the bus stop by at least 3 PM. This is a real-life example of using logic, which many people would call "common sense."

There are many different types of statements which are commonly used to describe mathematical principles. However, using the rules of logic, the truth of any mathematical statement must be evaluated. Below is a list of tools used in logic to evaluate mathematical statements.

Logic is the discipline that studies valid reasoning. There are many forms of valid arguments, but we will review just a few here.

A **proposition** is usually a declarative sentence which may be true or false.

An **argument** is a set of two or more related propositions, called **premises**, that provide support for another proposition, called the **conclusion**.

Deductive reasoning is an argument which begins with general premises and proceeds to a more specific conclusion. Most elementary mathematical problems use deductive reasoning.

Inductive reasoning is an argument in which the truth of its premises make it likely or probable that its conclusion is true.

21.2 Arguments

Most of logic deals with the evaluation of the validity of arguments. An argument is a group of statements that includes a conclusion and at least one premise. A premise is a statement that you know is true or at least you assume to be true. Then, you draw a conclusion based on what you know or believe is true in the premise(s). Consider the following example:

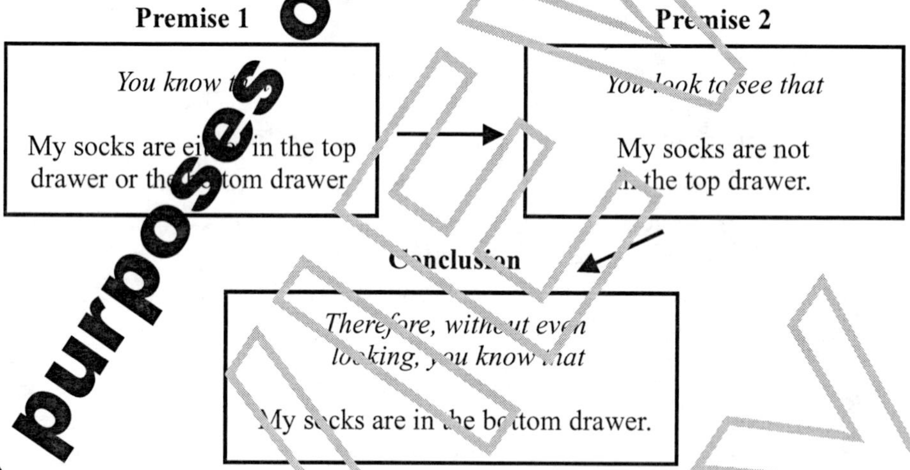
Premise 1
You know that
My socks are either in the top drawer or the bottom drawer.
Premise 2
You look to see that
My socks are not in the top drawer.
Conclusion
Therefore, without even looking, you know that
My socks are in the bottom drawer.

This argument is an example of deductive reasoning, where the conclusion is "deduced" from the premises and nothing else. In other words, if Premise 1 and Premise 2 are true, you don't even need to look in the bottom drawer to know that the conclusion is true.

21.3 Deductive and Inductive Arguments

In general, there are two types of logical arguments: **deductive** and **inductive**. Deductive arguments tend to move from general statements or theories to more specific conclusions. Inductive arguments tend to move from specific observations to general theories.

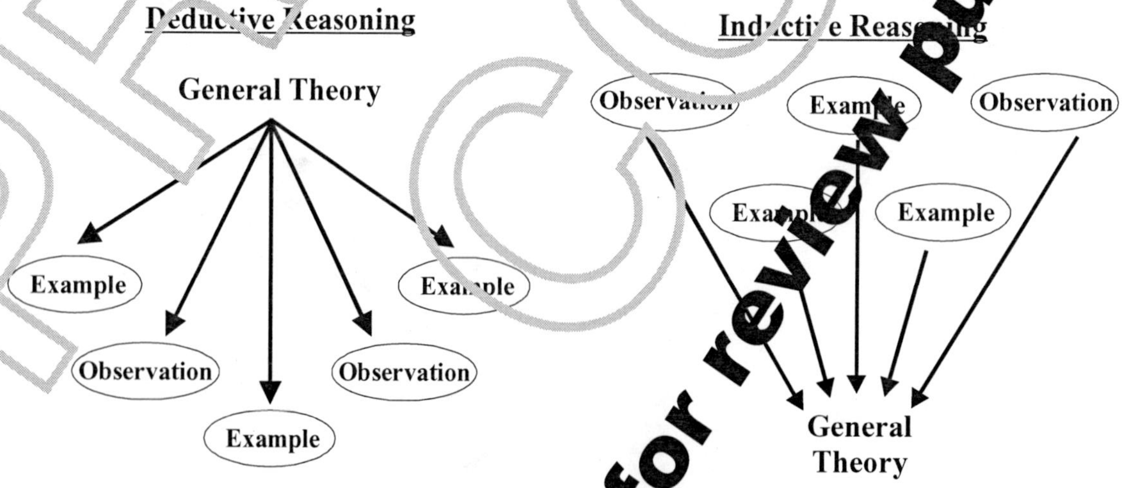
Deductive Reasoning
General Theory
Example
Observation
Example
Observation
Example
Inductive Reasoning
Observation
Example
Observation
Example
Example
General Theory

Compare the two examples below:

Deductive Argument

Premise 1	All men are mortal.
Premise 2	Socrates is a man.
Conclusion	Socrates is mortal.

Inductive Argument

Premise 1	The sun rose this morning.
Premise 2	The sun rose yesterday morning.
Premise 3	The sun rose two days ago.
Premise 4	The sun rose three days ago.
Conclusion	The sun will rise tomorrow.

An inductive argument cannot be proved beyond a shadow of a doubt. For example, it's a pretty good bet that the sun will come up tomorrow, but the sun not coming up presents no logical contradiction.

On the other hand, a deductive argument can have logical certainty, but it must be properly constructed. Consider the examples below.

True Conclusion from an Invalid Argument

All men are mortal.
Socrates is mortal.
Therefore Socrates is a man.

Even though the above conclusion is true, the argument is based on invalid logic. Both men and women are mortal. Therefore, Socrates could be a woman.

False Conclusion from a Valid Argument

All astronauts are men.
Julia Roberts is an astronaut.
Therefore, Julia Roberts is a man.

In this case, the conclusion is false because the premises are false. However, the logic of the argument is valid because *if* the premises were true, then the conclusion would be true.

A **counterexample** is an example given in which the statement is true but the conclusion is false when we have assumed it to be true. If we said "All cocker spaniels have blonde hair," then a counterexample would be a red-haired cocker spaniel. If we made the statement, "If a number is greater than 10, it is less than 20," we can easily think of a counterexample, like 35.

Example 1: Which argument is valid?

If you speed on Hill Street, you will get a ticket.
If you get a ticket, you will pay a fine.

(A) I paid a fine, so I was speeding on Hill Street.
(B) I got a ticket, so I was speeding on Hill Street.
(C) I exceeded the speed limit on Hill Street, so I paid a fine.
(D) I did not speed in Hill Street, so I did not pay a fine.

Solution: C is valid.
A is incorrect. I could have paid a fine for another violation.
B is incorrect. I could have gotten a ticket for some other violation.
D is incorrect. I could have paid a fine for speeding somewhere else.

Example 2: Assume the given proposition is true. Then determine if each statement is true or false.

Given: If a dog is thirsty, he will drink.

(A) If a dog drinks, then he is thirsty. T or F

(B) If a dog is not thirsty, he will not drink. T or F

(C) If a dog will not drink, he is not thirsty. T or F

Solution: A is false. He is not necessarily thirsty; he could just drink because other dogs are drinking or drink to show others his control of the water. This statement is the **converse** of the original. The converse of the statement "If A, then B" is "If B, then A."

B is false. The reasoning from A applies. This statement is the **inverse** of the original. The inverse of the statement "If A, then B" is "If not A, then not B."

C is true. It is the **contrapositive**, or the complete opposite of the original. The contrapositive says "If not B, then not A."

For numbers 1–5, what conclusion can be drawn from each proposition?

1. All squirrels are rodents. All rodents are mammals. Therefore,

2. All fractions are rational numbers. All rational numbers are real numbers. Therefore,

3. All squares are rectangles. All rectangles are parallelograms. All parallelograms are quadrilaterals. Therefore,

4. All Chevrolets are made by General Motors. All Luminas are Chevrolets. Therefore,

5. If a number is even and divisible by three, then it is divisible by six. Eighteen is divisible by six. Therefore,

For numbers 6–9, assume the given proposition is true. Then, determine if the statements following it are true or false.

All squares are rectangles.

6. All rectangles are squares. T or F
7. All non-squares are non-rectangles. T or F
8. No squares are non-rectangles. T or F
9. All non-rectangles are non-squares. T or F

21.4 Geometry Logic

A **conditional statement** is a type of logical statement that has two parts, a **hypothesis** and a **conclusion**. The statement is written in "if-then" form, where the "if" part contains the hypothesis and the "then" part contains the conclusion. For example, let's start with the statement "Two lines intersect at exactly one point." We can rewrite this as a conditional statement in "if-then" form as follows:

$$\underbrace{\text{If two lines intersect}}_{\text{hypothesis}}\text{, then }\underbrace{\text{their intersection is at exactly one point.}}_{\text{conclusion}}$$

Conditional statements may be true or false. To show that a statement is false, you need only to provide a single **counterexample** which shows that the statement is not always true. To show that a statement is true, on the other hand, you must show that the conclusion is true for all occasions in which the hypothesis occurs. This is often much more difficult.

Example 2: Provide a counterexample to show that the following conditional statement is false:
If $x^2 = 4$, then $x = 2$.

To begin with, let $x = -2$.
The hypothesis is true, because $(-2)^2 = 4$.
For $x = -2$, however, the conclusion is false even though the hypothesis is true.
Therefore, we have provided a counterexample to show that the conditional statement is false.

The **converse** of a conditional statement is an "if-then" statement written by switching the hypothesis and the conclusion. For example, for the conditional statement "If a figure is a quadrilateral, then it is a rectangle," the converse is "If a figure is a rectangle, then it is a quadrilateral."

The **inverse** of a conditional statement is written by negating the hypothesis and conclusion of the original "if-then" conditional statement. Negating means to change the meaning so it is the negative, or opposite, of its original meaning. The inverse of the conditional statement "If a figure is a quadrilateral, then it is a rectangle" is "If a figure is **not** a quadrilateral, then it is **not** a rectangle."

The **contrapositive** of a conditional statement is written by negating the converse. That is, switch the hypothesis and conclusion of the original statement, and make them both negative. The contrapositive of the conditional statement "If a figure is a quadrilateral, then it is a rectangle" is "If a figure is not a rectangle, then it is not a quadrilateral."

Example 4: Given the conditional statement "If $m\angle F = 60°$, then $\angle F$ is acute. Write the converse, inverse and contrapositive.

Step 1: The converse is constructed by switching the hypothesis and the conclusion: If $\angle F$ is acute, then $m\angle F = 60°$.

Step 2: The inverse is constructed by negating the original statement: If $m\angle F \neq 60°$, then $\angle F$ is not acute.

Step 3: The contrapositive is the negation of the converse: If $\angle F$ is not acute, then $m\angle F \neq 60°$.

Answer the following problems about geometry logic.

1. Rewrite the following as a conditional statement in "if-then" form: A number divisible by 8 is also divisible by 4.

2. Write the converse of the following conditional statement: If two circles have equal radii, then the circles are congruent.

3. Given the conditional statement: If $x^4 = 81$, then $x = 3$. Is the statement true? Provide a counterexample if it is false.

4. Given the statement: A line contains at least two points. Write as a conditional statement in "if-then" form, then write the converse, inverse, and contrapositive of the conditional statement.

5. "If a parallelogram has four congruent sides, then it is a rhombus." Write the converse, inverse, and contrapositive for the conditional statement. Which are true? Which are false?

6. "If a triangle has one right angle, then the acute angles are complementary." Write the converse, inverse, and contrapositive for the conditional statement. Indicate whether each is true or false. Can all the statements be either true or false? Explain.

7. "If a rectangle has four congruent sides, then it is a square." Write the contrapositive for the conditional statement and indicate whether it is true or false. Give a counterexample if it is false.

8. Show why a conditional statement and its inverse are always logically equivalent. Similarly, show why a statement's converse and inverse are logically equivalent.

Chapter 21 Review

For numbers 1–4, assume the given proposition is true. Then determine if the statements following it are true or false.

All whales are mammals.

1. All non-whales are non-mammals.
2. If a mammal lives in the sea, it is a whale.
3. All mammals are whales.
4. All non-mammals are non-whales.

For numbers 5–8, determine whether the situation is showing deductive or inductive logic.

5. A group of students were given three descriptions about a person's job. They were then told to decide what type of job title the person has.
6. When traveling in a car on a family vacation, I noticed that I could see the ocean to my left and palm trees to my right. I concluded that my family and I were going to the beach.
7. Sammy asked her friend, Amy, to give her a good reason to get a summer job. Amy gave Sammy four good reasons to get a job.
8. The neighbor's cars are in the driveway and all of the lights in the house are off, so they must be sleeping.

Look at statements 9–12. Determine whether the statements are true always, sometimes, or never.

9. Quadratic equations have two solutions.
10. If you graph a linear equation, the graph will be a straight line.
11. When multiplying both sides of an inequality by a number, you must reverse the direction of the inequality symbol.
12. When you take the absolute value of a number, you are making the number negative.

Solve the following problems.

13. "If a triangle is isosceles, then its base angles are congruent." Write the contrapositive for the conditional statement. Is the statement true or false? Is the contrapositive true or false? If false, give a counterexample.
14. "If the radius of a circle is doubled, then the area of the circle is increased by a factor of four." Write the converse, inverse, and contrapositive for the conditional statement. Indicate which ones are true or false.
15. "If today is Tuesday, then it is raining." Write the converse, inverse, and contrapositive for the conditional statement. Could the statements be true? Give a counterexample to prove each statement false.

Chapter 21 Test

For 1–3, choose which argument is valid.

1. If I oversleep, I miss breakfast. If I miss breakfast, I cannot concentrate in class. If I do not concentrate in class, I make bad grades.
   - **A.** I made bad grades today, so I missed breakfast.
   - **B.** I made good grades today, so I got up on time.
   - **C.** I could not concentrate in class today, so I overslept.
   - **D.** I had no breakfast today, so I overslept.
   - **E.** I had no breakfast today, so I made good grades.

2. If I do not maintain my car regularly, it will develop problems. If my car develops problems, it will not be safe to drive. If my car is not safe to drive, I cannot take a trip in it.
   - **F.** I took a trip in my car, so I maintained it regularly.
   - **G.** If I maintain my car regularly, it will not develop problems.
   - **H.** If my car develops problems, I did not maintain it regularly.
   - **J.** If my car is safe to drive, it will not develop problems.
   - **K.** If my car develops problems, I did maintain it regularly.

3. If two triangles have all corresponding sides and all corresponding angles congruent, then they are congruent triangles. If two triangles are congruent, then they are similar triangles.
   - **A.** Similar triangles have all sides and all angles congruent.
   - **B.** If two triangles are similar, then they are congruent.
   - **C.** If two triangles are not congruent, then they are not similar.
   - **D.** If two triangles have all corresponding sides and angles congruent, then they are similar triangles.
   - **E.** If two triangles are congruent, then they are not similar.

4. Cynthia is asked to list five duties of the President. What type of logic is Cynthia using?
   - **F.** mathematical reasoning
   - **G.** inductive reasoning
   - **H.** intuitive reasoning
   - **J.** logical reasoning
   - **K.** deductive reasoning

5. All carnivores are meat eaters. Lions eat meat. Therefore, lions are carnivores. This kind of thinking is an example of ___________ reasoning.
   - **A.** applied
   - **B.** inductive
   - **C.** qualitative
   - **D.** deductive
   - **E.** logical

Chapter 22
Transformations

22.1 Drawing Geometric Figures on a Cartesian Coordinate Plane

You can use a Cartesian coordinate plane to draw geometric figures by plotting **vertices** and connecting them with line segments.

Example 1: What are the coordinates of each vertex of quadrilateral $ABCD$ below?

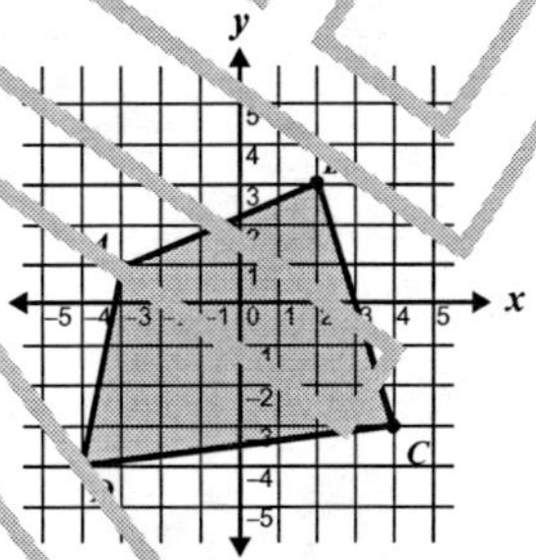

Step 1: To find the coordinates of point A, count over -3 on the x-axis and up 1 on the y-axis. point $A = (-3, 1)$.

Step 2: The coordinates of point B are located to the right two units on the x-axis and up 3 units on the y-axis. point $B = (2, 3)$.

Step 3: Point C is located 4 units to the right on the x-axis and down -3 on the y-axis. point $C = (4, -3)$.

Step 4: Point D is -4 units left on the x-axis and down -4 units on the y-axis. point $D = (-4, -4)$.

Example 2: Plot the following points. Then construct and identify the geometric figure that you plotted.

$$A = (-2, -5) \qquad C = (3, 1)$$
$$B = (-2, 1) \qquad D = (3, -5)$$

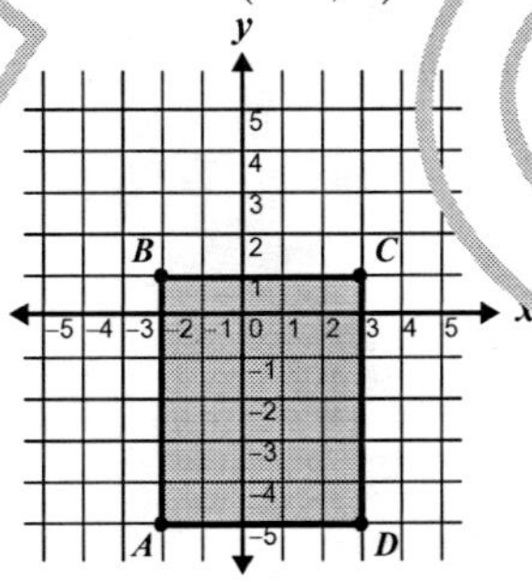

Figure $ABCD$ is a rectangle.

Find the coordinates of the geometric figures graphed below.

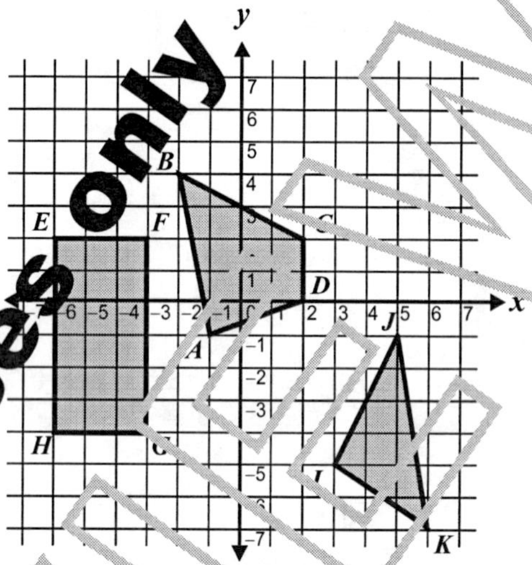

1. Quadrilateral $ABCD$
   $A =$ ________
   $B =$ ________
   $C =$ ________
   $D =$ ________

2. Rectangle $EFGH$
   $E =$ ________
   $F =$ ________
   $G =$ ________
   $H =$ ________

3. Triangle IJK
   $I =$ ________
   $J =$ ________
   $K =$ ________

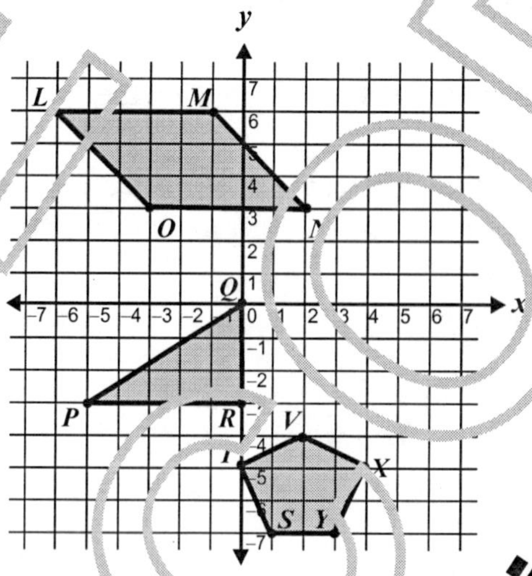

4. Parallelogram $LMNO$
   $L =$ ________
   $M =$ ________
   $N =$ ________
   $O =$ ________

5. Right Triangle PQR
   $P =$ ________
   $Q =$ ________
   $R =$ ________

6. Pentagon $STVXY$
   $S =$ ________
   $T =$ ________
   $V =$ ________
   $X =$ ________
   $Y =$ ________

Plot and label the following points. Then construct and identify the geometric figure you plotted. Question 1 is done for you.

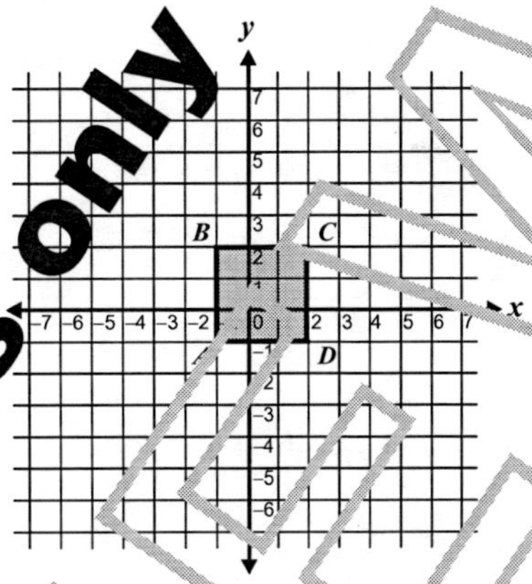

Figure | **Figure**

1. Point $A = (-1, -1)$
   Point $B = (-1, 2)$
   Point $C = (2, 2)$
   Point $D = (2, -1)$ **square**

2. Point $E = (3, -2)$
   Point $F = (5, 1)$
   Point $G = (7, -2)$ ________

3. Point $H = (-4, 0)$
   Point $I = (-6, 0)$
   Point $J = (-4, 4)$
   Point $K = (-2, 4)$ ________

4. Point $L = (-1, -3)$
   Point $M = (4, -6)$
   Point $N = (-1, -6)$ ________

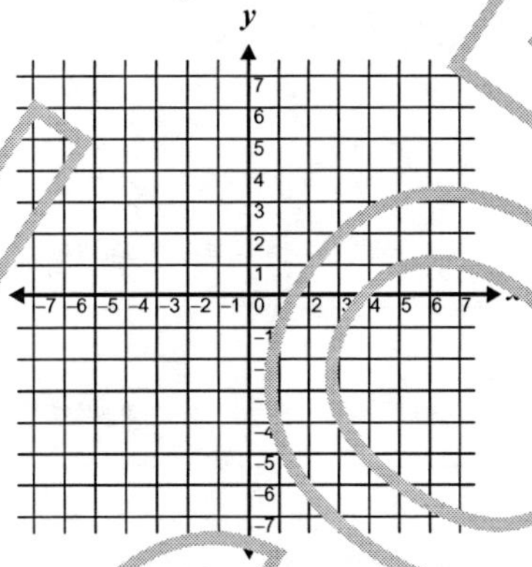

Figure | **Figure**

5. Point $A = (-2, -3)$
   Point $B = (-3, 5)$
   Point $C = (-1, 6)$
   Point $D = (1, 5)$
   Point $E = (0, -3)$ ________

6. Point $F = (-1, -3)$
   Point $G = (-3, -5)$
   Point $H = (-1, -7)$
   Point $I = (1, -5)$ ________

7. Point $J = ($[illegible]$, 2)$
   Point $K = (-1, -1)$
   Point $L = (3, -2)$ ________

8. Point $M = (6, 2)$
   Point $N = (6, -4)$
   Point $O = (4, -4)$
   Point $P = (4, 2)$ ________

22.2 Reflections

A **reflection** of a geometric figure is a mirror image of the object. Placing a mirror on the **line of reflection** will give you the position of the reflected image.

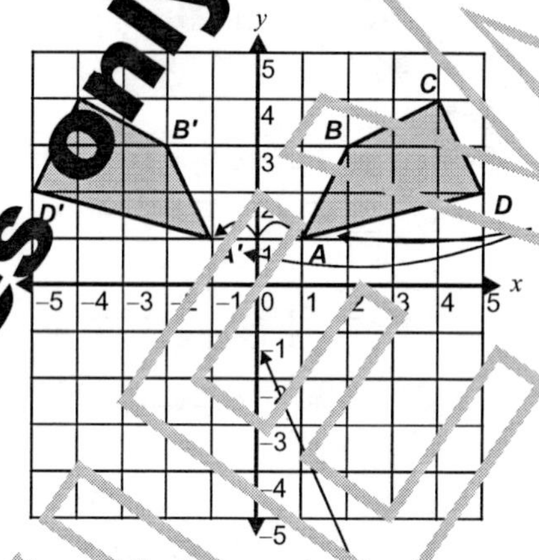

line of reflection: y-axis

Quadrilateral $ABCD$ is reflected across the y-axis to form quadrilateral $A'B'C'D'$. The y-axis is the line of reflection. Point A' (read as A prime) is the reflection of point A, point B' corresponds to point B, C' to C, and D' to D.

Point A is $+1$ space from the y-axis. Point A's mirror image, point A', is -1 space from the y-axis.
Point B is $+2$ spaces from the y-axis. Point B' is -2 spaces from the y-axis.
Point C is $+4$ spaces from the y-axis and point C' is -4 spaces from the y-axis.
Point D is $+5$ spaces from the y-axis and point D' is -5 spaces from the y-axis.

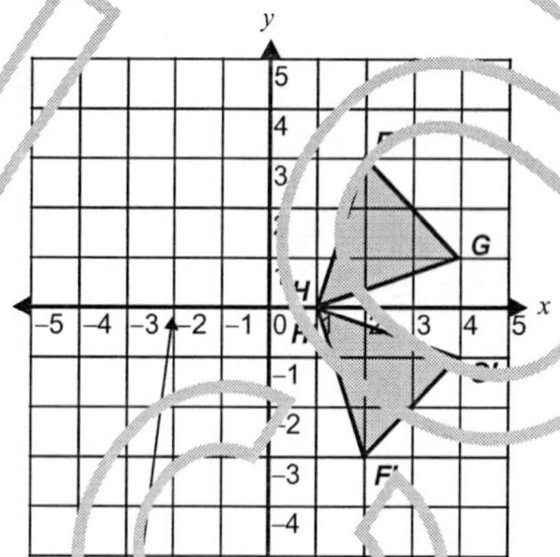

line of reflection: x-axis

Triangle FGH is reflected across the x-axis to form triangle $F'G'H'$. The x-axis is the line of reflection. Point F' reflects point F. Point G' corresponds to point G, and H' mirrors H.

Point F is $+3$ spaces from the x-axis. Likewise, point F' is -3 spaces from the x-axis.
Point G is $+1$ space from the x-axis, and point G' is -1 space from the x-axis.
Point H is 0 spaces from the x-axis, so point H' is also 0 spaces from the x-axis.

Reflecting Across a 45° Line

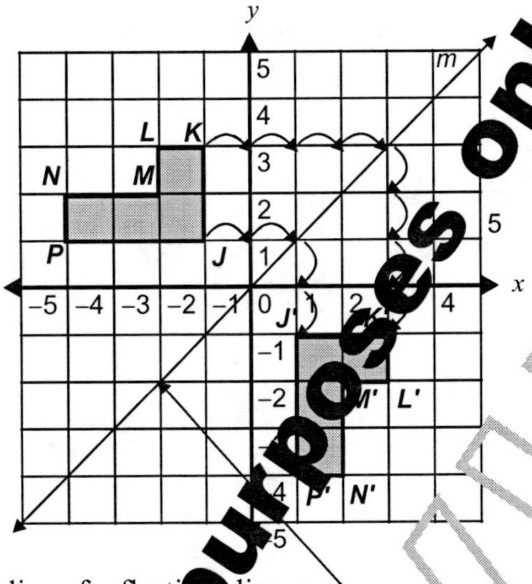

line of reflection: line m

Figure $JKLMNP$ is reflected across line m to form figure $J'K'L'M'N'P'$. Line m is at a 45° angle. Point J corresponds to J', K to K', L to L', M to M', N to N' and P to P'. Line m is the line of reflection. **Pay close attention to how to determine the mirror image of figure $JKLMNP$ across line m described below. This method only works when the line of reflection is at a 45° angle.**

Point J is 2 spaces over from line m, so J' must be 2 spaces down from line m.

Point K is 4 spaces over from line m, so K' is 4 spaces down from line m, and so on.

Draw the following reflections and record the new coordinates of the reflection. The first problem is done for you.

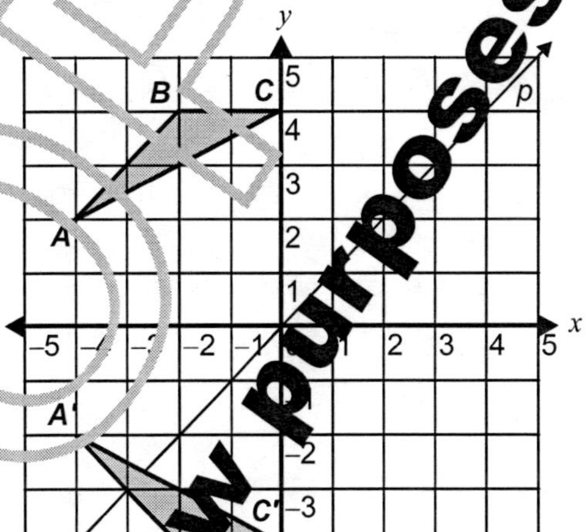

1. Reflect figure ABC across the x-axis. Label vertices $A'B'C'$ so that point A' is the reflection of point A, B' is the reflection of B, and C' is the reflection of C.
   $A' = \underline{(-4, -2)}$ $B' = \underline{(-2, -4)}$ $C' = \underline{(0, -4)}$

2. Reflect figure ABC across the y-axis. Label vertices $A''B''C''$ so that point A'' is the reflection of point A, B'' is the reflection of B, and C'' is the reflection of C.
   A'' = ______ B'' = ______ C'' = ______

3. Reflect figure ABC across line p. Label vertices $A'''B'''C'''$ so that point A''' is the reflection of point A, B''' is the reflection of B and C''' is the reflection of C.
   A''' = ______ B''' = ______ C''' = ______

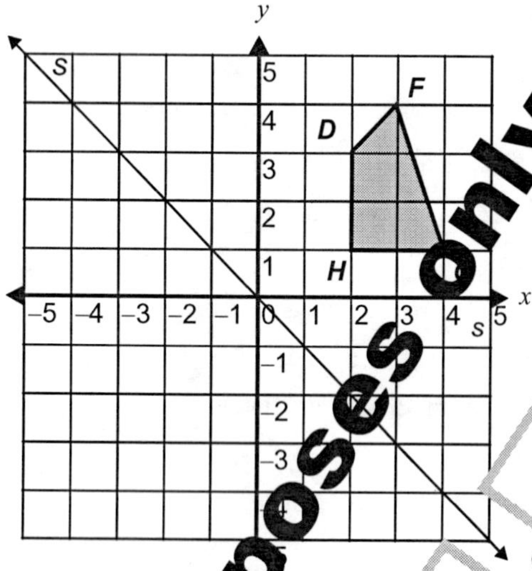

4. Reflect figure $DFGH$ across the y-axis. Label vertices $D'F'G'H'$ so that point D' is the reflection of point D, F' is the reflection of F, G' is the reflection of G, and H' is the reflection of H.
$D' =$ ______ $G' =$ ______
$F' =$ ______ $H' =$ ______

5. Reflect figure $DFGH$ across the x-axis. Label vertices D'', F'', G'', H'' so that point D'' is the reflection of D, F'' is the reflection of F, G'' is the reflection of G, and H'' is the reflection of H.
$D'' =$ ______ $G'' =$ ______
$F'' =$ ______ $H'' =$ ______

6. Reflect figure $DFGH$ across line s. Label vertices $D'''F'''G'''H'''$ so that point D''' is the reflection of D, F''' corresponds to F, G''' to G, and H''' to H.
$D''' =$ ______ $G''' =$ ______
$F''' =$ ______ $H''' =$ ______

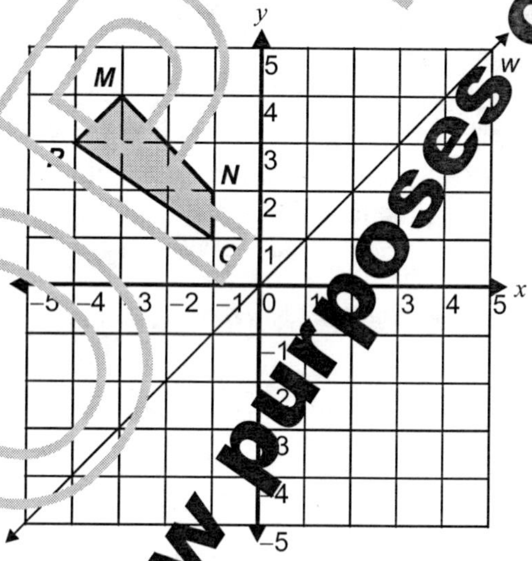

7. Reflect quadrilateral $MNOP$ across the y-axis. Label vertices $M'N'O'P'$ so that point M' is the reflection of point M, N' is the reflection of N, O' is the reflection of O, and P' is the reflection of P.
$M' =$ ______ $O' =$ ______
$N' =$ ______ $P' =$ ______

8. Reflect figure $MNOP$ across the x-axis. Label vertices M'', N'', O'', P'' so that point M'' is the reflection of M, N'' is the reflection of N, O'' is the reflection of O, and P'' is the reflection of P.
$M'' =$ ______ $O'' =$ ______
$N'' =$ ______ $P'' =$ ______

9. Reflect figure $MNOP$ across line w. Label vertices $M'''N'''O'''P'''$ so that point M''' is the reflection of M, N''' corresponds to N, O''' to O, and P''' to P.
$M''' =$ ______ $O''' =$ ______
$N''' =$ ______ $P''' =$ ______

22.3 Translations

To make a translation of a geometric figure, first duplicate the figure and then slide it along a path.

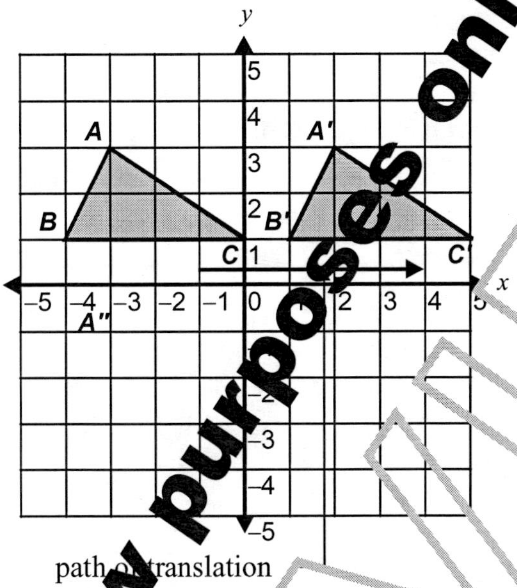

Triangle $A'B'C'$ is a translation of triangle ABC. Each point is translated 5 spaces to the right. In other words, the triangle slid 5 spaces to the right. Look at the path of translation. It gives the same information as above. Count the number of spaces across given by the path of translation, and you will see it represents a move 5 spaces to the right. Each new point is found at $(x+5, y)$.

Point A is at $(-3, 3)$. Therefore, A' is found at $(-3+5, 3)$ or $(2, 3)$.

B is at $(-4, 1)$, so B' is at $(-4+5, 1)$ or $(1, 1)$.

C is at $(0, 1)$, so C' is at $(0+5, 1)$ or $(5, 1)$.

Quadrilateral $FGHI$ is translated 5 spaces to the right and 3 spaces down. The path of translation shows the same information. It points right 5 spaces and down 3 spaces. Each new point is found at $(x+5, y-3)$.

Point F is located at $(-4, 3)$. Point F' is located at $(-4+5, 3-3)$ or $(1, 0)$.

Point G is at $(-2, 5)$. Point G' is at $(-2+5, 5-3)$ or $(3, 2)$.

Point H is at $(-1, 4)$. Point H' is at $(-1+5, 4-3)$ or $(4, 1)$.

Point I is at $(-1, 2)$. Point I' is at $(-1+5, 2-3)$ or $(4, -1)$.

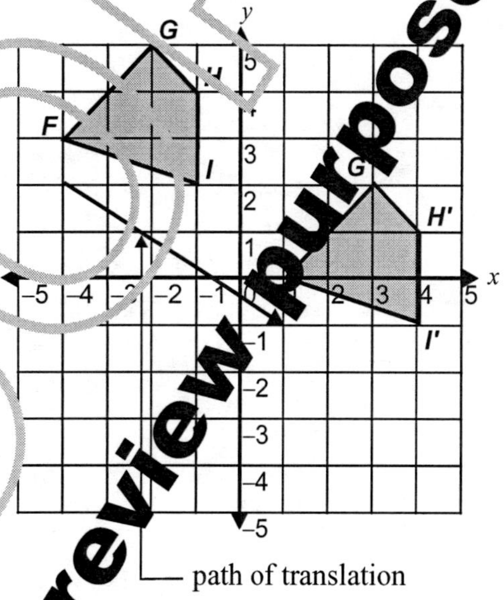

Draw the following translations and record the new coordinates of the translation. The figure for the first problem is drawn for you.

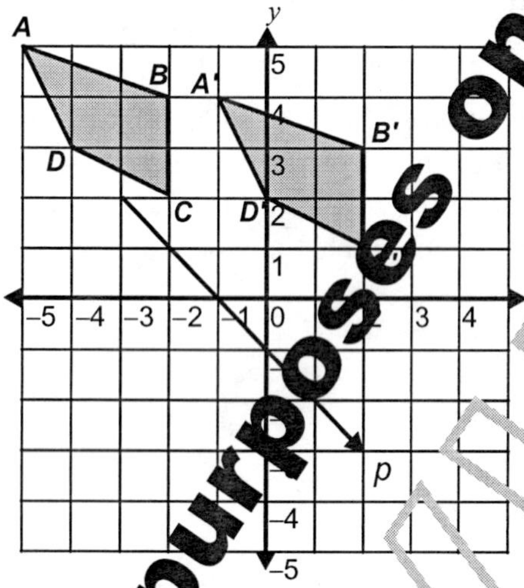

1. Translate figure *ABCD* 4 spaces to the right and 1 space down. Label the vertices of the translated figure *A′*, *B′*, *C′*, and *D′* so that point *A′* corresponds to the translation of point *A*, *B′* corresponds to *B*, *C′* to *C*, and *D′* to *D*.

   A′ = ______ *C′* = ______
   B′ = ______ *D′* = ______

2. Translate figure *ABCD* 5 spaces down. Label the vertices of the translated figure *A′′*, *B′′*, *C′′*, and *D′′* so that point *A′′* corresponds to the translation of point *A*, *B′′* corresponds to *B*, *C′′* to *C*, and *D′′* to *D*.

   A′′ = ______ *C′′* = ______
   B′′ = ______ *D′′* = ______

3. Translate figure *ABCD* along the path of translation, *p*. Label the vertices of the translated figure *A′′′*, *B′′′*, *C′′′*, and *D′′′* so that point *A′′′* corresponds to the translation of point *A*, *B′′′* corresponds to *B*, *C′′′* to *C*, and *D′′′* to *D*.

   A′′′ = ______ *C′′′* = ______
   B′′′ = ______ *D′′′* = ______

4. Translate triangle *FGH* 6 spaces to the left and 3 spaces up. Label the vertices of the translated figure *F′*, *G′*, and *H′* so that point *F′* corresponds to the translation of point *F*, *G′* corresponds to *G*, and *H′* to *H*.

   F′ = ______ *G′* = ______ *H′* = ______

5. Translate triangle *FGH* 4 spaces up and 1 space to the left. Label the vertices of the translated triangle *F′′G′′H′′* so that point *F′′* corresponds to the translation of point *F*, *G′′* corresponds to *G*, and *H′′* to *H*.

   F′′ = ______ *G′′* = ______ *H′′* = ______

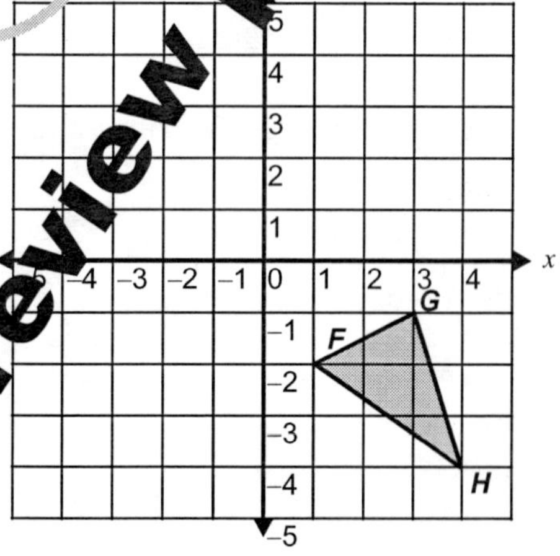

22.4 Rotations

A **rotation** of a geometric figure shows motion around a point.

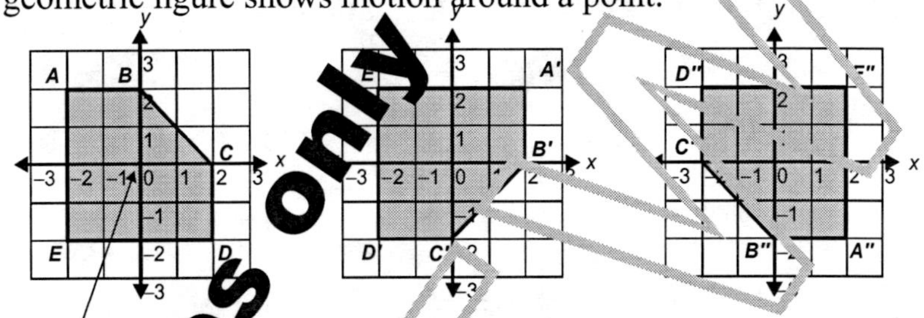

The origin is the point of rotation.

Figure $ABCDE$ has been rotated $\frac{1}{4}$ of a turn clockwise around the origin to form $A'B'C'D'E'$.

Figure $ABCDE$ has been rotated $\frac{1}{2}$ of a turn around the origin to form $A''B''C''D''E''$.

Draw the following rotations, and record the new coordinates of the rotation. The figure for the first problem is drawn for you.

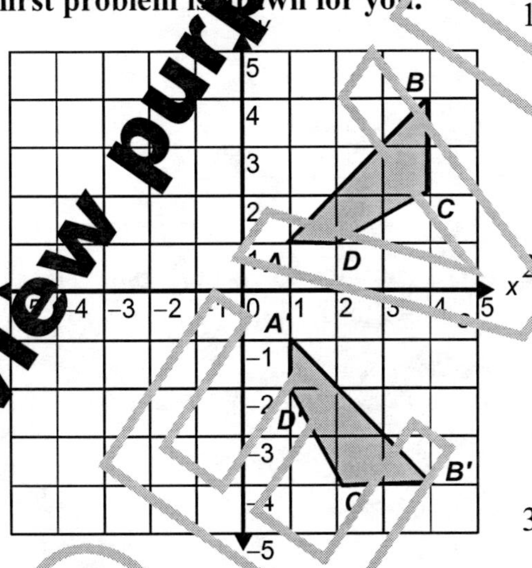

1. Rotate figure $ABCD$ around the origin clockwise $\frac{1}{4}$ turn. Label the vertices A', B', C', and D' so that point A' corresponds to the rotation of point A, B' corresponds to B, C' to C, and D' to D.
   $A' =$ ______ $C' =$ ______
   $B' =$ ______ $D' =$ ______

2. Rotate figure $ABCD$ around the origin clockwise $\frac{1}{2}$ turn. Label the vertices A'', B'', C'', and D'' so that point A'' corresponds to the rotation of point A, B'' corresponds to B, C'' to C, and D'' to D.
   $A'' =$ ______ $C'' =$ ______
   $B'' =$ ______ $D'' =$ ______

3. Rotate figure $ABCD$ around the origin clockwise $\frac{3}{4}$ turn. Label the vertices A''', B''', C''', and D''' so that point A''' corresponds to the rotation of point A, B''' corresponds to B, C''' to C, and D''' to D.
   $A''' =$ ______ $C''' =$ ______
   $B''' =$ ______ $D''' =$ ______

4. Rotate figure MNO around point O clockwise $\frac{1}{4}$ turn. Label the vertices M', N', and O so that point M' corresponds to the rotation of point M and N' corresponds to N.
   $M' =$ ______ $N' =$ ______

5. Rotate figure MNO around point O clockwise $\frac{1}{2}$ turn. Label the vertices M'', N'', and O so that point M'' corresponds to the rotation of point M, and N'' corresponds to N.
   $M'' =$ ______ $N'' =$ ______

6. Rotate figure MNO around point O clockwise $\frac{3}{4}$ turn. Label the vertices M''', N''', and O so that point M''' corresponds to the rotation of point M, and N''' corresponds to N.
   $M''' =$ ______ $N''' =$ ______

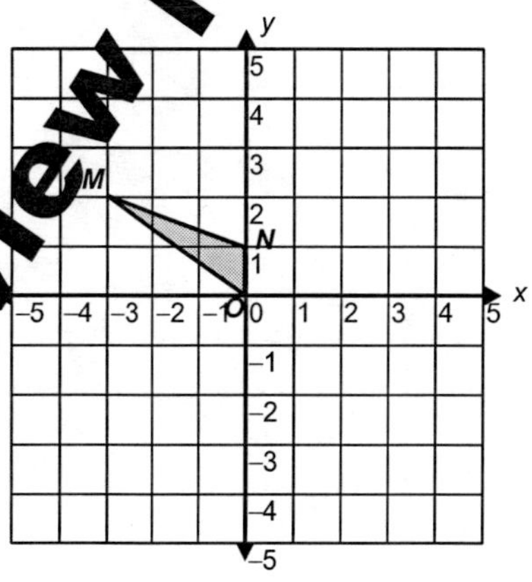

22.5 Transformation Practice

Answer the following questions regarding transformations.

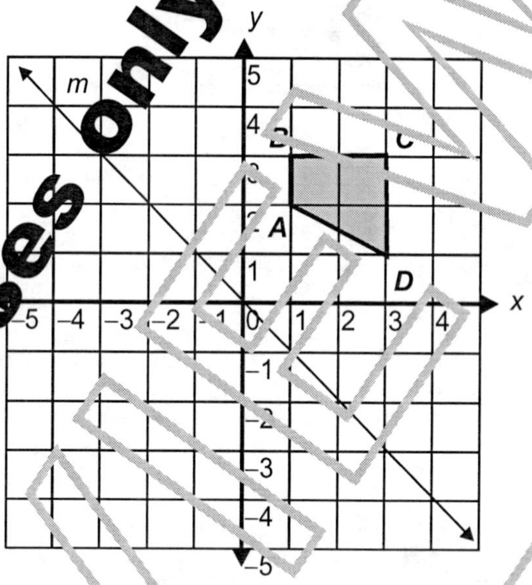

1. Translate quadrilateral $ABCD$ so that point A', which corresponds to point A, is located at coordinates $(-4, 3)$. Label the other vertices B' to correspond to B, C' to C, and D' to D. What are the coordinates of B', C', and D'?

   $A' =$ _____ $C' =$ _____

   $B' =$ _____ $D' =$ _____

2. Reflect quadrilateral $ABCD$ across line m. Label the coordinates A'', B'', C'', and D'', so that point A'' corresponds to the reflection of point A, B'' corresponds to the reflection of B, and C'' corresponds to the reflection of C. What are the coordinates of A'', B'', C'', and D''?

   $A'' =$ _____ $C'' =$ _____

   $B'' =$ _____ $D'' =$ _____

3. Rotate quadrilateral $ABCD$ $\frac{1}{4}$ turn counterclockwise around point D. Label the points $A'''B'''C'''D'''$ so that A''' corresponds to the rotation of point A, B''' corresponds to B, C''' to C, and D''' to D. What are the coordinates of A''', B''', C''' and D'''?

   $A''' =$ _____ $C''' =$ _____

   $B''' =$ _____ $D''' =$ _____

Chapter 22 Review

1. Draw the reflection of image $ABCD$ over the y-axis. Label the points A', B', C', and D'. List the coordinates of these points below.

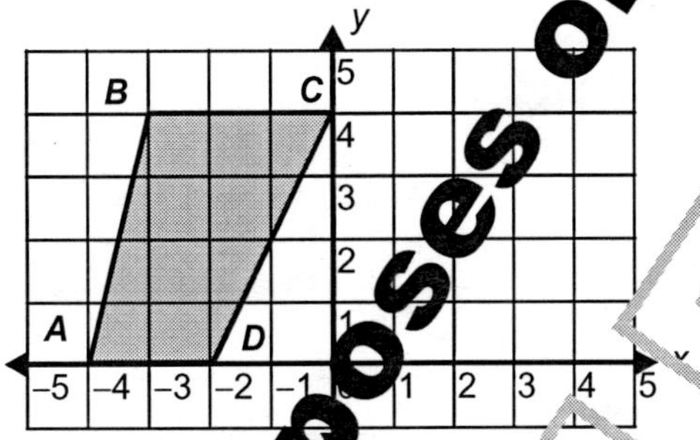

2. A' = _____
3. B' = _____
4. C' = _____
5. D' = _____

6. Rotate the figure above a $\frac{1}{2}$ turn about the origin, 0. Label the points A', B', C', D', E', and F'. List the coordinates of these points below.

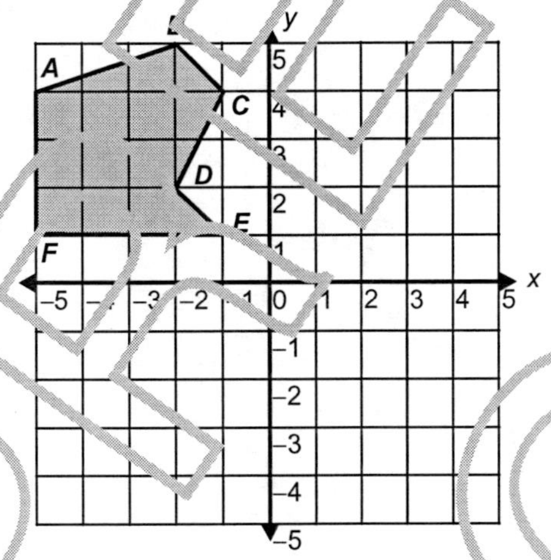

7. A' = _____
8. B' = _____
9. C' = _____
10. D' = _____
11. E' = _____
12. F' = _____

13. Use the translation described by the arrow to translate the polygon below. Label the points P', Q', R', S', T', and U'. List the coordinates of each.

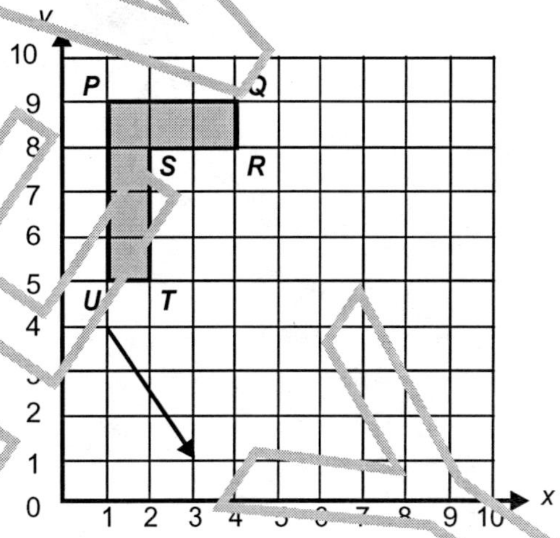

14. P' = _____
15. Q' = _____
16. R' = _____
17. S' = _____
18. T' = _____
19. U' = _____

Use the grid to answer the question that follows.

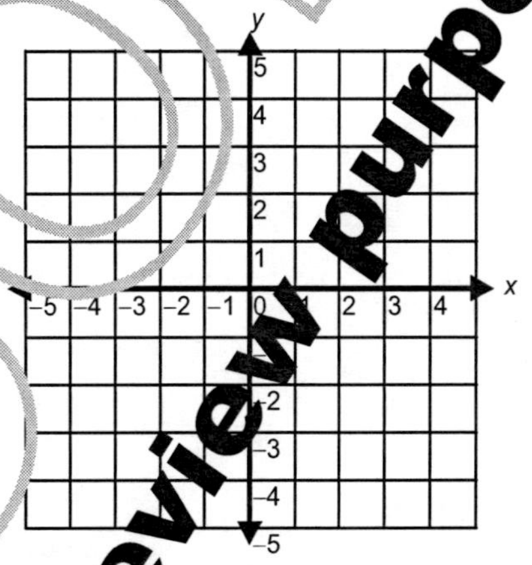

20. A point at $(-3, 2)$ is moved to $(0, 0)$. If a point at $(1, 1)$ is moved in the same way, what will its new coordinates be?

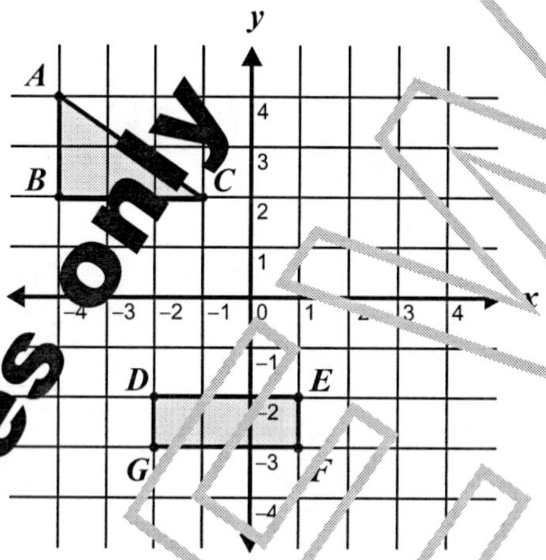

Find the coordinates of the geometric figures graphed above.

21. point A

22. point B

23. point C

24. point D

25. point E

26. point F

27. point G

Plot and label the following points on the same graph.

28. point $H = (1, 1)$

29. point $I = (3, 1)$

30. point $J = (4, -2)$

31. point $K = (2, -2)$

32. What type of figure did you plot?

Chapter 22 Test

1. If the figure below were reflected across the y-axis, what would be the coordinates of point C?

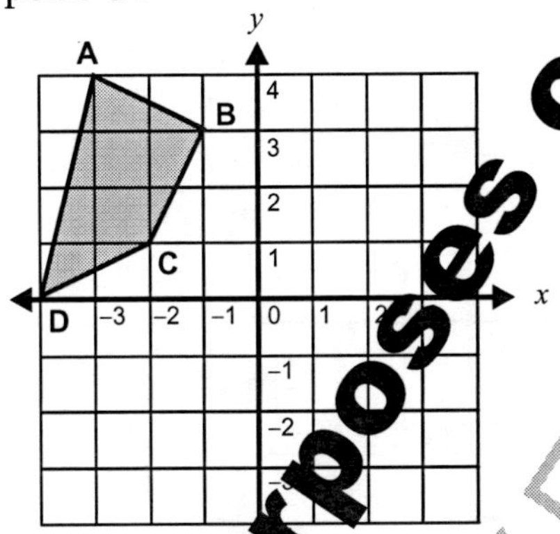

A. $(2, -1)$
B. $(2, 1)$
C. $(-2, -1)$
D. $(-2, 1)$
E. $(1, 2)$

2. If the figure below is translated in the direction described by the arrow, what will be the new coordinates of point D after the transformation?

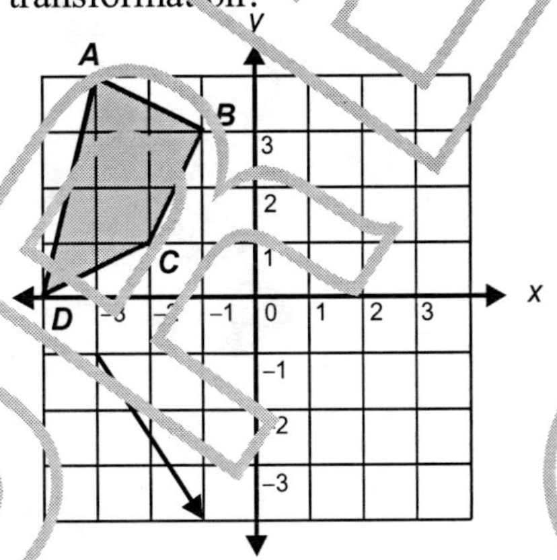

F. $(-2, -4)$
G. $(-1, -3)$
H. $(-1, -4)$
J. $(-2, -2)$
K. $(-2, -3)$

3. Figure 1 goes through a transformation to form Figure 2. Which of the following descriptions fits the transformations shown below?

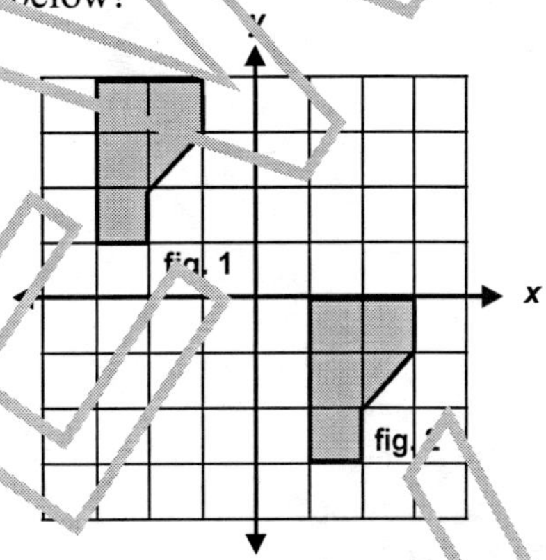

A. reflection across the x-axis
B. reflection across the origin
C. $\frac{1}{2}$ clockwise rotation around the origin
D. translation right 4 units and down 4 units
E. translation right 2 units and down 1 unit

4. Sammy plots the point $(-4, 3)$ on a coordinate grid. He reflects this point over the y-axis, then over the x-axis. What are the coordinates of the new reflected point?

F. $(-4, -3)$
G. $(-4, 3)$
H. $(4, -3)$
J. $(4, 3)$
K. $(-3, 4)$

5. What is the rule for the transformation formed by a translation 4 units down, then a rotation 90° clockwise around the origin?

A. $(x', y') = (x, -y + 4)$
B. $(x', y') = (x, y - 4)$
C. $(x', y') = (y - 4, -x)$
D. $(x', y') = (-y + 4, -x)$
E. $(x', y') = (y - 4, x)$

6. Randy plotted points G and H on the Cartesian coordinate graph below. Where could he plot points J and K if he wants to form a square $GHJK$?

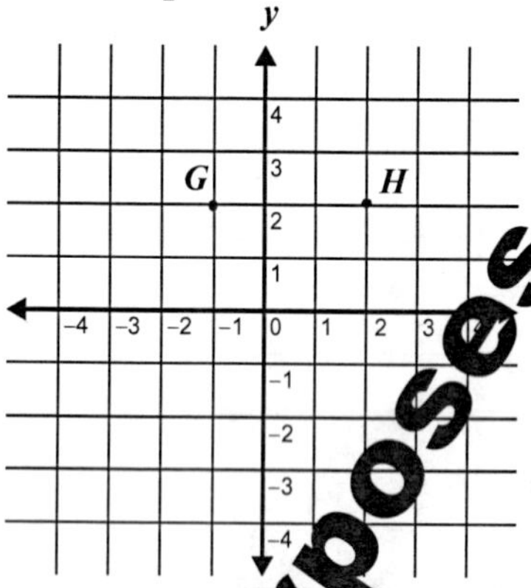

F. J at $(2, 4)$ and K at $(-1, 4)$
G. J at $(3, 6)$ and K at $(0, 6)$
H. J at $(2, 0)$ and K at $(-1, 0)$
J. J at $(2, -1)$ and K at $(-1, -1)$
K. J at $(-1, 0)$ and K at $(2, 0)$

7. Figure 1 goes through a transformation to form figure 2. Which of the following descriptions fits the transformation shown?

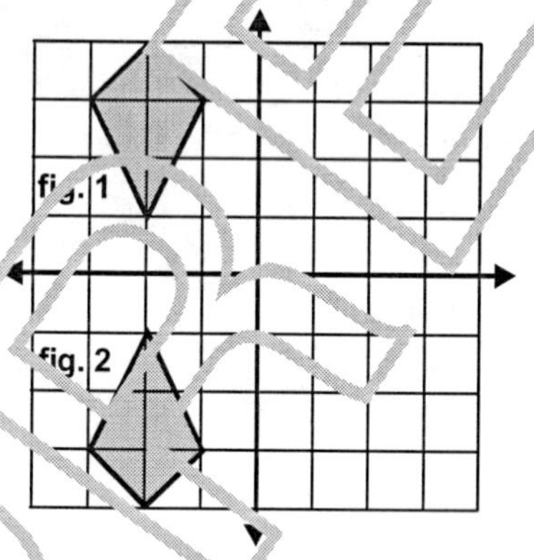

A. reflection across the x-axis
B. reflection across the y-axis
C. $\frac{3}{4}$ clockwise rotation around the origin
D. translation down 2 units
E. translation down 5 units

8. Figure 1 goes through a transformation to form figure 2. Which of the following descriptions fits the transformation shown?

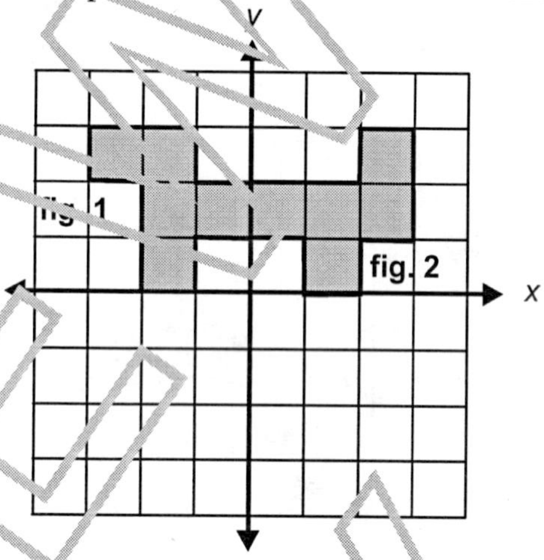

F. reflection across the x-axis
G. reflection across the y-axis
H. $\frac{3}{4}$ clockwise rotation around the origin
J. translation right 3 units
K. $\frac{1}{4}$ clockwise rotation around the origin

Chapter 23
Trigonometry

23.1 Trigonometric Ratios

Trigonometry involves the application of the relationships between sides and angles in right triangles. Recall that a right triangle has one 90° angle and two acute angles. Consider the right triangle shown below. Note that the angles are labeled with capital letters. The sides are labeled with lowercase letters that correspond to the angles opposite them.

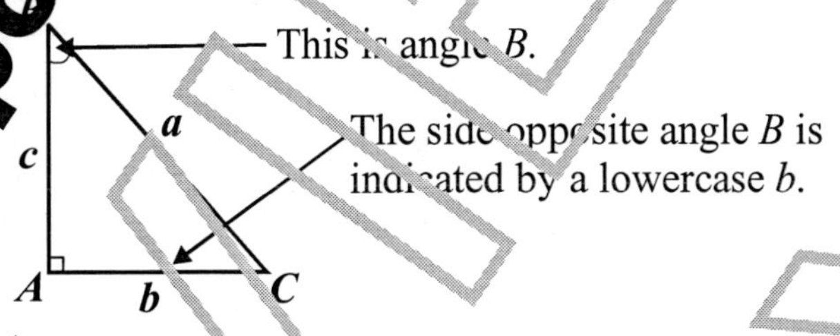

Trigonometric ratios are ratios of the measures of two sides of a right triangle and are related to the acute angles of a right triangle, not the right angle. Both of these angles have six trigonometric ratios associated with them: sine, cosine, tangent, cosecant, secant, and cotangent. The value of a trigonometric ratio is dependent on the size of the acute angle and the ratio of the lengths of the sides of the triangle.

Definitions and descriptions of the sine, cosine, and tangent functions are presented below.

Trigonometric Functions

$$\sin A = \frac{\text{length of side opposite } A}{\text{length of hypotenuse}} = \frac{\text{opp.}}{\text{hyp.}} = \frac{a}{c}$$

$$\cos A = \frac{\text{length of side adjacent to } A}{\text{length of hypotenuse}} = \frac{\text{adj.}}{\text{hyp.}} = \frac{b}{c}$$

$$\tan A = \frac{\text{length of side opposite } A}{\text{length of side adjacent to } A} = \frac{\text{opp.}}{\text{adj.}} = \frac{a}{b}$$

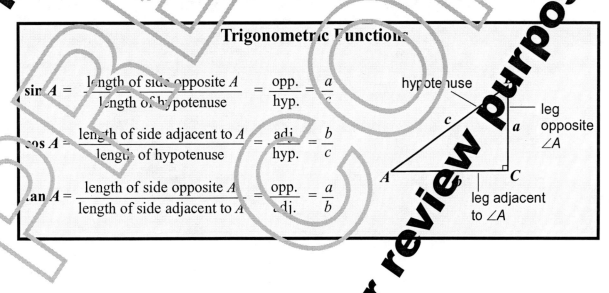

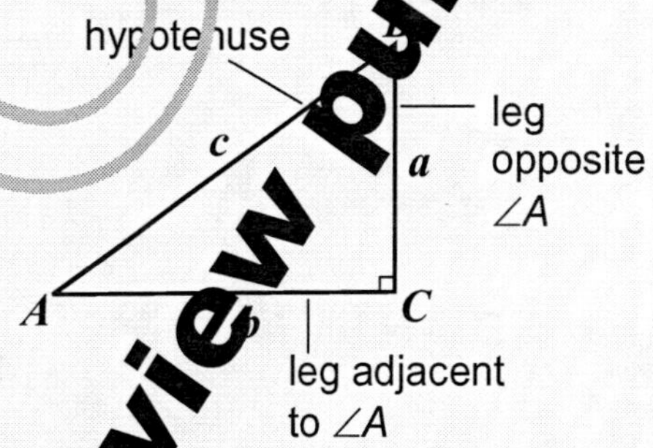

The three trigonometric ratios, sine, cosine, and tangent, can be written as follows for the angle θ:

$$\sin\theta = \frac{\text{opposite}}{\text{hypotenuse}} \qquad \cos\theta = \frac{\text{adjacent}}{\text{hypotenuse}} \qquad \tan\theta = \frac{\text{opposite}}{\text{adjacent}}$$

The cosecant, secant, and cotangent trigonometric ratios are the inverses of sine, cosine, and tangent, respectively. That is, for the angle θ:

$$\csc\theta = \frac{1}{\sin\theta} = \frac{\text{hypotenuse}}{\text{opposite}} \qquad \sec\theta = \frac{1}{\cos\theta} = \frac{\text{hypotenuse}}{\text{adjacent}} \qquad \cot\theta = \frac{1}{\tan\theta} = \frac{\text{adjacent}}{\text{opposite}}$$

Example 1: Suppose that $\triangle XYZ$ is a right triangle and that the lengths of two of its sides are as shown below. Find the six trigonometric ratios for $\angle Z$.

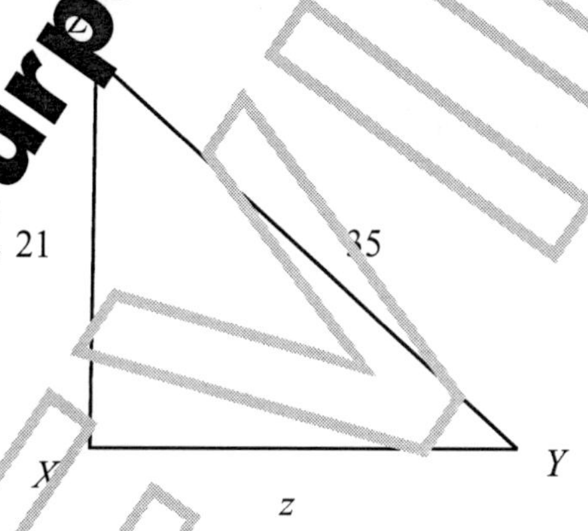

Step 1: First, the Pythagorean Theorem must be used to solve for z.

$21^2 + z^2 = 35^2$

$441 + z^2 = 1225$

$441 + z^2 - 441 = 1225 - 441$

$z^2 = 784$

$z = 28$

Step 2: Now, using the definitions given above, we can find the six trigonometric ratios for $\angle Z$.

$\sin Z = \frac{28}{35} = \frac{4}{5}$, $\cos Z = \frac{21}{35} = \frac{3}{5}$, and $\tan Z = \frac{28}{21} = \frac{4}{3}$

$\csc Z = \frac{35}{28} = \frac{5}{4}$, $\sec Z = \frac{35}{21} = \frac{5}{3}$, and $\cot Z = \frac{21}{28} = \frac{3}{4}$.

Similarly, these six trigonometric ratios could also have been found for $\angle Y$.

For each of the right triangles shown below, find the six trigonometric ratios for $\angle B$.

1.

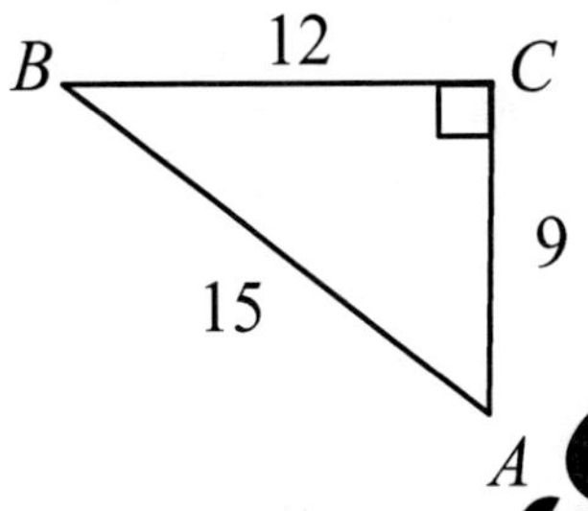

2.

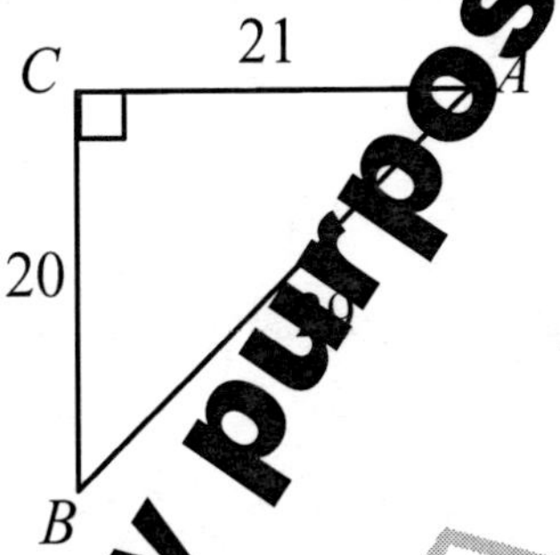

3.

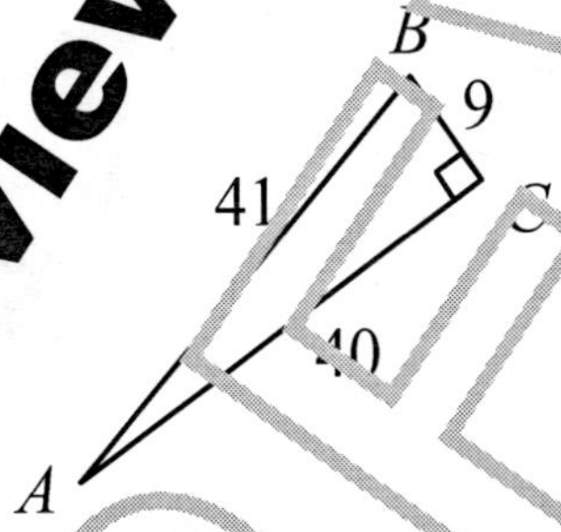

4.

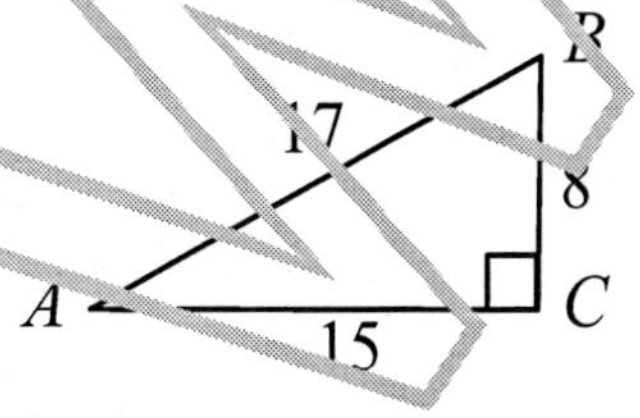

5.

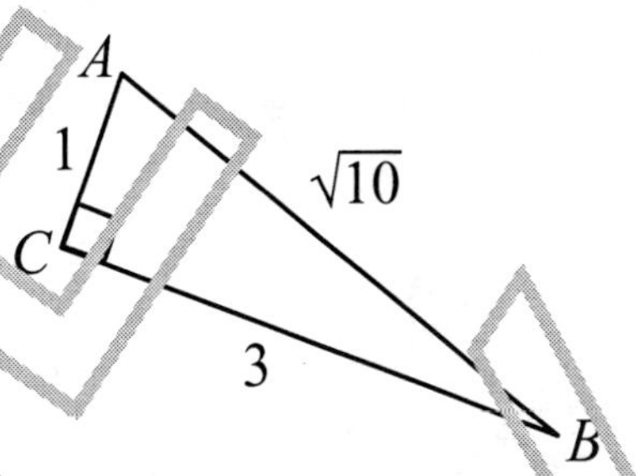

6.

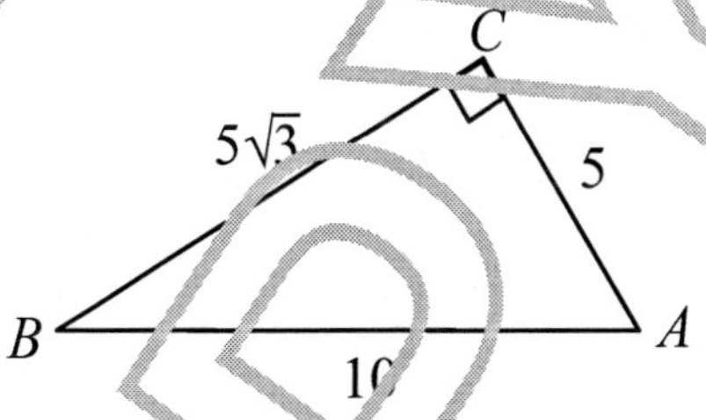

7. If the ratio of the lengths of the legs of a right triangle is $3 : 8$, what is the cosine of the angle formed by the longer leg and the hypotenuse?

8. If an acute angle in a right triangle has a cotangent of 3, what is the cosecant of the angle?

9. A right triangle has a hypotenuse that has a length quadruple that of one of its legs. What is the secant of the angle formed by the longer leg and the hypotenuse?

10. If the length of one of the legs of a right triangle is 65 percent the length of the other leg, what is the sine of the angle formed by the shorter leg and the hypotenuse?

Example 2: Suppose that $\triangle XYZ$ is a right triangle and that the lengths of two of its sides are as shown below. Find the measurement of $\angle Z$.

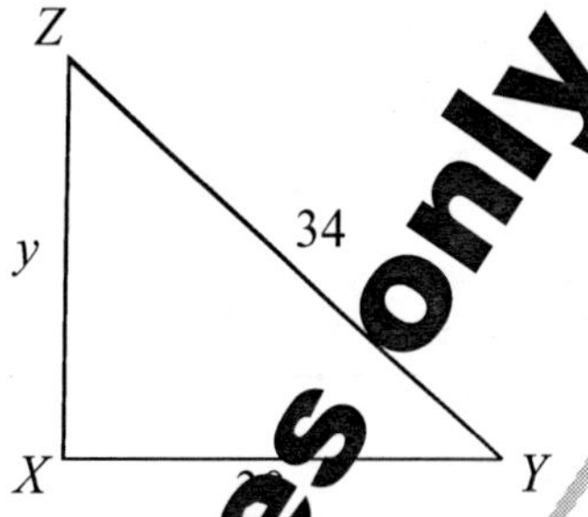

Since the length of the hypotenuse is 34 units and the length of the side opposite $\angle Z$ is 30 units,

$\sin Z = \frac{30}{34} = \frac{15}{17} \approx 0.8824$

Using the 2nd or INV button and the SIN button on a calculator, it can be determined that when the measurement of $\angle Z \approx \sin^{-1}(0.8824)$, $\angle Z \approx 62°$. Remember: When finding the measure of an angle in degrees, you must be in degree mode on the calculator.

Find the measurement of $\angle A$ to the nearest degree in questions 11–16. (Hint: $\angle C = 90°$)

11.
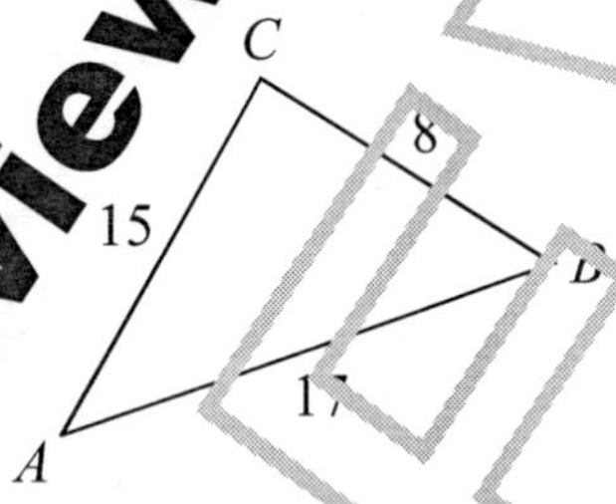

12.
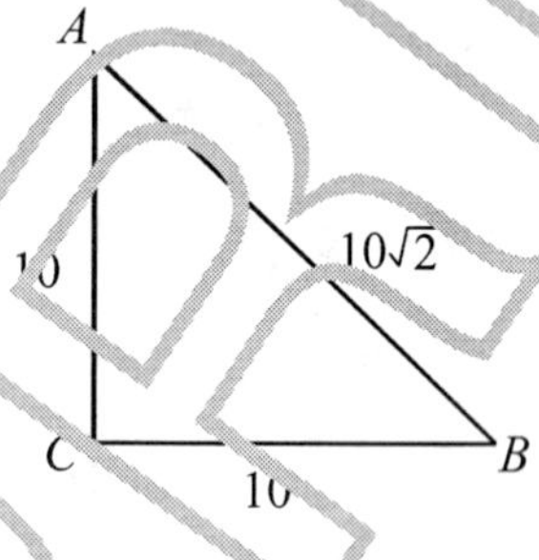

13.
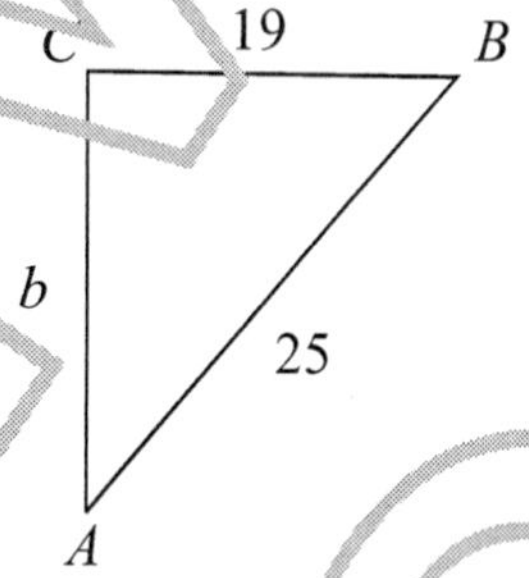

14.
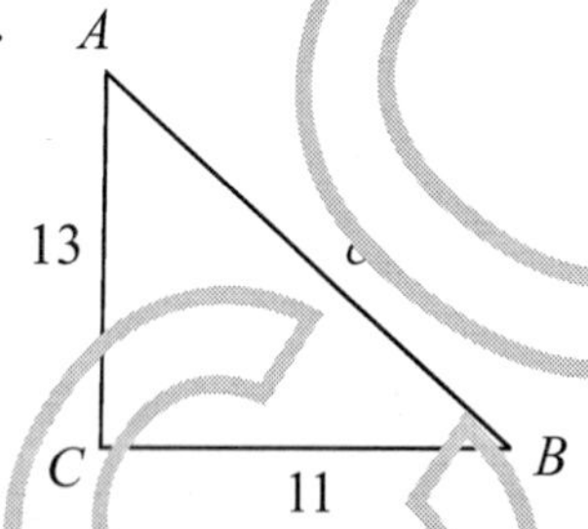

15.
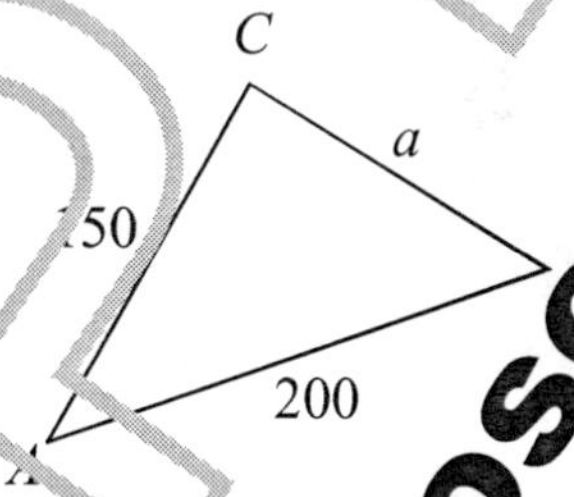

16.
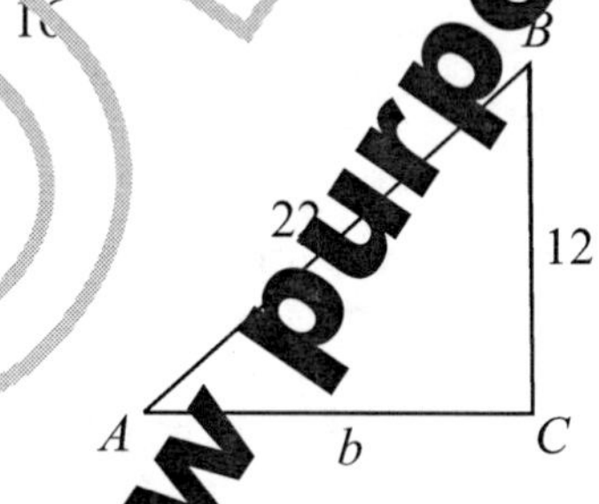

17. If the legs of a right triangle measure 5 units and 10 units, what is the measurement to the nearest degree of the angle formed by the leg measuring 10 units and the hypotenuse?

18. If the ratio of the length of a leg of a right triangle to the hypotenuse is 5 : 7, what is the measurement to the nearest degree of the angle formed by the leg and the hypotenuse?

19. The length of one leg of a right triangle is 6 times the length of the other leg. What is the measurement to the nearest degree of the angle formed by the shorter leg and the hypotenuse?

20. If the length of a leg of a right triangle is 40 percent of the length of the hypotenuse, what is the measurement to the nearest degree of the angle formed by the leg and the hypotenuse?

23.2 Radians

Given a circle on a coordinate plane, you can find **radians** using trigonometric functions.

Let an angle that has a vertex at the center of a circle, one leg on the x-axis, and the other leg that intercepts the circle. This angle measures 1 radian if the arc length formed by the angle equals the length of the radius. See the graph below. The graph shows an angle of 1 radian. ($\theta = 1$ radian)

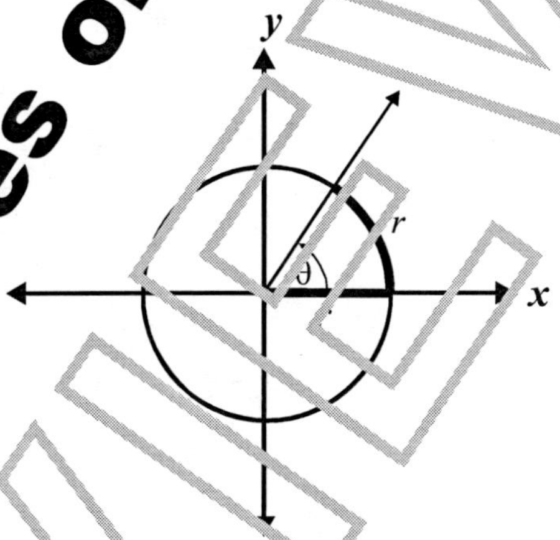

Additionally, an angle that measures 2 radians intercepts an arc of the circle equal in length to twice the radius of the circle, an angle that measures 3 radians intercepts an arc equal in length to three times the radius of the circle, and so on.

Using the circumference of a circle ($C = 2\pi r$), we can see that the radius of a circle goes around the circle 2π times. Also, we know that angle that forms a circle is $360°$. Therefore, $360° = 2\pi$ radians.

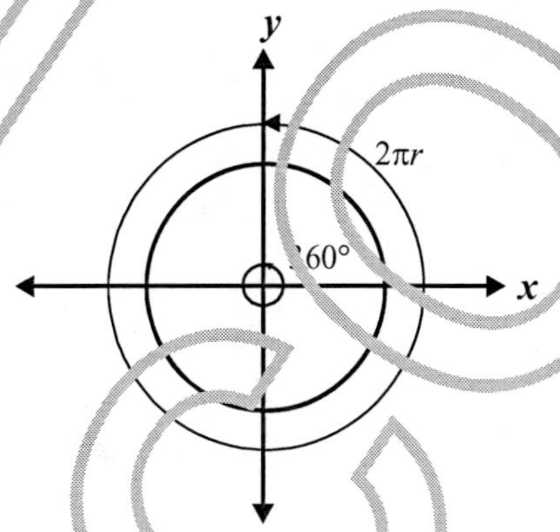

Since $360° = 2\pi$ radians, we can see that $180° = \pi$ radians by dividing both sides by 2. We can also use this fact to convert between radians and degrees.

To convert from degrees to radians: Multiply the degree by $\frac{\pi}{180}$ radians and simplify.

To convert from radians to degrees: Multiply the radian by $\frac{180}{\pi}$ degrees and simplify.

23.3 Values of Trigonometric Functions

The six trigonometric functions are functions of an angle and include $f(\theta) = \sin\theta$, $f(\theta) = \cos\theta$, $f(\theta) = \tan\theta$, $f(\theta) = \csc\theta$, $f(\theta) = \sec\theta$, and $f(\theta) = \cot\theta$. The angle θ can be expressed in either degrees or radians, where 360 degrees equal to 2π radians. The values of the six trigonometric functions for some angles are as follows:

θ **(degrees)**	θ **(radians)**	$\sin\theta$	$\cos\theta$	$\tan\theta$	$\csc\theta$	$\sec\theta$	$\cot\theta$
0	0	0	1	0	Undefined	1	Undefined
30	$\frac{\pi}{6}$	$\frac{1}{2}$	$\frac{\sqrt{3}}{2}$	$\frac{\sqrt{3}}{3}$	2	$\frac{(2\sqrt{3})}{3}$	$\sqrt{3}$
45	$\frac{\pi}{4}$	$\frac{\sqrt{2}}{2}$	$\frac{\sqrt{2}}{2}$	1	$\sqrt{2}$	$\sqrt{2}$	1
60	$\frac{\pi}{3}$	$\frac{\sqrt{3}}{2}$	$\frac{1}{2}$	$\sqrt{3}$	$\frac{(2\sqrt{3})}{3}$	2	$\frac{\sqrt{3}}{3}$
90	$\frac{\pi}{2}$	1	0	Undefined	1	Undefined	0
120	$\frac{2\pi}{3}$	$\frac{\sqrt{3}}{2}$	$-\frac{1}{2}$	$-\sqrt{3}$	$\frac{(2\sqrt{3})}{3}$	-2	$-\frac{\sqrt{3}}{3}$
135	$\frac{3\pi}{4}$	$\frac{\sqrt{2}}{2}$	$-\frac{\sqrt{2}}{2}$	-1	$\sqrt{2}$	$-\sqrt{2}$	-1
150	$\frac{5\pi}{6}$	$\frac{1}{2}$	$-\frac{\sqrt{3}}{2}$	$-\frac{\sqrt{3}}{3}$	2	$-\frac{(2\sqrt{3})}{3}$	$-\sqrt{3}$
180	π	0	-1	0	Undefined	-1	Undefined
210	$\frac{7\pi}{6}$	$-\frac{1}{2}$	$-\frac{\sqrt{3}}{2}$	$\frac{\sqrt{3}}{3}$	-2	$-\frac{(2\sqrt{3})}{3}$	$\sqrt{3}$
225	$\frac{5\pi}{4}$	$-\frac{\sqrt{2}}{2}$	$-\frac{\sqrt{2}}{2}$	1	$-\sqrt{2}$	$-\sqrt{2}$	1
240	$\frac{4\pi}{3}$	$-\frac{\sqrt{3}}{2}$	$-\frac{1}{2}$	$\sqrt{3}$	$-\frac{(2\sqrt{3})}{3}$	-2	$\frac{\sqrt{3}}{3}$
270	$\frac{3\pi}{2}$	-1	0	Undefined	-1	Undefined	0
300	$\frac{5\pi}{3}$	$-\frac{\sqrt{3}}{2}$	$\frac{1}{2}$	$-\sqrt{3}$	$-\frac{(2\sqrt{3})}{3}$	2	$-\frac{\sqrt{3}}{3}$
315	$\frac{7\pi}{4}$	$-\frac{\sqrt{2}}{2}$	$\frac{\sqrt{2}}{2}$	-1	$-\sqrt{2}$	$\sqrt{2}$	-1
330	$\frac{11\pi}{6}$	$-\frac{1}{2}$	$\frac{\sqrt{3}}{2}$	$-\frac{\sqrt{3}}{3}$	-2	$\frac{(2\sqrt{3})}{3}$	$-\sqrt{3}$
360	2π	0	1	0	Undefined	1	Undefined

Example 3: Evaluate the expression $\dfrac{\csc\theta}{\sec\theta}$ when $\theta = \dfrac{7\pi}{6}$ (radians).

Step 1: From the table above, $\csc\left(\dfrac{7\pi}{6}\right) = -2$.

Step 2: Likewise, $\sec\left(\dfrac{7\pi}{6}\right) = -\dfrac{2\sqrt{3}}{3}$.

Step 3: Therefore, $\dfrac{\csc\theta}{\sec\theta} = \dfrac{-2}{-\dfrac{2\sqrt{3}}{3}} = -2 \times -\dfrac{3}{2\sqrt{3}} = \dfrac{6}{2\sqrt{3}} = \dfrac{3}{\sqrt{3}} = \dfrac{3\sqrt{3}}{3} = \sqrt{3}$

Evaluate the expression $\csc\theta \times \cot\theta$ **for each of the following values of** θ.

1. $\theta = 45°$
2. $\theta = \frac{7\pi}{4}$ radians
3. $\theta = \frac{5\pi}{6}$ radians
4. $\theta = 300°$
5. $\theta = 240°$
6. $\theta = \frac{11\pi}{6}$ radians
7. Which of the six trigonometric functions are undefined at 180°?
8. For what values of θ does the function $f(\theta) = \cot\theta$ equal 0 if $0° \leq \theta \leq 360°$?
9. Which of the six trigonometric functions are never undefined?
10. For what values of θ does the function $f(\theta) = \sec\theta$ equal -2 if 0 radians $\leq \theta \leq 2\pi$ radians?

Example 4: A ray starting at the origin of a coordinate grid makes an angle of 120° with the positive half of the x-axis and intersects the unit circle as shown below. What are the coordinates of the point of intersection?

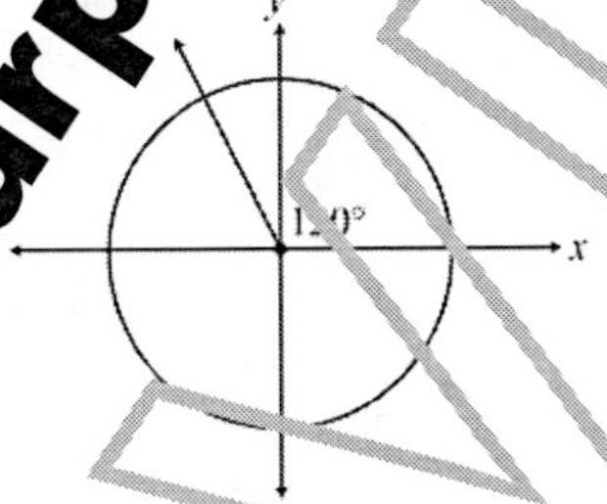

Step 1: When a ray starting at the origin of a coordinate grid makes the angle θ with the positive half of the x-axis, the coordinates of the point where it intersects a circle with radius r are $(r\cos\theta, r\sin\theta)$.

Step 2: Therefore, from the table above it can be determined that the coordinates of the point of intersection are $(1\cos 120°, 1\sin 120°)$, or $\left(-\frac{1}{2}, \frac{\sqrt{3}}{2}\right)$.

For each of the values of θ **listed in questions 11–16, a ray starting at the origin of a coordinate grid makes the angle** θ **with the positive half of the** x**-axis. Determine the coordinates of the point where each ray intersects the unit circle.**

11. $\theta = 45°$
12. $\theta = \frac{7\pi}{4}$ radians
13. $\theta = \frac{5\pi}{6}$ radians
14. $\theta = 300°$
15. $\theta = 240°$
16. $\theta = \frac{11\pi}{6}$ radians
17. A ray starting at the origin of a coordinate grid makes an angle of θ degrees with the positive half of the x-axis and intersects a circle with radius 3 at the point $\left(-\frac{3\sqrt{2}}{2}, -\frac{\sqrt{2}}{2}\right)$. What is the value of θ in radians?
18. A ray starting at the origin of a coordinate grid makes an angle of θ radians with the positive half of the x-axis and intersects a circle with radius 50 at the point $(0, -50)$. What is the value of θ in radians?

23.4 Properties of Graphs of Trigonometric Functions

Each of the six trigonometric functions has certain properties associated with it, just like other functions. Some of the most cited properties are domain, range, period, x-intercepts, y-intercept, minimums, and maximums.

The **domain** of the function $f(\theta)$ is all possible values of θ, while the **range** is all possible values of $f(\theta)$.

The **period** is the interval over which the function goes through one complete cycle, while its x-intercepts are the points where its graph crosses the x-axis, and its y-intercept is the point where its graph crosses the y-axis.

The function's **minimums** are its points that have y-coordinates of the least value, while its **maximums** are its points that have y-coordinates of the greatest value.

Finally, the graph of each of the six trigonometric functions is symmetric with respect to the origin or with respect to the y-axis.

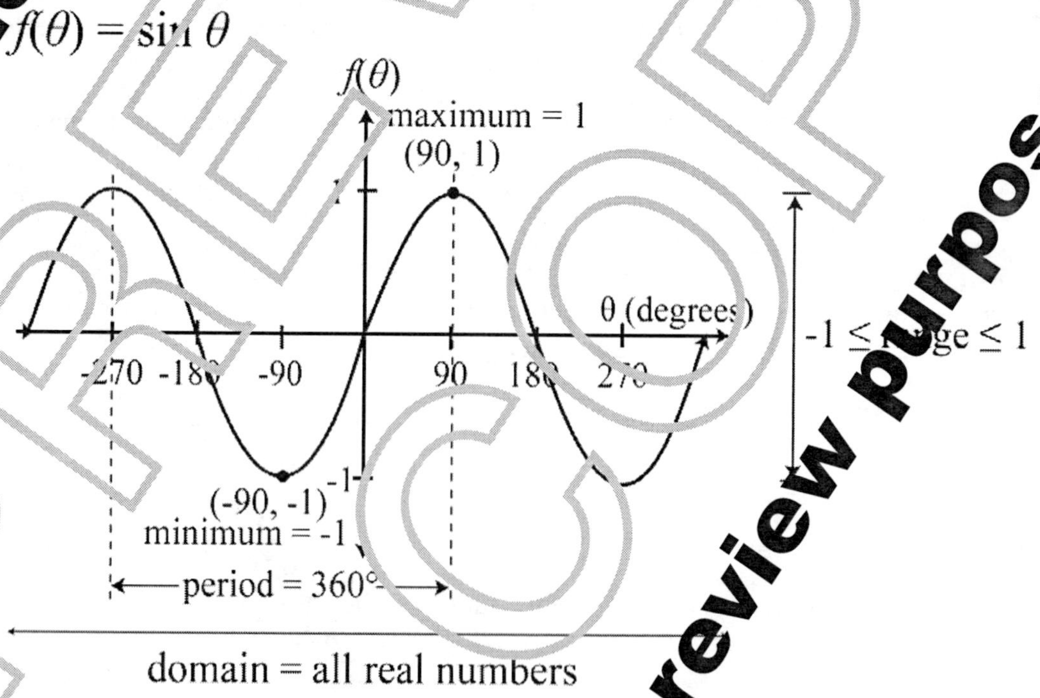

Determine the domain, range, minimum, and maximum for each of the following graphs.

1.

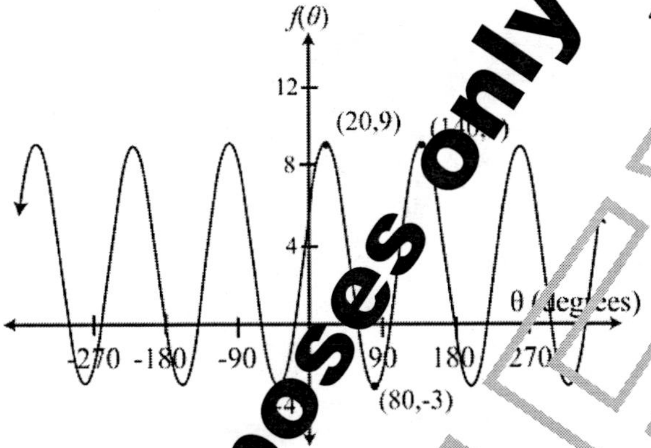

4.

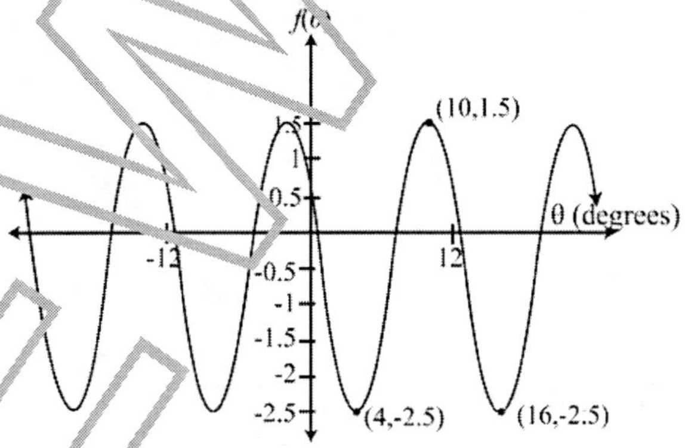

2.

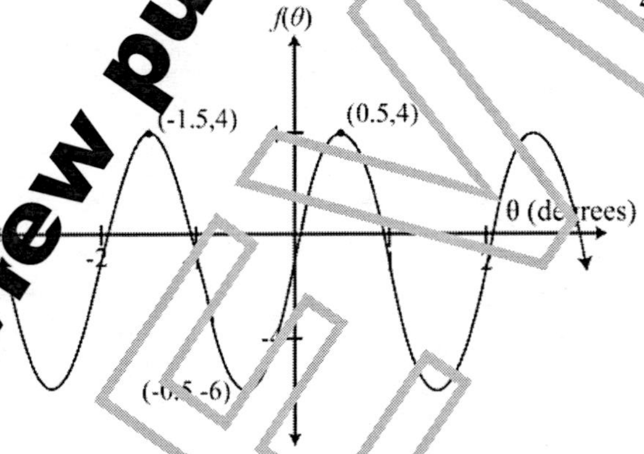

5.

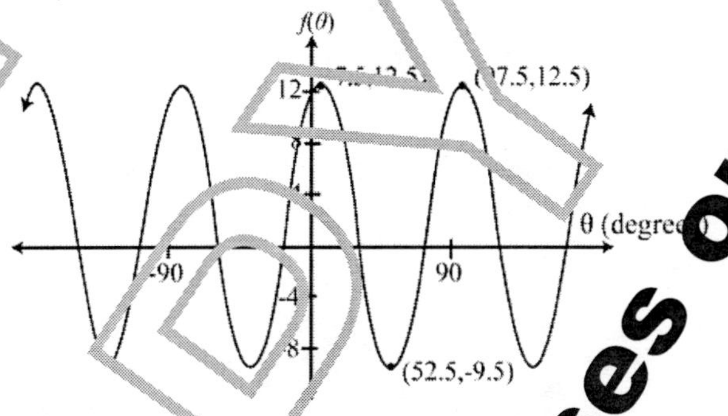

3.

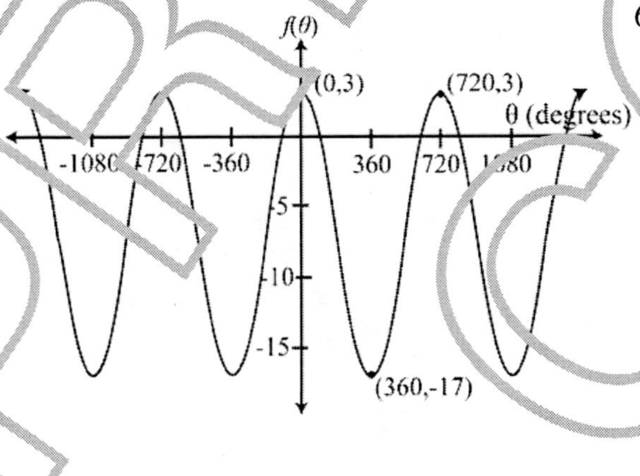

6.

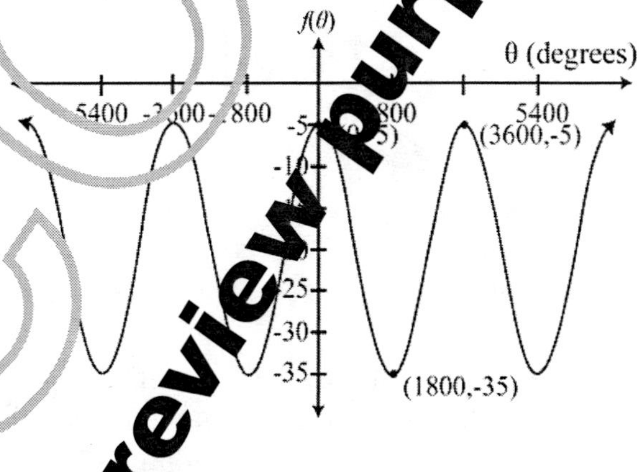

for review purposes only

The graphs of the six trigonometric functions are as follows:

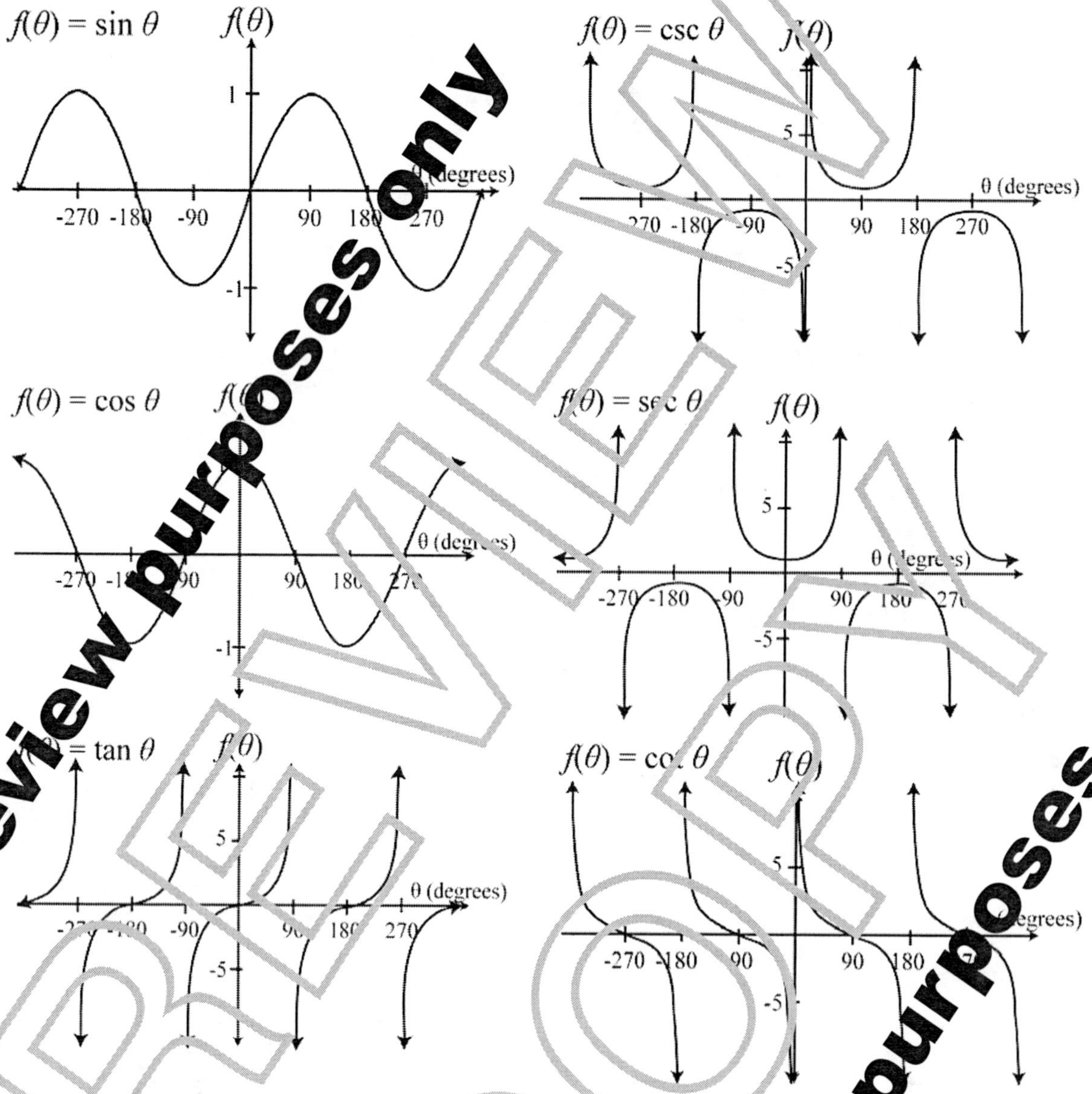

All six of the graphs are periodic, that is, they have a repeating pattern over a constant interval. In addition, the graphs of $f(\theta) = \sin\theta$ and $f(\theta) = \cos\theta$ are **sinusoidal**, that is, they are smooth, symmetrical waves. The graphs of the sinusoidal functions have both an **amplitude** and an **equation of the axis**.

The amplitude of the graph of a sinusoidal function is half the distance between the maximum and minimum values. Since the minimum is -1 and the maximum is 1 for the graphs of both $f(\theta) = \sin\theta$ and $f(\theta) = \cos\theta$, the amplitude for both is $\frac{1-(-1)}{2}$ or 1.

Also, the equation of the axis of a sinusoidal function is the equation of the horizontal line that is halfway between the maximum and the minimum values. The equation of the axis for both is $f(\theta) = \frac{1+(-1)}{2}$ or $f(\theta) = 0$.

The non-sinusoidal functions (i.e. $f(\theta) = \tan\theta, f(\theta) = \csc\theta, f(\theta) = \sec\theta$, and $f(\theta) = \cot\theta$) do not have amplitudes or equations of the axis, but they do have asymptotes. An **asymptote** is a line that a graph gets closer and closer to, but never touches. The asymptotes of the graphs of the non-sinusoidal functions occur where the functions are undefined. Therefore, the asymptotes of $f(\theta) = \tan\theta$ and $f(\theta) = \sec\theta$ occur at $\theta = \frac{\pi}{2} + k\pi$ radians or $\theta = 90 + 180k$ degrees, while the asymptotes of $f(\theta) = \csc\theta$ and $f(\theta) = \cot\theta$ occur at $\theta = k\pi$ radians or $\theta = 180k$ degrees.

Example 5: The graph of the trigonometric function $f(\theta) = \sin\theta$ has been vertically stretched, vertically translated up, horizontally compressed, and horizontally translated to the right as shown below. What is the amplitude, equation of the axis, and period of the graph?

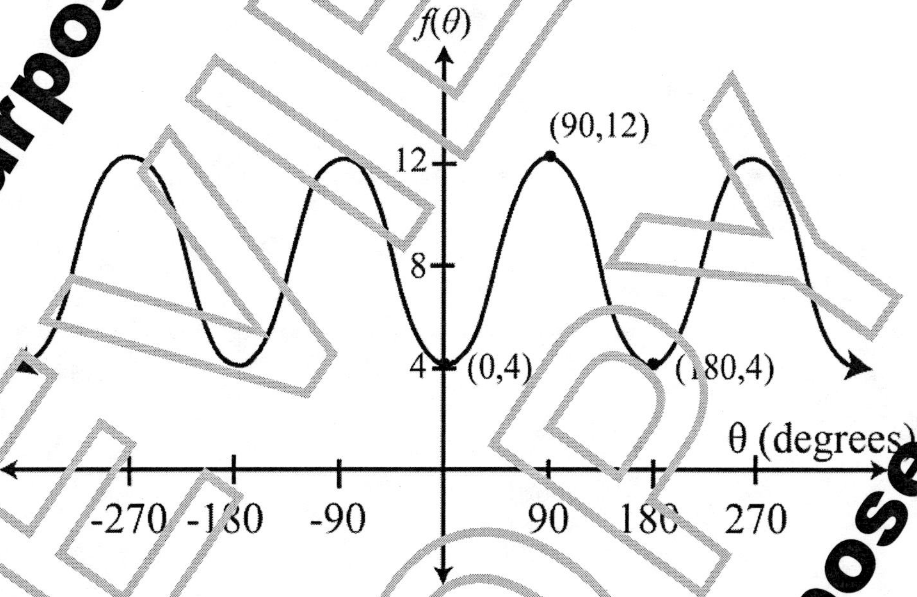

Step 1: The amplitude is half the distance between the maximum and minimum values. Since the minimum is 4 and the maximum is 12, the amplitude is $\frac{12-4}{2}$ or 4.

Step 2: The equation of the axis is the equation of the horizontal line that is halfway between the maximum and the minimum values. Again, since the minimum is 4 and the maximum is 12, the equation of the axis is $f(\theta) = \frac{12+4}{2}$ or $f(\theta) = 8$.

Step 3: Using the previous section, we know the period is the interval over which one complete cycle occurs. Since one complete cycle occurs from $\theta = 0°$ to $\theta = 180°$, the period is $180° - 0°$ or $180°$. (Remember: $180° = \pi$ radians)

Determine the amplitude, equations of the axis, and period for each of the following graphs.

1.

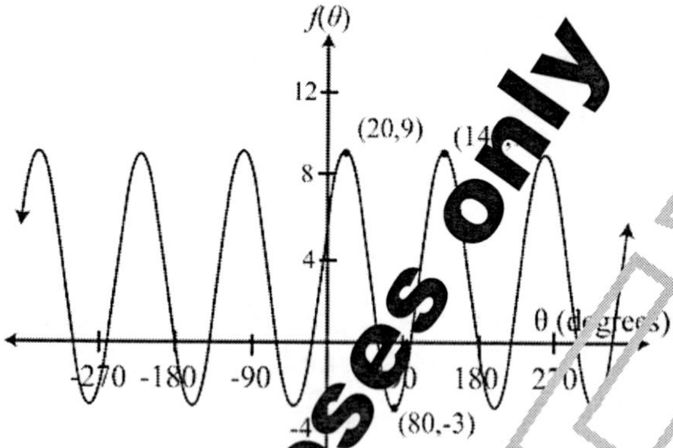

4.

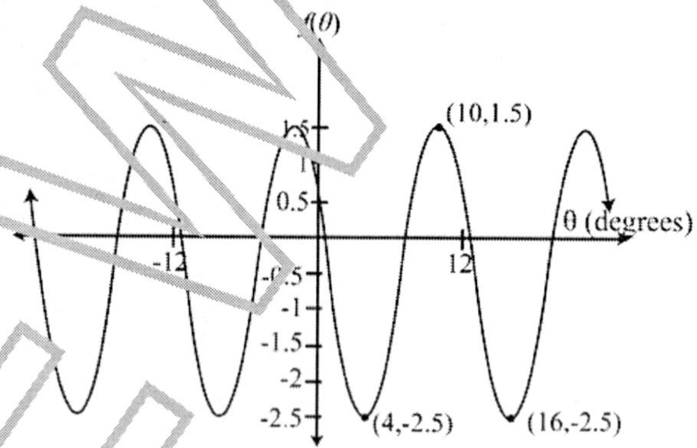

2.

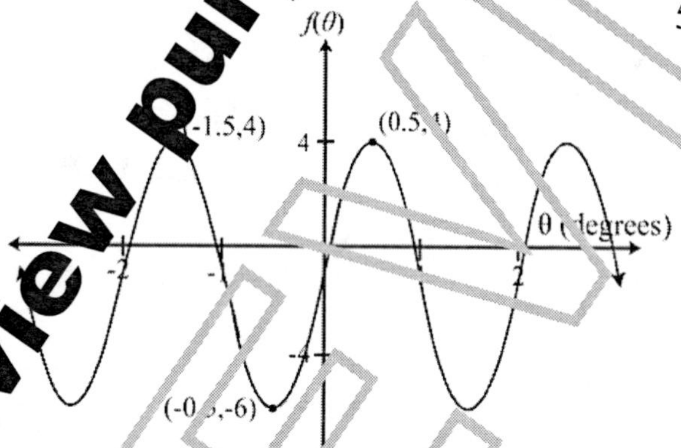

5.

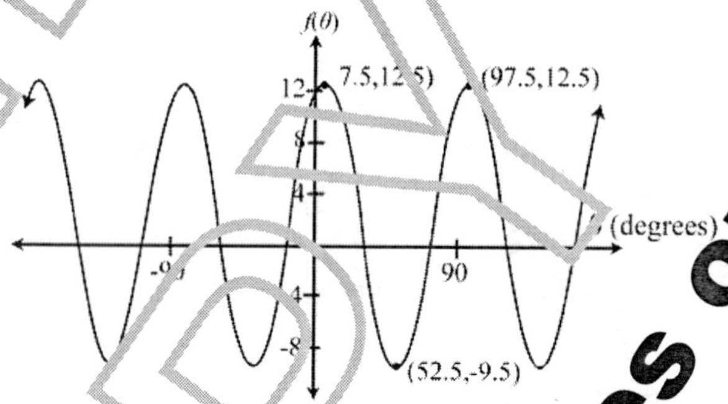

3.

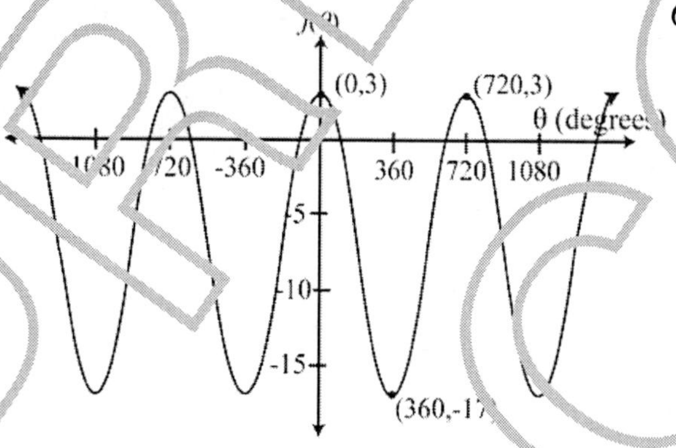

6.

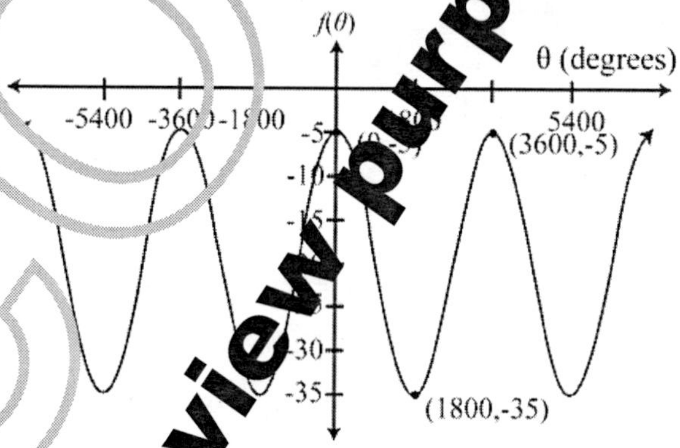

7. The graph of a sinusoidal function has been horizontally stretched and horizontally translated to the right. It has maximums at the points $(175, 1)$ and $(565, 1)$, and it has a minimum at $(370, -1)$. If the x-axis is in degrees, what is the period of the function?

23.5 Applications of Trigonometric Functions

The transformed graphs of sinusoidal functions (i.e. $f(\theta) = \sin\theta$ and $f(\theta) = \cos\theta$) are often used to model real-life situations in which an object is traveling in a circle.

Example 6: A clock is hanging on the wall, with the distance of the tip of the hour hand above the ground during one complete day. This is modelled by the graph below. What is the amplitude, equation of the axis, and period of the graph, and what does each represent in this situation? Also, at what speed is the tip of the hour hand traveling?

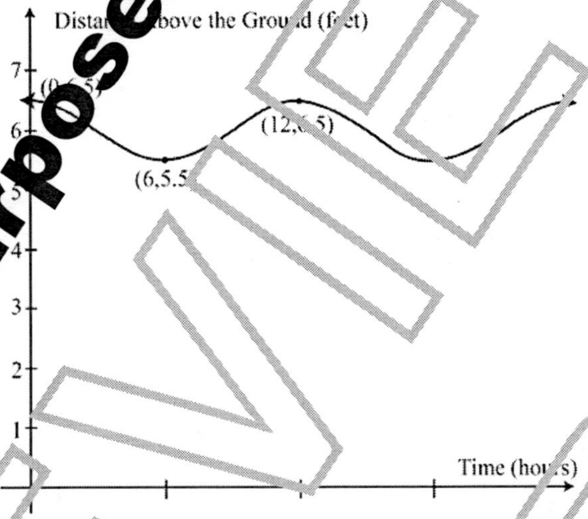

Step 1: The amplitude is half the distance between the maximum and minimum values. Since the minimum is 5.5 feet and the maximum is 6.5 feet, the amplitude is $\frac{6.5-5.5}{2}$ or 0.5 feet. In this situation, the amplitude represents the length of the hour hand.

Step 2: The equation of the axis is the equation of the horizontal line that is halfway between the maximum and the minimum values. Again, since the minimum is 5.5 feet and the maximum is 6.5 feet, the equation of the axis is $f(\theta) = \frac{6.5+5.5}{2}$ or $f(\theta) = 6$ feet. In this situation, the equation of the axis represents the distance of the center of the clock above the ground.

Step 3: The period is the interval over which one complete cycle occurs. Since one complete cycle occurs from $\theta = 0$ hours to $\theta = 12$ hours, the period is 12 hours. In this situation, the period represents the amount of time it takes for the hour hand to make one complete revolution.

Step 4: Finally, to calculate the speed at which the tip of the hour hand is travelling, it's first necessary to calculate the distance it travels during one revolution, or the circumference of the circle it traverses, which is $2\pi \times 0.5$ feet, or π feet. Since it completes one revolution in 12 hours, the speed at which it is travelling is π feet per 12 hours, or $\frac{\pi}{12}$ feet per hour.

A carnival has two Ferris wheels, with the distance of one of the seats on each Ferris wheel above the ground modelled by the graph below. Answer the following questions about the Ferris wheel.

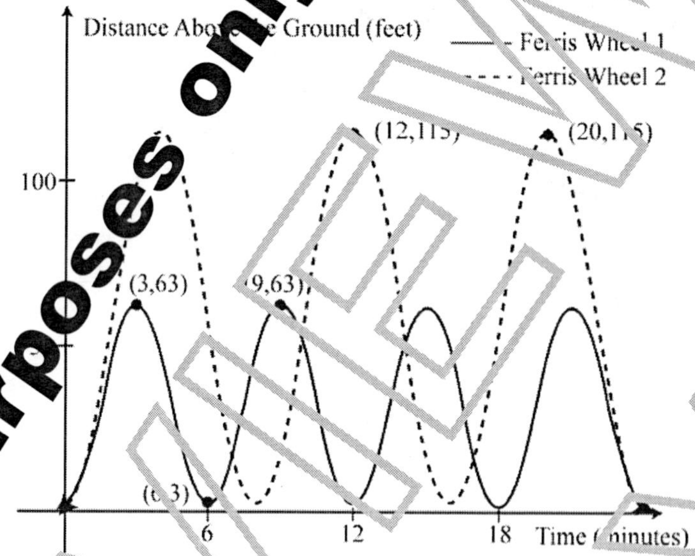

1. What is the radius of Ferris wheel 1?

2. What is the height of the axle above the ground in Ferris wheel 1?

3. How long does it take Ferris wheel 1 to make one complete revolution?

4. What is the speed at which the seat on Ferris wheel 1 is traveling?

5. What is the radius of Ferris wheel 2?

6. What is the height of the axle above the ground in Ferris wheel 2?

7. How long does it take Ferris wheel 2 to make one complete revolution?

8. What is the speed at which the seat on Ferris wheel 2 is traveling?

Two flies are on the blade of a rotating windmill. One fly on the tip of the blade, while the other fly is farther down on the blade. The graph below shows the distance above the ground of each of the flies as the windmill is rotating.

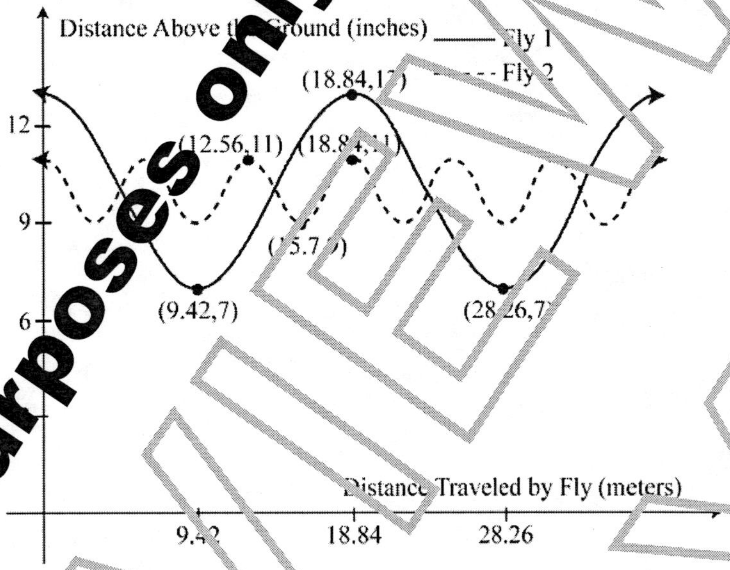

1. What can be determined from the graph about the length of the blade?

2. At what speed is the windmill rotating?

3. What is the height of the windmill?

4. What is the distance of the flies from each other?

Use the following to answer questions 5–8.

Darrell had a leak in the tire of his unicycle, and he had to get it plugged. The height above the ground of the plug as a function of the distance traveled by the plug was graphed. The tire has a radius of 29 inches, and the plug was at the top of the wheel when the graph began.

5. What is the amplitude of the graph?

6. What is the equation of the axis of the graph?

7. What is the period of the graph?

8. Which sinusoidal function could most easily be used to model this situation? Explain your answer.

23.6 Trigonometric Identities

The **trigonometric identities** can be broken down into the following categories: reciprocal identities, tangent and cotangent identities, Pythagorean identities, angle-sum identities, angle-difference identities, double-angle identities, and half-angle identities. Each of the identities is listed below.

Reciprocal Identities

$\csc\theta = \dfrac{1}{\sin\theta}$ $\sec\theta = \dfrac{1}{\cos\theta}$ $\cot\theta = \dfrac{1}{\tan\theta}$

Tangent and Cotangent Identities

$\tan\theta = \dfrac{\sin\theta}{\cos\theta}$ $\cot\theta = \dfrac{\cos\theta}{\sin\theta}$

Pythagorean Identities

$\cos^2\theta + \sin^2\theta = 1$ $1 + \tan^2\theta = \sec^2\theta$ $1 + \cot^2\theta = \csc^2\theta$

Angle-Sum Identities

$\sin(A+B) = \sin A\cos B + \cos A\sin B$
$\cos(A+B) = \cos A\cos B - \sin A\sin B$
$\tan(A+B) = \dfrac{\tan A + \tan B}{1 - \tan A\tan B}$

Angle-Difference Identities

$\sin(A-B) = \sin A\cos B - \cos A\sin B$
$\cos(A-B) = \cos A\cos B + \sin A\sin B$
$\tan(A-B) = \dfrac{\tan A - \tan B}{1 + \tan A\tan B}$

Double-Angle Identities

$\cos 2\theta = \cos^2\theta - \sin^2\theta$
$\cos 2\theta = 2\cos^2\theta - 1$
$\cos 2\theta = 1 - 2\sin^2\theta$
$\sin 2\theta = 2\sin\theta\cos\theta$
$\tan 2\theta = \dfrac{2\tan\theta}{1-\tan^2\theta}$

Half-Angle Identities

$\sin\dfrac{\theta}{2} = \pm\sqrt{\dfrac{1-\cos\theta}{2}}$ $\cos\dfrac{\theta}{2} = \pm\sqrt{\dfrac{1-\cos\theta}{2}}$ $\tan\dfrac{\theta}{2} = \pm\sqrt{\dfrac{1-\cos\theta}{1+\cos\theta}}$

Example 7: Simplify the expression $\dfrac{9\cos^2\theta + 9\sin^2\theta}{1+\tan^2\theta}$.

Step 1: If 9 is factored from the numerator, the expression becomes $\dfrac{9(\cos^2\theta + \sin^2\theta)}{1+\tan^2\theta}$.

Step 2: Then, using the Pythagorean identities $\cos^2\theta + \sin^2\theta = 1$ and $1+\tan^2\theta = \sec^2\theta$, the expression becomes $\dfrac{9(1)}{\sec^2\theta}$ or $\dfrac{9}{\sec^2\theta}$.

Step 3: The expression can subsequently be factored further to become $9 \times \dfrac{1}{\sec^2\theta}$.

Step 4: At this point, the reciprocal identity $\sec\theta = \dfrac{1}{\cos\theta}$ can be rewritten as $\cos\theta = \dfrac{1}{\sec\theta}$ and used to simplify the expression to $9 \times \cos^2\theta$ or $9\cos^2\theta$.

Simplify each of the following expressions.

1. $\dfrac{50}{1+\cot^2\theta}$
2. $\dfrac{\tan\theta}{7+7\tan^2\theta}$
3. $\dfrac{\sin^2\theta + \cos^2\theta + \tan^2\theta}{\sec^2\theta}$
4. $\dfrac{\cot\theta}{\sin\theta} + \sec\theta$
5. $\dfrac{10}{\cot\theta} + 10\cot\theta$
6. $\dfrac{\csc^2\theta + \sec^2\theta - 2}{\tan^2\theta + \cot^2\theta}$
7. $\dfrac{\sin\theta}{26\cos\theta} + \dfrac{\cos\theta}{26\sin\theta}$
8. $\dfrac{2-\sin^2\theta + \tan^2\theta}{\cos^3\theta + \sec^2\theta\cos\theta}$
9. $\dfrac{\cot\theta\sec\theta\sin\theta - 3}{\sec^2\theta - \tan^2 + 5}$

Example 8: Jessica needs to find the sine of 510°. She doesn't know what it is, but she does know the sine and cosine of 240°, as well as the sine and cosine of 270°. How can she find the sine of 510° with the information that she knows?

Step 1: Jessica can find the sine of 510° by using the angle-sum identity $\sin(A+B) = \sin A\cos B + \cos A\sin B$.

Step 2: The sine of 240° is $-\frac{\sqrt{3}}{2}$, while the cosine of 240 is $-\frac{1}{2}$.
Also, the sine of 270° is -1, while the cosine of 270° is 0.

Step 3: $\sin 510° = \sin(240° + 270°) = \left(-\frac{\sqrt{3}}{2} \times 0\right) + \left(-\frac{1}{2} \times -1\right) = 0 + \frac{1}{2} = \frac{1}{2}$

Calculate each of the following values using an appropriate trigonometric identity and the table on page 324.

10. $\cos 15°$
11. $\tan 22.5°$
12. $\sin 105°$
13. $\cos 285°$
14. $\tan 465°$
15. $\sin 255°$
16. $\cos 420°$
17. $\tan 345°$
18. $\sin(-165°)$

23.7 Solving Trigonometric Equations

Trigonometric equations can usually be solved by collecting like terms, finding square roots, factoring, substitution, or a combination of these methods. These types of equations are usually valid for certain ranges of angle values, so after solving a trigonometric equation, it's often necessary to go back and check the range of angle values the equation is valid for to see if there are any additional answers to the equation.

Example 9: Solve the trigonometric equation $3\sin^2\theta - 6 + 9\sin^2\theta + 4 + 6\sin^2\theta = 4\sin^2\theta + 5$ for 0 radians $\leq \theta < 2\pi$ radians.

Step 1: First, it's necessary to collect like terms and isolate $\sin^2\theta$ on one side of the equation.

$3\sin^2\theta - 6 + 9\sin^2\theta + 4 + 6\sin^2\theta = 4\sin^2\theta + 5$

$18\sin^2\theta - 2 = 4\sin^2\theta + 5$

$14\sin^2\theta = 7$

$\sin^2\theta = \dfrac{7}{14}$

$\sin^2\theta = \dfrac{1}{2}$

Step 2: Next, the square root of both sides of the equation should be taken.

$\sqrt{\sin^2\theta} = \sqrt{\dfrac{1}{2}}$

$\sin\theta = \pm\dfrac{1}{\sqrt{2}}$

$\sin\theta = \pm\dfrac{\sqrt{2}}{2}$

Step 3: Finally, the inverse sine function should be applied to both sides of the equation.

$\sin^{-1}(\sin\theta) = \sin^{-1}\left(\pm\dfrac{\sqrt{2}}{2}\right)$

$\theta = \sin^{-1}\left(\pm\dfrac{\sqrt{2}}{2}\right)$

Step 4: From the table on page 324, when 0 radians $\leq \theta < 2\pi$ radians, $\theta = \sin^{-1}\left(\dfrac{\sqrt{2}}{2}\right)$ at $\dfrac{\pi}{4}, \dfrac{3\pi}{4}, \dfrac{5\pi}{4}$, and $\dfrac{7\pi}{4}$ radians. Therefore, the solution to the trigonometric equation is $\theta = \dfrac{\pi}{4}, \dfrac{3\pi}{4}, \dfrac{5\pi}{4}$, or $\dfrac{7\pi}{4}$ radians.

Solve each of the following trigonometric equations for 0 radians $\leq \theta < 2\pi$ radians. Refer to the table on page 324 as needed.

1. $14 + 17\cos\theta - 13 = 18\cos\theta$
2. $50 + 12\tan\theta + 3 = 10\tan\theta + 54 + 3\tan\theta$
3. $17 + 8\tan^2\theta + 7 = 9\tan^2\theta + 21$
4. $7 + 3\sin^2\theta - 10 = -\sin^2\theta$
5. $15\tan^2\theta + 6 - 13\tan^2\theta = 7 - \tan^2\theta$
6. $3\cos^2\theta + 7 - 14\cos^2\theta = 9 - 15\cos^2\theta - 1$
7. $14\sin\theta + 150 + 7\sin\theta = 75 + 22\sin\theta + 76$
8. $61 - 33\csc^2\theta = -23\csc^2\theta + 59 - 9\csc^2\theta$

Example 10: Solve the trigonometric equation $\sec^2\theta - \sec\theta\sin\theta = 2\sin\theta$ for 0 radians $\leq \theta < 2\pi$ radians.

Step 1: First, it is necessary to move all the terms to one side of the equation and factor $\sin\theta$ from each of the terms on the left side of the equation.
$\sec^2\theta\sin\theta - \sec\theta\sin\theta = 2\sin\theta$
$\sec^2\theta\sin\theta - \sec\theta\sin\theta - 2\sin\theta = 0$
$\sin\theta(\sec^2\theta - \sec\theta - 2) = 0$

Step 2: Next, let $\sec\theta = x$ and factor the left side of the resulting equation. Then set each of the terms on the left side of the equation equal to 0, solve for x, and substitute $\sec\theta$ for x.
$\sin\theta(x^2 - x - 2) = 0$
$\sin\theta(x - 2)(x + 1) = 0$
$\sin\theta = 0$ or $x - 2 = 0$ or $x + 1 = 0$
$\sin\theta = 0$ or $x = 2$ or $x = -1$
$\sin\theta = 0$ or $\sec\theta = 2$ or $\sec\theta = -1$

Step 3: Finally, the inverse sine or inverse secant function should be applied to the appropriate equation.

$\sin^{-1}(\sin\theta) = \sin^{-1}(0)$ $\sec^{-1}(\sec\theta) = \sec^{-1}(2)$ $\sec^{-1}(\sec\theta) = \sec^{-1}(-1)$
$\theta = \sin^{-1}(0)$ $\theta = \sec^{-1}(2)$ $\theta = \sec^{-1}(-1)$

Step 4: From the table on page 324, when 0 radians $\leq \theta < 2\pi$ radians, $\theta = \sin^{-1}(0)$ at 0 and π radians, $\theta = \sec^{-1}(2)$ at $\frac{\pi}{3}$ and $\frac{5\pi}{3}$ radians, and $\theta = \sec^{-1}(-1)$ at π radians. Therefore, the solution to the trigonometric equation is $\theta = 0, \frac{\pi}{3}, \pi$, or $\frac{5\pi}{3}$ radians.

Solve each of the following trigonometric equations for 0 radians $\leq \theta < 2\pi$ radians. Refer to the table on page 324 as needed.

9. $12\sec^2\theta\sin\theta = 16\sin\theta$
10. $2\cos^2\theta + \cos\theta = 1$
11. $7\csc^2\theta + 7\csc\theta = 14$
12. $\tan^2\theta\sin\theta + \sin\theta = 2\tan\theta\sin\theta$
13. $16\cot^2\theta + 32\sqrt{3}\cot\theta = -48$
14. $\cos^3\theta + \cos\theta = 2\cos^2\theta$
15. $-\sqrt{2}\sec^2\theta - 4\sec\theta = 2\sqrt{2}$
16. $15\cot^2\theta\cos\theta = 5\cos\theta$

Chapter 23 Review

For both of the right triangles shown in questions 1 and 2, find the six trigonometric ratios for $\angle A$. (Hint: $\angle C = 90°$)

1.

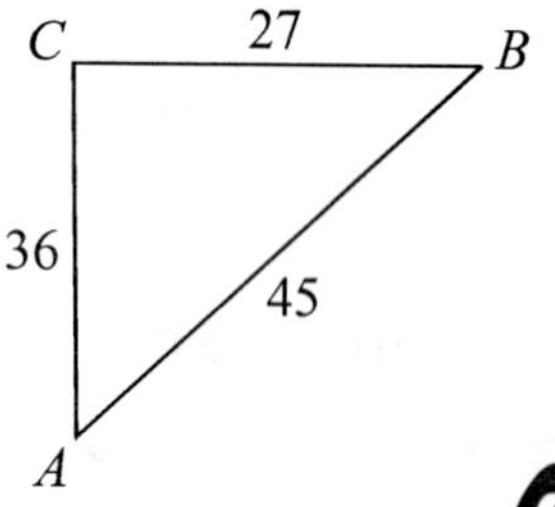

2.

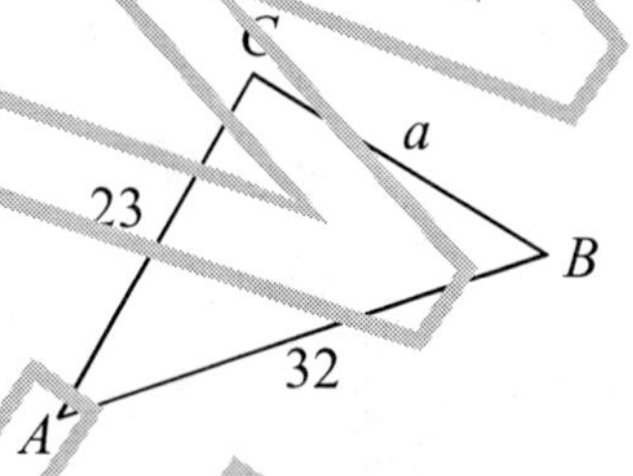

3. If the ratio of the lengths of the legs of a right triangle is 7 : 13, what is the sine of the angle formed by the shorter leg and the hypotenuse?

4. A right triangle has a hypotenuse that has a length triple that of one of its legs. What is the cotangent of the angle formed by the shorter leg and the hypotenuse?

5. The length of one leg of a right triangle is 9 times the length of the other leg. What is the measurement to the nearest degree of the angle formed by the longer leg and the hypotenuse?

6. If the length of a leg of a right triangle it 55 percent of the length of the hypotenuse, what is the measurement to the nearest degree of the angle formed by the leg and the hypotenuse?

Evaluate the expression $\sec\theta \times \tan\theta$ **for each of the following values of θ in questions 7–9.**

7. $\theta = 135°$

8. $\theta = 120°$

9. $\theta = 225°$

10. Which of the six trigonometric functions are undefined at 270°?

11. A ray starting at the origin of a coordinate grid makes an angle of θ with the positive half of the x-axis and intersects the unit circle at the point $\left(\frac{\sqrt{3}}{2}, \frac{1}{2}\right)$. What is the value of θ?

12. A ray starting at the origin of a coordinate grid makes an angle of θ radians with the positive half of the x-axis and intersects a circle with radius 18 at the point $(9\sqrt{2}, -9\sqrt{2})$. What is the value of θ?

Determine the amplitude, equation of the axis, and period for both of the following graphs.

13.

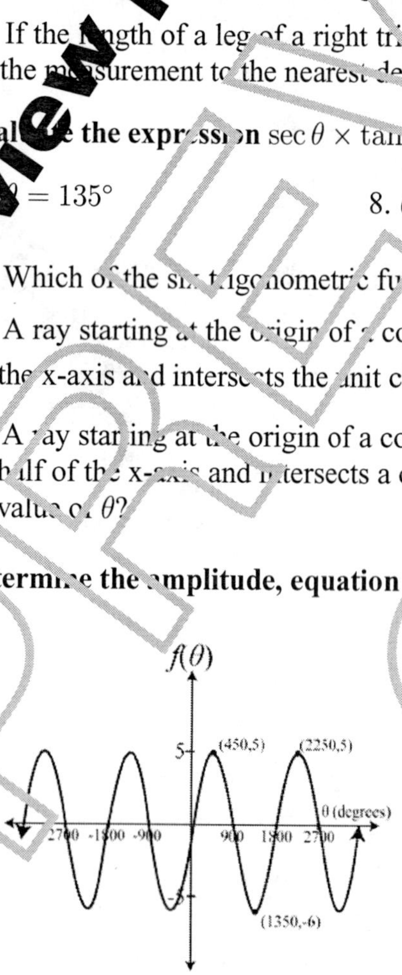

14.

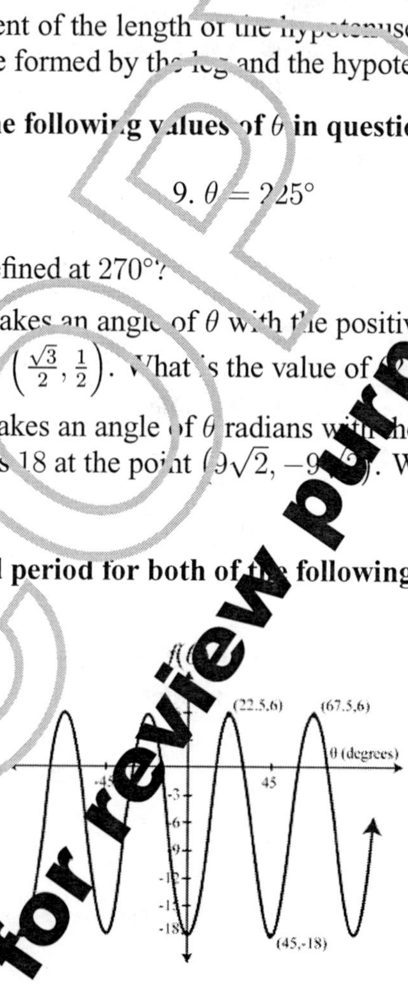

Use the following to answer questions 15–18.

Of two nails that were used in constructing a water wheel, one is on the circumference of the wheel. while the other is on one of the spokes. The graph below shows the height relative to the water level of the two nails as the wheel is rotating.

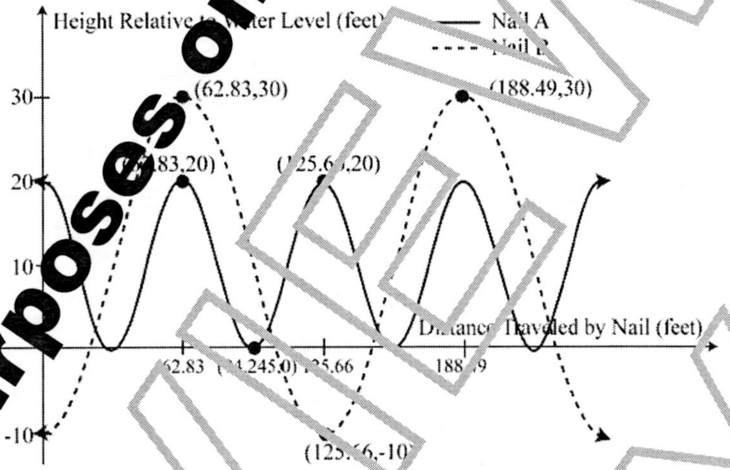

15. What can be determined from the graph about the size of the wheel?

16. At what speed is the wheel is rotating?

17. What is the height relative to the water level of the axel of the wheel?

18. What is the distance of the nails from each other?

Simplify each of the following expressions.

19. $\dfrac{\cos^2\theta + \sin^2\theta + 5}{\csc^2\theta - \cot^2\theta + 1}$

20. $\dfrac{2 + \tan^2\theta + \cot^2\theta}{2\sec^2\theta + 2\csc^2\theta}$

21. $\dfrac{\sin\theta}{\csc\theta - \cos^2\theta\csc\theta}$

Calculate each of the following values using an appropriate trigonometric identity. Refer to the table on page 324 as needed.

22. $\cos -105^\circ$

23. $\tan 645^\circ$

24. $\sin 195^\circ$

Solve each of the following trigonometric equations for 0 radians $\leq \theta < 2\pi$ radians.

25. $11\cos^2\theta + 8 - 9\cos^2\theta = \cos^2\theta + 9$

26. $44 - 75\cot^2\theta + 8 = 51 - \cot^2\theta + 1$

27. $4 + 3\sec^2\theta + 3 = 9\sec\theta + 1$

28. $1 + 9\sin^2\theta + 2 = 12\sin\theta - 1$

Chapter 23 Test

1. Solve for x. Round your answer to the nearest degree.

   $\tan x = 0.5$

   A. 27°

   B. 30°

   C. 60°

   D. 63°

   E. 0°

2. Harrison steps outside his house to see the hot air balloon pass by. He raises his eyes at a 35° angle to view the balloon. If the balloon is 5,000 feet above the ground, about how far is it from Harrison?

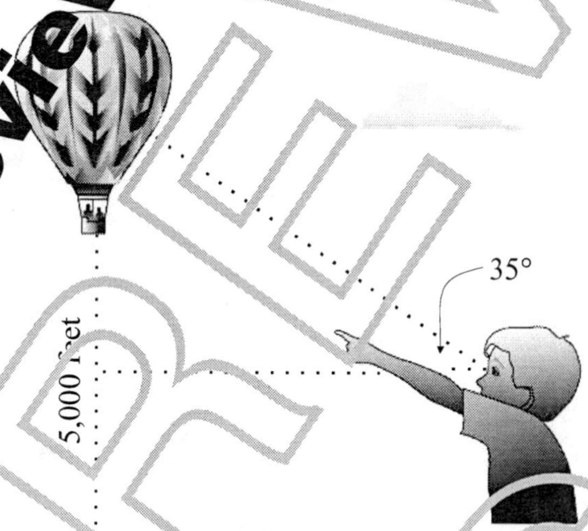

HINT: Harrison's eye level is 5.2 feet from the ground. $\sin(35°) \approx 0.57$ and $\cos(35°) \approx 0.82$

   F. 6,100 feet

   G. 8,700 feet

   H. 7,100 feet

   J. 2,900 feet

   K. 3,500 feet

3. What is the cotangent of $\angle Z$?

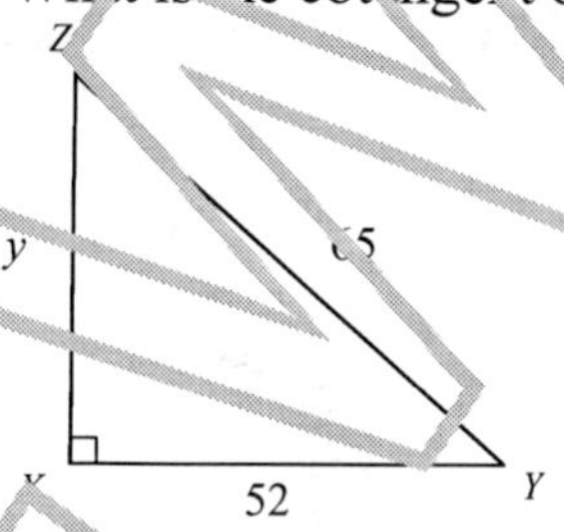

   A. 0.6

   B. 0.75

   C. 0.8

   D. 1

   E. 1.25

4. What is the value of the expression $\sin\theta \times \cos\theta$ when $\theta = 45°$?

   F. $-\frac{\sqrt{2}}{2}$

   G. $-\frac{1}{2}$

   H. $\frac{1}{2}$

   J. $\frac{\sqrt{2}}{2}$

   K. 1

5. Which of the following solutions is correct for the trigonometric equation $22\cot^2\theta + 9 = 17 - 2\cot^2\theta$ when 0 radians $\leq \theta < 2\pi$ radians?

   A. $\theta = \frac{\pi}{3}, \frac{2\pi}{3}, \frac{4\pi}{3}$, or $\frac{5\pi}{3}$ radians

   B. $\theta = \frac{\pi}{6}, \frac{5\pi}{6}, \frac{7\pi}{6}$, or $\frac{11\pi}{6}$ radians

   C. $\theta = \frac{\pi}{4}, \frac{3\pi}{4}, \frac{5\pi}{4}$, or $\frac{7\pi}{4}$ radians

   D. $\theta = \frac{\pi}{2}, \frac{7\pi}{6}$, or $\frac{11\pi}{6}$ radians

   E. $\theta = 0$ or radians

6. $1 - \sin^2\theta + \tan^2\theta - \sin^2\theta\tan^2\theta = ?$

F. $\sin^2\theta$
G. $\cos^2\theta$
H. $\tan^2\theta$
J. $\frac{1}{2}$
K. 1

7. What would be the amplitude of the sinusoidal function used to model the height above the ground of a patch on a rotating bicycle tire if the tire's circumference is 45π inches?

A. 22.5 inches
B. 22.5π inches
C. 45 inches
D. 45π inches
E. 506.25π inches

8. What is the approximate measure of $\angle D$ in $\triangle ADE$?

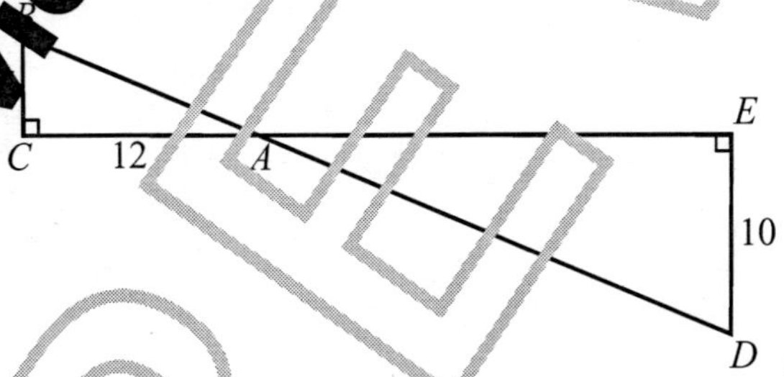

F. 23°
G. 25°
H. 36°
J. 65°
K. 67°

9. $\sin 59° = ?$
Use the formula $\sin(A+B) = \sin A\cos B + \cos A\sin B$.

A. $(\sin 48° \times \cos 11°) - (\cos 48° \times \sin 11°)$
B. $(\cos 48° \times \sin 11°) - (\sin 48° \times \cos 11°)$
C. $(\sin 48° \times \sin 11°) - (\cos 48° \times \cos 11°)$
D. $(\sin 48° \times \cos 11°) + (\cos 48° \times \sin 11°)$
E. $(\sin 48° \times \sin 11°) + (\cos 48° \times \cos 11°)$

10. A ray starting at the origin of a coordinate grid makes an angle of θ radians with the positive half of the x-axis and intersects a circle with diameter 64 at the point $(16\sqrt{3}, -16)$. What is the value of θ?

F. 30°
G. 60°
H. 120°
J. 210°
K. 330°

11. What is the measurement of $\angle Z$ to the nearest degree?

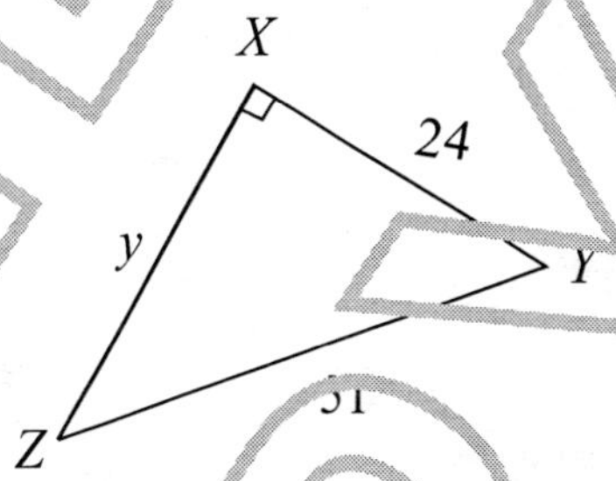

A. 25°
B. 28°
C. 30°
D. 62°
E. 65°

12. A light pole is located just outside of a circular race track with a diameter of 1 mile, and the center of the race track is directly north of the light pole. What would be the period of the sinusoidal function used to model a race car's distance north of the light pole as it travels around the track if the race car's distance north of the light pole is graphed as a function of its total distance travelled?

F. 0.5 miles
G. 1 mile
H. 2π miles
J. 0.5π miles
K. π miles

Practice Test 1

60 Minutes – 60 Questions

DIRECTIONS: Solve each problem and then choose the correct answer.

Do not linger over problems that take too much time. Solve as many as you can, then return to the others in the time you have left for this test.

You are permitted to use a calculator on this test. You may use your calculator for any problems you choose, but some of the problems may best be done without using a calculator.

Note: Unless otherwise stated, all of the following should be assumed.

1. Illustrative figures are NOT necessarily drawn to scale.
2. Geometric figures lie in a plane.
3. The word *line* indicates a straight line.
4. The word *average* indicates arithmetic mean.

---

1. A 52 foot building casts a 21 foot shadow onto the ground. If the shadow of a tree measures 9 feet, how tall is the tree to the nearest tenth of a foot?

A. 12.6 feet
B. 20.2 feet
C. 21.6 feet
D. 22.3 feet
E. 23.1 feet

PA

2. Which of the following expressions is equivalent to $\dfrac{x - \frac{1}{x}}{\frac{1}{x} - 1}$, $x > 0$?

F. $x + 1$
G. $x - 1$
H. $\dfrac{x^2 - 1}{x}$
J. $\dfrac{x^2 - x}{x + 1}$
K. $-1 - x$

IA

3. Given the set of data $\{1, 2, 2, 3, 3, 3, 4, 4, 4, 4\}$. Let X be the mean of the data set and Y be the mode. Find $|X - Y|$.

A. 0
B. $\frac{1}{2}$
C. 1
D. $\frac{4}{3}$
E. $\frac{3}{2}$

PA

4. A large group of friends went to a restaurant and had a bill of \$531.00. An 18% service charge was added on top to the bill. How much was the service charge?

F. \$29.50
G. \$34.88
H. \$53.10
J. \$95.58
K. \$106.20

PA

5. $|2^3 - 3^2| - 2\left|\sqrt{16} - 3\right| = ?$

A. -1
B. 0
C. 1
D. 2
E. 3

PA

6. $1.5 \times 10^{-3} = ?$

F. -1500
G. -4.5
H. 0.00015
J. 0.0015
K. 1500

PA

7. $3\frac{1}{6} - 2\frac{5}{12} = ?$

A. $\frac{1}{3}$
B. $\frac{3}{4}$
C. $1\frac{1}{16}$
D. $1\frac{1}{4}$
E. $1\frac{2}{3}$

PA

8. What is $\frac{3}{4}$% of 50?

F. 0.0375
G. 0.375
H. 3.75
J. 37.5
K. 375

PA

9. What is the prime factorization of 280?

A. $2 \times 5 \times 7$
B. $5 \times 2^2 \times 7$
C. $2^3 \times 5 \times 7$
D. $14 \times 2^2 \times 5$
E. 35×2^3

PA

10. Six cans of beans costs \$4.50. How many cans can be purchased with \$12.00?

F. 9
G. 12
H. 15
J. 16
K. 20

PA

11. What is the value of $3x^2 - 2x + 1$ when $x = -1$?

A. -4
B. 0
C. 2
D. 4
E. 6

PA

12. What is the average of $\frac{1}{5}$ and 0.5?

F. 0.30
G. 0.35
H. 0.40
J. 0.45
K. 0.50

PA

13. What is the solution to $3x + 2 = x - 6$?

A. $x = -4$
B. $x = -2$
C. $x = 0$
D. $x = \frac{8}{3}$
E. $x = 8$

PA

14. What is the solution to the inequality $x^2 + 2x > 3$?

F. $x > 1$ or $x < -3$
G. $-3 < x < 1$
H. $x < -1$ or $x > 3$
J. $-1 < x < 3$
K. No solution

EA

15. There are X students in Ms. Henderson's science class. $(X - 10)$ of the students are boys. If 40% of the class is female, how many boys are in the class?

A. 5
B. 10
C. 15
D. 20
E. 25

EA

16. While preparing a pitcher of lemonade, Hana realizes that she has put too much lemonade powder into the mixture. If 35% of the 140 gram pitcher is lemonade powder, how many grams of water should be added to the mixture so that the powder makes up 25% of the lemonade mixture?

F. 35
G. 40
H. 49
J. 50
K. 56

EA

17. $(x^2)(x)(x^2)$ is equivalent to

A. x^2
B. x^4
C. $2x^4$
D. x^5
E. $3x^5$

EA

18. Which of the following is equivalent to $(x^2 - 1)^2$?

F. $x^4 - 1$
G. $x^4 - x^2 + 1$
H. $x^4 - 2x^2 + 1$
J. $x^4 + 1$
K. $x^4 + 2x^2 + 1$

EA

19. If $3x = \frac{5 - y}{y}$, then $y =$?

A. $\frac{5}{3x + 1}$
B. $\frac{5}{3x - 1}$
C. $\frac{5}{3x + 5}$
D. $5 - 3x$
E. $5(3x - 1)$

EA

20. Raina is making a pie with nuts. The pie she is making has a flavor, one type of frosting, and one type of nut. If there are five pie flavors, three types of frosting, and two different nuts to choose from, how many different pies can be made?

F. 10
G. 15
H. 20
J. 25
K. 30

PA

21. There are n boys and m girls in a class at the beginning of the year. Midway through the year b more boys join the class. Which of the following expressions represents the fraction of boys in the class midway through the year?

A. $\frac{b}{n}$
B. $\frac{b}{n + m}$
C. $\frac{n}{n + m}$
D. $\frac{n + b}{n + m}$
E. $\frac{n + b}{n + m + b}$

EA

22. How many positive integers less than or equal to 100 are either multiples of 4 or multiples of 5?

F. 20
G. 30
H. 35
J. 40
K. 50

EA

23. Bindi traveled four miles on foot and six miles by car. If she traveled at a rate of 6 miles per hour by foot and 36 miles per hour by car, what was her average speed in miles per hour throughout the entire trip?

A. 8
B. 10
C. 12
D. 15
E. 2[illegible]

EA

24. The number of bacteria in a dish is dependent upon the surrounding temperature. The chart below shows the number of bacteria, b, at the corresponding temperature, T, measured in degrees Fahrenheit (°F). What is the linear function that models b in terms of T?

b	Number of bacteria	64	48	32	16
T	Degrees Fahrenheit	10	20	30	40

F. $b = \frac{5}{32}T - 10$
G. $b = -\frac{5}{8}T + 10$
H. $b = -\frac{5}{8}T + \frac{281}{4}$
J. $b = -\frac{8}{5}T + 64$
K. $b = -\frac{8}{5}T + 80$

IA

25. Which of the following is a factored form of the quadratic polynomial $3x^2 + 10x - 8$?

A. $(3x - 2)(x + 4)$
B. $(3x + 2)(x - 4)$
C. $(3x + 4)(x - 2)$
D. $(3x - 4)(x - 2)$
E. $(3x - 4)(x + 2)$

IA

26. What is the next term in the sequence 3, 5, 9, 15, 23, __ ?

F. 29
G. 30
H. 31
J. 33
K. 39

IA

27. What are the values of a and b, if any, where $|a| - b < 0$?

A. $-b < a < b$ and $b > 0$
B. $a < -b$ or $a > b$
C. $a < b$
D. $a < b$ and $b > 0$
E. There are no such values of a and b.

IA

28. If a and b are distinct prime numbers greater than zero, which of the following must always be true about the number $c = ab + 1$?

F. c is a prime number.
G. c is an even number.
H. c is an odd number.
J. c is a composite number.
K. None of these must be true about c.

IA

29. Find the real solution(s) to the equation $2|x| - x = 3$

A. $x = -1$ and 3
B. $x = -1$ and -3
C. $x = 1$ and -3
D. $x = 1$ and 3
E. $x = \pm 1$ and ± 3

IA

30. Fabian is traveling by car from Sunnyville to Littletown. The first hour of his trip he travels at a constant speed X miles per hour. The second hour of his trip, he travels twice the speed, $2X$ miles per hour. Which of the following graphs relates the distance traveled vs. time?

F.

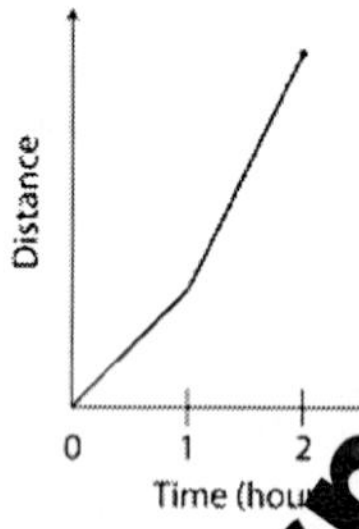

G.

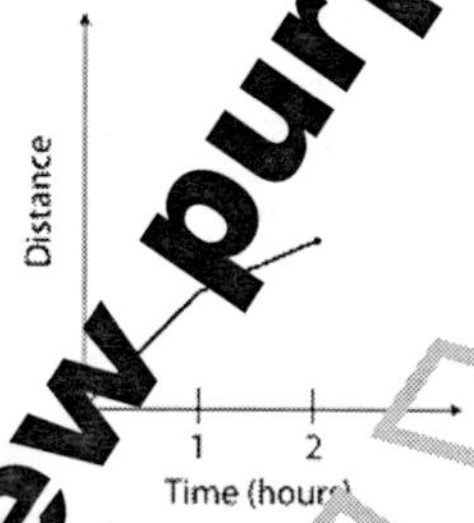

H.

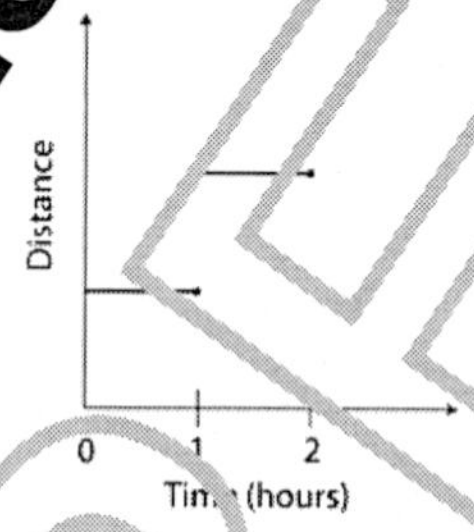

J.

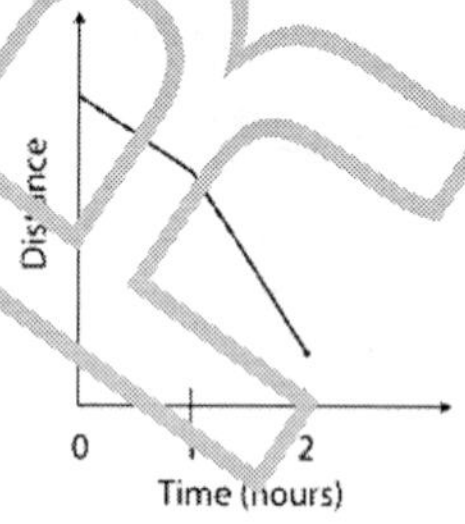

K.

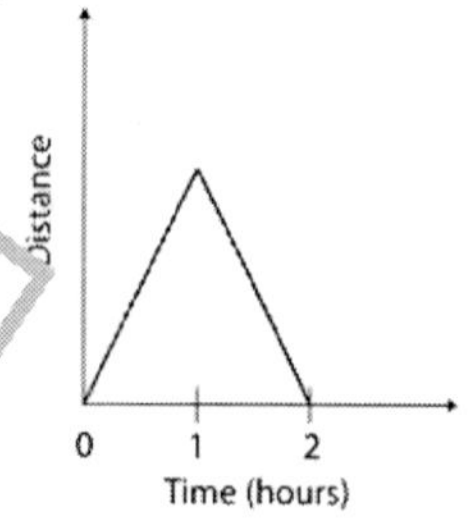

EA

31. If m is any negative even number and n is any positive odd number, which of the following statements must be true?

A. $m + n$ is a positive odd number.

B. $\frac{n}{m}$ is a negative even number.

C. $m \cdot n$ is a positive even number.

D. $n - m$ is a positive odd number.

E. $m^2 + n^2$ is a positive even number.

IA

32. Of the 30 students in Mr. Hancock's history class 30% own a cat, 80% own a dog, and 20% have both a cat and a dog. How many students have neither a cat nor a dog?

F. 3
G. 5
H. 6
J. 8
K. 9

PA

33. $\frac{1}{x+2} - \frac{1}{x^2+5x+6} = ?$

A. $\frac{x}{x+2}$

B. $-\frac{1}{x^2+4x+4}$

C. $\frac{x+1}{x^2+5x+6}$

D. $\frac{x+4}{x^2+5x+6}$

E. $\frac{1}{x+3}$

IA

34. Shown below is the line $\overleftrightarrow{AB}$ graphed below in the Cartesian Plane as the form $y = mx + b$, where m and b are real numbers. Which of the following are true about the values of m and b?

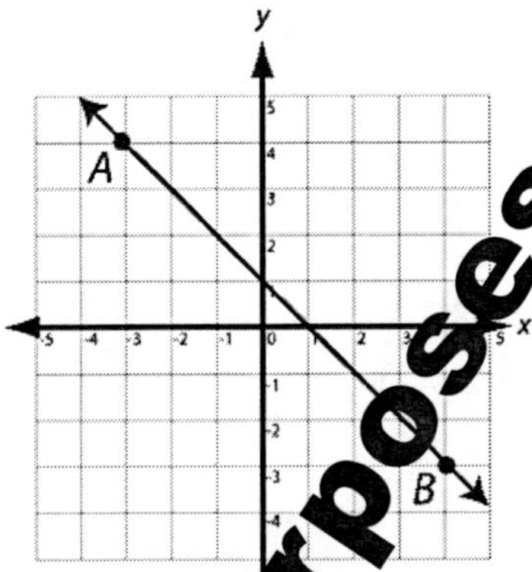

F. m is negative and b is positive.
G. m is positive and b is negative.
H. m and b are both positive.
J. m and b are both negative
K. Nothing can be determined with the following information.

PG

35. In the following figure lines $\overleftrightarrow{AB}$ and $\overleftrightarrow{CD}$ are parallel. The numbers represent the angle formed. Which of the following statements is not true?

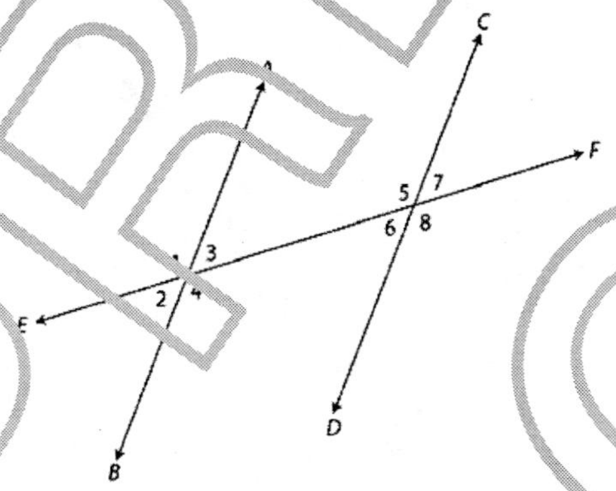

A. $\angle 1 = \angle 4 = \angle 5 = \angle 8$
B. $\angle 1 + \angle 5 = \angle 2 + \angle 6$
C. $\angle 3 + \angle 5 = \angle 1 + \angle 7$
D. $\angle 2 + \angle 3 = \angle 6 + \angle 7$
E. $\angle 3 + \angle 4 = \angle 7 + \angle 8$

PG

36. In the figure below, $\overline{BC} = 3$, $\overline{AE} = 2$, $\angle B = 135°$, $\angle C = 150°$, $BCFE$ is a rectangle, $\overline{AD}$ is parallel to $\overline{BC}$. Find the area of trapezoid $ABCD$.

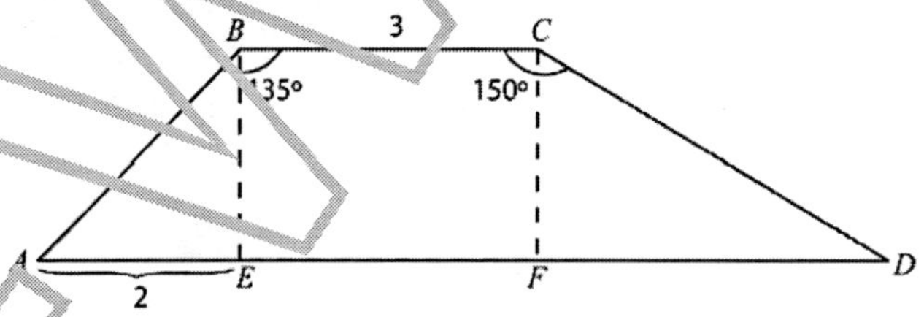

F. $4 + \sqrt{3}$
G. $8 + \sqrt{3}$
H. $4 + 2\sqrt{3}$
J. $8 + 2\sqrt{3}$
K. $16 + 2\sqrt{3}$

PG

37. Given the figure with the following lengths: $\overline{CD} = 1$, $\overline{FC} = 1$, $\overline{AH} = 3$, $\overline{GH} = 2$, and $\overline{FG} = 1$. What is the length of segment $\overline{DH}$?

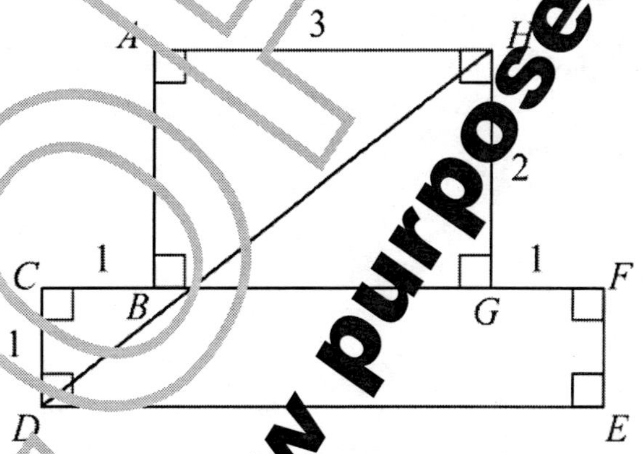

A. 4
B. $3\sqrt{2}$
C. 5
D. $4\sqrt{2}$
E. $3\sqrt{3}$

PG

38. In the given figure $\overline{AC} = 3$, $\overline{BC} = 5$, and $\overline{BD} = 2$. What is the area of triangle BDE?

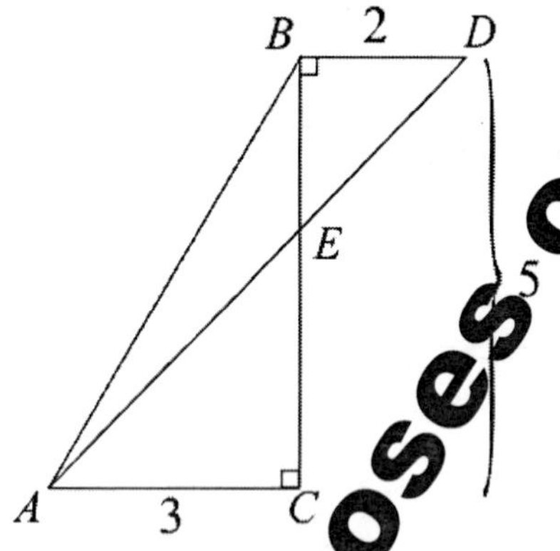

F. 1
G. 2
H. 3
J. 4
K. 6

PG

39. Two intersecting lines form four non-overlapping regions in two dimensional space as shown. What is the maximum number of non overlapping regions that can be formed by three intersecting lines? (Note: The lines do not need to all intersect at the same point.)

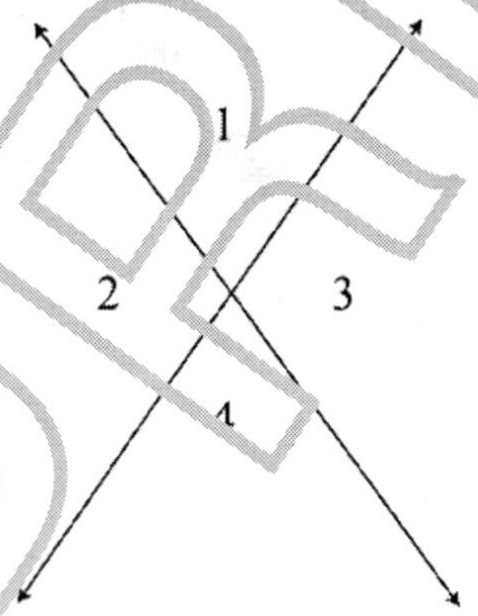

A. 6
B. 7
C. 8
D. 10
E. 12

PG

40. An isosceles right triangle is inscribed within a semicircle of diameter 4 as shown. The diameter of the semicircle is the same as the hypotenuse of the right triangle. What is the area of the shaded region?

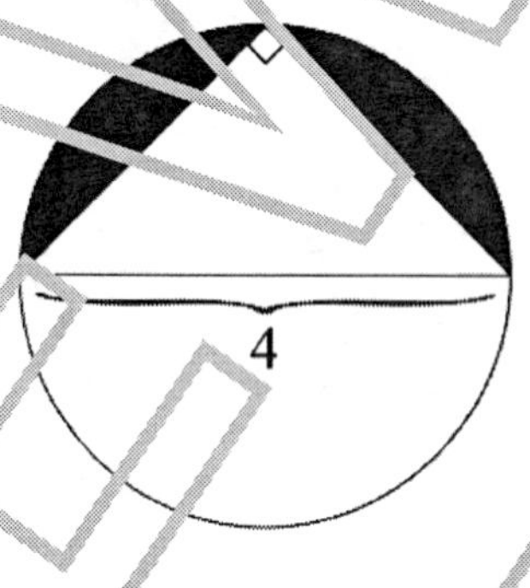

F. $2(\pi - 2)$
G. $2\pi - 1$
H. 2π
J. $4(\pi - 1)$
K. $2(\pi - 1)$

PG

41. How many triangles can be found in the given diagram?

A. 12
B. 16
C. 17
D. 20
E. 21

PG

42. A circle of radius r has the same area as a square of side length s. Which equation relates r and s?

F. $s = r \cdot \pi$
G. $s = \dfrac{r}{\pi}$
H. $s = \dfrac{r}{\sqrt{\pi}}$
J. $s = \sqrt{r \cdot \pi}$
K. $s = r\sqrt{\pi}$

PG

43. Which angle is complementary to $\angle FCG$?

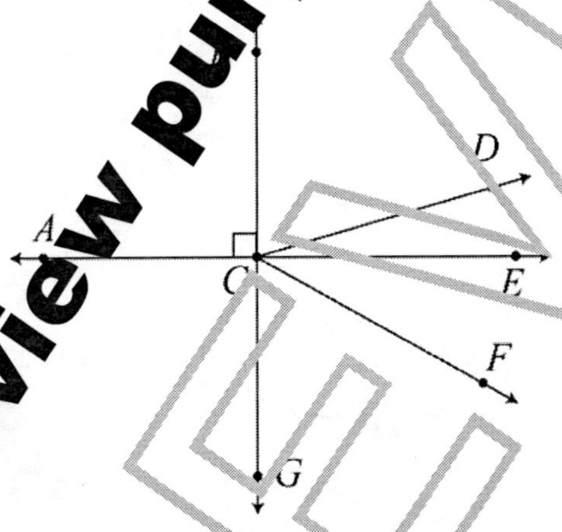

A. $\angle ECF$
B. $\angle DCE$
C. $\angle BCF$
D. $\angle BCD$
E. $\angle ACF$

PG

44. The hypotenuse of a right triangle is 8 units long and one leg is 6 units long. What is the length of the second leg?

F. 2
G. $[illegible]\sqrt{2}$
H. $2\sqrt{7}$
J. 6
K. 10

PG

45. Which of the following statements is true?

A. The sum of the angles of a triangle is 360°.
B. The square is the only quadrilateral having all equal angles.
C. A parallelogram must have four equal sides.
D. The area of an equilateral triangle is one-half times one of the sides squared.
E. The sides of an equiangular triangle are all the same length.

PG

46. A triangle has three angles, each of which can be classified as acute, right, or obtuse. Of the given scenarios for triangle angles, which of the following cannot exist?

F. A triangle has 3 acute angles.
G. A triangle has 2 acute angles and 1 obtuse angle.
H. A triangle has 2 acute angles and 1 right angle.
J. A triangle has 1 acute angle, 1 right angle, and 1 obtuse angle.
K. All these scenarios are possible.

PG

47. What is the volume of the cylinder?

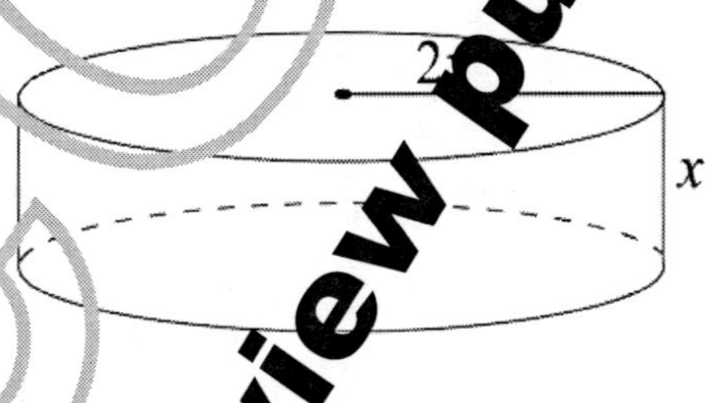

A. $2\pi \cdot x^2$
B. $4\pi \cdot x^2$
C. $2\pi \cdot x^3$
D. $4\pi \cdot x^3$
E. $8\pi \cdot x^3$

PG

48. Given the two functions $f(x) = x^2$ and $g(x) = 2x - 1$. The graphs of $f(g(x))$ and $g(f(x))$ intersect at one point, (a, b). Find $a + b$.

F. 0
G. 2
H. 3
J. 4
K. 6

CG

49. Which of the following lines is parallel to $4x - 2y = 9$?

A. $y = 2x -$ [illegible]
B. $y = -2x + 1$
C. $y = \frac{1}{2}x - 4$
D. $y = -\frac{1}{2}x - 4$
E. $y =$ [illegible] $x + 5$

CG

50. Three vertices of a square are $(1, 1)$, $(-2, 0)$, and $(2, -2)$. What is the fourth vertex?

F. $(-3, 1)$
G. $(-1, -3)$
H. $(-1, 3)$
J. $(3, -1)$
K. $(3, 1)$

CG

51. What is the radius of the circle $x^2 + y^2 - 4x + 2y = 4$?

A. 1
B. 2
C. 3
D. 4
E. 5

CG

52. Which of the following graphs describes the equation $\frac{x^2}{9} + \frac{y^2}{16} = 1$?

F.

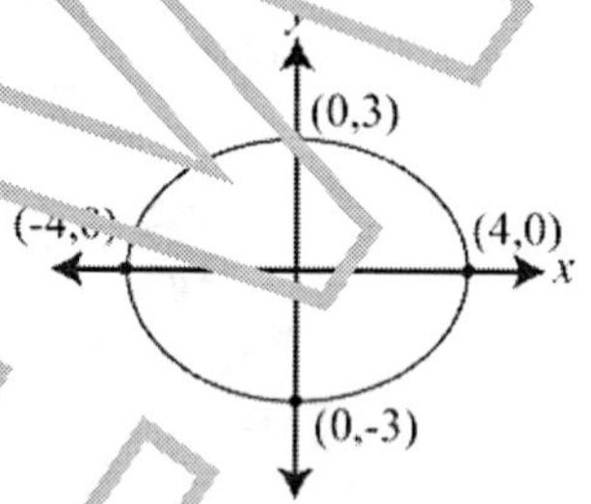

G.

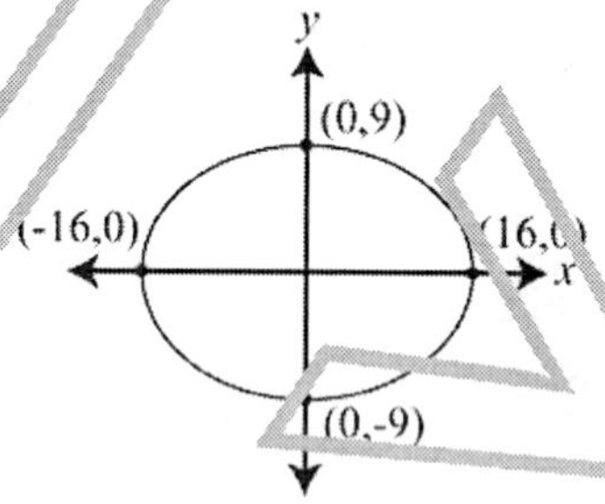

H.

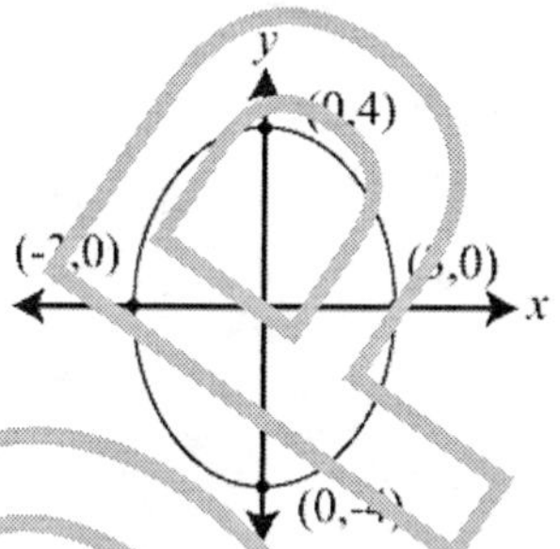

J.

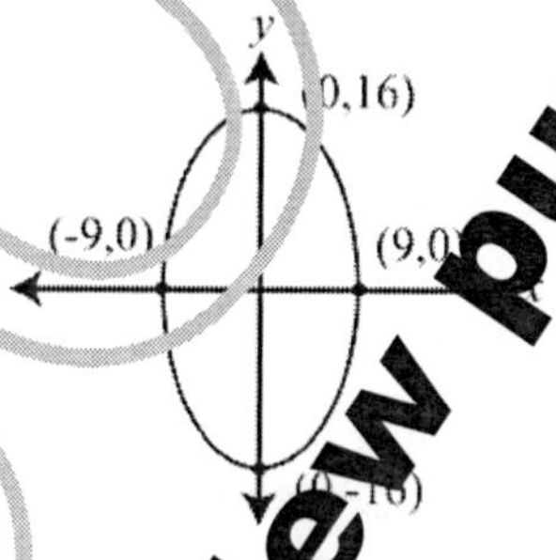

K.

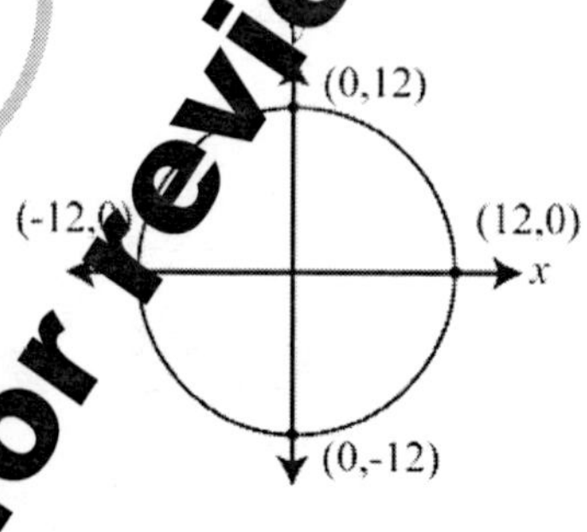

CG

53. Given the two functions $f(x) = \sqrt{x} + 1$ and $g(x) = (x-1)^2$. In the coordinate plane, the function $y = f(g(x))$ passes through the point $(a, 4)$. Which of the following is a possible value of a?

A. -4
B. -2
C. 0
D. 2
E. 4

CG

54. The two lines $y = ax$, $y = bx$, where a and b are real numbers, are plotted on the (x, y) plane, which are both drawn to scale. Which of the following statements is true?

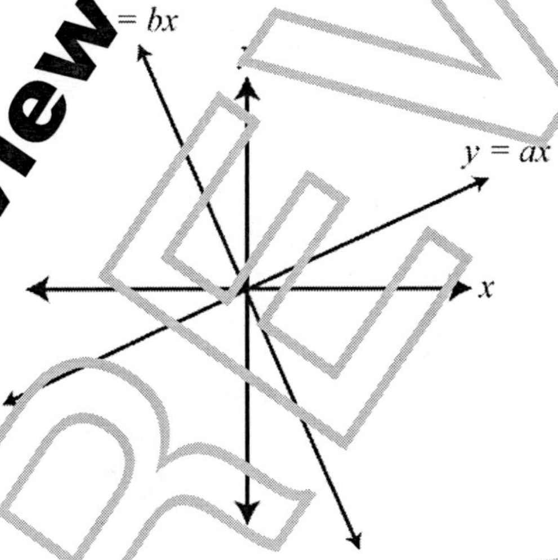

F. $|a| < |b|, a < 0, b > 0$
G. $|a| < |b|, a > 0, b < 0$
H. $|a| < |b|, a > 0, b > 0$
J. $|a| > |b|, a < 0, b > 0$
K. $|a| > |b|, a > 0, b < 0$

CG

55. Which of the following most accurately describes the translation from $f(x) = 4 + (x-1)^3$ to $g(x) = -1 + (x+1)^3$?

A. Up 2 units and 5 units to the left.
B. Down 2 units and 3 units to the right.
C. Down 5 units and 1 unit to the right.
D. Down 5 units and 2 units to the left.
E. Up 5 units and 2 units to the right.

CG

56. Two points, A and B, lie in the (x, y) plane where $A = (-3, 4)$ and $B = (6, -5)$. Let C be the midpoint of segment $\overline{AB}$ where $C = (a, b)$. Find $a + b$.

F. -1
G. 0
H. $\frac{1}{2}$
J. 1
K. 2

CG

57. In the right triangle ABC, $\angle A$ and $\angle B$ are acute angles and $\tan A = \frac{8}{15}$. What is $\cos B$?

A. $\frac{8}{17}$
B. $\frac{8}{15}$
C. $\frac{8\sqrt{141}}{141}$
D. $\frac{\sqrt{141}}{15}$
E. $\frac{15}{17}$

T

58. Barry wants to attach a wire from the ground to the top of a wall that is perpendicular to the ground as shown. He positions the end of the wire 12 feet away from the bottom of the wall and such that $\cot\theta = \frac{4}{3}$. What length wire will he need for this project?

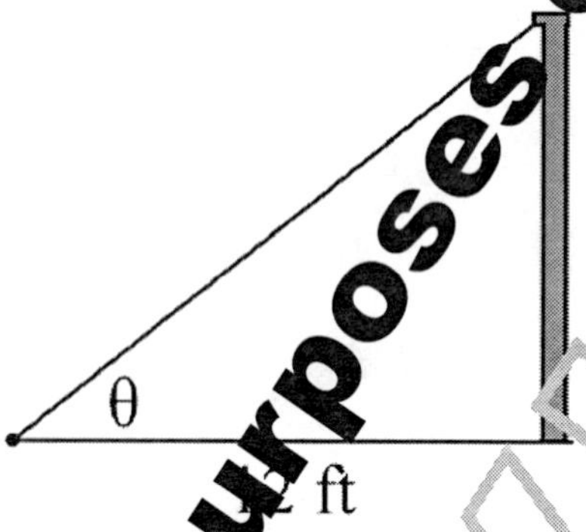

F. 12 feet
G. 15 feet
H. 16 feet
J. 18 feet
K. 20 feet

T

59. Which of the following expressions is equivalent to $\dfrac{1+\sin^2 x}{1-\sin^2 x}$ for $0 \le x < \dfrac{\pi}{2}$?

A. $\tan^2 x - \cos^2 x$
B. $(\cos^2 x)(\cot^2 x)$
C. $\sec^2 x + \tan^2 x$
D. $1 + \sec^2 x$
E. -1

T

60. Which of the following statements is false?

F. $\sin^2 x + \cos^2 x = 1$
G. $\sin(x+\pi) = \sin(x-\pi)$
H. $\cos(x+\pi) = \cos(x-\pi)$
J. $\sin(-x) = \sin(x)$
K. $\cos(-x) = \cos(x)$

T

Evaluation Chart for Practice Test 1

Directions: On the following chart, circle the question numbers that you answered incorrectly. Then turn to the appropriate topics (listed by chapters), read the explanations, and complete the exercises. Review the other chapters as needed. Finally, complete Practice Test 2 for further review.

		Questions	Pages
Chapter 2:	Pre-Algebra Review	4, 7, 8, 9, 11, 15, 19, 22, 27, 28, 31	22–42
Chapter 3:	Exponents and Square Roots	5, 6, 17	43–55
Chapter 4:	Solving Multi-Step Equations, Inequalities, and Patterns	13, 26, 29	56–79
Chapter 5:	Ratios and Proportions	1, 10, 16, 21, 23	80–85
Chapter 6:	Matrices		86–100
Chapter 7:	Polynomials	18	101–107
Chapter 8:	Factoring	2, 25, 33	108–117
Chapter 9:	Solving Quadratic Equations and Inequalities	14	118–133
Chapter 10:	Relations and Functions	48, 53	134–157
Chapter 11:	Graphing and Writing Linear Equations and Inequalities	34, 54, 56	158–173
Chapter 12:	Applications of Linear Graphs	24, 49	174–184
Chapter 13:	Graphing Non-Linear Equations	30, 51, 52	185–204
Chapter 14:	Systems of Equations and Systems of Inequalities	48	205–222
Chapter 15:	Statistics	3, 12	223–231
Chapter 16:	Probability and Counting	20, 32	232–243
Chapter 17:	Angles	35, 39, 43	244–251
Chapter 18:	Triangles	38, 41, 44, 46	252–263
Chapter 19:	Plane Geometry	36, 37, 40, 42, 45	264–281
Chapter 20:	Solid Geometry	47	282–296
Chapter 21:	Logic and Geometric Proofs		297–304
Chapter 22:	Transformations	50, 55	305–318
Chapter 23:	Trigonometry	57, 58, 59, 60	319–341

Practice Test 2

60 Minutes – 60 Questions

DIRECTIONS: Solve each problem and then choose the correct answer.

Do not linger over problems that take too much time. Solve as many as you can, then return to the others in the time you have left for this test.

You are permitted to use a calculator on this test. You may use your calculator for any problems you choose, but some of the problems may best be done without using a calculator.

Note: Unless otherwise stated, all of the following should be assumed.

1. Illustrative figures are NOT necessarily drawn to scale.
2. Geometric figures lie in a plane.
3. The word *line* indicates a straight line.
4. The word *average* indicates arithmetic mean.

---

1. After the advanced screening of a new movie, each of the members of the movie's audience was asked if he/she strongly agreed, agreed, disagreed, or strongly disagreed with the following statement: "I loved this movie!" The results of the survey are shown in the pie chart below:

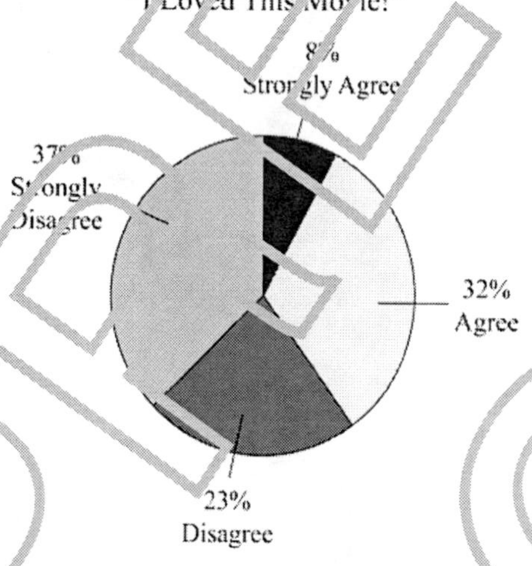

What percentage of the people who loved the movie strongly agreed with the statement?

A. 8 percent
B. 20 percent
C. 23 percent
D. 32 percent
E. 37 percent

PA

2. Simplify: $\dfrac{\csc^2\theta + \sec^2\theta}{18\csc^2\theta\sec^2\theta}$

F. $\dfrac{1}{18}$

G. $\dfrac{1}{18\csc^2\theta\sec^2\theta}$

H. $\dfrac{\csc^2\theta + \sec^2\theta}{18}$

J. $18\csc^2\theta\sec^2\theta$

K. 18

3. If $2x + 9y = -14$ and $5x - y = 12$, what are the values of x and y?

A. $x = \frac{1}{2}; y = -2$
B. $x = \frac{1}{2}; y = 2$
C. $x = 2; y = -2$
D. $x = 2; y = 2$
E. $x = -2; y = 2$

IA

4. A triangle with vertices at the points $(2, 0)$, $(8, 8)$, and $(8, -8)$ is rotated 270° clockwise about the origin of a coordinate grid. Which of the following points represents a vertex of the transformed triangle?

F. $(2, 0)$
G. $(0, 2)$
H. $(-2, 0)$
J. $(-8, -8)$
K. $(8, -8)$

PG

5. For vacation the members of the Johnson family are driving in a straight line from their hometown of Jamestown, which is 45 miles south and 16 miles east of their state capitol, to Kent. When they are halfway to Kent, they are 3 miles south and 44 miles west of their state capitol. Where is Kent located relative to their state capitol?

A. It is 14 miles south and 24 miles west of their state capitol.
B. It is 24 miles south and 14 miles west of their state capitol.
C. It is 39 miles north and 104 miles east of their state capitol.
D. It is 39 miles north and 104 miles west of their state capitol.
E. It is 39 miles south and 104 miles west of their state capitol.

CG

6. If $8x^2 - 39x + 45 = 0$, then $x =$?

F. $-\frac{15}{8}$ or -3
G. $-\frac{15}{8}$ or 3
H. $\frac{3}{8}$ or 15
J. $\frac{15}{8}$ or -3
K. $\frac{15}{8}$ or 3

EA

7. For $-180° \leq \theta \leq 180°$, the graph of which of the following trigonometric functions does not contain at least two asymptotes?

A. $f(\theta) = \csc\theta$
B. $f(\theta) = \cos\theta$
C. $f(\theta) = \sec\theta$
D. $f(\theta) = \tan\theta$
E. $f(\theta) = \cot\theta$

T

8. A company rented out a roller-skating rink for its holiday party. It paid \$1850 to rent out the rink and \$3.50 per employee to rent each a pair of roller skates. If the party was attended by m employees, and the company spent a total of \$28.50 per employee on the party, which of the following equations can be used to solve for m?

F. $\dfrac{1850 + 3.5}{m} = 28.5$

G. $\dfrac{1850 + 3.5}{m} = 28.5m$

H. $\dfrac{1850}{m} + 3.5 = 28.5$

J. $\dfrac{1850}{m} + 3.5 = 28.5m$

K. $1850 + 3.5m = 28.5$

PA

9. Which of the following statements accurately describes the quadratic equation $9x^2 + \dfrac{1}{49} = 0$?

A. It has one rational root.
B. It has two rational roots.
C. It has one irrational root.
D. It has two irrational roots.
E. It has two imaginary roots.

IA

10. A weather forecast states that there is a 20 percent chance of snow on Monday, a 10 percent chance of snow on Tuesday, and a 40 percent chance of snow on Wednesday. What is the probability that it snows on Monday and Tuesday, but not on Wednesday?

F. 0.02 percent
G. 0.012 percent
H. 0.8 percent
J. 1.2 percent
K. 12 percent

PA

11. The value of Michele's 401(k) account is increasing. Two months ago its value was $\frac{3}{16}$ of her annual income, one month ago its value was $\frac{1}{4}$ of her annual income, and now its value is $\frac{1}{3}$ of her annual income. If the pattern continues, what fraction of Michele's annual income will the value of her 401(k) account be in one month?

A. $\frac{1}{5}$
B. $\frac{4}{9}$
C. $\frac{1}{2}$
D. $\frac{16}{27}$
E. $\frac{4}{3}$

IA

12. $\sqrt{x^{36}y^{-16}z^{-\ldots}} \div (x^{-4}y^{10}z^{5})^{\frac{5}{2}} = ?$

F. $x^{8}y^{17}$
G. $x^{8}y^{17}z^{25}$
H. $\frac{x^{26}y^{-54}z^{-20}}{2}$
J. $x^{28}y^{-33}$
K. $x^{28}y^{-33}z^{25}$

EA

13. For which of the following statements is the following figure a counterexample?

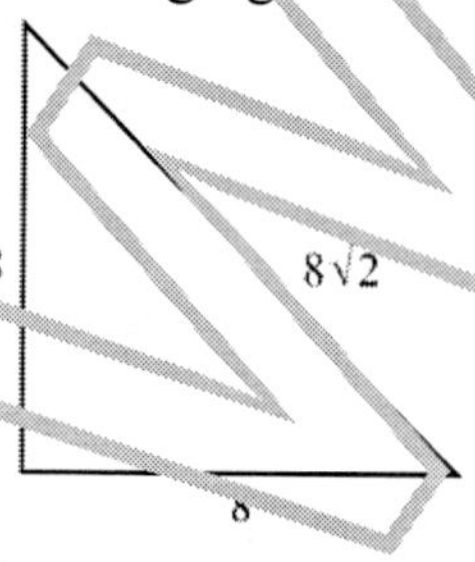

A. A right triangle cannot be isosceles.
B. A right triangle cannot be equilateral.
C. A right triangle cannot be scalene.
D. A right triangle cannot be acute.
E. A right triangle cannot be obtuse.

PG

14. Go-cart A and go-cart B are racing, and each has a tire with a pebble stuck in the tread. The following graph shows the distance of each of the pebbles above the ground as the tires of the two go-carts are rotating:

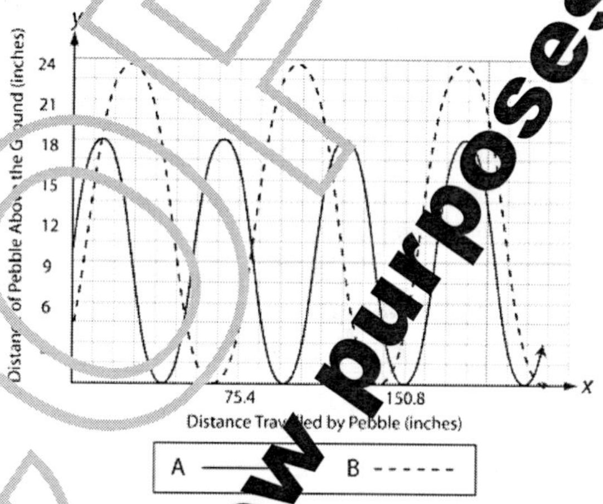

Which of the following statements about the two go-carts can be determined from the graph?

F. A is going faster than B.
G. B is going faster than A.
H. A and B are traveling at the same speed.
J. A has bigger tires than B.
K. B has bigger tires than A.

T

15. The equation $y = ax^2 + bx + c$ is graphed on a coordinate grid as shown below:

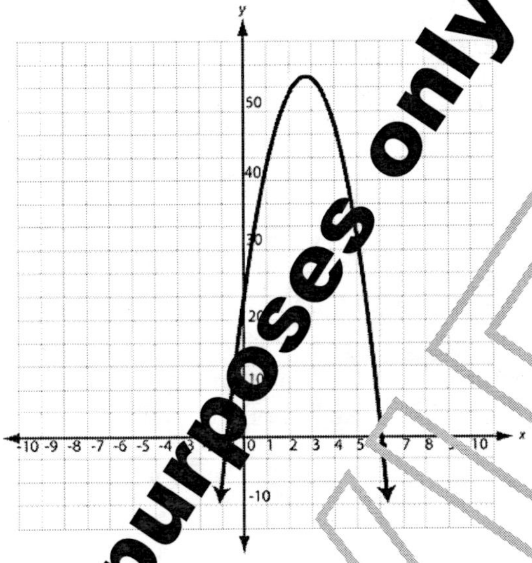

Which of the following scenarios is possible for a, b, and c?

A. $b^2 - 4ac = 0$
B. $b^2 - 4ac < 0$
C. $a > 0; b > 0; c > 0$
D. $a > 0; b > 0; c < 0$
E. $a < 0; b > 0; c > 0$

CG

16. A slide on a playground begins above the edge of a sandbox. If the slide goes in a straight line all the way to the ground, and its angle of depression is 60 degrees, how far from the edge of the sandbox does the slide end if it begins 26 feet above the ground?

F. $\frac{13\sqrt{3}}{2}$ feet
G. $\frac{26\sqrt{3}}{3}$ feet
H. $\frac{26\sqrt{3}}{4}$ feet
J. $13\sqrt{13}$ feet
K. $26\sqrt{3}$ feet

T

17. A bank offered online bill pay to its customers during a beta testing period, and 475 people signed up. Online bill pay was then officially launched, and since then, the bank has noticed that the total number of customers signed up has quadrupled every m months. If the bank has offered online bill pay for a total of y years since the end of the beta-testing period, which of the following expressions represents the current number of customers signed up?

A. $475^{(12y \div m)}$
B. $475 \times 4^{(y \div m)}$
C. $475 \times 4^{(12y \div m)}$
D. $1900^{(y \div m)}$
E. $1900^{(12y \div m)}$

EA

18. Which of the following inequalities is represented by the graph shown below?

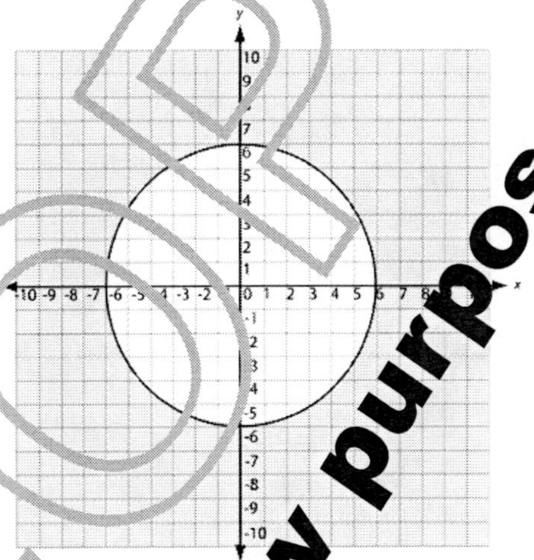

F. $\frac{x^2}{6} + \frac{y^2}{6} > 36$
G. $\frac{x^2}{6} + \frac{y^2}{6} < 36$
H. $\frac{x^2}{6} - \frac{y^2}{6} > 36$
J. $x^2 + y^2 > 36$
K. $x^2 + y^2 < 36$

CG

19. The cross section of a cylindrical tub of Neapolitan ice cream consists of an outer ring of chocolate ice cream, a middle ring of vanilla ice cream, and an inner circle of strawberry ice cream. The 30 centimeter diameter of the tub is partitioned as shown below:

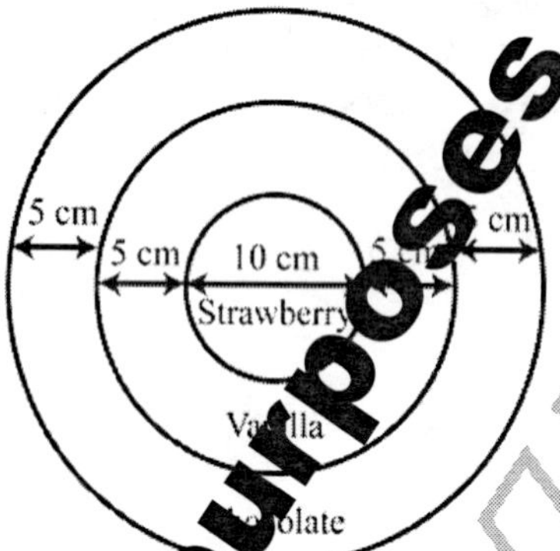

If the height of the tub is 40 centimeters, how many liters of ice cream that isn't vanilla are in the tub? (1 L = 1000 cm^3)

A. 5π
B. 6π
C. 9π
D. 10π
E. 24π

PG

20. Choose the best approximation for the expression $\dfrac{\sqrt{258} - \sqrt{119}}{\sqrt{440} + \sqrt{17}}$.

F. $\frac{1}{5}$
G. $\frac{5}{24}$
H. $\frac{3}{13}$
J. $\frac{6}{25}$
K. $\frac{1}{4}$

PA

21. Which of the following relations is not a function?

A. $y = 8x^2 + 53x - 21$
B. $y = -\frac{7}{2}$
C. $x = 15y + 11$
D. $y = 18x - 25$
E. $x = 3$

IA

22. A cylindrical water tank with a diameter of 5 feet and a height of 10 feet is being replaced by a new tank with diameter of 10 feet. If the two tanks have equal volume, what is the height of the tank?

F. 1.8 feet
G. 2.5 feet
H. 3 feet
J. 3.6 feet
K. 2.1 feet

PG

23. Which of the following lines is the steepest?

A. $5x + 7y + 6 = 0$
B. $y - 9 = \frac{2}{3}(x + 11)$
C. The line passing through the points $(3, 10)$ and $(-8, 1)$.
D. $y = -\frac{4}{5}x - 18$
E. The line that is perpendicular to the line $y = -\frac{4}{3}x + 13$

CG

24. One of the linear equations of motion states that $v^2 = u^2 + 2ad$, where v is the final velocity, u is the initial velocity, a is the constant acceleration, and d is the distance travelled. Which of the following expressions is equal to the distance travelled, d, if $\dfrac{v - u}{a} = t$ for time?

F. $0.5(u - v)t$
G. $0.5(v - u)t$
H. $0.5(u + v)t$
J. $0.5(u + v)(u - v)t$
K. $0.5(u + v)(u + v)t$

EA

25. The six employees of a small company have salaries of $\$38,000$, $\$29,000$, $\$49,000$, $\$41,000$, $\$26,000$, and x. If the median salary at the company is $\$36,500$, what is the value of x?

A. $\$34,500$
B. $\$35,000$
C. $\$35,500$
D. $\$36,000$
E. $\$36,500$

PA

26. The values of the volume of a cone were plotted on a coordinate grid as one of the dimensions of the cone was changed. The graph is shown below:

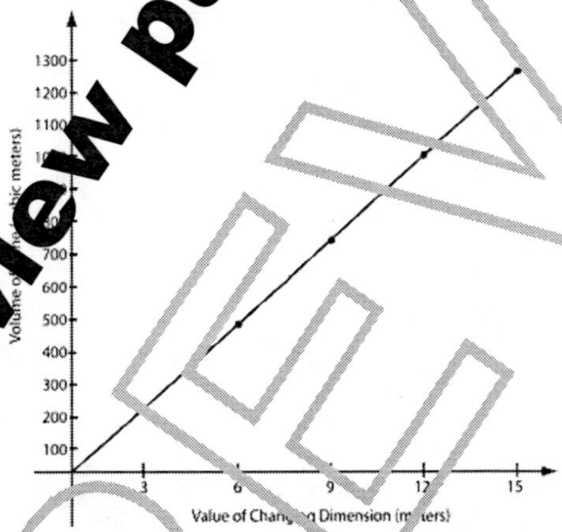

Which of the following statements accurately describes the situation shown by the graph?

F. As the height of the cone increased, its volume increased.
G. As the height of the cone increased, its volume decreased.
H. As the radius of the cone increased, its volume increased.
J. As the radius of the cone increased, its volume decreased.
K. As the circumference of the base of the cone increased, its volume increased.

PG

27. If $|-12x+5| \geq 41$, which of the following statements is true?

A. $x \geq -3$
B. $x \leq \frac{23}{6}$
C. $-12x+5 \leq 41$
D. $-12x+5 \leq -41$
E. $-(-12x+5) \leq 41$

IA

28. By definition the determinant $\begin{vmatrix} a & b \\ c & d \end{vmatrix}$ is $ad-bc$. What is the value of $\begin{vmatrix} 10 & -5 \\ -3 & 12 \end{vmatrix}$?

F. 105
G. 135
H. 7
J. 37
K. 120

IA

29. $(2x-1)(x+2)(2x+1)(x-2) = ?$

A. $4x^4+17x^2-4$
B. $4x^4+17x^2+4$
C. $4x^4-17x^2-4$
D. $4x^4-17x^2+4$
E. $-4x^4-17x^2-4$

EA

30. Which of the following equations is that of a hyperbola?

F. $x = 6y^2+3y+3$
G. $\dfrac{(x-5)^2}{49} - \dfrac{(y+9)^2}{36} = 1$
H. $\dfrac{(x+8)^2}{81} + \dfrac{(y-1)^2}{225} = 1$
J. $y = \frac{1}{2}x^2+4x-10$
K. $(x+12)^2+(y-7)^2 = 144$

CG

31. A men's clothing store sells 15 types of pants, 8 types of belts, 12 types of shirts, and 40 types of suspenders. However, store employees have determined that not all of the possible combinations of pants, belts, shirts, and suspenders go together. The ratio of the number of combinations that go together to the number of combinations that don't go together is 3 : 2. How many of the combinations don't go together?

A. 11, 520
B. 17, 280
C. 23, 040
D. 28, 800
E. 34, 560

PA

32. A trapezoid with vertices at the points $(-11, -10)$, $(-8, 3)$, $(-5, 3)$, and $(-2, -10)$ is first translated 5 units down and 3 units to the right and then reflected over the x-axis. In which quadrant(s) is the resulting trapezoid located?

F. Quadrant 1 only
G. Quadrant 2 only
H. Quadrants 1 and 2
J. Quadrant 3 only
K. Quadrants 3 and 4

PG

33. For which of the following sequences is the general term $t_n = \frac{1+3n}{6+n} \times (-1)^{n+1}$, where n is a whole number greater than or equal to 1?

A. $-\frac{1}{6}, \frac{4}{7}, -\frac{7}{8}, \frac{10}{9}, -\frac{13}{10}, \ldots$
B. $\frac{1}{6}, -\frac{4}{7}, \frac{7}{8}, -\frac{10}{9}, \frac{13}{10}, \ldots$
C. $\frac{4}{7}, \frac{7}{8}, \frac{10}{9}, \frac{13}{10}, \frac{16}{11}, \ldots$
D. $-\frac{4}{7}, \frac{7}{8}, -\frac{10}{9}, \frac{13}{10}, -\frac{16}{11}, \ldots$
E. $\frac{4}{7}, -\frac{7}{8}, \frac{10}{9}, -\frac{13}{10}, \frac{16}{11}, \ldots$

IA

34. If the following graph represents the equation $y = a^x$, what is the value of a?

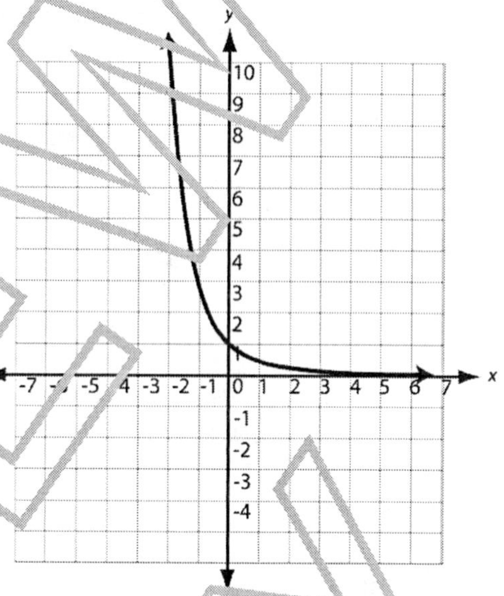

F. -3
G. $-\frac{1}{3}$
H. 1
J. $\frac{1}{3}$
K. 3

CG

35. Rex, Lex, and Tex are quarterbacks for their respective football teams. Rex has four times as many touchdown passes as Lex, and Lex has $\frac{9}{8}$ as many touchdown passes as Tex. If Rex has t touchdown passes, how many touchdown passes does Tex have?

A. $\frac{2t}{9}$
B. $\frac{9t}{32}$
C. $\frac{9t}{8}$
D. $4t$
E. $\frac{9t}{[illegible]}$

EA

36. Blue, green, red, black, and white chips are worth 1, 4, 16, 64, and 256 dollars, respectively. Smaller chips must be traded for larger chips whenever possible. After all trades are made, which of the following chip combinations will result in four chips?

F. 4 blue, 3 green, and 3 red
G. 4 blue, 4 green, and 3 red
H. 3 green, 3 red, and 3 black
J. 3 green, 4 red, and 3 black
K. 4 green, 4 red, and 4 black

PA

37. A regular octahedron is a three-dimensional geometric object composed of eight equilateral triangles, four of which meet at each vertex. How many edges does a regular octahedron have?

A. 6
B. 8
C. 12
D. 16
E. 24

PG

38. A public library wants to determine how many hours per year the average citizen in its community utilizes its services, so it will ask a random sample of citizens to fill out a questionnaire. Which of the following techniques will most likely produce a random sample?

F. Choose every third person currently in the library.
G. Have a computer program randomly choose people from a list of library-card holders.
H. Choose all people who currently have one or more overdue books.
J. Choose every hundredth person listed in the local phone book.
K. Have the head librarian choose twenty of her closest friends.

PA

39. A sphere with its center at the origin of a three-dimensional coordinate grid has a radius of 9 yards. The center of the sphere and the points at which the sphere intersects the positive portions of each of the three axes are connected to form a three-dimensional object. What is the volume of the object?

A. 121.5 yards^3
B. 243 yards^3
C. 364.5 yards^3
D. 729 yards^3
E. 2187 yards^3

PG

40. Which of the following equations does the graph below represent?

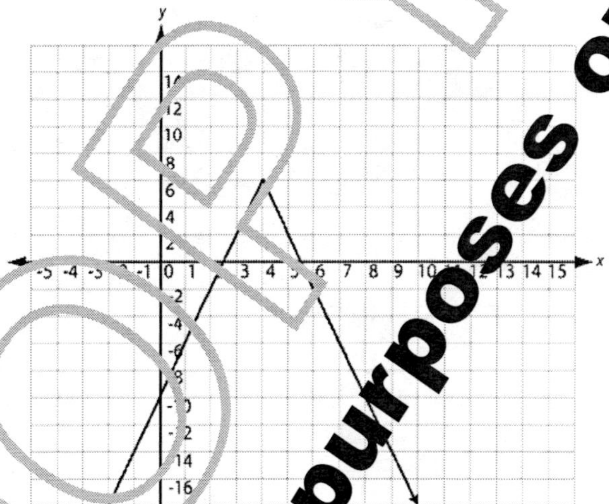

F. $y = -6|x - 4| + 4$
G. $y = -4|x - 6| + 4$
H. $y = -6|x - 4| + 6$
J. $y = 4|x - 6| + 4$
K. $y = 4|x - 4| + 6$

CG

41. Which of the following groups of numbers is in order from least to greatest?

A. $-\frac{10}{11}, -1, -\frac{12}{11}, -\frac{13}{11}, -\frac{14}{11}$

B. $\frac{7}{24}, \frac{3}{8}, \frac{1}{3}, \frac{5}{12}, \frac{11}{24}$

C. $-\frac{10}{3}, -\frac{7}{2}, -\frac{19}{6}, -3, -\frac{17}{6}$

D. $-\frac{17}{4}, -4, \frac{17}{4}, 4, 5$

E. $-\frac{13}{16}, -\frac{3}{4}, -\frac{11}{16}, -\frac{5}{8}, -\frac{9}{16}$

PA

42. Which of the following statements is correct about the logical validity of a geometric proof assuming no errors are made?

F. If it uses deductive reasoning, then its conclusion must not be logically valid.
G. If it uses deductive reasoning, then its conclusion might not be logically valid.
H. If it uses inductive reasoning, then its conclusion must not be logically valid.
J. If it uses inductive reasoning, then its conclusion might not be logically valid.
K. If it uses inductive reasoning, then its conclusion must be logically valid.

PG

43.

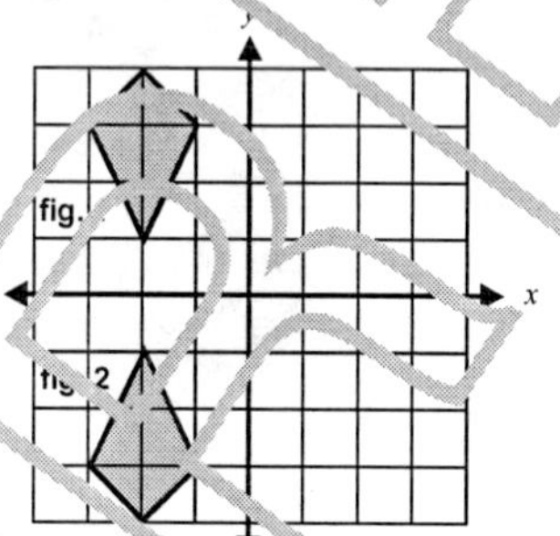

Figure 1 goes through a transformation to form figure 2. Which of the following descriptions correctly describes the transformation shown?

A. reflection across the x-axis.
B. reflection across the y-axis
C. $(x', y') = (x - 5, y)$
D. $(x', y') = (x, y - 5)$
E. $(x', y') = (x, y - 2)$

PG

44. The number of distinct colors that can be represented by a pixel when the color depth is 24 bits per pixel (bpp) is $16,777,216$. Which of the following values best represents the number of distinct colors that can be represented by a pixel at 24 bpp in scientific notation?

F. 1.7×10^{-8}
G. 1.7×10^{-7}
H. 1.7×10^{-6}
J. 1.7×10^{7}
K. 1.7×10^{3}

PA

45. If $11x^2 + 31x - 6 > 0$, which of the following solutions for x is correct?

A. $x > -3$
B. $x < \frac{2}{11}$
C. $x < -3$ and $x > \frac{2}{11}$
D. $x < -\frac{2}{11}$ and $x > 3$
E. $x = -3$ and $x = \frac{2}{11}$

IA

46. A plane parallel to the base of a right circular cone with a radius of 15 inches and a height of 10 inches intersects the cone $10 - a$ inches above the base. The radius of the circle formed by the intersection of the cone and the plane is 6 inches. What is the ratio of the volume of the portion of the cone below the plane to the portion above the plane?

F. $630\pi + 12\pi a : 120\pi - 12\pi a$
G. $630\pi + 12\pi a : 12\pi a$
H. $750\pi - 12\pi a : 120\pi - 12\pi a$
J. $750\pi - 12\pi a : 12\pi a$
K. $750\pi : 12\pi a$

PG

47. The scientists at a pharmaceutical company have just discovered the cure to widely prevalent disease, and the company's share price increased 40,000 percent at the open of today's trading. If the company's share price closed yesterday at \$6.50 per share, what was the share price at the open of today's trading?

A. \$2600.00 per share
B. \$2606.50 per share
C. \$26,000.00 per share
D. \$26,006.50 per share
E. \$260,000.00 per share

PA

48. If $a = 40$ and $b = \frac{1}{50}$, which of the following expressions is equivalent to $\sqrt{\sqrt{\frac{a}{b}}}$?

F. $2 \times 5^{\frac{1}{4}}$
G. $2 \times 5^{\frac{1}{2}}$
H. $2 \times 5^{\frac{3}{4}}$
J. $4 \times 5^{\frac{1}{2}}$
K. $4 \times 5^{\frac{3}{4}}$

EA

49. Line A and line B are located in plane P, and the two lines intersect. If line C is also located in plane P, which of the following statements must be true?

A. Line C must intersect only line A.
B. Line C must intersect only line B.
C. Line C must intersect both line A and line B.
D. Line C must intersect either line A or line B, but not both.
E. Line C must intersect either line A or line B, or possibly both.

PG

50. Two sides of a triangle measure 19 centimeters and 29 centimeters, respectively. Which of the following statements is correct about the length of the third side of the triangle?

F. It must be less than 10 centimeters.
G. It must be equal to 48 centimeters.
H. It must be greater than 48 centimeters.
J. It must be greater than 10 centimeters or less than 48 centimeters.
K. It must be greater than 10 centimeters and less than 48 centimeters.

PG

51. What are the coordinates of the points where the following two circles intersect if the centers of the two circles are at points A and B, respectively?

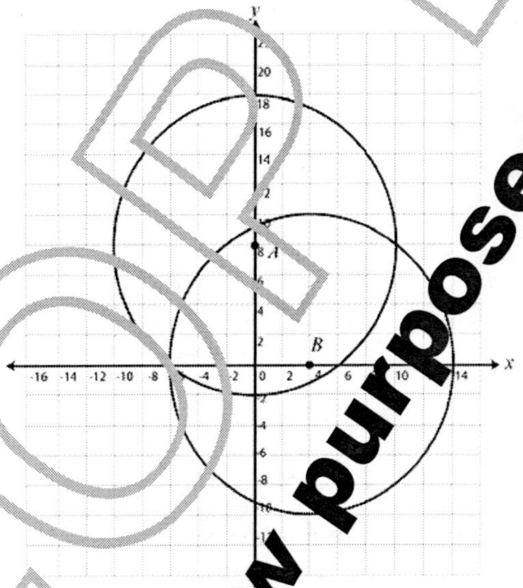

A. $(-6, 0)$ and $(10, 7)$
B. $(-6, 0)$ and $(10, 8)$
C. $(-6, 0)$ and $(10, 9)$
D. $\left(-\frac{11}{2}, 0\right)$ and $(10, 8)$
E. $\left(-\frac{11}{2}, 0\right)$ and $(10, 9)$

CG

52. Which of the following values does not represent the y-intercept of one of the lines shown below?

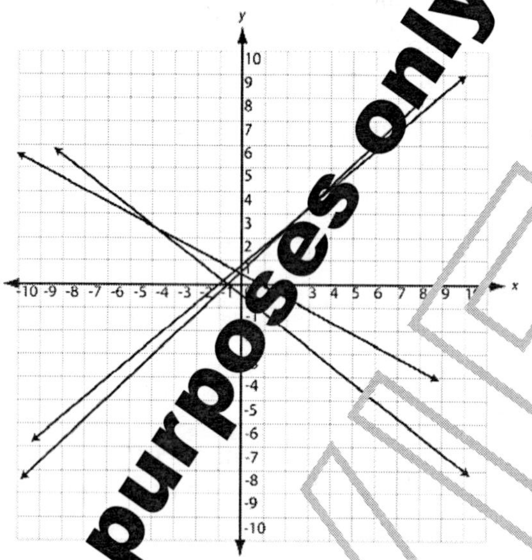

F. $-\frac{[illegible]}{3}$

G. $-\frac{1}{2}$

H. $\frac{1}{2}$

J. $\frac{3}{5}$

K. 1

CG

53. Solve the following expression:

$$2^3 + 2^3 \times 2^3 + 2^{-3} \times 2^{-3} - 2^3 \div 2^{-3} - 2^3$$

A. $\frac{1}{64}$

B. $\frac{1}{8}$

C. 1

D. 8

E. 64

EA

54. A recent newspaper poll revealed that 71 out of every 100 registered voters in a particular state intend to vote in the upcoming election. If there are 11,000,000 people in the state, and 52 percent of them are not registered voters, which of the following proportions can be used to determine the number of people in the state expected to vote in the upcoming election?

F. $\frac{29}{100} = \frac{x}{5280000}$

G. $\frac{29}{100} = \frac{x}{5720000}$

H. $\frac{71}{100} = \frac{x}{5280000}$

J. $\frac{71}{100} = \frac{x}{5720000}$

K. $\frac{71}{100} = \frac{x}{11000000}$

PA

55. A 50-meter-long rectangular swimming pool has a shallow end and a deep end. The shallow end is 0.5 meters deep, while the deep end is 5.5 meters deep. As the pool goes from shallow to deep, its bottom descends at a constant slope. A side view of the pool is as follows:

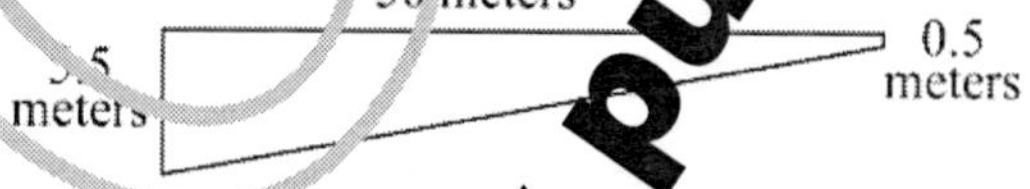

If the width of the pool is 30 meters, how many liters of water does the pool hold? (1 L = 0.001 m^3)

A. 150,000

B. 450,000

C. 1,500,000

D. 4,125,000

E. 4,500,000

PG

56. If the completing the square technique is to be used to solve the quadratic equation $x^2 + 16x + 1 = 0$, which of the following numbers should be added to both sides of the equation?

F. 8
G. 16
H. 32
J. 64
K. 256

EA

57. $(5.87 \times 10^{-5}) + (5.87 \times 10^{-6}) + (5.87 \times 10^{-7}) =$

A. 0.000000065157
B. 0.00000065157
C. 0.0000065157
D. 0.000065157
E. 0.00065157

PA

58. $(4)(6 - 5i)\left(\dfrac{8 + 3i}{2}\right) = ?$

F. $\dfrac{33 - 22i}{2}$
G. $2(33 - 22i)$
H. $2(33 + 22i)$
J. $2(63 - 22i)$
K. $2(63 + 22i)$

IA

59. In which of the following ways can the quadratic equation $a^2 + 2ab + b^2 = 676$ be rewritten?

A. $(a + b - 26)(a - b + 26) = 0$
B. $(a + b + 26)(a - b - 26) = 0$
C. $(a + b - 26)(a + b - 26) = 0$
D. $(a + b - 26)(a + b + 26) = 0$
E. $(a + b + 26)(a + b + 26) = 0$

EA

60. Leonard is training for a 50-mile bicycle race. His five-month training plan requires that each day he ride either 0 miles, 10 miles, 20 miles, or 40 miles. His training plan is represented as follows:

	0 miles	10 miles	20 miles	40 miles	Total
Jan.	8	23	0	0	31
Feb.	7	19	2	0	28
March	4	22	4	1	31
April	4	17	7	2	30
May	6	17	7	1	31
Total	29	98	20	4	

Which of the following statements does not accurately describe the training plan?

F. 350 miles are to be ridden in May.
G. 25 percent of the days in February will be off days.
H. The mean number of daily miles to be ridden in April is 13.
J. The median number of daily miles to be ridden in March is 10.
K. The range in the number of daily miles to be ridden in January is 40.

PA

Evaluation Chart for Practice Test 2

Directions: On the following chart, circle the question numbers that you answered incorrectly. Then turn to the appropriate topics (listed by chapters), read the explanations, and complete the exercises. Review the other chapters as needed.

		Questions	Pages
Chapter 2:	Pre-Algebra Review	8, 36, 41, 47	22–42
Chapter 3:	Exponents and Square Roots	20, 44, 48, 53, 57	43–55
Chapter 4:	Solving Multi-Step Equations, Inequalities, and Patterns	11, 24, 27, 33	56–79
Chapter 5:	Ratios and Proportions	54	80–85
Chapter 6:	Matrices	28	86–100
Chapter 7:	Polynomials	12, 29	101–107
Chapter 8:	Factoring		108–117
Chapter 9:	Solving Quadratic Equations and Inequalities	6, 9, 45, 56, 58, 59	118–133
Chapter 10:	Relations and Functions	17, 21	134–157
Chapter 11:	Graphing and Writing Linear Equations and Inequalities	52	158–173
Chapter 12:	Applications of Linear Graphs	23	174–184
Chapter 13:	Graphing Non-Linear Equations	15, 18, 30, 34, 40, 51	185–204
Chapter 14:	Systems of Equations and Systems of Inequalities	3, 35	205–222
Chapter 15:	Statistics	1, 25, 26, 38, 60	223–231
Chapter 16:	Probability and Counting	10, 31	232–243
Chapter 17:	Angles	49	244–251
Chapter 18:	Triangles	5, 50	252–263
Chapter 19:	Plane Geometry	19, 37, 55	264–281
Chapter 20:	Solid Geometry	22, 39, 46	282–296
Chapter 21:	Logic and Geometric Proofs	13, 42	297–304
Chapter 22:	Transformations	4, 32, 43	305–318
Chapter 23:	Trigonometry	2, 7, 14, 16	319–341

Index

American Book Company
Meeting Standards, Exceeding Expectations

ACT

Please fill out the form completely, and return by mail or fax to American Book Company.

Purchase Order #: ____________ Date: ____________

Contact Person: ____________

School Name (and District, if any): ____________

Billing Address: ____________ Street Address: ☐ same as billing ____________

Attn: ____________ Attn: ____________

Phone: ____________ E-Mail: ____________

Credit Card #: ____________ Exp Date: ____________

Authorized Signature: ____________

Order Number	Product Title	Pricing* (10 books)	Qty	Pricing (30+ books)	Qty	Pricing (30 books + e-book)	Qty	Total Cost
ACT-E0708	ACT English Test Preparation Guide	$129.90 (1 set of 10 books)		$299.70 (1 set of 30 books)		$328.70 (30 books + e-book)		
ACT-M0708	ACT Mathematics Test Preparation Guide	$139.90 (1 set of 10 books)		$329.70 (1 set of 30 books)		$358.70 (30 books + e-book)		
ACT-R0708	ACT Reading Test Preparation Guide	$129.90 (1 set of 10 books)		$299.70 (1 set of 30 books)		$328.70 (30 books + e-book)		
ACT-S0608	ACT Science Test Preparation Guide	$129.90 (1 set of 10 books)		$299.70 (1 set of 30 books)		$328.70 (30 books + e-book)		
SAT-M1205	New SAT Math Test Preparation Guide	$169.90 (1 set of 10 books)		$329.70 (1 set of 30 books)		$358.70 (30 books + e-book)		
SAT-R1205	New SAT Reading Test Preparation Guide	$169.90 (1 set of 10 books)		$329.70 (1 set of 30 books)		$358.70 (30 books + e-book)		
SAT-W1205	New SAT Writing Test Preparation Guide	$169.90 (1 set of 10 books)		$329.70 (1 set of 30 books)		$358.70 (30 books + e-book)		
GR-1007	Basics Made Easy: Grammar and Usage Review	$119.90 (1 set of 10 books)		$269.70 (1 set of 30 books)		$298.70 (30 books + e-book)		
MR-1000	Basics Made Easy: Mathematics Review	$139.90 (1 set of 10 books)		$329.70 (1 set of 30 books)		$358.70 (30 books + e-book)		
RR-1001	Basics Made Easy: Reading Review	$129.90 (1 set of 10 books)		$299.70 (1 set of 30 books)		$328.70 (30 books + e-book)		
WR-0305	Basics Made Easy: Writing Review	$139.90 (1 set of 10 books)		$329.70 (1 set of 30 books)		$358.70 (30 books + e-book)		
PS-L0710	Projecting Success! Language Arts Digital Version			$39.00 (1 digital set)				
FLASH-P0808	Periodic Table Flash Cards			$59.00 (1 set)				
FLASH-M0106	Mathematics Flash Cards			$69.00 (1 set)				
FLASH-0804	Science Flash Cards (English Version)			$59.00 (1 set)				
FLASH-B0906	Science Flash Cards (English/Spanish Version)			$79.00 (1 set)				
Call for Order #	Core Knowledge Software with CMS (Single Subject)✶			$499.00 (site license)				
MDVD-1005	Virtual Math Tutor - 1 DVD**			$199.00 (1 license)				

8-1-10

*Minimum order is 1 set of 10 books of the same subject.
**Call for site license pricing.
✶Available in Grammar, Math, Reading, Science, and Social Studies.

Subtotal ____________
Shipping & Handling 12% ($10 for software) ____________
Total ____________

merican Book Company • PO Box 2638 • Woodstock, GA 30188-1383
oll Free Phone: 1-888-264-5877 • Toll-Free Fax: 1-866-827-3240
/eb Site: www.americanbookcompany.com